MANAGING SMALL BUSINESSES

MANAGING
SMALL
BUSINESSES

Robert L. Anderson
COLLEGE OF CHARLESTON

John S. Dunkelberg
WAKE FOREST UNIVERSITY

WEST PUBLISHING COMPANY
Minneapolis/St. Paul • New York • Los Angeles • San Francisco

COVER DESIGN: Randy Miyake/Miyake Illustration
COPYEDITING: Maggie Jarpey
INTERIOR DESIGN: Paula Schlosser/Paula Schlosser Design
COMPOSITION: Carlisle Communications, Inc.
ILLUSTRATIONS: Precision Graphics
Production, Prepress, Printing and Binding by West Publishing Company.
Photo Credits appear following the index.

LIBRARY OF CONGRESS CATALOGING-IN-PUBLICATION DATA

Anderson, Robert Lloyd, 1942-
    Managing small businesses / Robert L. Anderson, John S.
  Dunkelberg.
      p.   cm.
    Includes index.
    ISBN 0-314-01163-3 (hard)
    1. Small business--Management.   I. Dunkelberg, John S.
  II. Title.
  HD62.7.A515   1993
  658.02'2--dc20
                                                          92-26315
                                                     CIP

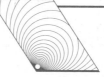

CONTENTS IN BRIEF

v

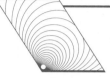

CONTENTS

PART THREE
EMPLOYEES AND OTHER ESSENTIAL PEOPLE   227

CHAPTER 10   Motivating and Compensating Employees   266

PART FOUR
MARKETING PRODUCTS AND SERVICES 327

CHAPTER 17   Controlling Inventory and Shrinkage   468

PART SIX
SPECIAL TOPICS   495

PREFACE

Small businesses are the backbone of the American economic system. They employ more people, create more jobs, and account for more sales than do larger companies. Yet the focus of most business schools' curriculum is on large corporations that comprise the Fortune 500. This book is for those courses, which are becoming more numerous and popular, that concentrate on the workings of small businesses.

This book enables students to acquaint themselves with small businesses from start-up to sell-off and all the stages in between. There is sufficient material in this text to allow interested students to plan, start, grow, manage, and expand a business, and if desired, take the company public or sell it to a larger company. We also identify and discuss the problems and pitfalls inherent in small business management, and show how to avoid them or rectify them if they cannot be avoided.

Our book is written not only for people with an academic interest in small business management, but also for those who may in fact intend to start their own businesses in the near future. We assume that students have some basic understanding of business fundamentals; however, even those who have not completed the required business courses such as marketing and finance will understand and benefit from the material in this book.

TEACHING METHOD

This text is intended to have a strong experiential and applications orientation. We do not want students to be passive bystanders who do not internalize what they read. Instead, we want them to be involved in the start-up process and the management of small businesses. Wherever possible, we demonstrate how real business owners apply theory to their own companies by recording their activities in The Way It Is boxes within the chapters.

To keep students involved, we offer activities at the end of each chapter that measure their skills, judgment, and ability to handle business problems. Each chapter also includes a short case study of a situation relating to that chapter's material. Finally, we have included four comprehensive cases that cover more complex situations than those found in the chapter cases. These cases, found at the end of the text, can only be analyzed adequately after students have studied several chapters.

TEXT ORGANIZATION

In an effort to present small business material in a logical sequence, we have organized this text into six major sections. The first discusses small business owners and their characteristics and origins. We present a case for either buying a business or starting one from scratch, and we devote a chapter to business ethics and social responsibility. We do not think that small business owners are less ethical than their counterparts at larger companies; however, we do recognize that there will be many occasions when it is easier for small business owners to "cut corners" or "look the other way" in their dealings with suppliers, customers, and so on.

In the second section, we concentrate on the start-up process. The four chapters of this section include: business planning, site selection and facility layout, capital requirements and funding sources, and the legal environment of small business. We move on, in the third section, to a small business's people matters. We discuss internal personnel functions such as selecting, training, motivating, and compensating workers. External personnel matters are covered in a chapter about selecting and using key outsiders. Here, we explain how small business owners choose and use lawyers, accountants, consultants, suppliers, and other advisors.

From people concerns, we move on to the fourth section in which we discuss the importance of marketing for small and growing businesses. Most marketing-related functions are discussed with special emphasis on market research and promotion. The next section of the text relates to the more quantifiable functions to which business owners must attend. This is the section that contains material about small business accounting records and procedures, profit planning and cash flow management, budgets, and controlling inventory and shrinkage. Finally, in the sixth section, we discuss international trade and government relations, management development and succession, and taking a company public or selling the business.

SUPPLEMENTS

Consistent with our desire to make this an experiential and applications oriented text, we are making several student and teacher aids available with this book.

For the Student

BIZPLAN: Strategic Business and Marketing Plan Template on Diskette. This complete commercial software package helps students create a business plan. The program helps users accumulate and organize material that is needed to complete a realistic and usable business plan. It runs on IBM PCs and compatibles and Macintosh computers. BIZPLAN is available packaged with the text for those instructors who will want their students to have access to a quality Basic Planning package.

The Marketing Plan Project Manual by William J. Quain and Glen R. Jarboe is a self-contained project manual that presents a step-by-step approach to writing a marketing plan. It includes selecting a client, preparing a situation analysis, and developing specific plans.

For the Instructor

"Strengthening America's Competitiveness: Resource Management for Small Business Success" is a four-volume video library developed by The Blue Chip Enterprise Initiative, sponsored by the Connecticut Mutual Life Insurance Company, the U.S. Chamber of Commerce and *Nation's Business* magazine. The library consists of 51 video profiles of successful small businesses. Each one-hour videotape provides case histories of at least 12 businesses from a range of industries and provides tried-and-true insights on maximizing Marketing, Financial, Technological, Human, Quality and Community resources. The complete library is available to qualified adopters.

Instructor's Manual and Test Bank, written by the authors, includes chapter summaries, answers to Questions for Review and Discussion, Case Teaching Notes, Instructor's Notes for the videos, and a Test Bank of True-False and Multiple Choice questions.

A set of 50 Transparency Masters is also available.

ACKNOWLEDGEMENTS

Very few people who have ever spent two or three years creating a textbook can claim that the end product was the result of individual effort. We certainly cannot. We have had the good fortune to have been assisted by countless competent people who gave us their time, encouragement, and support. Our deans made this project possible by protecting us from nonessential duties. Our secretaries helped prepare the manuscript, and our students "field-tested" some of the cases and check lists found in each chapter. We would also like to thank all of our colleagues at other institutions who reviewed portions of this manuscript and made cogent recommendations for its improvement. Reviewers of the manuscript include:

Don Bradley, III
University of Central Arkansas

W. R. Brown
Towson State University

Filemon Campo-Flores
California State University-
Long Beach

Anthony J. Cupo
County College of Morris

Brenda Geren
Cleveland State Community College

Paul Harmon
University of Utah

Freda Z. Hartman
University of Maryland

Jerry Jones
Spokane Community College

Rudolph Kagerer
University of Georgia

Lawrence H. Krantz
Henry Ford Community College

John Lea
Arizona State University

John G. Maurer
Wayne State University

Frank McDaniels
Delaware County Community College

Lynda Jo McGlamory
North Harris County College

John McGowan
Anoka Ramsey Community College

Carl E. B. McKenry
University of Miami

Douglas Naffziger
Ball State University

James K. Seeck
William Rainey Harper College

Victor E. Sower
University of Georgia

Charlotte Sutton
Auburn University

James Swenson
Moorhead State University

Nancy Upton
Baylor University

John B. Vinturella
Tulane University

Trudy Verser
Western Michigan University

Frederick C. Volker
Texas Tech University

Harold Wilson
Southern Illinois University

The support we received from West Educational Publishing was generous, timely, appropriate, and greatly appreciated. Our editors, Rick Leyh and Esther Craig, guided and assisted us throughout the creation of this text. They willingly spent the time with us that we needed, and they kept us on course and on schedule. Our production editor, Clifford Kallemeyn, has done a marvelous job making this book "say" what we intended it to say. We congratulate and thank him and his staff for turning out such a presentable product.

Finally, this book could not have been written without the support and encouragement of our wives. As our deans shielded us from some academic responsibilities, so did our wives excuse us from some of our familial responsibilities. We dedicate this book to our wives, Kathi and Lu, because their prodding, guidance, assistance, and encouragement made it a reality.

PART ONE

SMALL BUSINESS AND SELF-EMPLOYMENT

1

SMALL BUSINESSES AND THEIR FOUNDERS

Small businesses can be found in every industry and in every state, and every year several hundred thousand new ones are formed. These companies perform vital services or manufacture needed products. They provide jobs, contribute to the gross national product, and provide a living for their owners. Those are the positive aspects of small businesses, but there is also a negative side. Small businesses can consume their owners and have a relatively high failure rate. For employees, small firms offer lower pay than larger companies and other benefits are usually limited. Fortunately, the positive aspects of small businesses outweigh the negative factors, encouraging thousands of people to start their own companies.

In this chapter, we will examine the basic characteristics of small businesses and the people who own them. We will look at the traits of people who start businesses and how they come up with ideas for new companies. We will examine causes of small business failure and what can be done to increase the probability of survival. Part of this chapter will also be devoted to future trends and prospects for small businesses.

SMALL BUSINESSES

Accurately estimating the number of new businesses that are formed each year is virtually impossible; however, the Small Business Administration and such experts as David Birch believe that approximately 600,000 businesses are started each year. Some grow rapidly, some remain relatively small, and some fail in the first year. These small businesses created about 64 percent of the 10.5 million new jobs created in the American economy between 1980 and 1986, and they employ approximately half of the people in the work force. According to the SBA, from 1992 to 2007 about 71 percent of employment growth in the nation's fastest growing industries is likely to come from small firms. There can be no question that small businesses are a vital and productive part of our economy—but what is a small business?

Definition of Small Business

Small Business Administration (SBA)

small business

The **Small Business Administration (SBA)** tries to define a **small business** by the number of employees and annual revenue of the company; however, it makes so many exceptions and qualifications that the definition is sometimes meaningless. For our purpose, any company that meets the following criteria is considered small: the business is financed and managed by the owner (friends and relatives may also provide some of the financing); the business is independent (it cannot be a subsidiary of another company or a franchise); the business is local (most small businesses are usually confined to one city or county); and the company is small relative to others in the same industry.

Number of Small Businesses

Although the number of small businesses in existence is hard to determine precisely, one would be safe in saying that a great majority of businesses could be classified as small. In the 1990 Report of the President on the State of Small Business, the SBA reported that in 1989, an estimated 20 million business tax returns were filed with the Internal Revenue Service, an increase of 5 percent from 1988. Returns were filed by 13.8 million nonfarm sole proprietorships, over 1.9 million partnerships, and 4.3 million corporations. Fewer than 7,000 of the businesses represented by these tax returns are large businesses with more than 500 employees. In the same report, the SBA notes that there were over 677,000 incorporations recorded in 1989.

Advantages of Small Businesses

Small businesses have difficulty competing head-to-head with larger companies that enjoy the benefits of economies of scale. However, smaller firms can find niches in many industries where they can compete and prosper. Small companies tend to do well (1) where technological innovation is economical on a small as well as large scale; (2) in businesses dependent on a specialized skill or service; (3) in small, isolated, overlooked, or "imperfect" markets; (4) in little proven or unstable markets, or by filling marginal, fluctuating demand; (5) by being closer to the marketplace and responding quickly and cleverly to changes in it; and (6) in small communities.[1]

Although small businesses do have advantages over larger companies, determining how successful small businesses really are is difficult. In an attempt to track small business and failure (which we will discuss in more detail later in the chapter), the SBA maintains a **Small Business Health Index (SBHI).** The SBHI (see Exhibit 1–1) combines information about movements in new incorporations, business failures, and small business sector employment in relation to movements in small business profits into a single measure of the current state of small business. Positive values of the Small Business Health Index mean that small business profits are estimated to be growing at a faster-than-average rate.

Small Business Health Index (SBHI)

As can be seen in Exhibit 1–1, the index declined for the third consecutive quarter in the fourth quarter of 1989. The SBA reported that the second-, third-, and fourth-quarter declines reflected increasingly sluggish growth in the number of new business incorporations and small business sector employment. Slow growth in these areas was moderated somewhat by below-average growth in business failures.

EXHIBIT 1–1 Small Business Health Index First Quarter 1980 Through Fourth Quarter 1989

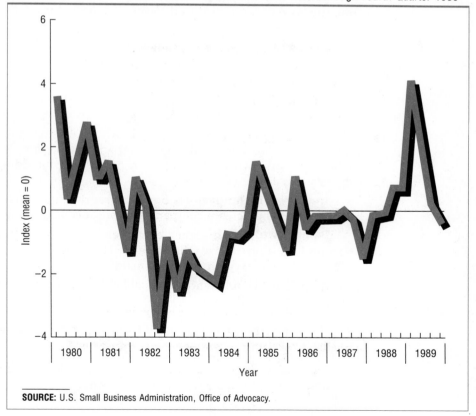

SOURCE: U.S. Small Business Administration, Office of Advocacy.

SMALL BUSINESS OWNERS

The "typical" business owner is nearly impossible to profile. Men and women of all races, religions, and ethnic backgrounds own small businesses. Women are now starting businesses at a faster rate than men, and immigrants are more likely than American-born men and women to be self-employed. Blacks were underrepresented in the ranks of the self-employed, but in the past few years more have decided to start their own companies. We do not know all the traits that differentiate business owners from others, but we have identified some characteristics of the self-employed.

Types of Business Owners and Entrepreneurs

Not everyone agrees about the differences between small business owners and entrepreneurs. Some researchers and academicians believe that only those people whose business is based on innovative products or services are truly entrepreneurs, all others are simply business owners. We believe that anyone "brave" enough to start a business is an entrepreneur. In the start-up phase of a new business, we use the term **entrepreneur** more than business owner; however, once a business is operational, we use the term **business owner** more frequently. Even the terms entrepreneur and business owner are not sufficiently descriptive for some researchers. For example, after researching the current literature, Karl Vesper[2] identified the following types of self-employed people:

entrepreneur

business
owner

Solo Self-employed Individuals. These include mom-and-pop operators; tradespeople such as agents, repairers, and brokers; and high-hourly-rate professionals such as accountants and physicians.

Deal-to-Dealers. These are people who start a business and sell it if it is successful or close it if it is not and then start other businesses.

Team Builders. These are people who start small and through effective hiring and delegation build larger companies. An example would be a janitor who starts his own business, which he grows by bidding on and winning increasingly larger contracts.

Independent Innovators. Some entrepreneurs invent new products or services and then create companies to produce and market their inventions.

Pattern Multipliers. Some entrepreneurs spot an effective business pattern and multiply it many times over. These people are usually franchisors such as Ray Kroc, creator of McDonald's.

Acquirers. People who buy established businesses and expand them are included in this category.

Characteristics of Business Owners and Entrepreneurs

Business owners and entrepreneurs must be

- Motivated to achieve. Entrepreneurs have clearly defined objectives, and they work diligently to achieve them.

- Calculated risk takers. Owners and entrepreneurs are willing to take moderate, calculated risks if they feel that they can affect the outcome of their decisions.
- Self-confident. Only by being confident in themselves can business owners make their companies successful.
- Orderly. Owners must be able to see order in chaos. They should be able to organize their time and priorities.
- Willing to work long hours. Anyone who wants to own a business cannot expect to work eight hours a day, five days a week.
- Healthy. Business owners cannot "afford" to be sick. They do not have sick leave, and they often have no one to replace them.
- Committed. Business owners must remain focused on their objectives. They cannot afford to deviate from their planned activities.
- Antistatus. Business owners may have to sweep floors or clean windows. They should do whatever it takes to make their business successful. Status comes later.
- Superior in conceptual ability. Business owners need to be able to "see the big picture" while at the same time being aware of the details.
- Optimistic. Business owners tend to look on the bright side. They are not unrealistic, they just tend to be more optimistic than others.

Origins of Small Business Owners

People from any walk of life can and do start businesses. Men and women leave their corporate positions, either voluntarily or involuntarily, to start new businesses; young people with little or no business experience start businesses because they perceive a need for a product or service; professionals decide that they want to be self-employed; and people coming to the United States start a business, often because it is their only vocational option.

CORPORATE REFUGEES. An ever-increasing number of men and women are foresaking the corporate world for a business of their own. Challenger, Gray & Christmas, a Chicago-based consulting company, estimates the number of laid-off executives who start their own business has tripled in the past five years from 7 percent to about 20 percent. "There is no question that a prime factor in the decision to become an entrepreneur is concern over another discharge," said James Challenger. "These people are hoping to guarantee that they will never again hear an employer tell them they no longer have a job."[3] Even if they are not laid off, some executives prepare for that eventuality by starting part-time businesses (see The Way It Is 1–1).

Many people who leave the corporate world to start their own business do it voluntarily. They do it because they believe they are more capable than their boss; they want the challenge and excitement of having their own business; they want to be independent; they want to create a legacy; or any

The Way It Is

1–1 PART-TIME BUSINESS

defensive
entrepreneurs

Frank Rekasi is preparing for doomsday. The 39-year-old auto worker is not hoarding canned food or building a bomb shelter. Instead he has begun a second career as a designer and producer of clothing for people with freer cash than his daytime associates. Mr. Rekasi hopes to keep his regular blue-collar job as a statistical processor at General Motors Corporation for a long time, but he knows layoffs are a fact of life. Mr. Rekasi turned a sewing hobby into a second job, laying a foundation for a future without GM. He is among a growing number of what are being called **defensive entrepreneurs:** people who, while continuing in their regular jobs, are developing new careers—for psychic as well as financial reasons. They are sacrificing weekends and vacations to moonlight as small-scale landlords, innkeepers, studio photographers, mechanics, and owners of hardware stores and hair salons.[4]

number of other reasons. Many of these corporate "refugees" are like Dallen Peterson. When his company decided to move from Omaha to Houston, he decided to quit so he could remain in Omaha. He noted that he had also "become disenchanted with corporate life. I saw that the closer you got to the top, the more vulnerable your position became." Peterson decided to start his own snack foods company. He cashed in his profit-sharing retirement benefits, obtained a loan at a local bank, and drew on his savings.

After seven years, Peterson's business became unprofitable and he sold it for a loss. Rather than return to the corporate fold, he took six months to figure out what to do next (he is an example of a deal-to-dealer entrepreneur). With the help of his wife, Glennis, Peterson decided to open a new business—a professional cleaning service for the homes of working women. His business was so successful that he franchised it and now has nearly 400 franchisees. He says that more than half of his franchise owners have come out of corporate life, just as he did.[5]

Those choosing to leave the corporate world for their own business should heed the following advice from consultants Robert W. Bly and Gary Blake:

1. Analyze the reasons you are unhappy with organizational life. When you leave, will you be ready to take charge of your life? Do you realize that a positive attitude, hard work, and challenging goals can probably bring you success?

2. Assess the options. Decide whether to buy a business, start one, or purchase a franchise. Get advice from people you trust and make a list

of the pros and cons of each option. Decide early if you are willing to go into debt and how much debt you can stand.

3. Plan your escape. Start saving money as an income cushion. Learn all you can from your current job, and begin planning exactly what you will do with the new business.

4. Escape! Do not resign until you are financially and emotionally ready. Give a month's notice and leave in good standing—you may need your employer for a customer, supplier, advisor, or lender.

5. After escape, keep active, be businesslike, print a brochure, and get your company listed in directories.[6]

YOUNG BUSINESS OWNERS. There is no age requirement for small business owners. A survey of business owners led to the conclusion that "the probability of switching into self-employment is roughly independent of age and total labor-market experience." Also it was noted that "the fraction of the labor force that is self-employed increases with age until the early 40s and then remains constant until the retirement years."[7] Young business owners are starting and growing successful companies. Recently, Gary Goralnick, the 19-year-old president of Teen Care, became the first teenager to sell a business to one of the 500 largest industrial companies. Colgate Palmolive bought his service for cleaning dental braces.[8]

For many young business owners, Steve Jobs (founder of Apple Computer) and Bill Gates (founder of Microsoft Corporation) are successful role models. In addition to role models, young business owners have organizations such as Junior Achievement, Distributive Education Clubs of America, and the Association of Collegiate Entrepreneurs (ACE) for advice and support. Each year ACE lists its top 100 young (under 30) entrepreneurs. The following are the top ten young entrepreneurs and their company's sales:

1. Michael Dell, 25
   Dell Computer Company
   $385,000,000

2. Arlene Krok, 30
   Loren Krok, 24
   EPI Products
   $100,000,000

3. Neil Balter, 29
   California Closet Company
   $64,825,000

4. Silvane DiGenova, 27
   Tangible Investments
   $42,825,000

5. Michael Avatar, 30
   Coral, Inc./System 800
   $37,320,000

6. Keith McCluskey, 30
   McCluskey Chevrolet
   $33,023,000

7. Brian Hinman, 27
   Picturetel Corporation
   $18,600,000

8. Tony Visone, 28
   Visone Corvette/First
   City Acceptance
   $18,000,000

9. Jack Hertzberg, 25
   Hertzberg Rare Coins
   $16,561,000

10. Ron Grey, 27
    Energy Enterprises
    $10,500,000

All these young people founded their companies before they were 30 years old and grew them to multimillion-dollar businesses. Not all these companies continue to be successful or continue to grow, however. For example, EPI Products, founded in 1987 by Arlene, Sharon, and Loren Krok, quickly became a multimillion-dollar company selling the Epilady leg-hair remover. The Krok sisters began appearing in glamorous photo spreads alongside magazine stories praising their marketing wizardry. Then, suddenly, it was over. On August 23, 1990, EPI filed for Chapter 11 bankruptcy in New York. Court papers show the company had $77 million in liabilities and $73 million in assets. EPI's demise illustrates the perils that threaten any single-product company that tries to grow too fast.[9] Some young people are great at starting a business but not so good at managing one.

IMMIGRANT BUSINESS OWNERS. People who migrate to the United States are more likely to become business owners than are those born in America. The national average is 48.9 self-employed persons per 1,000 of population; however, people of foreign ancestry surpass that rate. Census data indicate the following self-employment rates per 1,000 population for people of foreign ancestry:[10]

Ancestry Group	Business Ownership Rate
Russian	117.4
Lebanese	106.6
Rumanian	104.3
Swiss	104.2
Greek	94.9
Armenian	94.5
Danish	93.2
Syrian	92.7
Norwegian	88.2
Austrian	85.7

Much of the success of immigrant business owners can be attributed to networking and community support. They are willing to work long hours and keep their profits in their businesses, and they often come to dominate some industries.

FEMALE BUSINESS OWNERS. Historically absent from the ranks of the self-employed, women are now starting businesses at a greater rate than men. Although they have overcome some of the barriers that discouraged them from opening a business, women continue to have problems growing their businesses. In a recent survey of 450 women business owners the following professional and personal obstacles were identified: low self-esteem and/or fear of risks (cited by 40 percent of respondents); not taken seriously in nontraditional female fields such as manufacturing and construction (33 percent); balancing work and time spent with family (32 percent); lack of support from family and colleagues (28 percent); and raising capital (21 percent).[11]

People who migrate to the United States are more likely to become business owners than are those born in America.

Women are overcoming startup obstacles and are opening businesses in record numbers. A recent study done for the National Foundation for Women Business Owners revealed that 28 percent of U.S. businesses were owned by women in 1990. Women-owned businesses employed close to 11 million workers, only 1.3 million fewer than the Fortune 500 companies.

By 1995, women-owned businesses are expected to employ more workers than the Fortune 500, and the businesses will not be the small companies historically associated with women owners. We should expect to see more companies like those owned by Susie Tompkins (Esprit de Corp., 1991 revenues of $900 million), Jenny Craig (Jenny Craig International, 1991 revenues of $412 million), and Mary Kay Ash (Mary Kay Cosmetics Inc., 1991 revenues of $1 billion).

BUSINESS FAILURE

In an ideal world, every new business would be successful, but this is not an ideal world. Businesses fail despite their owners' best intentions and hard work. We know that businesses fail, but we do not know the actual annual rate, the precise causes, or even exactly what failure means.

Defining Business Failure

business
failure

To get widespread agreement on a definition of business failure is virtually impossible. Some experts believe that failure occurs only when a company files for bankruptcy protection. Others argue that merger or acquisition also constitutes failure. The following are some other definitions of failure: firms that liquidate and go out of business without ever filing for bankruptcy protection; firms that collapse and reduce to a fraction of their former size; firms that seek a merger partner under conditions of financial distress; firms that cannot pay their bills when due; and firms that are technically insolvent (the realizable value of all assets is insufficient to meet total liabilities).[12]

From these definitions of failure, we conclude that a business has failed when its liabilities exceed its assets, its cash flow is insufficient for normal operations, and the owner decides that the company should be closed, liquidated, or sold to another individual or company. Even if the business continues operating under new management or as part of a healthier company, the original firm has failed and should be included in the annual business-failure statistics.

Small Business Failure Rate

Because there is little agreement on a definition of business failure, it stands to reason that there is also little agreement on the number of businesses that fail annually. The general rule of thumb has been that 50 percent of all new businesses fail in the first year and 75 percent will not survive beyond their seventh year. Recent evidence indicates that these numbers are inaccurate and that the situation may not be so gloomy after all. An American Express Small Business Services study determined that 77 percent of all new businesses survive the first three years of operations. This study tracked 2,994 start-up companies nationwide for three years and found that most were still in business. Of the industries surveyed, manufacturing showed the greatest success rate, at 82 percent, whereas retailers showed the least success, at 73 percent.[13]

Other studies demonstrate similar, but not so optimistic, survival rates as the American Express study. Using a data source developed by the Small Business Administration, researchers found that an average of 39.8 percent of new firms survive six or more years. Manufacturing has the highest rate at 46.9 percent, and construction has the lowest, 35.3 percent.[14] The business failure rate is increasing after a decline in the late 1980s. According to the SBA, there were 700,000 bankruptcies from 1980 to 1990 and approximately 90 percent of those were small business. The bankruptcy rate is be increasing—business bankruptcies increased by 10.4 percent for the first three quarters of 1991 when compared with the same period in 1990.

Causes of Business Failure

Businesses fail for many reasons, and they usually do not operate independently. A combination of two or more of the most common problems may exist, which if not corrected, can cause business failure. The following are some of the primary causes of business failure:

- *Lack of management skills.* Successful employees do not necessarily make successful managers. Employees are often unaware of all the management skills they need to master before they can successfully operate their own business.
- *Inadequate capital.* People planning a new venture often underestimate the amount of money they will need to open and operate a business. It is not enough to have adequate capital to cover start-up costs; owners should be prepared to use their own money to cover business expenses for the first year or two.
- *Underestimation of the competition.* Most businesses, unless they have a unique product or service, need to take customers away from established competitors if they are to survive. Competitors do not willingly relinquish their customers to a start-up just to insure its survival.
- *Inadequate planning.* Some business owners believe that they do not need a business plan. They will just "wing it." Unfortunately, winging it can result in failure.
- *Legal problems.* Nearly all business owners need the advice of qualified attorneys. Failing to get advice or ignoring it can lead to a company's demise.
- *Accounting problems.* Any business that does not have an appropriate, not necessarily complicated, accounting system is a prime candidate for failure.
- *Location.* Selecting the wrong location for a business is one mistake that owners can rarely overcome.
- *Personnel problems.* Business owners need to devote much of their time to the personnel selection and training process. Incapable or dishonest employees can ruin a business in very little time.
- *Economic conditions.* A weak economy or one that is in recession can have a disastrous effect on small businesses. The economy can aggravate other existing problems and cause a business to fail.

Why Bother?

If so many problems can cause a business to fail, why do so many people accept the risk and start their own companies? Why leave the security of the corporate world or other established small businesses for the uncertainty of starting a business? That question was put to small business owners by Paul Reynolds, an entrepreneurship professor at Marquette University, who provided the following reasons for starting their own company: self-employment/autonomy (cited by 29 percent of respondents); income/wealth (19 percent); the challenge (12 percent); to pursue an idea (8 percent); utilize skills (7 percent); build estate for family (5 percent); and no better alternatives (4 percent).[15]

Once they start a business, do owners derive satisfaction from its operations? The following survey, published in *Inc.* magazine,[16] identifies the sources of satisfaction of owning a business:

Source of Satisfaction	Importance on a Scale of 1 to 10
Pride in product/service	8.7
Control	8.2
Freedom	8.1
Flexibility	8.1
Self-reliance	7.8
Customer contact	6.9
Income	6.8
Employee contact	6.3
Recognition	5.9
Privacy	5.9
Security	5.5
Status	5.2

PREVENTING FAILURE

Knowing that some businesses do fail and why they fail, can we write a "prescription" to avoid failure? That is the purpose of this book. The remaining chapters provide would-be business owners with the tools they will need to create and manage successful businesses. In this section we present some "commandments" and "suggestions" from various sources for preventing business failure.

Ten Steps to Business Success

To be successful in small business, you must

1. Be an entrepreneur, a manager, and a technician.

2. Know your competition and your field inside out.

3. Trust yourself and your own judgment, above all. But take the time to truly know your market well and the products it values. To stay one step ahead, constantly evaluate your business to add new ideas.

4. Take pride in your business—it is an extension of yourself. Understand your weaknesses and strengths, your product, and the market. Provide customers with the right product.

5. Serve the needs of the customer. Be sensitive, know their needs and how to reach them, and most of all, know what will convince customers to buy your product or service. Advertising is essential. The yellow pages are an excellent source in which to advertise to attract new customers.

6. Put together an effective and detailed business plan—it is the blueprint to your success. Update your business plan; it should be flexible

enough to adjust to changing circumstances. Plan your cash flow—insufficient working capital can be hazardous.

7. Know yourself and be willing to work day and night to make it work. Do not do it all yourself. Get moral support and the right kind of help to run your business. Professional consultants can help you tap the full resources of your business.

8. Carefully select your staff. They are the face customers put to your business. Reward them for a job well done.

9. Treat employees as individuals. Each has his or her own personality.

10. Read newspapers every day; become familiar with the financial pages. Keep up to date so that you understand the big picture.[17]

Ten Commandments to Prevent Business Failure

1. Thou shalt not tap the till for temptations.

2. Thou shalt not make big personal expenditures to show off, indulge whims, or cover up intemperate purchases.

3. Thou shalt avoid hiring relatives and friends because they are in need and thus place your business in jeopardy just to be "a nice person."

4. Thou shalt not be tempted to buy more goods than you can realistically sell at a profit, for slow-moving inventory can choke you into bankruptcy quickly.

5. Thou shalt not reinvent the wheel, but acknowledge that outside counsel can get your problems resolved despite your pride and ego.

6. Thou shalt not borrow more money than is absolutely needed, because interest and repayment schedules constrict cash flow.

7. Thou shalt not be a savior and supplier to everyone, but shall focus your business to your proper market niche and yourself to what you can do best.

8. Thou shalt not play music all by yourself, once your business requires a band.

9. Thou shalt not relax on top of the mountain, for there you will not know what is going on in the valley.

10. Thou shalt not crawl into a shell when you are needed to guide the growth of your business through staffs that are properly trained in quality and quantity and service that is composed of quality, quality, and quality.[18]

Much of the advice from these sources is repetitive, indicating that there are a few "rules" that any new business owner should abide by. Reducing good business advice to a few basic suggestions is really quite difficult, because the process of starting and managing a new business is complicated. It is, however, a good idea to concentrate on a few basic principles that can guide business growth.

FUTURE TRENDS

Predicting the future is more difficult and risky than trying to reduce good business advice to a few basic suggestions; however, there are a few trends that can be predicted that will affect small businesses. Also some predictions are not universally accepted, which will also have an impact on small businesses. In this section, we will discuss a few of the trends that most people expect to continue.

Demographic Changes

Two major demographic changes will affect small business through the end of this century. First, the population will become older, with the most growth in the prime working-age population between the ages of 35 and 54. Second, the rate of population growth is expected to decline to nearly its lowest level in the twentieth century, from an average annual growth rate of 1.14 percent during the 1980s to just 0.73 percent between 1990 and 2000.[19]

baby boomers   **Baby boomers,** those people born between 1946 and 1964, will create an older population and work force. The average age of the population will increase from 30 years in 1980 to just over 36 years in the year 2000. The number of older Americans, those over age 65, will grow less rapidly than in the past (see Exhibit 1–2). The number of young people in the population will decrease both relatively and absolutely. The age distribution of the population will affect the demand for goods and services in this country. Small business owners will have to cater to the needs of an aging population.

The aging of the population affects the composition of the labor force. The average age of the working population will increase from 35.3 years in 1986 to 38.9 years in the year 2000 (see Exhibit 1–2). Workers between the ages of 16 and 24 will decrease by 3.2 percent, and those between the ages of 25 and 34 will decrease by 8.5 percent. These changes are important to small businesses because they tend to hire relatively more younger and older workers than large businesses. Small businesses may have to raise wages, accept more marginal workers, increase the purchase and use of labor-saving technology, or improve employee training.

Women and Minorities in the Work Force

Women are the fastest growing portion of the work force. The labor force participation rate for women between the ages of 25 and 54 will increase from 70.8 percent in 1986 to 80.8 percent in 2000. The number of working-age women in the labor force will increase by 12.6 million by 2000, accounting for a major portion of the expected growth in the labor force of 20.9 million.[20] Other groups experiencing relatively large increases in the labor force throughout this decade will include Asians and Hispanic Americans. Asians in the work force will increase by 2.4 million, a gain of 71.2 percent. Hispanics will account for an increase of 6 million, or 74.4 percent.

The increasing number of women and minorities in the work force will benefit small businesses, which hire relatively more of these workers than

EXHIBIT 1-2 Projected Population Growth and Labor Force Growth by Age Group, 1986-2000

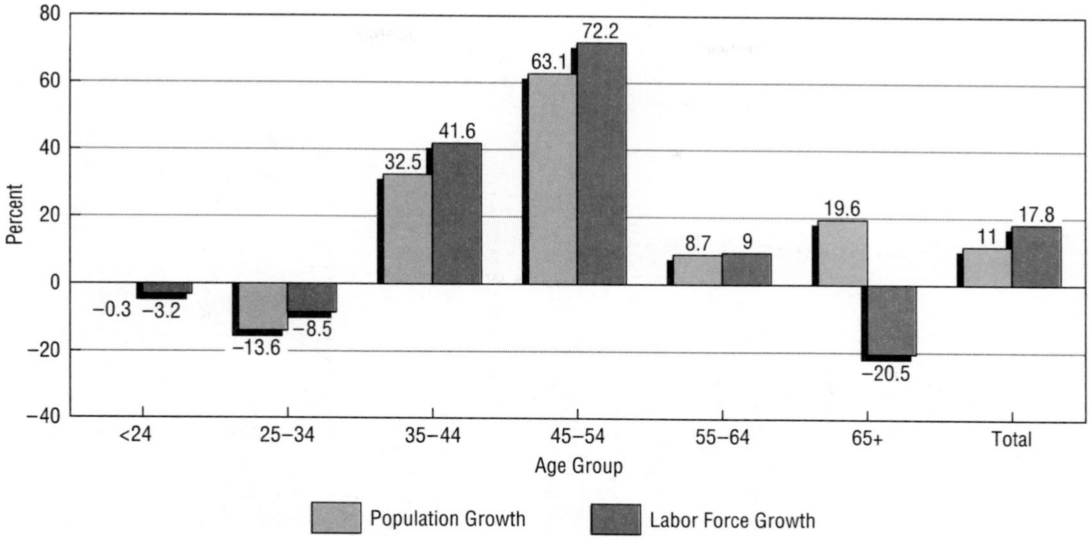

Bureau of the Census, Bureau of Labor Force Statistics.

larger businesses. Because women and minorities are creating businesses at a faster rate than white males, the start-up rate of small businesses should increase in this decade. That might also drive up the failure rate because more small businesses will be competing for the same resources.

Globalization

globalization

We are constantly being told that the world is "shrinking" and that the United States must learn to compete internationally. That advice is as appropriate for small businesses as it is for large companies. Many small businesses have ignored the international marketplace. On the import side, small retail and wholesale businesses welcome imports such as stereos, compact disc players, and televisions, which are imported, distributed, serviced, and sold primarily by small businesses.

Except for a minority of small businesses that choose to specialize in overseas markets, few small companies export their goods or services. Many small manufacturing and service firms may find valuable opportunities in foreign markets, if they choose to look for them. The decline of the dollar makes American goods cheaper overseas, and the world economy is expected to expand faster than the domestic economy. Small business owners should consider becoming active in international trade.

Computers

Computers have become a necessity for most companies; however, small businesses have lagged behind in their acceptance and utilization of comput-

EXHIBIT 1–3 Computer Use by Firm Size

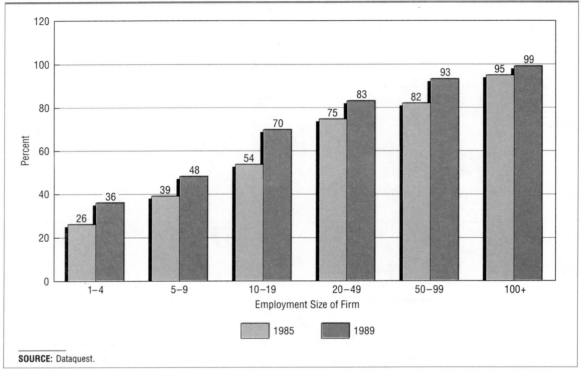

SOURCE: Dataquest.

ers. As of 1989, businesses with fewer than twenty employees were generally far behind larger firms in computer use (see Exhibit 1–3). However, small businesses will face increasingly difficult competition from larger competitors unless they increase their computer use.

Demand for Quality Products

There will be a continuing demand throughout the decade for better quality goods and services. The United States imports more than it exports primarily because foreign goods are perceived to be superior to domestic products. If manufacturers, both large and small, cannot improve the quality of their goods, they will be driven out of business by foreign competitors. The same can be said for service. Efficient and friendly service will be routinely expected and poor service will not be tolerated. Small businesses that are unable or unwilling to improve the quality of their goods and services will not survive.

The Environment

Concern for the environment will increase. Our garbage landfills are nearing their capacity, our forests and lakes are suffering, and people are concerned about nuclear plants. We can expect to see changes in packaging (more reusable or recyclable packaging will be used), different methods of disposing our waste, and a continuing search for alternate fuels. Small businesses will have to adapt to these changes. They need to become more fuel efficient and more involved in the recycling movement. Small firms such as auto paint shops and dry cleaners that emit pollutants have been largely ignored by government regulators. Those companies will be increasingly regulated by the government in order to reduce pollution. Small businesses will have to become "good citizens" and do their part in the fight against environmental degradation.

Preparing for the Future

With all the changes that are likely to occur before the end of the century, small business owners need all the help they can get. The remaining chapters of this book provide information that will help small business owners start and manage successful companies. We will examine, in more detail, business planning, marketing, financing, staffing, internationalizing, and other topics important to small business owners.

SUMMARY

The number of business start-ups continues to increase. Many men and women who leave their corporate jobs, voluntarily or involuntarily, choose to start their own business. They become self-employed because they want to be their own boss, they want flexibility, they believe they will make more money than in the old job, they want to be challenged, or for a number of other reasons. Many of the people who start a business see it fail within the first few years. Those companies do not survive because of one or more of the following reasons: lack of management skills; inadequate capital; underestimation of the competition; inadequate planning; legal and accounting problems; poor selection of a location or employees; or economic conditions.

Businesses do not have to fail. By avoiding the causes of failure, small business owners can expect their companies to grow and prosper. Successful business owners cannot simply avoid fatal mistakes, they must also be prepared for future changes. Some of the trends that will affect small businesses include the following: the aging of the population; the greater participation of women and minorities in the labor force; the increasing importance of the international community; the more widespread use and availability of computers; the demand for quality goods and services; and the need to protect the environment.

QUESTIONS FOR REVIEW AND DISCUSSION

1. How can you determine if a company is small?
2. What advantages do small businesses have over larger firms?
3. What are the traits of business owners?
4. Why do you think more women than men are starting new businesses?

5. Why do immigrants and people of foreign ancestry, as a percentage of their total population, start more businesses than other Americans?
6. When do you believe a business has failed?
7. What causes businesses to fail?
8. What causes so many women and men to choose self-employment?
9. What future trends do you expect to have an affect on small business?
10. How important are baby boomers to small businesses?

KEY TERMS

baby boomers
business failure
business owner
defensive entrepreneur
entrepreneur

globalization
small business
Small Business Administration (SBA)
Small Business Health Index (SBHI)

CASE
Mary Devlin, Inc.

Mary Devlin turned 26 the day she received her MBA from a prestigious Ivy League school. Before she entered graduate school, she had worked three years for a major bank in New York City. Her MBA proved to be her ticket to a well-paying job with a large Boston investment bank. Three-and-a-half years after starting her job Mary was informed that her department was being eliminated and that there would be no other position for her. Mary was devastated. She had been an exemplary employee and had enjoyed several promotions and raises. Mary's boss assured her that she was losing her job through no fault of her own—it was just a matter of "downsizing."

Once Mary got over the shock of losing her job, she began to ponder her future. She felt sure that she could find another job in the banking industry or, at least, one in a similar industry. Mary also considered starting her own company. She had always been interested in gourmet food and fine wines and was quite a good cook. Mary knew that her severance pay would almost cover her start-up costs, and if it did not, she could borrow from her family. Mary believed that she had what it takes to be a successful business owner—she was aggressive, smart, healthy, self-confident, and committed. Despite her strong business background, Mary was not absolutely sure that she would be a successful entrepreneur.

QUESTIONS
1. Would you advise Mary to start her own company?

2. If she starts a business, what kind of business should it be?

3. What advice would you give Mary about starting her own company?

ACTIVITIES

1. Make a list of future trends (other than those mentioned in the chapter) that you think might affect small business.
2. Take the "Quiz for Small Business Success." You may have to "assume" you have a business, or use your experience from previous part-time or full-time jobs.

Quiz for Small Business Success

Choose the answer you think is best for each question.

1. What is the key to business success?
   a. business knowledge
   b. market awareness
   c. hands-on management
   d. sufficient capital
   e. hard work

2. If a relative ever asks me for advice about starting a business, I will tell him or her to
   a. work for someone else in the field first
   b. write a business plan
   c. study marketing
   d. give up the idea
   e. learn about budgeting

3. Which is the largest potential trouble spot?
   a. too much growth
   b. too little growth
   c. too fast growth
   d. too slow growth
   e. sporadic growth

4. I trust (select as many as apply)
   a. nobody
   b. myself
   c. my partner
   d. a few key employees
   e. my customers

5. I am unhappy when my employees are
   a. late
   b. unhappy
   c. abrupt with customers
   d. resigning
   e. less dedicated than me

6. My customers are (select as many as apply)
   a. always right
   b. too fussy

    c. demanding

    d. worth listening to

    e. dumb

7. Rank these in order of importance for small business marketing success.

    a. word-of-mouth

    b. advertising

    c. signs

    d. location

    e. community events

8. When it comes to money, I am

    a. careful

    b. too carefree

    c. emotional

    d. shrewd

    e. hard-nosed

9. Financially my firm

    a. has trouble with cash flow

    b. has a good line of credit

    c. is financed totally by receipt—no credit

    d. is making better profits this year than last

    e. knows exactly where it is all the time

10. In hiring people,

    a. I take far too long

    b. I look for the cheapest person

    c. personality is more important than experience

    d. I look for the best person, and am willing to pay

    e. I only hire at the trainee level

11. With my employees,

    a. I treat everybody the same

    b. I try to talk privately with everybody once a week

    c. to whatever extent possible, I tailor assignments to personalities

    d. I encourage them to talk to me about the business

    e. I try to work alongside them whenever possible

12. The real key to business success is

    a. hard work and perseverance

    b. fine products and service

    c. advertising

    d. knowing the fundamentals of business

    e. employees

13. Competition is

    a. dumb

    b. smart

    c. cunning

d. everywhere
e. a constant threat

14. The best competitive advantage is
    a. experience
    b. understanding what the market wants
    c. confidence
    d. conducting a business ethically
    e. a detailed plan

15. I keep
    a. careful financial records
    b. in touch with my customers
    c. in touch with my employees
    d. trying new techniques
    e. wanting to retire

16. My dream is
    a. to grow a business until someone else can run it
    b. to work until I drop
    c. to give up these headaches and have more fun at work
    d. to try another business
    e. to take a vacation

17. I think business plans are
    a. for the birds
    b. nice but not necessary
    c. something I can do with my accountant
    d. useful and informative
    e. essential—wouldn't do business without one

18. What makes a terrific entrepreneur?
    a. creativity
    b. discipline
    c. consumer orientation
    d. technical proficiency
    e. flexibility

19. What does a business need most?
    a. money
    b. market share
    c. help
    d. time
    e. a solid business plan

20. What is essential to marketing?
    a. "a sixth sense"
    b. market research
    c. customer awareness
    d. experience
    e. testing

SCOREBOX

Question	Points
1.	a = 5, b = 4, c = 3, d = 2, e = 1
2.	a = 5, e = 4, b = 3, c = 2, d = 1
3.	c = 5, a = 4, b = 3, d = 2, e = 1
4.	b = 5, e = 4, d = 3, c = 2, a = 1
5.	b = 5, d = 4, c = 3, a = 2, e = 1
6.	d = 5, c = 4, a = 3, b = 2, e = 1
7.	a = 5, d = 4, c = 3, b = 2, e = 1
8.	a = 5, d = 4, e = 3, b = 2, c = 1
9.	e = 5, d = 4, b = 3, a = 2, c = 1
10.	d = 5, a = 4, c = 3, b = 2, e = 1

Question	Points
11.	c = 5, d = 4, e = 3, b = 2, a = 1
12.	e = 5, d = 4, a = 3, b = 2, c = 1
13.	e = 5, d = 4, c = 3, b = 2, a = 1
14.	a = 5, b = 4, c = 3, e = 2, d = 1
15.	b = 5, a = 4, c = 3, d = 2, e = 1
16.	e = 5, a = 4, b = 3, c = 2, d = 1
17.	e = 5, d = 4, c = 3, b = 2, a = 1
18.	c = 5, a = 4, b = 3, e = 2, d = 1
19.	b = 5, e = 4, a = 3, d = 2, c = 1
20.	c = 5, b = 4, e = 3, d = 2, a = 1

Score	Your Business Success Quotient
75–100	You are a successful entrepreneur whose operations reflect tried-and-true business practices.
50–74	Your business is probably headed for long-term success. But success will come sooner if you sharpen your awareness of solid management skills and marketing techniques.
25–49	Although you may be enjoying customer loyalty and repeat business, never forget that savvy competition is always looking for ways to take the lead. Don't let comfort lull you into false security. Be creatively assertive!
0–24	You may well have the right product, but to sell it successfully, you need to increase your market awareness and improve your operating philosophy. Reach out for practical classes, seminars, and advice from people who have good business track records. And—keep persevering. It's the key ingredient to winning!

SOURCE: "Quiz for Small Business Success," *Small Business Success,* 1988 Edition, 2–3. Used by permission. Reprinted with permission from *Small Business Success,* Volume I, Published by Pacific Bell Directory in partnership with the U.S. Small Business Administration (To obtain free copy of entire publication, call (800) 848-8000.)

2 BUYING A BUSINESS OR A FRANCHISE

Some entrepreneurs know that they want a business of their own but are unwilling to invest the time and effort to start a new business. They opt, instead, to purchase an established business. For these entrepreneurs, the major decision to be made is whether to buy an independent business or a franchise. Both options have advantages and drawbacks that must be evaluated by prospective business owners.

Although purchasing either an independent business or a franchise reduces an entrepreneur's risk of failure, the new owner has no firm guarantees that he or she will be successful. Considerable effort is required to effectively plan the acquisition, find the right business to buy, determine the right price, and successfully negotiate the "deal." Buying the business is only the first step in what will become perhaps the most challenging event in a person's life—successfully operating and growing a business.

In this chapter we will examine the purchasing process. We will concentrate on the process of buying a business—planning the acquisition, establishing criteria for appropriate acquisition candidates, valuing the business, negotiating the deal, and structuring the deal. We will also look at the concept and current state of franchising.

THE ADVANTAGES OF BUYING A BUSINESS

People interested in becoming self-employed often consider the option of buying a business rather than starting their own from scratch. The following are some of the advantages of buying an established business: it takes less time to buy than to start from scratch; it might be less expensive to buy;

capital is often easier to acquire to buy than to start a business; established businesses often have the best locations; inventory, personnel, control systems, etc., are already in place; and the business already has an image and market share. To make sure that these advantages really exist, buyers must thoroughly analyze any business that interests them.

BUYING A BUSINESS

caveat emptor

Buying a business is like buying any other product or service. The old adage **caveat emptor** (let the buyer beware) is particularly appropriate in this situation. Buyers who do not do their "homework" are likely to buy someone else's problem, and no amount of hard work will rescue a doomed business. Fortunately for most entrepreneurs, the task of purchasing the right business can be simplified by paying attention to the basic rules of the buying process.

The steps in the buying process include the following: develop a sound acquisition plan, establish criteria for acceptable acquisition candidates, search for companies that meet the criteria, determine the value of the company selected, negotiate the deal, and structure the deal. Buyers also need to determine if they should undertake the process alone or if they might benefit from the services of professionals.

Planning the Acquisition

Very few individuals would undertake any major project without first developing a plan for accomplishing that project. Similarly, would-be buyers should consider the purchase of a business to be a major project that requires substantial planning before the process begins. The acquisition plan should be sufficiently detailed to guide a person through the buying process but should not be so inflexible that it excludes unanticipated opportunities. For example, if a search uncovers a particularly attractive company that does not meet all the criteria established in the plan, the criteria should be reevaluated rather than rejecting the company outright.

acquisition plan

An **acquisition plan** should lay out the steps to be followed in the purchasing process and indicate the time and cost allowed for each step. At a minimum, an acquisition plan should address the following questions: what kind of company (manufacturing, retailing, etc.) do I want? what criteria should I use to select the right company? where should I look for suitable companies? what documents should the seller be willing to provide? how can I establish the right price for the selected company? how will I negotiate with the seller? how will I finance the purchase of the company? and how do I close the deal? An example of one person's acquisition plan can be seen in Appendix 2-1.

Establishing Criteria

Once the acquisition plan has been developed, a buyer is ready to establish criteria that will allow for the selection of the best business to purchase. We establish criteria—size, color, price, age, etc.—for every purchase we make;

therefore, entrepreneurs should be able to stipulate the criteria that acquisition candidates must meet. Suitable criteria will be different for each buyer, but the following are some general criteria that should be considered:

- Type of business
- Price range
- Location of business
- Company reputation
- Age of company
- Size of business
- Position of company in its market
- Reason company is for sale
- Company's profitability
- Condition of company's assets
- Seller financing

This short list of criteria would be lengthened to suit each buyer's needs. Longer lists facilitate the elimination of unsuitable candidates, but they also might cause buyers to neglect "good buys."

Searching for Businesses to Buy

Having established acceptable criteria, buyers can proceed to look for companies that meet those criteria. Where a person looks for a business to buy depends to a large extent on the price range of the company being sought. For example, relatively inexpensive companies might be listed for sale in the local newspaper, or they might be advertised by business brokers (see Exhibit 2–1). Buyers could also contact attorneys, accountants, bankers, the Small Business Administration, and acquaintances for leads about available small businesses.

To find larger, more expensive businesses to purchase, entrepreneurs could read the ads in the *Wall Street Journal* or similar national publications. Information about businesses for sale could also be obtained from venture capitalists, merger and acquisition consultants, investment bankers, or commercial banks. A buyer also might approach a business that is not for sale. If a business that meets the established criteria has been identified but is not for sale, an entrepreneur could approach the owner with a tentative purchase offer.

Many buyers may choose to let brokers or merger and acquisition consultants assist them with the purchase of the right business. Selecting the right broker or consultant may be a difficult task in itself; however, the following questions suggested by Lawrence Tuller will simplify the selection process:[1]

1. Is he or she listed in the telephone book (it's amazing how many are not)?
2. Has the Better Business Bureau and the Chamber of Commerce ever heard of him or her?

EXHIBIT 2–1
Business Broker Advertisement

Businesses For Sale
- Taverns
- Fast Food
- Restaurants
- Laundromats
- Liquor Stores
- Serv. Business
- Misc. Retail
- Franchise
- Convenience Stores
- Distribution
- Day Care Centers

● ● ● ● ● ● ●
● NEW LISTINGS! ●
Long Est'd & Very Profitable Accounting Business, W. Ashley Restaurant/ Lounge/Raw Bar, Convenience Store, North Area & W. Ashley Sports Bars, Long Est'd Large Plant Nursery, Johns Island Restaurant, and Sign Company.
WE NEED

Businesses to Sell!
Thinking about selling your business? Put Charleston's most experienced and knowledgeable brokerage company to work for you. Our staff has been marketing businesses in the Charleston area since 1981. We guarantee professional attention to detail and strict confidentiality. If you desire information on how the sales process works, please feel free to give us a call.

(803) 572-5702

3. To which professional organizations does she or he belong?

4. How many deals has he or she closed in the past 12 months? (If fewer than three, go elsewhere.)

5. Will those sellers named give her or him a reference?

6. Will the banks which closed the deals give him or her a reference?

7. Has she or he ever closed a deal involving a company of similar size and industry?

8. How will he or she locate a target? Networking? Advertising? Personal contacts?

9. How long does she or he estimate it will take to find a viable target? To close the deal?

10. Does she or he insist on an exclusive listing? (He or she should.)

11. What information are you expected to provide? You should be asked for bank and trade references.

12. What is the fee arrangement?

13. What type of contract are you expected to sign? It should be inclusive and guarantee how much time he or she will spend on your deal—five days per month, one week or whatever. If he or she refuses to commit his or her time, go somewhere else.

Once a broker or consultant has been selected, the buyer should enter into a formal agreement with that person. The brokerage agreement should include

- An exact description of the parties to the agreement.
- The terms of the agreement.
- The exclusivity or nonexclusivity of the agreement.
- A confidentiality protection clause.
- A protection clause against claims for payment to other intermediaries.
- The terms of cancellation of the agreement.
- The amount of the commission to be paid.
- When the commission will be paid.
- Who pays the commission (buyer or seller).
- A determination of what portions of the purchase price the commission will be paid on.
- The form of commission payment (cash, stock, etc.).
- A statement of what the intermediary will do to bring about the sale of the business.[2]

Valuing the Business

A basic marketing maxim is that an item can be sold only if there is a willing buyer, a willing seller, and an agreed-upon price—the condition that often scuttles the sale of a business. Buyers must consider all aspects of the business they wish to purchase before determining the price they are willing to pay for the company. There are a number of different methods of valuing a business, and astute buyers will use them all before arriving at their offering price. The following are the principal **valuation techniques:** a **multiple of cash flow generated in the past,** a **multiple of future cash flow, asset value,** and the **comparison of other similar companies.**

valuation techniques

multiple of cash flow generated in the past

MULTIPLE OF PAST CASH FLOW. In a fairly stable economy, a buyer can use past cash flow as an indicator of how well a company will do in the future. Even if only minimal growth is anticipated, a buyer should be able to earn a profit on a company that has been profitable in the past. The following is an example of using past cash flow as a method of valuing a company.

ACCOUNT CATEGORY	YEAR 1	(DOLLARS) ACTUAL YEAR 2	YEAR 3
Profit before taxes	2,100	2,340	2,560
Add:			
Owner's draw	350	370	370
Interest expense	700	680	655
Depreciation	900	900	900
Adjusted before-tax profit	4,050	4,290	4,485
Less: taxes @ 34%	(1,377)	(1,458)	(1,525)
Adjusted after-tax cash profit	2,673	2,832	2,960
Add:			
Decrease in working capital*	1,350		
Less:			
Increase in working capital		(1,575)	(1,730)
Purchase of fixed assets*		(800)	(960)
Net cash flow	4,023	457	270
Average three-year cash flow		1,583	
Multiple†		×5	
Historic cash-flow valuation		7,915	

*Changes in working capital and fixed assets are part of normal operating expenditures.
†This is an arbitrary number which indicates that the original investment would be recovered in five years.

multiple of future cash flow

MULTIPLE OF FUTURE CASH FLOW. The principal difference between this and the previous method is that this method uses forecasted earnings rather than historic earnings. This approach is somewhat more realistic, because it recognizes that a business is likely to have future earnings greater than past earnings. Buyers using this method should use their own earnings forecast rather than the seller's, which is likely to be more optimistic. Because cash earned three years from now is not worth as much as cash earned today, some entrepreneurs will apply a discount rate to arrive at a company's present value.

asset value

ASSET VALUE. This method is not as useful as using earnings to value a business, but it does give an indication of the amount and strength of the company's hard assets. The asset value of the business is usually used when the company's income stream is small relative to its investment in assets. A company's assets can be valued using the following definitions: replacement cost—new (buying new items), replacement cost—used (buying used items), value in place (the value of assets as part of the ongoing business, i.e., replacement cost—new, minus depreciation), orderly liquidation value, forced liquidation value, and borrowing value. The following is an example of asset value disregarding seller's long- and short-term debt and goodwill.

ASSET/LIABILITY CATEGORY	(DOLLARS) AMOUNT
Cash	125
Accounts receivable	4,600
Inventory	5,250
Net fixed assets	3,600
Total assets	13,575
Less:	
Accounts payable	(1,300)
Accrued expenses	(1,375)
Net asset value	10,900

comparison of other similar companies

COMPARISON METHOD. Comparing a target business with other similar businesses is the easiest and perhaps the least accurate method of valuing the target company. The major problem with this technique is that no two businesses are exactly alike; therefore, it is unreasonable to assume that two similar companies should sell for the same price. If this method is used, considerable leeway should be allowed for different company characteristics and operating conditions.

RULES OF THUMB. In some industries there are accepted formulas or rules of thumb that can be used by buyers to value a business. These rules of thumb are usually stated as some multiple of income, revenue, or capacity. In the movie theater industry, the formula used is a multiple of the number of seats, whereas gas stations value the business by applying a multiple to the number of pumps. A more complete listing of rules of thumb and some danger signals to watch for can be found in Exhibit 2–2.

Negotiating the Deal
Once buyers have satisfied themselves that they know the value of their target business, they should begin formal negotiations with the seller. At this point a decision needs to be made as to whether the buyer or the buyer's agent will be the negotiator. We have already noted that brokers or consultants can be used to locate a target company; likewise, they can negotiate the

EXHIBIT 2–2 Costs and Red Flags

Type of Business	Price Offering Range	Watch Out for . . .
Apparel shops	.75 to 1.5 times net + equipment + inventory	Location/competition company image/specialization/shopping patterns/obsolete inventory/parking
Auto dealerships	1.25 to 2 times net + equipment	Type or brand/factory allocation policy/location/reputation/reliability of mechanics
Auto service stations	$1.25 to $2 per gallon pumped each month, including equipment	Traffic pattern/length of lease/lease terms/location/competition/gas supplier relations/gallons per month
Beauty salons	.25 to .75 times gross + equipment + inventory	Staff turnover/image/location/reputation/ age of equipment
Fast-food stores	1 to 1.25 times net	Street traffic/service space/seating space/location/competition/lease terms/franchise/maintenance
Grocery stores/ Supermarkets	.25 to .33 times gross, including equipment	Nearby competition/lease terms/location/ condition of facilities/alcoholic beverage permit/percentage of nongrocery lines
Insurance agency	1 to 2 times annual renewal commissions	Agent turnover/client mix/carrier characteristics/demographics of clients/transferability of clients
Local newspapers	.75 to 1.25 times gross, including equipment	Economic profile of circulation area/ demographics/economic conditions/ competition/advertiser loyalty
Manufacturers	1.5 to 2.5 times net, including equipment + inventory	Single major customer/competition from abroad/relations with dealers or distributors/condition of plant and equipment/market position/labor relations
Personnel agency	.75 to 1 times gross, including equipment	Staff turnover/reputation/specialization/ client relations
Real estate office	.75 to 1.5 times net + equipment + inventory	Intensity of competition/tenure of sales associates/reputation/franchise agreement
Restaurants	.25 to .50 times gross, including equipment	History of previous failures/location/ reputation/competition/lease/liquor license
Retail stores	.75 to 1.5 times net + equipment + inventory	Chain competition/lease term/location/ competition/company image/specialization/ shopping patterns/obsolete inventory/parking
Travel agencies	.04 to .10 times gross, including equipment	Where revenue comes from/general climate for travel (international)/reputation/location/ relationships with key employees/memberships (IATA, ASTA, etc.)
Video stores	1 to 2 times net + equipment	Obsolescence of tapes/chain store competition/location—traffic/customer match to inventory

SOURCE: Gustav Belle, *The Small Business Information Handbook* (New York: John Wiley & Son, 1990), 30–32. Used by permission.

deal for the buyer. Whoever is selected to negotiate should meet some basic conditions. He or she should not be emotionally involved in the sale; know the buyer's goals and objectives; know the seller's goals and objectives; have negotiating experience and skill; be persuasive; be someone the seller will trust; be creative; and be able to satisfy the needs of both buyer and seller.

Negotiating the deal is likely to be the most sensitive phase of the purchase process because buyer and seller usually have placed a different value on the business. Because negotiations could be terminated if the owner is not serious about selling the business, the following issues should be judged before proceeding:

- Does he or she *really* want to sell the business? Some owners realize, after negotiations commence, that they really do not want to sell the business.
- What are the seller's motivations? The seller may want to retire, buy another business, relocate, or any of a variety of other reasons. Knowing why he or she wants to sell gives the buyer a negotiating advantage.
- Does the seller personally need a large cash settlement? If the buyer cannot purchase with all cash, the negotiations should be terminated.
- What are the seller's plans after the sale? Is he or she willing to stay and train the new owner, or is retirement likely?
- Is the seller basically honest in her or his dealings? The need for honesty in such a major transaction is obvious. Buyers who have any doubts about a seller's integrity should break off negotiations and start searching for another business.[3]

Offer to Purchase

A buyer who is satisfied that the seller is serious and honest should now be prepared to present a formal **Offer to Purchase** document. Without this document most sellers will not provide buyers with privileged information such as customer lists and tax returns. The Offer to Purchase need not be a lengthy, complex document that covers all eventualities; however, it should state the buyer's intentions and conditions of sale. The offer should include the price, terms of payment, documents to be provided by seller, a covenant not to compete to be executed by seller, and any other conditions that might invalidate the purchase of the business.

Once the Offer to Purchase has been presented and accepted, the seller is obligated to provide the buyer with pertinent business information; however, the seller does not have to volunteer any information. The buyer should know what is needed to accurately gauge the health and value of the target business. Buyers or their agents should request that the seller provide the following information:

- Copies of business licenses, permits, etc.
- Tax returns for the last three to five years
- Audit letter from the most recently audited financial statements
- All financial statements for the last three to five years
- Current and long-term budgets

- Any copies of appraisals of fixed assets
- Past bank statements and canceled checks
- Copies of loan agreements
- Copies of insurance policies
- Copies of all leases and rental agreements
- A complete customer list
- Catalogs, price lists, and other company sales literature
- Payroll roster and records
- Information about retirement programs
- Job descriptions and employee responsibilities
- Details of current or past litigation
- Copies of patents, trade marks, or copyrights
- Policy and procedures manuals
- Copies of all existing contracts
- Copies of any other documents relating to any debts, obligations, liabilities, or commitments of the company[4]

Reluctance on the part of the seller to provide any of these documents could indicate that she or he was not being completely honest with the buyer or the buyer's agent.

noncompete agreement

One document all buyers should insist on is a **noncompete agreement** (see Exhibit 2–3). This agreement limits the seller's right to start the same kind of business in the buyer's territory for a specified amount of time. Although helpful, this document is not a panacea because at least twelve states have statutes that limit noncompete agreements. If the prohibition against starting a new business is not reasonable, the document will most likely be useless. Even if it is reasonable, the noncompete agreement may be useless if the new company has not caused irreparable harm to the other business (see The Way It Is 2–1). In general, most courts recognize two legitimate reasons for creating noncompete agreements—to protect customer contacts and to protect confidential information.

Structuring the Deal

structuring the deal

Having completed negotiations, the buyer and seller must finalize their agreement. **Structuring the deal** means agreeing on the method of payment and signing an Agreement to Purchase and Sell document. The following are the most common forms of payment: cash, notes payable, payments of stock, an earn out, or some combination of these methods.

Cash. This transaction simply involves the transfer of cash from the buyer to the seller to pay for the purchase of the business.

Notes Payable. The buyer asks the seller to accept a note, payable sometime in the future, for all or a portion of the selling price. The buyer and seller negotiate the payment schedule, the interest, and collateral needed. It is

EXHIBIT 2–3 Covenant Not to Compete

Name of Business _____

Address: _____

_____

_____

Phone Number _____

Seller does convenant to the Buyer, his or her successor and assigns, that he or she will not engage, directly or indirectly, in any business similar to or in competition with the business hereby being sold within a radius of _____ miles from the premises at (address) _____ for _____ years from the date of Buyer's possession thereof, either as a principal, agent, manager, employee, owner, partner, stockholder, director or officer of a corporation, trustee or consultant, or otherwise in any other capacity or be connected therewith in any other mannter.

The value placed on this convenant is the sum of $ _____

Executed on _____ , 19___ at (address) _____

X _____ Dated _____ , 19____
Seller(s)

_____
Print name(s) and title(s)

X _____ Dated _____ , 19____
Buyer(s)

_____
Print name(s) and title(s)

customary to secure a note with assets of the business, keeping the seller concerned about the well-being of the business for a few years after its sale.

Stock. Stock sales are most common among public companies; however, it is possible for an individual to offer a seller stock in the purchased company. Sellers who agree to accept stock for full or partial payment assume some risk if the company fails. Unlike a note payable, stocks carry no guarantee that the seller will receive a predetermined amount of cash in the future.

earn out

Earn Out. This is a contingent payment that obligates the buyer to pay the seller cash in the future. The amount of cash is based on the achievement of some specified objectives. Earn outs are usually contingent on a company's future revenue or profits. Like stock transactions, earn outs give sellers a vested interest in the future profitability and growth of the companies they sell.

2–1 COMPETING WITH A FORMER EMPLOYER

Because of differences with the owners of the company, Robert Agnes, president of ABC Trans National Transport, left to form his own competing company. Before leaving, Agnes and several other employees who would leave with him used ABC's equipment and time to prepare for the start up of their own business. Agnes started Aeronautics Forwarders Inc., lured several ABC employees to his company, and offered inducements to ABC's customers to shift their accounts to his company. ABC sued Aeronautics for $5 million and asked for an injunction that would prohibit Aeronautics from doing business with its principal customers.

ABC won—sort of. The court found that Agnes and his associates had breached their fiduciary duties by promoting Aeronautics's interests while working for ABC. However, ABC was awarded only $255,000 and the injunction was not issued because the judge determined that ABC had not suffered irreparable harm.[5]

In most cases the purchase of a business could involve several different types of payment. Most sellers expect some cash payment and will accept notes, stocks, or an earn out for the remainder of the price. It is in the buyer's best interest to keep the seller concerned about the well-being of the business, so he or she is likely to offer an earn out or stock for a substantial portion of the price.

Agreement to Purchase and Sell

The purchase process concludes with buyer and seller signing an **Agreement to Purchase and Sell.** This formal document contains the sale price and all the conditions and contingencies agreed on by both parties. The buyer absolutely must have a competent attorney draft the agreement so he or she is protected from any future liability.

Avoiding Buying Mistakes

The buying process is not without certain inherent risks. Some buyers, through errors of commission and omission, undermine their chances to succeed as owners. The following are some of those errors:

- Buying a company that is a poor personal fit.
- Paying too much money up front, leaving insufficient working capital.
- Placing too much faith in existing management.
- Assuming that sales will remain stable after the acquisition. Competitors see new ownership as an opportunity for them to raid the company's customer base.
- Assuming that the technology is proprietary and therefore cannot be duplicated.

- Underestimating how difficult it is to change an established company's culture.
- Failing to realize that there are few growth opportunities in a mature market.
- Relying too heavily on a contract with the seller, leaving the legal system as the main recourse in disputes.[6]

BUYING A FRANCHISE

franchise

Some people who choose to be self-employed may not be willing to accept the risk of buying an independent small business. To minimize their risk, those people could purchase a well-known, established **franchise.** There are more than 500,000 franchise operations in the United States, which accounted for more than one-third of all retail sales. The International Franchise Association (IFA) estimates that franchising's share of retail sales during the 1990s will increase to nearly 50 percent.[7] Owning a franchise is being self-employed, but it is not the same as owning an independent business (see The Way It Is 2–2). There is a boss-employee relationship in that franchisees (franchise buyers) must abide by the rules and regulations established by franchisors (franchise sellers).

What Is a Franchise?

One of the first franchises (a French term that means "free from servitude") was started around 1863 by the Singer Sewing Machine Company, but most major franchises were established in the 1940s and 1950s. Some of the major franchises started in those two decades include McDonald's (1955), Burger King (1955), Carvel Ice Cream (1945), Putt-Putt Golf (1954), Midas Muffler (1956), Hanna Car Wash (1955), Manpower Temporary Services (1955), Kentucky Fried Chicken (1952), Pizza Hut (1959), Pepperidge Farm (1941), Dunkin' Donuts (1955), Holiday Inn (1954), Quality Inn (1950), and H&R Block (1958). Today, only fifty-five companies, or just less than 4 percent of all

The Way It Is

2–2 FRANCHISEES NOT ENTREPRENEURS

To a true entrepreneur, franchising is like a Pittsburgh Steeler playing touch football. He still does a lot of running, but the danger of getting hurt is much less. As is the prospect of glory. Like an entrepreneur, the franchisee invests his or her money and owns the business, but he or she does not have to develop a new product, create a new company, or test the market. In return, the franchisee gives up some independence and pays the franchisor anywhere from 1.5 to 12 percent of gross sales. It is a hybrid form of entrepreneurship that appeals to a lot of Americans.[8]

franchisors, account for nearly half of all sales and for 51 percent of all franchise establishments.[9] The following is a generally accepted definition of franchising:

> A long-term, continuing business relationship wherein for a consideration, the franchisor grants to the franchisee a licensed right, subject to agreed-upon requirements and restrictions, to conduct business utilizing the trade and/or service marks of the franchisor and also provides to the franchisee advice and assistance in organizing, merchandising, and managing the business conducted pursuant to the license.[10]

The definition of franchising is relatively simple; however, not all franchises are alike. There are three basic types of franchises that can be bought. The first is **product franchise,** the second is **manufacturing franchise,** and finally there is **business format franchise.**

product
franchise

Product franchise. This type of franchise sells goods produced by the franchisor that carry the franchise trademark. The franchisee pays the franchisor a fee for the right to sell the trademarked goods in a designated area. Some swimming pool distributors and tire dealerships are product franchises.

manufacturing
franchise

Manufacturing franchise. In some industries, such as soft drink bottling, franchisors license their franchisees to manufacture and distribute trademarked products. For example, the formula for Coca Cola syrup is a highly guarded secret known only to a few people. Coca Cola sells its syrup to its franchisees who proceed to produce and bottle the final product for distribution to local customers.

business
format
franchise

Business format franchise. This is the most common form of franchising whereby the franchisor licenses the franchisee to open a retail shop, store, or chain to sell its trademarked products to the public. The franchisee's operating methods are controlled by the franchisor who provides specified assistance and guidance to the franchisee.

piggyback
franchise

conversion
franchise

master (area)
franchise

multiunit
franchise

subfranchise

A few other franchising terms also need to be defined. A **piggyback franchise** is two or more franchises sharing space or a franchise located within an established nonfranchised business. A **conversion franchise** is an independent business that becomes a franchised outlet of an existing franchise. A **master** or **area franchise** gives the franchisee exclusive rights to expand within a given city, state, or region. A **multiunit franchise** means the franchisee has the right to open several franchise units. **Subfranchises** are sold by a master franchisee to others within the master franchisee's trade area.

Why Buy a Franchise?

Being a franchisee is not particularly entrepreneurial, and franchisees cannot exercise their creativity. Operating methods are supervised by franchisors, and income potential is limited. So why would anyone buy a franchise? The following are some advantages of owning a franchise:

Franchisees

- Benefit from well-known trademarks and the goodwill associated with them.
- Receive the standard quality and uniformity of the franchisor's product or service.
- Have access to a proven system of marketing and bookkeeping.
- Are assisted with site location, facility layout, marketing, and operations.
- Receive a business framework that minimizes start-up problems.
- Receive proven operating methods and procedures for creating and selling a product.
- Enjoy instant name recognition because consumers are already familiar with the franchisor's products.
- Receive information about competitors, product demand, and community attitudes.
- Can realize cost savings by taking advantage of franchisor discounts and centralized buying.
- Receive well-tested sources of supply and service.
- May receive financial assistance from some franchisors to purchase the franchise.

These advantages of owning a franchise generally offset the disadvantages, which include the following: earning less money than anticipated; incurring hidden costs; being overcontrolled by franchisors; having the franchise agreement terminated by the franchisor; having franchisors sell too many franchises in the same area; and losing the business because the franchisor goes bankrupt. Anyone who is aware of the disadvantages of being a franchisee can compensate for them and become a successful franchise owner.

Who Buys Franchises?

A profile of the "typical" franchisee is virtually impossible to construct, because people from literally all walks of life buy franchises (see The Way It Is 2–3). Most franchisors can probably identify the type of individual most likely to succeed with their franchise, but there is no list of traits or characteristics that differentiates successful from unsuccessful franchisees. Jack Lentz, the franchisor of PostalAnnex +, has determined that the people most likely to succeed with one of his franchises would be retired management executives as well as women in their 40s with working spouses.[11] The franchisors of Docktor Pet Centers found that they were "getting more professional people: veterinarians, lawyers, teachers, computer people, and corporate people. They bring their own flair and training, and they understand the value of business systems."[12]

A study of 229 franchisors conducted by DePaul University and Francorp[13] found that most franchise buyers fell into one of five categories. The following

2–3 A BEAUTICIAN BUYS A FRANCHISE

"I was a beautician for 11 years, a Tupperware manager for four years, and a receptionist at a country inn for several years before I decided that I needed to get serious about losing weight," says Ann Andre, 43, owner of three Formua-3 International franchises. Andre went to a Formua-3 center to lose 70 pounds and liked the establishment so much that she decided to buy one. She told the manager that she would like to buy his franchise, but he was not ready to sell. Instead, Andre was hired to work as a counselor in the Formua-3 center. She became assistant manager, then was promoted to manager, and in less than one year she and her husband purchased the center from the owner. Now the Andres own three centers, all within 19 miles of their home. Ann advises franchise buyers to be prepared to work hard and to work "long, long hours."[14]

are the categories and the percent of franchisees in them: blue-collar worker with little or no management experience (14.3); white-collar worker with little or no management experience (30.5); professional with little or no management experience (11.2); professional or executive with management experience (35.1); and investor or entrepreneur with other business interests (21.1).

Women are taking advantage of franchising to help them become self-employed. A survey by Women in Franchising (WIF) found that women, either alone or in partnership with men, own 30 percent of the nation's franchised businesses. Franchising is helping women break the barriers to business ownership, and women are also creating their own franchises. Gymboree, A Choice Nanny, Jazzercise, Careers USA, Little Professor Book Centers, Women at Large, Decorating Den, and others are, at least in part, owned by women.[15] The built-in support systems, the proven business methods, and the chance to have total responsibility for growing a business are attracting women to franchising as a way to achieve business ownership with a minimum of risk.

Although it is possible for people with varying backgrounds to buy franchises, not all would-be purchasers are automatically accepted by franchisors. The DePaul University/Francorp study found that 76.2 percent of franchisors questioned had turned down franchisees. The following are the most commonly indicated reasons for rejection and the percent of companies giving that reason: personality, attitude (27.6); unsuitable background (13.5); would not operate franchise (11.7); and too entrepreneurial (8.6). Men and women who do not have these problems are likely to be allowed to purchase a franchise if they can locate one that suits them, and if they can acquire the needed capital.

Women, either alone or in partnership with men, own 30% of the nation's franchised businesses.

Finding a Franchise

There are thousands of franchise opportunities available to prospective franchisees. They represent virtually every kind of business, and they can cost from less than $1,000 to more than $300,000. To find the right franchise, people should investigate various sources for information about available franchises. There are books written specifically to inform people about franchise opportunities. For example, Robert Laurance Perry wrote *The 50 Best Low-Investment, High-Profit Franchises* (Prentice-Hall, Inc., 1990) in which he describes desirable low-cost franchises. There are many other books that provide information about franchise opportunities.

Organizations have been established to provide franchise information to interested parties. The International Franchise Association (IFA) in Washington, D.C., has numerous books and pamphlets available for potential franchisors and franchisees. A person looking for the right franchise might purchase *How To Select a Franchise* and *Investigate Before Investing, A Guide for Prospective Franchisees* from the IFA. The International Trade Administration (U.S. Department of Commerce) publishes its *Franchise Opportunities Handbook,* which can be purchased from the U.S. Government Printing Office.

Many magazines, such as *Nation's Business* and *Entrepreneur,* have advertisements (see Exhibit 2–4) for franchises that can be purchased. Newspapers such as the *Wall Street Journal* and the *New York Times* also advertise franchise

EXHIBIT 2—4 Franchise Advertisements

opportunities. There are also franchise trade fairs held in major cities several times a year that bring franchisor and prospective franchisees together. These fairs provide an ideal opportunity for interested persons to compare a number of available franchises at the same time.

To limit the time involved in searching for franchise opportunities, prospective franchisees should know which media franchisors favor and find most effective. Franchisors who participated in the DePaul University/Francorp study used large metropolitan and small city newspapers more than any other media. The least used media were radio, television, and outdoor advertising. The most effective media used (generated the most sales) were *Entrepreneur* and the *New York Times,* and the least effective media were local radio and local television.

Evaluating Franchises

An effective search of franchise opportunities should identify several suitable franchises for sale. The prospective franchisee should carefully evaluate each opportunity to determine which one is right for her or him. The following are some critical points that should be considered before buying a franchise:[16]

The franchisor. Look at the company's profile, financial statements, and officers' backgrounds. This plus all the obligations of both parties are laid out in a Federal Trade Commission Franchise Disclosure Statement (or **Uniform Franchise Offering Circular**), required to be given to a potential franchisee ten days before signing an agreement.

Uniform
Franchise
Offering
Circular

Marketability. Investigate the long-term demand for the franchise's products or services, and the competition.

Support services. Critical areas are initial and ongoing training, site selection, lease negotiations, advertising and marketing materials, volume discounts on equipment and inventory, customer leads, private label products, and accounting systems.

The cost. Initial fees and ongoing royalties vary. Royalties may slide based on volume. Start-up costs include working capital, leasehold improvements, equipment, and inventory.

Return on investment. To find out what a typical franchise earns, talk to as many existing franchisees as possible.

Investment opportunities. Many franchisors offer area franchises, or discounts on multiple units.

Financing. Some franchisors offer direct financing, help prepare loan packages, or have financial arrangements with lenders.

Territorial protection. Determine if territorial exclusivity will be granted or if other franchisees can operate in the same territory.

Franchisee-franchisor relationship. Are there open lines of communications—such as newsletters, meetings, an advisory council? Existing franchisees are the best source for this information.

Disclosure Statement

All franchisors are required to provide potential franchisees with a copy of their **disclosure statement.** This document provides some of the information franchisees need to evaluate the franchise opportunity; however, it does not contain all the information needed. The content of disclosure statements is stipulated by federal law so they all look pretty much alike. The following is a fairly typical list of information that should be disclosed:

- Identification of the franchisor and any predecessors
- Identity and business experience of persons affiliated with the franchisor
- History of litigation (current and past) against the franchisor, its directors, and top managers
- History of bankruptcy of the franchisor, its directors, and top managers
- Amount of initial franchise fee or other initial payment
- Existence of other fees franchisee must pay
- Amount of franchisee's initial investment
- Obligations of franchisee to purchase or lease in accordance with specifications
- Description of the financial assistance franchisor offers franchisees
- Area or territory in which franchisee can operate
- Description of franchisor's trademarks, service marks, trade names, logos, and commercial symbols
- Description of franchisor's patents or copyrights
- Obligation of the franchisee to participate in the actual operation of the franchise
- Restrictions on goods and services offered by franchisees
- Renewal, termination, repurchase modification, and assignment of the franchise agreement and related information
- Existence of any arrangements with public figures
- Information about existing franchisees
- Description of existing contracts or those that must be signed by franchisee
- Copy of franchisor's financial statements

What Does a Franchise Cost?

Franchises can be purchased for less than $1,000, or they could cost $300,000 or more. The cost depends on the franchise fee and any additional investment the franchisor requires. The following are a few franchises that have fees of $5,000 or less: Jazzercise, Inc., Packy the Shipper, Almost Heaven Hot Tubs Ltd., and Novus Windshield Repair. Franchises with fees in excess of $20,000 include the following: Hampton Inn, Econo Lodge, McDonald's, General Business Services, Inc., Jack-in-the-Box, and Round Table Pizza.

The franchise fee is only the first cost a franchisee must pay. There are many other costs that can significantly increase the total cost of becoming a franchisee. Two types of expenses franchisees will encounter are common or expected costs and "extras" or hidden costs. The following is a partial list of common and hidden costs:[17]

COMMON COSTS OF STARTING A FRANCHISE

- Franchise fee, paid up front and nonrefundable
- Royalties and advertising fees (ongoing after start-up)
- Equipment purchases or leases
- Rents/leases and deposits
- Leasehold improvement costs
- Purchase of furniture and fixtures
- Start-up product inventory and supplies
- Personal and product liability insurance
- Utility and security deposits
- Legal, accounting, and professional fees
- Operating expenses for several months
- Grand opening promotional and advertising expenses

HIDDEN OR EXTRA COSTS

- Construction management fees
- Membership in professional, business, or franchise organizations
- Variable interest rate loans
- Umbrella or unusual types of liability insurance
- Option fees to buy the rights to open additional franchises
- Excess advertising and marketing costs for the grand opening
- Franchisee's salary and payroll costs for managers during the construction, training, and pre-grand opening periods
- Employment agency fees to hire managers and employees
- Extra costs for signage if larger than normal
- Fees paid to local planning, zoning, architectural review, or sign commissions and boards

The money to cover all these costs should be available before the franchise fee is paid. Prospective franchisees who do not have sufficient personal savings to cover start-up and early operating costs will need to acquire capital from other sources.

Paying for the Franchise

Once the total price of a franchise has been calculated, buyers need to line up their acquisition capital. Experts advise that prospective franchisees should have enough money to pay all start-up costs and six months of operating costs. Finding the money to cover these costs is not always easy, but it can be done if buyers approach the right sources. The first source of cash is from the buyer's own savings. Very few lenders are willing to provide prospective franchisees with capital if they have not first committed their own funds to the purchase of a franchise. Another informal source of funds is family and friends. If money is received from family or friends, franchisees should structure the loan just as they would one from a bank. In some cases, family and friends may prefer an equity stake in the business. They become part owners of the business rather than creditors.

If funds from personal savings and family and friends are insufficient, franchisees can approach banks or savings and loans for the remainder of the needed money. Being quite conservative, banks normally expect a franchisee's real assets to serve as collateral for the loan if it is granted. Franchisees would do well to solicit funds from commercial lenders such as Money Store Investment Corporation and ITT Small Business Finance Corporation, which specialize in new businesses requiring less than $1 million. These lenders consider new franchisees to be preferred borrowers. "Because they're taught how to operate the business profitably and are given proven systems to stay on top of costs and quality, there is far less risk to lenders," says Rosemary Dente of the Money Store's Union, New Jersey, office.[18] Of the $106 million in business loans that the Money Store Investment Corporation made in one year, nearly half went to new franchisees.

The Small Business Administration might guarantee a bank loan to purchase a franchise. In addition, landlords, construction companies, equipment suppliers, and related vendors may be interested in offering some type of financing assistance because they have a financial interest in the long-term success of the franchise. If these sources cannot provide all the funds needed to purchase a franchise, buyers can approach the franchisor to assist in the purchase of the franchise (see The Way It Is 2–4). Some franchisors will offer

The Way It Is

2–4 FRANCHISOR FINANCING

With annual sales from his two Docktor Pet franchises totaling about $1.4 million, Bill Diller decided to open a third shop. Despite the success of his first two stores, banks were unwilling to lend him money for the new shop. Diller was able to open his third store with a $98,000 bridge loan from the franchisor. Les Charm, president of Docktor Pet Centers Inc., says giving franchisees temporary financing through Docktor Pet Corporation, the finance subsidiary that lends money to franchisees, has helped slash the time it takes to open new stores. When Bill Diller refinanced his $98,000 loan through Allied Lending Corporation, Docktor Pet guaranteed 100 percent of the loan.[19]

direct financing to their franchisees, and others have good working relationships with regional and national lenders. Most potential franchisees who approach a variety of funding sources should be able to acquire the capital needed to purchase a franchise.

Franchising Problems

Once a franchise has been purchased and is operational, most franchisees and franchisors enjoy a good working relationship and both make money. However, there are some aspects of franchising that can strain relationships between franchisor and franchisee. The following are some of the potential causes of conflict between both parties:[20]

1. **Accounting procedures and requirements.** Franchisees occasionally neglect accounting and management reporting requirements stipulated in the franchise agreement. Sometimes franchisees even file false reports, which are discovered when the franchisor audits its franchises.

2. **Discount and coupon practices.** Franchisors are more willing than franchisees to offer consumers coupons or discounts that reduce the latters' income while having little effect on the formers' royalties. The franchise agreement should stipulate if and when franchisees must accept coupons and discounts offered by franchisors.

3. **Diversion of advertising funds.** Most franchisors require their franchisees to use a percentage of their revenue to pay for business advertising. In some instances, franchisees may use their advertising money for other purposes.

4. **Competition with company-owned stores.** Many franchisors operate company-owned stores that might compete with franchised stores. If competition is significant, franchisees can encourage franchisors to sell the company-owned stores to them or to other franchisees.

5. **Rebates and kickbacks.** A possibly illegal practice is for franchisors to accept rebates or kickbacks from suppliers or vendors of goods to franchisees. Franchisees can prevent this from happening by carefully watching their invoices and by making calls to suppliers for price quotes.

6. **Territory division.** Franchisees who have not acquired exclusive territorial rights might find new franchisees encroaching on their territory and diluting their customer base.

7. **Lack of support.** After a contract is signed, the most common cause of conflict is lack of support. Most lack-of-support complaints arise when field representatives fail to help during grand openings, do not respond to franchisee's requests for help, and do not make clear new requirements established by franchisors.

8. **Lack of financial support.** Franchisees increasingly look to franchisors for financial support to open new outlets. Conflict arises when franchisors cannot or will not provide their franchisees with financial support.

9. **Payment schedules.** A potential source of conflict concerns payment schedules for royalties, advertising fees, rental payments, and equipment leases that franchisees must comply with and sales quotas that they must meet. Franchisees should negotiate for a grace period for payments and should resist unrealistic sales quotas.

10. **Failure of the franchisor.** If the franchisor fails, franchisees could be left out in the cold with no image, no business goodwill, no reputation, no supplier, no support, and a mountain of debt.

Living Happily Ever After

For most franchisees the potential problems of owning a franchise are far outweighed by the benefits. Problems can be avoided by understanding and abiding by the franchise agreement. In cases where the franchisor appears to have too much power, franchisees can form an association to represent their interests. Franchisees also acquire power by purchasing multiple franchise units. In both cases, the concept of power in numbers applies and helps franchisees and franchisors "play on a level field." As long as the field is level, owning a franchise is the best way for some people to become self-employed and enjoy most of the fruits of their labor.

SUMMARY

Some people who choose to become self-employed are not really interested in starting their own business. For them, buying a business or a franchise is the most logical way to become their own boss. Before buying a business, people should establish the criteria that a suitable business should meet. Then the process of finding the best business begins. Buyers can contact attorneys, bankers, business brokers, suppliers, advertisers, chambers of commerce, or friends and acquaintances to assist them in their search for a suitable business. Once located, businesses should be thoroughly inspected and valued. Finally, buyers or their brokers need to negotiate the purchase with the seller and then structure the deal in a mutually agreeable manner.

People unwilling to accept the risk of buying an independent business might opt for the purchase of a franchise. Franchising continues to increase in popularity, and it is the safest way for a person to become self-employed. Available franchises are listed in magazines, books, newspapers, with brokers, and with franchise organizations. Buying a franchise requires almost as much work as buying an independent business; however, there is usually less room for negotiating or structuring the franchise deal than there is with the purchase of a business. Once the purchase has been agreed to, new franchisees move into a controlled business environment. They must follow the rules and regulations of the franchisor or risk losing their franchise. Although franchisees can, with hard work and long hours, enjoy a respectable income, they are never completely free of the boss-employee relationship.

QUESTIONS FOR REVIEW AND DISCUSSION

1. What should be included in an acquisition plan?
2. What are some appropriate criteria for selecting a business to buy?
3. What should you know about a business broker before selecting him or her to help you buy a business?
4. What are the different methods of valuing a business? Which do you think is the best? Why?
5. What are the desired characteristics of a person who will negotiate the purchase of a business?
6. What are the different ways of structuring a deal?
7. Do you think franchisees are "real" entrepreneurs? Explain your answer.
8. If you were going to buy a franchise, where would you look to find the best one available?
9. What are the different kinds of franchises?
10. How would you evaluate a franchise before deciding on which one to buy?
11. What subjects are usually covered in a disclosure statement?
12. What are some of the sources of possible conflict between franchisees and franchisors?

KEY TERMS

acquisition plan
Agreement to Purchase and Sell
asset value
business format franchise
caveat emptor
comparison of other similar companies
conversion franchise
disclosure statement
earn out
franchise
manufacturing franchise
master (area) franchise

multiple of cash flow generated in the past
multiple of future cash flow
multiunit franchise
noncompete agreement
Offer to Purchase
piggyback franchise
product franchise
structuring the deal
subfranchise
Uniform Franchise Offering Circular
valuation techniques

CASE
To Buy or Not to Buy

Jack Ferguson had been working for a large accounting firm since his graduation from a midwestern college six years ago. He passed the CPA exam soon after he graduated and has been doing well professionally ever since. His accounting services have involved him with a number of people who own their own companies. Jack has been impressed by the enthusiasm and excitement most business owners have for their companies, despite the long hours they devote to their work. Jack believes that his academic knowledge, practical experience, and entrepreneurial nature make him a perfect candidate to be self-employed.

If Jack left his accounting firm, he would probably have about $20,000 in deferred benefits that he would collect. He has also saved some money, and he has some equity in his house. Jack's wife, Emily, has a good job with the local school system and they have no children. Jack estimates that he would have about $37,000 to invest in a business of his own, but he is not interested in starting a business from scratch. The long hours, hard work, and possibility of failure associated with starting a business convinced Jack that it would be wise for him to purchase a business. Through his accounting colleagues and contacts, Jack was aware of a number of established businesses that were currently for sale.

Jack also wanted to evaluate a number of franchises that he knew were available in his area. He knew a little about franchising, but Jack was not sure that he would be able to manage a business according to someone else's prescribed method. Being a franchisee seemed too much like having a boss, but Jack knew that very few franchises ever failed. He also knew that he would have more support with a franchise than with an independent business, and borrowing money to buy a franchise would also be easier than borrowing for an independent business.

Jack decided to start searching for established businesses and available franchises. He would decide which to buy after thoroughly evaluating all his options. The selection criteria Jack established for a business included the following: total price should be less than $100,000; it should be a service rather than product business; the business should be within twenty miles of his home; the owner should be willing to provide some training; the business should have reasonable growth potential; and there should be few or no existing competitors. These criteria would apply to both independent businesses and franchise opportunities.

QUESTIONS

1. Should Jack quit his job before he finds a business to buy?

2. Given that most of his experience has been in accounting, do you think Jack should buy an independent business or a franchise? Why?

3. If Jack were to choose to buy an independent business, how would you suggest he locate some that meet his criteria?

4. Because Jack only has about $37,000, how would you suggest he finance the remainder of the price?

5. If Jack decided to purchase a franchise, which ones would you advise him to investigate?

ACTIVITIES

1. Search as many sources as possible to find a business you might want to buy.
2. Vist a local franchise and try to determine what it takes to be a franchisee and if you would be interested in owning one or more franchises.

APPENDIX 2–1

Acquisition Plan Outline

Action	Start Date	Finish Date	Estimated Cost
A. Survey Industry/Market/Product	10/31	1/1	$2,000
1. Economic growth curves—historical and future			
2. Market dominance—pricing and competition			
3. Foreign competition			
4. Economics of user applications			
5. List of companies			
6. Sales literature and financial data of companies in industry			
7. Trade association interviews			
B. Target Search	1/1	4/1	$3,000
1. Brokers, lawyers, accountants, consultants			
2. Investment bankers, venture capital firms, banks			
3. *Wall Street Journal*, trade journals			
4. Unsolicited mailings			
5. Personal contacts			
C. Preliminary Due Diligence	4/1	4/15	$ 800
1. Target #1			
a. Meet with seller			
b. Facilities tour			
c. Obtain financials and sales literature			
2. Target #2	4/15	5/1	$ 800
a. Same sequence as #1			

3. Target #3 a. Same sequence as #1	5/1	5/15	$800

D. Negotiate Price and Payment Terms for the Best of the Three Targets
  1. Valuation of the business
  2. Earn outs, contingencies, hold backs
  3. Buyer paper
	5/15	6/15	$ 800

E. Perform Detailed Due Diligence
  1. Financial—three years historical audit reports and monthly internal reports
  2. Prepare pro forma financial statements
  3. Organization chart
  4. Meet management and second facilities tour
  5. Customer data—competitors, pricing, market size and share
  6. Outstanding lawsuits or claims—government, employees, customers
  7. Contracts in force—union, vendor, customer, employee, leases
	6/15	8/15	$ 5,000

F. Source Financing
  1. Prepare comprehensive business plan
  2. Commercial banks
  3. Finance companies— commercial and asset-based lenders
  4. Investment banks and venture capital firms
  5. Others
	6/15	9/15	$ 5,000

G. Final Due Diligence
  1. Update pro forma financial statements
  2. Appraisal of equipment and real estate
  3. Audit review by CPA firm
	9/1	9/25	$20,000

H. Write Buy/Sell Agreement and Other Closing Documents	9/15	10/15	$7,000
1. Engage legal counsel			
2. Negotiate final language and terms of sale			
3. Coordinate with financing parties			
I. Attend Closing	10/31		

3 STARTING A NEW BUSINESS

For thousands of people who choose to become self-employed, buying a business or a franchise is just not the answer to their dreams. They want to start their own business from scratch and grow it to the size that meets their own personal needs. These people often underestimate the effort and expense of starting a new business, but when they finally open the doors of their new business, the feeling of accomplishment and pride is overwhelming. These people, the start-up entrepreneurs, often fulfill long-standing dreams when they leave someone else's employ and start a business that will become an extension of themselves.

Starting a business is not a quick and easy process that leads instantaneously to fame and fortune. The process is tedious, labor intensive, and time consuming, but the rewards that accrue to those who do it right are enormous and gratifying. In this chapter we will examine the process of starting one's own business. We will look at the initial phases of starting a business—the choice of the "right" business, market research, and initial financing. The next section of this book deals with more start-up activities and will cover more extensively funding and funding sources.

WHY START A BUSINESS?

Starting a business from scratch is more difficult than buying an established business or franchise, and it is more risky. Start-ups consume entrepreneurs' time, money, and energy, yet thousands of people prefer starting to buying. The following are a few of the advantages of starting a new business:

1. **Challenge.** Start-ups challenge entrepreneurs' creativity, stamina, and ability to meet their objectives. Start-up entrepreneurs can take pride in their ability to create a business from the ground up. Business creators take credit for accomplishing their goal while recognizing the efforts and contributions of others.

start-up
entrepreneur

2. **No existing errors. Start-up entrepreneurs** do not have to live with someone else's mistakes. If the owner of a business chose the wrong location, hired unsuitable people, or bought inferior equipment, a purchaser of that business would have to rectify those problems. Business creators have the opportunity to avoid mistakes made by those who started businesses before them.

3. **Everything is new.** Business creators can take advantage of state-of-the-art technology, new equipment, new systems, and so on when they design and plan their business. Start-up entrepreneurs can select their own site, suppliers, and employees without concern for what a previous business owner might have considered optimal.

4. **Job creation.** When people create businesses, they also create new jobs. New businesses typically cannot compete with established companies for employees, because they are not able to offer comparable wages and benefits. Therefore, the jobs created usually give younger and less skilled people, those who often have difficulty finding employment, the chance to work for a company that has growth potential.

5. **Social responsibility.** In addition to creating new jobs, start-up entrepreneurs often provide services not available in an area, and they start businesses that help their community environmentally, socially, and economically.

6. **Ego gratification.** People who are able to "put it all together" and start a business from the ground up take considerable pride in their accomplishment. The business becomes an extension of themselves, and they are proud when friends, acquaintances, or even strangers compliment the company.

Starting a new business is obviously not always a bed of roses. There are some distinct negatives and disadvantages associated with the creation of a new venture. Most of these disadvantages are recognized by new business creators, but they try to suppress them and concentrate on the advantages and anticipated rewards. The following are some of the more prominent disadvantages of starting a business:

1. **Failure.** People who want to be self-employed can reduce their chances of failure by buying rather than starting a business. For start-up entrepreneurs, every decision has a right and wrong option, and enough wrong decisions can lead to business and personal failure. Those people who cannot accept failure should plan to buy an established business or franchise.

2. **Competition.** Independent businesses and franchises usually "own" a portion of the market and can compete successfully with comparable businesses. Start-ups, however, have to carve out their own market share or risk

failure. Most established businesses are not going to simply make room for one more competitor just to keep the new entrant from failing.

3. **Fatigue.** Planning and starting a new business is a person-consuming job. Friendships often deteriorate, families may be unintentionally ignored, leisure is nonexistent, and other interests are abandoned when people commit themselves to starting a new business. It is not a pursuit for the weak-hearted.

4. **Frustration.** Bureaucracy and the "system" can frustrate even the most dedicated start-up entrepreneur. Permits and licenses are issued by bureaucrats who are not time oriented; construction is always delayed; bankers would rather deal with long-standing customers; newly selected employees find better-paying jobs; and so the start-up process goes. New venture creators need to be physically and mentally fit to cope with these "minor" irritants.

STARTING A BUSINESS

For many people, the most difficult part of starting a business is deciding where to begin. It is not possible to provide precise business-starting guidelines for every person; however, the Small Business Administration has a good checklist (see Exhibit 3–1), which everyone planning a business should

Most businesses are started because someone decides to turn a hobby such as baking, needlework, or carpentry into a "real" business.

EXHIBIT 3–1 Checklist for Starting a Business

CUSTOMER ANALYSIS
- Have you estimated the market share your company might capture? _____
- If you concentrate on a segment, is it large enough to be profitable? _____
- Can you foresee changes in the makeup of your company's neighborhood? _____
- Are incomes in the community apt to be stable? _____
- Have you joined your trade association? _____
- Have you subscribed to relevant trade publications? _____
- Have you visited market shows and conventions to help anticipate customer wants? _____

YOUR BUILDING
- Have you found a suitable building? _____
- Will you have enough room when your business gets bigger? _____
- Did you fix the building the way you want it without spending too much money? _____
- Can people get to it easily from parking spaces, bus stops, or their homes? _____
- Did a lawyer check the lease and zoning? _____

EQUIPMENT AND SUPPLIES
- Have you purchased or leased the equipment you need at a reasonable cost? _____
- Has the equipment been installed to maximize efficiency? _____
- Have you purchased adequate amounts of supplies? _____
- Have you established systems to replace your supplies when needed? _____
- Your Merchandise
- Have you decided what products you will make or sell? _____
- Have you stocked your business with enough merchandise to see you through the first few weeks of business? _____
- Have you found suppliers who will sell you what you need at a reasonable price? _____
- Have you compared the prices and credit terms of different suppliers? _____
- Do you have a system for reviewing new items coming into the market? _____
- Have you considered using a basic stock list and/or a model stock plan in your buying? _____
- Will you use some type of unit control plan? _____

PRICING
- Have you established pricing policies? _____
- Have you determined whether to price below, at, or above the market? _____
- Will you set specific markups for each product? _____
- Will you use a one-price policy rather than bargain with customers? _____
- Will the prices you have established earn planned gross margin? _____
- Do you understand the market forces affecting your pricing methods? _____

EXHIBIT 3–1 *Continued*

- Do you know the maximum price customers will pay for your products?   _____
- Are you sure you know all the regulations affecting your business, such as two-for-one sales?   _____

YOUR RECORDS

- Have you planned a system of records that will keep track of your income and expenses?   _____
- Have you worked out a way to keep track of your inventory so that you will always have enough on hand for your customers but not more than you can sell?   _____
- Have you determined how to keep your payroll records and take care of tax reports and payments?   _____
- Do you know what financial statements you should prepare?   _____
- Have you retained an accountant to help you with your records and financial statements?   _____
- Your Business and the Law
- Have you acquired the licenses and permits you need?   _____
- Do you know what business laws you need to obey?   _____
- Have you executed all the contracts you need to start your business?   _____
- Have you retained a lawyer you can go to for advice and for help with legal papers?   _____

PROTECTING YOUR BUSINESS

- Have you made plans for protecting your business against thefts of all kinds—shoplifting, robbery, burglary, and employee stealing?   _____
- Do you have up-to-date fire coverage on your building, equipment, and inventory?   _____
- Does your liability insurance cover bodily injuries as well as such problems as libel and slander suits?   _____
- Are you familiar with your obligations to employees under both common law and workers' compensation?   _____
- Have you looked into other insurance coverage, such as business interruption insurance or criminal insurance?   _____

ADVERTISING

- Are you familiar with the strengths and weaknesses of various promotional methods?   _____
- Have you decided how you will advertise? (Newspapers, posters, handbills, radio, mail, etc.)   _____
- Have you arranged for help with your ads?   _____
- Have you watched what other stores do to get people to buy?   _____
- Do you know which of your items can be successfully advertised?   _____
- Do you know which can best be sold through personal selling?   _____
- Do you know what can and cannot be said in your ads (truth-in-advertising requirements)?   _____
- Are cooperative advertising funds available from your suppliers?   _____
- Will you tie your local efforts to your suppliers' national programs?   _____

EXHIBIT 3–1 *Continued*

- Have you looked for guidelines or ratios to estimate what comparable firms are spending on promotion? _____
- Have you studied the advertising of other successful firms as well as your competitors? _____
- Have you some way of measuring the success of the various promotional programs you will use?

CREDIT FOR YOUR CUSTOMERS _____

- Have you decided whether to let your customers buy on credit? _____
- Do you know the good and bad points about joining a credit-card plan? _____
- Can you tell a deadbeat from a good credit customer? _____
- Have you discussed credit operations with your local credit bureau? _____
- Would a credit program be a good sales tool? _____
- Is a credit program of your own desirable? _____
- Do you know about the Fair Credit Reporting Act? _____
- Are you familiar with the truth-in-lending legislation? _____
- Have you discussed your credit program with your accountant and attorney? _____

MANAGEMENT

- Have you developed a set of plans for the first year's operations? _____
- Do your plans provide methods to deal with competition? _____
- Do they contain creative approaches to solving problems? _____
- Are they realistic? _____
- Have you written realistic job descriptions? _____
- Will your employees know how they will be rated for promotion and pay increases? _____
- Will training help your employees achieve better results? _____
- Have you provided for good working conditions? _____
- Do you have a plan to avoid all forms of discrimination in your employment practices? _____
- Do you have a formal program for motivating workers?

SOURCE: Most questions are from a checklist developed for the Small Business Administration by George Kress and R. Ted Will and from the SBA document *Checklist for Going Into Business*, Management Aid Number 2.016.

consult. The development of a new business usually begins with an idea of a product or service that would meet consumer needs. Once entrepreneurs know what they "think" consumers need, they should research their market to be sure that consumers "really" need and want the product or service. If there is genuine need, the planning process can go forward. (Most of the steps leading to the opening of a new business are discussed in more detail in the next section of this book.)

3–1 TURNING A HOBBY INTO A BUSINESS

Lynn Gordon's favorite pastime was baking. Her principal asset is a recipe for old-fashioned bread much appreciated by her friends and family. Because her family liked the bread so much, Gordon decided that others might also. She started a business making bread from a fermented mix of grains and water. She sold her bread, forty loaves a week, to local co-ops as a health food. One day she made a cold call to a local gourmet shop whose owner decided to sell the bread. Then grocery stores agreed to sell the bread, and now French Meadow Bakery has moved from Gordon's kitchen to a 13,500 square foot bakery and employs fifteen people.[1]

How Businesses Start

Some entrepreneurs have known since childhood that they wanted to own their own business, and the process of starting that business began when the decision was made. Others choose to be self-employed when they lose their corporate position, and they compress the start-up process into just a few months. Many people design and start their business while still employed by someone else. If the part-time business is successful, they leave their jobs and devote all their time to the business they created. Most businesses are started because someone decides to turn a hobby into a "real" business (see The Way It Is 3–1). Entrepreneurs who enjoy sports, cooking, needlework, carpentry, or any other activity find ways to turn their hobby into a profitable business.

Not all hobbies should be turned into full-time businesses, and not all hobbyists are qualified to run a business. The following are some tips for turning a personal fancy into a bona fide business:

1. **Be realistic.** Do you really want to turn your hobby into a business? Once it becomes a business, a hobby may cease to be fun. Thousands of people started restaurants because they loved to cook only to discover the distinct difference between entertaining and satisfying paying customers.

2. **Research the market.** Is there a market for your idea? People who enjoy a hobby have to do some objective research to ascertain whether enough other people enjoy the same hobby to make it a viable business.

3. **Test the waters.** Until you have convinced yourself and your banker that there is a market for your idea, keep your regular job. If demand is sufficient, leave the regular job and turn your hobby into a full-time business.

4. **Trust your instincts.** Many people who turn hobbies into businesses often have an unusual ability to see hidden opportunities. Learn as much as you can from others, but do what your instincts dictate.

5. **Crunch some numbers.** Determine your capital needs, decide how much time you need to devote to the business, and calculate your return. The figures may convince you to leave your hobby as just that.[2]

The Business Idea

business idea

Every year hundreds of thousands of new businesses are opened by people who believe they have found products or services needed by the public. Some of the products are innovative and unique, whereas others have been available for years. Creative entrepreneurs who produce new products and services are those who are attuned to their environment and trends that will change that environment. The following are just a few trends that might change the way we do business in the 1990s:

- Many large companies will continue to downsize. More released executives will start their own companies.
- The electronics industry will continue to experience more breakthroughs in computer and laser technology.
- Companies will place more emphasis on advertising and sales promotion.
- The information age will become more sophisticated, thus making it more difficult for uninformed entrepreneurs to succeed.
- Americans will demand that more be done about crime, disease, the homeless, and other problems of the 1990s.
- Women will have more influence in buying decisions.
- Minority and immigrant populations will grow in percentage.
- Dual-income families will increase.
- There will be a significant increase in home-based businesses.
- Concern for the environment will cause changes in business operations.
- Foreign ownership of American business will increase.[3]

aging of
America

The trend that is likely to have the most significance for the new business creator is the **aging of America.** The number of people aged 65 and over will increase from about 32 million in 1990 to nearly 40 million in 2020 and then to approximately 62 million in 2030. These older people will have more money to spend and more leisure time than younger people. People considering new ventures should consider a business that caters to older people. Older people tend to dominate some product and service markets. For example, people over 50 account for approximately 80 percent of leisure travel purchases; 50 percent of domestic car purchases; 50 percent of silverware purchases; and 37 percent of cosmetic and bath product purchases.[4]

Older consumers have varying life-styles and needs. George Moschis, director of the Center for Mature Consumer Studies at Georgia State University, has identified four classifications of older consumers.[5] The four classifications and the products and services that are likely to do well for each group include the following:

The trend that is likely to have the most significance for the new business creator is the aging of America.

Healthy Hermits. Their health is good, but they are psychologically withdrawn from society. They are consumers of domestic-assistance products and services such as housecleaning, meal preparation, shopping, and household-management activities.

Ailing Outgoers. Though in relatively poor health, these people are socially active. It is a market for planned retirement communities, medical and health services, and travel and entertainment services.

Frail Recluses. They are in poor health, and they are withdrawn from society. These people need home health care, domestic-assistance products and services (such as those mentioned for Healthy Hermits), and home entertainment products.

Healthy Indulgers. They enjoy good health, are socially active, and are relatively wealthy. This is a good market for financial services, clothes, high-technology products, and services focusing on leisure, travel, and entertainment.

In some instances successful companies are developed from products or services that start a trend or industry. There was no personal computer industry until Steve Jobs and Stephen Wozniak invented the first Apple computer, and there was no overnight package delivery until Fred Smith started Federal Express to do just that. A number of other less-well-known, unique

EXHIBIT 3–2 Unusual Businesses

Company	Product
Shoes for Moos Inc.	Black-and-yellow shoes for cows which prevent hoof rot, corns, or ulcers (with these problems, cows are put on antibiotics and cannot give milk).
Poultry Bowlers Association	Using a frozen turkey as a bowling ball and plastic cola bottles for the pins.
Laid Back Lifestyle Gifts Inc.	Humorous and unique gifts such as rubber skis that strap to a person's backside, thongs with cleats on the bottom, and the Rubber Duffer Stress Wedge golf club.
F.C. Scobie Inc.	Sells Dr. Stork's Pregnant Tummy Cast Kit—a kit molded around pregnant women's bellies which they keep as a reminder of their pregnancy.
Bug Sucker	The Bug Sucker is a miniature vacuum shaped like an anteater that sucks bugs. It comes with a disposable cartridge and special attachments.
Seat Down	A device that automatically lowers a toilet seat a few minutes after the toilet has been flushed.

SOURCE: Lynn Allison, "Entrepreneur's 4th Annual Report on Bizarre Businesses," *Entrepreneur*, December 1990, 120–127.

products and services have led to the formation of new businesses in the past few years. Some of those include the following: automated parking garages that allow customers to keep their keys; a business that provides leeches to the medical community; diet ice cream for dogs; a ranch that raises ostriches; home For Sale signs lighted by solar power; and a bicycle designed specifically for women (see Exhibit 3–2 for some other unusual businesses). People who do not have ideas for original products or services can turn to several other sources for their new business ideas.

sources of new business ideas

Sources of New Business Ideas

Not all start-up entrepreneurs are creative enough to invent a new product or service. Some of them need to locate a product or service they can use to build their business around. Knowing where to look for usable products helps reduce the time it takes to start a business. The following are some sources of products and services around which new businesses can be built:

- **Trade shows.** Many products are developed by people unwilling or unable to manufacture and market them. These products can be acquired by entrepreneurs for their own business.
- **Patents.** Some products are patented but not produced. It is possible to buy the rights to these patents and manufacture the product.
- **The federal government.** Many new products are the result of government-funded research. These products can be acquired and produced by private business people.
- **Large corporations.** Some large companies develop products for which they have no use. Entrepreneurs can buy the rights to manufacture and market those products.

- **Licensing brokers.** A corporation or individual with a new product may charge smaller companies a fee in exchange for the right to manufacture that product.
- **Nonprofit organizations.** Some institutions, such as universities and nonprofit research organizations, sell product ideas to entrepreneurs who want to start a new business.
- **Foreign companies.** Products being manufactured in other countries can be produced by new companies in the United States.
- **Competitors.** Entrepreneurs may see products or services produced by competitors that they can modify and sell more economically.

Which Business Is Best?

Being aware of trends and knowing where to look for products and services is not enough to help entrepreneurs select the best business. New business creators can narrow their decision by knowing which industries and services have the highest growth potential, because selecting a business in a high-growth industry increases one's chance of success. The U.S. Commerce Department identifies the following manufacturing and service industries as those with the greatest growth potential: metal cutting machine tools, semiconductor devices, paper industries machinery, metal forming machine tools, computer software, electronic databases, computer professional services, airlines, and data processing (see Exhibit 3–3 for more good businesses to start).

Growth potential is one factor to consider when choosing the right business to start, but it also helps to know which businesses have the greatest survival rates. The following businesses have the highest survival rates: veterinary services, funeral services, dentists, hotels and motels, campgrounds and trailer parks, physicians, barbershops, and bowling and billiards. Once entrepreneurs have decided on the business they want to start, they need to test the market in their area to determine if a need for their product or service really exists.

MARKET RESEARCH

market
research

Market research may be the most important step in the start-up process for most entrepreneurs. This is the way new business creators can determine if their product has a market, how large it is, how competitive it is, and so on. Most entrepreneurs would not consider starting a business without thoroughly testing the market; however, some have started with no research and have seen their businesses grow and profit.

For example, Kathryn Falk, the high priestess and chronicler of romance writing, noticed that no newsletter existed to serve readers' needs. Falk began *Romantic Times,* a newsletter service, without a second thought. "I've never done market research in my life," she declared. "If I set my mind to anything and follow my intuition, I can make anything happen."[6] Unfortunately, most people do not have Ms. Falk's intuition; therefore, they need market research.

EXHIBIT 3–3 23 Hottest Businesses for the 1990s

1. Temporary help
2. Microbreweries
3. Body shops (fragrances, makeup, skin care products, etc.)
4. Pasta stores
5. Computer learning for children
6. Baseball card stores
7. Import/export
8. Underwear
9. Gift basket shops
10. Men's ties
11. Mail order
12. Senior day care
13. Oriental fast-food delivery
14. Kids' fitness
15. Medical claims processing
16. Drinking water (bottled water, treatment systems, etc.)
17. Utility/phone bill auditing
18. Turkey-only stores (they cater to America's craving for the low-fat, healthful food)
19. Recycling broker
20. Coffeehouses
21. Home health care
22. Audio bookstores
23. Mobile frozen yogurt

SOURCE: "23 Hottest Businesses for 1992," *Entrepreneur*, December 1991, 73–83.

Although market research may not guarantee success, it certainly lowers the odds against business failure.

The Market Research Process

The market research process (see Exhibit 3–4) is deceptively simple. Novices know that "all" an entrepreneur needs to do is ask a few questions and use the responses to determine whether the business should be opened. Although the process is relatively straightforward, it is not easy and should not be undertaken without sufficient planning. The key to successful market research is the quality of the questions asked and the evaluation of the responses to those questions. Market research can be done by start-up entrepreneurs or by professionals hired to study the market for them.

EXHIBIT 3−4 Market Research Process

Define Objectives

↓

Plan Market Study

↓

Collect Data

Primary   Secondary

Process and Analyze Data

↓

Forecast Future Demand

↓

Is Market Analysis Favorable?

No   Yes

↓   ↓

Terminate   Plan New Business

Defining the Objectives of the Study

The first step in any decision-making process is a definition of objectives. Most new business creators usually face one or two major decisions—they either have a new product that must be test marketed, or they have an accepted product but their chosen market must be tested. In the first case, if the product is accepted, it is likely that the business will be created; likewise, if there is enough demand for an existing product, the business will probably be created.

PRODUCT TESTING. Many inventors and creative entrepreneurs thrive on the creation of new products. Newly created products are useless until they have been developed and test marketed. Some inventions are in the developmental stage for years before they are formally tested. For example, Ban deodorant was conceived in 1948 and tested in 1954; Maxim coffee was conceived in 1954 and tested in 1964; and the idea for Xerox was born in 1935 and not test marketed until 1950. Test marketing of new products should be done as soon after creation as possible so no other company reaches the market first.

Because little secondary data (that which has already been collected and analyzed) is available for new products, creators will have to rely more on primary sources (information that is collected for that particular study). This means collecting responses for a series of questions such as the following:

- Is there a real need for the product?
- Will enough people need the product to support a successful business?
- Are there similar products currently available?
- Can this product be produced?
- Is the product legal and safe?
- Are product-development costs reasonable and fundable?
- Will the pay-back period be fast enough to cover research and development costs?
- If the product is successful, can related products be easily introduced?
- Can the product be protected with a patent or copyright?
- Are the necessary raw materials available at reasonable costs?
- How long will it take other companies to introduce competitive products?

The answers to these and similar questions will indicate whether the product can support a new company. Favorable responses will not necessarily guarantee success because other factors can cause products to fail. A product can fail because the market is too small, the product is not new or different, the product provides no real benefit, competitors respond faster than expected, there is little support from distributors, consumers' taste changes, or there is insufficient return on investment. Chances of failure can be reduced by thoroughly test marketing a new product.

MARKET TESTING OF ESTABLISHED PRODUCTS. Defining the objectives of a market study is usually simpler for established products than for new ones. The questions deal primarily with potential consumers, their location, their buying habits, and competitors' reactions to a new entrant. If an entrepreneur can determine that there is in fact room in the market for a new company, then a business can be started to satisfy consumer demand. Having stated objectives for market research, entrepreneurs then have to plan their study.

Planning Market Research

Without a well-developed plan, market researchers may spend unnecessary time and effort learning about the market for their product. An acceptable market research plan should address the following questions:

1. **Why?** Why is market research being done? The objectives and expected outcome of market research should be articulated in the research plan. The ultimate purpose of market research is to determine whether to start a business; however, entrepreneurs may wish to identify other objectives that market research can achieve.

2. **Who?** Who is going to do the market research? In most cases people planning to start a business will do their own research. They will gather and analyze pertinent information and make the decision to start the business or to abandon the idea. In some instances entrepreneurs may decide to rely on professional market researchers to analyze their market for them (see The Way It Is 3–2). Consultants can collect and analyze data, but they cannot make the final decision about starting or not starting a business—that is the entrepreneur's decision.

3. **When?** This question pertains to the amount of time that should be devoted to market research. Many entrepreneurs become so engrossed in data collection and analysis that they allow the process to consume too much of their time. People planning to start a business should determine how much time they can allocate to market research and make their decision about the business at the end of that period.

4. **What?** What information is needed before a go/no-go decision can be made? At the very least entrepreneurs will need information about the best location for the business, need for the product, demographics of the area, target consumers, suppliers, future demand for the product, and established competitors. Collecting unnecessary information lengthens the market research process and adds nothing to the final decision.

The Way It Is

3–2 MARKET RESEARCH CONSULTANTS

In 1990, Charles Jenkins began thinking of leaving his job as a corporate personnel director and starting a private personnel consulting service. Charles had neither the expertise nor the time to analyze his target market, so he hired a professional market research firm to do it for him. Within three weeks the research firm's representative had collected information about potential locations for the business, most likely customers, established competitors, availability of start-up capital, and a number of other important factors. The firm analyzed the data and recommended that Charles start the business within six months. Charles left his job and started his own company, which was profitable after eight months of operations. One year after starting his business Charles said "I never would have had the confidence to start my own business if someone else had not studied the market and told me I would be successful."

5. **Where?** Where will the information come from? There are two basic sources of market information—secondary and primary. Secondary information, from libraries, trade journals, city halls, and so on, should be considered; however, primary information, collected for a specific study, is usually more valuable.

Secondary Information

secondary
information

Anyone planning a new business should start with secondary sources for information that has already been collected and published. This information is readily available, and it might be sufficient to convince the entrepreneur not to start the business, thereby, saving time and allowing her or him to consider another business. The following are some of the better known sources of secondary information:

1. **Small Business Administration.** This organization is the principal government repository of small business information. It has numerous publications, which can be acquired by anyone planning to start a new business.

2. **Trade Associations.** Most businesses are represented by a trade association, which can provide abundant information about that specific industry.

3. **U.S. Bureau of the Census.** This federal agency counts everybody in the United States once every ten years with the census, and it monitors ongoing changes with the monthly Current Population Survey and the Survey of Income and Program Participation.

4. **National Federation of Independent Businesses.** The NFIB can provide a tremendous amount of information about all aspects of starting and operating a small business.

5. **The Chamber of Commerce.** Local chambers collect and maintain information about business conditions in their area, and they are more than willing to make that information available to anyone considering a new business.

6. **Realtors.** Real estate companies can provide information about available locations, land and building prices, and other factors important to start-up entrepreneurs.

7. **City Hall.** This is the agency that can provide information about traffic patterns, new business start-ups, zoning regulations, business licenses, and other important matters.

These secondary sources possess far more information than any prospective business owner could possibly use; therefore, it is important to know what information is needed to make a decision about starting a business. What most entrepreneurs need is demographic, consumer, and competitor information (other information about such items as best location and suppliers is discussed in subsequent chapters).

DEMOGRAPHICS. Most prospective business owners usually start their market research by studying and defining the people in the target market. Some demographic data that is needed includes the following:

- Number of people in the area
- Number of families in the area
- Average size of families
- Average age of family members
- Educational level of the population
- Average income
- Distribution of income and purchasing power
- Primary purchasers of products
- Amount consumers typically spend for different products
- Major employers in the area

CONSUMERS. Although information about the population in the target area is important, prospective business owners are more concerned with the people who are expected to buy their product. Answers are needed for the following kinds of questions:

- Who is the likely consumer?
- How many potential consumers are there?
- Where do they live?
- What are consumers' quality expectations?
- How much will consumers buy?
- How often do consumers purchase the product?
- When do consumers buy?
- How will consumers learn about the product?
- What motivates consumers to purchase the product?
- How much will consumers pay for the product?
- Why will consumers purchase products from a new business?

COMPETITION. This is one of the aspects of market research most neglected by entrepreneurs. They tend to underestimate the tenacity and aggressiveness of established competitors. No decision to start or buy a business should be made without a thorough analysis of the competition. The following questions should be answered before deciding to start or buy a business:

- How many competitors are in the target market?
- Where are competitors located?
- What are competitors' strengths and weaknesses?
- How many competitors have failed in the last year or two?
- How many competitive businesses have opened in the last year or two?
- What is the approximate sales volume of each competitor?
- What sort of sales effort does the competition make?

- What is each competitor's market share?
- What is the general physical appearance of competitors' establishments?
- What customer services do competitors provide?
- What is the pricing structure of each competitor?
- How do competitors advertise their products?
- Why will consumers leave competing businesses to buy from a new entrant?

Recognizing the need for competitor information is often easier than actually collecting that information. Competitors do not voluntarily divulge sensitive information to potential new business owners; however, that information can often be acquired indirectly. The following methods of acquiring competitive information are legal and acceptable:

"Competitive Intelligence" File. A competitive intelligence file should be organized so that all pertinent information collected about competitors' operations can be stored in one place. The information in this file will allow entrepreneurs to develop plans for entering a new market with products or services that can compete with those of established businesses.

Industry Publications. Entrepreneurs should scrutinize industry publications for information about competitors. Industry publications often provide vital information about the operations of established businesses.

Trade Shows. Potential business owners should attend trade shows, exhibits, and conferences for their industry. Competitors or their agents at trade shows are willing to divulge considerable information to attendees as long as they are not aware that the recipient is a potential competitor.

Local Newspapers. Entrepreneurs should habitually read local newspapers to learn anything they can about their competitors. Business people being interviewed by reporters may reveal more about their current and future business plans than they would if they had more time to ponder their responses.

Competitors' Literature. Much information can be acquired by simply reading literature circulated by established businesses. Sales, product, and service brochures reveal how competitors relate to their customers, and they announce product modifications or the introduction of new products.

Independent Distributors and Dealers. Sometimes dealers and distributors of competitors' products will provide entrepreneurs with information about the plans and policies of those companies.

Suppliers. Suppliers can reveal substantial information about competitors' buying policies, credit policies, and other operating procedures that could be helpful to start-up entrepreneurs.

Credit Reports. It is possible to obtain credit reports about most competitors. Dun & Bradstreet, the world's largest business credit information company, has data on about nine million public and private companies.[7]

Entrepreneurs should not spend too much time collecting secondary data because, although it is important, it is not as critical to the final decision as is primary information.

Primary Information

primary
information

Most entrepreneurs make their decision to start or buy a business after they have collected and analyzed primary data—information they collect specifically about their own proposed business. Primary information is a compilation of the opinions of friends, relatives, potential customers, suppliers, lawyers, accountants, consultants, and any other relevant individuals or organizations. The keys to collecting meaningful primary data are the questionnaire and the survey techniques used.

QUESTIONNAIRES. A well-developed questionnaire (see Exhibit 3–5 for an example of an effective questionnaire) is essential to the collection of primary data.

EXHIBIT 3–5 Questionnaire

This questionnaire is designed to measure the interest in handmade goods imported from Turkey. Thank you for your candid responses.

1. Have you ever seen any handmade items imported from Turkey? Yes _____ No _____
2. Have you ever purchased any handmade Turkish items? Yes _____ No _____
3. Have you ever received any handmade Turkish items as gifts? Yes _____ No _____
4. If you have purchased or received as gifts any handmade Turkish items, what type of items were they?
   Copper _____ Brass _____ Carpets _____
   Jewelry _____ Other _____
5. Would you purchase the above-mentioned types of items? Yes _____ No _____
   If Yes, would the item be used:
   a. In your home for your or your family's enjoyment _____
   b. As a gift _____
   c. Other _____ Please explain _____
6. Approximately how much money would you expect to spend each year on such items? _____
7. Where would you expect to buy handmade Turkish items?
   a. Pier 1 type store_____
   b. Department store_____
   c. Discount store_____
   d. Specialty store_____
   e. Other _____ Please specify _____
8. When buying handmade items, what do you value the most? On a scale of 1 to 4, list in order according to preference beginning with number 1 as your most valued choice:
   Craftsmanship _____ Cost _____ Uniqueness _____ Other _____ Please specify _____

effective
questionnaires

If it is too short, important data will be omitted; however, if it is too long, it will be ignored by needed respondents. The following are a few general suggestions for designing **effective questionnaires:**

1. Questions should be brief and clear. Avoid long or ambiguous questions that lose or confuse respondents.
2. Questions should be direct.
3. Questions should be easy to answer and should usually be followed up with a request to explain yes or no answers.
4. Questions should be constructed in such a way as to ensure that answers can be easily interpreted.
5. Questions should be understandable to a wide range of people.
6. Questions should not be offensive.
7. Entrepreneurs should be honest about the intent of the questionnaire.

survey
techniques

SURVEY TECHNIQUES. A well-designed questionnaire is useless if it is improperly delivered to respondents. There are three ways to deliver questionnaires to prospective respondents—by mail, by telephone, or in a personal interview. Because each of these delivery methods has advantages and disadvantages, entrepreneurs may choose to use a combination of two or all three. The following are a few advantages and disadvantages of each of the survey methods:

1. **Mail**
   A. Advantages

   - The least expensive survey method because no "questioner" is involved with each respondent
   - No "questioner" involvement also eliminates interviewer bias
   - Respondents, who can complete the questionnaire at their leisure, may provide more accurate answers than those responding to interviewers
   - Can often reach people who may otherwise be unaccessible
   - Sensitive questions can be asked because respondents are not in the presence of an interviewer
   - It is not necessary to train interviewers

   B. Disadvantages

   - Complex questions generally yield poor results
   - Questionnaires are often ignored by recipients
   - There is a good possibility of biased or nonrepresentative returns
   - Lack of control of who completes the questionnaire
   - There is no opportunity to clarify confusing information
   - The slowest way to collect information

2. **Telephone**
   A. Advantages

- Fast, convenient way of acquiring information
- A relatively low-cost method of collecting data
- Can contact respondents at particular times of the day
- Can determine who is responding to questions
- Complex questions can be explained
- Minimal time and effort required to train interviewers

   B. Disadvantages

- Respondents can easily hang up
- Respondents can be asked only a limited number of questions before they terminate the interview
- Obtaining a random sample is sometimes difficult
- Cannot present any visual materials to solicit responses to product style, design, etc.
- Possibility of interviewer bias exists
- Cannot see respondents to observe nonverbal communication

3. **Personal interview**
   A. Advantages

- Face-to-face contact makes this the most reliable survey method
- Can usually select a representative sample
- Complex questions that might require explanation can be asked
- Follow-up questions can be asked to make sure original questions are completely answered
- Can use visual materials
- Fairly fast data-collection method
- Can observe nonverbal communication

   B. Disadvantages

- This is the most expensive survey method
- Interviewer bias may affect responses
- It is expensive and time consuming to train interviewers
- Poorly trained interviewers can have a negative affect on responses
- May have difficulty scheduling some key respondents
- Asking sensitive questions is difficult

Processing and Analyzing Data
Secondary and primary information is useless until it has been processed and analyzed by potential business owners. Unnecessary information should be

quantitative
analysis

qualitative
analysis

discarded, and what remains should be organized in a meaningful manner. Once organized, information can be analyzed both quantitatively and qualitatively. A number of statistical techniques can be used to determine the representativeness of the samples used, the reliability of responses, and the size of sampling error. **Quantitative analysis** alone will not allow entrepreneurs to decide whether or not to start or buy a business.

Qualitative analysis of market research information is a critical part of the decision process. Prescribing specific qualitative analysis techniques is quite difficult because much depends on individual preference and competence. Entrepreneurs who "know" they want to start a business are likely to interpret data differently than those not so committed. In the final analysis, entrepreneurs should use their interpretive and intuitive skills to determine what the data is "telling" them.

Forecasting Future Demand

The problem with market research results is that they are based on historic data. Entrepreneurs can learn what has happened in the past, but what they really need to know is what will happen in the future. Entrepreneurs do not have to be soothsayers or fortune-tellers; however, they should try to use their market research results to forecast future events. For example, if potential business owners have sales figures for a particular product for the past ten years or so, they can use that data to project sales into the future. One caveat for all would-be forecasters is that most forecasts are usually inaccurate, but that is preferable to having absolutely no idea of future demand for a product.

Entrepreneurs can use simple forecasting techniques such as straight-line forecasting (projecting next year's sales on a line created by previous years' sales), or they can use more technically exacting techniques such as time-series analysis or regression analysis. However forecasts of future demand are developed, they should be used guardedly by entrepreneurs who are trying to decide whether they should start a business.

Making the Decision

At some point, when relevant information has been collected and analyzed and forecasts of future demand and conditions have been made, entrepreneurs must decide to go forward with their new business plan, search for a different business concept, or abandon the idea of self-employment. No one can guarantee success, but entrepreneurs who have thoroughly researched their markets should have better-than-even chances of starting and growing a successful business. The decision to start a business does not depend solely on the outcome of market research. It also depends to a large extent on the availability of **start-up capital**.

start-up capital

START-UP FINANCING

If the results of market research are encouraging, entrepreneurs need to know their start-up costs and the likelihood of acquiring that capital before they can decide to go into business for themselves. (Start-up financing is covered more completely in a subsequent chapter, so we will only briefly discuss the topic in this chapter.) Most entrepreneurs underestimate the actual costs of starting a business, and they tend to be overly optimistic about their ability to acquire funds from other people and institutions. To maximize their chances of success, entrepreneurs should carefully determine how much money they will need to start and sustain their business until it becomes profitable.

Determining Start-up Costs

The cost of starting a business and sustaining it for the first few months is derived by creating three financial statements (discussed more completely in Chapter 7)—pro forma income statement, balance sheet, and cash-flow statement. The cash-flow statement is a listing of cash available, revenue, and all expenses such as wages, taxes, rent, equipment expense, advertising, and so on. It is this document that indicates how much money an entrepreneur needs to start a business. Entrepreneurs can combine the information from

EXHIBIT 3-6 Business and Personal Money Needs for First Three Months

Living Expenses	From last paycheck to opening day	$ _____
	Moving expense	_____
	For three months after opening day (from cost-of-living budget)	_____
Deposits, Prepayments, Licenses	Last month's business rent (first three months in operating expenses below)	_____
	Telephone and utility deposits	_____
	Sales tax deposit	_____
	Business licenses	_____
	Insurance premiums	_____
Leasehold Improvements	Remodeling and redecorating	_____
	Fixtures, equipment, displays	_____
	Installation labor	_____
	Signs—outside and inside	_____
Inventory	Service, delivery equipment, and supplies	_____
	Merchandise (approximately 65% of this amount to be invested in opening stock)	_____
Total Operating Expenses for Three Months (from Projected Profit and Loss Statement)		_____
Reserve to Carry Customers' Accounts		_____
Cash for Petty Cash, Change, etc.		_____
	TOTAL $	_____

Money for living and business expenses for at least three months should be set aside in a bank savings account and should not be used for any other purpose. This is a "cushion" to help get through the starting period with a minimum of worry. If expense money for a longer period can be provided, it will add to peace of mind and help the entrepreneur concentrate on building the business.

their pro forma statements into one document (see Exhibit 3–6), which will allow them to project their start-up capital needs.

The amount of start-up capital needed is difficult to specify, but the results of a recent survey reported in *Inc.*[8] should be encouraging to entrepreneurs with limited funds. The question was "How much capital did you need to start your business?" The responses from 1,650 business owners are as follows: less than $10,000 (29 percent), $10,000 to $25,000 (19 percent), $26,000 to $100,000 (26 percent), $101,000 to 500,000 (17 percent), $501,000 to $1,000,000 (5 percent), and more than $1 million (4 percent). Even though nearly 75 percent of the owners started their businesses for less than $100,000, entrepreneurs should have more money than they expect to need. Because entrepreneurs tend to underestimate costs and overestimate revenue, they should add 10 to 15 percent to their anticipated start-up cost just to be safe.

Capital Sources

capital sources

Most entrepreneurs are unable to start or buy a business with only personal funds; therefore, they need to acquire funds from some other source. These sources (discussed in Chapter 7) include the following: loans from friends and relatives, trade credit, loans or credit from equipment sellers, mortgage loans, commercial banks, other financial institutions, the Small Business Administration, suppliers, venture capitalists, or by selling stock in the business. These sources make money available to start-up entrepreneurs only after the entrepreneurs have committed as much of their own money as possible.

SUMMARY

Some people who choose self-employment do not want to buy an existing business or a franchise. They prefer to start their own business from scratch. Start-up entrepreneurs want the challenge and excitement of starting a new business. They like the idea that everything will be new and the way they want it, and they like to create jobs and give something to the community. Many start-up entrepreneurs turn their hobbies and pastimes into new businesses, which they hope will survive and prosper. Others look for unique products or services around which they can build a company. Regardless of how they get the idea for a new business, start-up entrepreneurs should conduct market research to determine if there is a genuine need for such a business.

Market research usually involves the following steps: defining the objectives of the study; planning the market study; acquiring both primary and secondary information; organizing and analyzing the information; forecasting future demand; and making the decision to start or not start a business. If market research is favorable, entrepreneurs need to determine how much money they need to start the business and how to acquire the necessary capital. Once some of the preliminaries have been worked out, entrepreneurs are ready to begin the challenging but rewarding process of creating their own business.

QUESTIONS FOR REVIEW AND DISCUSSION

1. What factors might persuade a person to start rather than buy a business?
2. What are some of the disadvantages associated with starting a new business?
3. How can a person decide if a hobby could be turned into a successful business?
4. Why are older Americans becoming a more important target market?
5. Where can entrepreneurs look for ideas for new businesses?
6. Why is market research important to start-up entrepreneurs?
7. What factors should be considered when planning market research?
8. What are some of the sources of secondary information?
9. How can entrepreneurs acquire information about competitors?
10. What are the characteristics of effective questionnaires?
11. If you had to collect primary information, would you use mail, telephone, or personal interviews?

KEY TERMS

aging of America

business idea

capital sources

effective questionnaires

market research

primary information

qualitative analysis

quantitative analysis

secondary information

sources of new business ideas

start-up capital

start-up entrepreneur

survey techniques

CASE
Alexander Inc.

When Ted Alexander retired from the army in 1989, he had given the United States twenty-three years of his life. He was 46 years old and was not ready for inactive retirement. During most of his active duty time Ted had flown helicopters and served as a supply officer. He now wanted to put his experience to work in a civilian occupation, but he did not want to work for someone else—Ted had been bitten by the "entrepreneur bug." Besides not wanting to work for someone else, Ted also decided that he did not really want to buy an existing business (mainly because he was unable to find one that excited him).

Ted thought that his city was ready for a commercial helicopter service and that he was just the person to start such a business. He did some preliminary market research and determined that there was only one other existing helicopter company and that it was underfinanced and poorly managed. From both secondary and primary sources Ted learned that there was a need for helicopter services, that he could buy some used equipment, and that he should be able to hire some competent maintenance people. Ted was not sure about how much money he would need to start the business, but he felt that his own savings, money from friends and relatives, and a bank loan (he had not talked to any bankers) would be sufficient to start his business. Ted thought that he now knew enough to start his business.

QUESTIONS

1. Do you think a person who has only had military experience could be entrepreneurial enough to start a business?

2. Has Ted done enough market research to decide whether he should start a business?

3. What information sources would you advise Ted to use before making his decision about starting a business?

4. Should Ted pay for the services of a professional market researcher?

ACTIVITIES

1. Try to identify some creative or unique products or services around which you might be able to build a business.
2. Answer the "Should You Start a Business?" questions to learn if starting a business is right for you.

Should you Start a Business?

Under each question, check the answer that says what you feel or comes closest to it. Be honest with yourself.

1. Are you a self-starter?
   ____ I do things on my own. Nobody has to tell me to get going.
   ____ If someone gets me started, I keep going all right.
   ____ Easy does it. I don't put myself out until I have to.

2. How do you feel about other people?
   ____ I like people. I can get along with just about anybody.
   ____ I have plenty of friends—I don't need anyone else.
   ____ Most people irritate me.

3. Can you lead others?
   ____ I can get most people to go along when I start something.
   ____ I can give the orders if someone tells me what we should do.

_____ I let someone else get things moving. Then I go
along if I like it.

4. Can you take responsibility?
_____ I like to take charge of things and see them
through.
_____ I'll take over if I have to, but I'd rather let someone
else be responsible.
_____ There's always some eager beaver around wanting
to show how smart he is. I say let him.

5. How good an organizer are you?
_____ I like to have a plan before I start. I'm usually the
one to get things lined up when the group wants
to do something.
_____ I do all right unless things get too confused. Then I
quit.
_____ You get all set, and then something comes along
and presents too many problems. So I just take
things as they come.

6. How good a worker are you?
_____ I can keep going as long as I need to. I don't mind
working hard for something I want.
_____ I'll work hard for a while, but when I've had
enough, that's it.
_____ I can't see that hard work gets you anywhere.

7. Can you make decisions?
_____ I can make up my mind in a hurry if I have to. It
usually turns out OK, too.
_____ I can if I have plenty of time. If I have to make up
my mind fast, I think later I should have decided
the other way.
_____ I don't like to be the one who has to decide things.

8. Can people trust what you say?
_____ You bet they can. I don't say things I don't mean.
_____ I try to be on the level most of the time, but some-
times I just say what's easiest.
_____ Why bother if the other fellow doesn't know the
difference?

9. Can you stick with it?
_____ If I make up my mind to do something, I don't let
anything stop me.
_____ I usually finish what I start—if it goes well.
_____ If it doesn't go OK right away, I quit. Why beat
your brains out?

10. How good is your health?

_____ I never run down.

_____ I have enough energy for most things I want to do.

_____ I run out of energy sooner than most of my friends seem to.

Now count the checks you made.

How many checks are there beside the first answer to each question?   _____

How many checks are there beside the second answer to each question?   _____

How many checks are there beside the third answer to each question?   _____

If most of your checks are beside the first answers, you probably have what it takes to run a business. If not, you're likely to have more trouble than you can handle by yourself. Better find a partner who is strong on the points you're weak on. If many checks are beside the third answer, not even a good partner will be able to shore you up.

SOURCE: *Checklist for Going into Business* (Washington, DC: U.S. Small Business Administration), 1981.

4 BUSINESS ETHICS AND SOCIAL RESPONSIBILITY

LEARNING OBJECTIVES

After you have read this chapter, you will be able to do the following:
- Decide what activities might be unethical
- Explain how codes of ethics help small business owners and their employees remain ethical
- Develop a code of ethics for a small business
- Explain social responsibility and the need for good company citizenship

S ome say that if something is legal it is moral. Others say that the business of business is business. However, most people expect business people to behave ethically and be socially responsible. The problem faced by many business owners and managers is deciding what is and what is not ethical. For example, taking office supplies home for personal use may be acceptable, but padding an expense account is not acceptable. Some people might think nothing of padding an expense account but would consider payoffs or bribes to be unethical.

We know that people have personal codes of ethics that govern their actions, but what happens when personal and organizational values conflict? In large companies, values are often part of the corporate culture, which evolves over time. In small businesses, however, the values are often those of the owner. If the owner is unethical, the company is also likely to be unethical. Ethical business owners pass their values on to their employees, their suppliers, and their customers.

In this chapter, we will discuss ethics and social responsibility. We will look at some basic ethics concepts and determine how business owners can operate ethically. Codes of ethics and policies of social responsibility will also be discussed. Although we are devoting a separate chapter to ethics, we do not mean to imply that this topic should be isolated from other aspects of business. We will discuss ethics as they apply to other business functions such as marketing, finance, and so forth.

ETHICS

Hardly a day goes by that the media do not report on some unethical business activity. Stockbrokers and investment bankers seem to get the most attention, but others such as hotel executives and lawyers also make the news. It seems that most Americans believe that business people are somewhat unethical. When asked whether people are unethical in their business dealings, senior executives gave the following answers: occasionally, 66 percent; seldom, 16 percent; often, 15 percent; and more often than not, 3 percent.[1]

It seems a sad state of affairs when only 16 percent of the executives polled consider that business people are basically ethical. Business people apparently are not the only people considered to be somewhat unethical. The last question of a Harris poll[2] was "Finally, I'd like to ask you to compare the ethical standards of people who work on Wall Street with those in other lines of work. If you had to choose, which one of these groups do you think has the lowest ethical standards?" The following groups and percentages were listed:

Those who work on Wall Street	7 percent
Politicians	43
Doctors	5
Reporters	10
Lawyers	16
Corporate executives	8
None and not sure	11

Business people may take some comfort in the fact that politicians and lawyers are perceived to be more unethical than they, but everyone should strive to be ethical.

When we hear about insider stock trading, expense account padding, and other similar activities, we usually believe that those activities occur only in large companies. The truth is that even owners of new and small businesses are sometimes unethical (see The Way It Is 4-1). Owners of small businesses need to be especially careful to be ethical because their values are often mirrored by their employees.

Definition of Ethics

Sometimes business owners are unethical without even knowing they are doing wrong. Part of the problem can be traced to definitions of ethics, morals, and so forth. It is fairly common to hear owners state that they conduct their business according to the Golden Rule; however, the Golden Rule is interpreted differently by business owners. For the vast majority it is: Do unto others what you would have them do unto you. A minority of business owners believes the Golden Rule means: He who has the gold rules, or do unto others before they do it to you.

There are numerous definitions of ethics and other related terms. We will use the following definitions throughout this chapter:

The
Way
It Is

4-1 UNETHICAL ACTIVITY

Robert L. Miller and Paul V. Fenton were both product managers at C. R. Bard, Inc., a leading medical device company in Murray Hill, New Jersey. Miller was in charge of developing and marketing an improved pump-driven system to deliver intravenous drugs to patients. As members of their division's management team, Miller and Fenton had access to top-secret technical documents and production-cost figures for Bard's pumps. In 1984, Miller and Fenton abruptly left Bard to start their own company, Strato Medical Corporation, to manufacture a competing pump. Bard sued Strato, its officers, and its backers, aiming to permanently enjoin them from marketing the pump. The judge who heard the case issued a one-year injunction against Strato's sale of its pump. Strato could probably have avoided the suit if its founders had been forthright with Bard from the outset, had quit the company sooner, and had developed their pump without relying on feedback from Bard's market trials.[3]

ethics

ideal

moral

value

Ethics. A system of moral principles and the methods for applying them.

Ideal. An ultimate aim of an individual or a society; a standard of perfection.

Moral. Dealing with or capable of distinguishing right from wrong.

Value. A lasting belief that a certain mode of conduct or goal is better than the opposite conduct or goal.[4]

Ethical Decision Making

Even when business owners can define ethics and values, they do not always make ethical decisions because of the many variables that affect ethical decision making. To make ethical decisions, business owners must first evaluate their own ethics and then those of subordinates and society. Situational elements such as opportunity and presence of others will also affect decision making, as will the rewards or punishments associated with the various decisions. Other variables such as occupation, education, and age also seem to affect ethical decision making.

In a recent study,[5] 2,156 managers and professionals were asked to respond to sixteen different vignettes about ethical situations. The following are examples of the vignettes:

- An executive earning $50,000 a year padded his expense account about $1,500 a year.

- A small business received one-fourth of its gross revenue in cash. The owner reported only one-half of the cash receipts for income tax purposes.

- A comptroller selected a legal method of financial reporting that concealed some embarrassing financial facts, which would otherwise have become public knowledge.
- An owner of a small firm obtained a free copy of a copyrighted computer software program from a business friend rather than spending $500 to obtain the program from the software dealer.

These vignettes were scored on a seven-point scale, ranging from 1, "never acceptable," to 4, "sometimes acceptable," to 7, "always acceptable." In most cases, younger professionals and managers were less ethical than older ones. The conclusion was that younger professionals apparently have a greater tendency to "bend the rules."

constituent
groups

Ethical decision making would be relatively simple if all parties were similarly affected by the outcome. However, business owners have to consider several **constituent groups** when making decisions. Decisions made by owners will affect employees, suppliers, competitors, customers, and society; therefore, some trade-offs need to be made to satisfy the most constituents. We will examine the effect of decision outcomes on each group, with emphasis on employees.

Ethics and External Constituents

External constituents are stockholders (if the company is a corporation), suppliers, competitors, and customers. Each group of constituents expects companies to be ethical and honest. Businesses that engage in unethical activity soon lose the trust and support of their constituents. Customers who believe that they have been unfairly treated can easily patronize other companies. If suppliers believe that they are dealing with unethical companies, they can discontinue servicing those firms. Stockholders can sell the stock of companies they consider to be unethical. For example, individual and institutional stockholders have sold stock in companies doing business in South Africa because of the treatment of blacks by the white government.

Business owners may not believe that they have any obligation to be ethical in their dealings with competitors—all's fair in love and war. Every business has competition, and how they interact determines the nature of their competition. Getting ahead legally and ethically is the accepted method of doing business.

Companies attempt to communicate their ethical beliefs in many different ways. Some make their constituents aware of the companies' nondiscrimination policies, whereas others publicize their commitment to fair prices and excellent service. Many companies have recently made their commitment to the environment public knowledge (see Exhibit 4-1). Protecting the environment is in the best interest of all a company's constituents.

Ethics and Employees

One of the most important constituent groups a business has is its employees. Employees are the prime ingredient of business success, and they deserve to be treated ethically. Because most small businesses are not unionized, em-

EXHIBIT 4-1 Example of a Company's Ethical Beliefs

WORKING FOR A CLEANER, SAFER ENVIRONMENT

BI-LO has launched a company-wide environmental awareness plan directed at protecting and preserving our environment. **BI-LO** will support legitimate and definable action which will preserve our land, air and water. We believe that if **BI-LO** works together with our suppliers and customers we can make a better world.

It seems a new spirit of working together is building in America. A spirit that says we are ready to tackle the task of cleaning up and protecting the environment. While the issues are very involved and the solutions complex, there are positive steps that can be taken now. Each family, community and business can preserve the environment by **reducing, reusing** and **recycling** solid waste.

At **BI-LO**, we have taken the following steps to reduce solid waste. These are only the first steps and certainly not the last in BI-LO's commitment to environmental awareness.

- All large paper shopping bags used by the stores will contain 20% recycled newspaper.
- **BI-LO** will initiate **IMMEDIATELY** a program wherein customers can return both paper and plastic shopping bags for recycling at every **BI-LO** Store.
- **BI-LO** will pay customers 5¢ for each large paper grocery bag returned to the store for reuse on their shopping trip.
- **BI-LO** will begin offering **IMMEDIATELY** an assortment of environmentally friendly paper products under the **"Tree Free"** label. These items have been manufactured 100% from recycled paper.
- **BI-LO** will encourage all manufacturers to become involved in source reduction and recycling efforts with their products.
- **BI-LO** will take steps to insure that all of its private label products are as environmentally friendly as possible–reduction of packaging material and the use of recycled packaging material will be emphasized.
- **BI-LO** will continue its program of recycling cardboard from each of its store locations. Currently, this program is recycling over 43 million pounds of cardboard on an annual basis.
- **BI-LO** will continue its program of distributing all used motor oil from its truck fleet to recycling firms.
- **BI-LO** will continue its program of using **"waste"** heat generated by refrigeration compressors to provide heat and hot water to its stores.

We encourage your participation in the extremely worthwhile effort to make our world cleaner and safer.

TOGETHER WE CAN MAKE A BETTER WORLD!

Marshall J. Collins, Jr.
President & CEO

ployees have no outside group to represent them in disputes with management. Therefore, business owners should create an ethical environment in which all employees are treated fairly and with respect. Employers should establish internal ethical principles to protect employees' rights. The following are some of those principles:

1. Performance evaluations more than four years old should be removed from employees' files.
2. Employees should have access to most material in their files and should know the kind of information kept in their files.
3. Employees' desks or workspaces should not be searched if they are not present.
4. Employee phone calls should not be monitored without the employee's knowledge.
5. Employees should be notified if information from their files is given to outside agencies or individuals.[6]

This list of principles is by no means complete, but it gives an idea of the type of rights employees should have. Employees who believe that their own sense of personal morality is at odds with the owner's ethics have several alternatives. The following are some of their alternatives:

- Not think about it. Employees can simply ignore unethical behavior and hope it will not be repeated.
- Go along and get along. Employees are pressured to conform and go along with the unethical activity. Conforming may cause an individual to change his or her own code of ethics.
- Protest. The advantage of the protest option is that employees can feel good about attempting to stop unethical behavior; however, protesting might also cost employees their jobs.
- Leave. Employees who cannot rationalize the difference between personal and company ethics can resign and look for other employment.
- Negotiate and build consensus for a change in the unethical behavior. It is possible for employees to discuss ethical differences with the business owner and try to resolve those differences.
- Secretly threaten to blow the whistle. If threatening to report unethical behavior causes the owner to discontinue those practices, the company does not have to be hurt by bad publicity.
- Secretly blow the whistle. If threats do not work, employees may have to inform some external source about unethical activities. In some cases employees may choose to report unethical activities without identifying themselves.
- Publicly blow the whistle. The major disadvantage of publicly informing on a company is that the business owner can retaliate against the whistle-blower.[7]

Code of Ethics

code of ethics

The best way to avoid conflicts between individual and company morals is to create and publicize a **code of ethics.** A code of ethics can eliminate undesirable practices that might cause a business to lose customers. A code of ethics could also ensure that employees are treated fairly, and it can inform employees of disciplinary action they can expect if they violate the code. Finally, a code of ethics informs external constituents what a company will and will not do. Before business owners can develop a code of ethics, they need to know what ethical issues should be covered.

ETHICAL ISSUES. Not everyone agrees on what constitutes ethical issues for business (see Exhibit 4-2); however, studies have been done that indicate the major points to cover in a code of ethics. One such study[8] found that codes could be placed in three clusters. The first cluster is "Be a dependable organization citizen." Examples in this cluster include the following statements: comply with safety, health, and security regulations; do not use abusive language or actions; follow directives from supervisors; and demonstrate courtesy, respect, honesty, and fairness in relationships with customers, suppliers, competitors, and other employees.

The second cluster is "Don't do anything unlawful or improper that will harm the organization." Sample statements in this cluster include the following: maintain confidentiality of customer, employee, and corporate records and information; do not accept any form of bribe; comply fully with antitrust laws and trade regulations; do not use company resources or property for personal benefit; and be personally accountable for company funds over which you have control.

The third cluster, "Be good to our customers," is the shortest with only the following statements: strive to provide products and services of the highest quality; perform assigned duties to the best of your ability and in the best interest of the corporation, its shareholders, and its customers; and, convey true claims for products.

CODE CONSTRUCTION. Business owners need to sift through all the ethical issues and construct a code dealing with the issues important to their business. A code of ethics can be simple or elaborate depending on the number of issues covered. The length of the code has nothing to do with the size of the company. Some large companies have brief codes, whereas others tend to include all the ethical behavior and practices they expect from employees and managers.

Each business owner will individualize her or his code of ethics so it is difficult to specify what items should be included. However, the following items should be included to eliminate illegal and unethical behavior:[9]

A. Illegal behavior on behalf of the company
   1. Price fixing and other monopolistic practices
   2. Bribery or payoffs
   3. Environmental laws
   4. Product safety and quality

EXHIBIT 4-2 Ethical Issues?

Executives at 300 companies worldwide were asked whether the following constituted ethical issues for business. The percentage of affirmative responses is listed next to the issue.

Issue	Percentage
Employee conflicts of interest	91
Inappropriate gifts to corporate personnel	91
Sexual harassment	91
Unauthorized payments	85
Affirmative action	84
Employee privacy	84
Environmental issues	82
Employee health screening	79
Conflict between company's ethics and foreign business practices	77
Security of company records	76
Workplace safety	76
Advertising content	74
Product safety standards	74
Corporate contributions	68
Shareholder interests	68
Corporate due process	65
Whistle-blowing	63
Employment at will	62
Disinvestment	59
Government contract issues	59
Financial and cash management procedures	55
Plant/facility closures and downsizing	55
Political action committees	55
Social issues raised by religious organizations	47
Comparable worth	43
Product pricing	42
Executive salaries	37

SOURCE: Ronald E. Berenbeim, ''The Corporate Ethics Test,'' *Business and Society Review* (Fall 1987): 22–25. Used by permission.

B. Illegal behavior against the company
   1. Proprietary information
   2. Embezzlement
   3. Conflict of interest
   4. Insider trading
C. Penalties for infractions
   1. Reprimand
   2. Demotion
   3. Firing
   4. Legal prosecution
D. Compliance and enforcement procedures
   1. The individual's integrity
   2. Company's legal counsel
   3. And most important—the ethics committee

We tend to think that codes of ethics are only for large businesses. However, all companies, regardless of size, should have at least an informal code for their employees to follow. Other organizations and groups also have codes of ethics to guide their members. Attorneys and accountants have written codes of ethics, and even the National Beer Wholesalers Association of America (NBWA) has a Code of Fair Practices (see The Way It Is 4-2). Although these codes of ethics are not a cure-all for unethical behavior, they have made employees and company owners more aware of accepted business practices.

Teaching Ethics

Codes of ethics help employees make ethical decisions, but most employers expect to hire people who already have acceptable ethical values. Someone has to teach people to be ethical. Ethics education should begin at birth and

---

The Way It Is

4-2 NBWA CODE OF FAIR PRACTICES

I shall refrain from selling malt beverages to any retail outlet which chronically engages in unlawful actions or undesirable practices offensive to members of my community.

I shall neither personally, nor through any other agency, attempt to procure special favors or privileges from a government official.

I shall never divulge any information obtained legitimately from a wholesaler in confidence to an unauthorized third party.

I shall not engage in illegal bar spending and will take appropriate measures to minimize this practice in my market.

I shall not solicit the franchise of another beer wholesaler without notice to the wholesaler.

continue at least through high school and college. Many business schools have decided to include business ethics courses in their curricula; however, some problems must be overcome before business ethics courses can be successful. The first problem is the reluctance of some faculty members to accept the need for ethics courses at the college level. Second, there is disagreement as to where ethics courses belong in the curriculum (should ethics be a separate course or included in other basic courses?). Finally, there is the problem of deciding who should teach ethics.

One managerial ethics professor who believes that ethics can be taught at the college level is LaRue Tone Hosmer of the University of Michigan. He says, "It is hard to change habits, beliefs, and values. But such change is not the primary function of a course on managerial ethics. The primary function is to teach ethical systems of analysis, not moral standards of behavior. This distinction . . . may be clearer if we consider the nature of the ethical dilemmas faced by managers, the source of the moral standards they hold, and the basis of the underlying principles that can be used for analysis."[10] Exhibit 4-3 depicts these relationships which Hosmer believes enable faculty to effectively teach managerial ethics.

Justification for Unethical Behavior

Despite codes of ethics and ethics courses, some people continue to be unethical. People use a number of "excuses" to justify or rationalize unethical behavior. The excuses used include the following:

- The act is not "really" illegal or immoral. If the act were "truly" unethical it would be illegal, and then I would not do it.

EXHIBIT 4-3 The Relationships among Managerial Dilemmas, Moral Standards, Personal Criteria, and Ethical Systems of Analysis

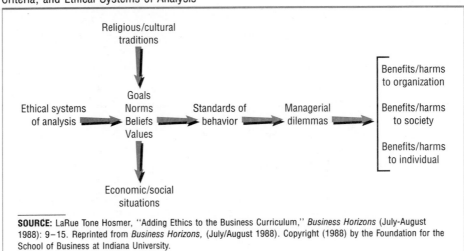

SOURCE: LaRue Tone Hosmer, "Adding Ethics to the Business Curriculum," *Business Horizons* (July-August 1988): 9–15. Reprinted from *Business Horizons*, (July/August 1988). Copyright (1988) by the Foundation for the School of Business at Indiana University.

- Unethical behavior is in the individual's or the company's best interest. Employees contend that any act or "deal" that improves the company's "bottom line" is acceptable even if it is unethical.

- The act will never be discovered or punished. Even business owners who implement codes of ethics may have employees who engage in unethical activity because they believe that they "can get away with it."

- Unethical activities are acceptable if "everyone" does them. Personal use of company property or padding an expense account is okay because everyone else does it.

All small business owners have the right to expect ethical behavior from their employees. To promote ethics, owners should develop and implement an effective code of ethics that all employees understand. Owners should also be willing to set the example for their employees. Ethics education and good codes of ethics cannot compensate for a business owner whose ethics are questionable.

SOCIAL RESPONSIBILITY

social
responsibility

All companies, from the largest corporations to the smallest sole proprietorships, are expected to be socially responsible. Companies, like people, are supposed to be good "citizens." The essence of this concept is that businesses have societal obligations which may not contribute to the firm's profitability. Business owners should contribute money, goods, or services to their constituents without regard to the "bottom line." This concept is not universal (Milton Friedman, for example, believes that a company's only responsibility is to make profits for its stockholders); however, most companies subscribe to the need to be socially responsible.

Constituents

Businesses have several constituent groups that make different demands of the company. Often, these groups make conflicting demands, which must be resolved by business owners. The constituents with whom business owners usually deal include the following:

Employees. These are probably the most important constituents business owners have because the success of the business is determined in large part by them. The welfare of employees is a major responsibility of small business owners.

Customers. Like employees, customers affect the success of any business. Dissatisfied customers find other businesses that can serve their needs.

Investors. Stockholders or other individuals who have invested in a company have a financial interest in the business. These constituents expect to receive monetary gain from the company's success.

Suppliers. Most companies are dependent on several suppliers for goods and services. Cordial, honest relationships with suppliers are essential to continued success and profitability.

Governments. Small business owners have continuing relationships with government officials who can affect the company's ability to operate and be profitable.

Interest groups. This group includes all individuals and organizations such as environmental groups and charitable agencies that expect something from the business.

Business owners who try to be socially responsible often have a difficult time reconciling opposing constituent concerns. For example, many communities are home to older companies that pollute the environment. The solution to environmental pollution seems to be simple—eliminate the cause of the pollution. However, the solution is never that simple because of the opposing needs of different constituents. Environmental groups would favor closing the business to end the pollution; employees need the business to remain open to protect their jobs; customers believe that the cost of any cleanup will be passed on to them; investors want no changes made that will decrease their return; suppliers oppose closing because they would lose a source of revenue; and finally, the government might accept reducing, not eliminating, the pollution. There are no simple solutions for social responsibility problems, but some companies develop their own guidelines for dealing with their different constituents.

One company, for example, has made the following commitments to its different constituent groups:

Commitment to Customers. The first commitment is to provide our customers with quality products and services which are innovative and technologically responsive to their current requirements, at appropriate prices.

Commitment to Employees. The second commitment is to establish an environment for our employees which promotes professional growth, encourages each person to achieve his or her highest potential, and promotes individual creativity and responsibility.

Commitment to Community. The company will constantly strive to improve the quality of life through its support of community organizations and projects, through encouraging service to the community by employees, and by promoting participation in community services.

Commitment to Stockholders. The final commitment of the company is to its stockholders. The company will strive to provide consistent growth and a superior rate of return on stockholders' investments, to protect stockholder investments, and to provide full and timely information.

Social Issues

Business owners encounter many different social issues; the following are some that most business owners consider legitimate.

Laws. All business owners recognize that they can only be good business citizens if they abide by established laws. Breaking laws results in civil and criminal penalties, and a company's image and reputation can be severely damaged.

Treatment of employees. Numerous laws govern employee treatment; however, in the absence of such laws, owners should treat their employees humanely and with respect.

Fair dealings. All constituent groups expect to have honest, truthful, and fair dealings with small businesses.

Financial reporting. All businesses are responsible for accurately reporting their financial condition. Business owners should not conceal financial information from any of their constituents.

Return on investment. Business owners have a responsibility to provide a fair return on investment for all investors.

Product safety. All products sold to the public should be of the highest standard possible and should be safe to use.

Contributions. Most small business owners accept the responsibility of donating something to their constituents. Owners who cannot afford cash contributions can donate goods, services, or their time. Donations on the scale of those from large corporations are not expected from small companies; however, constituents expect small firms to contribute their "fair share."

Environment. All constituent groups expect businesses to be environmentally concerned. Intentional pollution, such as illegally dumping toxic wastes, is punishable by law, but more subtle cases such as noise and visual pollution are often not covered by laws. Business owners should do whatever they can to protect the environment.

neglected
social issues

Neglected Social Issues

Although many companies try to be socially responsible by giving to charities, protecting the environment, and so on, many serious social ills are being neglected. In some instances, businesses believe that there is nothing they can do about the problem; however, in other instances, the causes either do not offer any payback or they are just "unfashionable." Causes that have been neglected or minimally addressed by business include the following:

substance
abuse

Substance abuse. Companies are battling drug abuse among their own employees, but they do little to combat the problem at its source: in the community. Too many business owners seem to think that other groups such as churches, schools, or the government are responsible for ridding communities of illegal drugs.

homelessness

Homelessness. Both large and small companies have done very little to eliminate homelessness. Again, they believe that churches, community organizations, and governments should bear the responsibility of housing and feeding needy citizens.

the arts

The arts. It seems to be "unfashionable" for businesses to donate funds to the arts. Business donations to the arts have declined as a result of the recent debate about the social value and acceptability of some art. Small business owners can support the arts by contributing to local theater groups, ballet companies, and other artistic endeavors.

higher
education

Higher education. Companies still contribute to colleges and universities, but a greater portion of education funds seem to be going to primary and secondary public schools.

Companies cannot be expected to contribute money or services to every worthy cause. There is simply not enough discretionary money to solve all our problems. To maximize the benefits of contributions, business owners should develop **"giving plans."** They should determine how much money they can afford to contribute and what agencies and organizations should receive those funds. There are more requests from charitable organizations than there are funds available. Business owners might want to consider the procedure used by Borden, Inc., to determine which charities it will support.

giving plans

Borden sends to all charities that approach it for support a booklet outlining the information it needs to know before making a decision, and the general policy criteria it adopts in choosing charities to support. The following is some of the information requested:

- A specific contact person in the organization
- The age of the charity, and a description of the geographical area and number of people it serves
- Names of the staff and board members, and frequency of board meetings
- Whether board members receive payment for their services
- Other sources of income
- A breakdown of how much money was spent on program services, fund-raising, administrative and general expenses
- Full details of the project. Is the problem area clearly defined?
- Why does the project need to be done by this organization? What significance will it have to the recipients and the community?
- What distinguishes this proposal from similar proposals?
- What is the budget for this particular project?
- How will the program be sustained once the company's support is terminated?[11]

Employee Rights

Employees are very important constituents; therefore, their rights should be part of a company's social responsibility program. We will discuss employee rights more extensively in future chapters; however, one important aspect, privacy, is discussed here in the context of social responsibility. The **right to privacy** is becoming a major concern of employees. They want to know what information about them is collected and how it is used. Sensitive information should be available only to those people who need it and who will keep it confidential. Business owners should develop a policy for safeguarding private information. A good guide for such a policy is the following policy adopted by a group of Business Leaders called the US Round Table:

right to privacy

1. The collection, use, and dissemination of employee information should be conducted in an open, understandable manner, with rules and reasoning behind such collection use and dissemination being available to all employees.

2. Companies should establish formal policies outlining the proper handling of employee information and communicate these to their employees.

3. All employees should be permitted to inspect those basic personnel documents that directly impact their individual employment status except for those documents that have been specifically excluded from disclosure.

4. A formal means should exist for employees to point out and request correction of errors in those records they have been permitted to inspect. And, the opportunity to inspect and obtain correction of one's record should be clearly available and communicated.

5. All releases of personal information within and beyond the boundaries of the employing organization should be strictly controlled by written procedures and closely monitored for compliance. Further, releases beyond the boundaries of the employer should be carefully circumscribed and should in general take place only with the employees' consent.

6. Only relevant and accurate information should be used to make decisions impacting the employment status of individuals.

7. Employee understanding and knowledge of company practices are crucial ingredients for the success of an employee information policy. Explanations of company practices should be clear. Remedies should be easily accessible. Communication should be encouraged.

SUMMARY

Very few people still believe that if an act is legal it must also be ethical or moral. We know that unethical acts can be legal but not acceptable. Small business owners should strive to treat all their constituents ethically. Ethical behavior is expected of business owners, and in the long run, it is good for business. By being ethical, owners set an example for their employees and customers. To help employees differentiate ethical from unethical behavior, business owners can develop and implement a formal code of ethics. The following are some items to include in a code of ethics: illegal behavior on behalf of the company; illegal behavior against the company; penalties for infractions; and compliance and enforcement procedures.

Closely related to ethics is the concept of social responsibility. Society expects businesses, large and small, to be good citizens. It is difficult to always be a good citizen because small businesses have a number of constituents to try to please. Employees, customers, investors, suppliers, governments, and interest groups are the constituents of small businesses, which make different, and sometimes conflicting, claims on a company. Although businesses have attempted to satisfy constituents' needs for a clean environment, fair dealings, and so forth, they have not done much to eliminate drug abuse, homelessness, and other persistent social ills.

QUESTIONS FOR REVIEW AND DISCUSSION

1. Why do you think 66 percent of surveyed executives believe that people are occasionally unethical in their business dealings?
2. Do you agree that all legal acts are also ethical?
3. What internal ethical principles to protect employees should business owners establish?
4. If an employee's and employer's ethics conflict, what can the employee do?
5. Do you believe that small businesses need codes of ethics? Why or why not?
6. How do unethical business people justify their behavior?
7. Do you believe that ethics can be taught in schools and universities?
8. Who are the constituents of a typical small business?
9. Do you believe that small business owners have a duty to be socially responsible? Defend your point of view.
10. What can businesses do about drug abuse and homelessness?

KEY TERMS

code of ethics	moral
constituent groups	neglected social issues
ethics	right to privacy
giving plans	social responsibility
higher education	substance abuse
homelessness	the arts
ideal	value

CASE
Ethical Dilemmas

Laura Frazier's six-year-old clothing boutique had just passed the half-million-dollar revenue mark. The clothes sold in her shop were quite fashionable and were bought primarily by professional women. The merchandise sold at Laura's Boutique was purchased four times a year in New York, Atlanta, and Dallas. The buying trips, which usually lasted two or three days, were made by Laura or two of her employees. Because the trips were purely business, the company paid all travel, food, and lodging expenses. Laura and her employees kept written logs of all their business-related expenses. Because all the cities visited were some distance from Laura's Boutique, the trips were all made by airplane.

The two buyers, Mary and Sarah, were at odds with Laura over the use of the frequent-flyer miles they earned when they made business trips. Laura contended that because the miles were earned for business trips, they should be used to offset the costs of other buying trips. Mary and Sarah, however, argued that the miles they earned should be theirs to use as they pleased. They intended to use their frequent-flyer miles to pay for their vacation trips.

Another problem associated with buying trips that Laura noticed was the difference in expense accounts for the three women. Laura observed that her expenses and Mary's were usually quite comparable, but Sarah's expenses were consistently higher. Laura had not confronted Sarah about this discrepancy, but she was sure that Sarah was padding her account by overstating her meal costs. Laura's Boutique had no formal policy manual that required receipts for *all* expenses, so Laura did not know whether she could ask Sarah to justify all her travel-related costs.

While she was struggling with those ethical problems, Laura was apprised of another possible breach of ethics. One of her sales clerks, Betty Clark, had accepted a part-time job to supplement her income from Laura's Boutique. The job Betty accepted was with another women's clothing store less than two miles from Laura's Boutique. Laura asked Betty to find another part-time job in a business not related to hers, but Betty's response was that the other store's clothes were less expensive than Laura's Boutique's, therefore, the two were not really competitors. Laura did not accept Betty's explanation and told her that she thought Betty had a conflict of interest that had to be resolved.

QUESTIONS

1. How would you resolve the frequent-flyer miles problem?

2. What would you do about Sarah's expense account?

3. Should Betty be allowed to continue her part-time job and her full-time job at Laura's Boutique?

4. Does Laura's Boutique need a written policy manual and code of ethics?

5. What would you include in a code of ethics for this type of small business?

ACTIVITY

Answer the questions in this "Evaluate Your Ethics" quiz to determine your primary and secondary ethical sets.

Evaluate Your Ethics

To identify your dominant value set(s) assign the numbers 4, 3, 2, and 1 to each of the phrases that completes the eight self-descriptive statements below. Use 4 for the ending that best describes you; 3, next most like you; 2, next; and 1, least like you.

1. In relating to a boss, I may
   a. express a lack of concern if a lack of concern is expressed to me. (S)
   b. convey impatience with ideas that involve departures from procedures. (R)
   c. show little interest in thoughts and ideas that show little or no originality or understanding of the company. (I)
   d. tend to get impatient with lengthy explanations and direct my attention to what needs to be done right now. (C)

2. When circumstances prevent me from doing what I want, I find it most useful to
   a. review any roadblocks and figure out how I can get around them. (C)
   b. rethink all that has happened and develop a new idea, approach, or view of my job. (I)
   c. keep in mind the basics, pinpoint the key obstacles, and modify my game plan accordingly. (R)
   d. analyze the motivations of others and develop a new "feel" for those around me. (S)

3. If I must deal with an unpleasant customer, I would probably try to
   a. clarify the problem and explore the alternatives. (R)
   b. highlight in plain language what I want, need, or expect the customer to do. (C)
   c. explain the "big picture" and how the situation relates to it. (I)
   d. express empathy by putting myself in his/her shoes. (S)

4. In terms of such things as personal phone calls on the job, a company should probably
   a. be understanding of the employees if they do not overdo it. (S)
   b. make the rules clear and see that they are followed. (R)
   c. do what is best for company profits. (C)
   d. explore company policies that are consistent with personal needs. (I)

5. If a friend told me he was "padding" the expense account for $10, I would probably
   a. advise the person not to; that he is stealing and should not do it. (R)
   b. figure this is common practice even if it is not right. (I)
   c. figure each person is trying to survive the best he can. (C)
   d. try not to be judgmental and see if I can help. (S)

6. If I have done something that goes against the company policy and procedures, I probably
   a. would have done so to help others in the company. (S)
   b. would be upset and need to reexamine my actions. (R)
   c. would have done so to get results in the most practical way. (C)
   d. would consider how the policies and procedures could be modified in the future. (I)

7. When I start a new job, I feel it is preferable to
   a. learn what is expected—what the rules are—and follow them. (R)
   b. see where the company is and what its orientation really is. (I)
   c. make a name for myself based on competitive results. (C)
   d. make friends and show that I am a "regular" person. (S)

8. When workmates take shortcuts, my actions will probably depend on
   a. whether the workmates are good friends or not. (S)
   b. whether they knew the rules; if they did not, I would explain them. (R)
   c. whether their actions would hurt me and my department. (C)
   d. whether such shortcuts would significantly affect results. (I)

After each statement there is a letter—S, R, I, or C. Make four categories, one for each of these letters; place your numbers for each statement in the appropriate column and total the figures. The category in which you scored highest corresponds to your primary value set; the second highest score shows your backup system.

* S: Socially oriented values are characterized by deep concern for the welfare of others. Someone meeting this profile might not see a conflict in stealing company resources to help indigent people.

* R: Rational values center on commitment to rules and regulations. A rationalist might be indecisive in a crisis not covered by specific rules or procedures.

* I: Individualistic values are expressed in autonomous thinking and the belief that people should evaluate rules rather than obeying them blindly. Under stress, an individualist may become rigid and dogmatic, ignoring others and putting his or her cause above the established codes.

*C: Competitive values are typical of someone motivated by the desire "to win the game." If this means bending the rules or cutting corners, so be it.

SOURCE: Paul Mok, SPOT (Situational Perceptions-Observations Test) Copyright by Paul P. Mok, Training Associates, Dallas, Texas 1985. Used by permission.

PART TWO

GETTING STARTED

5 BUSINESS PLANNING

LEARNING OBJECTIVES

After you have read this chapter, you will be able to do the following:
- Explain why business plans are necessary
- Decide what information should be included in business plans
- Decide who should receive plans and how they should be packaged
- Explain why planning does not end with the business plan

Many excited entrepreneurs are so intent on starting their business that they ignore one of the most important pre-start-up functions—planning. Everyone who wants to own a new business should take the time necessary to develop a workable business plan. Once completed, the business plan should not be relegated to a shelf to collect dust. Planning is an integral part of business from pre-start-up to maturity, and entrepreneurs who learn early to plan will be able to cope with the process as their businesses become more complex. For those who do not plan, "ready, fire, aim" becomes their modus operandi.

In this chapter we will discuss the relevance and the process of planning. We will identify the recipients of a business plan and present some information that should be included in a business plan. (An example of a complete business plan is presented as Appendix A at the end of this text). Finally, we will discuss successful techniques for packaging a plan and presenting it to the appropriate recipients.

Also in this chapter, we will examine the planning process in growing businesses. The needs for planning are the same, but the techniques become somewhat more sophisticated. Post-start-up planning is sometimes referred to as strategic planning because it attempts to determine what a company will do for the next five or so years. Unless they create and implement sound strategies, entrepreneurs could see their businesses stagnate or fail.

THE NEED TO PLAN

planning

Few people would take a vacation without **planning** where they were going, where they would stay, how much the trip would cost, or how they would travel. Yet many people feel that they can start a business without creating a plan to guide their efforts. Some entrepreneurs who "wing it" without a plan are successful, but more nonplanners fail than succeed with their new ventures.

Nonplanners

The major reason given by nonplanning entrepreneurs for not creating a business plan is that their plan is "in my head" and, therefore, does not need to be committed to paper. They also claim that they do not need a plan and point to the fabulous success of entrepreneurs such as James Barclay (Reebok International Inc.), Randy and Debbie Fields (Mrs. Fields Cookies), Frank Carney (Pizza Hut), and Gordon Segal (Crate & Barrel) who started their businesses without formal plans. Other reasons for not writing a formal business plan include insufficient time to plan; plans are notoriously inaccurate; no one pays attention to plans; planning is too difficult; and doing is much more important than planning. The Way It Is 5-1 illustrates the two possible outcomes of not planning.

Planners

There are no precise figures about businesses started with or without formal plans; however, it appears that planners outnumber nonplanners. Many entrepreneurs realize that they need a **business plan** which, according to small business expert David Gumpert, is "a document that convincingly demonstrates that your business can sell enough of its product or service so as to make a satisfactory profit and be attractive to potential backers."[1] Entrepreneurs who plan their businesses want a document that forces them to organize their thoughts and gives them a way to communicate their thoughts to others. The plan does not need to be lengthy, but it does need to be complete and as realistic as possible. The Way It Is 5-2 provides an example of a confirmed business planner.

business plan

Entrepreneurs who plan do so for a number of reasons. They need a "road map" for their business, but they know that the plan also serves other purposes. Other reasons for having a business plan include the following:

- The plan makes it easier for bankers to understand the business, which makes them more willing to lend the company money.
- Private investors and venture capitalists need a plan to determine whether they care to invest in the company.
- Suppliers need to see a business plan before they can decide whether it is in their best interest to do business with the new company.
- Principal customers may be more inclined to do business with a new company after seeing a formal business plan.

5-1 STARTING WITHOUT A BUSINESS PLAN

Success

Linda Schneider, publisher of Greater Houston Women's Yellow Pages, started her business without a formal plan. While working as a volunteer at a women's business conference, she decided to distribute a questionnaire to participants to see if there was a need for a women's networking directory. She found there was. A few months later, Schneider met a private investor and asked him to help her create a business plan so she could qualify for a bank loan. Instead, he offered to invest in her idea himself. Without a business plan, any publishing background, or even much forethought, Schneider started her company with $10,000 in personal funds and $20,000 from the investor. Today, her 144-page directory is in its fourth edition. "With my type of business, if I had had a business plan, I would have been tied to one market," says Schneider. "I always had a plan in my head, and that's what worked for me."

Failure

When Faith Maybury started her San Diego-based catering company, At Your Service Catering, she made two mistakes. First, she started with only her own money; second, she did not have a business plan. A year into the business, Maybury had depleted her savings and was forced to apply for a loan. She decided to write a business plan that took her one month to complete and was twenty-five pages long. Maybury's loan was rejected by several banks, but on her sixth try, she found a bank willing to make the loan. "In the plan, I included what I had done wrong and how I planned to correct it," explains Maybury. "I think that's what the bank liked." "Think out your plan carefully because it's a road map to success," advises Maybury.[2]

- Key managers may want to see a business plan before deciding whether to work for a new business.
- Start-ups that are planning joint ventures should be willing to show venture partners a business plan.

Planning Problems

One reason given by nonplanners for their unwillingness to create a business plan is that planning is too difficult. The planning process is not necessarily difficult; however, there are some common problems that make the endproduct unusable. Raymond Loen, a consultant with over thirty years of experience helping small businesses, identifies the following problems to avoid in the planning process:

5-2 THE NEED FOR A BUSINESS PLAN

"A business plan is critical for starting a business," says Susan Anderson, owner of the Kit Company, a Minneapolis company that manufactures cleaning kits for office equipment. "It establishes where you're going and what you're doing with your business." Anderson created her first business plan by reading books and seeking assistance from the Minneapolis Small Business Development Center. After a few rough drafts, she presented her plan to the National Association of Female Executives (NAFE) and received a $50,000 loan. That loan plus $35,000 of her own money was all the capital Anderson needed to start her business. Anderson has just written another business plan, which she hopes will lead to an expansion loan from the Small Business Administration. "I've learned so much from writing a business plan," says Anderson. "It was quite a task putting one together—but now I'm assessing, budgeting and projecting sales."[3]

Single-Purpose Use. Owners prepare a business plan to acquire capital and demonstrate little regard for how to implement the plan.

Benign Neglect. The business plan is left on the shelf, with the assumption that preparing it was the real value of the planning process.

Unworkable Document. Business plans, particularly those prepared by someone other than the entrepreneur, may end up being bulky, hard-to-follow documents.

Unbalanced Application. Sometimes a disproportionate amount of attention is given to one part of the plan, such as marketing or the financial statements.

Disillusionment. Entrepreneurs tend to get disillusioned when they find that reality does not match business plan projections.

No Performance Standards. Many entrepreneurs cannot tell how well their plans work because they did not include any performance standards in the original document.

Early Consumption. The business plan gets used up because no one is updating it as time passes.[4]

Developing a Business Plan

The problems often associated with planning can be minimized if entrepreneurs follow a few simple rules that can lead to sound, functional business plans. The following guidelines will help planners develop a useful business plan:

- Keep it short and crisp without compromising the description of the new business.

- Keep it simple. Entrepreneurs should be able to describe their business in one or two sentences.
- Organize the plan properly, with a table of contents, an executive summary, logically arranged chapters, and any necessary appendices.
- Select the appropriate target market. Businesses cannot cater to everyone.
- Demonstrate the benefits of the product or service to the users or customers.
- Orient the plan toward the future. Entrepreneurs should concentrate on what is projected to happen, not on what has already happened.
- Avoid overly optimistic sales forecasts. It is helpful to develop worst case, best case, and most likely sales projections.
- Highlight current and potential problems because investors will be aware of them anyway.
- Demonstrate that an effective management team is in place or will be at the appropriate time.
- Explain how investors can recover their investment over the next three to seven years.
- Allow ample time to develop an effective plan. (It is not possible to state how much time each plan will require, but Appendix 5-1 is an example of the steps in the planning process and the time allocated to each. The steps in this plan are not necessarily sequential; e.g., steps such as developing an initial product description and researching trade journals could be done simultaneously.)[5]

PLAN RECIPIENTS

plan recipients

Having decided to create an effective business plan, entrepreneurs next must decide who is to receive their plan. If the plan is to be read by multiple recipients, it may be necessary to create different documents. The information in the plans would be the same, but the focus of the plans may be different. For example, plans sent to investors would emphasize the financials and the time necessary to recoup the investment, whereas plans sent to potential key employees would stress growth opportunities. The needs of each recipient should be considered while a business plan is being written. Exhibit 5-1 presents a synopsis of the important business plan issues to emphasize and deemphasize for different recipients.

Friends and Family

Most entrepreneurs rely on their friends and families for some of their start-up capital. These lenders may provide money because they have faith in the entrepreneur; however, it would be more businesslike and reassuring to family and friends if they could see the entrepreneur's formal business plan. A well-documented plan may even convince family and friends to increase the amount of money they are willing to lend to the new venture.

EXHIBIT 5-1 Business Plan Targeting Summary

Recipient	Issues to Emphasize	Issues to Deemphasize	Length
Banker	Cash flow, assets, solid growth	Fast growth, hot market	10–20 pages
Investor	Fast growth, potential large market, management team	Assets	20–40 pages
Strategic partner	Synergy, proprietary products	Sales force, assets	20–40 pages
Large customer	Stability, service	Fast growth, hot market	20–40 pages
Key employees	Security, opportunity	Technology	20–40 pages
Merger and acquisition	Past accomplishments	Future outlook	20–40 pages

SOURCE: David E. Gumpert, *How to Really Create a Successful Business Plan*, (Boston, MA: *Inc.* Publishing, 1990), 149. Reprinted with Permission, *Inc.* Magazine. Copyright © 1990 by Goldhirsh Group, Inc., 38 Commercial Wharf, Boston, MA 02110.

Lenders

Funds secured from family and friends usually have to be supplemented with money from lenders before a business can be started. Lenders include commercial banks, savings and loans, insurance companies, finance companies, and other institutions that lend money for new ventures. Lenders are not investing in a company in anticipation of growth providing future profits; instead they are providing funds that they expect to be repaid by a specified date at a stipulated rate of interest. A business plan must convince lenders that the company will have the capacity to repay loans in a timely fashion. The business plan should also show that the entrepreneur has assets that can be used to collateralize loans if necessary. Finally, lenders want to see realistic financial statements, particularly cash-flow projections.

Investors

Investors, those institutions and individuals taking an equity position in a new venture, expect to share in the company's success. Venture capitalists, Small Business Investment Corporations, and individual investors need to be convinced that the business is truly market driven and has fast-growth potential. They also need to know that the business has or will have capable management and that the entrepreneur has created realistic financial projections. Investors are unlikely to commit their funds to a new venture if the cash out

business plan does not explain how and when they will be able to **"cash out"** (recover their investment and profit) of the business.

Major Customers

Some new companies have one or only a few major customers. For example, a computer software company might choose to have its products distributed with the computers manufactured by one or two major computer companies. Or a wholesaler may have only a few retailers to serve in its market area. Potential customers are more likely to be receptive to a new venture's products if they are provided with a copy of the business plan. Customers want to know that the new venture's products meet their quality standards, will be available when needed, and will be competitively priced. Customers also need to be convinced that the new company will be stable and will provide services they require.

Suppliers

When entrepreneurs solicit the services of established suppliers, they should be prepared to show the suppliers a copy of their business plan. Suppliers want to know that a new business will exist long enough to justify the time and effort required to establish a working relationship. Because most new ventures are on a cash-on-delivery payment basis, suppliers want to see evidence that the company will be able to pay for merchandise it receives. Entrepreneurs who expect to negotiate with their suppliers for favorable credit terms should present them with a business plan that demonstrates their creditworthiness.

Key Employees

A business plan can be effectively used to recruit key employees for a new business. These employees, many of whom will be leaving secure jobs, need to see evidence of profitable growth and opportunity for personal advancement. Key employees need to be convinced that revenue and growth projections are accurate and that they will be rewarded for their commitment to the company.

Key Outsiders

Most entrepreneurs will need assistance and advice from such key outsiders as lawyers, accountants, consultants, and insurance agents. These people should be instrumental in developing the business plan and providing important information to the entrepreneur. Key outsiders should also be given the opportunity to critique the finished business plan before it is submitted to any other recipients.

Helping Agencies

As with key outsiders, entrepreneurs may need assistance from organizations dedicated to providing such assistance. Agencies such as the Small Business Administration, Small Business Development Centers, and Service Corps of

Retired Executives require a business plan before they agree to advise a new venture. These agencies can also suggest modifications that could make the business plan more appealing to other recipients.

Strategic Partners

Some new ventures, especially those that are technology oriented, seek to form alliances with larger, established companies. The new venture receives funds, distribution channels, and research assistance from the partnership, and the large company receives access to proprietary products, a substantial return on its investment, and a company to possibly acquire. Strategic partnerships cannot be formed unless the established company is impressed by the new venture's business plan.

BUSINESS PLAN CONTENTS

Business plans are not standardized, mass-produced documents; rather, they are customized products that accurately depict a unique venture. This means that there is no single format that must be slavishly adhered to in order to be acceptable. However, there are guidelines that suggest the kind of information entrepreneurs should include in their plans to make them acceptable to different recipients.

Cover Page

The cover page, which should be personalized for each recipient, should include the following information:

- The name of the business and a logo, if available
- The name of the plan recipient
- Names, addresses, and telephone numbers of the principals
- Copy number of the business plan
- Confidentiality statement

Table of Contents

Like any multipage document, a business plan should have a complete table of contents including section headings and page numbers. Different readers have particular sections of the plan that are especially important to them, and they tend to read those sections first. If readers cannot easily locate their "favorite" section in the table of contents, they may simply return the business plan unread.

Executive Summary

The most critical part of a business plan is the **executive summary,** because it determines whether the remainder of the plan will be read or not. The summary should be written twice—before any other sections of the plan and again when the plan has been completed. The first writing provides an outline of the information the entrepreneur will expand in the plan, and the second writing reflects what has actually been included in the plan. The summary should generally be no more than two pages and should provide readers with the following information: a brief description of the company and its product; the background and qualifications of the principals; the size and growth prospects of the market; the investment needed and the amount contributed by the principals; the amount of money needed from outside sources and when they will be repaid or be able to recoup their investment.

Purpose and Background

The purpose and background section of the business plan provides readers with information about the company and its intentions. Entrepreneurs who have not yet started their company cannot provide much concrete information about their business; however, they can provide information about the concept of the company, the product, the industry, and the long-range goals of the business. This section should answer the following kinds of questions:

- What is unique about this business?
- What are the company's strengths?
- What are the company's weaknesses?
- Can the weaknesses be eliminated or minimized?
- What will make this business successful?
- What is the nature of the industry?
- How large is the market for this product?
- Is the market growing?
- Does the company have a competitive pricing strategy?
- How was the company's location selected?
- Who will manage the business?
- When will the company be profitable?

mission
statement

The purpose section of the plan should explain what a company is expected to do in the long run. This is the place to include a mission statement that lets readers know what the company is all about. **Mission statements** are brief and quite general, yet they should capture the essence of the company. The mission statement of Pizza Hut, Inc., for example, is "to increase our share of the pizza market and be a leader to the food service industry." That is certainly not elaborate, but it does tell readers what the company expects to do.

The Market

Entrepreneurs who cannot demonstrate that a market exists for their product and that they thoroughly understand the market and the competition should not expect outside support for their business. Most new businesses provide products or services already available to consumers; therefore, they are really not in a position to "create" a market for their product. Businesses without new products will survive only if they can take customers from established companies. To do that, start-up entrepreneurs should address three issues in the market section of the plan.

First, the target market absolutely must be defined. Entrepreneurs should be able to identify characteristics such as age, gender, education, occupation, and income of their primary customers. If the business is to serve more than one type of customer, entrepreneurs should segment their market and explain why different customers will purchase their company's product or service. Having defined the target market, entrepreneurs' second task is to measure the market. This can be done most effectively by relying on secondary data sources. Census data, information from chambers of commerce, traffic studies, business permits, and so forth help entrepreneurs determine how many customers make up the target market.

The third issue that should be addressed in this section is how the new business will attract and keep customers. Essentially, entrepreneurs should demonstrate how they will differentiate their business from competitors' businesses. Many business owners dismiss the competition by proposing to be smarter or "better" than the established companies. In fact, competitors are probably doing a good job satisfying their customers and will not likely greet new competitors with open arms. Start-up entrepreneurs should carefully study their major competitors and be able to answer the following questions:

- Where are the competitors located?
- How long have they been in business?
- Are the major competitors' businesses stable, growing, or declining?
- What are the strengths and weaknesses of the competition?
- What has been the failure rate of competitors in the last few years?
- Why have they failed?
- How will the new business take customers from competitors?

The last question is probably the most important to readers of the business plan. If entrepreneurs cannot show that they will do something better—quality, price, service, etc.—than the competition, then they will not be able to convince readers that their company will attract enough customers to survive.

The Product and Production Process

The business plan must describe the product and how it will be manufactured; however, it need not provide elaborate details about both. Very few business plan readers have a keen interest in production details; in fact, many readers refuse to support new businesses because they are too "product oriented." Entrepreneurs should describe their product, explain how it works and how much it costs to make, show how they arrived at the selling price, and explain what benefits customers will derive from the product. They should also state whether the product or any of its parts can be patented, how long the product will last, whether it will be guaranteed, and whether it can be easily duplicated by competitors.

The production process should be explained in rudimentary terms that laypeople can understand. Entrepreneurs should outline the basic steps their company uses and briefly explain each step. They should explain the raw materials needed and their cost, the skills needed by employees involved in the process, the equipment needed and its cost, and how the raw material is converted into the end product. Finally, entrepreneurs should justify the need to produce rather than purchase their products.

Marketing

Many companies with excellent products or services have failed because they had weak marketing strategies. Business plan readers need to be convinced that a new company has an effective marketing plan in place before it starts business. The following information should be included in this section:

Image. There should be a description of the image the company wants to project. For example, will the business emphasize low price, high quality, personal service, an unquestioned product-return policy, courteous employees, or some combination of these qualities?

Pricing. Entrepreneurs should be prepared to explain how they developed their pricing strategy. For example, do prices depend on some set markup, on cost-plus pricing, or on competitors' prices? It is also important to explain when the company will break even given its pricing strategy.

Channels of Distribution. Business plan readers want to know how the product will be delivered to the consumer. Will the product go from manufacturer to wholesaler to retailer then to the customer, or will some other channel such as door-to-door selling be used?

Promotion. Entrepreneurs should show how they intend to promote and advertise their products. They should describe the selling techniques, such as trade shows, direct calling, telephone, or mail, that they will use to attract customers. They should also indicate which advertising media—print, broadcast, point of sale, etc.—will be used to reach the most customers and create the image the company wants for itself.

Warranties and Guarantees. Customers often choose the business they will patronize on the basis of product warranties and guarantees of service after the purchase. For example, some retailers guarantee the lowest price in town. They back this guarantee by offering to refund the difference between their price and the advertised price of similar products sold by competitors.

Financial Plans

One of the most important sections of the plan—the financial section—is also one of the most difficult to prepare. Virtually every reader of the business plan is interested in the company's financial condition and its future projections. Some people read this section first, and read no more if they are not satisfied with the financial plans. Other people may not place that much importance on the financials; nevertheless, they do expect entrepreneurs to have given sufficient thought to their basic financial plans. The financial forecasts for most companies are usually inaccurate—entrepreneurs nearly always overestimate income and underestimate expenses. Even though accuracy cannot be guaranteed, financial plans should be as realistic as possible.

The financial information required by most plan readers is contained in three documents—a **pro forma income statement,** a **pro forma balance sheet,** and a **cash-flow forecast.** Each business is unique; however, financial statements should not be unique. This is not the place to demonstrate creativeness, nor is it the place to try to cover up weaknesses. Standard financial statements should be used to convey entrepreneurs' best projections of their business for the next few years.

Appendix 5-2 contains examples of the needed pro forma statements for King Construction Company. This company is changing from one that builds single-family homes to one that specializes in renovating older homes. Therefore, the income of $100,000 listed in the income and cash-flow statements for the first month reflects cash already in the old company. Sales for the following months reflect the money the company expects to earn from renovations.

The financial section of the plan should also detail how much money is needed, how it will be used, and when it will be repaid. Investors want to know when they will recoup their investment, and lenders need to know when and how their loan will be repaid. A fairly detailed break-even analysis will make it easier for investors and lenders to determine when they will receive their money.

Key People

Another important section to business plan readers is the key people section because it identifies key managers and details their experience and backgrounds. Although both product and managers are important, investors and lenders are more willing to provide capital to companies with strong managers and a mediocre product than vice versa. Key functional areas within the business should be identified, and the qualifications of the person in charge of those areas should be presented. Entrepreneurs should include enough information about key people to convince readers that each is capable of doing his or her job and has the capacity to grow with the company.

After key people have been identified and described, it is then appropriate to identify other personnel. How many employees have already been hired? How many need to be hired in the next few years? What are the responsibilities and skill requirements of employees? How will employees be recruited and trained? How will performance be assessed and rewarded? Will the employees have an opportunity to share in the ownership of the company?

Summary

The summary section highlights the important items included in the business plan. It should summarize the main points that have been discussed in detail in each of the previous sections. A short summary paragraph for each of the sections might be useful, or several sections could be consolidated into one paragraph. The summary section is also a good place to repeat key arguments

(margin notes)

pro forma
income
statement

pro forma
balance sheet

cash flow
forecast

in favor of the venture's potential. Finally, the summary gives entrepreneurs an opportunity to review each section of the plan and make sure that the sections make sense and are accurate. This section also prepares entrepreneurs for the second writing of the executive summary.

Appendices

To hold the interest of most readers, a business plan should probably not exceed forty pages; however, in some instances, it is necessary to provide more than forty pages of information. If additional information is needed for specific readers, it should be placed in the appendices. Appendices should include detailed descriptions and diagrams of the product; market research methodology and results; sample advertisements; break-even analysis calculations; resumés of key people; letters of recommendation or commitment to do business with the company; and any other vital information.

PACKAGING AND PRESENTING BUSINESS PLANS

"You can't judge a book by looking at its cover," or so the saying goes, but many of us do just that. Therefore, a business plan absolutely must be packaged in a professional manner. The plan should look professional and presentable, but it should not look so "slick" that readers immediately become skeptical and question its authorship. Entrepreneurs should write and package their own business plans because those done by consultants or other outsiders often do look too slick. Also, plans created by others give readers the impression that the entrepreneur was either unwilling or unable to prepare her or his own plan.

This is not to say, however, that entrepreneurs should not solicit advice and assistance to prepare and package their plans. Assistance can be provided by the Small Business Administration, Small Business Development Centers, Service Corps of Retired Executives, consultants, and other experienced entrepreneurs. Entrepreneurs should take advantage of all the plan-writing assistance that is available; however, the final document should reflect their own ideas and plans.

Packaging Business Plans

Small business expert, David Gumpert, makes the following packaging suggestions:[6]

Make it Businesslike. The plan should look neither too slick nor too shabby. Too slick could be leather binding and Linotronic typesetting. Too shabby could be faded Xerox pages stapled together. Using simple desktop publishing, entrepreneurs can create a plan that is interesting and readable.

Look for Ways to Make the Plan Stand Out. People such as bankers and investors receive numerous business plans each year and read only a few. The ones they tend to read are those that have some distinguishing feature. Creative use of photographs or drawings, or the inclusion of a sample of the product, make plans more noticeable.

Tend to the Details. Be sure to include a cover page with the company's phone number and a table of contents with page numbers. The plan must have been proofread by the writer and an outsider to catch any typographical and spelling errors. Minor errors may cause readers to ignore the plan.

Limit Access. Business plans are not for general consumption. Rather, they are sent to specific people who have been identified as decision makers. The following techniques help entrepreneurs limit the circulation of their business plan:

- **Number the plans.** Place the number, preferably below 10 or 12, of each plan prominently on the cover. This indicates that there are only limited copies of the plan and that each one's reader has been identified.

- **Include a statement that copying is prohibited.** Included on the cover or the table of contents should be a simple statement such as "The contents of this plan are proprietary and confidential. It is not to be copied or duplicated in any way."

- **Have readers sign confidentiality statements.** Most readers will not object to signing a statement that prohibits them from discussing a business plan with unauthorized people.

Presenting Business Plans

Many investors and lenders will request a written business plan before they agree to meet with an entrepreneur to discuss the plan. This is not advantageous for entrepreneurs because they will not have the opportunity to explain any potentially confusing sections of the plan. It is better in all instances to try to present the business plan in person. Entrepreneurs fortunate enough to be able to present their plans personally should keep the following points in mind:

Keep It Short and to the Point. Entrepreneurs should be prepared to present their plan in less than one hour. Like the written plan, the presentation should be concise and easy to understand. Entrepreneurs need to emphasize the executive summary and highlight only the critical areas of the plan.

Use Visual Aids. In our visually oriented society, aids such as slides, overheads, graphs, flip charts, and so on, keep people focused on the important points of the plan presentation.

Involve Other Key Personnel. If there is a management team starting the company, each should present the part of the plan for which he or she will be responsible. This lends credibility to the plan and convinces those in the audience that the company is not a "one-person band."

Try to Demonstrate the Product or Service. If possible, bring a sample that listeners can hold and touch or watch being demonstrated. Few of us would buy a product or service if we had not had the opportunity to "test" it or "try it on" before we parted with our money.[7]

Oral presentations are frightening to many entrepreneurs who are afraid of making fools of themselves or of making a mistake that will "kill the deal."

When presenting a business plan, bring a sample of your product that listeners can hold and touch or watch being demonstrated.

The fear of presentations, particularly to lenders and investors, can be minimized if entrepreneurs know what people expect of a presentation. Investors and lenders base their decisions on answers to the following questions:

- Has the entrepreneur fully prepared herself or himself to make an oral presentation of the plan?
- How well does the entrepreneur explain the company's product and market?
- How well does the entrepreneur sell the company and its concept?
- Is the entrepreneur really market oriented, or is he or she too product oriented?
- Does the entrepreneur have the necessary experience and expertise to operate a company?
- Does the entrepreneur respond intelligently to questions from the audience?
- Is the entrepreneur physically presentable?
- Can the entrepreneur accept constructive criticism?
- What is the interpersonal "chemistry" between the entrepreneur and the investors? [8]

BEYOND BUSINESS PLANS

A complete business plan is only the first document produced in the continuing planning process. Start-up entrepreneurs write their business plan for a specific purpose—to acquire the resources needed to start the business. Once started, businesses will require additional plans or strategies to continue growing. Some occasions requiring **strategic plans** include the following: acquiring expansion capital, adding new products to the company's product line, relocating to larger facilities, vertically integrating, acquiring another company, and so forth.

strategic plans

Strategies can be formulated and implemented if entrepreneurs collect and analyze information that helps answer the following questions:

1. What business am I in?
2. What are my five greatest expenses, and how can I reduce them?
3. Who are my customers; how can I reach them most effectively; and how are they changing?
4. What market segment(s) do I want?
5. What new products, or manufacturing techniques, or suppliers, are available in the near term? Within a year? Within three to five years?
6. How well is my management performing? How well can they cope with growth?
7. Which of my major investments are most nearly obsolete? Machinery? Buildings? Key personnel?
8. How much do my key financial indicators vary from month to month?[9]

Business owners who create a successful initial business plan gain the experience needed to continue planning and developing effective strategies. The **strategy development process** (see Exhibit 5-2) starts with an analysis of the company and an identification of goals and objectives. Then owners select the best strategies, consistent with company policies and the external environment, to achieve their objectives. As companies grow, this process becomes more complex and requires input from key executives and employees.

strategy development process

EXHIBIT 5-2 The Strategy Process

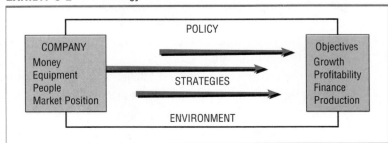

Company Analysis

Determining where a company should go without knowing where it has been is virtually impossible, so the first step in the strategy creation process is a company analysis. This analysis includes evaluation of past activities and the company's current status. A successful analysis requires owners to identify the strengths and weaknesses of critical elements within their company. Money, equipment, people, and market position are some of the key factors that should be evaluated.

MONEY. A company's financial position and its access to and utilization of capital provide crucial information around which to develop sound strategies. Internal scanning usually focuses initially on financial condition because it is so vital to a company's continued existence. If, for example, analysis revealed that a company's financial condition was very tenuous, the only rational strategy to adopt would be one aimed at survival. However, if the financial condition were sound, then the company's strategy might be one of growth, acquisition, new product development, or any of a number of other possibilities.

EQUIPMENT. Once a company's financial position has been analyzed, focus should be shifted to facilities and equipment. The condition of a company's physical plant and equipment should be periodically evaluated to make strategic remodeling or replacement decisions. After all, if the building is in poor condition, strategies that ignore restoration would be inappropriate and impractical. Besides considering the condition and suitability of the physical plant, owners should also analyze the quality and reliability of their machinery and other equipment.

PEOPLE. For most businesses, people are often the key to success or the cause of failure. Business owners should evaluate the strengths and weaknesses of their employees before creating any long-range strategies that involve their services. Companies that have been in existence for only a year or two usually have just a few employees who are often treated as part of the family. The company owner works long hours, and the employees are expected to do likewise. There is a sense of excitement and enthusiasm, and everyone pulls together to make the company a success. However, once the business stabilizes and then begins to grow, some of the enthusiasm and camaraderie are replaced by more formal working relationships.

MARKET POSITION. Before business owners can formulate long-range strategies, they should assess the company's basic market and its position in that market. For small companies, the geographic scope of their market is quite limited; however, growth will probably extend a company's market area to other states and regions. Entry into each new region requires careful planning and strategy formulation. In addition to developing an awareness of geographic markets, owners will have to assess their company's position in its market. A growing company will usually control a small but increasing share of the market. If market dominance is a viable objective, then the company's strategies should be formulated to achieve this goal.

Company Objectives

If companies are to have effective strategies, they need well-defined, measurable objectives that conform to the basic mission. Business owners should initially develop objectives, some of which may already be part of the business plan, for such areas as finance, sales, personnel, and production.

FINANCE. The company should have clearly stated and realistic profitability goals. It should also have plans for how funds will be acquired and dispersed. Without specific profit objectives, a company's progress cannot be accurately measured.

SALES. Owners should establish realistic sales targets for their business. Sales objectives may be stated as a percentage increase over last year's sales or as a discrete dollar amount.

PERSONNEL. Growing businesses need to acquire new employees. Objectives should be established for how many people will be needed, where they will be recruited, how they will be trained, and so forth.

PRODUCTION. Most companies strive for efficiency in their general operations. Production objectives specify acceptable levels of efficiency based on employee productivity, quality assurance, etc.

Growth Strategies

Analyzing company strengths and setting objectives are precursors to developing viable strategies that will achieve the stated objectives. For many companies, growth and profitability are principal objectives that can be achieved by employing such strategies as internal growth, vertical integration, diversification, and merger or acquisition.

INTERNAL GROWTH. The most common form of growth for small businesses is to simply produce or sell more of the original product. Owners often select strategies that enable them to sell more than their competitors, expand their facilities or move to larger ones, or become the dominant factor in the market.

vertical
integration

forward
integration

backward
integration

VERTICAL INTEGRATION. If internal growth stalls, business owners might consider integrating their company. Vertical integration can be either forward or backward. **Forward integration** involves the development of wholesaling or retailing activities by a company that used to rely on independents for these functions. **Backward integration** occurs when a manufacturer or other type of business acquires its source of supplies or raw materials.

diversification

DIVERSIFICATION. **Diversification** entails the introduction of new or different products or services to a company's traditional customers or to a new market. If a company is not able to develop a new item to add to its product line, it may consider purchasing another company that has the desired product.

MERGER OR ACQUISITION. For many young companies, normal internal growth may be too slow or opportunities may be limited. For these companies, **merger** or **acquisition** may be the strategy necessary to realize growth objectives. Owners who choose to acquire or merge with other companies need to carefully analyze the target company to insure a good strategic fit with their own business.

merger

acquisition

Strategy Constraints

Without constraints, owners could conceivably create an infinite number of strategies that might meet their objectives. However, there are internal and external constraints that limit the number of acceptable strategies. Internal constraints are company policies and external constraints are environmental factors.

POLICIES. Policies are essentially guides to carrying out actions or strategies. They define the parameters or boundaries within which strategies can be created. Policies that have been developed and accepted by a company determine which strategies are acceptable and which are not. For example, if company policy required a commitment to high ethical standards, growth strategies that included bribes or kickbacks would be unacceptable. Small businesses may function for years with only implicit policies; however, as they grow, it may be necessary to make company policies more explicit.

THE ENVIRONMENT. The environment in which a company exists constrains strategy creation. The following are just some of the environmental factors that affect a company's strategy creation process: economic factors such as interest rates, unemployment, inflation, and so forth; technological forces; sociocultural and demographic factors; political forces; and competitive forces. These factors all limit a company's strategic choices. For example, if a recession seemed imminent, business owners would not be likely to create optimistic growth strategies.

Evaluation of Strategies

Before implementing strategies, business owners should evaluate those they have created to determine which are most likely to be successful. Establishing criteria for evaluating strategy can be difficult but needs to be done. A number of different measures could be used to determine how successful a strategy is likely to be. One way to evaluate strategies is to ask several pertinent questions such as the following:

- Is the strategy identifiable, and has it been made clear in words or in practice?
- Is the strategy consistent with company competence and resources?
- Are the major provisions of the strategy and the program of major policies of which it is comprised internally consistent?
- Is the chosen level of risk feasible in economic and personal terms?
- Is the strategy appropriate to the personal values and aspirations of the key managers?
- Is the strategy appropriate to the desired level of contribution to society?
- Does the strategy constitute a clear stimulus to organizational effort and commitment?

These questions might help owners discard unsatisfactory strategies; however, the real evaluation of a strategy can only be conducted after it has been implemented.[10]

SUMMARY

Business planning is a crucial part of the start-up process that can get overlooked by busy entrepreneurs intent on opening a new business. Entrepreneurs should prepare a business plan that covers at least the following aspects of the company: purpose of the business; the market and marketing; the product and production process; key managers; and financial plans. A well-developed business plan will help lenders, investors, suppliers, customers, and others determine whether they care to associate with the proposed business. The formal business plan also becomes the basis for most future planning once the company is operational.

Planning never ends, it just becomes more sophisticated and complex. Business owners will have occasion to develop strategies to enable their companies to overcome obstacles and take advantage of opportunities. Strategies should be created to increase internal growth, evaluate diversification opportunities, compare merger or acquisition candidates, and avoid mistakes that could lead to the company's decline. To create effective strategies, owners and their key managers should study the company's history, evaluate environmental factors, select the strategy most likely to succeed, implement it, and evaluate the relative success of the selected strategy.

QUESTIONS FOR REVIEW AND DISCUSSION

1. Do you think most entrepreneurs should have a formal business plan?
2. Why do some people refuse to write a business plan?
3. What are some of the problems associated with business planning?
4. Who should be given a copy of an entrepreneur's business plan?
5. Why is the executive summary such an important part of a business plan?

6. How can entrepreneurs package their plans to make them appealing to recipients?
7. How can an entrepreneur's oral presentation of the business plan be evaluated?
8. How do most business owners create strategies that help their companies achieve goals and objectives?
9. What occasions in a company's growth process usually require the creation of formal strategies?
10. How can business owners evaluate strategies?

KEY TERMS

acquisition	mission statement
backward integration	plan recipients
business plan	planning
cash flow forecast	pro forma balance sheet
cash out	pro forma income statement
diversification	strategic partners
executive summary	strategic plans
forward integration	strategy development process
merger	vertical integration

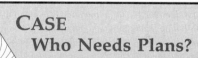

CASE
Who Needs Plans?

For eight years after graduating from technical school, Tom Johnson had worked for Hansen's Appliance Company. His chief responsibilities were to deliver and repair major appliances sold by Hansen's sales staff. Occasionally, Tom was allowed to sell appliances, but the commissioned salespeople frowned on that practice because it reduced their take-home pay. Besides, Tom was not a particularly good salesperson. He did not have the confidence or product knowledge that other salespeople did, nor was he very comfortable with customers. Tom realized that his strength was appliance repair.

After eight years with Hansen's, Tom decided that he could just as easily be self-employed. With very little serious thought or planning, he informed Jim Hansen that he intended to leave and gave the required two weeks' notice. Tom was told by his friends and former instructors that he should develop a business plan before he started his own business, but he ignored the advice. Why did he need a plan when he was completely familiar with the repair business? Besides, he was going to offer another service that most appliance repair businesses did not—he would rent appliances to people who could not afford to buy them.

During his final two weeks at Hansen's, Tom found a location for his business and decided to name his company Johnson's Appliance Rentals and Repairs. He had enough money to see him through the first two or three months of operations by which time he expected to be making a profit. He saw no need to advertise because he was sure the people whose appliances he serviced while at Hansen's would continue to use his services. Tom did not plan to use the services of an attorney or accountant because his business was a sole proprietorship and he knew a little about bookkeeping. There was no need to plan for personnel because Tom had friends who could help him during busy periods. At the completion of his final two weeks Tom left Hansen's, moved to his new location, put out a sign, and was "ready" for business.

QUESTIONS

1. Does a business as small as the one proposed by Tom need a business plan?

2. If Tom had written a business plan, what information should it have contained?

3. Do you think people whose appliances Tom repaired when he was at Hansen's will become his customers?

4. Given Tom's limited finances, is his rental business idea realistic?

5. Do you think Tom's new business is likely to succeed?

6. If you answered no, do you think a business plan would have made a difference?

ACTIVITY

1. Executive Summaries. The following four executive summaries are composites based on real executive summaries. Read each carefully, and then answer the following questions:
   a. Which two are the most effective summaries?
   b. Which two are the least effective summaries?
   c. In the best executive summaries, describe the three most important strengths.
   d. In the worst executive summaries, list the three most significant weaknesses.

Executive Summary: Rodney Foster Associates

Rodney Foster Associates is a highly qualified group of public relations executives based in Indianapolis, Indiana. The president is Mr. Foster, who is highly experienced, first as a business reporter with the Associated Press and then as chief of public relations for PepsiCoke. All five of the firm's top representatives have experience at Fortune 500 companies in either public relations or corporate communications.

At Rodney Foster Associates we pride ourselves on our ability to write clearly and design attractive media kits. This combination of skills enables us to produce excellent public relations materials that make our clients look their best to the outside world.

We expect our growing reputation to lead to the new clients necessary to support our anticipated growth. As clients see the attractive news releases and media kits that we produce, we are certain that word about our skills will spread, leading to new contracts via referrals. This approach will allow Rodney Foster Associates to concentrate on producing the best-quality media materials, without being diverted by the need to spend time and resources on marketing and sales.

In our first three years we have received seven small contracts, but we expect that as our reputation spreads, our work load will increase. When this occurs, we will need additional well-qualified public relations representatives.

In addition, our skills are expanding. We are preparing to organize seminars for clients and train them for television appearances. We expect Rodney Foster Associates to become a full-service public relations firm, capable of taking on any assignment. We will work with any type of client, preferring not to limit ourselves to any one industry or type of company.

As our public relations reputation and skills expand, we expect to add four more public relations professionals to the six we now have and two administrative assistants to the three we now have, all within the next four years.

Rodney Foster Associates has operated at near break-even during its first three years, but we expect the local corporate world to seek out our services and enable us to achieve our growth objectives over the next four years.

SOURCE: David E. Gumpert, *How to Really Create a Successful Business Plan* (Boston, MA: *Inc.* Publishing, 1990), pp. 50–54. Reprinted with permission, *Inc.* Magazine. Copyright © 1990 by Goldhirsh Group Inc., 38 Commercial Wharf, Boston, MA 02110.

Executive Summary: The Kansas City Architectural Group

The Kansas City Architectural Group is a nine-person firm that includes six well-trained and experienced architects supported by two drafters and an administrative assistant. Gross revenues have averaged $550,000 annually, mainly in medical office design, over the past three years. During the last year, sales began to increase.

The firm's goal is to pass the $1 million mark within three years and the $1.3 million mark in five years. We will require fourteen people to handle the $1 million sales.

The Kansas City Architectural Group expects to achieve its revenue goals through an aggressive marketing program that includes

· Direct contacts provided by existing clients and networking
· Regularly planned publication of newspaper and magazine articles describing its work and its viewpoints

- Seminars for existing and prospective clients on new architectural approaches for improving the operations of systems in aging facilities
- An expanded public relations effort that includes news releases announcing contracts received and human interest stories about our personnel

All employees consider themselves an important part of the firm's marketing effort. This attitude and approach has enabled the firm to grow to its present size in only three years and is expected to lead to a near doubling in size over the next three years.

By concentrating on designing medical facilities, the Kansas City Architectural Group does not allow itself to be distracted from what it does best. The firm intends to continue in the area of medical facilities in an effort to undertake larger projects.

The firm encourages its staff members to improve their professional skills by sending them to professional meetings and contributing to the cost of additional education. Because of its efforts to recognize and stimulate employee growth, the Kansas City Architectural Group has had minimal employee turnover. Its employees truly are and will remain its most important asset as the firm continues its rapid growth.

The firm now has a $200,000 revolving line of credit with the First National Bank of Kansas City. It seeks to increase that by $100,000 in each of the next three years, in line with expected revenue growth.

Executive Summary: The Green Thumb

The Green Thumb is a highly successful garden center that is rapidly outgrowing its existing Chicago facilities. The company plans to renovate and expand its facilities to increase per-customer sales to existing customers and to attract more new upscale customers.

Such expansion and renovation will enable the company to achieve sales over the next three years of $3.1 million and over the next five years of $4 million from expected 1990 sales of $1.8 million. Moreover, pretax profit margins are expected to increase to between 17 and 22 percent from the current 5 percent.

The renovation and expansion will enable the company to capitalize further on its premier location on Broadway on the north side serving an urban market not extremely knowledgeable about horticultural products and thus open to sales upgrades. The facilities improvement will also enable the company to build sales during traditionally slow periods and fill in the gaps between the three existing peaks of spring, fall, and Christmas.

The company also seeks to reduce high work-force turnover brought on by the seasonal sales fluctuations. The Green Thumb in its improved facilities will be able to capitalize on its more even sales by retaining a highly trained work force. This work force can use its knowledge about horticultural products to improve sales effectiveness.

Similarly, the company seeks to sell high-priced, high-margin containers, lawn furniture, and gift items it does not have space to stock in its existing facilities; such items are necessary to substantially increase revenues and profits. The new facilities will enable management to take advantage of its superior knowledge of the intricate supply side in horticultural products to expand its product line. The company has already taken steps to guarantee an increase in low-cost annual and perennial supplies by leasing 43 acres of land in Palos Heights.

The company has built an experienced and expert management team to work with its founder and chief executive officer, Bradley Turner, to take maximum advantage of the expanded facilities. Moreover, the company plans to provide intense training and equity incentives to upgrade its entire staff and motivate it to aspire to management positions.

The Green Thumb seeks a $500,000 bank loan to finance the facilities upgrading. The renovation and expansion will involve three phases to be completed over a year. Substantial revenue growth should become apparent within two years. The company seeks an agreement that will provide for loan repayment over eight years.

Executive Summary: Cherry Tree Technologies

Cherry Tree Technologies publishes ONLINE, a widely recognized disk monthly for Compaq computers. Periodical disk publishing is in its infancy, and Cherry Tree Technologies has the opportunity to become a market leader for all PC disk publications. ONLINE has proved the viability and potential profitability of its magazine on a disk or disk monthly concept and has expanded its success on Compaq computers.

Some of the primary benefits to subscribers of ONLINE are

1. Variety or programs
2. Entertainment value
3. Overall usefulness
4. Low cost
5. Ease of use

The ONLINE publications by Cherry Tree Technologies are the primary source of revenue for the company at this time. However, there are additional software sales through ONLINE's catalog of products to which it has the rights and a small amount of sales of software from other vendors. The company plans to expand its software sales area as it grows to provide more complete services to the PC aftermarket subscriber base.

The ONLINE Disk Monthly is not a concept unique to Cherry Tree, but the success it has achieved in recent months is unparalleled. The competition to date in this field has been weak or unsuccessful, and ONLINE currently has the opportunity to capture the leadership position for all disk publications.

The company, founded in 1984, spent 1985 determining the best path for success and can now concentrate on a dramatic growth opportunity currently available to it. Through the first eight months of 1986, the company achieved $350,000 sales; for the rest of this year the company expects $600,000 revenue. Next year the company projects $4 million revenue, with $6 million in 1988, $10 million in 1989, and $20 million in 1990.

These projections are based on proven formulas for success in marketing the ONLINE for Compaq so far in 1986. The formula was developed by the new management teams, which reorganized in February/March. Projections have been exceeded in every month since March. The company is thus a new business situation with an unusual growth opportunity over the next five years.

APPENDIX 5-1

Business Plan Time Line

1. Prepare Product Description	**19 Days**
Develop initial description	1 day
Interview potential customers	3 days
Hold brainstorming session #1	3 days
Write product description	2 days
Have laypersons evaluate product description for readability	7 days
Revise product description	3 days
2. Prepare Market Description	**89 Days**
Research trade journals	5 days
Gather industry statistics	5 days
Conduct customer interviews	10 days
Hold brainstorming session #2	3 days
Collect market data	50 days
Hold brainstorming session #3	3 days
Write market description	5 days
Have laypersons evaluate market description for readability	5 days
Revise market description	3 days
3. Define Your Objectives	**2 Days**
What does the venture need?	1 day
What do the founders want?	1 day
4. Analyze the Management Team	**4 Days**
List management skills needed	1 day
Inventory skills available	2 days
Map available skills against those needed	½ day
Define management skills needed	½ day

5. **Analyze the Final Strategy**   **3-½ days**
   Identify what can be done without outside help   1 day
   Identify how much outside help is needed   2 days
   Choose the audience for this version of the plan   ½ day

6. **Assess the Fundamentals**   **1-½ Days**
   Review the product and the market   ½ day
   Review the founders and what is needed   ½ day
   Review the audience   ½ day

7. **Prepare the Business Plan**   **30 Days**
   Prepare the financial analysis   5 days
   Produce visuals for the plan   5 days
   Write and assemble final text   3 days
   Have laypersons evaluate readability   5 days
   Revise plan if needed   2 days
   Duplicate and bind copies of plan   5 days
   Produce visuals for presentation of plan   5 days

8. **Present the Business Plan**   **20 Days**

9. **Evaluate Results**   **2 Days**

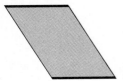

APPENDIX 5-2

King Construction Company—Pro Forma Statements

<table>
<tr><td colspan="7" align="center">**1991 King Construction**
Income Statement</td></tr>
<tr><td></td><td colspan="6" align="center">ESTIMATES 1991</td></tr>
<tr><td></td><td>MONTH
1</td><td>MONTH
2</td><td>MONTH
3</td><td>MONTH
4</td><td>MONTH
5</td><td>MONTH
6</td></tr>
<tr><td>NET SALES</td><td>100000</td><td>17273</td><td>17000</td><td>27000</td><td>37273</td><td>47273</td></tr>
<tr><td>COST OF SALES:</td><td></td><td></td><td></td><td></td><td></td><td></td></tr>
<tr><td>Goods/Mat'ls</td><td>0</td><td>38500</td><td>6650</td><td>6545</td><td>10395</td><td>14350</td></tr>
<tr><td>Production Exp</td><td>11400</td><td>1969</td><td>1938</td><td>3078</td><td>4249</td><td>5389</td></tr>
<tr><td>Direct Labor</td><td>37100</td><td>6408</td><td>6307</td><td>10017</td><td>13828</td><td>17538</td></tr>
<tr><td>   GROSS PROFIT</td><td>51500</td><td>(29604)</td><td>2105</td><td>7360</td><td>8801</td><td>9996</td></tr>
<tr><td>EXPENSES:</td><td></td><td></td><td></td><td></td><td></td><td></td></tr>
<tr><td>GENERAL & ADMIN</td><td></td><td></td><td></td><td></td><td></td><td></td></tr>
<tr><td>Payroll Expense</td><td>2427</td><td>2427</td><td>2427</td><td>2427</td><td>2427</td><td>2427</td></tr>
<tr><td>Payroll Taxes</td><td>1516</td><td>1516</td><td>1516</td><td>1516</td><td>1516</td><td>1516</td></tr>
<tr><td>Rent</td><td>450</td><td>450</td><td>450</td><td>450</td><td>450</td><td>450</td></tr>
<tr><td>Util/Tel</td><td>125</td><td>125</td><td>70</td><td>70</td><td>80</td><td>130</td></tr>
<tr><td>Ins/Legal/Acct</td><td>417</td><td>417</td><td>417</td><td>417</td><td>417</td><td>417</td></tr>
<tr><td>Office & Supply</td><td>50</td><td>50</td><td>50</td><td>50</td><td>50</td><td>50</td></tr>
<tr><td>Maintenance</td><td>0</td><td>0</td><td>0</td><td>0</td><td>0</td><td>40</td></tr>
<tr><td>Auto/Truck Exp</td><td>90</td><td>87</td><td>87</td><td>87</td><td>87</td><td>87</td></tr>
<tr><td>Other</td><td></td><td></td><td></td><td></td><td></td><td></td></tr>
<tr><td>SELLING EXPENSE</td><td></td><td></td><td></td><td></td><td></td><td></td></tr>
<tr><td>Payroll Expense</td><td>1667</td><td>1667</td><td>1667</td><td>1667</td><td>1667</td><td>1667</td></tr>
<tr><td>Advertising</td><td>513</td><td>513</td><td>513</td><td>513</td><td>513</td><td>513</td></tr>
<tr><td>Travel/Entert</td><td>33</td><td>33</td><td>33</td><td>33</td><td>33</td><td>33</td></tr>
<tr><td>Auto Expenses</td><td>90</td><td>87</td><td>87</td><td>87</td><td>87</td><td>87</td></tr>
<tr><td>License/Permits</td><td>385</td><td>50</td><td>50</td><td>100</td><td>125</td><td>200</td></tr>
<tr><td>OTHER EXPENSES</td><td></td><td></td><td></td><td></td><td></td><td></td></tr>
<tr><td>Interest</td><td>500</td><td>500</td><td>500</td><td>500</td><td>500</td><td>500</td></tr>
<tr><td>Depreciation</td><td></td><td></td><td></td><td></td><td></td><td></td></tr>
<tr><td>TOTAL EXPENSES</td><td>8263</td><td>7922</td><td>7867</td><td>7917</td><td>7952</td><td>8117</td></tr>
<tr><td>NET PROFIT/LOSS</td><td>43,237</td><td>(37,526)</td><td>(5762)</td><td>(557)</td><td>849</td><td>1879</td></tr>
</table>

			ESTIMATES 1991			
	MONTH 7	**MONTH 8**	**MONTH 9**	**MONTH 10**	**MONTH 11**	**MONTH 12**
NET SALES	57273	25908	30000	20000	11000	10000
COST OF SALES:						
Goods/Mat'ls	18200	22050	9975	11550	7700	4235
Production Exp	6529	2954	3420	2280	1254	1140
Direct Labor	21248	9612	11130	7420	4081	3710
GROSS PROFIT	11296	(8708)	5475	(1250)	(2035)	915
EXPENSES:						
GENERAL & ADMIN						
Payroll Expense	2427	2427	2427	2427	2427	2427
Payroll Taxes	1556	1556	1556	1556	1556	1556
Rent	450	450	450	450	450	450
Util/Tel	125	110	65	80	100	120
Ins/Legal/Acct	417	417	417	417	417	417
Office & Supply	50	50	50	50	50	50
Maintenance	0	0	0	0	0	0
Auto/Truck Exp	87	87	87	87	87	87
Other						
SELLING EXPENSE						
Payroll Expense	1667	1667	1667	1667	1667	1677
Advertising	2392	513	513	513	513	513
Travel/Entert	33	33	33	33	33	33
Auto Expenses	87	87	87	87	87	87
Other						
OTHER EXPENSES						
Interest	500	500	500	500	500	500
Depreciation						
TOTAL EXPENSES	9791	7897	7852	7867	7887	7917
NET PROFIT/LOSS	1505	(16,605)	(2377)	(9117)	(9922)	(8832)

1991 BALANCE SHEET

		ESTIMATED	
	1991	**1992**	**1993**
ASSETS			
CURRENT ASSETS			
Cash & Equivalents	50000	6605	88451
A/R - Progress Billings	293850	407133	456452
A/R - Current Retention	154000	269492	224840
Inventory	0	0	0
FIXED ASSETS			
Auto & Truck Equipment	20000	20000	20000
Office Furniture & Equip	3000	3000	3000
TOTAL ASSETS	520850	706230	792743
LIABILITIES AND NET WORTH			
Current:			
Short-Term Notes Payable	6000	6000	6000
Accounts Payable	154000	269492	224840
Accounts Pay. - Retention	287,850	407133	456452
Income Taxes Payable	0	0	18973
Long-Term Debt Due	0	0	50000
Net Worth/Equity	73000	23605	36478
TOTAL LIABILITIES/NET WORTH	520850	706230	792743

1991 CASH-FLOW STATEMENT

	ESTIMATES 1991					
	MONTH 1	MONTH 2	MONTH 3	MONTH 4	MONTH 5	MONTH 6
CASH SOURCES:						
FROM OPERATIONS						
Cash Sales	100000	17273	17000	27000	37273	47273
A/R Collections	38500	6650	6545	10395	14350	18200
Other Cash Coll	0	61500	10623	10455	16605	22923
OTHER SOURCES						
Interest Income						
Loan from Bank	50000	0	0	0	0	0
Investment						
SUBTOTAL	188500	85423	34168	47850	68228	88396
CASH USES:						
TO OPERATIONS						
Accts Payable						
Goods/Mater'ls	0	38500	6650	6545	10395	14350
Services	37100	6408	6307	10017	13828	17583
Payroll Expense	5650	5650	5650	5650	5650	5650
Travel/Entert	33	33	33	33	33	33
Rent	450	450	450	450	450	450
Util/Tel	125	125	70	70	80	130
Advertising	513	513	513	513	513	513
Auto/Truck Exp	180	174	174	174	174	174
Maintenance	0	0	0	0	0	40
Ins/Legal/Acct	417	417	417	417	417	417
License	385	50	50	100	125	200
Office & Supply	50	50	50	50	50	50
OTHER USES						
Interest Exp	500	500	500	500	500	500
Loan Payoff	0	0	0	0	0	0
Reserve for Tax						
SUBTOTAL	45403	52870	20864	24519	32215	40090
CASH INCR/DECR	143097	32553	13304	23331	36013	48306
BEGINNING BAL	0	143097	175650	188954	212285	248298
ENDING BALANCE	143097	175650	188954	212285	248298	296604

	ESTIMATES 1991					
	MONTH 7	MONTH 8	MONTH 9	MONTH 10	MONTH 11	MONTH 12
CASH SOURCES:						
FROM OPERATIONS						
Cash Sales	57273	25908	30000	20000	11000	10000
A/R Collections	22050	9975	11550	7700	4235	3850
Other Cash Coll	29073	35223	15933	18450	12300	6765
OTHER SOURCES						
Interest Income						
Loan from Bank	0	0	0	0	0	0
Investment						
SUBTOTAL	108396	71106	57483	46150	27535	20615
CASH USES:						
TO OPERATIONS						
Accts Payable						
Goods/Mat'ls	18200	22050	9975	11550	7700	4235
Services	21248	9612	11130	7420	4081	3710
Payroll Expense	5795	5795	5795	5795	5795	5795
Travel/Entert	33	33	33	33	33	33
Rent	450	450	450	450	450	450
Util/Tel	125	110	65	80	100	120
Advertising	2392	513	513	513	513	513
Auto/Truck Exp	87	87	87	87	87	87
Maintenance	0	0	0	0	0	0
Ins/Legal/Acct	417	417	417	417	417	417
License	100	100	100	50	25	25
Office & Supply	50	50	50	50	50	50
OTHER USES						
Interest Exp	500	500	500	500	500	500
Loan Payoff						
Reserve for Tax						
SUBTOTAL	49397	39717	29115	26945	19751	15935
CASH INCR/DECR	58999	31389	28368	19205	7784	4680
BEGINNING BAL	296604	355603	386992	415360	434565	442349
ENDING BALANCE	355603	386992	415360	434565	442349	447029

6 SITE SELECTION AND FACILITY LAYOUT

LEARNING OBJECTIVES

After you have read this chapter, you will be able to do the following:
- Determine important location factors
- Select the "best" site for different businesses
- Decide whether it is better to lease or buy a facility
- Explain the basic facility layout considerations
- Specify the best layout for different businesses

S electing the best location is one of the most important decisions a small business owner has to make. Although businesses that do not rely on customer traffic in their establishments are not as affected by location selection as are retail and service businesses, any business that is in an unsuitable location can fail or at least be only a marginal firm. People do not go out of their way to do business with companies. They want convenience as well as fair prices and good service. Customers tend to do business with those companies that are conveniently located and are easily accessible.

Besides selecting the best location, business owners should also select the best design or layout of their building. Well-designed buildings attract customers, and they are comfortable places for the employees. Manufacturers lay out their buildings to make the production process as efficient as possible. Store owners lay out their buildings to attract customers and to make their merchandise as attractive as possible. Other business owners have to design their offices to be comfortable for employees in order to maximize production and efficiency.

In this chapter, we will examine some site-selection techniques used by small business owners or their agents. We will also discuss the merits of buying a facility or building one, and we will examine the pros and cons of owning or leasing a building. Finally, we will look at the different ways of laying out facilities to make them attractive, comfortable, and efficient.

SITE SELECTION

site selection

Because most small business owners are committed to a certain city, their major decision involves locating the most suitable site in that city. However, some people who intend to open a new business may be willing to relocate to another city or even another state. Therefore, we will discuss methods of selecting the best state and city before we concentrate on specific site selection. Fortunately, there are numerous agencies and organizations that can simplify the business owner's decision-making process.

Selecting the State

For the person with a plan for a new business who is willing to relocate to the "best" state, selecting that state may seem to be a difficult task. Analyzing the strengths and weaknesses of the states for particular types of businesses is not too difficult. Some states cater to small businesses whereas others prefer to court big business or even foreign companies. A new business owner might want to locate in a state that has a high concentration of small businesses. Conversely, it might be advantageous to locate the new business in a state with a smaller percentage of small businesses. The following list depicts the ten states with the highest and lowest percentage of small businesses (fewer than ten workers):[1]

Ten Highest		Ten Lowest	
Wyoming	83.0	Indiana	72.1
South Dakota	82.1	Virginia	73.1
Montana	81.4	Wisconsin	73.1
North Dakota	80.5	Utah	73.3
Alaska	79.0	Illinois	73.6
California	78.9	North Carolina	73.8
New York	78.9	Tennessee	74.1
Oklahoma	78.9	Missouri	74.1
Vermont	78.4	Pennsylvania	74.2
Colorado	78.4	Michigan	74.2

RANKING STATES. All states will provide information about their labor force, taxes, land prices, and so forth, but the information is usually presented in a favorable light. To get a better idea of the attractiveness of each state, business owners should obtain information from a disinterested source. One such source is the annual *Inc.* "Report on the States." The editors of *Inc.* evaluate job generation, new businesses, and young-company growth; they then rank each of the fifty states. The ten best states are Nevada, New Hampshire, Virginia, Maryland, Georgia, Florida, Delaware, North Carolina, Tennessee, and California.[2]

FACTORS TO EVALUATE. Business owners should do some analysis on their own before they select the state that is best for them. The following factors are a few that need to be evaluated:

EXHIBIT 6-1 Financial Incentives and Tax Programs from States

Financial Help	**Tax Programs**
Industrial revenue bonds	Corporate tax exemption
General obligation bonds	Excise tax exemption
Private development credit	Moratorium or exemption on goods in transit (free port)
Loans for building construction	Moratorium or exemption on land and capital improvements
Loans for machinery and equipment	Exemption on manufacturer's inventories
Incentives for investments in high unemployment areas	Stabilization agreements for specified industries
Plant expansion assistance	Exemption on raw materials used in manufacturing
Guarantees for machinery and equipment loans	Accelerated depreciation for pollution control
Guarantees for building construction loans	Tax credits for the use of specified state products
Free land for industry	Credits against corporate income tax for pollution control facilities
State matching funds for local industrial financing programs	
State-owned industrial parks	
University R&D available to industry	
Employee training programs	

SOURCE: U.S. Department of Commerce.

- Availability and price of land
- State taxes (income, sales, etc.)
- Quantity and quality of labor
- Transportation systems
- State laws and regulations
- Environmental-control regulations
- Ability of government officials
- Prevailing economic conditions
- Quality of educational institutions
- Financial incentives (see Exhibit 6-1)
- Quality of life

Other factors that business owners could include in their evaluation of the states may be industry-specific or personal (availability of leisure activities, proximity to ski areas, etc.) and should be carefully analyzed by owners.

Selecting the City

Many people may be willing to start their business in a new city if it has advantages over their home town. People willing to relocate should evaluate cities as carefully as they would the different states. Information about cities is offered by chambers of commerce, city halls, and real estate agents. Many cities have departments that are responsible for promoting the advantages of locating in that city. Some advertisements are quite flamboyant; others are

EXHIBIT 6-2 Sample Advertisement Promoting City

reserved and more factual (see Exhibit 6-2). Like data provided by states, information provided by city agencies can be somewhat biased. Therefore, business owners should obtain as much unbiased data from sources not directly affiliated with cities. Once again, *Inc.* magazine is a good source for unbiased data. The magazine's editors evaluate and rank cities on the basis of their attractiveness to small businesses. In 1990, the following were the top and bottom ten cities:[3]

Top Ten	Bottom Ten
1. Las Vegas, NV	1. Colorado Springs, CO
2. Washington, DC	2. Amarillo, TX
3. Orlando, FL	3. Shreveport, LA
4. Tallahassee, FL	4. Springfield, IL
5. San Jose, CA	5. Davenport-Rock Island, IL
6. Atlanta, GA	6. Monroe, LA
7. Charleston, SC	7. Tacoma, WA
8. Lincoln, NB	8. Terre Haute, IN
9. Raleigh-Durham, NC	9. Wichita Falls, TX
10. Anaheim, CA	10. Wheeling, WV

Although *Inc.* and other magazines provide information about cities, business owners will still have to collect and evaluate their own data. Before locating in a given city, a person should know about its taxes, land prices, availability and cost of labor, availability of capital, schools, and cultural events. Knowing about the city's infrastructure would also be helpful. Interested owners should evaluate crime statistics, transportation systems, condition of roads, ability of elected officials, competence of city managers and employees, and the general condition of buildings.

Selecting a Rural Location

rural locations

Sometimes the best location may not be in a city at all. **Rural locations** offer advantages not found in most cities. For example, rural areas have less crime, little traffic congestion, less pollution, and possibly a better quality of life. The following businesses are most frequently started in remote places:[4]

- Miscellaneous business services
- Eating and drinking places
- Miscellaneous shopping goods
- Automotive repair shops
- Miscellaneous repair shops
- Grocery stores
- Miscellaneous retail stores
- Residential construction
- Women's clothing stores
- Retail furniture and furnishings

These businesses generally provide services or products to the people in the surrounding area. However, remotely located companies such as L.L. Bean and Lands' End sell merchandise throughout the country. The major drawback of a rural location is that businesses started there often remain small—the growth potential is considerably less than in cities.

Choosing the Site

Once the city or rural location has been selected, business owners have to make a critical decision. Which specific site within a chosen city or rural area is best for the business? For all retail businesses and most service and manufacturing companies, site selection is one of the most crucial decisions owners must make. If the wrong location is selected, a business is very likely to fail. On the other hand, selecting the best site gives the business a real chance to survive. The site-selection process is so important that many people use experts to help make the decision.

USING CONSULTANTS. Some business owners will turn to city officials, friends, or real estate agents for help in selecting the best site. However, to be sure that the site selected is the most appropriate, small business owners should retain a site-selection consultant. The prudent owner will select a consultant who is a **Certified Industrial Developer (CID).** These people must satisfy certain requirements before they can be certified. Management consultant Otto P. Geier suggests the following reasons for using consultants:[5]

Certified Industrial Developer (CID)

- Consultants will maintain the confidentiality needed to keep competitors or real estate firms from finding out which sites are being considered.
- Consultants are usually unbiased and objective.
- Consultants are likely to make important business issues other than real estate considerations a part of their recommendations.
- Consultants know local professionals and experts who can provide relevant information.
- Consultants who have had years of site-selection experience can do the job in less time than inexperienced new business owners.

environmental audit

ENVIRONMENTAL AUDIT. Whenever sites are being considered, owners or their consultants should have an **environmental audit** performed. The audit is to check for hazardous wastes that may have been left behind by previous owners. The person who owns the land when waste is discovered is the one who pays for cleanup, not the person who created the waste (see The Way It Is 6-1). Some states require an environmental audit before purchasing a site, and some lenders also require an audit. Some courts have recently held lenders liable for cleanup if they foreclose on contaminated property.

SELECTION QUESTIONS. Site selection involves answering a number of questions about each site being considered. Listing here all the questions that should be answered is not possible; however, the following are a few important questions:

- Is there adequate transportation?
- Is there good visibility?
- How many potential customers pass the site daily?

6-1 POLLUTED SITES

It was the ultimate nightmare for any company buying a piece of land. A lubricating-oil company bought property for $48,000 and finalized plans to build a warehouse. But bulldozers soon uncovered an awful surprise: The prior owner, a solvent-recycling company, had polluted the soil with toxins. The estimated cost to eliminate the pollutants was $2 million. According to the federal law which established Superfund, liability for hazardous-waste cleanup follows land ownership. The owner of the land, not the polluter, is responsible for cleanup. Therefore, pollution experts are urging companies to do their homework before buying land. Before signing any papers, many companies are testing the soil for evidence of toxic waste. It is also prudent to require an indemnification clause protecting buyers from liability if toxic waste is discovered later.[6]

- Is the site accessible?
- What is the price of the site?
- Is there sufficient parking?
- What is the crime rate in the immediate vicinity?
- Is there a fire station nearby?
- Is the neighborhood stable?
- Are competitors located nearby?
- What are the zoning restrictions?
- Are city services adequate?
- Can the site be easily resold in the future?

This is only a small sample of the questions that need to be answered before deciding on a specific site. The longer the list of questions, the greater the probability of selecting the best site.

Choosing Special Locations

Special locations in cities and rural areas are making the site-selection process a little easier for new business owners. These locations are designed to make start-up easier and to provide small businesses with low-cost services. Although these sites do not insure success, they do make it easier for small businesses to be successful.

recycled sites   RECYCLED SITES. In many cities, particularly large ones in industrial states, large facilities abandoned by major corporations are being recycled and used by smaller companies (see The Way It Is 6-2). The major attraction of these sites is the low cost to purchase or rent part of the building.

6-2 OLD BUILDINGS, NEW BUSINESSES

A few years ago, Dennis Oleksuk was working in B. F. Goodrich's facilities-management office. His job was to get the company's many divisions out of the aging factories. The buildings would then be demolished. His colleague, Michael Owen, in the company's real estate department, was considering ways to save the buildings. Owen and Oleksuk, with the city's approval, sold the buildings to Covington Capital Corporation, a developer that had rehabilitated smaller industrial facilities in other cities. Covington would turn the buildings into a mammoth mixed-use complex: housing, shops, offices, and sizable amounts of industrial space. The company has rented space to an architecture-engineering firm, a day-care center, a desktop publishing company, and many others. About half of the available space is leased, and Owen and Oleksuk are confident that the rest will be used soon. "Benjamin Franklin Goodrich brought a struggling company here and watched it grow and diversify," says Owen. "We can do the same thing with many businesses. So much of what I perceive as Akron's future is coming through these doors."[7]

incubators

INCUBATORS. Some large corporations such as Control Data, AT&T, GTE North, and Coopers & Lybrand have established or are promoting **incubators.** These are buildings that offer space at below-market rent to new businesses. Some incubators, particularly those affiliated with city governments or other public agencies, are quite selective. Others will accept any small business as long as it meets some basic criteria. In addition to below-market rent, small companies receive the following benefits:

Support services. A receptionist, telephone answering, and secretarial help may come with the rent. Renters also have access to fax machines, copiers, computers, and conference rooms, which they pay for only if they use them.

Discounted fees. The center may negotiate discounted rates with local professionals, such as accountants and lawyers.

Networking. Joint ventures are frequently encouraged between tenants and with other local businesses.

Financing. The center alerts tenants to local, state, and federal funding sources. It may offer its own seed-funding programs.[8]

The approximately 400 incubators have been quite beneficial to many businesses (see The Way It Is 6-3). A study by the National Business Incubation Association (NBIA) of 120 incubators found that they are successful at "graduating" businesses (small businesses leave the incubator when they reach a predetermined size).[9] Though most of the incubators were less than

6-3 STATE-OF-THE-ART BUSINESS INCUBATOR

In 1980, June Lavelle used a portion of a $1.7 million federal grant to buy a building in the inner city of Chicago. The old factory was renovated and turned into an incubator. Nine years later, Lavelle points with satisfaction to the incubator's following accomplishments:

- Forty-two healthy start-ups have outgrown their space and moved to bigger locations.
- Of the 143 companies that have been launched there, only 23 (just 16 percent) have failed.
- The bad-debt rate has averaged four percent.
- Full capacity was reached within two years of acquisition.
- Today seventy-seven companies are housed in the facilities; about thirty are owned by women or minorities.
- A total of 1,171 jobs have been created at a cost to taxpayers of $1,452 each.
- Since the Fulton-Carroll Center for Industry opened in 1980, surrounding industrial property has quintupled in market value.[10]

four years old, 63 percent of those studied had "graduated" 270 businesses in 1989 after a stay of two to three years in the sheltered environment. And 18 percent of the companies applied for 185 patents. The association concluded that it was too early to compare the success of graduates with the 1-in-5 survival rate of small businesses after five years, but their chances look good.

ESTABLISHED STORES. Finding small businesses located in larger stores is not unusual now. The bigger, national stores are "downsizing" in an effort to become more profitable. A downsized store has space that it cannot use, but it must still pay rent for the whole building. The store subleases space to other businesses thereby reducing its own costs. For example, Montgomery Ward rents space to Toys R Us in ten of its stores. Other examples include car telephones being sold in automobile dealerships, cookies being sold in fast-food restaurants, and package-mailing franchises being set up in retail establishments.

TWO-FOR-THE-PRICE-OF-ONE. Some small business owners have found that they can increase business by using part of their existing space for a complementary business. For example, Steve Beninati and his partner, Richard Nicotra, took their 500-square-foot mall space and divided it in two. Part one houses their original Everything Yogurt shop, and the second part houses a new business, Bananas, in which they started to sell "frosty fruit shakes."[11]

The two businesses, usually owned by the same person, attract more business jointly than they would individually. In other words, one plus one equals more than two. The developers of this strategy caution that the following things should be kept in mind:

- **Synergy.** This is one place where it actually exists. If you cannot save money on staff, signage, and supplies, you might as well open your second store across town.
- **Compatibility.** Because the two stores will be side by side, they must be complementary. The idea is to get customers who would normally visit your first store to come to the second one as well.
- **Create real-life Doublemint twins: Cross-train.** Hopefully, the peak times at shop one will be balanced by shop two. Cross-trained employees can work both stores without affecting customer service.
- **Focus.** Like store one, store two should stand for something. If you want to add a third product line, open a third store.[12]

MALLS AND SHOPPING CENTERS. Many new business owners will choose to locate in a mall or shopping center. Rents in these facilities may be higher than at other locations, and some of the rules may be cumbersome; however,

Some business owners have found that they can put their business in a van or small truck and go to the customer.

these facilities do offer advantages for new businesses, such as heavy traffic, ample parking, other complementary businesses, security, professional management, attractive surroundings, shared advertising support, space modifications to meet tenants' needs, high visibility, and prestige location.

mobile sites

MOBILE AND TEMPORARY LOCATIONS. Not all new businesses require a fixed or permanent location. Some owners have found that they can put their business in a van or small truck and go to the customer. Services such as house washing, pet grooming, and blood collecting are offered from **mobile sites.** There are even dentists and physicians who practice from mobile sites. Other businesses, particularly food sellers, use pushcarts set up on sidewalks as their primary location. Many people are making money from small businesses set up in kiosks temporarily located in malls (see The Way It Is 6-4). Vans, pushcarts, and kiosks are relatively inexpensive, and if the location is not satisfactory, it is easy to move to another.

Site Selection Trends

Site selection will always be very important, but there are some changes predicted for the next ten years that will affect the process. Those anticipated changes will make it more necessary than ever for small business owners to rely on experts when selecting a suitable site. Some of the most significant changes include the following:

- A number of developer/broker firms will establish global operations, owning and operating business parks of uniform quality in many nations.
- Product life cycles will get shorter, requiring customized buildings to be amortized over short spans.
- Environmental regulations will assume greater significance.
- Communities will compete vigorously for high-tech, high-value-added companies.
- Computer networks will speed site selection.

The
Way
It Is

6-4 VANS, PUSHCARTS, AND KIOSKS

Last Christmas a Minneapolis couple made $25,000 in seven weeks selling sheepskin slippers at kiosks in three shopping malls. The man who set them up in business, Barry Silverman, earned more. He grossed more than $1.25 million in that same period from forty-five kiosks, earning 15 percent in profits. Four years ago he averaged just 5 percent from the four shoe stores he owned. In one Christmas season, "I did more business from a kiosk the size of my desktop than in my whole store that season," said Silverman. The experience converted him from a conventional retailer to a temporary tenant.[13]

- Multiuse buildings with great flexibility will be in demand.
- There will be increased interest in portable industrial buildings, such as air-supported domes.
- Amenities and aesthetic factors will play an ever-increasing role in the design of business facilities.[14]

FACILITY LAYOUT

Once new business owners have chosen the best location, they need to make several other important decisions. Should they buy or lease the building? What should they do about designing or remodeling their building? Whom should they contact about lighting, noise control, and so forth? What equipment will they need for their business? Some business owners will choose to work from their homes; they also will have problems to solve and decisions to make. We begin this section with a comparison of leasing or buying a store, factory, office, or restaurant.

Purchasing or Leasing Facilities

One of the most important decisions new business owners need to make is whether to purchase or lease facilities. Too many owners hastily agree to buy a building only to learn that they cannot afford the costs associated with ownership. On the other hand, some owners lease when they probably should have purchased their building. Some lease then purchase the building. For example, an art gallery owner leased his building for many years while he was growing his business. In 1989, he decided to buy the facility and use the upstairs for framing and the downstairs for art display. In 1992, he realized that he had more space than he needed and his mortgage costs were burdensome. His solution was to lease half of the downstairs to another business which sells ladies clothes. Before deciding whether to buy or lease, owners should consider the advantages and disadvantages of both options.

ADVANTAGES OF BUYING. New business owners who are interested in purchasing a facility should consider the following advantages:

- Owners can make whatever modifications they deem necessary.
- Mortgage costs remain relatively stable.
- Depreciation, interest payments, and property taxes are treated as business expenses for tax purposes.
- Building owners cannot be evicted by a landlord.
- The property usually appreciates in value.

ADVANTAGES OF LEASING. Although purchasing a building may be an attractive option, leasing also has some advantages including the following:

- There is usually no large initial capital outlay.
- Landlords are often responsible for some maintenance.

- It is easier for business owners to relocate if they do not have a building to sell.
- Most lease expenses are tax deductible.
- The building owner usually pays the insurance premiums for the facility.
- If the value of the building declines, it does not directly affect the lessor.

DISADVANTAGES OF BUYING. To decide between purchasing or leasing, business owners must also consider the disadvantages of both options. The disadvantages of buying a building include the following:

- The initial capital outlay needed to buy a building is usually considerably greater than that required to lease.
- Owning a building can limit a business owner's mobility.
- The owner of a building pays for maintenance and repairs.
- If a neighborhood begins to deteriorate, the value of a building will decline.

DISADVANTAGES OF LEASING. The following are some of the drawbacks of leasing a building:

- The rent paid to landlords is usually increased on a regular basis.
- Tenants can be evicted if the landlord wants the building for other purposes.
- Some landlords allow their buildings to deteriorate.
- Landlords may restrict tenant activities.
- Long leases make it nearly impossible for owners to relocate until the lease expires.

Layout and Design Considerations

Most buildings selected by business owners need to be remodeled to meet specific needs. Remodeling usually entails decisions about lighting, noise control, appropriate color schemes, position of equipment, and so forth. Business owners want their facilities to be attractive and aesthetically pleasing, but the facilities should also be functional. Well-designed workspaces increase productivity. A survey of about 10,000 workers by the Buffalo Organization for Social and Technological Innovation (BOSTI) found a direct relationship between workplace environment and productivity. Conditions identified that affect productivity include: temperature, lighting, sound, and the degree of enclosure.[15]

ENVIRONMENTAL CONCERNS. Today's offices, stores, restaurants, and factories are not always environmentally "friendly." Pollutants such as asbestos, radon, and formaldehyde have been found in workplaces. There is also considerable controversy about smoking in the workplace. Since the Surgeon General's announcement that even second-hand smoke is hazardous, many companies are banning smoking altogether. By installing adequate ventilation systems and selecting nonpolluting materials, business owners can develop environmentally safe workplaces. There is also considerable pressure from the government to design safe and comfortable workplaces.

CLIMATE CONTROL. Workspaces that are either too hot or too cold decrease productivity and contribute to employee discomfort. In general, room temperatures should be between 68 and 76 degrees and humidity should be from 40 to 60 percent. Rooms should have sufficient fresh air, and drafts from fans or ventilators should be eliminated. Determining the right temperature and amount of fresh air is difficult because people react differently to climatic conditions.

NOISE CONTROL. Workplaces where noise is minimized are conducive to employee efficiency. Experts contend that high noise levels in offices can lead to increased blood pressure, accelerated heart rate, decreased digestive activity, tension, mental stress, irritability, and inability to think and work efficiently. To protect workers' hearing, the government limits the number of hours they can be exposed to various levels of noise (see Exhibit 6-3). These requirements can be met by selecting appropriate materials such as carpeting and curtains. When considering the use of carpets, curtains, and so forth, it is important to know their **Noise Reduction Coefficient (NRC).** The NRC is a number between zero and one that represents the amount of energy absorbed by the material. The higher the number, the more energy absorbed.

Noise Reduction Coefficient (NRC)

LIGHTING. Good lighting is a vital component of the workplace environment. Inadequate or improper lighting may cause eyestrain or headaches, whereas appropriate lighting increases employees' efficiency and productivity. The selection and placement of lights is best left to experts because of the

EXHIBIT 6-3 U.S. Government Standards for Exposure to Sound

Maximum Hours Exposure per Day	Sound Level (Decibels)
No limit	60 Average office/store
8	90 Loud street noise
6	92
4	95
3	97
2	100 Noisy industrial plant
1.5	102
1	105
0.5	110
0.25 or less	115
?	120 Thunder
?	130 Threshold of feeling

technical expertise required. Lighting experts can determine how to maximize natural light, find ways to minimize glare, select the most efficient kind of lights, and place lights in the best location. Designing acceptable ambient or general lighting systems is important, but more attention should be focused on task lighting systems. Task lighting should possess the following qualities:

- Appropriate employees should be able to vary and adjust the light level.
- The position of the light should be flexible on both horizontal and vertical planes.
- The illumination pattern should be rectangular or elliptical rather than round.
- Desk space needed for manual activities should not be taken up by the task light.[16]

COLOR. Color affects employees' moods, attitudes, and feelings of comfort. If appropriate colors are selected (see Exhibit 6-4), a comfortable environment that increases productivity can be created. Before deciding on the best color, business owners should determine what work will be done in the room, whether the room is exposed to natural light or needs artificial light, and what effect (stimulative, relaxing, etc.) is to be achieved.

Store Layout

Effective layout is probably more important to retail establishments than to any other workplace. If customers feel that a store is cluttered, illogically arranged, or physically unattractive, they will shop elsewhere. To prescribe a general layout for all stores would be virtually impossible, because each is unique; however, certain merchandise can be placed to maximize revenue.

EXHIBIT 6-4 Color's Effect

Color	Positive	Negative
Black	accomplished/worldly	empty/desolate
Blue	secure/peaceful	depressing
Brown	dependable/logical	plain/boring
Gray	secure/calm	colorless
Green	calm/natural	jealous
Pink	sweet/soft	overly feminine
Red	powerful/exciting	aggressive
Tan	calm/natural	ordinary
Violet	regal	oppressive
White	pure	lifeless
Yellow	happy/sunny	stagey

SOURCE: David Iushewitz, ''Sudden Impact,'' *Entrepreneur*, November 1990, 114.

Different types of merchandise should usually be placed in the following areas of a store:

Impulse goods. Attractive visual displays encourage customers to buy these items. In a small store they should be near the entrance, but in larger stores they should be on the main aisle.

Convenience goods. Customers purchase these items in small quantities quite frequently. Convenience goods should be placed in easily accessible locations along the main aisle.

Necessities or staple goods. These items are purchased because people need them. They should be located at the rear of the store or on upper floors of multilevel stores.

Utility goods. These items, such as brooms and dustpans, are usually purchased for the home and should be placed along the main aisle.

Luxury and major expense items. People shop around before deciding to purchase these items. These types of goods should be located some distance from the store's entrance.[17]

Stores should be designed so customers can move about easily and so that merchandise is attractively displayed. In most cases, store owners should rely on design professionals to select the best layout for the facility. Whoever designs a store should

1. Know the product lines: size, quantity, and quality.
2. Know the target market: demographics, income, age, sex, buying patterns, and so forth.
3. Analyze the products to be sold for their best features, and devise the most cost-effective and appealing means of display.
4. Develop a coordinated plan for graphics and signage.
5. Use appropriate colors and materials.
6. Create a storefront and window design to communicate a statement of the store's uniqueness.
7. Install good theft and security systems.
8. Eliminate areas hidden from visual surveillance by employees.
9. Place cash-wrap counters so staff have a clear view of the entrance and other critical areas.
10. Make sure receiving and storage areas are adequate.[18]

Factory Layout

Even though customers do not normally visit factories, effective layout is still an important consideration. Well-designed factories increase worker productivity, use space effectively, and minimize waste. New business owners will choose one of the following types of basic factory layout: product, process, or fixed.

product layout

PRODUCT LAYOUT. A business engaged in the mass production of single or limited numbers of products would use a **product layout.** In this layout, all the equipment used to produce goods is arranged sequentially, as in an assembly line. Products are moved, usually by a conveyor system, to each machine until the manufacturing process has been completed. This layout offers the following advantages: uses floor space efficiently, reduces manufacturing costs, minimizes product handling time and costs, reduces production time, reduces employee-training time, and reduces waste.

The major disadvantage of this layout is that machines are dependent on each other. If one machine breaks down, the assembly line comes to a halt. The machines are also expensive and often are idle. Finally, assembly line jobs tend to be very tiring and quite boring.

process layout

PROCESS LAYOUT. Small plants with a varied product line often use a process or "job shop" layout. This layout groups similar machines together. For example, products that need to be sanded and painted are taken first to an area where all sanding machines are located and then moved to a different place where they are painted. Process layout has the following advantages: greater utilization of machines, ability to shift work when a machine is not functioning, better control of intricate processes, less initial capital investment, lower costs for small production runs, and easier maintenance.

fixed layout

FIXED LAYOUT. In manufacturing plants with **fixed layouts,** the product is stationary and workers and machinery move to it to perform necessary functions. This layout, which is rarely found in small plants, is used for large products such as airplanes and locomotives.

Office Layout

Most small businesses have space that is used for one or more offices. A well-designed office should accomplish two goals. The design should facilitate the smooth flow of work between various people, and it should minimize movement and noise. The following are some principles of efficient office layout:

- Keep people who communicate frequently with each other in the same location.
- Keep files and other equipment close to the people who use them.
- Common destinations (toilets, photocopy machines, and so forth) should be close together and accessible by direct routes.
- Workstations should be away from sources of intermittent sounds and areas of frequent conversations.[19]

closed offices

CLOSED OFFICES. Offices traditionally have been small, enclosed rooms designed to segregate management from employees. Each person worked in an office separated from others by fixed walls. The size of the office often signified a person's rank or importance in the company. This layout provided

open offices

privacy, but it also allowed employees to waste time unobserved by management. The common closed office has been replaced to a large extent by **open offices.**

OPEN OFFICES. Early open offices reflected a basic bull-pen design. Workers were placed together in one large room that was bordered by smaller private offices for the managers. Modern open offices give workers a little more privacy. Employees now have identifiable workspaces separated from each other by some type of partition. Business owners who choose open offices should be aware of the following requirements:

- The design of the workplace should be flexible enough to accommodate the formation of new work groups.
- All work groups should be identifiable as groups.
- Acoustical systems should be able to accommodate user arrangement.
- Employees should be able to communicate confidentially.
- There should be adequate lighting for areas in which conventional tasks are performed.
- Storage areas in each workplace should be within a worker's reach when he or she is seated at the desk.
- Work surfaces should be nonreflective.[20]

home offices

Home Offices

Many people, nearly 11 million in fact, work at home. Some of these people work for major corporations; however, many are self-employed workers, freelancers, and contract workers. A home office can be equipped with computer, printer, facsimile machine, and so forth for less than $4,000, and expenses can be deducted from a person's federal taxes. To take a home office deduction, the following factors must be considered: (1) the amount of time spent working in the home office; (2) the business reasons for having a home office; (3) whether the functions performed in the home office are essential to the conduct of a person's business; (4) whether the office is suitable for all the essential business functions performed there; and (5) the appropriateness of the furnishings.[21]

SUMMARY

One of the most important decisions facing new business owners is where to locate their company. Some will search for the "best" city for their business, others will decide to locate in their home town. All business owners need to select a specific site within a city, small town, or rural area for their business. Most owners will select the site themselves; however, some will rely on specialized consultants to make the selection. Some of the site-related factors that owners or consultants should consider include: transportation, visibility, accessibility, land cost, expansion possibilities, competing businesses, complementary businesses, and city services.

Once a location has been selected, owners will have to decide whether they should buy or lease their building. The advantages of buying the facility include the following: owners can make necessary modifications; mortgage costs are relatively constant; interest, taxes, and so forth are tax deductible; and owners cannot be evicted by a landlord. The advantages of leasing a facility include the following: less initial capital is required to lease than to buy; landlords are usually responsible for some maintenance; leasing does not limit a business owner's mobility; most lease expenses are tax deductible; and declining property value does not affect the lessor.

When the building has been chosen, most owners will need to remodel it or design it to suit their needs. Facility layout is best done by experts who can design lighting systems, climate control systems, and noise control systems to maximize the comfort of employees and customers. Good building layout facilitates smooth traffic flow and allows for attractive merchandise display.

QUESTIONS FOR REVIEW AND DISCUSSION

1. What makes some states more attractive than others to small businesses?
2. What are some of the major factors to consider before selecting a city in which to locate a business?
3. What businesses do well in rural locations or in small towns?
4. Why is an environmental audit important to the site-selection process?
5. What advantages do incubators offer new businesses?
6. What advantages do shopping malls offer new businesses?
7. What are the advantages of buying a building? What are the advantages of leasing?
8. Why are noise and climate control important in stores and offices?
9. Why is color an important consideration in the design of a facility?
10. What are the advantages of product and process layouts?
11. What are the advantages and disadvantages of working at home?

KEY TERMS

Certified Industrial Developer (CID)	Noise Reduction Coefficient (NRC)
closed offices	open offices
environmental audit	process layout
fixed layout	product layout
home offices	recycled sites
incubators	rural locations
mobile sites	site selection

CASE
Fine Furniture Company

Frank Boyd had spent much of his life making and selling furniture. His furniture was not ordinary, machine-made furniture. Frank made high-quality, expensive furniture. He specialized in tables and chairs and usually made these items to customers' specifications. Because Frank worked alone, his output was not great, but he was able to sell everything he made. For the past six years, Fine Furniture Company has been located in a small building in the downtown section of a medium-size city. Frank's lease expires in three months, and his landlord informed him that he needs the building. Frank will have to find a new site for his company.

The requirements for Frank's new building include the following: there must be a minimum of 2,000 square feet; lighting and ventilation systems should be better than average; there should be parking for customers; the location should be convenient for customers; and the neighborhood should be safe. Frank had been paying $16 per square foot a year for his building, which contained approximately 2,150 square feet of usable space. From newspapers, real estate agents, and other sources, Frank had identified several possible sites.

Frank knew of an available building three blocks from his current site, which he could rent for $18.50 per square foot. The only drawback of this site was that he would have to pay for 2,500 square feet. He would have 500 square feet that he did not need. Another possibility was a 2,100-square-foot building on the fringe of downtown that Frank would have to purchase. The building met most of Frank's

requirements, but he was not sure he could finance the $200,000 purchase price. A third alternative was to rent space in the city-run incubator. Frank could custom design his own space and the rent would only be $11 per square foot. This location might be ideal, but Frank was not sure if his customers would come to an incubator, and he knew that he would have to leave the incubator in three to five years.

A final alternative was to share space in a building owned by one of his friends. Frank's friend owned a machine shop about six blocks from the downtown area. He had more space than he needed and agreed to rent 2,000 square feet to Frank for $17 per square foot. The machine shop was not in the best section of town, and Frank worried that his customers would not be willing to visit his new location. Frank was also concerned that his friend's business might grow and he would need all of his space. Frank knew that he only had three months to find a new location, but he was having difficulty selecting the best location.

QUESTIONS

1. Should Frank use the services of a location consultant?

2. Would Frank be better off buying or leasing?

3. If Frank had to select one of the sites he has identified, which one should it be? Why?

4. Should Frank continue his search for a new location?

Go to an average-size retail store and use the Checklist for Interior Arrangement and Display to determine if the layout is as good as it could be.

Checklist for Interior Arrangement and Display

LAYOUT

	Yes	No
1. Are fixtures low enough and signs placed so that customers have a bird's-eye view of the store and can see where to go for desired goods?	—	—
2. Do aisle and counter arrangements tend to stimulate a circular traffic flow through the store?	—	—
3. Do fixtures, signs, lettering, and colors all create a coordinated and unified effect?	—	—
4. Is the use of hanging signs limited to special sale events?	—	—
5. Are counters and aisle tables overcrowded with merchandise?	—	—
6. Are ledges and cashier-wrapping stations kept free of boxes, unneeded wrapping materials, personal effects, and odds and ends?	—	—
7. Are trash bins kept out of sight?	—	—

MERCHANDISE EMPHASIS

	Yes	No
1. Do signs referring to specific items contain important information rather than general facts such as the names and prices of the products?	—	—
2. Are advertised and nonadvertised specials prominently displayed at the ends of counters as well as at the point of sale?	—	—
3. Are national and private brands highlighted in arrangements and window displays?	—	—
4. Wherever feasible, is the more colorful merchandise given preference in display?	—	—

5. In the case of apparel and home furnishings, do the items that reflect the store's fashion sense or fashion leadership get special display attention at all times?   _____ _____

6. In positioning merchandise in the store, is the productivity of space (vertical as well as horizontal) considered?   _____ _____

7. Is self-service merchandise arranged to attract customers and assist them in their selection by the following means:
   a. Is each category grouped under a separate sign?   _____ _____
   b. Is the merchandise in each category arranged according to its most significant characteristic—color, style, size, etc.?   _____ _____
   c. In apparel categories, is the merchandise arranged by price lines or zones to assist customers in making a selection quickly?   _____ _____
   d. Is horizontal space usually devoted to different items and styles within a category (with vertical space used for different sizes—smallest at the top, largest at the bottom)?   _____ _____

SOURCE: J. Wingate and S. Helfant, *Small Store Planning for Growth* (Washington, DC: Small Business Administration, 1977), 100–101.

CAPITAL REQUIREMENTS AND FUNDING SOURCES

LEARNING OBJECTIVES
After you have read this chapter, you will be able to do the following:
- Determine how much capital is needed to start a business
- Identify potential sources of capital
- Know what role the commercial bank plays to the start-up firm
- Learn how to package a loan request

N o aspect of starting and managing a small business is given more coverage in both the popular and the financial press than acquiring start-up capital and financing the business through its early growth stages. Most of the articles written are either case studies of particular small business owners and their sources of capital or a listing of the generic sources. Both serve a purpose. A case study indicates how an individual, or firm, developed capital funding sources and helps readers believe that they, too, can overcome various hurdles that abound in locating capital. The disadvantage of cases is that each is focused on a specific situation that probably will never be faced by the reader. On the other hand, lists give small business owners an idea of where to start their search for capital. The problem with lists is that they are sterile and give little idea of how each item may be used or what problems may be encountered with each.

This chapter will combine both of the popular approaches by examining the various sources of start-up capital and providing several case studies focusing on how these sources can be exploited.

DETERMINING CAPITAL NEEDED FOR START-UP

Many small business owners do not take the time to plan how much capital is needed to start up their enterprise and to keep it operational until it reaches the break-even phase. The most common approach is to raise enough money from personal savings and/or borrowing to start the business and then attempt to raise operational capital only as the need arises.

This approach is typical because most small business owners are so immersed in the details of getting their new business off the ground that they seldom take time for financial planning. Their primary objective is to get the business open and then to worry about where the money will come from to keep it open.

start-up capital

The capital required to start a business will vary greatly depending on the type of industry the business is in. Manufacturing concerns normally require the most **start-up capital.** Retail businesses require less start-up capital than manufacturing firms, and service firms usually require the least start-up capital. Capital requirements for manufacturing are high because of several factors, but the primary reason is the length of time required to establish a production operation. All the equipment and the labor required to set up the facility is a cash outflow without any corresponding cash inflow to help to offset it during the initial period. In addition, once the plant is operational, it takes time for it to become efficient. A well-known example of this was General Motors' new Saturn plant; over five years and two billion dollars of expenditures were required before the first car was produced, and then the production rate was less than one-third of what had been planned for the first six months of operation. Just as General Motors can have these kinds of problems, many small businesses also can easily encounter delays and additional costs.

Retail businesses generally require less start-up capital for a number of reasons. First, most will rent or lease, rather than build, their primary place of business. For most retail businesses, finding an existing unoccupied building or space in a mall that is suitable for their particular enterprise is fairly easy. In addition, much of the inventory may be purchased on terms that allow sixty days or more before payment is required. The major expenditure may be the leasehold improvements (shelves, display cases, painting, etc.) that must be completed before the inventory arrives.

Some service businesses, such as consulting, may be started with almost no initial capital requirements, but others, such as the motel or restaurant business, may require a large capital outlay. Initial capital requirements may, therefore, vary greatly between industries and even within an industry. Although the capital requirements do vary greatly from start-up to start-up, a survey of three thousand small business owners showed that 72 percent of them started with less than $50,000 in initial capital.[1]

Types of Start-up Capital

To most small business owners start-up capital is generic, and they do not think about the fact that there are many different types of capital; however, the distinction can greatly aid them in their search for start-up capital. There are several ways capital may be defined. Capital may be classified as either

debt

debt or **equity.** Debt capital is the funds that have been borrowed from creditors who expect interest payments on the amount borrowed and expect to have the loan repaid at some point in the future. Debt may be secured or

collateral

unsecured. When a creditor requires that **collateral** be pledged as a condition for the loan, then the debt is secured. The collateral used to secure a loan is usually the tangible assets (buildings, equipment, inventory, accounts receivable, or even personal assets) of the firm or its owners. Unsecured debt is that debt which is not secured by any collateral other than the promise to repay. Debt may be either short term or long term; short-term debt has a maturity of less than one year, and long-term debt has a maturity of more than one year.

equity

Equity capital is the capital that has been invested in the firm by investors expecting a return on their investment that is primarily based on the increase in the value of their investment rather than from a specific return in the form of dividends. There is a legal obligation to repay creditors, but there is no legal obligation to repay equity investors.

risk capital

Start-up capital may also be divided into the capital needed to purchase a business, or open the doors, and the capital needed to operate for one operating cycle or about six months. This type of capital is sometimes known as **risk capital.** The providers of risk capital are those investors willing to take the inherent risk of starting a new enterprise with all the uncertainties of business success or failure. Start-up capital may be further divided into capital needed to purchase capital assets such as the building and equipment and the capital needed to purchase inventory. The sources for this type of capital are those willing to lend money only if the loan is secured by tangible assets. In their search for capital, small business owners must recognize the difference because there are sources of capital for capital assets (those assets with a life of more than one year) and the capital needed for shorter term assets such as inventory. This distinction will be noted in the following section as each different source of capital is presented. The capital needed to open the doors and for the first six months of operation is much harder to obtain from outside sources than is the capital backed by tangible assets.

The business plan should determine the amount of initial capital needed to start a business. The complete business plan (see Chapter 5) should contain a section on the capital requirements to open the business and a section showing the cash flows over the start-up period. The start-up period could be as short as three months or as long as several years, with the typical period ranging from six to nine months.

Cash Budgets

cash budget

The **cash budget,** which must be part of the business plan, should cover the first year of business and should be updated after each turnover period. The cash budget, therefore, needs to cover two different periods. The first period is the time necessary to set up the business and to ready it for opening. The second period is the time expected to cover at least one complete inventory turnover. The inventory turnover period is the time between opening and the cash collection from sales from one complete "turnover" of a firm's inventory. For example, if inventory turnover is expected to be four times per year (i.e., sales are expected to be four times the retail value of total inventory), then the new owner should prepare a cash budget that will carry the firm through the first three months of operation.

The objective of this cash budget is to determine how much cash will be needed until money received from sales is sufficient to cover future purchases and the firm is, in effect, supporting itself. A quick method of making this determination is to multiply the expected sales figure by the assumed gross margin. Thus, if the annual sales are expected to be $340,000, and the inventory turnover is expected to be four, the average inventory should be $340,000/4 = $85,000. If the gross margin is expected to be 35 percent, then the inventory cost would be $85,000 × (1 − .35) = $55,250. The new owner then must plan to cover all operating expenses through the first three months plus the cost of purchasing all new inventory. (Cash budgeting is presented in greater detail in Chapter 15.)

SOURCES OF CAPITAL

A recent study by the Federal Reserve and the Small Business Administration revealed some interesting facts on where small firms obtain their financing. The firms surveyed were in a diversified group of industries, with 25.6 percent in the retail industry, 18.7 percent in the service industry, 13.4 percent in the construction industry, and 10.2 percent in wholesaling. Firms with ten or fewer employees made up 77.7 percent of the surveyed firms, and 54.2 percent had annual sales of less than $250,000. Of this group, almost 97 percent used their local (within thirty miles of the firm's location) commercial bank to provide some of their financing. The services provided by the commercial bank included checking accounts, lines of credit, motor vehicle loans, mortgage loans, and equipment leasing. Nonbank financial institutions, however, were the main providers of leasing services.[2]

Entrepreneurs often waste valuable time seeking funds from the wrong sources.

The primary sources of capital include

- Personal funds
- Family, relatives, friends
- Partners
- Private investors
- Venture capitalists
- Going public

The key to effectively locating the sources of capital for the new firm is to know which sources to approach for particular types of capital. This section presents the primary sources of capital together with an explanation as to the type of business that each source typically considers before providing funds. In addition, the advantages and disadvantages of each source will be discussed.

Personal Funds

Small business owners should expect to provide start-up capital for their own firm. Many owners feel that they are providing not only the idea but also the time and energy to get their firm started; therefore, they should not also be expected to provide start-up funds from their own personal assets. Looking at the same situation from the investors' (sources) standpoint, they are seldom willing to provide capital to the new firm if the primary beneficiaries of those funds are not willing to risk some of their own capital. In fact, personal funds are the most important source of start-up capital—not only in the United States, but worldwide.[3]

Typically most small business owners have access to more capital than they realize. The cash in their checking and savings accounts is the capital most recognize as readily available, but they can usually borrow even greater sums using other personal assets. Among these assets are their house, stocks, bonds, cash value of life insurance policies, and many other assets that may be used as collateral. A risky source of capital can even be cash advances from several credit cards. The use of credit cards as a source of capital is very risky because of the high interest charged and the short term of the loan. Although not a recommended source, credit cards have been used to give the cash infusion needed to start many businesses. The capital provided by the small business owner should be used to pay for all the normal start-up expenses except the purchase of tangible assets such as buildings, equipment, and inventory. The primary advantage of using personal funds is that the owner is in total control of how those funds are used. A major disadvantage of using personal funds is that, for most small business owners, these funds are very limited.

Family, Relatives, and Friends

Almost all small business owners will need to look to both family and friends as potential sources of capital. In fact, this is the second most popular source after the use of personal funds.[4] Family and friends are much more willing to invest in a new enterprise than most other sources of capital because they either know the entrepreneur and the product or service that will be produced or are willing to take a chance on someone they know because they want to help him or her succeed. Capital raised from family and friends could be either debt or equity and is usually used in the start-up phase of the business.

Funds obtained from family and friends should be treated as a business transaction, not as a simple handshake loan between friends. Few things can sour a friendship or ruin a family relationship as quickly as a misunderstanding over money. If the funds are in the form of debt, the lender should be given a document that states the amount of the loan, the interest rate on the loan, when the interest payments are due, and when the principal will be repaid. If the funds represent equity, the investor should be given a document as to the number of shares purchased, when, if ever, dividends will be paid, and how the shares may be valued and sold. All investors should be kept up to date on how the company is doing. This may be accomplished through periodic meetings with all investors or through periodic reports to them. News about the company, even bad news, will help the small business owner's relationship with these investors and reduce a potentially debilitating situation.

The primary advantage of obtaining funds from family and friends stems from the increase in the amount of funds that may be raised. The small business owner has only her or his own funds, but the potential sources increase as more individuals are involved. The major disadvantage with this source is that family and friends, because they know the small business owner personally, may tend to give unrequested or unneeded advice on how the firm should be run. If the firm fails, this group may hold the small business owner responsible for their losses for a very long time, straining family and personal relationships.

Partners

In addition to family and friends, other people may be interested in investing in a new business. By taking on a partner or partners, the entrepreneur may gain several important advantages. The first and most obvious advantage is that a partner may bring additional financial resources into the enterprise. Partners have assets that normally will total much more than those of a single individual, and, thus, the initial financial strength of the business will be stronger. In addition, if each individual small business owner has family and friends as potential sources of capital, then partners, together with their family and friends, would be able to extend the number of this potential source of funds. Partners can be "limited" partners, which means that they have limited liability and limited control. (For more on limited partnerships, see Chapter 8.)

Finally, a partner may bring to the organization a particular type of business expertise that can complement the small business owner's skills. One partner may have a good background in manufacturing whereas another may have excellent marketing skills. This could make a combination that increases the overall management skill level of the business. However, with these potential advantages comes the potential disadvantage of having to share the decision making with a partner. If a partner puts resources into a firm, he or she is normally going to want to participate in the decision-making process. Thus, if the owner wishes to obtain a partner or partners, she or he is going to have to relinquish some control, which is not always easy to do.

Private Investors

Private investors are usually local successful business people who invest in new companies within their own industry or related industries. In fact, private investors have been particularly active in financing high-technology firms.[5] In addition to providing financial help, private investors can help the small business owner by providing advice, local contacts, and introductions within their sphere of influence. In addition, private investors can help in obtaining better terms with suppliers or in obtaining the services of an accountant who "does not take on new customers."

Private investors usually understand the risks they are taking and are willing to invest in the start-up phase of a new business. Their investment usually will be in equity capital, but sometimes they will loan a new firm funds for an extended period of time without the typical collateral require-

| The Way It Is | **7-1 ANGELS** |

Finding an angel can be the quickest way to obtain start-up capital. *Angel* is a term sometimes used to describe private investors who provide new companies with start-up and/or operating capital. Finding an angel is not an easy task, and it takes a lot of work and perseverance. An example of how this system functions may be the best way to explain it.

ICOM Simulations, Inc., was an early-stage software company looking for operating capital. William Weaver is a partner in a Chicago law firm who, with a group of twenty to twenty-five potential investors, continually looks for promising growth companies in need of capital. Mr. Weaver heard about ICOM from a contact at a major accounting firm. He visited the firm several times, talked to the founder, Tod Zipnick, and had some people who were familiar with the technology ICOM employed evaluate the firm. He then asked Mr. Zipnick to make a presentation to seventeen potential investors. The result was an investment of $2 million in ICOM. For this capital infusion, Mr. Zipnick gave up almost 20 percent of ICOM's equity, but he maintained control and obtained the capital boost needed to continue the development of a promising technology.[6]

ments of most lenders. A disadvantage of private investors is that they may start making managerial demands of the firm, particularly if the firm runs into early problems. They have a stake in the firm, and when things go bad, they tend to want to have a hand in turning the company around. Private investors are sometimes called angels (see The Way It Is 7-1).

Venture Capitalists

venture
capitalists

There is an almost mystical air about **venture capitalists.** The popular press has portrayed this group as a swashbuckling group of adventurers who are always looking for the next Apple or McDonalds and are willing to "bet" large sums of their money on firms seeming to have unlimited potential for growth. Like so many things, the reality differs greatly from the myth. Venture capitalists are individuals or firms that invest primarily in companies having a potential for fast growth. Venture capitalists typically invest between $500,000 and $2 million in firms in those industries in which they have some knowledge. In fact, most venture capitalists will only invest in specific industries, such as high technology, real estate, or medical technology, although some will invest in a diversified group of new firms. Venture capitalists are, therefore, willing to take the high risk that is inherent in a new or fast-growing business, but they hope to obtain a very high return for taking these risks.

Venture capitalists usually do not invest in the start-up phase of a firm but wait until the firm has a record that indicates the potential for fast growth. When they invest, they usually take an ownership (equity) position and, in effect, become much like a financial partner to the entrepreneur. Typically, they plan to sell their stock, either to the public or to the small business owner, in three to five years after it has appreciated greatly. Thus, their goal is to promote the growth of the firm over a relatively short period of time and then get out. They are not interested in investing in the firm over a long period of time but in obtaining a high return on their investment. To the small business owner, venture capitalists have the advantage of investing equity capital in their firm at a point in time where raising additional capital to promote growth may be critical to the future of the firm. The primary disadvantage to the small business owner is that venture capitalists are looking for a return on their investment through selling their stock in a few years; thus, the owner may be forced to either repurchase his or her shares or to go public. Therefore, by accepting venture capital, the small business owner is accepting the fact that the firm will be on a fast track to becoming a publicly held firm with the resulting dilution of ownership position to the original owner.

Many entrepreneurs face a difficult decision before accepting capital from venture capitalists or before selling shares to any other potential investors. Giving up any ownership control for financial assistance is not a decision that should be taken lightly. Some entrepreneurs indicate that they would rather have a small part of a big firm, than all or a big part of a small one. The decision, however, is one that the entrepreneur should consider very carefully before accepting additional shareholders, for once in, they are also owners and will have some say in managerial decisions affecting the future of the company.

Going Public

going public

Going public is the process through which a privately held (all equity held by a small group of individuals) firm sells a portion of its equity to the public through a stock offering. There are two major reasons for going public. First, the original investors have a chance to cash in on their investment. If a firm is privately held, then the owners control the firm, but their investment is tied up in the assets of that firm. If some of their shares are sold to the public, then they have a chance to realize a return on their investment through selling their shares to others. Until a firm goes public, the market value (value of the stock to public investors) of the firm is very hard to determine. Certainly the book value is known with some certainty, but the book value only shows the accounting value of the assets minus the liabilities. For most growth firms, the market value is much greater than the book value.

The second reason for going public is that it allows the firm to raise equity capital from a much broader group of potential investors. When a firm goes public, the original owners sell not only some of their shares, but also additional shares to the public. Thus, in the typical initial public offering (IPO), a combination of owners' shares and new shares are sold to the public. Once a firm has gone public, raising additional equity capital through additional public offerings is much easier than attempting to raise capital through personal contacts. (Going public is discussed in greater detail in Chapter 20.)

The major disadvantages of going public are that ownership control is diluted, the firm must issue public financial statements, the cost of selling common stock (flotation costs) is very high (up to 25 percent), and there is a significant increase in the liability exposure of the directors and officers.

BANKS

Banks are in the business of lending money. However, they have a fiduciary responsibility to their depositors, which means that they have a legal obligation to take care of the monies entrusted to them and not to take unnecessary risks. Banks will evaluate a loan request on whether the business will generate enough cash flow to meet the interest obligations.

To determine whether a new firm will be able to meet its interest obligations, there are three fairly standard financial documents that bankers will require from the small business owner. First, bankers will request the last three years of the small business owner's tax returns. They will also request the tax returns from the small business owner's firm if she or he has been in business that long. The second document will be the business plan with financial projections. The business plan was thoroughly covered in Chapter 5, but this section indicates that someone beside the small business owner will be reading it. The final document that may be requested is the firm's and/or the small business owner's latest financial statements including a personal financial statement. See The Way It Is 7-2 for more on how to obtain a bank loan.

Personal Financial Statement

The personal financial statement is one of the primary statements that a banker will be interested in viewing. Unfortunately, many small business owners will not have developed one of these statements previously and may not know exactly what the banker is requesting. The personal financial statement is a statement of the owner's net worth. Physically, the personal financial statement is no more than a balance sheet of personal assets and liabilities. The assets are listed in order of liquidity, starting with cash and monies in checking and savings accounts. Other assets include certificates of deposits, marketable securities such as stocks and bonds, any receivables due from goods or services sold or performed, and any notes (loans) that are due. Long-term assets are listed next including the market value of all real estate, personal property (household goods), cash value of life insurance, automobiles, boats, planes, and other assets such as an art/coin collection or jewelry. All these items must be listed at the present prevailing market value, not what they originally cost.

After assets, the liabilities must be listed. Current liabilities include a list of all the bills that are currently due and a notation as to whether they have been billed to the small business owner. Thus, all store charge accounts, credit card purchases, doctor's or other professional charges, and any other payments paid on a monthly basis but that are not necessarily paid off each

7-2 BANK LOANS WHEN TIMES ARE TOUGH

Jack Asher is the CEO of Chester A. Asher, Inc., a Philadelphia-based company that bakes and sells chocolate and fudge. The company had banked with the same bank for forty-five years and had never reneged on a loan. Yet when he recently asked for a letter of credit to back up $5.5 million in bonds that the company wanted to purchase a new plant, the bank balked. Later the bank refused a $115,000 loan the company wanted to purchase a smaller candy company. Mr. Asher was able to obtain the letter of credit and the loan from another bank based on the strong financial statements of his company.

To obtain loans when times are tough requires that small business owners be prepared for the following:

1. The company will need income projections produced by a CPA.
2. The bank may request that the firm submit audited financial statements.
3. Banks may require more frequent financial reports, sometimes even requesting monthly statements.
4. More banks are asking the firm for more collateral than in the past.
5. The owner should be prepared to submit more personal income statement information, sometimes including copies of the owner's income tax returns.

When times are tough, owners must be prepared to prove their credit worthiness with each loan request.[7]

month should be included as a liability. Long-term liabilities include the balance still due on any loans that are payable to a bank, other financial institution, or even a friend. The balance on any mortgage secured by real estate and any other liabilities such as court-ordered judgments or the settlement of a lawsuit should also be included.

The difference between the total of all assets and all liabilities is known as net worth. Thus, net worth is the total market value of everything the small business owner owns minus the total value of all liabilities. What the banker is looking for is the size of the small business owner's net worth, because this is the value on which most loans will be based. In a nutshell, this means that bankers are willing to lend funds to the small business owner's firm, but these funds will be based on the collateral (security) of his or her personal assets.

The Five Cs of Credit

In addition to the collateral the small business owner may have in either personal assets or the firm's assets, bankers also look at five other aspects of

**five Cs of
credit**

the small business owner's background before extending a loan. These elements are sometimes called the **five Cs of credit** and include character, capacity, credit rating, collateral, and conditions.[8] Character is the small business owner's record of fulfilling commitments. A banker wants to be comfortable with his or her decision to lend the small business owner money, and it is easier to lend money to a person known for keeping his or her word. Capacity refers to the ability of the small business owner to make periodic interest payments and to repay the principal when due. This differs from character in that a person could have a history of fulfilling his or her commitments, but this loan request may be considered to be over his or her financial ability to repay.

Credit rating is the small business owner's and her or his firm's corporate reputation within the financial community for paying financial obligations on time. Typically a banker will check the local credit bureau and/or a national credit agency, such as Dun and Bradstreet, to obtain a credit report on the person or firm requesting a loan. These reports show the history of the individual or the firm in repaying both financial institutions for loans and in paying their suppliers. In addition, these reports contain the firm's financial statements, and special emphasis is placed on analyzing the firm's risk ratios—the debt-asset ratio, the current and quick ratios, and the times-interest-earned ratio.

Collateral has been discussed above, but there is more to the value of the asset than book value. A building could be worth several hundred thousand dollars but be located in an area that could make finding a buyer a very long and difficult process.

The final C is the current economic condition. Bankers tend to lend money more freely during economic expansions and are more likely to be tighter in their lending practices during economic recessions. From a purely economic standpoint, however, banks should actually be trying to slow down the speed of some economic expansions by making money harder to obtain during the expansion and should try to help their customers out of the recession during economic downturns. That is good economic philosophy, but the cash flows (ability to make interest payments) are just not there during economic recessions and that is the main reason bankers are reluctant to make loans at that time.

Types of Bank Loans

What types of loans should the small business owner expect to obtain from the bank? Banks make two basic types of loans: secured and unsecured. The unsecured loan is usually made for relatively small amounts and is granted to only the bank's most creditworthy customers. This type of loan is usually for a short time period (typically less than one year), and the interest and principal are both paid at maturity.

Secured loans are backed by specific types of assets. These assets are fixed assets such as machinery, automobiles, trucks, furniture and fixtures, or real estate. The term of these loans generally ranges from one to ten years. Usually interest is paid on a periodic basis (monthly, quarterly or semiannually), whereas the principal may be amortized over the life of the loan or due at maturity. Although the bank is securing the loan with a lien on specific assets, it is looking at the expected cash flows from the business as the source of funds with which the loan will be paid off. Thus, collateral is good, but the loan will only be granted if the business seems sound because the bank does not wish to recover its money by foreclosing. The Way It Is 7-3 gives a little more insight on obtaining a loan.

Besides those secured by fixed assets, several other types of secured loans are granted by banks. Banks will sometimes set up a line of credit that is secured by the firm's accounts receivable or its inventory. A line of credit means that a bank will allow a customer to borrow up to a specified amount over a relatively short period of time, typically six months to a year. With accounts receivable financing, the bank will grant a line of credit based on a percentage (usually 50 to 85 percent) of the firm's acceptable accounts receivable. Typically a bank will define acceptable as those receivables from customers with a certain credit rating, and they will reject receivables from lower-rated customers, customers that are overdue on their payments, and foreign customers. The line of credit will be constantly reviewed by the bank and may be revised either up or down depending on the quality and dollar amount of the receivables.

The Way It Is

7-3 SELLING YOURSELF TO A BANKER

Although many start-up firms have trouble obtaining a line of credit from a bank, Stephen Kenda of Kenda Systems Inc. found a way. Kenda Systems provides temporary computer consultants to a growing group of blue-chip commercial and military clients. Stephen's problem is that he must pay his employees before he receives money from his clients. Knowing that cash flow would always be a problem as long as his billings were growing, Stephen courted his banker from his company's inception. He took out small loans and paid them back on time and gave his banker copies of his financial statements. Still his original banker capped Kenda's line of credit at $100,000.

The search for a bank willing to extend a larger line of credit was long and frustrating. Stephen wrote a three-year business plan and used his clients (Digital Equipment, Honeywell, and Wang) as his calling card. Finally Shawmut Bank agreed to extend a line of credit based on 80 percent of Kenda System's accounts receivable. The loan, however, did require a personal guarantee from Stephen, and the loan was secured by the total assets of the company. Stephen believes he was finally successful due to his willingness to explain his service to his banker and his clean credit history.[9]

Inventory financing is similar to accounts receivable financing. Inventory financing is also a line of credit granted a firm, but the line of credit is based on a percentage of the value of a firm's inventory. Like accounts receivable financing, inventory financing is short term in maturity. Small business owners should realize that both inventory financing and accounts receivable financing are considered more risky than other types of bank loans and, therefore, will carry a higher interest rate. This type of financing is considered risky because a financially strong firm can borrow on its own strength (unsecured loan) or on its expected cash flows especially when the loan is backed by fixed assets. When a firm has exhausted these stronger sources of loans, then it turns to weaker sources such as its accounts receivable or inventory.

One of the main advantages of borrowing from the bank as a source of capital is that banks offer several types of financing and, in effect, offer a sort of one-stop shopping for the small business owner who usually does not have the time to shop for several sources of funds. In addition, banks offer miscellaneous services that other sources may not provide. Among these are credit checks, data processing, tax advice, letters of credit, export credit insurance, foreign bank drafts, and general business advice. The primary disadvantage of borrowing from a bank is that it can become very adamant in its efforts to collect its interest. Sometimes it is quick to force a delinquent payer to pay off the entire loan and to discontinue or reduce lines of credit.

OTHER CREDIT SOURCES

In addition to the better known sources of capital discussed previously in this chapter, several excellent but lesser known types exist. These include the use of trade credit, finance companies, leasing companies, factoring, and warehousing. Another potential source of capital is the government. Each source has its own fairly unique set of circumstances, which a small business owner can explore as a potential funding source. The characteristics of each source with its advantages and disadvantages will be presented.

Trade Credit

trade credit

Trade credit is really nothing more than asking the firm's suppliers to extend their credit terms. If supplies (raw materials, finished goods, machine components, catalogs, supplies, etc.) are purchased from a trade supplier on credit, the supplier is, in effect, lending the purchaser the amount of the purchase. Without this credit, the small business owner would have to obtain the funds and pay for the supplies as they arrived. There may be a cost to this credit if the supplier offers discounts. Terms of a typical discount could be 2/10 net 40. This means that the purchaser can take a 2 percent discount from the total invoice amount if the bill is paid within ten days, but the full amount is due in forty days.

One advantage to the purchaser is that the firm has forty days in which to obtain the necessary funds. It is even possible during this interval to sell and receive payment for the goods. Another advantage is that this type of financing is on an informal arrangement and usually no formal (written) agreements are made. A final advantage of this type of financing is that it is possible to ask the supplier to grant an extended period before the supplies must be paid for. Showing a supplier a business plan or just explaining the business to the supplier could be a method of obtaining extended terms. Suppliers can sometimes be very understanding and helpful to the new firm, particularly if this empathy could mean more business in the future.

The disadvantage is that there is a cost to not taking the discount. The cost of not taking the discount can be indicated two ways. The first is the difference in the amount that must be paid. For example, with terms of 2/10 net 40 on a $10,000 invoice, there is a $200 difference in paying on the tenth or fortieth day. Thus, the purchaser is paying $200 to keep from borrowing $10,000 for thirty days. The second method indicates the percentage cost. This cost may be calculated from the following equation:

$$\text{Cost} = \frac{\text{discount \%}}{(100 - \text{discount \%})} \times \frac{365}{(\text{final due date} - \text{discount period})}$$

For terms of 2/10 net 40, the cost would be

$$\text{Cost} = \frac{2}{(100 - 2)} \times \frac{365}{(40 - 10)} = .248 \text{ or } 24.8\%$$

This means that if the purchaser can obtain a thirty-day loan at a lower rate than 24.8 percent, then it is better to obtain that loan than to use trade credit. Thus trade credit, although easy to obtain, may have a relatively high cost if discounts are offered. These costs should be calculated and weighed against the costs of other sources of financing.

Finance Companies

finance companies

Finance companies are different from commercial banks in a number of distinct ways. Whereas banks obtain the funds that they lend from their depositors, finance companies obtain their funds from their owners (stockholders) and from borrowing. Thus, finance companies raise most of their funds by borrowing (based on the financial strength of the finance company) from other sources, including selling their own commercial paper. They make their money by lending these borrowed funds at a higher rate than their costs. Finance companies are not regulated by the same state and federal laws as commercial banks and operate in a different business environment. Generally, they tend to make riskier loans than commercial banks and, therefore, charge higher rates. Finance companies grant asset-based loans, inventory loans, and accounts receivable loans just as banks do, but they also arrange equipment leasing financing and will factor accounts receivable.

Leasing Companies

leasing companies

Leasing companies are one of the fastest growing sources of funds in the United States. There are some financial institutions that specialize in leasing, and leasing is very popular as a method of financing vehicles and equipment.

Many equipment suppliers and their leasing companies offer generous lease and lease-purchase agreements to encourage sales of their equipment.

In a leasing agreement, the user (lessee) selects the equipment needed and makes periodic payments to the owner (lessor). The lessee obtains the use, and therefore, the benefits of ownership but without the large outlay of funds usually required in purchasing the equipment or without having to arrange financing based on the financial strength of the firm. The lessor is able to purchase the equipment based on the lessor's financial strength and for this reason may be able to obtain lower financing costs than the lessee would have been able to obtain. For this reason, leasing may cost less than purchasing. The two major sources of lease financing are leasing companies and commercial banks.

The two basic types of leases are operating leases and financial leases. Operating leases, sometimes called service leases, are usually used for office equipment such as computers, copying machines, telephone equipment, and motorized vehicles such as cars, trucks, and planes. Operating leases normally call for the lessor to provide maintenance and service for the leased equipment. In addition, operating leases typically are not fully amortized over the term (life) of the contract. This means that the payments are not high enough to cover the full cost of the equipment, usually because the contract is written for a shorter period of time than the economic life of the equipment. Finally, operating leases, unlike financial leases, may be canceled. This is an important feature because it means that the equipment may be returned if there is a decline in business or if the equipment is rendered obsolete by newer technology.

Financial leases, sometimes called capital leases, cannot be canceled and are fully amortized over the economic life of the asset. Fully amortized means that the payments cover the full price of the leased equipment plus a return to the lessor. Normally with a financial lease, the lessee will provide equipment maintenance and service.

Factoring

factoring

Factoring is similar to accounts receivable financing in that the accounts receivable of the firm are used as the asset against which funds are being provided. The major difference is that with factoring the lending company takes complete title of the accounts receivable and collects directly from the customer. In effect, the firm sells its accounts receivable to the factor. Factors charge a processing fee (factoring fee) of 1 to 1.5 percent of the net invoiced billings that they accept. In addition they usually charge around 3 to 4 percent over the prime rate on advances the firm takes against the invoices. With factoring, the firm gets its money faster (the advances against the invoices) but at a high cost. In addition, some customers dislike being billed by the factor.

Factoring can save the company the cost of having a credit department because the factor will check the credit of potential customers before it will accept their invoices. Once the factor accepts the invoice, it assumes the risk

The
Way
It Is

7-4 FACTORING FOR IMPROVED CASH FLOW

Factoring can help a new firm grow fast. Magnetic Sportswear started with $350,000 in capital, but the manufacturer of women's apparel had sales of $7 million in its first year and $27 million two years later. To help finance this growth, Magnetic Sportswear used a nonbank factor who was willing to finance 80 percent of its accounts receivable. Thus, as sales grew, the factor provided the financing that enabled the firm to continue growing.

Although factoring is fairly common in the textile and apparel business, We Care Nurses Inc. used factoring to promote its growth in the temporary employee business. We Care places temporary employees in hospitals. The company needs cash to pay the nurses weekly, but the hospitals pay in 30 to 90 days. To obtain the cash to pay the nurses and, therefore, to be able to place even more nurses, We Care turned to a factor. The factor was willing to purchase 70 percent of the receivables, and We Care started transferring its invoices to the factor twice a week.

In both of these cases, a growing firm was able to obtain cash much quicker than if it had waited to collect its own receivables. The improved cash flow allowed these firms to grow faster than would have been possible otherwise.[10]

of collecting, and the seller has no further liability. In a typical sale in which the customer wishes to buy a product on credit, the seller has the factor check the customer's credit rating. The factor will either accept the sale or reject it. If accepted, the customer leaves with the product and is later billed by the factor. The seller receives the money for the sale from the factor. As can be seen from this description, factoring would work best for those firms that sell few but high-priced goods such as large appliances or cars. Factoring fits some types of businesses better than others, and it is prevalent in the textile, furniture manufacturing, clothing manufacturing, toy, shoe, and plastic industries. For an example of how one firm used a factor, see The Way It Is 7-4.

Warehousing

warehousing

Warehousing is a method of obtaining short-term funds on inventory that is stored in a warehouse but that is not for immediate processing or sale. The warehouse may be either a public warehouse or a field warehouse. When the inventory is stored in a public warehouse, the firm storing the goods must have no affiliation with the owners of the goods. In effect, it is a public warehouse in the terms of being in the business of storing goods for others. When the goods are placed in a public warehouse, a receipt may be obtained and used as collateral for inventory financing. An example of a public warehouse could be a peach cannery that must process a crop of peaches over a relatively short period of time. The farmers bringing their crop to the canner want to be paid on, or shortly after, delivery. The canner needs to pay the farmers but will only be able to sell the canned goods over the next few months. Using the public warehouse as a storage facility for the canned peaches allows the canner to borrow money on the finished product, pay the farmers, and thus buy enough peaches to stock enough inventory to satisfy the expected sales.

A field warehouse is set up on the premises of the borrower and is usually a specified area that is partitioned from the other inventories. Within the partitioned area, inventory belongs to the lender rather than the borrower. For example, a boat manufacturer could set up a field warehouse for storing motors. The motors would be stored in the partitioned area until needed by the manufacturer for installation in a completed, or nearly completed boat. The motors would be the property of the seller until they were taken from the partitioned area, at which time the manufacturer would be responsible for the purchase of the motors. This arrangement allows the manufacturer to inventory a range of motors without the immediate cost of paying for them. From the seller's standpoint, they are providing an incentive for the manufacturer to use their products rather than those of a competitor.

Government Sources

There are several potential sources of funds from state, local, and federal government. Unfortunately funding from these sources tends to come and go with the various political and economic tides that sweep the country. Both state and city officials have at one time or another seen the need to provide funding for small businesses and entrepreneurial firms within their borders. They recognize that small firms need help to get started and that after starting, they tend to be major sources of job growth.

THE SMALL BUSINESS ADMINISTRATION (SBA). The SBA was created by Congress in 1953 to aid small businesses. The aid provided by it can be either managerial advice or financial assistance. Although the SBA seldom grants direct loans to start-up businesses, it does generally participate with banks through a loan guarantee program. In this program the SBA will guarantee up to 90 percent of a loan, which helps banks grant loans that they otherwise may not have undertaken. Each year, the SBA guarantees loans worth about $4 billion; these represent about 50,000 separate loans, which makes it the largest single source of financial assistance in the United States. The typical SBA-arranged loan is for about $100,000 with a maturity of seven to ten years.

The SBA has provided financial assistance for many firms that have become household names today including Winnebago, Apple Computer, Nike, Federal Express, and Godfather Pizza. Obtaining an SBA loan, however, requires a lot of paperwork, and the small business owner will probably still be required to secure the loan with either personal or company assets. Other requirements include the following:

- Loan application—SBA form (See Exhibit 7-1)
- Personal history of principals—SBA form
- Personal financial statement—SBA form

The Small Business Administration, created in 1953, provides both managerial advice and financial assistance to small businesses.

- Current balance sheet for the firm
- Pro forma income statement for one year
- Business plan
- Business lease and terms (if applicable)
- Income statements of business to be purchased (if applicable)
- Federal tax returns (previous two years)
- Proposed bill of sale and schedule of inventory, equipment, furniture, and fixtures to be purchased with the loan

Although this list of forms and statements may seem like a lot of paperwork to most first-time entrepreneurs, it is a fairly accurate indication of the requirements almost all providers of capital will request.

STATE AND LOCAL GOVERNMENTS. Many state and local governments have economic development centers that encourage and sometimes provide financial assistance to new and innovative firms in their area. State and local governments know that small firms provide the majority of new jobs in their area, that small firms tend to grow and provide even more jobs, and that homegrown firms tend to stay put. For these reasons, many local govern-

EXHIBIT 7-1 U.S. Small Business Administration Application for Business Loan

Applicant	Full Address	

Name of Business	Tax I.D. No.

Full Street Address	Tel. No. (Inc. A/C)

City	County	State	Zip	Number of Employees (Including subsidiaries and affiliates)

Type of Business	Date Business Established	At Time of Application _____

Bank of Business Account and Address	If Loan is Approved _____

Subsidiaries or Affiliates _____
(Separate from above)

Use of Proceeds: (Enter Gross Dollar Amounts Rounded to Nearest Hundreds)	Loan Requested	SBA USE ONLY
Land Acquisition		
New Construction/Expansion/Repair		
Acquisition and/or Repair of Machinery and Equipment		
Inventory Purchase		
Working Capital (Including Accounts Payable)		
Acquisition of Existing Business		
Payoff SBA Loan		
Payoff Bank Loan (Non SBA Associated)		
Other Debt Payment (Non SBA Associated)		
All Other		
Total Loan Requested		
Term of Loan		

Collateral

If your collateral consists of (A) Land and Building, (D) Accounts Receivable and/or (E) Inventory, fill in the appropriate blanks. If you are pledging (B) Machinery and Equipment, (C) Furniture and Fixtures, and/or (F) Other, please provide an itemized list (labeled Exhibit A) that contains serial and identification numbers for all articles that had an original value greater than $500. Include a legal description of Real Estate offered as collateral.

	Present Market Value	Present Loan Balance	SBA Use Only Collateral Valuation
A. Land and Building	$	$	$
B. Machinery & Equipment			
C. Furniture & Fixtures			
D. Accounts Receivable			
E. Inventory			
F. Other			
Totals	$	$	$

PREVIOUS SBA OR OTHER GOVERNMENT FINANCING: If you or any principals or affiliates have ever requested Government Financing, complete the following:

Name of Agency	Original Amount of Loan	Date of Request	Approved or Declined	Balance	Current or Past Due
	$			$	
	$			$	

SBA Form 4 (2-85) Previous Editions Obsolete

EXHIBIT 7-1 *(continued)*

INDEBTEDNESS: Furnish the following information on all installment debts, contracts, notes, and mortgages payable. Indicate by an asterisk (*) items to be paid by loan proceeds and reason for paying same (present balance should agree with latest balance sheet submitted).

To Whom Payable	Original Amount	Original Date	Present Balance	Rate of Interest	Maturity Date	Monthly Payment	Security	Current or Past Due
	$		$			$		
	$		$			$		
	$		$			$		
	$		$			$		

MANAGEMENT (Proprietor, partners, officers, directors and all holders of outstanding stock — <u>100% of ownership must be shown</u>). Use separate sheet if necessary.

Name and Social Security Number	Complete Address	% Owned	*Military Service From	To	*Race	*Sex

* This data is collected for statistical purposes only. It has no bearing on the credit decision to approve or decline this application.

ASSISTANCE   List the name(s) and occupation(s) of any who assisted in preparation of this form, other than applicant.

Name and Occupation	Address	Total Fees Paid	Fees Due
Name and Occupation	Address	Total Fees Paid	Fees Due

Signature of Preparers if Other Than Applicant

THE FOLLOWING EXHIBITS MUST BE COMPLETED WHERE APPLICABLE. ALL QUESTIONS ANSWERED ARE MADE A PART OF THE APPLICATION.

For Guaranty Loans please provide an original and one copy (Photocopy is Acceptable) of the Application Form, and all Exhibits to the participating lender. For Direct Loans submit one original copy of application and Exhibits to SBA.

Submit SBA Form 1261 (Statements Required by Laws and Executive Orders). This form must be signed and dated by each Proprietor, Partner, Principal or Guarantor.

1. Submit SBA Form 912 (Personal History Statement) for each person e.g. owners, partners, officers, directors, major stockholders, etc.; the instructions are on SBA Form 912.

2. Furnish a signed current personal balance sheet (SBA Form 413 may be used for this purpose) for each stockholder (with 20% or greater ownership), partner, officer, and owner. Social Security number should be included on personal financial statement. Label this Exhibit B.

3. Include the statements listed below: 1, 2, 3 for the last three years; also 1, 2, 3, 4 dated within 90 days of filing the application; and statement 5, if applicable. This is Exhibit C (SBA has Management Aids that help in the preparation of financial statements.) All information must be signed and dated.

1. Balance Sheet   2. Profit and Loss Statement
3. Reconciliation of Net Worth
4. Aging of Accounts Receivable and Payable
5. Earnings projections for at least one year where financial statements for the last three years are unavailable or where requested by District Office.
   (If Profit and Loss Statement is not available, explain why and substitute Federal Income Tax Forms.)

4. Provide a brief history of your company and a paragraph describing the expected benefits it will receive from the loan. Label it Exhibit D.

ALL EXHIBITS MUST BE SIGNED AND DATED BY PERSON SIGNING THIS FORM.

SBA Form 4 (2-85) Previous Editions Obsolete

ments have worked hard to encourage new firms and to support them in their early and formative years.

New Jersey, for example, provided $6 million for an advanced food technology center, and New York has started a $200 million biotechnology-research park. Several states, including New York and Ohio, now permit a small portion of state-held pension funds to be invested in small business ventures. Many cities have small business incubators, which are buildings where several new businesses have their offices and/or labs. The grouping of new businesses saves money in shared office equipment and staff support and in the sharing of new ideas among the entrepreneurs. Many universities have also started small business centers with the stated purpose of providing financial assistance and, more importantly, research and technical expertise. For the entrepreneur interested in exploring state, local, or university assistance, a good starting point is the state economic development office or the local SBA office.

SUMMARY

The small business owner must determine how much capital is needed before attempting to raise the funds to start a firm and finance it through at least one operating cycle. The best method for making this determination is through the use of a well-developed business plan or a cash budget. The amount of capital needed, however, may vary greatly depending on the type of industry. Small business owners should also be aware of the different types of start-up capital needed and what sources tend to supply each. Among the many sources of start-up capital are the small business owner's personal funds, family and friends, partners, private investors, venture capitalists, sale of stock, and banks. Before approaching any of these sources, the small business owner should carefully consider the advantages and disadvantages of each.

Banks are in the business of lending money, and small business owners need to understand what type of loans banks make and how they should approach a bank for a loan. The three documents that may be required are copies of the small business owner's personal and/or business tax returns, the firm's business plan, and the small business owner's personal financial statement. Banks grant both secured and unsecured loans, but the unsecured loans will go only to the financially strongest individuals or firms. In addition to the collateral that may be required as security for a loan, banks may consider five intangible aspects, known as the five Cs of credit, before extending a loan.

Several additional sources of capital are available to the small business firm; these include the use of trade credit, finance companies, leasing companies, factors, and warehousing companies. Seldom are all these sources available to a single firm, but each provides its own unique set of circumstances that should be considered. Finally, potential government sources of funds include state and local governments and the SBA.

QUESTIONS FOR REVIEW AND DISCUSSION

1. Briefly describe the difference between debt and equity capital.
2. Why must small business owners be willing to commit their personal funds in a business before approaching other sources?
3. What are the disadvantages of obtaining start-up and/or operating funds from family and friends?
4. Why is a bank more interested in the cash flow a firm is expected to generate than the value of any assets that the firm uses as collateral for a loan?
5. What are the five Cs of credit? Give a brief description of each.
6. What is the difference between a secured and an unsecured loan? Under what circumstances would an entrepreneur expect to be able to obtain an unsecured loan?
7. How is trade credit a source of funds?
8. If a supplier offers terms of net 30, is there any cost of trade credit?
9. When should a firm consider an operating rather than a financial lease?
10. What is the major difference between accounts receivable financing and factoring?

KEY TERMS

cash budget	going public
collateral	leasing companies
debt	risk capital
equity	start-up capital
factoring	trade credit
finance companies	venture capitalists
five Cs of credit	warehousing

CASE
Cindy's Cakes

Jim Sinclair has worked as an engineer for a large paper mill company in Virginia for almost twenty years, but during the last few years he had thought more and more about having his own business. In the last few months, Jim has actively explored various opportunities ranging from start-ups to the purchase of a going business. Last week, a business broker introduced Jim to Cindy Allstair, the sole owner of Cindy's Cakes. Cindy had started her company over thirty years ago baking small individual-size cakes primarily for the vending machine business. She had developed five different types of cakes that sold well throughout the state of Virginia. According to the business broker, Cindy wanted to sell her business and move to Maine and retire. She was asking $1 million.

After doing a fairly intensive marketing study of the potential for individual cake sales and looking at the past four years of Cindy's financial statements, Jim was very interested in purchasing the business and being his own boss. His problem was how to pay for the business. The two most obvious sources of assets were those of the business and his own personal assets. Jim's personal assets consisted of $120,000 equity in his home, $175,000 in stocks and bonds, and $50,000 in his checking account. The financial statements for Cin-

dy's Cakes are attached. Cindy made it very clear that she was not interested in financing the purchase and wanted a cash offering.

QUESTIONS

1. Assume that Cindy agrees to a price of $900,000. Can Jim finance the purchase based on his personal assets and those of the firm? Explain your answer and list the assumptions you made.

2. In addition to the existing asset base, what other sources of capital could you suggest that Jim explore?

3. Do you think that Jim can obtain bank financing based on the potential cash flow from the business?

4. If you had money to invest, would you invest as a limited partner?

Cindy's Cakes

Income Statement, December 31

Sales		$1,098,000
Cost of sales		723,000
Gross profit		375,000
Expenses:		
Compensation of officers	$95,000	
Salaries and wages	73,945	
Repairs	5,500	
Utilities, office	12,700	
Contributions	715	
Advertising	3,300	
Pension, profit-sharing	55,700	
Employee benefits	28,300	
Office expenses	18,100	
Interest	540	
Depreciation	19,700	
Total expenses		$ 313,500
Income before taxes		61,500
Income taxes		11,500
Net income		$ 50,000

Cindy's Cakes

Balance Sheet, December 31

Current assets		Current liabilities	
Cash	$110,000	Accounts payable	$ 14,500
Marketable securities	30,000	Notes payable	12,400
Accounts receivable	58,400	Salaries payable	28,000
Inventories	48,300	Total current liabilities	$ 54,900
Total current assets	$246,700		
		Liabilities & stockholders' equity	
Fixed assets		Long-term debt	$ 0
Plant & equipment	$577,300	Stockholders' equity	
Less depreciation	204,000	Capital stock	59,900
Net plant & equipment	373,300	Retained earnings	505,200
		Total liabilities &	
Total assets	$620,000	stockholders' equity	$620,000

ACTIVITIES

1. Based on your own assets or assets you think you would have before starting a business, fill out the information requested in the U.S. Small Business Administration's "Application for Business Loan" (See Exhibit 7-1). Do you think you could obtain a loan based on this application? What are the primary strengths and weaknesses of your application?
2. Obtain and complete a business loan application from a local bank. Present this loan request to the class and have them critique the application's strengths and weaknesses. Ask the class if they would grant you the loan.

8 THE LEGAL ENVIRONMENT OF SMALL BUSINESS

Most entrepreneurs have very little legal experience or acumen, yet the very success of their businesses depends on operating within the laws of the country, state, and community. Business owners need the services of qualified attorneys before they start or buy a business, while they operate the business, and when they choose to sell the business or go public. In fact, entrepreneurs should seek legal advice whenever they make major decisions that determine the direction of their business. Small business owners usually do not have full-time lawyers in their employ, but they do have arrangements with lawyers and pay them for services rendered. We will discuss the selection and evaluation of attorneys more fully in Chapter 11; however, in this chapter we will discuss some of the more important services performed by attorneys.

Entrepreneurs should consult their attorneys about ownership form of the business—sole proprietorship, partnership, or corporation. Attorneys should also provide advice about contracts, leases, and warranties. We will also discuss the ways lawyers can help business owners protect proprietary and intellectual property.

OWNERSHIP FORMS

In the early stages of planning a business, entrepreneurs need to choose the form of ownership of the company. Should it be a sole proprietorship, a partnership, a C corporation, or an S corporation? Each form has advantages and disadvantages, which should be considered and discussed with an attorney and an accountant. Accountants and attorneys are needed because one of the major criteria used to select the best form of ownership is the tax treatment under each form (Exhibit 8-1 contains a few of the ways to measure different tax treatments). Fortunately for new business owners, the selection of a form of ownership need not be permanent. As situations change, owners can elect to change their company's legal structure.

Sole Proprietorship

sole
proprietorship

A **sole proprietorship** is the oldest, simplest, and most common form of doing business in the United States. A sole proprietorship is a business enterprise with a single owner who personally holds title to the business and its assets. This form is so simple that it does not require the assistance of a lawyer to

---

EXHIBIT 8-1 A Dozen Ways to Measure Different Tax Treatments

1. *Taxability of income.* Look at the tax rates, the brackets, and whether you will save by having a separate entity that pays relatively low rates on its first increments of profits.

2. *Deductibility of losses.* Can losses generated by the business be used to offset all other sources of income, just active or passive income, or active and portfolio income? Is the use of losses deferred through a mandatory carryforward?

3. *Organization of the business.* Can assets be transferred to the business without tax? Can the organizational expenses be amortized or written off as deductions against ordinary income without waiting for a liquidation of your interest?

4. *Family planning.* Does the form of the business make it possible to split the income with other family members in order to achieve savings in income, gift, and estate taxes?

5. *Special allocations.* In a group enterprise, can certain individuals receive the benefit of an allocation of a disproportionate amount of income, deductions, or losses?

6. *Fiscal year.* Can the business choose a different fiscal year from that of its owners? If so, can income or loss be accelerated or deferred advantageously as between individual owners and the business?

7. *Fringe benefit deductions.* Are expenses for medical reimbursement plans, group term life insurance, and accident and health insurance plans fully deductible against business income?

8. *Loans.* On the loans from the owners, will the business be able to deduct interest against income from all sources?

9. *Leases.* Will lease rental payments on property leased from owners of the business be deductible against business income from all sources? Can the owners take accelerated depreciation deductions on the leased property?

10. *Liquidation.* Will there be a double layer of taxes on gains upon liquidation, one layer at the level of the business itself and another at the owner's level?

11. *Passive losses.* Can passive losses be deducted in the year they are incurred and against active or portfolio income as well as against passive income?

12. *Alternative minimum tax.* Is the tax position of the business clouded by the book income preference on corporations and other factors relating to the alternative minimum tax?

SOURCE: Reprinted by permission of publisher, from The Legal Handbook for Small Business (revised) by Marc J. Lane, © 1989 AMACOM, a Division of American Management Association. All rights reserved.

begin operations. A sole proprietor needs to obtain necessary licenses and register the name of the business if it is not his or her name. Most states require the business name to be registered with a "doing business as" certificate. For example, Jacki Boyd owns a business known as "In Good Taste." She must register it as Jacki Boyd d/b/a In Good Taste. There are several other advantages and disadvantages associated with sole proprietorships that should be considered.

ADVANTAGES. The following are some of the advantages of sole proprietorships:

1. **Ease of Formation.** There is very little formality and few legal restrictions associated with establishing a proprietorship. It needs little or no government approval and is usually less expensive to start than a partnership or corporation.

2. **Retention of Profits.** The proprietor need not share any business profits with partners or stockholders.

3. **Tax Advantages.** If a business produces losses instead of profits, those losses can be deducted from the owner's personal income tax.

4. **Control of Decision Making.** Business decisions are the responsibility of the sole proprietor. However, proprietors should consult outsiders, such as lawyers, accountants, and management consultants, when making crucial decisions.

5. **Flexibility.** Owners can react quickly to changes or opportunities that could affect the profitability of their business. Group decisions and the consent of partners or stockholders can delay action and let opportunities slip away.

6. **Few Government Regulations.** Sole proprietorships are relatively free from government control and regulation. There are very few reports that must be made, and proprietorships are not subject to some of the laws that apply to partnerships and corporations.

DISADVANTAGES. Before selecting this form of ownership, entrepreneurs should evaluate the following disadvantages of being a sole proprietor:

1. **Unlimited Liability.** This is probably the most significant disadvantage of sole proprietorships. The owner is responsible for all business debt, which might be greater than his or her total investment. Creditors have access to all the owner's assets such as house, car, and boat to satisfy any loans that cannot be paid by the business.

2. **Unstable Business Life.** The illness or death of the owner can terminate a business unless transfer arrangements have been made.

3. **Limited Availability of Capital.** Owners may have difficulty raising the capital needed to start and operate a sole proprietorship. Owners can usually only acquire capital by pledging their personal assets as collateral for loans from banks or other financial institutions.

4. **Limited Operating Skills.** Very few individuals have all the functional skills needed to operate a business. An owner might be good at innovation and production and have no marketing or management skills. This problem can be remedied by having partners with complementary skills.

Partnership

partnership

Many entrepreneurs realize that they do not possess all the functional skills required to successfully operate a business, so they decide to form a partnership. A **partnership** is defined in Section 6 of the Uniform Partnership Act (UPA) as "an association of two or more persons to carry on as co-owners a business for profit." In this definition, "persons" is not only human beings because corporations or other partnerships can own a partnership. Also, the partners must expect to profit personally from the business; therefore, charities and other nonprofit organizations cannot be organized as partnerships. Those persons considering partnerships should weigh the advantages against the disadvantages.

ADVANTAGES. Partnerships have the following advantages:

1. **Ease of Formation.** Partnerships, like proprietorships, can be formed without legal counsel or assistance; however, prudent business owners should have a partnership agreement written or examined by an attorney.

2. **Complementary Skills.** People with complementary skills form a partnership to benefit from their combined expertise. One owner with innovative and production skills might take partners with marketing and management skills to form a competitive business.

3. **Access to Capital.** Two or more partners have more assets to collateralize loans than proprietors have.

4. **Tax Advantages.** Partnerships are taxed like sole proprietorships. Partners report income and deduct losses from their individual tax returns.

5. **Group Decision Making.** Partners can discuss problems and opportunities and reach a consensus decision, which might be superior to one made by an individual.

6. **Minimal Government Control.** As with proprietorships, partnerships file few reports with the government and are not closely regulated by federal, state, or local governments.

DISADVANTAGES. The following are disadvantages associated with partnerships:

1. **Unlimited Liability.** All partners are liable for the debts of the partnership. An additional liability is that one partner can generate debt that all partners are liable for even though they were unaware of the debt. For example, Frank Cihlar found that after leaving his law firm that was formed with three other partners he was being sued for five months of office rent that had not been paid. He, along with his partners, was liable for past and future rent even though he was no longer affiliated with the company.[1]

2. **Uncertain Duration.** Partnerships dissolve with the death or withdrawal of a partner unless transfer provisions have been agreed to prior to such an event.

3. **Conflict.** There is potential for conflict among partners unless a partnership agreement exists that eliminates or mitigates sources of conflict.

4. **Dissolution.** Dissolving or terminating is more difficult with a partnership than with a proprietorship.

IDENTIFYING PARTNERS. Because a partnership agreement is not legally required, people can simply form partnerships with an oral agreement. A partnership may even be implied from the conduct and activities of the parties. It is also possible for a partnership to be created even though the parties did not intend or know of its creation. This problem is addressed in the **Uniform Partnership Act (UPA)** where it outlines what constitutes evidence that a person is a partner in a business:

Uniform Partnership Act (UPA)

> The receipt by a person of a share of the profits of a business is prima facie evidence that he is a partner in the business, but no such inference shall be drawn if such profits were received in-payment:
> (a) As a debt by installments or otherwise,
> (b) As wages of an employee or rent to a landlord,
> (c) As an annuity to a widow or representative of a deceased partner,
> (d) As interest on a loan, though the amount of payment varies with the profits of the business,
> (e) As the consideration for the sale of a goodwill of the business or other property by installments or otherwise.

TYPES OF PARTNERS. Not all people in a partnership perform the same function. Some people manage the partnership, whereas others only lend the partnership money or their name. The following are the different types of partners:

active partner

Active partner. Also known as a general partner, this person is responsible for the actions of the partnership and actively participates in the partnership's operations.

secret partner

Secret partner. This is an active partner who may not be readily identifiable as a partner.

silent partner

Silent partner. This person is an inactive partner who usually only has a financial interest in the partnership. Silent partners are usually known to be involved in the partnership.

dormant partner

Dormant partner. This is a silent partner who is not generally known to be a member of the partnership.

limited partners

Limited partners. Essentially silent partners, limited partners' personal liability is limited to the value of her or his investment.

SELECTING PARTNERS. Like marriages, partnerships are only successful if all partners are compatible and committed to the same goals and objectives.

The old adage, "Don't go into business with a friend because you will very likely lose that friend," can be true if friends are not also compatible business partners. Partners should be selected for their skill and competence, not because they are friends or relatives. When searching for partners, potential business owners should consider people who

- Have similar or compatible business objectives
- Are capable
- Are honest and honorable
- Are predictable
- Have suitable credentials and experience
- Have appropriate business contacts
- Will be committed to the new business
- Are not actively engaged in other businesses
- Can assist in capital acquisition

Even if partners are compatible, having a formal partnership agreement is advisable; it can delineate the responsibilities of each partner and protect everyone with an interest in the business.

PARTNERSHIP AGREEMENTS. The Uniform Partnership Act does not specifically require written Articles of Partnership; however, such a document can prevent numerous interpartner problems and provide remedies for problems that do occur. Articles of Partnership can be as informal or as complex as desired, but the following topics are usually addressed in the document:

- **Legal name of the partnership.** An attorney should verify that the name selected by the partnership is not already being used.
- **Nature of the business.** The scope of the activities planned for the partnership should be delineated.
- **The duration of the partnership.** Partnerships can be established to last indefinitely, or they may be expected to be dissolved on a certain date.
- **Contributions.** The financial and other contributions of each partner should be recorded. Partners usually receive benefits in proportion to their contributions.
- **Sales, loans, and leases.** All sales, loans, and leases made by partners to the partnership should be documented.
- **Withdrawals and salaries of partners.** Unless agreed upon otherwise, no partner will be entitled to a guaranteed salary from the partnership. How much income each partner is entitled to draw from the partnership should be spelled out.
- **Responsibility and authority of each partner.** Each partner's managerial duties and responsibilities should be carefully delineated, and procedures to resolve conflict should be established.

- **Dissolution.** When partners no longer care or are able to continue the partnership, it should be dissolved. There should be established mechanisms for terminating a partnership.
- **Arbitration.** Some conflict-resolving procedure should be agreed upon by all partners.

Corporations

corporations

Entrepreneurs who want to limit their personal liability can choose to incorporate their business. **Corporations** are recognized as entities unto themselves. They are separate and distinct from the owners; therefore, a corporation can own property, enter into contracts, and sue and be sued in its own name. Corporations are composed of shareholders who contribute capital in exchange for an opportunity to share in the profits, directors who manage the corporate board, and officers who manage the day-to-day activities of the corporation. The **Model Business Corporation Act (MBCA)**, adopted by two-thirds of the states, regulates incorporation procedures and corporate operations. The MBCA allows a corporation to maintain perpetual succession, sue and be sued in its own name, have a corporate seal, acquire and sell both real and personal property, lend money, and make and alter its bylaws. Approximately 17 percent of all businesses are corporations, but they account for about 87 percent of all sales.

ADVANTAGES. Entrepreneurs who choose the corporate form do so to negate some of the inherent disadvantages of both proprietorships and partnerships. The primary advantages of corporations include the following:

1. **Limited Liability.** This is the most significant advantage of the corporate form for business owners, because it allows them to protect their personal assets. Stockholders' liability is limited to the amount of their investment in the corporation. In some cases, creditors may require stockholders to personally guarantee corporate debt thereby negating limited liability protection.

2. **Transfer of Ownership.** Transferring ownership of a corporation from one person to another is quite easy. Stock is sold to the buyer who becomes one of the new owners of the corporation, and the seller relinquishes her or his ownership position.

3. **Stability.** In theory, corporations can last indefinitely. Death or withdrawal of one or more stockholders does not cause the corporation's demise or dissolution.

4. **Acquisition of Capital.** Capital is acquired through the sale of stock and long-term bonds. Corporations also can secure long-term financing from lending institutions by pledging their assets as collateral for loans.

5. **Skilled Managers.** Most stockholders empower their corporation's board of directors to seek the best qualified managers to operate the business. In some corporations managers have no, or only a small, ownership position in the corporation.

6. **Stockholders as Customers.** People who own a corporation's stock tend to purchase that company's goods or services. They are also a good source of advertising for the corporation.

DISADVANTAGES. Before selecting the corporate form, entrepreneurs should weigh the following disadvantages against the advantages of corporations:

1. **Taxes.** A principal disadvantage of corporations is that their income is taxed twice. Income earned by a corporation is taxed, and income distributed to stockholders in the form of dividends is taxed again.

2. **Rigidity.** Proprietorships and partnerships are easier to start than corporations because the latter requires more forms, registrations, and permissions. Corporations are quite structured, and their activities are restricted unless their charter is written in very general terms.

3. **Shared Ownership.** Entrepreneurs who want to own the whole company should probably not consider incorporating. To attract capable management and acquire capital, entrepreneurs have to give up ownership of part of the company. They may even have to relinquish a majority share of their business.

4. **Regulations.** Corporations are closely regulated entities and must file numerous reports with federal, state, and local governments.

TYPES OF CORPORATIONS. The following are the different types of corporations:

domestic
corporation

Domestic corporation. A corporation organized under the laws of a particular state where its corporate charter is registered.

foreign
corporation

Foreign corporation. A corporation chartered in a different state from the one in which it is operating.

publicly held
corporation

Publicly held corporation. A corporation that has outstanding shares owned by a large number of people.

closely held
corporation

Closely held corporation. This type of corporation has very few shareholders.

S Corporations

S corporations

Entrepreneurs who like the limited liability of corporations but not the double taxation can choose to form an **S corporation** (so called because it was provided for in Subchapter S of the tax code). This is a hybrid corporate form that was created especially for small businesses (see The Way It Is 8-1).

ADVANTAGES. The advantages of S corporations include the following: Lower "current" income tax (the current maximum tax rate is lower for individuals than for corporations); exemption from the corporate alternative minimum tax; and flexibility in the use of different accounting methods (S corporations, for example, generally are free to use the cash method of accounting).

8-1 WHEN AN S CORP MAY SPELL TAX RELIEF

The 1986 tax law closed a vast array of favored loopholes, but it left a major one for owners of closely held companies—S corporation status. Small businesses set up as traditional corporations have converted in droves into S corporations, which are taxed like partnerships, thus eliminating corporate-level taxation. The tax status is especially attractive to start-ups. For the first time ever, corporate tax rates, which peak at 39 percent, exceed the highest individual tax rate of 33 percent. In the past, when individual rates were higher than corporate rates, it made sense to retain earnings in the company. Now S corporation status makes more sense because earnings can be distributed directly to owners.[2]

DISADVANTAGES. Not all owners will select S corporation status because of some inherent disadvantages, which include the following: Multistate S corporations must deal with state laws that are inconsistent, complex, and sometimes inequitable; banks may be reluctant to lend to S corporations that distribute all their earnings; and some rigid restrictions apply to S corporations, including:

- A limit of 35 stockholders
- No corporations, partnerships, or nonresident aliens can be stockholders
- Only one class of stock can be issued
- The business cannot be a subsidiary of any other company
- Certain states do not permit S corporation status
- The company cannot be an ineligible corporation, which is defined as
    a. a member of an affiliated group
    b. a financial institution
    c. an insurance company subject to tax under Subchapter L

Whether the advantages of S corporations outweigh the disadvantages may not be easy to determine, but most tax experts advise companies that expect annual earnings to exceed $152,273 (see Exhibit 8-2) to elect the S corporation form. If *all* stockholders elect S status, the company files Form 2553 with the Internal Revenue Service. If an S corporation terminates its election, it cannot become an S corporation again for five years.

INCORPORATING A SMALL BUSINESS

Entrepreneurs who choose the corporate form can, in most states, complete and file the necessary documents themselves. Although attorneys are not required to sign incorporation documents, using their services before filing

EXHIBIT 8-2 Minimum Break-even Point

	Taxable Income	Regular Corporation		S Corporation Taxed at Individual Level		Savings of S Corp Election
		Rate	Tax	Rate	Tax	
First	$ 50,000	15%	$ 7,500	28%	$14,000	$(6,500)
Next	25,000	25	6,250	28	7,000	(750)
Next	25,000	34	8,500	28	7,000	1,500
Next	52,273	39*	20,386	28	14,636	5,750
Total	$152,273		$42,636		$42,636	

SOURCE: *A 5 percent surcharge is assessed on corporate income between $100,000 and $335,000.

with the appropriate state agency is a good idea. Attorneys can ensure that entrepreneurs do not omit any relevant information that might invalidate the corporate charter at a later date. Entrepreneurs who choose to do their own incorporation should use a preincorporation checklist similar to the one in Appendix 8-1.

Articles of Incorporation

articles of incorporation

Most states have standard **articles of incorporation** (see Appendix 8-2), which can be supplemented with information pertinent to particular corporations. At a minimum, entrepreneurs must provide the following information about their companies:

- The corporate name
- Location of the company
- Purpose of the company
- Duration
- Names and addresses of incorporators
- Amount and type of stock to be issued
- Capital required at time of incorporation
- Provisions for stockholder preemptive rights
- Names and addresses of initial directors and officers
- Provisions for regulation of the affairs of the company
- Right to amend, alter, or repeal corporate provisions
- Bylaws

THE CORPORATE NAME. The name chosen for a new corporation cannot be too similar to that of an already established business, and it cannot be deceptive or intentionally misleading. To reserve the selected name, most states require corporations to file the name with the secretary of state and pay the appropriate filing fee. The secretary of state will reserve the corporation's name for thirty days and will not allow any other company to incorporate using that name. If the incorporating paperwork cannot be completed within thirty days, most states allow corporations to pay an additional fee and file for a thirty-day extension.

A company's name, which might very well be one of its most valuable assets, should be carefully selected and protected. People identify the company's products, image, and reputation with its name; therefore, entrepreneurs should select a company name only after considerable deliberation. A name should be selected that is easy to spell and pronounce; easy to recognize and remember; adaptable to packaging and labeling needs; unique; informative; not offensive; short; and related to the product or service. The following are some clever business names that have appeared in the *New Yorker:* Prints of Peace (Christian book center); Able to Cane (chair-repair business); Kosher Nostra (restaurant); The Marquis de Sod (landscaper); Wooden It Be Nice (cabinetmaker); and Ash Kickers (chimney cleaners).

LOCATION OF THE COMPANY. A company can incorporate in a state in which it does not intend to do business. For example, many corporations with headquarters in New York, Chicago, or elsewhere are incorporated in Delaware. Delaware offers tax concessions and other favorable laws to corporations that make it an attractive state in which to incorporate (see Exhibit 8-3). Entrepreneurs selecting the state of incorporation should do the following:

- Compare the corporation laws of the contending states for their requirements for capitalization, powers of directors, and flexibility of operations.
- Compare incorporation fees and related taxes.
- Compare the cost of qualifying a foreign corporation in states where the company will do business with the cost of incorporating there in the first place.
- Compare rules dealing with tender offers, if the stock of the corporation will be widely held.
- Check on annual fees and taxes in each state.
- Check on state stamp taxes applicable to the original issue of the stock and on any later transfers.[3]

PURPOSE. Care should be taken when specifying the purpose of the corporation so that the language does not unnecessarily restrain the company's activities. If the purpose section of the corporate charter is too limiting, the document will have to be amended if the company chooses to change its focus. Some states allow the purpose to be described in broad terms, such as "the purpose of the corporation is to engage in any lawful act or activity for which corporations may be organized." However, the use of fairly precise language to explain the purpose of the company is preferable. A nonspecific clause that allows for territorial, market, or product expansion can be added.

EXHIBIT 8-3 Ten Good Reasons to Pick Delaware (or a State with a Delaware-type Corporation Law)

1. There is no corporate income tax in Delaware for companies doing no business there, no tax on shares held by nonresidents, and no inheritance tax on nonresident shareholders.

2. The private property of shareholders is protected from liability for corporate debts (shareholders' liability is limited to their stock investment) and officers and directors may be indemnified.

3. Shareholders and directors may meet outside Delaware, or meet by conference telephone calls, and keep corporate books and records outside the state.

4. Only one incorporator is required, and that incorporator may itself be a corporation.

5. A Delaware corporation may be perpetual, and it can operate through voting trusts and shareholder voting agreements.

6. Directors may make and alter bylaws, and they may act by unanimous written consent in lieu of formal meetings.

7. Delaware has no minimum capital requirements. A corporation may issue shares—common and preferred, even in serial classes—without par value, fully paid, and nonassessable, for consideration or at a price fixed by the directors. And the directors' judgment about the value of the property or services is conclusive. They may determine what portion of the consideration received goes to capital and what part to surplus.

8. A Delaware corporation can hold the securities of other corporations and all kinds of other property, both in Delaware and outside the state, without limit. It can also purchase its own stock and hold, sell, or transfer it.

9. Any different kinds of business can be conducted in combination.

10. Dividends can be paid out of profits as well as out of surplus.

SOURCE: Reprinted, by permission of publisher. From The Legal Handbook for Small Business (revised) by Marc J. Lane, © 1989 AMACOM, a division of American Management Association. All rights reserved.

DURATION. Most corporations are expected to operate "in perpetuity"; however, some corporations are created to accomplish a specific task. When that task has been accomplished, the corporation is dissolved.

NAMES AND ADDRESSES OF INCORPORATORS. The incorporators and their addresses must be identified. Some states require that at least one incorporator be a resident of the state of incorporation.

AMOUNT AND TYPE OF STOCK TO BE ISSUED. The capital structure of the corporation should be delineated. Officers will have to stipulate the number and classification of the shares of stock to be issued, as well as the rights, preferences, and limitations of each class of stock.

CAPITAL REQUIREMENTS. Some states require that a specified percentage of the par value of the capital stock be paid in cash and banked to the credit of the corporation before the certificate of incorporation is submitted to the state for official approval. In some cases, payment can be made just after the business is incorporated but before it starts business.

PROVISIONS FOR STOCKHOLDER PREEMPTIVE RIGHTS. Preemptive rights give existing stockholders the right to purchase new stock before it is offered to other buyers. This section might also include any restrictions on the transfer of the corporation's shares.

NAMES AND ADDRESSES OF DIRECTORS AND OFFICERS. The principal corporate officers should be identified, and the names and addresses of the persons serving as directors should be included. These directors serve until the first meeting of the stockholders or until their successors are elected and qualify (the same directors are usually elected by the stockholders).

PROVISIONS FOR REGULATION OF THE AFFAIRS OF THE COMPANY. Provisions for amending the corporation's bylaws, determining the number of directors, and so forth can be included either in the corporate charter or in the company's bylaws. The articles of incorporation usually require stockholder action to be amended, but the bylaws can be changed by the directors.

RIGHT TO AMEND, ALTER, OR REPEAL CORPORATE PROVISIONS. This right is generally statutory, reserved to a majority or two-thirds of the stockholders.

BYLAWS. The bylaws of the corporation may repeat some of the provisions of the charter but also cover the following items:

1. The location of the principal office and other offices of the corporation.
2. The time, place, and required notice of annual and special stockholder meetings. Also the number of stockholders required for a quorum and their voting privileges.
3. The number of directors, their compensation, their term of office, the method of electing them, and the method of filling vacancies on the board of directors.
4. The time and place of regular and special director's meetings, as well as the notice and quorum requirements.
5. The method of selecting officers and their titles, duties, terms of office, and salaries.
6. The issuance and form of stock certificates, their transfers, and their control in the company books.
7. When and by whom dividends may be declared.
8. The fiscal year, the corporate seal, the authority to sign checks, and the preparation of the annual statement.
9. The procedures for changing the bylaws.

CONTRACTS

People planning a new business and those operating established businesses will be expected to sign contracts with a variety of individuals and companies. There will be contracts with suppliers, contracts (leases) with landlords, contracts with key employees, and contracts (warranties) with customers. All these contracts should be scrutinized by a competent attorney before they are consummated because, as with other aspects of law, poorly drafted contracts can come back to haunt entrepreneurs.

Elements of Contracts

contract

A **contract,** "a promise or a set of promises for the breach of which the law gives a remedy, or the performance of which the law in some way recognizes as a duty," has certain elements that make it valid. The following prerequisites are needed to create a legally binding contract:

- It must involve two or more parties having the capacity to contract.
- It must show agreement, including offer, acceptance, and mutuality.
- It must be made for consideration.
- It must be for a legal purpose.
- It must be in the correct form (some contracts, for example, must be in writing).

CONTRACTING CAPACITY. Not everyone has the capacity or ability to enter into a contract. To be a fair contract, all parties should be able to participate in and understand the bargaining process that culminates in a contract. People lacking capacity are protected from their own actions and those of others who would take advantage of them. The following individuals are considered to lack capacity to enter into a binding contract:

- **Minors.** Under common law, a person ceases to be a minor after his or her twenty-first birthday; however, most states have lowered that age to 18. The assumption behind the view that minors are not competent to make contracts is that adults and children have unequal bargaining power.
- **Mentally infirm.** Mental incompetency is either the inability "to understand in a reasonable manner the nature and consequences of the transaction" or the inability "to act in a reasonable manner in relation to the transaction and the other party has reason to know of this condition." This condition covers problems caused by mental illness or retardation, brain deterioration in old age, drunkenness, and drug use.

AGREEMENT. All parties must agree to the contents of a contract before it can be binding. The contract usually contains an offer, which is simply a promise to do or refrain from doing something in the future, and the acceptance of that offer by the other party or parties. The offer must be intended, specific, and communicated before it can be considered a bona fide offer. Acceptance is an overt act by the person receiving the offer that demonstrates his or her assent to the offer.

CONSIDERATION. Consideration is something valuable that changes hands between the parties to a contract. In legal terminology:

1. To constitute consideration, a performance or a return promise must be bargained for.
2. A performance or return promise is bargained for if it is sought by the promisor in exchange for her or his promise and is given by the promisee in exchange for that promise.
3. The performance may consist of
    a. an act other than a promise,
    b. a forbearance, or
    c. the creation, modification, or destruction of a legal relation

This means that the law does not usually enforce gratuitous or free promises. As long as the consideration has some value, it is legally sufficient to support a contract.

LEGALITY. Illegal contracts cannot be enforced. For example, a contract to purchase any prohibited drug such as cocaine cannot be legally enforced. Small business owners should determine whether any contracts they sign violate federal or state law. Most states have laws that protect consumers from harmful or misrepresented products; therefore, any business owner who signed a contract to buy harmful products for resale to the public would be party to an illegal contract.

CORRECT FORM. Verbal contracts are acceptable and enforceable; however, written contracts are preferable and, in some instances, required. There must be written evidence of the terms of the following business-related contracts: contracts for the sale of land; contracts for the sale of goods (this usually refers to tangible, movable property sold for more than $500); contracts that will be valid for more than one year (see The Way It Is 8-2); and, surety contracts, which are promises to be responsible for or guarantee another person's debt.

Leases

Most small business owners will need facilities and equipment that they cannot afford to purchase. Facilities and equipment that cannot be purchased can be leased from their owners. A **lease** is a valid contract between two parties for the use of specified property for a certain amount of time at a stated fee. Most entrepreneurs will enter into a lease for the building they use for their business. A building lease is a complex, lengthy document (Exhibit 8-4 is the first two pages of a 21-page lease), which spells out the responsibilities of tenant and landlord. Most leases will contain at least the following information:

lease

8-2 ORAL CONTRACTS

Robert Montgomery, a producer of videotapes used to train salespeople, agreed to produce twenty-five tapes for Futuristic Foods Inc., a New York company. The company promised it would use the tapes only for training its own people and would never sell the tapes to anyone else. The tapes were produced in the allotted time, and Montgomery received the agreed-upon price of $1,600. A few months later, Futuristic formed Mind Trek Inc. to market Montgomery's tapes. Montgomery sued to stop Futuristic's subsidiary from selling the tapes, but he lost the case. The judge explained that the courts do not enforce an oral agreement that covers more than one year. Therefore, the proviso that Futuristic could never sell the tapes was invalid.[4]

- Location and description of the property
- Amount and frequency of rent payments
- Amount of any required security deposits
- Identification of common spaces
- Acceptable building modifications
- Allowable uses of premises
- Tenant and landlord maintenance responsibilities
- Duration of the lease and renewal options
- Penalties for vacating building before expiration of lease
- Conditions for subletting space

In addition to building leases, business owners may also lease operating equipment, vehicles, and even employees. These leases are usually less complex than building leases and can often be consummated without consulting an attorney. Entrepreneurs who enter into lease agreements should be certain that they understand and accept all the conditions of the lease. If in doubt, owners should have their attorney read the lease and translate it into nontechnical language.

Warranties

warranty A **warranty** is essentially a guarantee or an assurance that is made to the purchaser of a product. The warranty provisions of the Uniform Commercial Code (UCC) provide alternative grounds of recovery for people who are injured by the products they use. The two primary types of warranties are express and implied.

EXHIBIT 8-4 Shopping Center Lease for Orange Grove Plaza

THIS SHOPPING CENTER LEASE, made and entered into as of the _____day of _____198 ___ , by and between ORANGE GROVE ASSOCIATES, A SOUTH CAROLINA PARTNERSHIP, (hereinafter sometimes referred to as "Landlord") and Tenant as hereinafter defined.

WITNESSETH:

In consideration of the rent to be paid, the mutual covenants and agreements herein contained, and of other good and valuable considerations, the receipt and legal sufficiency of all of which are hereby acknowledged by both parties hereto, Landlord hereby demises and rents unto Tenant, and Tenant hereby leases from Landlord, certain premises in Landlord's shopping center known as Orange Grove Plaza, upon the terms, covenants and conditions hereinafter contained.

ARTICLE 1 FUNDAMENTAL LEASE PROVISIONS AND EXHIBITS
Section 1.1 *Fundamental Lease Provisions.*

A. LANDLORD (including mailing address):
Orange Grove Associates
c/o Bailey & Associates
114 Doughty St.
Charleston, SC 29401

B. TENANT (including mailing address): In Good Taste

C. LEASED PREMISES: A portion of the Orange Grove Plaza shopping center premises identified and/or outlined in red on Exhibit "B," having dimensions of approximately _____feet × _____feet, and containing approximately _____square feet, known as space number _____ .

D. PERMITTED USES:

E. LEASE DURATION: _____years (original term).

F. FIXED RENT: $ _____ per year in equal monthly installments of $ _____ .

G. (i) PERCENTAGE RENT RATE: _____(%) percent.
(ii) BASE GROSS SALES AMOUNT: _____ .

H. COMMON AREA MAINTENANCE CONTRIBUTION: $ _____ per year, adjusted annually.

I. RENTAL COMMENCEMENT DATE: March ___ , 198_ .
In the event the leased premises have not been constructed or completed the Rental Commencement Date shall be determined pursuant to ARTICLE XIV.

J. RENTAL PAYMENT PLACE: Bailey & Associates
114 Doughty Street
Charleston, SC 29401

K. PRO RATA SHARE: _____percent, representing the percentage of the total rentable space in the shopping center represented by the number of rentable square feet in the Leased Premises as of the date of this lease.

L. SECURITY DEPOSIT: _____ .

M. RENEWAL OPTIONS:

N. BASE YEAR: 199_ .

Note: The entire lease is twenty-one pages long.

express
warranties

EXPRESS WARRANTIES. **Express warranties** are obligations that are voluntarily assumed by the seller, rather than duties imposed by the law. They are frequently created by oral or written statements about the nature of a product, although they need not include the words *guarantee* or *warranty.* A description of the goods may also be interpreted as a claim about their characteristics and hence an express warranty.

implied
warranties

IMPLIED WARRANTIES. **Implied warranties** are created by law as a matter of public policy. These warranties do not represent any written agreement between buyers and sellers of products. A merchant might sell a product without any written guarantee of its condition; however, the act of selling the product infers an implied warranty that the product is in good condition and safe. The implied warranty is a binding contract between buyers and sellers, and the courts tend to liberally construe implied warranties to protect buyers.

PROTECTING PROPRIETARY PROPERTY

When entrepreneurs invent new products, create literary or artistic works, or come up with unique names and logos, they want to be able to protect their creations. Attorneys can help entrepreneurs protect these items by securing a patent, copyright, or trademark for the new creation. Some small business owners may not need patent or copyright protection, but they will probably need to consider trademarking the name of their business.

Patents

patent

A **patent** is an exclusive property right to an invention and is issued by the Commissioner of Patents and Trademarks, U.S. Department of Commerce. It gives an inventor the right to exclude others from making, using, or selling an invention for a period of seventeen years in the United States. Of the 4.8 million patents issued by the U.S. Patent and Trademark Office since its inception in 1836, nearly 3.9 million have expired. In 1989 the Patent and Trademark Office granted 83,584 patents out of a total of 148,183 applications and is now grappling with a backlog exceeding 200,000.[5] Those that were rejected could not meet one or more of the following conditions for receiving a patent:

1. The product must fill a legally useful purpose.
2. The product must be a machine, a manufacturing process, a manufactured article, or a substance.
3. The product can be patented only by its inventor.
4. The product must be really novel. It cannot be a modification of an existing product or a copy of a foreign product.
5. The product cannot be an obvious extension of something that already exists.
6. The patent application must be pursued in the manner prescribed by law.

PATENT APPLICATION. A patent can be applied for by submitting the following items to the Commissioner of Patents and Trademarks: a written document that comprises a petition, a specification (description and claims), and an oath; a drawing of the product; and the filing fee of $170 for small businesses and $340 for corporations. The parts of the application can be seen in Exhibit 8-5, which is a copy of a patent granted in 1917, a year when applications were far less complex than are current ones.

PATENT SEARCH. When applications arrive at the Patent and Trademark Office, they are scanned to verify their completeness and accuracy. If applications are acceptable, they are assigned a serial number and filing date, which govern their position on the docket. Accepted applications are sent to an examiner who has expertise in the appropriate field. The initial review of a patent application may take anywhere from five to thirty hours of an examiner's time. Typically, examiners test the novelty of a product by scanning scientific and popular literature, as well as previous U.S. patents and those from eighty-one other countries. Any publication of an idea more than a year before the application, no matter how obscure, can kill or severely narrow a patent.[6]

PROTECTING PATENTS. While a patent application is being processed (which can take from six months to four years), entrepreneurs can protect their product by prominently displaying the words *patent pending* on the product. Once patents are issued, the patent holder has exclusive rights to produce and sell the patented product. Holders of patents often have to sue individuals or companies that introduce identical or exceptionally similar products. Patent litigation has soared 52 percent from 1980 to 1990. Prior to 1982, there were eleven regional courts that heard patent appeals; however, in that year, the Court of Appeals for the Federal Circuit was created to hear all appeals for patent cases. Small businesses can bring suit against large companies that infringe their patents, but it is a very expensive proposition.

One company, Windsurfing International Corporation, got its start back in the late sixties when a pair of inventors put together the first sailboards. In 1970 Windsurfing International secured a patent. Major firms began copying the sailboard and undercutting the pioneer's price. In 1981 Windsurfing sued and in 1985 a district court ruled that the Windsurfing patent was valid and that it had been infringed on. Two big companies—BIC Corporation and AMF Inc.—were enjoined from making sailboards. Those rulings were upheld by the Court of Appeals for the Federal Circuit.[7]

Copyrights

copyrights

Some unique items do not qualify for patent protection, but they can be protected by use of a copyright. **Copyrights** protect literary and artistic intellectual property, including computer software. A copyright relates to the exact form of expression, not the substantive idea it represents. Protection is

EXHIBIT 8-5 Patent Application

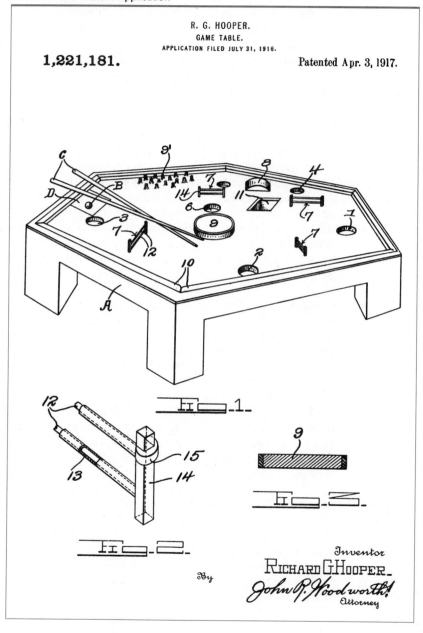

EXHIBIT 8-5 *(continued)*

UNITED STATES PATENT OFFICE.

RICHARD G. HOOPER, OF DELAWARE, OHIO.

GAME-TABLE.

1,221,181. Specification of Letters Patent. **Patented Apr. 3, 1917.**

Application filed July 31, 1916. Serial No. 112,323.

To all whom it may concern:

Be it known that I, RICHARD G. HOOPER, a citizen of the United States, residing at Delaware, in the county of Delaware and
5 State of Ohio, have invented new and useful Improvements in Game-Tables, of which the following is a specification.

This invention relates to a table for the playing of two games, namely, table golf
10 and hazard.

With the above and other objects in view this invention resides in the novel features of construction, formation, combinations and arrangements of parts to be hereinafter
15 more fully described, claimed, and illustrated by the accompanying drawing in which:—

Figure 1 is a perspective view of my table adapted for use in the playing of table golf
20 and hazard,

Fig. 2 is a fragmentary detail perspective view of one end of one of the bars, illustrating the application of the rubber cushion thereto, and,
25 Fig. 3 is an enlarged cross-sectional view through the disk, illustrating the application of a similar rubber cushion thereto.

Referring to the accompanying drawing by similar characters of reference through-
30 out the letter A designates in general my hexagonal table upon which may be played the two games table golf and hazard, through the medium of the customary cues and balls in present use upon the well-
35 known type of pool tables so familiar to those interested in such games and in every day use throughout the country.

To play the first game that of table golf each player has a ball. The play starts by
40 shooting the ball designated by the letter B with the cue designated by the letter C, from the rectangular space also designated by the letter D at one edge of the table to the hole indicated by the numeral 1. The ball
45 must be gotten into this hole. If this is accomplished in one shot, the player sets the ball at the edge of said hole 1 any where within one and a half inches from said hole, and tries for the hole indicated by the nu-
50 meral 2 and repeats at each hole consecutively. When the player first shooting fails to get his ball into the hole aimed for, his opponent beginning at the starting point with his own ball, tries for the hole indicated by
55 the numeral 1 following the process of play as given above.

The game is made more intricate by reason of the facts that a series of bars indicated in general by the numeral 7, a bunker 8, a disk 9, and woods 9′ protruding up-
60 wardly from the surface of the table a sufficient distance and suitably secured thereto, all of said objects being placed in such a position that it is necessary to use the cushions 10, which are made of rubber, as on the
65 customary billiard tables now in every day use. To reach the holes in most cases direct shots for said holes are not possible and the fact that a player at any time for a shot, instead of shooting his ball for the de-
70 sired hole, may, with his ball, knock his opponent's ball, to place said opponent at a greater disadvantage for his, the opponent's next shot, also the fact that of the pond indicated by the numeral 11, which
75 forfeits one hole for the player whose ball drops into it, this is if a player is trying for the hole indicated by the numeral 4 and his ball falls into said pond he will on his next shot have to shoot from the edge of said
80 pond for the hole indicated by the numeral 3. The player who places his ball in the hole indicated by the numeral 6, first, is the winner of said game.

In the second game, that of hazard, only
85 one ball is used as a cue ball, the same ball being used by all the players irrespective of the number in the game and each player has a ball, known as the playing ball. All the playing balls are placed near the center
90 of the table in a space to be designated and the player beginning the game shoots the cue ball from the rectangular space at the edge of said table, at the balls in the center of the same in an attempt to get his play-
95 ing ball into the hole indicated by the numeral 1. If he succeeds in this he then places his playing ball on the edge of said hole 1, within one and one-half inches of the edge of said hole, he then tries with the
100 cue ball to shoot his playing ball into the hole indicated by the numeral 2 and so on to each hole consecutively. A player at any time may drive his opponent's playing ball away from the position it may hold in order
105 to gain an advantage for himself or to put his opponent at a disadvantage, and not loose his shot thereby.

When the player first shooting fails to get his playing ball into the hole for which he
110 is aiming his opponent shoots the cue ball from the position such cue ball may occupy

EXHIBIT 8-5 *(continued)*

2 1,221,181

on said table, as left by the first player, at his playing ball, wherever it may be located as left by the first player, attempting to drive his ball into the hole indicated by the numeral 1 and to each hole consecutively, as above-described.

Either the cue ball or a playing ball dropping into the pond forfeits one hole to the player as previously described in the game of table golf. The player first placing his ball in the hole indicated by the numeral 6 is declared winner of the game same as in that of table golf as before described.

It may be further stated that the disk 9 is of a diameter equal to the length of the bars indicated in general by the numeral 7 and the height of said disk being equal to the height of the side of said table from the playing surface thereof to the top surface of the cushions 10, this feature being clearly illustrated in Fig. 1 of the accompanying drawing.

It may be still further stated that the bars indicated in general by the numeral 7 as illustrated by the drawing are made of steel, the cross bars 12 being round in cross-section and of any suitable diameter, covered with rubber or any suitable material as indicated by the numeral 13, while the supporting end posts 14 of said cross bars 12 are square in cross-section and also of any suitable thickness as clearly illustrated by Fig. 2 of the accompanying drawing. These end posts are also provided with a rubber cushion 15 of suitable design which is secured to the upper end of each of said posts and envelop the same on three sides thereof as clearly illustrated by the above-mentioned views. This cushion 15 is in close proximity to the upper cross bar 12 and in alinement with the cushions 10 of the table A proper.

It is now thought that the above description together with the accompanying drawing sufficiently sets forth the method to be adopted for successfully playing these two games, to enable those familiar with this art to readily understand the arrangement of objects used in connection with this table

and the necessary moves to make in order to play either of said games to advantage.

It should also be understood, however, in this connection that various minor changes in the details of construction may be resorted to within the scope of the appended claims, without departing from or sacrificing any of the advantages of this invention.

From the foregoing disclosure taken in connection with the accompanying drawing it will be manifest that I have provided a game table for use in connection with the two games, namely, table golf and hazard, which will fulfil all of the necessary requirements of such a table.

Having thus fully described this invention, what I claim, and desire to protect by Letters Patent, is:—

1. In combination with a game table, having a cushion surrounding its periphery in close proximity with the surface of said table, a series of bars mounted upon the surface of said table, a pond formed in the surface of said table, a disk mounted upon the surface of said table, a series of apertures formed in the surface of said table, a woods arranged upon the surface of said table and a bunker mounted upon the surface of said table as and for the purpose set forth.

2. In combination with a table, having an elastic cushion surrounding its periphery in close proximity with the surface of said table, a series of bars mounted upon the surface of said table and covered with elastic material, a plurality of posts supporting each of said series of bars, an elastic cushion substantially secured to each of said posts, a pond formed in the surface of said table, a disk mounted upon the surface of said table, a series of apertures formed in the surface of said table, a woods arranged upon the surface of said table and a bunker mounted upon the surface of said table as and for the purpose set forth.

RICHARD G. HOOPER.

Witnesses:
H. H. LOWRY,
E. J. POLLOCK.

unavailable for ideas, systems, concepts, or principles. Copyright law lets the owner of a copyright do the following:

- Reproduce the copyrighted work in copies or phonorecords
- Prepare derivative works based on the copyrighted work
- Distribute copies or phonorecords of the copyrighted work to the public
- Perform the copyrighted work publicly
- Display the copyrighted work publicly

No government agency is responsible for awarding copyrights, rather they are secured by the work's creator by satisfying the following requirements:

1. The material must be subject to copyright.

2. The material must be original. It can be any one of the following categories:

   • Literary works, including computer software
   • Musical works, including any accompanying words
   • Dramatic works, including any accompanying music
   • Pantomimes and choreographic works
   • Pictoral, graphic, and sculptural works
   • Motion pictures and other audiovisual works
   • Sound recordings

3. The material must be fixed in a tangible medium of expression (usually a copy or phonographic record).

4. The word *copyright*, the abbreviation *copr.*, or the the universally recognized symbol © must be displayed with the work.

5. The claim should be registered in the Copyright Office. For original registrations one of the following forms is required:

   • Form TX: For published or unpublished nondramatic literary works
   • Form SE: For serials, works issued or intended to be issued in successive parts (periodicals, newspapers, and so forth)
   • Form PA: For published and unpublished works of the performing arts
   • Form VA: For published and unpublished works of the visual arts
   • Form SR: For published and unpublished sound recordings[8]

Once a copyright has been registered, it is valid for the life of the owner plus fifty years after death. As with patents, copyright holders have to protect their literary or artistic work from other people or businesses. Some uses of copyrighted material are legally accepted, such as the private and incidental use of such material or a reasonable quotation in a review or biographical work.

Trademarks

For most small businesses, their name and logo is one of their most important assets. These assets cannot be protected by patents or copyrights; however, they can be protected by a trademark. **Trademarks** may be words, logos, or other symbols (see Exhibit 8-6). They may even be sounds, three-dimensional symbols, or colors. Technically, the word *trademark* means a symbol used to denote a particular source of goods, rather than services. A good trademark does not wear out or expire with the passage of time. A trademark actually becomes more valuable as goodwill is developed.

trademarks

EXHIBIT 8-6 Trademark

ACQUIRING TRADEMARKS. Anyone can use the symbol ™ to try to keep others from using their name, but the ® symbol may be used only if the trademark is federally registered. Companies may trademark their name and logo in their own state, or they can opt for wider protection by registering with the federal government. The place to register a trademark, after a thorough search of existing trademarks has been conducted, is with the U.S. Patent and Trademark Office. In the past, products had to be in use before a trademark could be registered; however, in November 1989 a change was made to trademark law. The new law allows businesses to file an application for trademark registration based on a bona fide intention to use the trademark within a reasonable time. A registered trademark is good for ten years but can be renewed for an indefinite number of ten-year periods.

Neil Balter is one person who found out that a company's name should be protected before the business starts operating. He says, "Hey, I was a kid when we started. I didn't know anything about a trademark. I just went out and built a business." At the time, the business was called Creative Closets, a reorganizer of existing closet and garage space. About five years after the company was founded, Balter applied for a trademark, only to find that a company in New Jersey and three other companies were using the same name. The New Jersey company was going to file an opposition to Balter's use of the name unless it was paid $200,000. Neil Balter changed the name of his company to California Closets.[9]

PROTECTING TRADEMARKS. As with patents and copyrights, trademark protection is the primary responsibility of the trademark owner. Whenever small business owners see or hear of other companies using their name or a

The Way It Is

8-3 PROTECTING TRADEMARKS

Until 1980, family owned Pace Foods, Inc., seemed to have it made. Its picante sauces were the best-selling Mexican sauces in Texas; it was moving into other states; and the big companies were not paying attention. During the 1980s, the Mexican sauce market exploded, growing 15 percent a year to nearly $300 million and Pace became the target of bigger companies. In late 1986, Pet Inc.'s Old El Paso took dead aim at its longtime rival. In Texas and a few other states, it started test marketing a new jar—that just happened to look a lot like Pace's. Pace went to federal court, charging its rival with, among other things, trademark infringement and unfair competition. In January 1988, the two companies reached an out-of-court settlement and Pet agreed to give up the new bottle and label.[10]

closely related name, they should take the matter to the appropriate court (see The Way It Is 8-3). Even unintentional use of another's trademark damages the reputation and goodwill of the infringed-on company.

SUMMARY

In the early start-up phase, business owners should seek the advice of qualified attorneys on several key issues. In conjunction with their attorneys, entrepreneurs should decide whether their business should be a proprietorship, partnership, or corporation. The advantages and disadvantages of each form of ownership should be evaluated before one form is selected as the most appropriate. If owners choose to structure their business as a partnership or corporation, they should have their attorney draw up the papers necessary to protect all parties' rights and delineate their responsibilities.

Attorneys should also be consulted whenever contracts or other legal documents need to be initiated. To be binding, contracts must meet certain conditions that can be verified and explained by a competent attorney. Business owners will also need their attorneys' advice about other legal documents such as contracts, leases, and warranties. Lawyers can explain the intricacies of express and implied warranties and inform business owners of their responsibilities for defective or unsafe goods. Finally, attorneys are needed to help business owners protect any proprietary property.

Proprietary property can be protected by patents, copyrights, or trademarks. Patents protect novel products, copyrights protect literary and artistic intellectual property, and trademarks give business owners exclusive rights to use and display protected company names and logos. Acquiring protection for proprietary property usually requires an exhaustive search of existing patents and trademarks, which should only be undertaken by a qualified patent attorney. Attorneys' services are usually quite expensive, but business owners who try to save money by avoiding lawyers may find that they are penny wise but pound foolish.

QUESTIONS FOR REVIEW AND DISCUSSION

1. What are the advantages of sole proprietorships?
2. What are the advantages of partnerships?
3. Is incorporation advisable for most small businesses? Why or why not?
4. If you were starting a business, would you choose S or C corporate status?
5. If your new business were to be a partnership, what would you include in your partnership agreement?
6. What conditions must a company satisfy in order to be an S corporation?
7. What should be included in a corporation's bylaws?
8. What makes a contract legal and binding?
9. What conditions must be met for a product to be patented?
10. How long are patents, copyrights, and trademarks valid?
11. How did the 1989 legislation change the way trademarks were issued?

KEY TERMS

active partner
articles of incorporation
closely held corporation
contract
copyrights
corporations
domestic corporation
dormant partner
express warranties
foreign corporation
implied warranties
lease

limited partners
partnership
patent
publicly held corporation
S corporations
secret partner
silent partner
sole proprietorship
trademarks
Uniform Partnership Act (UPA)
warranty

CASE
In Good Taste

Carol Tempel and Jacki Boyd were starting a business and knew they would need an attorney to assist them with some of the pre-start-up activities they would soon encounter. Like so many other start-up entrepreneurs, they failed to conduct an objective search for the best attorney for their proposed business. Instead, they decided to use the services of a friend. The attorney was first needed to advise Jacki and Carol about the structure of the business. The owners thought that the corporate form was probably most appropriate, because it would formalize their relationship, give them limited liability, and make it easier for them to borrow money. The attorney suggested a C corporation, but their accountant, who had been recommended by the lawyer, suggested an S corporation. Jacki and Carol decided to accept the advice of their attorney and become a C corporation (they later regretted that they had not followed the accountant's advice).

Because the lawyer was Carol's friend, he said, "let me do the incorporating as a friend" (a favor to Carol and Jacki). Neither owner could see how they had received any favors when the lawyer presented his bill. The next time Jacki and Carol called on their lawyer was to help them negotiate a lease on the building they had selected. The lawyer's negotiating efforts were not satisfactory, so Carol's husband stepped in and completed the negotiations (Carol and Jacki later changed lawyers).

Jacki and Carol planned a business that would have no proprietary products; therefore, they would not need to apply for any patents. Likewise, they had nothing that needed to be copyrighted. They did, however, have something that needed trademark protection. That was the name they had chosen for their shop. Jacki and Carol spent many hours trying to select a name for their business that would let customers know what merchandise the shop sold. They also wanted a name that would be easy to remember and would help create an "upscale" image. They finally decided to name their business IN GOOD TASTE, a name that they felt was descriptive of their business and was unique. Not totally unique, it turned out. There was another company in California that had already registered a similar name with the U.S. Commissioner of Patents. Jacki and Carol were able to register the name they had selected with the attorney general of South Carolina. Now they could legally use the name IN GOOD TASTE in their trade area.

QUESTIONS
1. How could Jacki and Carol selected a qualified lawyer?

2. Should the lease for the building have been negotiated by a professional?

3. When the name In Good Taste turned out to be trademarked in California, should Jacki and Carol have searched for another name for their business?

ACTIVITIES

1. Interview a patent attorney to find out what you would have to do to protect a product you invented.

2. Name Identification

   Match these businesses with the appropriate name.

Business	Name
1. Pet suppliers and groomers	A. Sweet Nothings
2. Fine jewelers	B. Pic-a-Flick
3. Gifts and collectibles	C. Straightlace
4. Ministorage	D. In Good Taste
5. Party and paper supply	E. Wedgies
6. Computer service center	F. A Pack Rat
7. Children's clothing	G. Murder by Design
8. Craft shop	H. Paper Chase
9. Dancing instruction	I. Beep One
10. Opticians	J. Dazzles
11. Day care	K. Electricities
12. Catering	L. Animal House
13. Car phones	M. My Favorite Things
14. Take-out food	N. Fete Accompli
15. China and glassware	O. If It's Paper
16. Consignment shop	P. Up-N Running
17. Dry cleaners	Q. Repeat Boutique
18. Furniture repair	R. Outer Vision
19. Video rentals	S. Strip-Ease
20. Cocktail lounge	T. Idle Knot
21. Seafood restaurant	U. Happy Feet
22. Lingerie	V. Out to Lonch
23. Theatrical production company	W. Gingerbread House
24. Gourmet shop	X. Crystal Clear

25. Pizza parlor   Y. Pressing Club

26. Rare bookstore   Z. Castaways

SOURCE: Answers: 1.L., 2.J., 3.M., 4.F., 5.O., 6.P., 7.C., 8.T., 9.U., 10.R., 11.W., 12.N., 13.I., 14.V., 15.X., 16.Q., 17.Y., 18.S., 19.B., 20.K., 21.Z., 22.A., 23.G., 24.D., 25.E., 26.H.

APPENDIX 8-1

Preincorporation Checklist

1. Who serves as the incorporators? Where do they live?
2. In what state will the business be incorporated?
3. Will the corporation's existence be perpetual or limited in duration?
4. What name do you want the corporation to have? Has it been reserved?
5. Where will the principal place of business be? Will it be owned or leased? Who owns it or has the lease now? Will it be transferred to the corporation? In exchange for what?
6. Where else will the corporation operate? Will it own property or have operations in other states? When?
7. What is the nature of the business to be conducted? Is that likely to change?
8. Will the new corporation receive any patents or copyrights? From whom and for what?
9. Does the corporation need any state or local licenses? Are any licenses to be transferred to it? By whom? How long will this take? Can the corporation hold such a license or permit?
10. What will be the initial investment in the corporation? Will it be in cash or in some other form?
11. How many shares will be authorized by the corporation? How many will be issued? To whom? For what consideration?
12. Will there be more than one class of stock? For each class of stock, will there be preemptive rights? Restrictions on transfer? Cumulative voting?
13. Who will subscribe to the initial issue of stock? How many shares will they get? What will they pay in terms of cash or property?
14. When will the corporation begin business?
15. Who executes the articles of incorporation and files them?

16. Will the articles of incorporation provide for indemnification of officers and directors? For the removal of directors by shareholders at any time, with or without cause?

17. How many directors will there be?

18. Who will serve on the first board of directors?

19. When will the directors hold their first meeting?

20. What will be done at the organizational meetings of the incorporators and the directors?

21. Who will be the initial officers?

22. When will the annual meeting of the shareholders be held? Where? On what notice?

23. How will special meetings of the shareholders be called?

24. What kind of quorum is needed for a meeting of shareholders?

25. How many days notice is needed to call a meeting of the directors? What is the quorum for a meeting of the directors?

26. What is the fiscal year of the corporation going to be?

27. How can the bylaws be amended: by the directors or the shareholders?

28. Where will the corporation open its bank account?

29. Who will keep possession of the minutes and records of the board and shareholders and prepare needed materials?

30. Who will keep the books and accounts of the business and be responsible for all tax filings?

APPENDIX 8-2

Articles of Incorporation

STATE OF SOUTH CAROLINA
OFFICE OF THE SECRETARY OF STATE
JOHN T. CAMPBELL

INSTRUCTIONS FOR PREPARING ARTICLES OF INCORPORATION

No. 1   **Name** -- must **NOT** be similar to existing corporation. The name must also contain the word **CORPORATION, INCORPORATION, LIMITED** or the abbreviation of one of these.

No. 2   Must have a complete street address (A POST OFFICE BOX IS **NOT** ACCEPTABLE) and it may be the address of the corporation or one of its officers.

The **agent** may be an officer or employee of the corporation or it may be an attorney.

No. 3   Self explanatory.

No. 4   **Class of shares** -- must be common and may include some preferred.

Authorized Shares -- is the number of shares which the corporation may issue.

Par Value -- will be the value of each share to be sold.

No. 5   **Authorized capital** -- is equal to number of shares times par value as shown by No. 4.

No. 6   Self explanatory.

No. 7   Name and **complete** address (street or box number) for the initial board of directors.

No. 8   **Must briefly** state the **SPECIFIC** purposes for which the corporation is organized.

No. 9   Usually not used.

No. 10 Must have name and address (street or box number) of **EACH** incorporator (may be one or more incorporators).

No. 10 **-Page 2.** Each incorporator must sign.

No. 10 **-Page 3.** Verification must be **completed** and **signed** by EACH incorporator.

No. 11 **Certificate of attorney** -- must be signed by an attorney **LICENSED** to practice in the **STATE OF SOUTH CAROLINA.**

FEES -- Authorized capital **NOT** exceeding $100,000, fee is $45.

Authorized capital exceeding $100,000, fee is **$45 PLUS $.40** for each $1,000 exceeding $100,000. MAXIMUN FEE IS $1,005.

When no par stock is used, a $10 par is assumed for the basis of computing the filing fee.

NOTE-- These articles are filed in duplicate and must be accompanied by the first report of corporations and check of $10, **MADE PAYABLE TO THE S. C. TAX COMMISSION.**

NAME AVAILABILITY SHOULD BE CLEARED IN WRITING. CLEARANCE BY TELEPHONE IS NOT RECOMMENDED AS IT IS NOT OFFICIAL.

APPENDIX 8-2 *(continued)*

STATE OF SOUTH CAROLINA
SECRETARY OF STATE
ARTICLES OF INCORPORATION

OF

_____

	(File This Form in Duplicate Originals) (Sect. 33-7-30 of 1976 Code) (INSTRUCTIONS ON PAGE 4)	This Space For Use By The Secretary of State
For Use By The Secretary of State File No. .... Fee Paid $ .... R. N. .... Date		

1. The name of the proposed corporation is _____

2. The initial registered office of the corporation is ....
   Street and Number

   located in the city of ...., county of .... and

   the State of South Carolina and the name of its initial registered agent at such address is ....

   ....

3. The period of duration of the corporation shall be perpetual (............. years).

4. The corporation is authorized to issue shares of stock as follows:

Class of shares	Authorized No. of each class	Par Value
....	....	....
....	....	....
....	....	....
....	....	....
....	....	....
....	....	....

If shares are divided into two or more classes or if any class of shares is divided into series within a class, the relative rights, preferences, and limitations of the shares of each class, and of each series within a class, are as follows:

5. Total authorized capital stock ....
   Please see instructions on Page 4.

6. The existence of the corporation shall begin as of the filing date with the Secretary of State or to be effective _____ .

7. The number of directors constituting the initial board of Directors of the corporation is .... , and the names and addresses of the persons who are to serve as directors until the first annual meeting of shareholders or until their successors be elected and qualify are:

.... Name	.... Address
.... Name	.... Address
.... Name	.... Address

....
Name

....
Address

....
Name

....
Address

8. The general nature of the business for which the corporation is organized is (it is not necessary to set forth in the purposes powers enumerated Section (33-3-10 of 1976 Code).

9. Provisions which the incorporators elect to include in the articles of incorporation are as follows:

10. The name and address of each incorporator is.

Name	Street & Box No.	City	County	State

....
(Signature of Incorporator)

Date ....

....
(Type or Print Name)

....
(Signature of Incorporator)

....
(Type or Print Name)

....
(Signature of Incorporator)

....
(Type or Print Name)

APPENDIX 8-2 *(continued)*

STATE OF ....

COUNTY OF ....

The undersigned ....
....

do hereby certify that they are the incorporators of .... Corporation and
are authorized to execute this verification; that each of the undersigned for himself does hereby further certify
that he has read the foregoing document, understands the meaning and purport of the statements therein contained and the same are true to the best of his information and belief.

....
(Signature of Incorporator)

....
(Signature of Incorporator)

....
(Signature of Incorporator)
(Each Incorporator Must Sign)

11. I, ..., an attorney licensed to practice in the State of South Carolina, certify that the corporation, to whose articles of incorporation this certificate is attached, has complied with the requirements of chapter 7 of Title 33 of the South Carolina Code of 1976, relating
to the organization of corporations, and that in my opinion, the corporation is organized for a lawful
purpose.

Date ....
(Signature)

....
(Type or Print Name)

Address ....

....

SCHEDULE OF FEES

(Payable at time of filing Articles of With Secretary of State)

Fee for filing Articles	$	5.00
In addition to the above, $.40 for each $1,000.00 of the aggregate value of shares which the Corporation is authorized to issue, but in not case less than		40.00
nor more than		1,000.00

NOTE. THIS FORM MUST BE COMPLETED IN ITS ENTIRETY BEFORE IT WILL BE ACCEPTED FOR FILING.
THIS FORM MUST BE ACCOMPANIED BY THE FIRST REPORT OF CORPORATIONS AND A CHECK IN THE
AMOUNT OF $10 PAYABLE TO THE SOUTH CAROLINA TAX COMMISSION.

Please see instructions on the reverse side.

PART THREE

EMPLOYEES AND OTHER ESSENTIAL PEOPLE

9 STAFFING AND TRAINING

"I can't find qualified employees," "My new employees can't do anything," "How can she sue me for firing her?" These are complaints and questions heard with increasing frequency from small business owners. We even hear about the weaknesses of our workers from foreigners. Japanese government officials have said that American workers are lazy, uneducated, and unproductive. Numerous surveys have shown that personnel problems are the primary difficulty faced by small business owners.

Finding suitable, capable, honest, trained, dedicated, and retainable employees can be a frustrating experience for any business owner, and it is especially so for small business owners. Small business owners often do not have the time or the expertise to recruit, test, interview, and select the best employees, and their inability to pay what larger firms can means they often select from a less desirable pool of applicants. However, small business owners can recruit and train people who become competent, dedicated employees.

Small business owners need to learn how to legally staff their businesses because mistakes can be costly—wrongful discharge settlements can easily reach the high six figures. Other costs resulting from faulty staffing include recruiting, testing, and training expenses for replacement employees. In this chapter, we will consider the government's role in protecting employees and examine the best methods of staffing a business. We will also discuss useful methods of evaluating and training employees.

EMPLOYMENT LAWS

From the founding of this country until the early 1960s employer-employee relations were affected primarily by economic factors and employer decisions were rarely questioned or reversed. However, the early 1960s saw the government become directly involved in employer-employee relations, usually to protect individuals from unfair or discriminatory hiring practices. Laws were passed to protect individuals not only from discriminatory hiring practices but also from discriminatory or unfair practices during their employment.

The Equal Pay Act of 1963

Equal Pay Act

The **Equal Pay Act** was passed to "prohibit discrimination on account of sex in the payment of wages by employers engaged in commerce or in the production of goods for commerce." This law requires that men and women doing the same job receive the same pay. Some employers try to circumvent the provisions of the Equal Pay Act by changing job titles or descriptions of work done by males and females, thereby justifying wage differentials.

The Civil Rights Act of 1964

Title VII of the Civil Rights Act

Title VII of the Civil Rights Act may be one of the most important and comprehensive laws guaranteeing employee rights. This law, which applies to businesses with more than fifteen employees, makes discrimination in any form illegal. Employers cannot refuse a person employment, promotion, pay increases, training, or other employment-related activities because of race, color, religion, sex, or national origin. As comprehensive as this law was, it still did not protect people who were discriminated against for other reasons, such as age or disability. Those oversights were rectified with later legislation.

The Age Discrimination in Employment Act of 1967

Age Discrimination Act

The **Age Discrimination Act,** as amended, states:

> It is therefore the purpose of this act to promote employment of older persons based on their ability rather than age; to prohibit arbitrary age discrimination in employment; to help employers and workers find ways of meeting problems arising from the impact of age on employment.

Not all employees or job applicants are protected by this law from age discrimination. Only those persons between the ages of 40 and 70 have protection under this law.

The Vocational Rehabilitation Act of 1973

Vocational Rehabilitation Act

Section 503 of the **Vocational Rehabilitation Act** stipulates that employers with federal government contracts of $50,000 or more and fifty or more employees must actively recruit and hire handicapped individuals. Employers cannot discriminate against mentally or physically handicapped persons for jobs they are qualified to do. Businesses must make efforts to accommodate physical and mental limitations of applicants and employees unless they can show that such accommodation would constitute an "unusual hardship."

Companies that violate the law can be penalized; however, those that abide by the law can also be penalized. For example, a Colorado state court ordered McDonald's to pay damages for negligent hiring. The $210,000 award was made to a mother and her three-year-old son, who was assaulted by a disabled worker at a McDonald's restaurant in Denver. Employment law specialists say the case could have far-reaching implications for companies that want to institute or maintain programs for hiring persons with addictions, handicaps, or mental impairment.[1]

Vietnam Era Veterans Readjustment Act of 1974

Vietnam Era
Veterans
Readjustment
Act

Section 402 of the **Vietnam Era Veterans Readjustment Act** requires contractors who have federal contracts in excess of $10,000 to take affirmative action to employ and advance in employment qualified disabled veterans and veterans of the Vietnam War.

Immigration Law of 1986

Immigration
Law of 1986

Form I-9

The **Immigration Law of 1986** requires employers to examine the documents of all new hires to certify that no illegal aliens are employed. Documents inspected must be listed on Immigration and Naturalization Service **Form I-9**, and the form must be kept for three years after the employee is hired. Simple paperwork violations are punishable by fines up to $1,000 per employee. Sanctions against employers actually hiring illegal aliens range from $250 to $10,000 per worker and prison sentences up to six months. A New Jersey man found out how costly it could be to violate this immigration law (see The Way It Is 9-1).

The U.S. Chamber of Commerce has published a detailed guide for complying with the new law. *The Immigration Law: An Employer's Handbook* is

The Way It Is

9-1 VIOLATING IMMIGRATION LAWS

Alfred Mizhir, of Spring Lake, New Jersey, was fined $20,000 and sentenced to three months in prison for employing more than 100 illegal aliens at his textile plant. Mr. Mizhir, the president of Piedmont Quilting Corporation, was also sentenced to three months in a halfway house and ordered to pay $5,960 in court costs. U.S. Immigration and Naturalization Service agents raided Piedmont Quilting's Walhalla (South Carolina) plant and deported 86 aliens to Mexico and Peru. The INS fined Piedmont Quilting $580,000, but that fine was reduced to $225,000 after the company appealed.[2]

targeted to small and midsized businesses. It addresses subjects such as recordkeeping, hiring practices, verification of eligibility, and penalties for noncompliance. It contains a copy of Form I-9 plus descriptions and photographs of documents commonly used for verification.

The Americans with Disabilities Act of 1990

Americans
with
Disabilities
Act (ADA)

The **Americans with Disabilities Act (ADA)** is effective as of July 26, 1992. For the first two years, the law affects employers with twenty-five or more employees; then businesses with fifteen or more employees are also affected. According to this law, employers may not

- Discriminate against disabled persons qualified for a job, in hiring or firing
- Inquire whether an applicant has a disability, but may ask about ability to perform a job
- Limit advancement opportunity or job classifications
- Use tests or job requirements that tend to screen out the disabled
- Participate in contractual arrangements that discriminate against the disabled
- Deny opportunity to anyone in a relationship with a disabled person

In addition to not discriminating against the disabled, employers must provide reasonable accommodations to the disabled, including

- Making existing facilities accessible
- Providing special equipment and training
- Providing readers for the blind

Civil Rights
Act of 1991

The Civil Rights Act of 1991

This piece of legislation, signed by President Bush, will have the following affect on employers and employees nationwide:

- The law will make it easier for certain workers to sue their employers over alleged job discrimination. It would also allow women and the disabled to collect monetary damages that are already available to racial minorities.
- Smaller businesses might feel new pressure to keep more detailed records, consult with lawyers, and consider whether they have overlooked potential employees who are not white and male.
- This legislation does not explicitly encourage quotas, but it shifts the legal burden back to the employer, who would have to defend its employment practices as necessary.
- Employers would have to prove that any allegedly discriminatory practices are "job-related for the positions in question and consistent with business necessity."[3]

This new civil rights law is expected to have an especially severe impact on small and medium-sized businesses. The law specifically exempts businesses with fewer than fifteen employees, but Lawrence Lorber, a labor attorney, notes that small businesses "are big enough to be affected by the issue but not big enough to have a staff to deal with it internally." The law will make it likely that small firms, faced with the possibility of damage payments and legal fees, will settle suits out of court. Under the law, punitive damages will be capped at $50,000 for companies with 100 or fewer employees and at $100,000 for those with 101 to 200 workers.[4]

STAFFING

employment-at-will

wrongful discharge

When **employment-at-will** (employees could quit or be terminated with no justification) was prevalent, hiring the wrong person was not a serious mistake. However, now that employees have some job protection and are willing to sue their employer for **wrongful discharge,** hiring mistakes can be extremely costly. Paying large settlements for a wrongful discharge suit could be disastrous for small businesses. Small business owners experience staffing problems because the labor pool is changing, and the selection process is still as much art as science.

The Labor Pool

The labor pool is shrinking and will continue to do so for the foreseeable future. William B. Johnston, author of the study "Workforce 2000," said that "the labor market of the next decade will be the 1970s turned on its head. There will be a spreading surplus of jobs and spreading shortages of workers to fill them."[5] The following are indicators that the shortage is already here in some areas of the country:

- By the late 1980s, Disneyland was unable to fill 200 of its 2000 jobs.
- In Danbury, Connecticut, the opening of a shopping mall was delayed by five weeks because of a severe shortage of workers.
- Texas' Zapata Gulf Marine, a supplier of offshore oil rigs, has had to mothball several ships because it cannot find chief engineers to operate them.
- In Hyannis, Massachusetts, owners of the popular Denny's restaurant were forced to close up shop just before the start of the summer beach rush because they could hire only thirteen of the seventy employees they needed.[6]

baby boomers

The nation's supply of young workers will continue to drop for seven or eight more years before bottoming out and starting up again. The decline in the number of young workers represents the passage into the workplace of the "baby bust" generation, born between 1965 and 1979. Its numbers are too small to replace all the **baby boomers,** those born between 1946 and 1964. The number of young people aged 16 to 24 will drop by half-a-million each year until 1995.[7] These shortages have forced business owners to adopt radical strategies to staff their companies. The following are some of the steps taken by employers desperate for employees:

- A Pawtucket, Rhode Island, pizza shop, strapped for order takers, advertises jobs at the previously unheard-of wage of $10 an hour.
- An electronics firm was moved from Bethany, Connecticut, to upstate New York because the owner could not find workers, even at high wages.
- Companies ranging from Wendy's to Stop & Shop to construction firms in booming Fairfax and Prince William counties in Virginia are busing in workers from surrounding areas, often up to two hours away, just to meet their hiring needs.
- In Des Moines, Washington, Wesley Homes, a retirement community with 430 employees, has such a severe shortage of registered and practical nurses that it is offering scholarships to encourage young women to enroll in nursing schools.[8]

The shortage problem is compounded by the lack of skills of those people who do want to work. Between 25 and 30 percent of the young people who start school do not complete high school. Of those that do graduate, only half go on to college. Anywhere from 17 million to 27 million American adults are functionally illiterate, and another 45 million are only marginally literate. Nearly one-half of the 17-year-olds in the United States cannot solve junior high math problems, and less than one-tenth can solve problems that require algebra. Finally, approximately 25 million current workers of all ages will need to have their skills upgraded to remain productive employees during the next decade.[9]

The Selection Process

Because the labor pool is shrinking, and those people who are available to work are less skilled, small business owners will have to put more effort into the selection process to hire and retain acceptable employees. In small businesses, the owner is usually the recruiter, interviewer, tester, and selector of employees; however, as companies grow, some of those functions may be delegated to other managers.

THE STAFFING PROCESS

The staffing process generally progresses in the following manner:

- Job audit
- Recruiting
- Interviewing
- Testing
- Interviewing

· Reference checking

· Selecting

Not all steps of the process are needed for all jobs. For example, some positions may not require employee tests, and others may require only one interview. In general, the more important the job, the longer and more detailed the selection process.

Job Audit

Determining how many employees are needed for a new business or an established one begins with a job audit or a needs assessment. Owners should analyze the positions they have to fill and project the number of new positions that might need to be filled in the future. By carefully describing jobs and the specifications that people should possess to do them, business owners will be able to select the best qualified people for each position.

job
descriptions

JOB DESCRIPTION. **Job descriptions** basically outline the most common functions performed by that job holder. Descriptions of job functions should be as simple and straightforward as possible. Owners should not attempt to list all the duties of a job; rather they should describe the most commonly performed functions. A job description should list the job title, identify the person the incumbent reports to, and detail how the incumbent will spend most of his or her time while at work.

Most good job descriptions include a clause stating that employees may be asked to perform functions not specifically included in the description. This clause eliminates the necessity to describe every function a person may be expected to do. It also allows owners to make minor job modifications without rewriting the job description. However, when additional duties are added that become a routine part of a job, the description should be rewritten.

job
specifications

JOB SPECIFICATIONS. Having determined what duties are performed by different job incumbents, business owners can then determine what qualifications employees need to fill that position. As with the job description, **job specifications** should be fairly general so as not to exclude people who would be competent employees. However, it is possible, for example, to write specifications that only one person, known to the employer, possesses. This would allow a business owner to hire a preselected individual without having discrimination charges filed by other applicants.

Specifications for most jobs usually include criteria such as education, experience, skill level, and advancement potential. If a more exhaustive set of specifications is required, owners could include analytic ability, creativity, communication skills, perseverance, assertiveness, enthusiasm, and interpersonal skills. The principal reason for not including some of these characteristics in a skills inventory is that objectively measuring them can be quite difficult and costly. On the other hand, a too general inventory of skills allows owners to hire people who can do that particular job but cannot progress to more responsible jobs.

Recruiting

Having determined how many positions need to be filled, a business owner can proceed to the next step in the staffing process—recruiting interested people. Owners need to find the best places to "look" for potential employees before they can continue the staffing process. There are various sources of potential employees that could be fruitful for small business owners.

FRIENDS AND RELATIVES. Many business owners, especially those whose business is just in the start-up phase, choose friends and relatives to be their employees. This may turn out to be a satisfactory arrangement, but it could be unworkable because personal relationships could bias decision making. In a survey conducted by *Venture,* respondents who chose not to hire friends cited the following reasons for their decision: 34 percent said they anticipated complications; 28 percent said it caused aggravation; 20 percent said it destroyed friendships; and 18 percent said they had been taken advantage of by friends.[10]

EMPLOYEE REFERRALS. Studies have shown that about one-third of the people hired by companies are referred by current employees. Current employees are generally familiar with requirements of vacant positions, and they

There are many ways in which business owners can look for potential employees.

know what kind of person would be most suitable for the job. If a reliable employee refers a friend for a job, it is quite likely that the referred person will prove to be a valuable employee. Similarly, if the referring employee is only a marginal worker, then the person being referred should be scrutinized more closely to be sure that she or he is qualified and competent. Business owners who have had good experiences with employee referrals can encourage the practice by rewarding employees who refer acceptable people (see The Way It Is 9-2).

WALK-INS. Some job seekers apply to companies where they think they would like to work. If this happens, and there are no jobs available, owners should keep the applications on file for six months to a year in the event that a position becomes vacant. Business owners should not forget to periodically purge their files of old applications.

PRIVATE EMPLOYMENT AGENCIES. Reliable private agencies are usually a good source of employees because they are familiar with the job market, the requirements of companies, and the abilities of prospective employees. Private agencies respond to requests for employees by referring only their qualified clients to the requesting company. If the referred person is hired, the agency receives a fee equal to 10 to 15 percent of the annual salary. The fee is paid either by the hiring company or by the person who is hired.

PUBLIC EMPLOYMENT AGENCIES. State employment offices, in conjunction with the U.S. Department of Labor, offer placement services for anyone actively seeking employment. The service provided by these agencies is free and available to all employers and job seekers. Public agencies are being used more now than in the past because businesses need to demonstrate that they are equal-opportunity employers.

The Way It Is

9-2 REWARDS FOR REFERRALS

At Integrated Microcomputer Systems Inc., a software development company in Rockville, Maryland, about 60 percent of its employees have been hired through an employee referral program. All jobs are posted, and employees make referrals by filling out a standard form and attaching the applicant's resumé. If the applicant is hired and remains with the company at least four months, the referring worker gets a bonus—from $300 (for administrative jobs) to $800 (for technical positions). The bonus for filling senior or skilled positions has been as much as $1,000. The company's turnover rate is only 3 percent.[11]

SCHOOLS. Colleges, universities, and vocational schools are good sources of qualified employees. Newly hired graduates usually need additional training before they can be productive, but even though they lack experience, they are usually enthusiastic and willing to work. Graduates of vocational and technical schools have already acquired the skills that employers seek; therefore, they need very little company-sponsored training.

A source often overlooked in the past that should be investigated by small business owners is the nation's business schools. Conventional wisdom has always been that people who receive an M.B.A. work only for large, prestigious institutions—conventional wisdom is wrong. Several placement officers at leading business schools report that more and more M.B.A. students want to work for small companies. Priscilla Greer, associate placement director of the Tuck School at Dartmouth, has started a direct-mail campaign to promising small companies requesting brief profiles from them to help students job hunt.[12]

TEMPORARIES. Some business owners postpone hiring decisions by using temporary or contingent workers. Temporaries work as long as the business owner needs them, and they usually receive no benefits from the business. A study commissioned by the SBA found that

- Independent contractors were the most common form of contingent staff employed by small firms.
- Contingent workers help small business owners reduce the paperwork and administrative costs associated with short-term labor needs.
- Relatively few contingent workers have medical insurance provided by the company that buys their services.[13]

Business owners who choose to use employees provided by a temporary agency may be relieved of the burden of evaluating workers' qualifications, but they cannot shed the burden of evaluating the agency itself. To insure receiving qualified workers when needed, business owners should evaluate the following agency-related factors:

Reliability. Is the service a well-established company with a history of success and financial stability?

Recruiting. The company should have an aggressive recruiting system that attracts the most qualified temporary employees.

Testing and Evaluating. Business owners should investigate a firm's testing and evaluating techniques and determine how thoroughly employees' references are checked.

Training. Firms should have ongoing training programs that are designed to keep their temporaries current and familiar with the latest technology.

Retention. Does the company have a good program to keep qualified employees for a longer period of time?

Prompt Service. Efficient temporary service firms should be able to supply business owners with needed temporaries without undue delay.

Guarantee. Does the firm guarantee satisfaction with each and every temporary employee placed in a client company?[14]

MISCELLANEOUS. Other sources and events that can be used by small companies to recruit employees include the military, other companies, other countries, school career days, trade journals, newspapers, and job fairs.

LEASED EMPLOYEES. Some small business owners may decide that they do not want to have the responsibility for permanent employees. For them, leasing employees from another company is the answer. The practice of leasing employees is about eighteen years old and is quite simple and appealing to some business owners. A leasing company provides employees to a small business for an agreed-upon fee and replaces them when necessary. Business owners determine who works for them at what wages, who gets promoted, who gets time off, and who gets fired. Leased employees are paid by the leasing company, which also finances their benefits.

APPLICATION FORM. Whether people have been recruited or are walk-ins, most will expect to complete a formal application form. This document has undergone considerable scrutiny in the past few years to purge it of discriminatory questions. Any business owner using an application form prepared in-house should have it carefully analyzed by an attorney who can eliminate potentially discriminatory questions. Specifying precisely what information can be considered discriminatory is difficult, but the following are some questionable subjects: racial or ethnic background, birthplace, age, religion, marital status, number and ages of children, a woman's maiden name, extracurricular affiliations, arrest record, height and weight, and persons to notify in case of emergency.

Bona Fide Occupational Qualification (BFOQ)

Information of a potentially discriminatory nature can be legally collected only if it can be proven to be a **Bona Fide Occupational Qualification (BFOQ).** If a characteristic such as height or weight can be proven to be an essential job requirement, that information can be included on an application form. Or if a person needs foreign-language capability in a job, that information can also be requested; however, owners should avoid asking how skill in that language was acquired. The list of what can and cannot be included on an application form may seem daunting, but business owners can create a document (see Appendix 9-1) that meets their needs without violating applicants' rights.

Interviewing

Once potential employees have been recruited and have completed the necessary paperwork, it is time to select some of the most promising to be interviewed. The number, depth, and length of interviews each candidate is subjected to usually depends on the importance and complexity of the job.

Entry-level hourly employees may be selected after a simple half-hour interview, whereas a marketing director may participate in several multihour interviews. Regardless of length or the type of questions asked, all interviews are expected to achieve the same results—identify the most suitable applicants. To be successful, interviews need thorough planning, and interviewers need to prepare for the meeting with applicants.

INTERVIEW PREPARATION. Business owners have individualized ways of preparing for job interviews; however, most will address the same factors to insure a comfortable and fruitful interview. The following questions will give most owners an idea of the factors they should consider when preparing for an interview:

- Have a suitable time and place been selected?
- If other managers are to attend the interview, have they been notified?
- Have all the necessary data and information been collected and organized for the interview?
- Have employees been advised not to interrupt the session?
- Has a list of points to cover been made?
- Are the objectives to be achieved clear and reasonable?
- Are the applicant's objectives known?
- What follow-up steps should be taken? Memos sent? Ideas pursued? Actions taken?
- Should there be a record made of the interview?
- If there are to be follow-up interviews, should there be a note made of the ideas gained that can be used in subsequent interviews?[15]

Adequate preparation enables the interview to be smooth and productive. As soon as the interview begins, the interviewer should establish rapport with the applicant before he or she begins asking relevant questions. The interviewer should listen to and possibly record the applicant's answers and should completely answer all applicant questions. The interviewer should know when the interview is over and should terminate it at the appropriate time. Finally, the applicant should be given some idea of when he or she will know the outcome of the interview.

QUESTIONS. The questions asked during an interview are perhaps the most important factor of the session. Poorly conceived questions fail to elicit responses that provide the desired information, and inappropriate questions can lead to charges of discrimination. Interviews can be structured (all applicants are asked the same questions) or unstructured. **Unstructured interviews** allow the interviewer to ask questions that are most appropriate for that session and applicant, and an applicant's answer to one question may call for a suitable follow-up question.

unstructured interviews

structured
interviews

Structured interviews often rely on closed-ended questions—those that can be answered with one or two words. Questions such as "Did you like your last job?" "Did you get along with your previous supervisor?" and "Can you work under pressure?" can be answered with a simple yes or no and do not provide much valuable information. Answers to open-ended questions such as "What do you see yourself doing in five years?" "How do you feel you respond to pressure?" and "What is your interpretation of success?" provide more information, but they may be harder to evaluate than answers to closed-ended questions.

DISCRIMINATION. The potentially discriminatory questions that should be eliminated from application forms should also be avoided in personal interviews. Some applicant characteristics such as age, gender, height, and weight can be determined in an interview, but others can only be determined by skillful questioning. Some interviewers may feel that they can ask discriminatory questions in a personal interview because any discrimination charges would be based on one person's word—there would be no written evidence that such questions had been asked. Some interviewers might inadvertently ask discriminatory questions, but lack of intent to discriminate is not an acceptable defense. The following list offers some guidelines of general areas of questioning to avoid:

It is discriminatory to suggest by statement or question that

1. A particular job has always been held by members of the same sex.
2. An applicant is not qualified because the job requires travel with members of the opposite sex.
3. Appropriate physical facilities are not available for one sex or the other.
4. An applicant is unqualified because she is female and subject to the following distractions:
   Plans to have a family
   Married, single, divorced, separated, widowed
   Has children
   Arrangements for child care
   Husband's reaction to working or travel
5. An applicant is not suitable because of regular, nonregular, or no church attendance.
6. An applicant's involvement in any church groups makes her or him unsuitable.
7. An applicant is unacceptable because the rest of the staff is much younger.
8. A person is unacceptable because of the nationality of his or her parents or spouse.

9. A candidate is not hired because of the clubs, societies, or lodges to which he or she belongs.[16]

INTERVIEWER TIPS. Interviewing job applicants may intimidate small business owners who have had very little experience with interviews in the past. However, the following tips should make interviewing easier for most owners: take a course on interviewing; do no more than 15 percent of the talking (concentrate on listening); ask open-ended questions; ask about personal goals and plans; ask what was easy and what was hard in school, in other jobs, and in other relationships; and, in judging a candidate, keep your own biases in mind.[17]

Testing

For years, testing has been one of the major methods of selecting the best-qualified applicant; however, recent laws and court cases have questioned the acceptability of some tests. For example, in the landmark case *Griggs v. Duke Power Company*, the court ruled that selection tests and other promotion criteria were unacceptable because they were not job related. Small business owners who use tests should thoroughly evaluate each test, use tests in conjunction with other selection instruments, use only validated tests, and set the cut-off score in advance.

Standardized tests can be acquired from companies such as Behavior Dyne in Palo Alto, California; London House/SRA in Park Ridge, Illinois; or The Personnel Laboratory, Inc. in Stamford, Connecticut. Even if these companies validate their tests, user companies must also validate them for their own employees. Business owners should have their own employees take tests to determine if they measure the qualities or capabilities claimed.

EVALUATING TESTS There are numerous companies selling hundreds of instruments to measure skills, values, personality, and many other variables. To receive the most for their money, business owners should carefully evaluate any instruments they might buy and use in the selection process. The following are some instrument constructs that should be considered:

Validity. What does the instrument measure? Will the data be useful?

Reliability. How accurate or stable are the test scores?

Objectivity. Is the scoring dependent on the judgments of the scorer, or is there a standard key?

Theoretical Base. Is the instrument based on a workable model?

Observability. Can the scores be related to the observable behavior of respondents?

Special Training. How much professional preparation is needed to use the instrument?

Language. Is the instrument written at an appropriate reading level? Does it use a special vocabulary or jargon?

Transparency. How obvious is the rationale underlying the items?

Fakeability. How easy is it for respondents to manipulate their scores?

Copyright Restrictions. Can the materials be copied or edited without special permission?

Time Required. How much time is required to prepare, administer, score, and interpret the instrument?

Familiarity. How likely is it that participants will have responded to this instrument before?[18]

KINDS OF TESTS. Business owners should determine which applicant characteristics are most important and then select the best tests to measure them. Tests can be purchased that measure intelligence, personality, aptitude, skills, honesty (not polygraph tests, which are not used because the results are often unreliable), and numerous other characteristics or traits. Most tests, other than skill tests, are paper-and-pencil instruments that are not overly complex and do not require an inordinate amount of time to complete. Some test-development companies are even using computer-based tests (see The Way It Is 9-3) that measure a person's ability to perform specific jobs. Because these tests do not rely on human scoring or interpretation, they are less likely to be challenged by those who fail them.

Reference Checking

One of the last steps in the staffing process is checking an applicant's references. If done correctly, reference checks provide valuable information; if mishandled, however, reference checks can lead to a negligent-hiring case.

The
Way
It Is

9-3 COMPUTER-BASED TESTS

Every day before he begins work at Ion Implant Services Inc., Robert Anguay lines up with his fellow delivery drivers, stands in front of a console, and "plays" a short video game. Unless the machine dispenses a receipt confirming that the drivers have passed the video test, they cannot climb behind the wheels of their trucks. Factor 1000, a software system developed by Performance Factors Inc. (PFI) tests a worker's hand-eye coordination to measure fitness for duty. When employees report to work, they go to the computer and type in an ID code. Then they take the test to determine if they can proceed with their jobs. To make the test accurate, employees perform the test many times to establish a base average; then they are measured against their average, which is stored in the computer. Most failures are caused by severe fatigue or illness rather than drug or alcohol problems.[19]

Business owners should consider the following facts before creating a reference-checking procedure: prospective employers check references on only 25 percent of job candidates; 79 percent of fired employees filing a defamation claim recover damages; and a study of 120 wrongful-discharge cases found that initial jury verdicts average \$272,064.[20] The possibility of being sued for providing personal and job information has made many employers extremely cautious.

To protect themselves from lawsuits, many employers give only minimal information about previous employees. For example, there are employers who will verify only the length of service of former employees. They will provide no salary information or reasons for termination or withdrawal from the company. To avoid legal problems, many business owners are turning to computerized data services for employee information. Companies such as Equifax, Fidelifacts Metropolitan New York, and Apscreen maintain databases comprised of information obtained from credit bureaus, police records, and other public sources. These companies mix information from various databases and produce summaries that describe the applicant's financial condition, criminal and driving records, and business relationships.

The information obtained from database companies is not always totally accurate, and it is not cheap. A background report from companies such as Equifax can cost thousands of dollars for a corporate officer or as little as \$100 for a lower level worker.[21] Business owners who choose to use these services should not rely completely on them for applicant information. They should also contact previous employers (applicants must give their permission for these contacts to be made), other listed references, and people who are not listed but who might have some information about the applicant.

Selecting

The preceding steps in the staffing process provide the information needed for this final step—selecting the best individual for the job. Throughout the staffing process, business owners should endeavor to be nondiscriminatory. Because employees are more inclined to sue their employers than they were in the past, business owners should take some precautions to protect themselves from discrimination charges. Peter M. Panken, a partner in a New York law firm, suggests the following:

1. Document the company's compliance posture in detail. Interviewers and interviewees should know that employment decisions are based solely on job-related criteria.

2. Avoid irrelevant questions during an interview. Questions not related to business matters could be viewed as evidence of hidden motives.

3. Do not offer applicants reasons for rejection unless forced to do so.

4. Do not tell applicants they were or were not qualified for the job. Only say that those selected had better qualifications.

5. Apply prerequisites consistently and even-handedly.

6. Require applicants to specify in their applications exactly what type of job they are seeking, and then have them document their own qualifications for that job.

7. Beware of making casual, shorthand comments on applications or in notes during an interview.

8. Review job descriptions. They should not contain irrelevant criteria that might exclude certain groups of people.

9. Be consistent.

10. Analyze hiring practices by race, sex, age, etc. If one category of applicant is being rejected disproportionately, changes should be made in the selection process.[22]

Once business owners are satisfied that they have conducted an objective, nondiscriminatory job search, they should make a formal offer to the successful candidate. The formal job offer should, at a minimum, contain a short congratulatory message from the business owner, the title of the job, the name of the applicant's immediate supervisor, hourly wages or annual salary, when the job is to begin, and the date by which a reply is expected.

PERFORMANCE APPRAISALS

Throughout their working lives employees want to know how they are performing. They want to be rewarded for doing good work, and they expect to be corrected if their work is not satisfactory. The formal performance appraisal is the basis for many personnel decisions in small companies. For example, appraisals indicate if additional training is necessary, determine employees' pay increases, determine who gets promoted, and so forth. Because so much depends on performance appraisals, business owners should do them frequently and objectively. Employees should be counseled after their performance has been evaluated, and they should receive positive suggestions for improvement.

Appraisal Methods

performance
appraisal
methods

A number of different **performance appraisal methods** can be used by small business owners to objectively evaluate their employees' performance. The following are the most appropriate methods for small companies: the **graphic rating scale, ranking, critical incidents,** and **essay appraisals.**

graphic rating
scale

GRAPHIC RATING SCALE. This scale, which can be either descriptive or numerical, evaluates a number of job-important attributes. Attributes such as job knowledge, leadership, motivation, and so on can be rated on a scale of "much below standard" to "much above standard" with a number assigned to each rating. The numbers for each attribute are totaled and employees' scores can be compared with their peers' scores. Employees who score low on evaluated attributes can be counseled and have personalized improvement regimens created for them.

ranking

RANKING. This method requires the rater to rank employees from "best" to "worst" on the basis of their performance. Although this method might be useful for determining pay raises and promotions, it is very demoralizing for those employees ranked low. Owners who use this method should be prepared to justify the criteria they used to arrive at their rankings; otherwise they may be open to charges of subjectivity and unfairness.

critical incidents

CRITICAL INCIDENTS. This might be the fairest and least criticized performance appraisal technique. Using job descriptions and specifications, the rater develops a list of requirements considered critical to particular jobs. Throughout the rating period—a quarter, six months, one year, and so on—the rater records these incidents for each employee being evaluated. The value of this method is that performance is evaluated for the entire rating period rather than on the last few weeks of the period. The incidents recorded can be negative and positive, and they can result in rewards or job-improvement counseling.

essay appraisals

ESSAYS. Some business owners may be uncomfortable with quantifiable lists of job attributes and may choose, instead, to simply write a relatively brief essay about an employee's performance. To insure consistency and objectivity, essays should describe comparable attributes and activities for all employees being evaluated. This can be accomplished by combining this evaluation method with the critical incidents technique.

Counseling Employees

In the past, employee performance was generally evaluated once a year, and the employee was not informed of the outcome of the appraisal. Today, it is rare to encounter a business owner who does not discuss appraisals with employees. After all, what performance-improvement value would an appraisal have if employees were not told how they were performing their jobs? The counseling session should be used to inform employees of their job performance. Counseling based on performance appraisals can change work habits; however, to be most effective, counseling should be an ongoing activity.

Counseling is not always easy, particularly when negative information has to be transmitted to employees. Business owners can become more comfortable with counseling sessions if they remember to do the following:

Provide Privacy. Counseling should take place in a private setting free from distractions so that confidentiality can be maintained. People receiving criticism do not want peers to be aware of their shortcomings.

Be Positive First. All employees perform some parts of their jobs well. Begin a counseling session by commending a person for what he or she has done well—then discuss weaknesses.

Avoid Negative Criticism. Substandard performance can more readily be improved when criticism is constructive rather than unnecessarily negative.

Be Specific. "You're doing a lousy job, Bill" does not really tell the employee what he is doing wrong or what it will take to improve his performance. Specific examples should be provided to illustrate which job functions are not satisfactory.

Provide Remedies. Giving examples of unsatisfactory performance illustrates but does not correct the problem. Employees should be told what they have to do and how to do it to improve their work.

Explain Consequences. Employees should be told exactly what to expect if their job performance does not improve within a specified period.

TRAINING

Even the most exhaustive selection process rarely identifies people who are able to begin a job with a new employer without some orientation and training. In the very early phases of business growth, training is often done by the owner or another designated employee. The training is usually unsatisfactory because the owner does not have the time, the experience, or the inclination to do it properly. The result is that new employees are minimally trained or the business relies on outside sources for periodic training. To capitalize on employee training, business owners or designated trainers should determine training needs, design effective training programs, present the programs, and evaluate training programs.

Determining Training Needs

Some companies train on a regularly scheduled basis, whenever they have available funds, or when they are sold a new training package, but rarely on an as-needed basis. However, training is most effective when it is performed as a result of a well-planned needs analysis. Training needs can be detected by examining a company's operations, by observing the employees, and by analyzing performance evaluations. The following are some of the events or observations that could signal a need for more training:

- Excessive waste
- High absenteeism and turnover rates
- Low employee morale
- A high product rejection rate
- Too much machine down-time
- The introduction of new technology
- The addition of new items to the product line
- Too many accidents

Designing Training Programs

Poorly designed training programs are worse than no program at all because they consume time and money that could be used more productively. Small businesses rarely operate with a surplus of people, and the pace of operations is fast and often frantic. Therefore, training, if recognized as a necessity at all, tends to be dealt with on an as-needed, if-we-can-afford-it basis. To be really effective, training should be an ongoing process consisting of well-designed, subject-specific programs.

Some business owners will choose to purchase off-the-shelf training programs designed by professionals for a generic audience. These programs might be satisfactory, but they are probably not as effective as programs designed for a specific industry or company. Small business owners should not automatically presume that they have neither the funds nor the in-house talent to create effective training programs (see The Way It Is 9-4). Business owners who choose to design their own training programs should consider the following points (see Appendix 9-2 for a checklist for developing training programs):

1. Because learning is accelerated by reducing restraints, design should focus on reducing these restraints rather than adding driving forces.
2. Training programs should help people convert experience into learning.
3. People should feel safe and capable in the early stages of the design.
4. A good design will allow for different learning styles and not be a projection of the leader's own style.
5. "Here and now" facets should be provided in the design.
6. A good design should provide opportunities for discovering "I'm not alone here!"
7. Transfer of learning depends on how similar experiences are to the "real world"; therefore, realistic role plays or situations should be built into training programs.

The Way It Is

9-4 IN-HOUSE TRAINING PROGRAMS

When a prospective client calls Backroads Bicycle Touring, a 39-employee travel company that provides cycling tours all over the world, the telemarketer who answers the phone is faced with a formidable task: find out how physically fit the client is—and then talk the client into a trip best suited to his or her fitness level and personality. To make sure her telemarketing staff asks the right questions the right way, Susan Parker, the sales and marketing manager, relies on ongoing in-house sales seminars that adapt selling techniques to their particular product. "The generic selling methods don't work for us," says Parker. "We once hired a telemarketing expert to conduct a seminar here, but we didn't feel it was very productive. Our product is so unique—and so are our problems."[24]

8. Some stress is necessary for learning to take place, so remember to design some stress into training programs.[23]

Training Employees

Training should begin the first day a new employee is on the job. Company orientations, which last from one hour to one or two days, are possibly the most important "training" new employees receive. The orientation session lets employees know what is expected of them and what they can expect from the company. Once orientation is over, new employees receive their "basic training" either on the job or in a classroom setting. Basic training should not signal the end of an employee's training; rather it should be the first phase of an ongoing training and development program.

ORIENTATION. Even very small businesses should have formal orientation programs that help make new employees comfortable with their new surroundings. Business owners should explain the company's rules and policies to new hires and should explain wage rates, benefits, and other items important to employees. To make the orientation session more meaningful, owners should develop an employee handbook or personnel manual that contains the information that is presented during an orientation. Personnel manuals need not be elaborate, but they should contain the information employees

Training should begin the first day a new employee is on the job.

need to do their jobs satisfactorily (see Exhibit 9-1 for relevant personnel manual topics).

BASIC TRAINING. After orientation, employees usually need skill-specific training to perform their jobs efficiently. For most small businesses, this means **on-the-job training (OJT),** which is relatively inexpensive and quite effective. The principal problem to guard against is allowing "seasoned" employees to pass on bad work habits to the new employees they are training.

on-the-job training (OJT)

EXHIBIT 9-1 Personnel Manual Table of Contents

A. General Introduction
1. Welcome to company
2. Brief history of company
3. Equal-opportunity statement
4. Probationary period
5. Ethical standards of company
6. Work hours
7. Employee rights
8. Hiring of relatives

B. Pay Policies
1. Regular paydays
2. Standard payroll deductions
3. Overtime pay
4. Severance pay
5. Performance review and merit increases

C. Benefits
1. Value of benefits
2. Available benefits
3. Eligibility requirements for benefits

D. Discipline System
1. Unacceptable behavior
2. Consequences of unacceptable behavior
3. Discharge procedures
4. Grievance procedure

E. Work Rules
1. Attendance policies
2. Vacations and sick leave
3. Excused absences (military service, jury duty, etc.)
4. Smoking
5. Alcohol and drug regulations
6. Work breaks
7. Safety procedures
8. Dress code
9. Moonlighting
10. Sexual harassment

Employers who have several employees to train or whose jobs are fairly complex may opt for classroom training.

vestibule training

Classroom, or **vestibule training** allows employees to learn in a simulated workplace without the actual stress or pressure of the workplace. Also an accomplished trainer can be used to train all new employees, thus insuring consistent work performance. The major drawback of this type of training is a transfer-of-training problem. Someone may be able to function well in a simulated environment but does not do well in the actual work setting.

CONTINUOUS TRAINING. Once basic training is over, employees will need additional, or refresher, training from time to time. More training will be needed when a person moves to another job, when new technology is introduced, when new products are made or sold by the company, and so forth. This training, like basic training, can be either on the job or in classrooms. Other useful training methods include job rotation, role playing, and formal courses offered by academic institutions.

Evaluating Training

Too many companies fail to evaluate the effectiveness of their training programs. Program evaluation should be conducted immediately upon completion of the training session to determine whether trainees learned and retained the desired information, the instructor was capable, and the program was cost effective. Trainees can be tested before and after the program to determine what they have learned. In addition to pretest-posttest evaluations, training programs can be evaluated by using subjective techniques such as questionnaires and observation. Owners can develop questionnaires that determine whether trainees' expectations were met, the trainer was capable, the material presented was useful, and so forth.

SUMMARY

Finding the right people to operate a small business is absolutely essential. The task is becoming more difficult because of the numerous federal laws regulating the selection process. Business owners must not discriminate against potential employees on the basis of race, color, creed, sex, or national origin. Many other factors such as age, physical condition, and so forth cannot be used as selection criteria. Once interested persons apply for announced positions, they should be allowed to complete a nondiscriminatory application form, which is then screened by the business owner or another designated employee. Acceptable applicants are then interviewed.

Application forms and interviews should be constructed and conducted in a nondiscriminatory fashion. Questions regarding racial or ethnic background, marital status, arrest record, and height and weight should be avoided as they are likely to be considered discriminatory. Another part of the selection process, testing, can also be discriminatory; therefore, owners using tests should be sure that each test is regularly validated. The final step in the selection process requires owners to accumulate all the data they have on applicants and decide which one is most suitable for the position.

Once hired, new employees will most likely need to be trained. First, they should be subjected to a well-organized orientation that explains their duties, work rules, compensation, and other important company features. Next, most new employees will need some skill-specific training to prepare them for their new job. Finally, ongoing training is needed to keep employees current and prepare them for more responsible and important jobs. Well-trained employees are motivated and loyal workers who become valuable company assets.

QUESTIONS FOR REVIEW AND DISCUSSION

1. What is the significance of Title VII of the Civil Rights Act of 1964?
2. Should employers be prosecuted if they unknowingly hire illegal aliens?
3. Why is it becoming more difficult to locate capable workers?
4. What do you think is the best employee recruiting source for small businesses? Why?
5. What should a business owner do to prepare for an interview with a job applicant?
6. Which selection tests do you think are not likely to be discriminatory?
7. What test constructs should be considered before creating or purchasing a selection test?
8. Do reference checks help much in the selection process?
9. Why are performance appraisals important?
10. What is the purpose of a company orientation for new employees?

KEY TERMS

Age Discrimination Act
Americans with Disabilities Act
baby boomers
Bona Fide Occupational
   Qualification (BFOQ)
Civil Rights Act of 1991
critical incidents
employment-at-will
Equal Pay Act
essay appraisals
Form I-9
graphic rating scale
Immigration Law of 1986

job descriptions
job specifications
on-the-job training (OJT)
performance appraisal methods
ranking
structured interviews
Title VII of the Civil Rights Act
unstructured interviews
vestibule training
Vietnam Era Veterans Readjustment
   Act
Vocational Rehabilitation Act
wrongful discharge

CASE
An Undisclosed Case of AIDS

George Ferguson owned a small mens' clothing store in a fashionable part of a medium-sized midwestern city. The business, Main Street Clothiers, employed six people full-time and two part-time. Because the customers were males and the product was for males, all the salespeople were also male (George had no policy of discriminating against women). The two part-time employees, who handled mainly secretarial and bookkeeping duties, were females. Working conditions at Main Street Clothiers were good and salespeople were able to make a comfortable living selling quality clothes.

George's business grew as the population of the city increased and, in early 1992, he decided to add another salesperson to his staff. Newspaper advertising had been successful in the past, so George placed an advertisement announcing his store's need for a salesperson in the local newspaper. The ad did not specify gender, age, or any other potentially discriminating qualifications. Applicants were expected to be high-school graduates with three years of retail experience who could work full-time for Main Street Clothiers.

The advertisement drew responses from five men who were interested in the job. Once they had completed the store's application form (which had been checked by George's lawyer for acceptability), George made interview appointments with four of the applicants—one person had no retail experience and was not considered. On the basis of education, experience, and personality, George offered the job to Harry Greene who gladly accepted the offer. Harry was to begin work the following Monday.

Harry arrived early on the appointed Monday so he could go through a brief orientation with George who explained the store's operations, compensation policies, and other appropriate procedures and policies. Harry received on-the-job training for three days and was then put on the sales floor to begin his career with Main Street Clothiers. Harry learned quickly and soon became one of George's best salespeople.

Three months after starting work, Harry inadvertently let one of his colleagues know that he had AIDS. The other employee advised George of Harry's condition, putting George in a very unenviable position. George did not want to fire Harry because he was a good salesperson, yet he was afraid that customers would start buying their clothes elsewhere if they knew about Harry's condition. To add to the dilemma, George did not even know if he could legally terminate Harry. George had to make a decision soon because, by now, all the other salespeople knew that Harry had AIDS.

QUESTIONS

1. Can George legally terminate Harry?

2. Should George terminate Harry?

3. If terminated, what recourse does Harry have?

ACTIVITIES

1. Take the "How Good an Interviewer Are You?" quiz below

How Good an Interviewer are You?

	True	False
1. Generalizations about people based on large-group categories, such as gender, nationality, hair color, and such can be seriously misleading.	___	___
2. I always stick with first impressions.	___	___
3. Preparation is the best antidote to panicking in a crisis.	___	___
4. It is possible to observe an interviewee's behavior and learn how he or she is feeling.	___	___
5. Stress interviewing is a tried-and-true technique.	___	___
6. A courtesy interview is called that because you should be especially courteous while conducting it.	___	___
7. Interviewing has a clear field in the sense that it doesn't overlap or conflict with other types of business communication.	___	___
8. Ending the interview and shaking the other's hand is a final wrap.	___	___
9. The big thing about the hidden agenda is that it must remain hidden.	___	___
10. The knockout factor idea can prevent needless continuation of a hiring interview.	___	___
11. Short and sweet is the best formula for an exit interview.	___	___
12. Extrasensory perception is fine in science fiction but has no place in interviews.	___	___
13. What happens in a subordinate's home life is of no concern to the manager, and still less a subject for an interview.	___	___
14. Pair dynamics is one of those impractical hot-shot phrases that has little meaning or use.	___	___
15. You can psych yourself up for an interview in the same way an athlete does before a contest.	___	___

SOURCE: Reprinted, by permission of publisher, from *88 Mistakes Interviewers Make and How to Avoid Them*, by Auren Uris, © 1988 AMACOM, A Division of American Management Association. All Rights Reserved.

Scoring for Interviewer Quiz

Preferred answers: 1.T, 2.F, 3.T, 4.T, 5.F, 6.F, 7.F, 8.F, 9.F, 10.T, 11.F, 12.F, 13.F, 14.F, 15.T.

Scoring: Give yourself 10 points for each correct answer.

What your score suggests:

        130–150: Your knowledge of interviewing is excellent.

        90–120: You're good, with only a slight susceptibility to mistakes.

        Below 90: Your knowledge of the field is shaky and probably lands you in hot water from time to time.

2. Take the "Equal Employment Opportunity Commission Discrimination" quiz.

Equal Employment Opportunity Commission Discrimination Quiz

True False

An employer

1. can refuse to hire women who have small children at home   ___ ___

2. can generally obtain and use an applicant's arrest record as a basis for nonemployment   ___ ___

3. can prohibit employees from conversing in their native language on the job   ___ ___

4. whose employees are mostly white or male, can rely solely on word-of-mouth to recruit new employees   ___ ___

5. can refuse to hire women to work at night because it wishes to protect them   ___ ___

6. may require all pregnant employees to take leave of absence at a specified time before their delivery date   ___ ___

7. may establish different benefits—pension, retirement, insurance, and health plans—for male employees than for female employees   ___ ___

8. may hire only males for a job if state law forbids employment of women for that job   ___ ___

9. need not attempt to adjust work schedules to permit an employee time off for a religious observance   ___ ___

10. only disobeys the Equal Employment Opportunity laws when it is acting intentionally or with ill motive   ___ ___

All answers are false.

3. Identify the potentially discriminatory items on the application form on pages 256–57.

APPLICATION FOR EMPLOYMENT
(All Information Treated Confidentially)

Date _____

Name (print) _____ Home Tel. No. _____

(First)   (Middle)   (Last)

Present Address _____ How long have you lived there? _____

No.   Street   City   State   Zip Code

In Case of Emergency
Please Notify _____ Address _____ Tel. No. _____ Area Code_____

Date of birth _____ 19____ ☐ Single ☐ Married ☐ Separated   Number of children _____ Ages _____

☐ Engaged ☐ Widowed ☐ Divorced

Height ____ ft. ____ in. Weight _____ lbs. Date of marriage _____ Number of other dependents _____

Soc. Sec. No. _____ How many times married? _____ Are you a citizen of U.S.? ☐ Yes ☐ No

per hr.

Position Applied for _____ Are you now employed ☐ Yes ☐ No Rate of pay expected $ _____ per week

Would you work full-time _____ Part-Time _____ Specify days and hours if part-time _____

Were you previously employed by us   ☐ Yes ☐ No If so, when? Where? _____

Names of friends or relatives presently
working for our company _____ How would you get to work? _____

EDUCATION

Type of School	Name of School	Address of School	Course Majored in	Check Last Year Completed				Graduate?		Last Year Attended
Elementary				5	6	7	8	☐ Yes	☐ No	19
High School				1	2	3	4	☐ Yes	☐ No	19
College				1	2	3	4	☐ Yes	☐ No	19
Business, Trade, Correspondence				1	2	3	4	☐ Yes	☐ No	19

PREVIOUS EMPLOYMENT HISTORY

	Date Started	Date Left	Employer's Name	Employer's Address	Job Hired For	Last Job Held	Starting Salary	Last Salary	Reason for Leaving
Last Place Worked									
2nd Last									
3rd Last									
4th Last									

GENERAL

Do you: ☐ Own your home? ☐ Rent? ☐ Live with Relatives ☐ Board ☐ Other _____

What monthly rent or home payments do you pay? $ _____

Occupation of wife (or husband) _____

If single, occupation of Parents _____

Have you ever been convicted of a crime other than minor traffic violations? ☐ Yes ☐ No if yes explain _____

_____ Date _____

Have you ever been refused bond? ☐ Yes ☐ No

Any special achievements in high school, college or business? Explain _____
_____

Why are you seeking employment with *our company* _____
_____

How far can you progress with *our company* _____
_____

REFERENCES

NAME	ADDRESS	PHONE	RELATION	YRS. KNOWN

MEDICAL HISTORY

Have you ever had or do you now have any of the following? (Check "Yes" or "No")

	Yes	No		Yes	No		Yes	No		Yes	No		Yes	No
Asthma			An Allergy			Heart Disease			Mental Disorder			Fits or Convulsions		
Diabetes			Back Trouble			Varicose Veins			Stroke			Weight Gain/Loss		
Epilepsy			Tuberculosis			Disease of Ear			Venereal Disease			Trick/Locked Knee		
Arthritis			Headaches			Disease of Eye			Painful Joints			Dis. of Nose/Throat		
Broken Bones			Skin Disease			Rupture (Hernia)			Hi or Lo Bl. Pres.					

(If answer to any of above questions is "Yes", give complete details, including dates and duration of condition.)
_____

Have you ever been refused employment or insurance or rejected for military service because of your health? ☐ Yes ☐ No
(If "Yes", state why)
_____

Have you ever been discharged from employment or the military service because of medical reasons? ☐ Yes ☐ No
(If "Yes", state why)
_____

What surgical operations have you had? (Give nature and date of each operation. If "None", so state.)
_____

Are you now receiving or have you ever received benefits or medical treatment from the Government, Insurance Companies, or Workmen's Compensation for Injuries, Illnesses, or Occupational Diseases? ☐ Yes ☐ No (If "Yes", explain)
_____

Are you now, or have you ever received treatment for a drug or alcohol habit? ☐ Yes ☐ No (If "Yes", explain)
_____

Do you smoke?

If your application is considered favorably, on what date will you be available for work? _____ 19____

Signature _____

APPLICANT SHOULD NOT WRITE BELOW THIS LINE

COMMENTS AND RECOMMENDATIONS OF INTERVIEWER: _____
_____
_____
_____

DATE: _____ INTERVIEWER: _____

REFERENCE CHECK INFORMATION

	Company or Person Contacted	RESULTS OF REFERENCE CHECK		Company or Person Contacted	RESULTS OF REFERENCE CHECK
1			3.		
2.			4.		

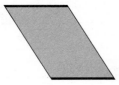

APPENDIX 9-1

Sample Employment Application

Baby SUPERSTORE

PO Box 16569
Greenville, SC 29606

APPLICATION FOR EMPLOYMENT

AN EQUAL OPPORTUNITY EMPLOYER

All applicants will receive consideration for employment without regard to race, color, religion, age, sex, national origin, handicap or veteran status.

INSTRUCTIONS: Please read this entire application before you answer any questions — Print all information in ink. Answer all questions accurately and completely. Print "N/A" in any space that does not apply to you. All applicants receive consideration for the position for which they apply and the application will remain active for a period of 30 days. Those applicants not employed within the 30 day period will be required to reapply for employment as job openings occur.

PERSONAL DATA (Please print)   Date ____ / ____ / ____

LAST NAME	FIRST	NICKNAME	MIDDLE	SOCIAL SECURITY NUMBER
ADDRESS	CITY	STATE	ZIP	AREA CODE/TELEPHONE NUMBER

Are you: Under 18 ☐   over 18 ☐   years of age?   NOTE: If you are under 18, Do Not Continue filling out application, see manager.
If under 18 years of age, employment is subject to verification of minimum legal age certificate or work permit.

Are you a U.S. Citizen?   ☐ Yes   ☐ No
If "No", do you have an alien registration card or valid U.S. work permit?   ☐ Yes   ☐ No

What position or type of work are you applying for? _____   Approximate starting pay (wage or salary) expected:
List job related skills you possess _____ $ _____ per _____ (hr., wk., mo., or yr.)
Will you be able to work overtime if required?   ☐ Yes   ☐ No   Provide this information only if you choose.

Date available for work	Have you previously applied to Baby Superstore? ☐ Yes ☐ No If yes, Where? _____ When? _____	Have you previously been employed by Baby Superstore? ☐ Yes ☐ No If yes, Where? _____ When? _____

How will you get to work? _____

Are you applying for: ☐ Full Time ☐ Part Time or ☐ Temporary work?

Will this be steady transportation?   ☐ Yes   ☐ No
What other way can you get to work? _____

Do you have a valid driver's license?   ☐ Yes   ☐ No
Driver's License # _____

Commercial or truck license?   ☐ Yes   ☐ No

Has your driver's license ever been revoked, suspended or reissue refused?   ☐ Yes   ☐ No
If yes, Why? _____

Do you smoke?   ☐ Yes   ☐ No
If so how many packs per day? _____

If you DO NOT smoke, when did you quit? Check one:
Within last month ☐   Within last 12 months ☐
Over one year ☐   Never smoked ☐

How many miles do you live from the store? _____

How did you learn of job opportunities at Baby Superstore?
_____

The position for which you are applying may require work on **Saturdays, Sundays, Holidays, and nights.**
Are you willing to work a schedule involving work during these periods of time? _____

Have you filed for unemployment compensation this year?   ☐ Yes   ☐ No

If "yes," please explain the circumstances. _____

Have you filed a law suit or other complaint against a former employer or its agents?   ☐ Yes   ☐ No. If "yes", please explain the circumstances. _____

EDUCATION Applicants may be asked to furnish transcripts of school or college work.

Name and Location of School	Class Standing		
High School	☐ Top 1/3 ☐ Middle 1/3 ☐ Lower 1/3 Date of Graduation _____ / _____ / _____		
College or University	Degree Received Date of Graduation _____ / _____ / _____	Major and Minor Subjects	Grade Point Average _____ out of possible_____
Graduate School	Degree Received Date of Graduation _____ / _____ / _____	Major and Minor Subjects	Grade Point Average _____ out of possible_____
Special Schooling — Business or Vocational	Degree or Certificate Received Date of Graduation _____ / _____ / _____	Major Subjects Subjects	Grade Point Average _____ out of possible_____

GENERAL INFORMATION

Ever injured on or off the job? ☐ Yes   ☐ No   Give nature and extent of such injuries _____

Will injury affect your ability to safely perform the job in question? _____ How many days absent from your job last year? _____

Explain absences _____

Do you have any impairments, physical, mental, or medical problems which would prevent you from performing in a reasonable manner the activities involved in the job or occupation for which you have applied?

☐ Yes   ☐ No   If YES, what can be done to reasonably accommodate your limitations? _____

Within the last seven (7) years, have you been convicted of a felony (crime(s) other than minor violations) which is related to the job for which you are applying?

NOTE: Conviction of a crime will not necessarily disqualify you from the job for which you are applying. Each conviction will be judged on its own merits with respect to time and job-relatedness.

☐ Yes   ☐ No

If YES, please explain (state date, court, type of crime, place of occurrence and disposition): _____

If required, are you and your family willing to relocate to a different city?   ☐ Yes   ☐ No

U.S. MILITARY SERVICE

Branch of Service	Date Entered _____ / _____ / _____ Date Discharged _____ / _____ / _____	Final Rank
Duties in Service		

ACTIVITIES

List Trade or Professional Organizations of which you are a member (excluding racial, religious or nationality organizations.)

List Hobbies and Recreational Interests (which may have a bearing on the job for which you are applying).

If offered a position with Baby Superstore, how would you be able to help us be successful?

EMPLOYMENT HISTORY List full time work only, attach additional sheet if necessary. Start with most recent position.

EMPLOYER (NAME OF COMPANY)	ADDRESS (CITY AND STATE)	PHONE NUMBER
DATE STARTED	STARTING SALARY/WAGE $ PER HOUR (MONTH) — STARTING POSITION (JOB TITLE)	MAY WE CONTACT? ☐ YES ☐ NO
DATE ENDED	ENDING SALARY/WAGE $ PER HOUR (MONTH) — POSITION AT LEAVING (JOB TITLE)	
NAME AND TITLE OF IMMEDIATE SUPERVISOR	REASON FOR LEAVING	
BRIEF DESCRIPTION OF YOUR RESPONSIBILITIES		

EMPLOYER (NAME OF COMPANY)	ADDRESS (CITY AND STATE)	PHONE NUMBER
DATE STARTED	STARTING SALARY/WAGE $ PER HOUR (MONTH) — STARTING POSITION (JOB TITLE)	MAY WE CONTACT? ☐ YES ☐ NO
DATE ENDED	ENDING SALARY/WAGE $ PER HOUR (MONTH) — POSITION AT LEAVING (JOB TITLE)	
NAME AND TITLE OF IMMEDIATE SUPERVISOR	REASON FOR LEAVING	
BRIEF DESCRIPTION OF YOUR RESPONSIBILITIES		

EMPLOYER (NAME OF COMPANY)	ADDRESS (CITY AND STATE)	PHONE NUMBER
DATE STARTED	STARTING SALARY/WAGE $ PER HOUR (MONTH) — STARTING POSITION (JOB TITLE)	MAY WE CONTACT? ☐ YES ☐ NO
DATE ENDED	ENDING SALARY/WAGE $ PER HOUR (MONTH) — POSITION AT LEAVING (JOB TITLE)	
NAME AND TITLE OF IMMEDIATE SUPERVISOR	REASON FOR LEAVING	
BRIEF DESCRIPTION OF YOUR RESPONSIBILITIES		

EMPLOYER (NAME OF COMPANY)	ADDRESS (CITY AND STATE)	PHONE NUMBER
DATE STARTED	STARTING SALARY/WAGE $ PER HOUR (MONTH) — STARTING POSITION (JOB TITLE)	MAY WE CONTACT? ☐ YES ☐ NO
DATE ENDED	ENDING SALARY/WAGE $ PER HOUR (MONTH) — POSITION AT LEAVING (JOB TITLE)	
NAME AND TITLE OF IMMEDIATE SUPERVISOR	REASON FOR LEAVING	
BRIEF DESCRIPTION OF YOUR RESPONSIBILITIES		

EMPLOYER (NAME OF COMPANY)	ADDRESS (CITY AND STATE)	PHONE NUMBER
DATE STARTED	STARTING SALARY/WAGE $ PER HOUR (MONTH) — STARTING POSITION (JOB TITLE)	MAY WE CONTACT? ☐ YES ☐ NO
DATE ENDED	ENDING SALARY/WAGE $ PER HOUR (MONTH) — POSITION AT LEAVING (JOB TITLE)	
NAME AND TITLE OF IMMEDIATE SUPERVISOR	REASON FOR LEAVING	
BRIEF DESCRIPTION OF YOUR RESPONSIBILITIES		

Is this a complete list of your employment?   ☐ Yes   ☐ No

PROFESSIONAL REFERENCES (If none, list personal references.)

NAME	TELEPHONE NUMBER	OCCUPATION	YEARS KNOWN
ADDRESS			
NAME	TELEPHONE NUMBER	OCCUPATION	YEARS KNOWN
ADDRESS			
NAME	TELEPHONE NUMBER	OCCUPATION	YEARS KNOWN
ADDRESS			

STATEMENT — READ THIS SECTION CAREFULLY

I understand that any misrepresentation on this application may constitute grounds for dismissal. I authorize initial and periodic investigative reports on my background including credit checks, driving record, lack of a criminal record, educational record and military record. I also accept the condition of submitting to and successfully passing a drug test.

I understand and agree that, if hired, my employment is for no definite period and under no contract relating to length of time of employment. I further understand that employment is at will and unless there is a contract labeled "Employment Contract" and signed by both me and an officer of Baby Superstore, my employment can be terminated by the Company or by me at any time.

If hired, Federal Law requires me to furnish documentation showing my identity and that I am legally authorized to work in the United States.

_____
Applicant's Signature

DO NOT FILL OUT THIS SECTION   (POST EMPLOYMENT INFORMATION)

Date of Birth		Are you a U.S. Citizen?	
Mo. Day Year		☐ Yes ☐ No	
Person to call in an emergency. Name:	Relationship	Home Phone	Work Phone

Form W-4 (Rev. Aug. 1987) Department of the Treasury Internal Revenue Service	EMPLOYEE'S WITHHOLDING ALLOWANCE CERTIFICATE (This certificate is for income tax withholding purposes only, it will remain in effect until you change it.)	
Type or print your full name	SOCIAL SECURITY NUMBER	NOTE TO STUDENTS You may qualify for exemption from federal income taxes. If interested ask your manager to obtain appropriate forms.
Home address (Number and street or rural route)	Marital Status ☐ Single ☐ Married	
City or Town, State and Zip Code	(If married, but legally separated, or wife (husband) is a nonresident alien, check the single block.)	
Total Number of Allowances you are claiming _____		
I certify that to the best of my knowledge and belief, the number of withholding allowances claimed on this certificate does not exceed the number to which I am entitled.	_____ Applicant's Signature	

TO BE COMPLETED BY STORE OR DEPT. MANAGER

Employment Date / /	JOB TITLE	MALE ☐ FEMALE ☐	EMPLOYMENT Part Time ☐ Full Time ☐	SALARY $ _____ Per _____
Employee's Signature			/ / Date / /	_____ per week
Baby Superstore Approval			Date	

APPENDIX 9-2

Checklist for Developing a Training Program

	Yes	No
What Is the Goal of the Training?		
1. Do you want to improve the performance of your employees?	___	___
2. Do you need to prepare employees for newly developed or modified jobs?	___	___
3. Is training needed to prepare employees for promotion?	___	___
4. Is the goal to reduce accidents and enhance safety practices?	___	___
5. Is the goal to orient new employees to their jobs?	___	___
What Does the Employee Need to Learn?		
6. Can the job be broken down into steps for training purposes?	___	___
7. Are there quality standards that employees can be taught?	___	___
8. Are there certain skills and techniques that trainees must learn?	___	___
9. Are there hazards and safety practices that must be taught?	___	___
10. Are there material handling techniques that must be taught?	___	___
11. Has the best way to operate equipment been determined?	___	___
12. Are there performance standards that employees must meet?	___	___
13. Are there attitudes that need improvement or modification?	___	___
14. Will product information help employees do a better job?	___	___
15. Will the employee need instruction about departments other than his or her own?	___	___
What Type of Training?		

16. Can employees be trained on the job so they can pro-
    duce while they learn? ___ ___

17. Should there be classroom training conducted by a paid
    instructor? ___ ___

18. Will a combination of on-the-job training and vocational
    classroom instruction work best? ___ ___
    What Method of Instruction?

19. Does the subject matter call for a lecture or series of lec-
    tures? ___ ___

20. Should the instructor follow up with discussion sessions? ___ ___

21. Does the subject matter lend itself to demonstrations? ___ ___

22. Can operating problems be simulated in a classroom? ___ ___

23. Can the instructor direct trainees while they perform
    the job? ___ ___
    What Audio-Visual Aids Will Be Needed?

24. Will a manual of instruction—including job instruction
    sheets—be used? ___ ___

25. Will trainees be given an outline of the training program? ___ ___

26. Can outside textbooks and other printed materials be
    used? ___ ___

27. Can appropriate videos, film strips, or slides be ob-
    tained for the training program? ___ ___

28. Are there drawings or photographs of the machinery,
    equipment, or products that could be enlarged and used? ___ ___
    What Physical Facilities Are Needed?

29. Is there a conference room or lunch room on-site that
    can be used for training? ___ ___

30. Should the training be conducted off premises, as in a
    nearby school, restaurant, hotel, or motel? ___ ___

31. Will there be sufficient seating and writing surfaces for
    the trainees? ___ ___
    What About the Timing?

32. Should the training be conducted part-time and during
    working hours? ___ ___

33. Can the length of each session and the number of ses-
    sions per week be established? ___ ___
    Who Will Be the Instructor?

34. Will the owner be the instructor? —— ——

35. Will a supervisor or department head handle the training? —— ——

36. Should a skilled employee be used as the instructor? —— ——

37. Will the instructor have to be trained? —— ——

38. Is there a qualified outside instructor available for employment on a part-time basis? —— ——
Who Should Be Selected?

39. Is the training for new employees? —— ——

40. Are there present employees who need training? —— ——

41. Is the training to be a condition for promotion? —— ——

42. Will employees be permitted to volunteer for the training? —— ——
What Will the Program Cost?

43. Should the program be charged for the space, the machines, and the materials used? —— ——

44. Will trainee wages be included? —— ——

45. If the instructor is an employee, will his or her pay be included in the costs? —— ——

46. Will preparation and administration time be part of the cost? —— ——

47. If usable products result from the sessions, should their value be deducted from program costs? —— ——

What Checks or Controls Will Be Used?

48. Can training results be checked against goals or objectives? —— ——

49. Can data on trainee performance be developed before, during, and after training? —— ——

50. Will records be kept on the progress of each trainee? —— ——

51. Will trainees be tested on the knowledge and skills acquired? —— ——

SOURCE: Leonard J. Smith, *Checklist for Developing a Training Program*, U.S. Small Business Administration, Management Aids, Number 5.001.

10 MOTIVATING AND COMPENSATING EMPLOYEES

Successfully operating a small business with unmotivated employees is quite difficult. If employees are basically clock-watchers, they tend to neglect customers, waste time, and perform poorly. Business owners should do whatever is necessary to keep their workers motivated and interested in their jobs. Owners also have a responsibility to compensate their workers adequately and equitably. Although some controversy still exists over a direct compensation-motivation link, workers who believe that their pay is equitable are likely to be productive and committed to their companies.

In this chapter we will review motivation theories and ways owners can keep their employees motivated. We will also discuss compensation practices that attract good employees and keep them striving for advancement and additional responsibility. Even though small business owners are often unable to match compensation packages offered by large companies, they can create a desirable working environment that attracts capable employees. Finally, in this chapter, we will discuss communication, the process that increases motivation and clarifies compensation programs.

MOTIVATING EMPLOYEES

Newly formed companies generate a sense of excitement and enthusiasm that affects everyone concerned with the firm's survival. Employees are not clock-watchers or personal profit maximizers; people are willing to work fifty or sixty hours a week for relatively little pay because they have a feeling of "we're all in this together" which sustains their effort. Employees want to see the company succeed, and they will make personal sacrifices to insure success. However, as the company matures, small business owners must devise new motivational methods and techniques to achieve maximum productivity.

Summary of Motivation Theories

Several theories of motivation attempt to explain why people do what they do and what can be done to entice them to do more. Most theorists stress a positive approach to motivation; however, in practice, using negative motivators to increase work and productivity is sometimes easier. Owners or managers threaten to fire nonproductive workers rather than explain to them that increased output will result in more recognition or praise. Although negative motivators might be easier to use, they do not have the long-term benefits that positive motivators produce. The basic theories discussed in this section stress positive motivation.

NEED AND DRIVE THEORY. Early motivational theorists tried to identify the needs that provoked certain behavior. They knew that eating was motivated by hunger and that sleep was motivated by exhaustion, but they were not sure what motivated some people to work harder than others. Eventually several hundred needs, a much too unwieldy number, were associated with certain actions. Some theorists, trying to avoid this lengthy list, conjectured that all behavior could be ascribed to one consuming drive. For example, Freud believed that all behavior was sexually motivated.

One of the most widely accepted need theories is that formulated by Abraham Maslow[1] (see Exhibit 10-1). Maslow believed that humans are wanting animals incapable of satisfying all their needs; therefore, he ranked people's needs in the order in which they are satisfied. The needs are usually satisfied in ascending order, that is, when one's physiological needs are satisfied, safety needs become primary. The following needs were identified by Maslow:

Physiological needs. These are the most basic bodily needs, such as food, water, and sleep, which are necessary to sustain life. If these needs are not satisfied, no other needs are important.

Safety needs. Once physiological needs have been satisfied, safety needs become dominant. The basic safety needs such as clothing and shelter have been satisfied for most Americans.

Belonging and love. The third-order need is the desire most people have to belong to and be accepted by one or more groups. This need leads people to join social, fraternal, and work groups, and it causes people to behave like other group members. Lack of group membership can lead to undesirable behavior. For example, the most dissatisfied employees and the ones with the highest absenteeism and turnover rates are those who work in isolation.

Esteem. People need the acceptance and recognition of others as well as self-recognition that one has contributed meaningfully to the organization

EXHIBIT 10-1 Hierarchy of Needs

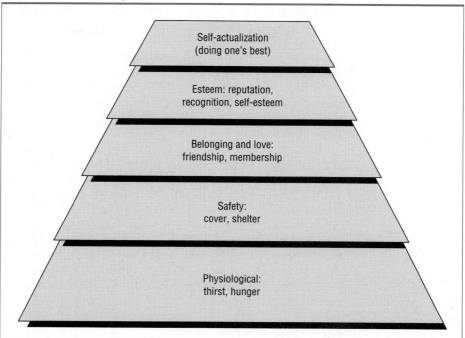

Self-actualization
(doing one's best)

Esteem: reputation,
recognition, self-esteem

Belonging and love:
friendship, membership

Safety:
cover, shelter

Physiological:
thirst, hunger

and to society. The need for self-esteem motivates individuals to exert maximum effort to achieve goals that will elicit praise and recognition from their peers and superiors.

Self-actualization. This need drives men and women to become what they are destined to be. It surpasses esteem needs, because the self-actualizer is not seeking recognition for being capable in his or her current profession, but rather is searching for the profession, occupation, or calling that is right for her or him. Self-actualization induces successful physicians to abandon medicine to enter the priesthood or causes lawyers to leave the bar to become artists.

Small business owners are likely to find that most of their employees are motivated by belonging and esteem needs. Most workers have probably satisfied their physiological and safety needs and are now interested in being accepted by their peers and in doing the best job they can. Owners who facilitate group formation and encourage team effort motivate their employees to do the best work they can.

DUAL FACTOR THEORY. This well-known theory is the result of research done by Herzberg and his associates[2] to determine what factors motivate people to do the best work they are capable of doing. Herzberg asked a sample of engineers and accountants to answer the following questions: "Can you describe, in detail, when you felt exceptionally good about your job? and "Can you describe, in detail, when you felt exceptionally bad about your job?"

Herzberg concluded from the responses that elements associated with good and bad jobs could be divided into two major categories, which he labeled motivation and hygiene factors. **Hygiene factors,** such as company policies, salary, and job security, will not increase motivation but will contribute to job satisfaction. The absence of hygiene factors can cause dissatisfaction and demotivation. However, **motivators,** such as responsibility, praise, and interesting work, cause people to strive to do the best work they are capable of doing.

hygiene factors

motivators

EXPECTANCY THEORY. Victor Vroom's[3] expectancy theory attempts to explain how people select needs to satisfy and how strongly they believe that certain actions will lead to need fulfillment. Expectancy theory assumes that individuals are inwardly motivated, that they have a number of needs or desires that they wish to satisfy, and that they will exert effort to satisfy those needs if they believe that their chosen activities are likely to lead to success. Vroom's theory emphasizes valence and expectancy. **Valence** refers to the value, either positive or negative, one places on specific needs. **Expectancy** is the probability that one assigns to the likelihood that selected activities will have successful outcomes.

valence

expectancy

Motivation Myths

Motivation theories help business owners understand what motivates employees, but the number of theories and their lack of specifics make it difficult to implement practical motivation programs. Some theories can confuse owners and leave them in doubt about the value of specific motivators. The following are some of the most common management misconceptions about motivation:

- Motivational techniques always lead to greater performance and productivity.
- Financial rewards are a foolproof motivator.
- Intrinsic rewards motivate more than money.
- All employees need to be artificially motivated.
- Some employees need no motivation.
- Most employees only respond to a kick in the pants.
- Employees are motivated only by fear.
- A happy worker is always a productive worker.
- Workers today are less motivated than in the past.[4]

Motivation Strategies

For small businesses to be efficient and productive, their employees need to be motivated to contribute their maximum effort to the firm's success. Selecting strategies to motivate employees is not always an easy task, and the task

10-1 THE PRIZE IS RIGHT

Phil Roberts, president of Premier Ventures Inc., discovered that his thirty-day employee-motivation contest was successful for only one week. "After that, they just ignored it," said Roberts. Finally, Roberts asked employees what he could do to motivate them, and he was surprised by the answers. Few, he learned, were motivated by cash, and rarely were all employees motivated by the same prize. Now, Roberts constantly monitors his employees' needs and offers a changing menu of prizes from which his employees can choose. "It gets complicated," he admits, "but it has also kept us ahead of the competition."[5]

is made even more difficult when owners realize that what motivates one employee may not motivate others (see The Way It Is 10-1).

The following are strategies that owners can consider to motivate employees.

extrinsic rewards

EXTRINSIC MOTIVATION. One of the first motivation strategies considered by business owners prescribes offering external or **extrinsic rewards** to employees for desired behavior. These rewards may include higher wages, incentive pay, better working conditions, more benefits, profit sharing, stock options, or a number of other tangible items. Although extrinsic rewards may provide short-term increases in effort and enthusiasm, most experts agree that they do not noticeably enhance productivity in the long run. The rewards become expected, and employees may require more of the reward at increasingly frequent intervals to become motivated.

intrinsic rewards

INTRINSIC MOTIVATION. To maintain motivation, employers should use intangible or **intrinsic rewards** more than extrinsic rewards. For example, designing jobs to give employees more responsibility for their own work is likely to motivate them more than offering them relatively small salary increases.

Many management observers believe that **intrinsic rewards** are more likely than extrinsic rewards to increase and sustain motivation. Business owners can use praise, recognition, advancement, and interesting work to motivate their employees to perform up to their capabilities. In essence, business owners should enrich their employees' jobs. Employees who are encouraged to take responsibility for their jobs and are appreciated for jobs well done are likely to be dedicated and committed to their company. Small business owners may find that some combination of intrinsic and extrinsic rewards contributes to sustained motivation. For example, bonuses or commissions given in conjunction with praise and recognition are likely to cause employees to strive to reach the pinnacle of their ability.

After reviewing the motivation literature, Raymond Katzell and Donna Thompson[6] arrived at the following conclusions about work motivation (see Exhibit 10-2 for more information): workers' motives and values must be appropriate for their jobs; jobs must be attractive; effective performance must be positively reinforced; work goals should be clear, challenging, attainable, and attractive; needed resources should be provided and constraints to performance should be eliminated; interpersonal and group processes must support goal attainment; and personal, social, and technological parameters should be harmonious.

Many small business owners have also found that the timing of reinforcement is important. For example, Dave Wiegand, president of Advanced Network Design Inc. (AND), found that when a program to motivate certain behavior stopped, so did the desired behavior. Wiegand's new motivation plan surprises employees—now his employees do not know who will get bonuses or what they will be. "Out of the blue we'll call a meeting and reward somebody for outstanding performance," says Wiegand, who gave fifteen awards worth $9,000 at two meetings in 1990. The size of the reward depends on the profitability of the activity being rewarded.[7]

Practical Motivation Techniques

Not all motivation methods or techniques work for all companies; however, the following practices suggested by William Cohen should be useful to owners or managers of most small businesses:

1. Care about your employees.
2. Take responsibility for your actions.
3. Be tactful for the people who work for you.
4. Give praise when a job is done well.
5. Foster independence in your employees.
6. Be willing to learn from your employees.
7. Be enthusiastic and confident.
8. Keep lines of communication open.
9. Give employees with problems help, not orders.
10. Set standards for the company.
11. Always let employees know where they stand.
12. Keep employees informed.
13. Encourage employee initiative, innovation, and ingenuity.
14. Be aware of your own prejudices and biases toward certain people.
15. Try to be flexible.[8]

COMPENSATING EMPLOYEES

Although money may not directly motivate employees, low salaries and wages make it very difficult for small businesses to attract and retain capable

EXHIBIT 10-2 Approaches to Improving Work Motivation

	Exogenous variables						
Imperative and programs	1. Personal motives and values	2. Incentives and rewards	3. Reinforcement	4. Goal-setting techniques	5. Personal and material resources	6. Social and group factors	7. Sociotechnical systems
Motivational imperative	Workers' motives and values must be appropriate for their jobs	Make jobs attractive, interesting, and satisfying	Effective performance must be positively reinforced, but not ineffective performance	Work goals must be clear, challenging, attainable, attractive	Provide needed resources and eliminate constraints to performance	Interpersonal and group processes must support goal attainment	Personal, social, and technological parameters must be harmonious
Illustrative programs	Personnel selection Job previews Motive training Socialization	Financial compensation Promotion Participation Job security Career development Considerate supervision Job enrichment Benefits Flexible hours Recognition "Cafeteria" plans	Financial incentive plans Behavioral analysis Praise and criticism Self-management	Goal setting Management by objectives Modeling Quality circles Appraisal and feedback	Training and development Coaching and counseling Equipment Technology Supervision Methods improvement Problem solving groups	Division of labor Group composition Team development Sensitivity training Leadership Norm building	Quality of work-life programs Sociotechnical systems designs Organizational development Scanlon plan

Raymond A. Katzell and Donna E. Thompson, ''Work Motivation,'' *American Psychologist*, February 1990, 144–153. © 1990 by the American Psychological Association. Reprinted by permission.

people. Most small businesses are unable to offer compensation packages comparable to those offered by large corporations; even their owners earn significantly less than their counterparts in larger companies. A recent study[9] found that the median pay for owners of companies with annual sales below $100 million was $151,000 compared with $508,000 for heads of large public companies. Owners of companies in primary metals industries earned median salaries of $264,000, whereas at the lower end of the scale, owners of building- and garden-supply companies earned $108,000.

Because owners of most small businesses earn less than their counterparts at larger companies, it stands to reason that their employees will earn less than workers at large companies. To attract and retain capable employees, owners need to be creative and flexible when developing compensation packages (see Exhibit 10-3). Using the best combination of wages and noncash benefits, small business owners can build creative, nontraditional compensation plans that fit the individual needs of their employees.

Compensation for Time Worked

By far the most common compensation method is payment for time worked. This requires employees to maintain accurate records, usually on the company time clock, of the hours worked during the pay period. Because employees are paid for the number of hours worked, their wages will vary from one pay period to the next because of overtime and holiday or weekend work. A disadvantage of this compensation scheme for the company is that employees can misrepresent the amount of time they actually worked, whereas employees are disadvantaged because they do not know what their income will be from one pay period to the next.

To stabilize wages for at least one year, some small businesses pay all employees on a salary basis. This means that the employee will be paid a stipulated sum regardless of the number of hours worked. Receiving a fixed salary reduces employee anxiety and insecurity; however, there is little evidence that productivity increases or that absenteeism is noticeably reduced.

Variable and Incentive Pay Systems

Business owners who choose not to pay on a salary or time-worked basis can select a pay-for-output or incentive plan. These plans are diverse, but they are all based on the assumption that it is possible and useful to tie pay directly to performance. A recent study by Hewitt Associates found that 51 percent of surveyed companies used some type of pay-for-performance program. Owners who choose to pay for performance should use one or a combination of the plans described below.

piecework system

PIECEWORK. One of the earliest incentive plans used, the **piecework system,** allows employees to earn daily wages based on the number of items or pieces produced. Some companies guarantee employees a minimum wage based on some predetermined standard output and then pay more for each piece produced above the standard. This type of payment plan is appropriate only for those companies that can accurately measure employee output.

EXHIBIT 10-3 Comparison of Compensation Options

Compensation Item	Large Company	Small Company
1. Sabbatical leave/leave without pay	In the early stages of use by a small number of companies.	Sabbatical leave needs more complex funding. But leave without pay is easily worked into the structure. Has been used for many years to attract and retain workers.
2. Flexible work schedules	Generally limited to flex time arrangements. Large production line operations often preclude arrangements as do union contracts.	Used regularly by the high tech firms and service companies. Others are realizing the compensation potential. Some small companies allow employees to do paper work at home (typing, report writing, etc.) when appropriate. Others utilize off-hours work time if the employee's presence is not mandatory during regular hours.
3. Cafeteria benefit system	Recent surge in popularity. Main restrictions lay in unionized settings.	Main setback is the lack of numbers to achieve discounts on selected items.
4. Retirement systems	Advantage appears to be with the larger company. Yet, without union coverage less than half of employees are covered by pension accounts.	The pension law changes have dealt this a serious setback, but there are other alternatives.
5. Profit sharing plans	Utilized frequently. Most fail because they become devices of expected compensation.	This can be the most readily accessible avenue to pursue retirement benefits through. Easily implemented due to the reduced number of participants.
6. Stock options	Available generally to key executives.	Unfortunately, most restrict to key employees. Appear to model large companies. Can be a useful motivator for all employees.
7. Leave with pay (e.g., vacations, holidays, etc.)	Well structured along industry norms. Difficult to be flexible with one person among a large work force. Unionization sharply restricts options.	Flexibility is present in selecting which days, the number of days, and holidays. Despite flexibility the figures do not reflect abuse.
8. Wages	The data suggest that large corporations may be able to afford more generous salary.	Creative small business people have used compensation time (e.g., time off the job) in lieu of overtime. Others offer bonus personal hours. That is, after every 100 hours worked, they get 2 hours credited to use as they please for time off or to accumulate toward an extended sabbatical.

SOURCE: Stephen J. Holoviak, "Compensation that Attracts and Retains Employees in Small Businesses," *NBDC Report,* October 1990, 1–4. Stephen J. Holoviak, Ph.D. is Director of the Frehn Center for Management at Shippensburg University in Shippensburg, Pennsylvania. Reprinted from the October 1990 issue of NBDC Report by permission of the Nebraska Business Development Center, College of Business Administration, University of Nebraska at Omaha.

Owners who use this kind of plan also have to guard against a deterioration of quality as workers attempt to maximize output. For example, Walter Riley, CEO of G.O.D. Inc., took his freight dock loaders off hourly wage scales and paid them for each shipment handled. Freight loss and breakage became epidemic. "All of a sudden, there were problems all over the place. This system just sped them up. The dock loaders thought, 'If there are mistakes, there are mistakes,' " said Riley. So Riley changed the system: on top of the shipment rate, freight loaders get weekly bonuses of 25 percent of their total week's earnings if all shipments go through with no breakage, misloading, or short cartons. Some 85 percent of dock workers meet the weekly bonus requirements.[10]

commissions

COMMISSIONS. **Commissions** are similar to piecework systems except they are usually paid to nonmanufacturing employees. People who sell products often receive a commission based on some percentage of the price of that product. It is customary to pay salespeople a minimal base-wage that is supplemented by a commission only if they achieve above-standard sales.

bonus

BONUSES. Rather than pay employees for each item produced, some owners pay them a lump sum **bonus,** in addition to other normal pay, for performance once or twice a year. To be effective, bonuses should be directly related to performance and they should be withheld in unprofitable years.

knowledge pay

KNOWLEDGE PAY. Employees can increase their value to a business by learning to do more than one job. As they become capable of doing multiple jobs, employees should see their overall compensation increase correspondingly. The **knowledge pay** system can reduce the number of job classifications in a company and create a team-oriented atmosphere.

profit-sharing plans

PROFIT-SHARING PLANS. Stock ownership and **profit-sharing plans** are also incentive plans, in that employees are rewarded for their performance with a share of the company's profits or stock. These plans may reward success in the year it occurs, or employees may have to wait until retirement or some other stipulated time before receiving their stock or share of profits.

performance unit plans (PUPs)

PERFORMANCE UNIT PLANS (PUPs). PUPs are appropriate for small businesses because, unlike year-end bonuses, they tie financial rewards to long-term, individual achievements. Yet they do not entail prolonged financial obligations the way some profit-sharing plans do. **Performance unit plans** are created in the following manner: (1) A company's owner selects the goal (usually stretched out over a three- to five-year horizon) that makes sense for each person; (2) owners attach numbers to the goal, which generally take the form of targeted percentages of change; then (3) a PUP document is created that gives the employee a number of performance units that have no value when they are issued. If the employee achieves his or her goal over a predetermined period, each unit will increase in value to the point where it can be redeemed for its new value, in effect as a cash reward.[11]

Administering Incentive Pay Systems

The reason so many small business owners choose time-based pay systems rather than incentive systems is that the former are much easier to administer. There are at least two major difficulties encountered in administering incentive pay systems. First, determining output is not always an easy task because it is not always obvious who contributed to the manufacture or sale of a product. Second, plans that attempt to reward individual rather than group effort often are counterproductive (see The Way It Is 10-2).

Pay-for-performance plans do not always reward employees for desirable performance while ignoring substandard performance. Some plans are designed to reward above-standard performance and penalize below-standard work. Baby Superstore, a retailer that has only recently left the ranks of small businesses, pays employees bonuses for increased sales and reduces that bonus for undesirable results such as excessive overtime or too high utility bills.

Successful Incentive Pay Programs

Pay-for-performance plans should be equitable and relatively easy to administer. To create successful plans, owners should ask themselves the following questions:

1. Does the system generate excitement? Most traditional pay programs are dull and boring and generate very little enthusiasm. Variable pay plans need to be just the opposite: loud and colorful.

2. Is the new plan understood? Good variable pay plans should be quite simple and fairly easy to explain. Highly technical plans that are a mystery to most employees have little motivational value.

3. Has the plan generated a "line of sight?" To be effective, variable pay plans should demonstrate that a direct link exists between employees' productivity and a company's bottom-line results.

The Way It Is

10-2 GROUP REWARDS

When the Solar Press owners decided to create a bonus plan for their employees, they decided to reward teams of workers for increased output. Employees were divided into teams of four or five people who received monthly bonuses based on the volume of material that the team shipped. Production shot up, but so did conflict between teams that earned different bonuses, and employees were so intent on raw production that quality suffered. Finally, Solar Press switched to a companywide plan based on quarterly profit targets. If the company exceeds the target, 25 percent of the gains are shared with all employees as a percent of their base pay. Employees feel that the companywide gain-sharing plan is a big improvement over team rewards, even though employees do not always earn bonuses.[12]

4. Does the system pay out when it should? Are incentives paid when objectives are met—and withheld when they are not?

5. Is the company or unit performing better? Companies that do not make sure that they are continuing to get results from their pay-for-performance program will end up with just another entitlement. That is, they will end up with base pay plus some amount expected every year, completely divorced from performance.[13]

Finally, to be successful, any pay plan should meet the needs of employees and small business owners. A pay-for-performance plan implemented by a business owner in a company whose employees want a steady, pay-for-time system will not be very effective. Conversely, employees who want to benefit from a company's financial success will be dissatisfied with a pay-for-time compensation system (see Exhibit 10-4 for pay systems that meet different employee needs and objectives).

Determining Wage Rates

Employees expect a fair day's pay for a fair day's work; however, determining precisely what employees are worth to a company is sometimes difficult. Employee worth is determined in part by experience, skill, and productivity. There are several other external and internal factors that determine wage rates.

EXTERNAL INFLUENCES ON PAY LEVELS. Business owners cannot unilaterally determine how much they should pay their employees. They must also consider several external variables when setting wage and salary levels. The following are some of those external variables:

Supply and demand. If supply and demand for workers are not in equilibrium, wages for a particular job will be higher or lower than justified. For example, a business owner may believe that a clerical position is worth $4.75 an hour; however, if workers with the necessary skills are earning $6.00 per hour, the supply of people willing to work for $4.75 will be insufficient to fill the owner's position. Therefore, the business owner will have to pay approximately $6.00 per hour to fill the position.

Area pay practices. In most communities there is a "going rate" for jobs, which is established by custom. Employers would rather not pay their workers more or less than similar employees receive at comparable jobs in other companies.

Industry pay practices. Some industries, because of their relatively high profit margin, are able to pay higher wages than less profitable industries can afford.

Type of work performed. Obviously, skilled jobs demand higher pay rates than unskilled jobs, but other adjustments are made to compensate for dangerous work, jobs performed in undesirable work environments, and jobs nobody wants to do.

Unions. Strong unions are able to bargain for high wages, whereas weak unions or nonunionized employees do not have the collective strength to command comparable wages.

EXHIBIT 10-4   Company and Employee Needs and Objectives Served by Different Forms of Compensation

Form of Compensation	Employee	Company
Salaries or wages	Sets standard of living Reflects employer's evaluation	Key to pay competitiveness Basis for administering other forms of compensation

Premium payments	Extra income, frequently permits
	    special purchases
		Legal requirement
		Induces employees to work longer
		    hours

Bonuses	Extra current income
	Reward for achievement of
	    short-term goals
	Opportunity for above-average
	    income
	Impact of lump-sum income on
	    lifestyle
		Variable cost
		Motivation for attainment of
		    short-term goals
		Attract key personnel
		Favorable short-term cash flow

Long-term income	Reward for achievement Opportunity for high income Possibly lower net tax Key estate-building mechanism	Favorable financial aspects Holding power Motivation for attainment of long-term goals Attracts key personnel
Pay for time not worked	Rest from work Recreational opportunities	For some employees, low-cost item of high value Competitive need
Benefits	Tax-sheltered income Protection against economic risks	Meet company's social responsibilities to employees
Extra pay plans	Leveraged savings High-level fund management	Flexible supplement to insurance programs Build favorable employee attitudes

SOURCE: Reprinted, by permission of publisher, from Compensation (5th Edition) by Robert E. Sibson, © 1990
AMACOM, A division of American Management Association. All rights reserved.

Government regulations. There is legislation (see Exhibit 10-5) to insure minimum wages, nondiscriminatory wages, and prescribed wage rates for firms doing business with the federal government.

INTERNAL INFLUENCES ON PAY LEVELS. For many small businesses, external factors determine the wages that must be offered to attract qualified employees. However, as businesses grow, owners or managers determine pay scales through a variety of objective methods. The most commonly used methods are (1) ranking systems, (2) job classification systems, (3) point systems, and (4) factor comparison systems. These systems are quite similar and are often blended together in actual practice.

1. **Ranking systems.** This relatively uncomplicated job evaluation method is used in businesses that do not have a great variety of jobs. In the **ranking**

EXHIBIT 10-5 Laws Affecting Compensation

Law	Essential Provisions
Davis-Bacon Act, 1931 (Prevailing Wage Law)	Contractors doing construction work in excess of $2,000 for the federal government must pay the area prevailing wage as determined by the Department of Labor.
National Labor Relations Act, 1935	This act provides employees with the right to bargain collectively for wages, benefits, and working conditions.
Walsh-Healy Act, 1936 (Public Contracts Act)	Employers with federal contracts in excess of $10,000 must pay the area prevailing wage as determined by the Department of Labor. All employees receive time and one-half pay for hours worked in excess of 40 per week.
Fair Labor Standards Act, 1938 (Wage and Hour Act)	This law, which applies to most companies engaged in interstate commerce, established the minimum wage and overtime pay for more than 40 hours of work per week. Employers must observe certain work rules for children under 18 years of age.
Equal Pay Act, 1963	Employers must pay men and women the same wage for jobs requiring equal skill, effort, and responsibility.
Economic Stabilization Act, 1970	Empowers the president of the United States to establish wage and price guidelines or controls.
Employee Retirement Income Security Act, 1974 (ERISA)	Benefit plans must meet certain minimum standards for employee participation, vesting rights, funding, and reporting.
Retirement Equity Act, 1984 (REA)	Because women have more gaps in their employment history, this act reduces allowed penalties that can be imposed under ERISA. This act provides for the sharing of pensions in the event of divorce.

ranking system   system, the evaluator is not expected to dissect each job into its subfunctions or assign any measurable scores or point values to jobs. Instead, the evaluator simply ranks the jobs in order of importance. For example, in a restaurant the chef's position might be ranked the highest, and a bus person's position might have the lowest ranking. The job's ranking would determine the wages paid for that position.

    2. Job classification system. Arbitrarily ranking one job above another may job be difficult, so the **job classification system** was designed to compare the importance of several classes or clusters of jobs. Once job clusters have been identified, general specifications are prepared, indicating the types of jobs that will be included in each cluster. Salary ranges can then be specified for each cluster.

job
classification
system

    3. Point systems. The **point system** is quite sophisticated yet relatively point system simple, and its objectivity makes it one of the most frequently used job evaluation techniques. First, business owners need to describe the elements or factors that will be measured and weighted for each job in the company. Second, the weights assigned to each factor are determined by the relative importance of each factor as it relates to different jobs. For example, some job factors to measure might include education, manual dexterity, responsibility, training, mental effort, and working conditions. Once identified, these factors are weighted according to importance and the degree required for each job. Generally, the more difficult jobs have higher total values and, consequently, higher wage levels.

factor
comparison
system

4. **Factor comparison systems.** This method of job evaluation is similar to the point system. In the **factor comparison system,** several key or "bench-mark" jobs are selected to be evaluated, and all other jobs are compared with these jobs to establish equitable pay rates. The factors selected to be evaluated for key jobs may be the same as those used in point systems (education, manual dexterity, and so forth). The rate of pay for key jobs is analyzed to determine what percentage of the total rate is attributable to each factor. For example, if a job is worth $6.50 per hour, how much of that amount is for mental requirements? How much is for education, and so on? Finally, all other jobs are assigned pay ranges by comparing them to the key jobs.

Wage-Determination Problems

Although there are external forces that set broad pay guidelines and internal methods of determining wage levels, objectively determining the value of each job is still quite difficult. There are, and will always be, employees who believe their coworkers receive more pay for less important jobs. Some variables that contribute to imagined or real wage inequity include the following:

Subjectivity. Personal bias, prejudice, leniency, and inconsistency are major factors affecting wage determinations. Too often, pay is based on the job incumbent rather than on the job itself.

Inadequate information. After wage scales have been developed, jobs can still be over or undervalued because of inadequate or incorrect information. For example, area wage surveys are intended to make known going rates for most jobs; however, because of misleading job titles or faulty reporting, wage scales may be developed that do not reflect the true going rate.

Inflexibility. The lack of flexibility in most job evaluation methods concerns many business owners. Once the wage scale has been established, making changes in response to unforseen circumstances is quite difficult.

Pay secrecy. Many businesses forbid employees to discuss wages and salaries. Some even consider pay disclosure to be a terminable offense. Without knowing what their coworkers earn, some employees will incorrectly assume that they are being underpaid and will react accordingly.

Benefits

During World War II, wage and price controls made it very difficult to retain workers because they could only increase their pay by moving to another company. Innovative employers introduced noncash items such as health insurance and pensions to entice their workers not to leave for other jobs. The cash value of these benefits was not great; therefore, the term *fringe benefits* was coined. Today, however, benefits are a substantial part of a worker's total compensation package and the term *fringe* is no longer appropriate. A study by the U.S. Bureau of Labor Statistics found that benefits cost employers $3.28 per hour and average wages were $10.15 per hour. Other surveys have found that benefits can be as much as 40 percent of total compensation costs.

There is another way to calculate the value of benefits—ask recipients what benefits are worth to them. A survey of 1,000 people conducted in September 1990 uncovered the following opinions: (1) Given a choice of two jobs—one with benefits, one without—52 percent of the respondents needed a median of $10,000 more per year to make up for the lack of benefits; (2) Benefits were an important issue in job selection to 84 percent of the respondents; and (3) Nearly 64 percent would not accept a job without benefits.[14]

Benefits Provided by Small Businesses

What benefits can and do small business owners offer to attract and retain qualified workers? All companies, regardless of size, must provide legally required benefits, which include social security, workers' compensation, and unemployment compensation. Of the average $3.28 per hour paid for benefits, legally mandated benefits cost $1.13 per hour. Beyond those benefits, business owners can offer any benefits they can afford, or they may offer none.

Employee benefits at small firms lag far behind those in bigger ones. The Bureau of Labor Statistics, in its first study of the benefits provided by small firms, found that medical care was offered to full-time workers by 69 percent of firms with fewer than 100 employees in 1990. Only 64 percent of the companies provided life insurance, and 42 percent offered retirement plans. Unpaid maternity leave was provided by 17 percent of small companies, whereas 83 percent gave paid holidays and 88 percent gave paid vacations.[15] Small business owners may not have the luxury of choosing which benefits to offer for very long. There is a move in congress to mandate that certain benefits, such as health insurance, be offered to all employees.

As meager as these benefit offerings may be, they are generous when compared with benefits offered to part-time workers. Small firms offered health and life insurance to only 6 percent of part-time employees, whereas 10 percent had a retirement plan and 29 percent received paid vacations. Some employers who depend heavily on part-time workers provide those workers with the same benefits offered to full-time workers (see The Way It Is 10-3).

There are many noncash benefits small business owners can offer their employees. The list of such benefits is too extensive to discuss in this chapter; however, we will examine some of the most desired benefits. Most surveys have found that people who work for small companies are most desirous of receiving health insurance and pensions. After those benefits, vacations and paid holidays head the list of desired benefits.

10-3 BENEFITS FOR PART-TIMERS

Ben Strohecker, chocolate maker, treats his part-time workers better than many companies treat their full-timers. The owner of Harbor Sweets Inc. pays his part-timers well, gives them part of his profits, opens his books to them, and solicits their suggestions. Strohecker's part-time workers also get paid vacations and promotions, and they are eligible for health insurance. Such policies have helped Harbor Sweets attain an annual revenue of $2.1 million using mostly part-time workers. Part-timers operate in every level of the company except top management.[16]

Health Insurance

Because the cost of health care has consistently risen faster than the general inflation rate, employees need company-provided health insurance more than any other benefit. Surveys have found that employees consider health insurance to be worth approximately $10,000 per year. Employees want health care insurance from their employers, yet only 39.2 percent of workers in companies with fewer than twenty-five employees receive health insurance from their employers (see Exhibit 10-6).

Reasons for not providing health insurance include the following: (1) With fewer employees to cover, small businesses pay higher premiums than larger companies; (2) Small companies tend to hire more young and old employees who are more likely to need health care services; (3) Sole proprietorships and partnerships do not receive the tax benefits of paying health insurance premiums that corporations receive; (4) Small businesses, which are not as profitable as large companies, cannot afford to offer health insurance; and (5) Small companies cannot afford to self-insure as some large companies have. Business owners who want to provide health insurance, but think they cannot afford it, might consider MEWAs and FSAs.

Multiple
Employee
Welfare
Arrangements
(MEWAs)

MULTIPLE EMPLOYER WELFARE ARRANGEMENTS (MEWAs). **Multiple Employer Welfare Arrangements (MEWAs)** are self-funded health insurance pools usually marketed to businesses with fewer than 300 employees. Most traditional carriers have judged these small companies as too risky to insure, but by joining an insurance pool, several small companies can reach economies of scale that qualify them for lower health care premiums. The problem is that the number of MEWA plans failing because of mismanagement or outright fraud is soaring. The principal complaint against MEWAs is that they pay small claims, but abandon companies with large claims, leaving a company's employees stuck with the bills. For example, the La Crosse Visiting Nurses Association in Wisconsin was liable for $100,000 in unpaid medical bills after its MEWA went broke. One $5.25-an-hour employee must pay a $26,000 surgery bill that the MEWA should have covered.[17]

EXHIBIT 10-6 Health Insurance Availability and Coverage among Wage-and-Salary Workers, by Firm Size, 1988

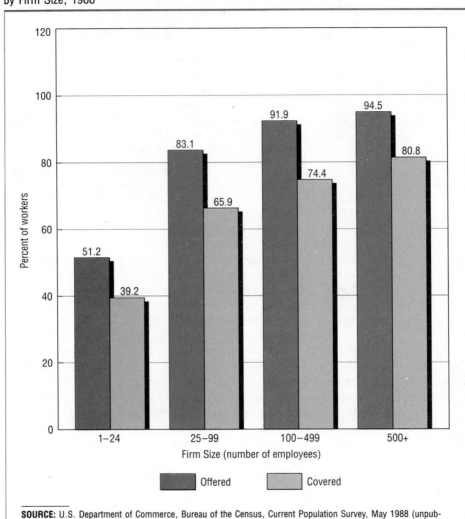

SOURCE: U.S. Department of Commerce, Bureau of the Census, Current Population Survey, May 1988 (unpublished data). *The State of Small Business—A Report of the President.* 1990, 47.

Flexible
Spending
Accounts
(FSAs)

FLEXIBLE SPENDING ACCOUNTS (FSAs). Because employer and employee decide who controls the program, **Flexible Spending Accounts (FSAs)** are safer than MEWAs. FSAs allow employees to direct part of their otherwise taxable income into accounts from which their medical and dental bills will be paid or reimbursed. The money put into an FSA is not taxed, thereby, giving employees funds to pay medical bills and higher take-home income. For example, a $25,000-a-year employee who deposited $1,640 into an FSA— instead of paying it out directly for premiums, deductibles, and so on—could expect to take home $19,782 after taxes. That is $370 more than a similarly paid employee with a standard health care plan.[18] Small businesses also benefit; since a company's payroll would be reduced by the amount of FSA contributions, its FICA taxes would also be less.

Small businesses realize benefits, other than federal tax advantages, from FSAs. First, any money remaining in individual FSAs at the end of the year reverts to the company. Second, before employee contributions are disbursed, employers can invest those funds and earn interest. Finally, some states compute unemployment taxes from the reduced employee salaries. FSAs are a win-win situation for both employees and small business owners.

Pension Plans

There has been, since the 1930s, a three-tiered philosophy about retirement income. Social security, available to most workers, should provide sufficient income to provide retirees with life's necessities. Next, income from company-sponsored pension plans should provide retirees with a comfortable standard of living. Finally, personal savings should provide discretionary income for retirees to purchase goods and services they want rather than need.

The system has not worked as intended because too many employees, in small and large companies, have no company-provided pension plans. The problem is worse in small companies (see Exhibit 10-7) where only 12.3 percent of workers in companies with fewer than twenty-five employees participate in pension programs. Small business owners who want to offer contributory or noncontributory pension plans have a few options.

Individual
Retirement
Accounts
(IRAs)

INDIVIDUAL RETIREMENT ACCOUNTS (IRAs). In 1974, the Employee Retirement Income Security Act (ERISA) established **Individual Retirement Accounts** to allow workers not covered by employer pension plans to set aside tax-deferred income for retirement. Eight years later, the Economic Recovery Tax Act (ERTA) extended IRAs to all workers. Then the Tax Reform Act of 1986 made IRAs less attractive by limiting the amount of money employees could contribute to their account. By 1988, only 12.5 percent of workers had IRAs compared with 17.5 percent in 1983.[19]

401(K) plans

401(K) PLANS. **401(K) plans** are similar to IRAs in that they allow employees to contribute tax-free dollars to their retirement plan. However, employers may also contribute to their employees' 401(K) plan. Employers with profit-sharing programs may contribute employees' portions of that program to their 401(K) plan, thereby sheltering profit-sharing income from federal taxes (the income is taxed when the money is withdrawn from the plan).

Simplified
Employee
Pension (SEP)
plans

SIMPLIFIED EMPLOYEE PENSION (SEP) PLANS. **Simplified Employee Pension (SEP) plans** were created for small business owners who could not afford the high start-up costs of traditional pension programs. The employer establishes the SEP plan through a financial institution and makes tax-deductible

EXHIBIT 10-7 Pension Plan Availability and Coverage among Wage-and-Salary Workers, by Firm Size, 1988

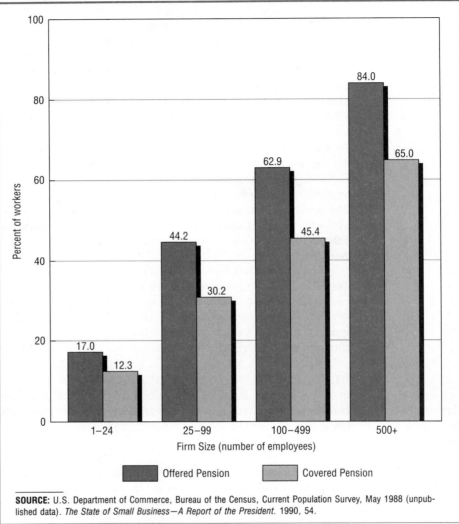

SOURCE: U.S. Department of Commerce, Bureau of the Census, Current Population Survey, May 1988 (unpublished data). *The State of Small Business—A Report of the President.* 1990, 54.

payments to each eligible participant's annuity contract. Payments each calendar year may be as much as $30,000 or 15 percent of an employee's compensation, whichever is less. All SEP payments made by the employer for employees are deductible as business expenses. However, an employer has no obligation to make annual payments.

As with most programs, there are advantages and disadvantages associated with SEPs. Advantages include the following: there are no set-up costs; there is no annual administrative cost to the employer; employers are not required to make annual contributions; there are no annual forms to be filed with the IRS; and there are no restrictions on withdrawals (tax and penalties do apply). The disadvantages that must be considered include the following: the plan is limited to twenty-five or fewer employees; funds cannot be used as collateral for loans; at least 50 percent of employees must participate; and special tax treatment such as five-year and ten-year averaging is not available.

Child Care

As more mothers with preschool children enter the work force, child care as a company-provided benefit assumes greater importance than in the past. Companies may soon be forced by the federal government to provide paid or unpaid maternity leave to employees whose jobs must be available when they return. This may not be as onerous to small businesses as it sounds; a recent study[20] found that 84 percent of companies with fewer than fifty employees offered maternity leave. Beyond this requirement, however, small business owners should also voluntarily provide leave and some form of child care (see The Way It Is 10-4) if they hope to attract and retain capable employees.

Any of the following plans make it easier for women to be both mother and employee: on-site child care; company-subsidized child care; flexible scheduling of hours worked; flextime for all workers; job sharing; or telecommuting. These and other innovative programs have been used successfully by many small businesses to keep good employees.

The Way It Is

10-4 SOME SMALL BUSINESSES' CHILD-CARE BENEFITS[21]

Company	Number of Employees	Benefits
Boward Business Services Inc. Answering service, FL	110	Subsidy
Bowles Corp. Engineering firm, VT	12	on-site center
Byrne Electrical Specialists Inc. Electrical systems maker, MI	110	on-site center
Chalet Dental Clinic Dental services, WA	45	on-site center
Lynchburg Hematology-Oncology Cancer treatment center, VA	16	flexible benefit plan
Sheehan, Phinney, Bass & Green Law firm, NH	150	dependent-care assistance plan
Stackpole Ltd. U.S.A. Metal bearings maker, TN	100	on-site center

Miscellaneous Benefits

Once business owners have offered benefits that satisfy the basic health and retirement needs of employees, they might add any of the following to their package of benefits:

- Disability insurance
- Life insurance
- Vacations
- Holidays
- Legal counseling
- Paid education
- Financial assistance
- Tax preparation
- Elderly care
- Subsidized food service
- Wellness programs
- Pay for time not worked (jury duty, civic duty, military duty, time off to vote, etc.)

Flexible Benefit Plans

flexible benefit plans

For small business owners, benefit packages are expensive and can be cumbersome to administer. Employees, on the other hand, may receive benefits from their employers that are duplicative or unwanted. To overcome these problems, some small businesses have "cafeteria" or **flexible benefit plans.** Owners identify the benefits they are willing to provide employees and the cost of each item. Employees are told how much they can "spend" on benefits and are then allowed to select the ones important to them. That way, for example, a female employee who is included in her husband's health insurance policy may substitute longer vacations for the company's health insurance. Employees should be allowed to alter their benefits mix as their situation changes.

Communication about Benefits

Although some small business owners consider benefit packages to be expensive and difficult to administer, employees often believe that they are not receiving enough benefits. According to International Survey Research Corporation, only 50 percent of American workers consider their benefits adequate, compared with 83 percent in the early 1980s.[22] Employees also appear to be unaware of the nature and cost of their benefits. For example, when asked what type of health insurance they had, 25 percent of surveyed employees did not know what kind of health coverage their employers provided.

Small business owners should not allow their employees to be confused about the benefits they receive or how expensive those benefits are to the company. Beginning with the orientation and continuing throughout an employee's tenure, owners should remind employees that most benefits are provided voluntarily, and they should be made aware of the cost of each benefit. Benefits will be appreciated by employees when they realize how much they cost and that they could lose those benefits.

COMMUNICATING WITH EMPLOYEES

Many employer-employee problems are the result of poor communication between both parties. Owners who constantly communicated with their employees when their business was young and growing tend to forget how important communication with employees really is once the business begins to mature. Employees want to know what is going on, what the company's goals are, how the company is performing, and how they are performing. Meaningful communication goes a long way toward keeping employees motivated and interested in the business and their jobs.

The Communication Process

The communication process (see Exhibit 10-8) is relatively straightforward and uncomplicated, yet many of us tend to be inadequate communicators—messages sent do not always have the same meaning to the receiver as they

Meaningful communication between employer and employee is important in keeping employees motivated and interested in their jobs.

EXHIBIT 10-8 The Communication Process

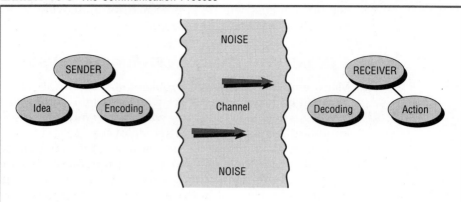

do to the sender. The sender and receiver (both can be either individuals or groups) are the key participants in the communication process. Senders have ideas they wish to transmit, which must be encoded or put into a meaningful message form and transmitted via an appropriate channel. The receiver receives the message, which must be decoded and responded to in some fashion. Complicating this process is "noise," a collection of elements that cause messages to be confusing or misunderstood by receivers.

Noise

Many messages, even the simplest ones, are often misunderstood because of communication barriers that are difficult to eliminate. The following are a few of the communication barriers that tend to garble messages:

Semantics. Commonly used words have varied meanings to different people. Words such as few, sometimes, occasionally, and frequently are imprecise and subject to interpretation.

Jargon. Many messages are confusing because they contain words that are meaningful only to people in similar professions or groups. Physicians, government employees, athletes, and others use words and phrases that mean nothing to "outsiders."

Interest. Lack of interest in subject matter, on the part of either the sender or receiver, can block the reception of ideas. For example, employees who are not particularly interested in efficiency will not be receptive to a business owner's exhortations to minimize waste.

Organization. Ideas that form a message may be so poorly organized that the receiver cannot decipher the communication.

Status. Superior-subordinate communications are often unsuccessful because subordinates are too intimidated to ask to have the message repeated or restated.

Poor listening. Too often, senders or receivers are too preoccupied or distracted to actively listen to communications. It takes effort and practice to be effective listeners.

Nonverbal barriers. Sometimes what is said is contradicted by how it is said. Voice inflection, facial expressions, posture, and a host of other movements or expressions can confuse messages or send conflicting signals.

Downward Communication

When business owners communicate with their employees, they are engaged in downward communication and can use the following media: memos, reports, bulletins, company magazines, orientation manuals, handbooks, letters to employees, and bulletin boards. These media can be used to accomplish the following objectives:

- To let employees know about company activities, problems, markets, mergers, profits, sales of new products, and diversification plans.
- To emphasize the company's dependence on the efforts, loyalty, and creativity of the employees.
- To remind employees of their responsibilities, achievements, and status in the business.
- To emphasize the value and usefulness of the benefits employees receive.
- To remind employees of new or rescinded government regulations.
- To keep employees abreast of changes in company operations, policy, or direction.
- To encourage employees to use company publications to express their needs and concerns.[23]

Upward Communication

Employees making their concerns and needs known to business owners are communicating upward. Employee messages may reach owners via letters, face-to-face communication, formal suggestion systems, quality circles, or formal employee councils. Business owners often have to encourage employees to initiate upward communication because employees may be too timid or insecure to tell management what they think. A healthy two-way flow of ideas and messages keeps employees informed and management aware of employee needs and concerns. Interrupting that flow can lead to employee dissatisfaction or disinterest, which could ultimately result in unionization.

SUMMARY

Motivated employees tend to be dedicated, enthusiastic workers who have the best interest of the company in mind. To motivate workers owners should care about their employees, be tactful, give praise and recognition, be enthusiastic and confident, set standards for the company, and keep employees informed. Motivating with negative factors such as threat of discharge may be easier, but that type of motivation can often be counterproductive. Although there is some disagreement about the motivational value of money, most people would agree that substandard wages can contribute to job dissatisfaction.

To keep wages and salaries adequate and acceptable, owners should decide how they want to pay their employees. Workers can receive wages for time worked or they can receive wages based on their individual or group output. Pay-for-output systems include the following: piecework, commissions, bonuses, profit-sharing, and knowledge pay. Any of these pay systems will be incomplete if they are not accompanied by desired benefits. Most employees want their company to provide health care insurance, dental insurance, sick leave, and paid vacations. Other benefits can be offered to employees if owners feel they are necessary. To be appreciated, benefit programs should be explained to employees, who should then have some choice in which benefits they receive.

Communicating with employees about compensation and other company activities is a necessary aspect of managing a small business. To communicate effectively, owners need to overcome communication barriers, which include semantics, jargon, lack of interest, poor listening, and nonverbal barriers. Keeping employees informed about all important company activities generates trust and loyalty, and keeps the employees motivated.

QUESTIONS FOR REVIEW AND DISCUSSION

1. What are the different need levels in Maslow's theory of motivation?
2. Briefly explain Herzberg's dual factor motivation theory.
3. Do you think intrinsic or extrinsic factors are better motivators?
4. If you owned a business, would you pay your employees by the hour or for their output? Why?
5. What are the different variable pay systems?
6. How does the federal government affect wage levels?
7. What are the different methods of determining wages or salaries?
8. Why are benefits no longer referred to as "fringe" benefits?
9. Do you believe the government should require companies to provide benefits such as child care, health insurance, and maternity leave?
10. What are "cafeteria" benefit plans?
11. What are the verbal barriers to effective communication?

KEY TERMS

bonus	factor comparison system
commissions	flexible benefit plans
expectancy	Flexible Spending Accounts
extrinsic rewards	401(K) plans

hygiene factors

Individual Retirement Accounts

intrinsic rewards

job classification system

knowledge pay

motivators

Multiple Employee Welfare
Arrangements

performance unit plans

piecework system

point system

profit-sharing plans

ranking system

Simplified Employee Pension plans

valence

CASE
Group or Individual Rewards?

Kent Bergstrom owned one of the best seafood restaurants in town. His eight-year-old business had developed a reputation for excellent service, high-quality food, and a reasonably priced wine list. Kent was proud of what he had accomplished, and he was gratified to be able to offer forty-six people steady employment. With the exception of the cooks, hostesses, and assistant managers most employees were students who worked to pay some of their college expenses. Most students started to work at the restaurant after their freshman year and remained until they graduated.

Employees were selected on the basis of their appearance, attitude, and motivation. Kent did not hire people who were not motivated to do a good job or who could not get along with customers and fellow employees. Once hired, employees received a few days of training before they were allowed to serve customers. Upon completing a three-month probationary period, employees were considered to be permanent and were eligible for full benefits. Benefits included health insurance (employees paid 15 percent of the pre-

mium), sick leave, vacations, and a $15,000 life insurance policy.

In addition to benefits, employees were paid $2.09 per hour. Waitpersons supplemented their wages with tips, which they shared with buspersons and barbacks who were not usually tipped by customers. On a good night, waitpersons could earn between one and two hundred dollars in tips if they were fast and courteous to customers. Of course, inefficient or unmotivated employees earned considerably less in tips. The disparity in tips received often caused problems among employees who occasionally let Kent know about their dissatisfaction.

Kent was not sure how to resolve the problems caused by differences in tip-generated income, but he was determined to find a solution. Kent decided to initiate a plan that required all tips to be pooled and then distributed equally among all employees. He reasoned that employees would continue to work hard and would not be envious of the tips received by fellow employees. Within a few days, service deteriorated and customer complaints increased significantly. Waitpersons were dispirited, absenteeism increased, and pilferage became a problem. Kent Bergstrom did not believe that all his problems could be caused by the new tip-pooling program, so he began searching for other causes.

QUESTIONS

1. Does this restaurant have an effective benefits plan?

2. Why would a tip-pooling plan cause problems in a restaurant?

3. Would reverting back to the original tip plan resolve all of Kent's problems?

ACTIVITIES

1. Interview several small business employees and determine what motivates them and how they would like to be compensated.
2. Read the brief situations below and decide how you would motivate each person described. Select two or three of the following inducements or conditions that you believe would motivate each person to perform better:
    1. Threat of termination
    2. More benefits
    3. Higher wages or salary
    4. Pay-for-performance plan
    5. More recognition and praise
    6. Less supervision
    7. Enhanced status—different title, etc.
    8. Group profit-sharing plan
    9. More decision-making power
    10. Job cross-training

SITUATION ONE

Tom Carson manages an antique shop that employs eighteen people. He is 39, single, and lives in a rented condominium. Tom has managed the shop for four years and now receives $35,000 per year. Because Tom is not part of the family that owns the shop, his promotion possibilities are almost nonexistent.

SITUATION TWO

Jeff Finney has been a carpenter all his life. He is now 61 years old and has been employed by the same contractor for the past nine years. Jeff lives with his wife in a modest home they have owned for twenty-seven years. They share their home with a 32-year-old daughter who cannot afford a place of her own. Jeff is paid $16.25 per hour and receives time-and-a-half for any hours worked beyond forty per week. During the summer building season he averages about fifteen hours of overtime each week.

SITUATION THREE

Elizabeth Harrison is a computer programmer for a large insurance company. She has been with the company for twelve years and hopes to be promoted soon. Elizabeth goes to school part-time and is working toward a master's degree in computer science. She and her husband and his dependent mother live in an average house in a middle-class neighborhood. Elizabeth and her fellow employees feel that their benefits are inadequate.

SITUATION FOUR

Jack Cassidy is a bright 32-year-old engineer with an aerospace company on the West Coast. He has twelve other engineers reporting to him, and he earns $62,000 per year. Jack drives a BMW, and he and his wife and three children live in a $200,000 house in a fashionable neighborhood. The company has several incompetent managers who are blocking Jack's advancement.

SITUATION FIVE

Judy Fairchild is a talented violinist who plays with a well-known orchestra. She is 26 years old and has been with the orchestra for three years where she earns $23,600. Judy lives with her boyfriend, a musician in a rock band, in an inexpensive apartment in the center of town. Judy wants to continue her formal education and save enough to buy her own house (she would also like to marry her boyfriend). The orchestra director, a German with many years of experience, does not believe that women perform as well as men.

11 SELECTING AND USING KEY OUTSIDERS

LEARNING OBJECTIVES

After you have read this chapter, you will be able to do the following:
- Explain why positive supplier relationships are so important
- Select and use lawyers and accountants
- Explain the functions and value of advisory boards and outside consultants
- Determine what business owners can and cannot do to keep their companies union free

The stereotype of the entrepreneur is that of a rugged individual who works countless hours to perform all the functions necessary to grow his or her business. Implicit in that stereotype is the notion that entrepreneurs are solo players who need no assistance from others. In fact, few entrepreneurs or small business owners could survive without the help of outside experts. New venture creators need the assistance of attorneys and accountants to establish the business. They may also need the assistance and advice of consultants and other business advisors. Business owners also need to select and maintain relationships with reliable suppliers. The need for outside experts continues as the business grows and prospers.

Although business owners need help from people with specialized skills, they do not have to make these experts full-time employees. Some small business owners keep lawyers and accountants on a retainer basis; however, others pay for legal and accounting services only when used. Consultants and other outside advisors are used on an as-needed basis and are paid only for services rendered. In this chapter we will discuss the ways business owners can select, use, and evaluate the outsiders they need to keep their businesses growing and profitable.

SUPPLIERS

Goods and services are necessary for the conduct of almost all small businesses. Retailers, for example, must purchase most of the goods they sell. Wholesalers also purchase most of the goods they stock for resale to retailers. Manufacturers purchase the raw materials needed to produce goods to sell to wholesalers. The quality of these goods and services and the dependability and reliability of suppliers is vital to the success of small businesses.

Frequently, purchasing in small businesses is based on hunches rather than on adequate information. Business owners who decide to deal with the first supplier they come in contact with may find that they have overlooked better supplier opportunities. Therefore, they need to carefully select their suppliers and maintain professional relationships with them.

Multiple or Single Suppliers

One of the first decisions business owners need to make is whether they want several suppliers to provide products or whether they want to rely on a single supplier. The advantages of using several, often competing suppliers, include the following: (1) If one supplier is out of needed products, they can be purchased from a supplier who has the goods in inventory; (2) Suppliers who compete for the right to supply small businesses keep their prices low and offer superior service; and (3) Multiple suppliers can offer small business owners more product variety and quality.

Some business owners may find that it is more prudent to rely on a single supplier than to purchase from several vendors. The advantages of using a single supplier include the following: (1) Using only one supplier allows business owners to establish a trusting relationship with that vendor; (2) In times of product shortage vendors usually service their "loyal" customers before they provide products to "casual" customers; and (3) Buyers can place larger purchase orders with their vendors, which might entitle them to a lower price. Once owners have made the multiple/single supplier decision, they need to locate acceptable vendors.

Locating Suppliers

Business owners can use several sources to locate suppliers with whom to establish long-term relationships. All these sources should be investigated because some are more useful than others. The following are some sources of reliable vendors:

Experience. Owners who have had relationships with vendors or have met them socially might choose to use the services of those suppliers. Owners should be sure that they are using suppliers for their competency rather than for personal or social relationships that might have been established.

Telephone Directories. Owners can quite easily peruse the business section or yellow pages of a telephone book to locate suppliers. Because owners are not likely to know much about the suppliers listed in the telephone book, they tend to make their selection by the size of the advertisement. Advertisement size may not be a very good indicator of vendor quality, reliability, and so on.

Salesperson Interviews. Salespeople who currently call on small businesses are valuable sources of information about suppliers of other products.

Catalogs. Many suppliers have catalogs describing the products that they can make available to prospective buyers. The caveat for business owners is that information prepared by vendors may not be as accurate as that prepared by a disinterested party.

Trade Journals and Shows. Most industries have trade journals that carry advertisements and articles by and about vendors and their products. Similarly, industries have periodic trade shows where suppliers display their products and provide prospective buyers with any pertinent information they need about the vendor's operations.

Chambers of Commerce. Business owners could get a listing of appropriate suppliers from their local chamber of commerce. Owners should realize that the list is incomplete because not all suppliers choose to be chamber members.

Selecting Suppliers

Having located a number of vendors, business owners need to establish criteria for selecting the most suitable ones. This decision should be made carefully because supplier-business relationships are critical to the success of most small companies. Although many owners consider price to be the most important selection criteria, they should also consider the following factors before making their selection:[1]

Location. Suppliers located near a business can deliver goods quicker and less expensively than those located some distance from the purchasing company. Nearby vendors might also be more willing to provide periodic personal service than their more distant competitors.

reserve capacity

Reserve Capacity. Reserve capacity is the ability of suppliers to provide sufficient goods if the purchasing company's business expands rapidly. Suppliers who are at or near their own capacity will be unable to fill orders for growing companies, causing the latter to search for substitute vendors at an inopportune time.

Labor Relations. Owners should be aware of relationships vendors have with their unionized employees. Poor relations could lead to production slowdowns or even strikes, which leave vendors unable to provide products to purchasers.

Guarantees and Warranties. Most suppliers guarantee the quality of the products they sell and should be willing to replace or repair defective items. Suppliers should also be willing to guarantee that goods will be delivered on time, in the quantity ordered, and at the specified place. Owners should be suspect of vendors who provide no guarantees or warranties or refuse to honor the ones they do make.

Financial Status. Long-term relations are difficult to establish with vendors who are financially insecure. Owners should check the Dun & Bradstreet report or similar reports to determine the financial well-being of prospective vendors.

Facility Visitations. Perhaps the most critical part of the vendor selection process is a visit to the company's facility where business owners can acquire the most information about the vendor's operations and ability to meet contractual obligations.

Maintaining Good Supplier Relationships

The success of most small businesses is dependent, to some extent, on good supplier relationships. The key to good supplier relations is the golden rule: Treat others as you would wish them to treat you. Be strong in requiring that the terms of a contract are met, then be fair by not making unreasonable demands on the supplier and by paying on time. Suppliers usually finance their receivables, and late payments increase their financing costs. Suppliers who are paid late often provide less service, increase prices, or simply decide to discontinue their relationship with the delinquent buyer.

If small business owners have suppliers bid on contracts, fairness dictates that no advance information be given on bids and that competitors' prices are not revealed. Unsuccessful bidders should be notified promptly, but they should not be given specific figures concerning the successful bid. After notifying the successful bidder, owners should maintain contact from the time that orders are placed until the goods are actually delivered.

reciprocal
buying

Another potential problem with supplier relations is that of **reciprocal buying,** where both parties agree to purchase goods or services from the other. As beneficial as a reciprocal buying agreement may seem to be to both companies, the practice is a dangerous one. The buyer loses control of the contract. What happens if the supplier is late, or if the quality is poor? What pressure can be exerted? The most prudent practice is to buy from the best source and to sell to the best source.

expediting

Expediting is also a potential problem that can exist between buyers and sellers. **Expediting** is requesting that a supplier ship an order or portion of an order by a specific date, usually earlier than originally specified. Expediting places a strain on relationships, because one company is requesting delivery before the other can reasonably expect to make delivery without incurring additional cost. To alleviate this problem, owners should help the supplier look for solutions—e.g., shipping part of an order, or shipping by air if the goods are critically needed.

Evaluating Vendors

Once business owners have established vendor relationships, they should periodically evaluate their vendors to determine whether the relationship should be continued. The following are a few factors that can be used to evaluate vendors:

- On-time delivery; number of times late.
- Percent of order shipped.
- Rejections—a quality rating.
- Technical service—Is it available? Is it good?

11-1 VENDOR EVALUATION

Small businesses that deal with multiple vendors need to attract and retain high-caliber suppliers. To decide which vendor relationships should be continued, business owners need effective performance evaluation methods to differentiate good from marginal suppliers. Miller Business Systems (MBS), a regional distributor of office products and furniture, developed a rigorous vendor rating program that used the following criteria to rate performance:

- Accounting: Credit policies and billing accuracy.
- Administration: Product-line acceptability, product quality, and responsiveness.
- Advertising: Promotion flexibility and advertising allowance.
- Purchasing: Fill percentage, lead time, representatives' performance, pricing, and minimum order.
- Receiving: Packing list accuracy and quality of shipments.

For each performance criterion, suppliers are rated on a scale of 1 to 5, with 5 being the highest rating. Ratings for each supplier are calculated, and suppliers are compared by product category. The top suppliers are notified and thanked for their excellent service; lower-ranked suppliers are also notified and given an opportunity to improve. Interestingly, suppliers' response to the program has been positive, as it gives them some insight into what kind of performance MBS expects.[2]

- Expediting—Will vendor expedite orders?
- Financial status—Will the company be around next year?
- Cost delivered—This should include rejections, lost time due to late deliveries, lost manufacturing time, and lost sales.

Companies can use any reasonable criteria to evaluate their suppliers (see The Way It Is 11-1). This information should be timely, but it does not need to involve complicated record keeping. A simple two-page form (see Exhibit 11-1) is sufficient to keep accurate records.

ATTORNEYS

Some business owners consider attorneys to be an avoidable expense. They know enough about legal matters to be their own lawyer and believe that they will consult an attorney when they or their company gets into trouble. The fact is that new laws are created almost daily and the government is meting

EXHIBIT 11.1 Vendor Evaluation Form

Side 1

Vendor Name: _____ Vendor No: _____ Items Handled _____

Orders

Date	P.O. No.	Quantity	Items	Dollar Amt.	Delivery Days Early + Days Late −	No. of Rejects

Six Months Totals: No. of Orders _____ Total Dollars _____ Avg. Days Early ____ Avg. Days Late ____ % of Rejects ____

Side 2

Expediting: No. of times _____ From _____ To _____ Average per order _____

Needs Routine Expediting: Yes _____ No _____

No. of Sales Calls _____ From _____ To _____ Salesperson Reachable in an Emergency: Yes _____ No _____

Extra Services Rendered: _____

_____

_____

_____

_____

Complaints: No. _____ By Customers _____ By In-House Personnel _____

Problems: _____

_____

_____

_____

_____

_____

_____

_____

out harsher penalties to lawbreakers. For example, during his 1990 trial, John Borowski was found guilty of having ordered his employees to dump toxic wastes down a sewer. The judge sentenced Borowski to two years in jail and fined him $400,000. The president of metal-finisher Borjohn Optical Technology Inc. thus became the first person ever convicted under the four-year-old "knowing endangerment" provision of the Clean Water Act.[3]

The following laws that are subject to stricter enforcement may directly or indirectly affect small business owners:

Antitrust. The Antitrust Amendments Act of 1990 increases the maximum penalties for price-fixing from $1 million to $10 million.

Banking. The Financial Institutions Reform, Recovery & Enforcement Act of 1989 ups fines to $1 million and prison sentences to twenty years for ten banking-related crimes such as lying to regulators and falsifying credit applications.

Environment. The Clean Air Act of 1990 authorizes fifteen-year prison terms for knowingly polluting and changes violations from misdemeanors to felonies.

Securities. The Securities Law Enforcement Remedies Act of 1990 lets the Securities & Exchange commission fine companies and bar persons convicted of financial fraud from ever serving as officers and directors of companies.[4]

Some business owners believe that these laws will never affect them because their companies are too small. Even if they are never involved in litigation, business owners should use the services of attorneys to ensure that their companies are operating legally.

The Need for Attorneys
When entrepreneurs make the decision to be self-employed, they need to determine whether it is more efficient to buy a business or start one from scratch. If the decision is to start a business, attorneys can examine licensing laws and zoning regulations, evaluate leases and other necessary contracts, and develop partnership agreements or incorporate the company. If the decision is to buy a company, a lawyer can verify the transferability of assets, ensure the legality and scope of patents and trademarks, study the rights and obligations under existing contracts and permits, and verify all documents transferring the business to the new owner.

Once started, businesses will need the services of attorneys on many occasions. Attorneys should develop contracts between owners and employees, vendors, and clients that are explicit and uncontestable. Lawyers should be counselors who provide owners with their best advice on business and personal matters. Finally, good attorneys should help businesses avoid litigation and should be able to present a credible defense if litigation cannot be avoided.

Selecting Attorneys

The first consideration in the attorney-selection process is whether to use the services of a large or small law firm. Advantages of large firms include the following:

1. Larger firms may intimidate opponents.
2. The prestige and influence of large firms makes it easier for small firms to schedule appointments with banks, underwriters, and so forth.
3. Attorneys with large firms have a broad range of expertise.
4. Some larger firms charge small businesses lower fees in order to make them long-term clients.

Sometimes small businesses might be better represented by small law firms, which can devote more time to their particular needs. To decide if smaller firms are preferable, owners should consider the following disadvantages of large law firms:

1. Attorneys in large firms may be too specialized and not very creative.
2. Large firms are not likely to refer clients to outside experts.
3. Large law firms may have very little small business experience.
4. Larger firms try to maximize billable hours.[5]

LOCATING ATTORNEYS. Business owners can begin their search for a lawyer by asking the bar association to make recommendations and by questioning friends and acquaintances about attorneys they may know or use. However, these are not the best sources because the bar association is not familiar with the particular circumstances of each small business, and friends may be biased about the performance of their attorney.

Business owners might rely on advertisements to locate a suitable attorney. It is now legal for attorneys to advertise their services, and many newspapers and telephone directories tout the ability and expertise of various lawyers. However, most attorneys who advertise appear to specialize in divorce, accidents, or other nonbusiness matters. In the legal profession there is still a feeling that the best lawyers rely on word-of-mouth advertising.

Other business owners are a good source of lawyer leads. Nonlawyer professionals, such as accountants and bankers, who deal with attorneys on a daily basis can recommend the best lawyers for small businesses. Lawyers who do not specialize in small business affairs, such as corporate and tax attorneys, could recommend suitable lawyers to small business owners. Finally, business owners can check the credentials of lawyers in the *Martindale-Hubbell Law Directory*, the only comprehensive directory of lawyers. People in a position to recommend lawyers to business owners have evaluated the competence of those lawyers using the following criteria:

Martindale-
Hubbell Law
Directory

- **Substantive knowledge.** Is the lawyer informed and up-to-date regarding major cases and legislation?
- **Fact-gathering ability.** Does the attorney know the level of factual research needed for each matter and the specific facts that are of importance?
- **Understanding problems.** Does the lawyer identify and address all the important aspects of the client's problems?
- **Communication with clients.** Does the lawyer communicate clearly and on a timely basis with his or her clients?
- **Negotiating judgment.** Does the attorney prioritize goals in handling negotiations so that concessions do not reveal the client's most important objectives?
- **Allocation of time and resources.** Does the lawyer use time and resources so as to maximize the returns on these investments?
- **Ethics.** Is the attorney ethical in all her or his professional and personal dealings?
- **Staying within areas of competence.** Does the lawyer refer clients to other lawyers or other professionals when a matter is beyond his or her field of expertise?[6]

INTERVIEWING ATTORNEYS. Once a few lawyers have been located, business owners need to interview them individually before making the final selection. The following are some questions that should be asked before and during the interview:

- **Before the Interview:**
  Will there be a charge for the exploratory session? If so, how much will it be?
  Do you have or do you expect any conflicts of interest?
  Have you or your law firm taken a position that is inconsistent with my position?

- **During the Interview:**
  Do you have clients of comparable size to my business and in a similar industry?
  In addition to client matters, what other experience do you have relevant to my situation?
  In what area do you and others in your firm specialize?
  Do you have recent experience with cases like mine? What were the outcomes and your fees? May I contact some of those other clients?
  Will you be doing all the work for my company? If not, will you introduce me to others who might do work for my business? Will you provide the necessary supervision of work performed by others?

What are your alternatives for fee arrangements? What fraction of an hour do you use in billing?

Will your bills identify each service performed, date of performance, and names of persons doing the work?[7]

Legal Fees

Fees can be one of the most common sources of misunderstanding between business owners and their attorneys (see The Way It Is 11-2); therefore, business owners must determine how attorneys will be paid and how much they will be paid. Hourly fees are the most common way of paying attorneys, but they can also be paid on a retainer or contingency basis.

HOURLY FEES. Attorneys and business owners should agree on the hourly rate the attorney will be paid and what portion of an hour is used for billing. Many lawyers bill in quarter-hour segments, which means a two-minute telephone call to a $200-an-hour attorney costs the business owner $50 in legal fees. Some lawyers bill in six-minute segments, which makes it easier for owners to justify short exchanges with them. Owners should determine if all

The Way It Is

11-2 UNEXPECTED LEGAL FEES

Jack and Margie Roberts own and operate Senoret Chemical Company, a small business that manufactures Brite-Blue toilet cleaner, Scent-Go house fresheners, and Terro Ant Killer. In 1987, the EPA raised questions about Terro's potential risk to children. To defend themselves against the charges, the Robertses hired a top law firm, because this was the most serious charge the company ever faced. Three years later, Senoret, which had never grossed more than $1.4 million a year in sales, was presented with a $457,000 bill for legal services, which it could not pay. The firm that Senoret had hired, 203-attorney firm Robins, Kaplan, Miller & Ciresi, lost the EPA suit and then filed a lawsuit against Senoret to recover its fees.

The Robertses selected their law firm because it was well known, it had Washington D.C. connections, and its advertising brochures stated that facing Robins Kaplan in court "was a little like encountering Genghis Khan on the steppes." Throughout the pretrial period, Robins Kaplan's fees were modest and their estimate of total costs was $100,000. However, when the case went to trial, the firm needed other lawyers, expert witnesses, and technical experts. Costs escalated rapidly, and the Robertses were not kept informed of the expenses Robins Kaplan was charging to their company. Now Senoret must find a substitute for the sodium arsenic in Terro Ant Killer and find the capital to pay its legal fees.[8]

members of their attorney's firm charge the same hourly rate, and how much services performed by others such as paralegals cost.

RETAINERS. There are several types of retainers—case retainers, advances against costs, and general-representation retainers, which are fees paid periodically for limited types and amounts of work agreed upon in advance. Business owners should negotiate a deal with an attorney whereby unused portions of a retainer can be used to reduce next year's retainer. If such a deal cannot be negotiated, owners are often tempted to use their attorney's services frivolously.

contingency
fee

CONTINGENCY FEES. In some instances, particularly in litigation cases, attorneys collect their fees from any payment made to the business owner. Before any case goes to court, owners should find out how many hours it might take to resolve and then decide whether a **contingency fee** is greater or less than an hourly fee. If a case is to be paid on a contingent basis, owners should make it clear that they are in charge of the case—they will decide on settlement or appeal.

STOCK. When companies are young and unable to pay standard attorney fees, their owners may offer lawyers stock in the business as partial payment for their fees. Many an attorney has become wealthy by accepting the stock of a struggling company that grows and becomes very profitable.

billable hours

BILLABLE HOURS. Regardless of how they choose to pay their attorneys, business owners need to be aware of the concept of **billable hours.** This is the way lawyers compute the amount of time they have worked for the client. The time may include direct discussions with the client, telephone calls, secretarial time, research time, and so on. In some cases, attorneys, particularly young ones intent on becoming a partner, may be too aggressive in calculating billable hours. The following scenario involving a young would-be partner and a senior partner was suggested by Russell R. Miller:[9]

- The client is charged for the conversation in which he explains the problem to the senior partner.
- The client is charged for the senior telling the junior what the client told him.
- The client is charged for the junior calling the client to clarify some points.
- The client is charged for the senior reviewing the work of the junior.
- The client is charged for the time the senior used to explain the work to the client.
- The client is charged for all the time it takes the involved lawyers to figure out how much time they should bill the client for the work.
- The client is sent the bill, and in two months is sent another bill for Xeroxing, telephones, delivery, etc.

CONTROLLING LEGAL FEES. Business owners should do whatever they can to negotiate the lowest legal fees possible, and they should ensure that they do everything possible to avoid being billed for unnecessary hours. The following are some techniques owners can use to minimize their legal fees:

- **Be prepared.** Whenever owners meet with their attorney, they should know the purpose of the meeting and should have all pertinent files and documents available for inspection.
- **Keep current.** Owners should learn about new developments in their industry and should consult with their lawyer only if those developments could have a serious impact on their business.
- **Be punctual.** Legal fees begin when a meeting is scheduled to begin. Owners who are a half-hour late to a meeting with their attorney pay for those unused thirty minutes.
- **Be frank and honest.** Owners should not withhold vital information from their attorney even if it is negative.
- **Practice preventive law.** Owners should contact their attorney about problems before they become serious and potentially expensive.
- **Avoid courts.** Whenever possible, owners should try to settle matters out of court or use some alternative dispute resolution (ADR) techniques.

preventive law   PREVENTIVE LAW. **Preventive law** has only recently been accepted by small business owners even though the concept is not new. Preventive law helps avoid lawsuits, bankruptcy, or even liquidation by spotting problems before they become serious. For example, Doak Jacoway, founder of a two-man investment firm, has a year-end planning meeting with his lawyer, Ned A. Minor, which costs $330 and lasts two hours. Over the years Minor has uncovered several legal time bombs, including rusty estate plans, poorly drafted contracts, no corporate minutes, and the absence of noncompetition clauses for key employees.[10] In most cases, fees incurred for yearly checkups save time and money in the long run for business owners.

alternative dispute resolution (ADR) techniques   ALTERNATIVE DISPUTE RESOLUTION (ADR). Not all disputes between two or more parties need to go to court. **Alternative dispute resolution (ADR) techniques** such as arbitration, mediation, minitrials, and so forth can be used to settle disputes. ADR techniques save time and money for all parties, and the outcome is usually the same as it would have been if the dispute had been taken to court. Approximately 95 percent of all suits settle before trial. The ADR movement attempts to settle those cases quicker and at lower costs. Small business owners who choose to use ADR should build it into their contracts. John H. Wilkinson, a litigation partner at Donovan Leisure Newton & Irvine in New York City, recommends including the following provisions in ADR contract clauses:

- There will be a period of negotiation before the start of formal ADR. ADR is less expensive than litigation, but it may even be possible for owners to avoid ADR as well.

- A third-party neutral will be appointed to resolve differences that arise in planning the ADR proceedings.
- The parties will choose the form of ADR to use, the rules and the format of the proceedings, and the extent of fact-finding before the proceedings begin.
- The parties will agree that the proceedings will be confidential and will be used for no other purpose.
- Either side may initiate a lawsuit if settlement is not reached within a specified time after the start of ADR.[11]

REDUCING LEGAL FEES. Preventive law and ADR help keep fees low, but they are not the only cost-saving techniques available to small business owners. The following are some fee arrangements owners can try to negotiate with their attorneys:

Flat Fees. The lawyer handles a legal matter for a specified price regardless of the number of hours involved.

Blended Rates. Owners pay a single hourly rate for the work of senior and junior lawyers alike, thereby ensuring that cases are staffed efficiently and economically.

Hourly Rate Discounts. Regular billing rates are cut for the owner.

Bidding. A business owner invites several lawyers to bid on a project.

Modified Contingency Fees. A portion of the lawyer's fee is pegged to her or his success in the case.[12]

ACCOUNTANTS

Small business owners use their attorneys intermittently; however, they need the services of accountants on a regular basis. The easiest way for an owner to get into financial trouble is to ignore record keeping, financial planning, tax preparation, and so forth—the services provided by an accountant. If owners do not need a certified public accountant, they can elect to use the services of bookkeepers or tax preparers. The following types of accountants can provide services to small business owners:

Certified Public Accountant (CPA). To sit for the Uniform CPA Examination, a candidate must have a degree from an accredited college or university. Upon completion of the CPA exam, candidates must complete at least two years of work experience before receiving a license to practice.

Accounting Practitioner (AP). To become an AP, a person must either have a baccalaureate degree from an accredited college or university with a major in accounting or pass the practice and theory parts of the CPA exam. No accounting experience is required. APs may not express an opinion on financial statements; however, they can prepare income tax returns and do bookkeeping work.

Accountants, who are usually hired on a retainer basis, should be fully utilized, but their time should not be wasted by owners who refuse to do any of their own record keeping. As with attorneys, small business owners can get the most from their accountants by doing the following: Knowing what assistance and advice an accountant can provide; explaining exactly what is expected from the accountant; keeping good records and avoiding fees by not using the accountant to do routine work, such as accumulating data; and keeping the accountant informed of changes and new directions.

Accountant Services

The services accountants provide correspond to the stage of development the small business is in (see Exhibit 11-2) and the resources available to the owners. For example, in the pre-start-up phase, accountants can help prepare a business plan and develop a credible loan package (for a more extensive list of services accountants can provide at start-up see Appendix 11-1). Later, they can develop reporting and control systems, prepare tax returns, and do estate planning.

More specifically, accountants can provide the following services to small businesses: prepare tax planning strategies; review a company's accounting system with recommendations for improvement; help set up internal control systems; assist with the design and installation of data processing and management information systems; make suggestions for cash management; make evaluations for risk management (insurance); do valuations of closely held businesses; design compensation and benefit plans; develop plans for family business ownership succession; make recommendations on mergers and acquisitions; and assist in ensuring compliance with government regulations.

Selecting Accountants

When selecting an accountant, owners should solicit recommendations from business acquaintances, lawyers, bankers, and the chamber of commerce. Accountants are listed in telephone directories, and most state societies of CPAs publish directories of practitioners. The qualifications that should be examined before selecting an accountant include the following:

- Reputation in the business community
- Quality and extent of education
- Breadth of small business experience
- Ability to understand the problems of small business owners
- Willingness to devote sufficient time to the business
- Ability to communicate clearly
- Other clients served
- Other professionals in his or her network
- Cost of services

OUTSIDE DIRECTORS

Many small business owners are turning to outside directors for advice and counsel. Boards of directors can do for small businesses the same things they

EXHIBIT 11-2 Evolution of a Business

Stage of Development	Key Characteristics	Critical Problems	Areas of Assistance
Pre-start-up	• Developing the business concept. • Deciding to "do it."	• Developing the concept. • Marshalling the resources. • Deciding to "do it."	• Assisting with the business plan. • Obtaining financing.
Existence	• Striving to gain enough customers or to produce enough quality products to be a viable business.	• Producing the product or selling the service. • Husbanding cash.	• Cash control. • "Rent a controller."
Survival	• Making less than "economic returns" on the labor and capital employed in the business. • Marginal cash flow.	• Cash flow. • Making a profit. • Evaluating the market niche.	• Cash control. • "Rent a controller." • Marketing studies.
Success	• At a juncture of remaining comfortably profitable (and perhaps deploying time and resources elsewhere) or marshalling the financial resources to "go for growth."	• Constructive disengagement. • Absentee management. • Tax minimization. • Investments.	• Reporting systems. • Control systems. • Tax and personal financial planning.
Take off	• Expanding the company's geographic coverage, its product lines or both. • Delegating and installing management controls and accountability. • May or may not be public.	• Delegation. • Hiring good people. • Cash for growth. • Management control. • Strategic management. • Strategies for growth.	• Management information systems. • Management control systems. • Strategic planning. • Mergers-acquisitions. • Initial public offering.
Resource mature	• A large corporation with all the resources and problems "appertaining thereto." • Usually a public corporation.	• Keeping the company customer oriented. • Ensuring that the company is innovative rather than ossifying.	• Taxes. • Systems. • Initial public offerings. • Mergers-acquisitions.

SOURCE: Bruce J. Harper and Neil C. Churchill, "Serving Small Business: What CPAs Should Know," *Journal of Accountancy* June 1987, 120–127. Reprinted with permission from the Journal of Accountancy, Copyright 1987 by American Institute of Certified Public Accountants, Inc. Opinions of the authors are their own and do not necessarily reflect policies of the AICPA.

do for large corporations, and they can can be a source of unbiased information for business owners. By being "outsiders," directors can tell a business owner that she or he is doing something wrong without fear of losing their jobs. Outside directors also bring expertise to small companies that is not readily available from its employees. A board of directors also lends a certain amount of prestige and credibility to small businesses.

Statutory Boards of Directors

statutory board
of directors

Companies that are incorporated need a formal **statutory board of directors.** These directors may be company employees, individuals with no relationship to the company, or a combination of both. The duties and responsibilities of board members are set forth in the corporation's bylaws, and the power and authority of the board of directors is delegated to management (see Exhibit 11-3). Men and women who serve as corporate directors are elected by the shareholders and are paid for their services. However, many people are reluctant to be corporate directors because of the legal problems they face while discharging their duties. For example, a survey of board members conducted by the National Association of Corporate Directors revealed the following facts:

- 85 percent believe that being named in a lawsuit related to service on a board of directors is more probable now than it was in the past.
- 46 percent served on boards of corporations where directors or officers have been sued.
- 93 percent recommended federal or state legislation establishing a cap on the liability of independent outside directors.
- 61 percent do not believe certification of directors would minimize the number of lawsuits brought against directors.
- 48 percent knew people who had refused a directorship offer because director and officer (D&O) insurance was not provided by the company.

EXHIBIT 11-3 Delegation of Board Authority

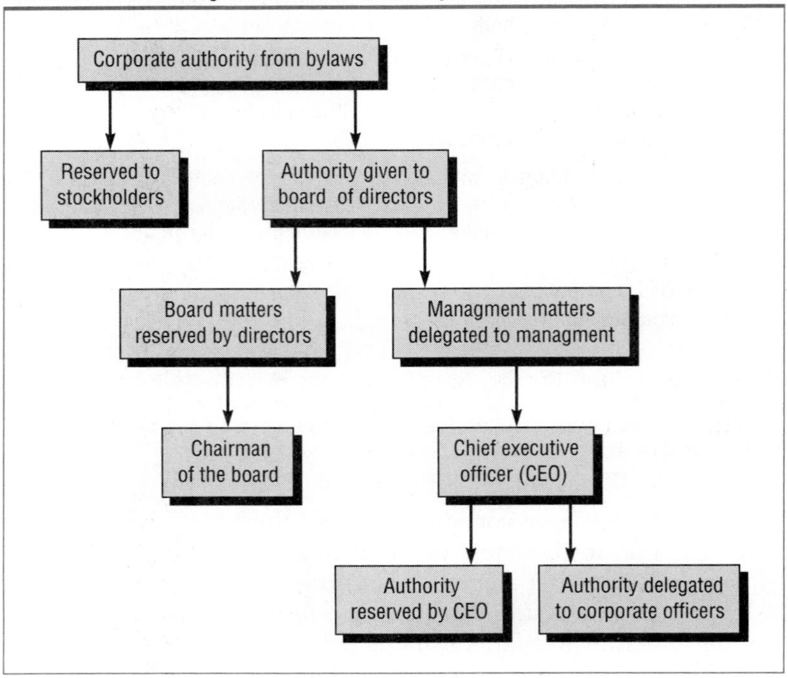

· 24 percent indicated willingness to serve as a director of a corporation that did not carry D&O insurance.[13]

The reluctance of many qualified people to serve on corporate boards and the fact that most small businesses are not corporations leaves many small firms without a statutory board of directors. Nevertheless, small businesses, even those that are partnerships or proprietorships, can establish advisory boards, which do not have the same power and authority as statutory boards.

Advisory Boards

advisory board

An **advisory board** is a group of outsiders who advise small business owners but do not have the legal right to depose management. Advisors supplement the expertise of company staff and perform a vital intelligence-gathering function for the owner. Advisors can also provide introductions to potential customers, suppliers, or clients and keep abreast of political, social, and technical developments in industry or government. More specifically, the role of an advisor is

1. To comment on the reasonableness and propriety of a proposed company decision.
2. To identify and analyze alternative courses of action not readily apparent to management.
3. To confirm or verify important factual data relating to a specific proposition, project, or policy request.
4. To provide independent assistance in the development of long-term goals and strategies.
5. To objectively evaluate the performance of the business owner and key managers.
6. To provide expertise and experience not available internally.
7. To watch for conflict of interest (real or perceived overtones of a proposed activity or transaction).
8. To provide a mechanism for monitoring the external environment.[14]

SELECTING ADVISORS. Business owners should choose advisors they can trust and with whom they can be comfortable, but with whom they will not necessarily always be in agreement. Advisors could include any of the following: a professional manager with broad business experience; a person with the integrity and courage to make decisions based on fact and need; a person who can add to the stature of the company; someone who has convictions and can stand up for them; a person whose knowledge and experience bring to the board the most current thinking; or someone who can be objective when dealing with principles, procedures, and practices—a person as free of conflicting loyalties as possible.

ADVISORY BOARD COMPOSITION. The most efficient advisory boards are those composed of true outsiders—those people who have nothing to lose if they disagree with the owner. People such as bankers, suppliers, customers, accountants, insurance agents, and attorneys (retained by the company) should not be advisors because they have a vested interest in the company. Instead, owners should seek the advice of prominent corporate executives, attorneys (not affiliated with the company), professionals, and other experts with no formal ties to the business.

BOARD GROUND RULES. To function efficiently and provide owners with meaningful advice, advisory boards need guidelines or ground rules to follow. The following ground rules can keep boards functioning efficiently:

- No advisory board member shall misuse the position for personal profit. And advisors must disclose any personal interests that could jeopardize their objectivity or cause personal conflict.
- No advisory board member shall serve concurrently on the board of a competing firm.
- Board members must attend meetings regularly and provide input by taking an active part in discussions, analyses, and proposals.
- Members shall be kept informed of all actions requiring their input. Any information from questionable sources must be verified.
- Board members shall inform the company of any business opportunities made available by their positions before pursuing the opportunities.
- All information received by the board members must be held in strictest confidence.[15]

These ground rules can be formalized in a written contract signed by advisors and the company owner. Contracts include information about how often advisors meet, where they meet, how much they are paid for each meeting, how long their term is, and so on.

LOSING ADVISORS. The maxim "Use it or lose it" applies to advisory boards. Business owners who create an advisory board primarily for show should not expect to attract capable advisors. The following are some of the reasons why advisors resign: they are not given timely information to meet their obligations; they are ignored and treated as "rubber stamps" for the owner's actions; meetings are dull, uninteresting, and unchallenging; they disagree with the owner too often; they have ethical conflicts with company operations; and owners do not act on their advice.

Entrepreneur Boards

entrepreneur boards

Some business owners are unable to establish advisory boards for their companies; however, they do not have to operate without any outside advice. Many small business owners are banding together in self-help groups, or **entrepreneur boards,** to talk out their problems. For example, Allen Fishman established The Alternative Board (TAB) in Aspen, Colorado, to assist small business owners. His company sets up advisory boards of about a dozen chief executives, usually owners of small, noncompeting companies. They meet one morning a month with a paid "facilitator" to discuss topics of mutual interest. Another provider of advisory-board services, The Executive Committee (TEC), has seen membership double in the last five years to 2,000 in the United States and hundreds more in other countries. Members pay $6,400 a year for monthly all-day sessions.[16]

CONSULTANTS

Nearly every small business needs the services of consultants at some point in their development. Consultants provide advice in areas such as general management, manufacturing, personnel, marketing, purchasing, and so forth. Consultants may be hired for one day or for several weeks or more, and they can end up being hired as permanent employees of the company they are advising. Business owners can turn to any of the following types of firms for consulting services: national general management firms such as McKinsey and Company; large accounting firms with consulting divisions; functionally specialized firms; industry-specific companies; local firms; and solo practitioners.

Need for Consultants

Some business owners overuse consultants whereas others do not hire them when needed. In his book *How to Make it Big as a Consultant*,[17] Willian Cohen suggests the following times when business owners might need consultants:

The Need for Personnel. As companies grow, they may not have enough employees with the needed skills to operate the business. Consultants can fill in temporarily, or they can locate people who can permanently fill the position.

The Need for Fresh Ideas. Sometimes a business has a problem, and management feels the employees are too close to it to be objective. Consultants can provide the necessary objectivity and detachment.

Company Politics. Sometimes the solution to a problem may actually be known, but for various political reasons it cannot be presented by those who understand the problem. For example, a longtime employee's poor performance might be cause for termination, but the owner cannot bear the discomfort of firing the person. A consultant, with no emotional ties to the business, can recommend terminating the employee.

The Need for Improved Sales. Small business owners may not be able to devise creative methods of increasing their company's sales. Consultants who specialize in marketing can use their experience with other clients to boost sales and increase profits.

The Need for Capital. Most companies need start-up capital, growth capital, and capital for a host of other reasons. Many small business owners turn to financial consultants to help them meet their capital requirements.

Government Regulations. Small business owners often complain that they "work for the government." The federal, state, and local rules and regulations that must be complied with are numerous and sometimes onerous.

Often, owners are unaware of or do not understand some of the regulations. Consultants with expertise in consumer credit, safety standards, equal employment opportunity, and so on can be very helpful to small businesses.

The Need for Maximum Efficiency. Small businesses that do not operate as efficiently as possible are likely to lose business to those that do. Consultants can observe internal operations and suggest ways to eliminate waste and improve overall efficiency.

The Need to Diagnose Problems and Find Solutions. Business owners who cannot separate their personal lives from their business lives often become so involved with the business that they are unable to identify and deal with problems. Disinterested consultants who have no personal attachment to a company are better able to discover and solve problems that could be costly to a small business.

The Need to Train Employees. As companies grow, owners usually find that they do not have the skills or the time to attend to all aspects of their business. One aspect of the business, employee training and development, is vital and can be performed best by consultants who are training and development experts.

The Need for a Complete Turnaround. There are times when problems become so serious that a business is in imminent danger of failing. When that happens, bankers, investors, or others with a vested interest in the company will call in a consultant who is a "workout specialist" to make the business healthy again.

There are, of course, other indicators of the need for a consultant. James E. Suatko, senior editor of *Small Business Reports*, has identified the following situations that signal the need for assistance from an outside consultant:

- Lack of a written business plan
- Unexplained low morale
- Steady, constant increases in cost
- Regular cash shortages
- Chronic delays or late deliveries of products
- Loss of market position
- Overworked staff
- Excessive rework without achieving objectives
- Continual supply deficiencies
- Lack of information about the competition or market[18]

Selecting Consultants

Recognizing the need for a consultant might be easier than selecting the best qualified consultant. When selecting a consultant, owners should use the same process they used to select an attorney and an accountant. They should ask business associates for recommendations of qualified consultants, and they should solicit recommendations from bankers, attorneys, professional associations, and so forth. Owners should look for consultants who have the ability to diagnose and solve problems, technical expertise, good communication skills, and above-average marketing and management skills.

Successful Consultant-Client Engagements

Business owners often feel that they did not receive their "money's worth" from consultants they hired to solve problems. The consultant did not tell them anything they did not know or told them what to do but not how to do it. Jeffrey Lant, a consultant based in Cambridge, Massachusetts, suggests the following guidelines to insure successful consulting relationships:

Agree on the Problem. The owner and the consultant should agree on the problem or problems that are to be solved. This can be done by both owner and consultant putting down, clearly and in writing, precisely what problem or problems exist. The key words here are *clearly* and *in writing*.

Agree on the Objective. After agreeing on the problem, the owner and the consultant need similar agreement on the objective to be accomplished. The objective is usually a precise outcome to be accomplished by a given time. The owner may want to have a short contract drawn up that stipulates what is to be accomplished, by what date, and at what cost.

Agree on the Method. When the objectives have been identified, the owner needs to know what methods the consultant will employ to achieve them. Methods should be specific and spelled out in the very beginning.

Agree on the Necessary Resources. To achieve objectives, the owner needs to commit relatively scarce resources such as personnel, money, and time to the agreed-upon process. A list should be created that describes resources needed, who will provide them, and when they will be needed. This list will keep the owner and the consultant aware of what is needed to complete the project.

Agree on the Date. Both parties in a consulting relationship should agree on the date by which a project is to be completed. If there is disagreement on the completion date, an owner may be able to speed up the process by committing more resources to the project.

Commit to Working with the Consultant. What makes a consulting relationship work is for the owner to be committed both to achieving the objective and to working with the consultant to do what is necessary to achieve the objective. Assigning another person to work with the consultant may doom the project to failure.

Hold Regular Meetings with the Consultant. Regular, structured meetings between owner and consultant are vital. These meetings should have an agenda, include a progress report, be recorded, and conclude with a list of tasks to be completed before the next meeting.

Have Regular Progress Checks. The owner needs to regularly ask the consultant for a review of how individual tasks are coming along and how things in general are developing.

Develop a Thick Skin. Some of the information provided by consultants is not what owners want to hear. However, if owners give the impression that favorable information is all they want to hear, their consultants will withhold vital but negative findings. Owners should encourage the consultant to tell the truth, the whole truth, and nothing but the truth.

Find Out What Happened—and Why. Each consulting relationship should end with a formal exit interview and a final summary report. The report should be divided into two parts: what went right—and why—and what went wrong—and why.[19]

UNIONS

In the previous sections we have discussed ways small business owners could locate and select outsiders with skills needed by the business. In this section we will discuss how owners can avoid unwanted outsiders, namely unions. Small businesses have historically been unattractive to unions; however, with fewer workers in large corporations choosing union membership, union organizers have turned their attention to smaller businesses. For example, for twenty years Jerry Goldstein operated a quiet business. His Jerry's Artarama, a discount art supplier, was run like most small businesses—as its owner saw fit. Then the Teamsters struck. A three-week strike by Local 810 brought Goldstein to the bargaining table, but during that time his warehouse locks were filled with glue and his truck was vandalized. His thirty employees won a first-year pay hike of 65 cents an hour and his business suffered its first loss ever.[20]

The Unionizing Process

The unionizing process is quite standardized and occurs in the following manner: First, employees may contact a union to represent them, or a union may take the initiative and contact small business employees who might be sympathetic to the union's cause; second, the union tries to get a minimum of 30 percent of eligible employees to sign a petition so it can ask the **National Labor Relations Board (NLRB)** to conduct an election; third, if the signatures on the petition are validated, the NLRB supervises an election usually within ninety days; and, finally, if a simple majority of those employees voting vote for the union, it becomes the certified bargaining agent for that business. During this process, owners should do whatever they legally can to convince their employees to reject the union.

National Labor Relations Board (NLRB)

Staying Union Free

To successfully combat a union, owners should first put an end to the following union myths:

- The union can guarantee better wages.
- The company must sign a contract if the union wins.
- The union can guarantee present benefits.

- The union can make the company remove unpopular managers.
- The union can guarantee job security.
- The union will protect jobs.
- The company will eliminate benefits if the union loses.

WHAT OWNERS CAN DO. In an effort to remain union free, business owners can do or say the following: stress that employees do not need to belong to a union to have company benefits; emphasize the benefits employees already enjoy; point out how expensive union membership could be (dues, fines, etc.); explain that union members cannot deal directly with management; ask employees not to sign authorization cards; make it clear to employees that they are not obligated to vote for a union; let employees know how difficult it is to eliminate (decertify) a union; and assure employees that the company will not be closed down if the union wins its campaign.

WHAT OWNERS CANNOT DO. Some of the things owners might like to do or say during a campaign are illegal. Owners should avoid doing or saying the following: employees cannot be asked to divulge their feelings about the union; owners cannot imply that employees will lose their jobs if the union wins its campaign; owners cannot attend, or have their agents attend, union meetings or other functions; owners cannot call or visit employees' homes to discuss the union campaign; employees who favor the union cannot be discriminated against; and all statements made by owners must be true and factual.

SUMMARY

Very few business owners can operate their companies without specialized outside help. The two outsiders that owners should retain first are an attorney and an accountant because these people can provide pre-start-up and start-up advice. An attorney can suggest the form of the business (proprietorship, etc.); secure necessary permits, licenses, leases, and so forth; and generally keep owners from making legal errors. Accountants can also advise on the most appropriate form of business ownership as well as develop satisfactory record keeping and reporting systems.

Also in the start-up phase, business owners need to carefully select their suppliers. Poor supplier relationships can cause a new business to fail; therefore, owners should solicit recommendations for suppliers from associates, attorneys, bankers, and others whom they trust. Once supplier relationships have been established, owners should periodically monitor their suppliers' performance and replace those suppliers who are performing below par.

Business owners can benefit from the advice of those not directly involved in the day-to-day operations of the company. An advisory board composed of other managers, bankers, attorneys, and others with needed skills can help owners with present business problems and develop strategies for the future. Consultants with specialized skills can also be retained to assist owners with specific problems or opportunities. Finally, owners need to be able to keep unwanted outsiders away from their companies. Union organizers are paying more attention to small businesses than they did in the past, and they are using more sophisticated organizing tactics. Business owners need to know how to keep their companies union free.

QUESTIONS FOR REVIEW AND DISCUSSION

1. How would you locate satisfactory suppliers for a new business?
2. What factors would you consider when selecting suppliers?
3. How can you evaluate supplier performance?
4. What are the advantages and disadvantages of using a large law firm?
5. What are the different methods of paying attorneys for their service?
6. What services can accountants provide small businesses?
7. What is the difference between a statutory board of directors and an advisory board of directors?
8. What functions can an advisory board perform for a small business?
9. In what situations could a business owner use the services of consultants?
10. How can small business owners keep their companies union free?

KEY TERMS

advisory board	Martindale-Hubbell Law Directory
alternative dispute resolution (ADR) techniques	National Labor Relations Board (NLRB)
billable hours	preventive law
contingency fee	reciprocal buying
entrepreneur boards	reserve capacity
expediting	statutory board of directors

CASE
Conflicting Advice

Eric Shaw's small manufacturing company, which he started eight years ago when he retired from the army, was becoming quite successful. His products were now being distributed throughout the Southwest, and his revenue was approaching $8 million per year. The sixty-two men and women employed by Shaw Manufacturing worked hard, were paid well, and were nonunionized. There was a family atmosphere in the factory because Eric believed that employees and management should be treated well, and that management should not feel superior to the workers.

When Eric decided to start his company, he retained an attorney with small business experience and a local accounting firm. His attorney and accountant recommended that the business be a proprietorship, and they offered other advice and assistance necessary to establish Shaw Manufacturing. Because the company was owned by Eric and his wife, Eric saw no need to have a board of directors. However, as the company began to grow, Eric decided that an advisory board might be useful and prestigious. Six men and two women were selected to be advisors to Shaw Manufacturing's president and management.

At their first formal meeting the advisors made the following recommendations: the company should become an S corporation; the stock should be owned by Eric and his family; two new managers should be hired to strengthen the management team; a profit-sharing plan should be developed for managers; employee rela-

tions should be more formal (the board felt that the prevailing family atmosphere caused workers to be unproductive); and the company should retain a larger law firm and a national accounting firm. Eric's attorney and accountant disagreed with all the board's recommendations, especially the last one. Eric needs to decide whose advice he will accept and what the reactions of the "losing" side will be.

QUESTIONS
1. Should Eric Shaw have created an advisory board for his company?

2. If you were in Eric's place, would you accept the recommendations of the board or the attorney and accountant?

3. Is there a "diplomatic" way to handle this situation?

ACTIVITIES

1. Assume you are going to start a business and search all available sources for the "best" attorney and accountant for your company. Explain how you would make your selection.

2. Interview the owner of a company that has a board of directors and ask him or her about the company's directors.

Questions about the Board of Directors

	Yes	No
1. Does the chairperson have a job description?	—	—
2. Does the chairperson perform his or her job well?	—	—
3. Do the directors review company objectives?	—	—
4. Do directors monitor the company's performance?	—	—
5. Do directors approve the operating budget?	—	—
6. Are most board members insiders?	—	—
7. Is there a formal compensation plan for directors?	—	—
8. Do directors attend meetings regularly?	—	—

9. Have performance standards been established for the business owner? ___ ___

10. Is there an established procedure for recruiting and compensating directors? ___ ___

11. Is there an accepted method for identifying acceptable board members? ___ ___

12. Are company bylaws specific and understood by all board members? ___ ___

13. Do board members advise the owner on all important matters? ___ ___

14. If so, does the owner usually accept the board's advice? ___ ___

15. Do board members approve employee pay and benefit programs? ___ ___

16. Do board members have liability insurance? ___ ___

17. Is there a mandatory retirement age for directors? ___ ___

18. Is there a method for removing noncontributing directors? ___ ___

19. Is there a mechanism for resolving conflicts between directors and the owner? ___ ___

20. Do you intend to keep your board of directors? ___ ___

APPENDIX 11-1

Checklist of Procedures for Start-up Business Planning Engagements

Company Name _____

Staff Assigned to Project _____ Date Completed _____

Procedure   Completed by (or N/A)

1. Conduct a pre-engagement meeting with the client:
   - Determine the nature and scope of the engagement, e.g., the nature of the product or service and proposed operations, whether the engagement will include other planning services, etc. _____

- Determine if the engagement will include preparation of prospective financial presentations and whether they will be intended for internal use vs. third-party use. _____

2. If this is a new client, determine that existing firm policies regarding accepting a new client have been followed. _____

3. Prepare a time estimate for the engagement. _____

4. Establish an understanding with the client regarding the nature, scope, and limitations of the services to be performed and the estimated fees in an engagement letter. Modify the letter as appropriate if preparation of prospective financial information will be included in the engagement plan. _____

5. Evaluate the client's plans and prospective information related to the following matters and consider whether they provide indications that the venture is not likely to succeed:
   - Forecasted revenue, _____
   - Marketing plans, _____
   - Forecasted costs, _____
   - Forecasted profit or loss, and break-even point if a loss is indicated, _____
   - Forecasted capital requirements, financing needs, and related costs, and _____
   - First-year cash flow. _____

6. If the analysis in Step 5 suggests that the venture is not likely to succeed, discuss the matter with the client and consider whether revised assumptions, additional information, or additional analysis is warranted; and whether to terminate the engagement. _____

7. If your analysis does not raise doubts about failure in the first year, obtain or prepare a forecast of operations and cash flow for an additional two to three years and consider whether it suggests failure during that period. If so, discuss the matter with the client and consider terminating the engagement. If it appears that the venture is worth pursuing, perform the remaining program steps to assist the client in setting up the business. _____

8. Evaluate whether the client has considered the following options relating to setting up the new business operations: (Answer Yes, No, or N/A in the "Completed by" column.)
   - Has the client considered purchasing an existing business rather than starting one? _____

- Has the client considered acquiring a franchise rather than starting a new business?   _____
- Has the client considered the various advantages and disadvantages of the following forms of legal entity: (1) sole proprietorship, (2) partnership, (3) C corporation, (4) S corporation.   _____

9. Determine whether the following administrative steps are made and information recorded by the client: (Answer Yes, No, or N/A in the "Completed by" column.)

- Has the client's site selection process included consideration of the following factors:
  Location with regard to the market?   _____
  Physical suitability of the site?   _____
  Lease or buy benefits?   _____
  If lease, type and cost of lease?   _____
  Provision for future expansion?   _____
  Long-term quality of the site?   _____
  Adequacy of utilities?   _____
  Parking facilities?   _____
  Availability of transportation?   _____
  Traffic flow   _____
  Tax burden?   _____
  Fire and police protection?   _____
- Has a certificate of occupancy been obtained?   _____
- Are any special permits necessary due to local ordinance or the nature of the business?   _____
- Will the client be in compliance with zoning regulations?   _____
- Will the client be in compliance with OSHA regulations?   _____
- Have security services or security techniques, e.g., alarms, been considered?   _____
- Have janitorial and maintenance services been considered?   _____

10. Determine whether the client has evaluated the need for the following various types of insurance coverage: (Answer Yes, No, or N/A in the "Completed by" column.)

- Worker's compensation,   _____
- General liability,   _____
- Product liability,   _____
- Malpractice,   _____
- Fire,   _____
- Business interruption,   _____
- Crime,   _____
- Burglary,   _____
- Glass breakage,   _____
- Contents,   _____

- Sprinkler damage, _____
- Key man, _____
- Money and securities, _____
- Fidelity and _____
- Employee benefits (life, health, disability). _____

11. Determine whether the client has considered staffing needs, including the minimum number and types of personnel to operate the business, the availability and capability of the owner or family members, or the need to hire outside employees. If appropriate, recommend that the client use the services of an employment agency, attorney specializing in labor matters, etc. _____

12. Determine whether the client has considered minimum recordkeeping requirements, including accounting records for the following areas:
- Sales and receivables, _____
- Purchases and payables, _____
- Cash receipts and disbursements and _____
- Payroll. _____

13. Determine whether the client has planned minimum procedures for safeguarding assets, e.g., a bank account and measures to protect physical equipment and inventory. _____

14. If additional business planning services are being provided as part of the engagement, be sure firm procedures for those services are followed. _____

15. Document the work performed. The level of documentation should be based on the complexity and duration of the engagement and firm policies. _____

16. Conduct progress meetings with the client at appropriate intervals during the engagement to discuss the status of the engagement, any problems encountered, etc. _____

17. Communicate the results of the business start-up engagement to the client, in a written report or closing letter, if appropriate. If prospective financial information is included, consider the reporting standards for such information. _____

18. Review the engagement workpapers and the draft of the report, if any, in accordance with firm review policies. _____

19. Comments: (This section may be used to document problems that were encountered or to bring unusual matters to the attention of the in-charge consultant or engagement partner.)

SOURCE: William J. Gole and Dennis R. Meals, ''How to Assist Start-up Businesses: The Basics,'' *The Practical Accountant*, November 1987, 112–126. Used by permission. Reprinted with permission from *The Practical Accountant*. Copyright 1987 Research Institute of America, Inc.

PART FOUR

MARKETING PRODUCTS AND SERVICES

12 MARKETING FUNDAMENTALS

LEARNING OBJECTIVES

After you have read this chapter, you will be able to do the following:
- Explain marketing's Four Ps
- Understand the importance of marketing research
- Determine appropriate channels of distribution
- Explain why packaging is a valuable marketing tool
- Understand the functions of packaging
- Decide which pricing strategies to use in given situations

N early every successful small business is market driven, which means that its owner is aware of the importance of marketing—packaging, pricing, and promoting. Products and services do not sell themselves. Someone has to create a needed product or service and then make sure that the customers know about that product and service. Someone also has to make sure that the product or service is priced competitively and distributed effectively. Finally, companies must create a need for their products, and they should provide customers with service after the sale.

Market-driven companies have proved Ralph Waldo Emerson's statement "If a man can write a better book, preach a better sermon, or make a better mousetrap than his neighbor, though he builds his house in the woods the world will make a beaten path to his door" to be inaccurate. Many potentially useful products have not been commercially successful because they were marketed poorly. Small business owners who follow the basics of effective marketing should have no problem selling their products.

In this chapter we will examine some basic marketing fundamentals. We will introduce the Four Ps and discuss three of them (the other P, Promotion, will be discussed in the following chapter). We will also present reasons for continuing to do market research, and we will see why selecting the correct channels of distribution is so important to the successful selling of products and services. Finally, we will discuss the importance of packaging and pricing to the overall marketing effort.

THE FOUR PS

Four Ps

Almost all marketing can be explained by the **Four Ps**—Product, Place, Price, and Promotion. Once a business owner has attended to these Ps, his or her marketing plan should be fairly well developed. We will briefly discuss the Ps here, saving more complete discussion for later.

Product

product

Most successful businesses are built around an innovative **product** (product and service are used interchangeably). However, not everyone can create new products, so successful businesses can also be created around modified products or products that now have a new use. Products sold should have built-in quality and should provide users with desired benefits. Customers need to receive value from the products they purchase if they are to become loyal, long-term patrons. Finally, manufacturers, wholesalers, and retailers should stand behind their products so customers can buy them with confidence.

Place

place

Place, sometimes referred to as channels of distribution, explains how products are conveyed to customers. In general, products are produced by manufacturers who sell them to wholesalers who, in turn, sell them to retailers who eventually sell them to consumers. There are some other arrangements which we will discuss later.

Price

price

Failing to accurately **price** a product can lead to the failure of a small business. If a product's price is too high, customers will not buy, and if it is too low, customers will buy in great quantities but the selling price will not cover the product's cost. In either case, the business will soon be unable to compete and will have to be sold. We will spend more time examining pricing strategies later in this chapter.

Promotion

promotion

Many people believe that **promotion** and advertising are the key to a company's success. Before start-up, small business owners should advertise the company's impending opening so consumers will know to look for the new business. Once open, the firm's advertising should be consistent enough to attract customers and make them regulars. All phases of promotion will be discussed more completely in the next chapter.

MARKETING RESEARCH

As we mentioned in Chapter 3, accurate marketing research is vital to the success of a new business. The same is true for operating companies whose owners want the business to continue to be successful and expand. Marketing research for the existing business deals with the following: products, competitors, sales, consumers, and promotion.

Mr. Coffee's Ice Tea Maker. In order to remain successful, most companies must introduce new or improved products.

Product Research

This is research done to create new products or improve old products. Very few companies can continue to be successful if they do not introduce new or improved products that meet consumer needs. This research should be done in conjunction with consumer research so that only needed products are created or added to the firm's product line. Very often, new products are variations of the ones that made the company successful (see The Way It Is 12-1).

The Way It Is

12-1 THE PEACE POP

Ben Cohen and Jerry Greenfield, the founders of Ben and Jerry's Home-made Inc., needed a new product to keep their extremely successful ice-cream business growing. They created the Peace Pop, an ice-cream bar on a stick that would compete in supermarket freezers against the likes of Dove Bars and Jell-O Pudding Pops. Aside from providing sorely needed diversification, the Peace Pop would be used to build awareness and raise funds for a movement called "1% for peace" cofounded by Ben and Jerry.[1]

Competitor Research

Any small business owner who is not aware of what the competition is doing is likely to lose business to those competitors. An analysis of competitors serves the following purposes:

1. **Holding market share.** Competitors are continually trying to lure away customers. How will they do it? Are their products superior? Are their products cheaper or marketed better? What is the competition doing differently that makes them successful?

2. **Increasing market share.** How can a business attract customers away from another business? Where are competitors vulnerable? What tactics will convince customers to switch to another firm?

3. **Preparing for contingencies.** Knowing what competitors are doing or planning allows a business owner to make plans or create strategies that will negate any competitive advantages.[2]

Sales Research

Sales research deals with the selling activities of the firm such as how the product is sold, how effective the sales force is, and whether sales are increasing or decreasing. Sales research also identifies the best place to sell a product. Selecting the wrong place to sell products can be disastrous (see The Way It Is 12-2, which is about the previously mentioned Peace Pops).

Consumer Research

Companies need to know who their customers are, where they live, where they shop, what they like, and how they choose the products they buy. Consumer research provides this kind of important information. Companies that cannot do their own research can hire consultants or other firms to

---

The Way It Is

12-2 WHERE TO SELL PEACE POPS?

After Ben and Jerry created their Peace Pop, they rushed the product to supermarkets and watched it languish. The company's low-budget, low-key, grassroots marketing strategy was no match for the marketing blitzes of competitors. Six months later Peace Pop sales were just 50 percent of projections. In studying the poor returns, however, Ben and Jerry's marketing people noticed one bright spot: the Peace Pop was doing well at local delis. They concluded that the product was really an impulse buy. Today, after months of fine-tuning, 70 percent of Peace Pops end up in convenience stores, and sales have increased 60 percent. And the lesson? "We learned that a product doesn't sell just because you're trying to do good in the world," says Greenfield. "You still have to have a healthy distribution, a good marketing strategy, and price the product properly."[3]

conduct the research for them. For example, Allen Kelson, a former publisher and food reviewer, formed Customer Satisfaction Systems Inc. to do customer surveys for Chicago restaurants. He charges clients up to $3,800 for individual restaurants and as little as $1,000 an establishment for large restaurant concerns. Most restaurant owners who hire Kelson's company are pleased with the changes made as a result of customer surveys.[4]

Promotion Research

Promotion research provides information about the most effective promotion strategies, what advertising appeals to customers, and what media is most cost effective. We will discuss promotion more completely in Chapter 13.

PRODUCTS

The product is where it all comes together. It is the culmination of the efforts of many creative individuals, and it is what makes the company. Products have a fairly predictable life cycle (see Exhibit 12-1), and when demand for these products begins to decline, they should be replaced or modified. In some instances it is possible to create companies to provide existing products in new and creative ways (see The Way It Is 12-3). At other times, companies need to create new products to continue to grow.

Product Development

New products are usually not just "discovered"; rather, they are the outcome of an orderly development process, which includes the following steps:

- Research to determine needs and wants
- Search for new or improved products

EXHIBIT 12-1 Product Life Cycle

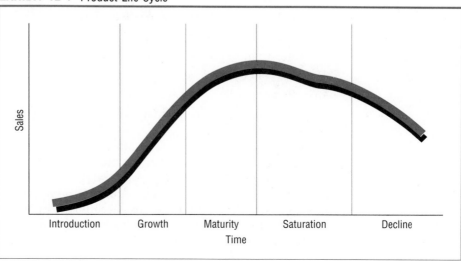

12-3 SELLING CREDIT CARD INSURANCE

Peter Halmos worked on Wall Street for five years before realizing he did not want to work for someone else. "I knew I wanted to do something on my own. But since I didn't have any money and didn't know how to get any, it had to be something simple to start." What Halmos did was create SafeCard, a company that records customers' credit card numbers for a $15 annual fee. If the cards are lost or stolen, clients make one call on the Hot Line to the company. Then SafeCard employees notify all of the client's credit card companies of the loss or theft. SafeCard was the first company to offer this service to the public. What did Halmos really do? He did not create a new concept. He took a proven idea—insurance—and applied it to a new area.[5]

- Analysis of potential profit for proposed product
- Feasibility testing of proposed product
- Development of product
- Market testing
- Mass production

Even firms that follow the above process create far more failures than successes. A few reasons for product failure include the following:

- Inaccurate market research
- Market potential was overestimated
- Product introduced at the wrong time
- Selected the wrong channel of distribution
- Inadequate advertising
- Stronger than expected competitor reaction
- Product was overpriced
- Insufficient service after purchase
- No need or desire for product
- Low quality and poor work

Developing a Creative Environment

The people charged with creating or modifying products need to be creative, resourceful, flexible, and original. Finding creative people is often quite difficult, especially for small businesses. Creativity can be stimulated by providing an environment that encourages it. The following are some of the ways to encourage creativity:

- Allow freedom for people to guide their own work.
- State that innovation is expected because it rarely happens spontaneously.
- Create an open, interactive climate in which people can stimulate greater awareness, excitement, and ideas in each other.
- Recognize individual differences.
- Realize that there is no single managerial style appropriate to and effective with all individuals.
- Promote responsible individuality in employees.
- Provide work that stimulates a feeling of personal and professional growth.
- Allow enough time for ideas to develop and mature.
- Actively recruit and reward those with special creative talents.
- Allow free play and encourage openness.
- Allow for errors or mistakes by not punishing them.
- Provide a safe atmosphere for failures.[6]

Stifling Creativity

We have mentioned some of the ways business owners can encourage creativity. Now let us look at some of the often-heard statements that can kill creative ideas. The following statements can quickly put an end to creativity:

- "Management would never buy it."
- "That's much too radical."
- "Be practical."
- "Probably costs too much."
- "You've got to be kidding."
- "Have you really thought that through?"
- "We need to follow the rules."
- "That's just your opinion."
- "Why stick our necks out?"
- "It's too much trouble."
- "We don't do that around here."
- "We tried it once, and it didn't work."
- "Where is the research to back it up?"[7]

Even when these statements are avoided and creativity is encouraged, it is not always possible to develop new or improved products within a company. When products cannot be created in-house, owners should look to other sources for ideas or products.

Sources for New Products

Sometimes business owners must look to other sources for new products or improvements of existing products. New products can come from many different sources, such as other companies (they should not be copied exactly), foreign companies (in some cases they can be copied if not patented in the United States), inventors or other manufacturers who do not want to produce them, government agencies, licensing brokers, or trade shows.

Whether products are developed in-house or acquired from some other source, they will be failures if a company cannot convince customers to buy them. Many products that business owners expected to be money-makers turned out to be losers because there was no way to effectively market them (see The Way It Is 12-4). All marketing people know that there is very little possibility of selling a product if the need or desire for it does not exist.

Classification of Products

Classifying products makes it easier to determine how to sell them, where to sell them, and to whom to sell them. The following are five basic categories of products:

convenience
goods

Convenience goods. Convenience goods such as cigarettes are needed by customers who are unwilling to spend much time shopping for them. Customers are normally brand-loyal (they always buy the same brand), but they are usually unable to distinguish their chosen brand from others.

shopping
goods

Shopping goods. People are willing to look for and evaluate **shopping goods.** These products, such as clothing, are compared with similar products for price and quality by customers who base their selection on perceived value.

speciality
goods

Speciality goods. Customers seek out **speciality goods,** which they usually buy from their favorite store.

12-4 A GOOD IDEA IS NOT ENOUGH

Marketers of unprecedented products rarely wonder why nobody developed a similar product before. If they did wonder, they would probably conclude that they have come up with a solution for which there is no real problem. A good product is not enough. Someone needs to pay for the product. Which means you have to have a way to market the product. That is not always an easy task. Ask yourself whether you could: convince the world to eat tuna hot dogs or market a chain of clinics that could tell people if they are really coming down with Alzheimer's disease. Talented people have created tuna hot dogs and Alzheimer-detection clinics, but they have had no success marketing them. Apparently the products were created before customers perceived a need for them.[8]

unsought
goods

Unsought goods. Unsought goods are products that customers do not even realize they want, thereby making it very difficult to promote and sell these types of goods. Life insurance and cemetery plots are examples of unsought goods.

new products

New products. New products that have recently been created are unknown to customers and need much promotion to sell them to often skeptical buyers.

PLACE

Another major marketing decision concerns channels of distribution. What is the best way to get products to customers at the least cost? Standard channels of distribution see manufacturers produce goods which they sell to wholesalers who sell them to retailers who finally sell them to customers; however, there are a number of other acceptable ways of getting products to customers. Manufacturers may choose to sell directly to consumers (note the increasing number of "factory" outlets) or they may choose to license a well-known name to let their product sell through a new distribution channel (see The Way It Is 12-5). Another way of bypassing wholesalers and retailers is direct mail or catalog sales. This method of distribution is becoming more popular because of the increasing number of women with full-time jobs.

Channel Choices

Choosing the appropriate channel of distribution is most important for manufacturers because wholesalers and retailers usually have that choice made

The
Way
It Is

12-5 LICENSING PRODUCTS

Gerry Rubin's company, Helen of Troy Corp., sells hair dryers and styling tools to beauty salons. The company was making $6 million a year, but there was no room to grow. The market was flat, competitors strong, and new products hard to come by. "Obviously," says Rubin, "retail was the place for us if we wanted to grow." Getting into retail meant taking shelf space from such giants as General Electric and Gillette, which Rubin estimated would cost at least $25 million in advertising. Because he had nowhere near $25 million, Rubin had to consider other alternatives. Rubin decided to license the Vidal Sassoon name for the products he would sell through retail establishments. Projections (which proved true) showed that first-year sales of Vidal Sassoon products would be greater than Helen of Troy's entire professional line.[9]

for them. The following are some of the distribution options available to manufacturers:

Direct salespeople. Some manufacturers choose to employ their own salespeople who sell only that company's products. These salespeople are paid by the manufacturer, and they report to the company's sales director.

Sales representatives. Known also as manufacturers' agents or representatives, these people are independent sellers. Because they work for themselves, sales representatives usually handle products from many manufacturers. It is often difficult to get representatives to emphasize or "push" a particular manufacturer's product because they concentrate on the most profitable item. The product that provides the highest profit margin is the one to which sales representatives devote the most time and effort.

Distributors. Distributors, unlike manufacturers' representatives, usually purchase the merchandise that they then resell to customers. An adequate inventory is maintained by distributors who want to fill customer orders without waiting for shipments from the manufacturer.

Retailers. Manufacturers may choose to sell their products directly to retail establishments. Retailers then increase the price, advertise the product, and sell it to consumers.

Wholesalers. Most manufacturers sell their products to wholesalers who in turn sell the products in smaller quantities to retailers. Some wholesalers sell directly to consumers, a practice that is illegal in some cases and unethical in most cases. The different kinds of wholesalers include: general merchandise wholesalers, single-line wholesalers, speciality wholesalers, cash-and-carry wholesalers, drop-shippers, mail-order wholesalers, and brokers.

MARKETING STRATEGY

Every small business should have a marketing strategy—where it wants to go and how it will get there. Marketing strategies let business owners know how effective their marketing program is and where improvement is needed. Strategies need not be complex plans that few people understand, but they should be well-thought-out plans that guide the firm's marketing program. Regardless of the length or comprehensiveness of a marketing plan, it should address long-range goals, marketing objectives, products, and the target market.

Long-Range Goals

Long-range goals state in general terms what marketing expectations a company has for the future. Business owners should include in the marketing plan statements about the firm's major markets, products that might be added, and customers to be targeted. Because these are long-range goals, they should be stated in fairly general terms. More specific language should be used for intermediate and short-term objectives.

Marketing Objectives

Marketing objectives are the intermediate (one to three years) and short-term (less than one year) marketing goals of the company. This is the section of the plan where specific, even quantitative, terms are most appropriate. Examples of marketing objectives include the following: introduce a new-flavored toothpaste by the end of the fiscal year; reposition our product so it appeals to children as well as adults; or prepare to enter the West Coast market within the next three years.

This is also the section of the plan where business owners can state their intermediate and short-term sales and profit goals. For example, an owner might state that her or his company should realize a 15 percent increase in sales over last year's figures. Another acceptable short-term goal would be to strive for a 10 percent increase in profits resulting from extra effort from the salespeople.

Products

The marketing plan should also include a comprehensive description of the company's current and potential products. The following are a few of the details that should be included in this section:

- Physical description of the products
- Position of products in their life cycle
- How products differ from competitors' products
- Market for which products are intended
- Features that induce customers to buy product
- Price of products
- User benefits of products
- Possible modifications that could improve products
- Other products that could enhance the product line
- Services provided to buyers of products

Target Market

New companies generally have a fairly narrow target market; however, as they mature, those companies might target broader markets to increase revenues and profits. For example, baby shampoo used to be just for babies, but the decline in the birth rate prompted manufacturers to sell the same product to adults. There were no changes in the product; only the advertising claims were changed to appeal to adults. Although broadening target markets may seem fairly simple, there are instances when it can be nearly fatal to companies (see The Way It Is 12-6).

PACKAGING

Creating distinctive packages can give products an edge over those of competitors. Although nobody believes that exceptional packaging can sell infe-

12-6 NEW TARGET MARKET

Charles E. Harlfinger had taken his company, TW Kutter Inc., from simply distributing blades for meat-processing machinery to actually manufacturing the equipment. Then Harlfinger recognized a new market for his state-of-the-art packaging equipment: applying the technology to wrapping medical devices to keep them sterile. But marketing this new product almost tore his company apart. TW Kutter's existing national sales force was told to call on medical supply companies in addition to the food companies they called on regularly. The salespeople did not speak the same language as their new customers. Harlfinger hired a separate sales force and technical support staff to service equipment in the field. The company was eventually split in two and both companies became profitable but remained separate. "I thought we could just roll the two businesses together and address another industry with very little cost," says Harlfinger. "We ended up having to duplicate our business."[10]

rior products, most people do believe that an attractive package can induce customers to buy products. Packaging is no longer simply for containment of products—it now serves other purposes.

Functions of Packaging

Besides containment and protection, packaging serves the following major functions:

Information. A label provides considerable information about the product in the package. Manufacturers can explain how to use the product, what ingredients constitute the product, remedies for misuse of the product, and warranty information. With all the regulations pertaining to labels, some products such as food and pesticides have very detailed information on them. Try reading the print on a container of weed killer without a magnifying glass.

Identification. Distinctive packages help customers identify products even if they cannot read the label. A classic case of distinctive packages is the Coca-Cola bottle. People all over the world are familiar with the Coca-Cola bottle and can distinguish that drink from all others without reading the label.

Convenience. Customers expect to be able to purchase products in suitable containers. What would happen to beverage sales if customers had to provide their own bottles or other appropriate containers? Why would a family of two need a giant economy-size box of detergent? How would customers' grocery shopping habits change if they had to take their own bags to the store? People simply expect to have the choice of several different size containers of the products they buy.

12-7 DESIGNING PRODUCTS AND PACKAGES

Package designers sometimes complain that their work often begins after a new product is nearly developed. Todd Hansen, a designer in Amston, Connecticut, is no longer surprised by eleventh-hour calls from harried manufacturers. "It's as if they didn't realize they were going to need a package for their products," says Hansen, who helped create the boxes housing Coleco's Cabbage Patch Kids. "Package design is part of the entire process of creating a product. It's not something you add on at the last moment. The consumer doesn't think of the package as a separate entity when he picks up the product but sees it as part of the product itself," says Hansen.[11]

Aesthetics. Attractive packaging can dress up even unexciting but necessary products. Because most laundry powders, paper towels, and dishwashing liquids are quite similar, customers often choose the product they buy for the aesthetic appeal of the package.

Safety. Packages should be constructed of safe material. Flammable or toxic materials should not be used in packaging, and packages should not have sharp corners or rough edges.

Package Development

Good packaging is not accidental, and it should not be an afterthought. When products are in the early development stage, design of the package should also begin. Too many manufacturers wait until the product is ready for market before they think about packaging (see The Way It Is 12-7). Creative packaging can enhance sales and should be given as much consideration as product development itself. Last-minute design can be expensive, and the end product may be unacceptable to consumers.

For product and package development to occur simultaneously, companies should follow a practical packaging development process (see Exhibit 12-2). During the marketing plan phase, a company needs to determine what objectives it expects its new or redesigned package to accomplish. Proposed packages should then be subjected to a careful cost analysis to make sure that the cost is acceptable. In the design step, the package's structural development and graphic design are evaluated. Technical package testing (strength, shelf life, and stackability) precedes consumer testing and distribution reactions, which can be done at the same time. Next, the package should be test marketed before final design based on test results is accepted.

Package Design

As we noted earlier, good packages help sell products. An appealing package is often the factor that causes customers to purchase one product and reject

EXHIBIT 12-2 Packaging Development Process

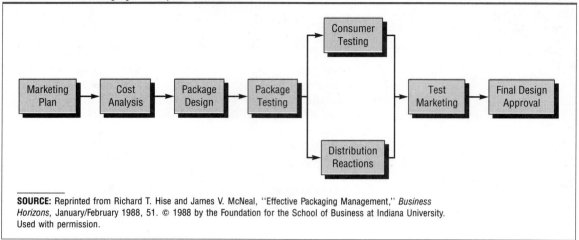

SOURCE: Reprinted from Richard T. Hise and James V. McNeal, "Effective Packaging Management," *Business Horizons*, January/February 1988, 51. © 1988 by the Foundation for the School of Business at Indiana University. Used with permission.

another. Not all package design involves new packages for new products; some design is actually redesign of an old package. In many instances redesigned packages cause a significant increase in sales. The following example shows how a redesigned package increased the sales of smoked salmon.

> Janice Ashby, managing director of the Siegel & Gale Package Design Group in New York, was approached by King Solomon Smoked Salmon to redesign its package. She believed that salmon was the only fish that looked good in its natural state so she decided to let shoppers see the product. The redesigned package made the salmon look like a new product. The new package
>
> · Contained a product packed in a clear vacuum pack
> · Featured a photograph of the salmon attractively arranged on a plate
> · Described the contents as slices rather than pieces
> · Rendered the product's name in italic script and provided translations in German and French for the export market
>
> The company's sales for the year following the introduction of the new package increased 380 percent from $300,000 to about $1 million. In addition, the company received its first export orders.[12]

Many small companies cannot afford their own package designers so they rely on professional firms such as the one mentioned above. The following are a few questions to ask when selecting package designers: How many clients does the firm have, and how long have they been customers? Can your friends in the same industry recommend the company? Will your marketing consultant recommend the firm? Can the firm be recommended by your trade association? Business owners can also contact the firm that has designed packages they find appealing.

EXHIBIT 12-3 What Colors Mean

Color	Meaning Associated with Color
Green	Green is symbolic of safety, fidelity, nature, and youth.
Violet	Violet denotes dignity, royalty, sorrow, despair, and wealth.
Red	Red is symbolic of danger. It is also associated with warmth, passion, virility, life, excitement, power, and bravery.
Blue	Blue is symbolic of achievement. It is also associated with coolness, calmness, freshness, cleanliness, melancholy, truth, purity, depth, and restraint.
Yellow	Yellow makes an object look large. It is exciting, cheerful, bright, youthful, and optimistic.
Orange	Orange has high attention value and indicates tastiness, abundance, harvest, and mid-life.
Black	Black denotes mourning, mystery, and strength.
White	White symbolizes cleanliness, fear, and purity.
Gray	Gray denotes depression, old age, and dignity.
Pink	Pink is associated with sweetness, tenderness, and poetry.

Using a designer is not going to be inexpensive; however, shopping around and comparing prices is advisable. Prices can range from $500 to $200,000 depending on what services are provided. For example, King Solomon Smoked Salmon paid Janice Ashby $10,000 to redesign the package for its smoked salmon.

A package design communicates through the following basic components: copy, illustration, typeface, color, and container.[13]

COPY. Good copy, consisting of a few well-chosen words or phrases, captures customers. Phrases such as "no additives," "only fresh ingredients," "no cholesterol," or "original family recipe" identify features customers are looking for today.

ILLUSTRATION. Designers do considerable research to make sure that the illustrations used on packages relay meaning and appeal to customers. For example, when Gerber Baby Food redid its Junior Juice line, the photo of the smiling baby was replaced with a watercolor of fruits against a backdrop of a country orchard.

TYPEFACE. Using different kinds of typeface reinforces the label's message and adds interest and distinction to the package.

COLOR. Colors, which create certain images (see Exhibit 12-3), help consumers identify products. For example, shoppers look for green labels when they want decaffeinated coffee—the regular coffee is red. Color can also be used to differentiate products from the same manufacturer (see The Way It Is 12-8).

If color is to help sell products, it must be selected and used properly. Joe Selame, founder and creative director of Selame Design/Boston, offers the following suggestions for choosing colors:

12-8 COLOR CODING BAGEL CHIPS

Warren Wilson is the president and founder of New York Style Bagel Chips Company in Princeton, New Jersey. He thought sales were good until he introduced a new product, New York Style Pita Chips. The pita chips were in a package much different from the bagel chips package, but sales of the new product took off fast. Wilson decided that bagel chips should be in a new package so he hired May Bender Design Associates to create a package similar to the one pita chips were in. Wilson and the designers realized that people outside the New York area were not familiar with bagel chips. Therefore, the package had a picture of a bagel chip on one side and instructions for their use on the other. The all-purpose yellow bag was replaced by five different colors: green for garlic, blue for plain, and so forth.[14]

- Avoid negative colors associated with different industries. For example, airlines do not have green interiors because the color reflects on passengers' faces, thereby contributing to airsickness.
- White makes a package look bigger and cleaner.
- Do not use black-and-white photos to advertise food. Taste buds react to color.
- White letters on a red background create a strong, noticeable image.
- Use different colors than those used by competitors—consumers will be drawn to your product.
- Do not "camouflage" your message with a color background that makes it hard to read.
- Use colors that are easy to describe and recognize. How many people know what color magenta is? Even the dictionary definition is confusing—Magenta–a moderate to vivid purplish red, or dark to strong reddish purple.
- Avoid fad colors.[15]

CONTAINER. Containers range from traditional to innovative. Some provide the convenience of easy disposal, whereas others suggest permanence and durability. In some industries, the container is often the main reason for purchasing the product.

Recognizing Good Design

Good design usually results in increased sales, but it is also recognized and rewarded by other companies. Du Pont Company recently sponsored a competition to honor companies that created innovative packages for food products. The following companies were recognized: Ocean Spray Cranberries and Monsanto for the first clear plastic container that can be filled with hot liquid; Courtesy Mold and Tool Corporation for tamper-evident packaging; Campbell Soup Company, Continental Can Company, and Reynolds Metals Company for a prepared soup that can be heated and served from the same container; and Swanson Frozen Dinners for crystalized polyester trays that can be placed in microwave ovens.[16]

Excessive Packaging

Companies like to receive awards for good design, but they are not thrilled when their packaging is criticized. Criticism today centers mainly on the use of nonbiodegradable or nonrecyclable materials, or for excessive packaging. For example, Colgate-Palmolive's Fab 1 Shot contains sixteen single-use packets of detergent placed in a segmented plastic tray, which is covered with plastic and encased in a cardboard box. The company agreed to change its package. Other companies that are cited for packaging mistakes do not change their packaging. For example, the Washington Citizens for Recycling Foundation awarded a "packaging booby prize" to the plastic egg that contains L'eggs panty hose. But Mary Gilbert, public relations manager with L'eggs Products, says the company will not give up the egg. "It's part of our total marketing concept," she says.[17]

New Package for New Products

The real challenge for designers is creating a new package for a new product. This approach enhances the overall performance of the product because it is in a package created to deliver exactly what the task requires. For example, Wagner Spray Tech developed Glass Mask, a liquid that is spread onto a window before it is painted allowing painters to work quicker. The package for Glass Mask has a dip tube and dispensing valve to fill the foam applicator pad with just the right amount of liquid. The built-in scraper leaves a clean line when removing the paint and solution from the window.[18]

Developing new packages for new products tests the designer's skill as well as his or her ability to cooperate with people in the production department. If identified consumer needs and expectations are satisfied, the new package will translate into increased sales and profits.

Graphic Design

Color, material, shape, and size are important packaging considerations; however, a package is not complete until a suitable label has been designed and tested. Creating an informative, appealing label is the function of graphic designers. The most attractive labels are those that do not appear to be cluttered or messy. Customers should be able to identify the product, its ingredients, and its uses quickly and easily. Innovative labels can increase sales and profits. For example, Welch Foods, Inc., watched its sales of jellies and juices decline for five years in a row. The label, which gave a cheap, generic look to what was an all-natural, high-quality product, was part of the problem. A new label, showing a stylish fruit basket labeled Welch's Way, was created, and consumers interpreted it as a symbol of simple, honest food.[19]

Brand Name

Choosing a brand name for a product is not a direct packaging function. However, those involved with packaging should assist in name selection because they will be expected to incorporate the name or logo into the package. The following are some suggestions for selecting a good brand name:

- It is short and simple.
- It is easy to spell and read.
- It should be easy to recognize and remember.
- It should be easy to pronounce.
- It should be timely (the name does not go out of date).
- It should be adaptable to packaging and labeling needs.
- It is legally available (it does not belong to another company).
- It is not offensive, obscene, or negative.
- It suggests the product benefits.[20]

Importance of Packaging

We close this section of our discussion of packaging with a few observations of the importance of packaging. Effective packaging is not a substitute for a high-quality product offered at a fair price. Good packaging can enhance the visibility of a product, reinforce the brand's image in the customer's mind, make marketing budgets more cost effective, and increase profits. Packaging is now estimated to be a $50 billion business. About 90 percent of packaging is done by independent design firms, most of which belong to the Package Design Council.[21] The work done by in-house and independent package designers results in a product that adds to a company's growth and profitability.

PRICE

The third P in the marketing mix is price. Manufacturing, packaging, and distributing products are important; however, if products are incorrectly priced, the company will lose money and eventually be forced to close. Many small businesses have very little choice about the price they charge for their goods. They simply must follow the price leader to remain competitive. Even companies that follow the price leader can be successful if they can compete on other factors such as cost cutting or customer service. Setting the right price for products requires considerable effort and a certain amount of luck.

Price Elasticity

price elasticity

Price elasticity measures the responsiveness of quantity demanded to changes in price. Basic economics teaches that demand for goods is usually either elastic or inelastic. If demand is elastic, changes in price will change the quantity of goods purchased. However, inelastic demand means that price changes have little effect on the amount purchased. As in all real-life situations, the effect of price on quantity of products purchased is not always easy to measure. Therefore, price setting is often a trial-and-error process. Small business owners can experiment with a number of price-setting strategies.

Pricing Strategies

The pricing strategies presented in this section can be used at different stages of a company's growth or at different stages in the product life cycle. In general, small business owners will most likely have to choose a competitive price strategy.

competitive
pricing

Competitive pricing. Competitive pricing means that products sold by most small businesses will be priced about the same as those offered by competitors. If an owner can demonstrate superior quality, greater durability, or personalized customer service, she or he may be able to sell products at higher prices than those of competitors. One mistake small business owners should avoid is selling inferior products at prices similar to the competitors'.

penetration
pricing

Penetration pricing. Companies introducing a product to a market that already has similar goods may choose a **penetration pricing** strategy. That is, introducing the product at a lower price than competing items. Once the product gains market share, the price will be gradually raised to compete with those of the competitors.

oddball pricing

Oddball pricing. Some companies have discovered that at certain times **oddball pricing** is effective: three items priced together at $0.99 may result in more sales than pricing the same items at $0.33 each.

prestige
pricing

Prestige pricing. Customers are generally unable to make objective quality judgments about some products and often associate high prices with better quality. Companies that desire a quality image might choose **prestige pricing**—setting relatively high prices for their products. In some instances, companies with high-quality products are unable to sell them at prices higher than their competitors' lower quality goods.

skimming

Skimming. Firms that have the only product or a significantly better product can afford to charge a high price for that item—called **skimming.** Once other companies offer similar products, the leader may have to change to a competitive price strategy.

leader pricing

Leader pricing. Some companies, especially grocery and retail stores, advertise very low prices for a few items to attract customers. Once in the store, customers will most likely purchase other items along with the low-price ones. This is referred to as **leader pricing.** Another similar strategy, bait-and-switch, should be avoided because it is illegal. In this situation, store owners advertise low-cost products which are conveniently unavailable when customers come for them, but the owner or salesperson offers a better product at a higher price.

odd-number
pricing

Odd-number pricing. Many products are priced using **odd-number pricing** such as $19.99 or $99.99 because customers "think" these prices are less than $20 and $100. Customers' resistance to purchase goods is supposedly reduced by using odd-number prices.

opportunistic
pricing

Opportunistic pricing. The less polite term for **opportunistic pricing** is price gouging. Some firms take advantage of product shortages or natural disasters and charge an artificially high price for their products. For example, hurricane Hugo devastated Charleston, South Carolina, in 1989. A few days after the storm it was fairly easy to find $600 chain saws, $1,500 generators, and $3 per gallon gasoline. Most of the purveyors of the chain saws and generators were not Charleston residents; rather they were out-of-staters who just wanted to "help." Needless to say, once the emergency passed, the sellers and their pickup or rental trucks vanished.

Setting Prices

The above pricing strategies can be used by small businesses, but owners may still not know exactly what price to charge for their merchandise. Setting the appropriate price for products requires consideration of a number of factors. A few of the important factors to consider include the following:

- The strength of consumer demand
- The ability of consumers to pay for the product
- Consumer knowledge, bargaining skills, and effort devoted to purchase products
- Availability and desirability of competing products
- Number and relative strength of competitors
- Competitors' pricing strategies
- Availability of substitute products
- Raw material costs
- Overhead
- Desired profit

Analyzing these factors might suggest price-setting plans such as cost-plus pricing or discounting. Some business owners may determine what profit margin they need and then set their prices accordingly.

COST-PLUS PRICING. This pricing system requires owners to determine direct and indirect costs of manufacturing and selling a product. The following are some of the major costs that must be determined and allocated to each unit produced:

- Product design and testing cost
- Cost of labor and materials
- Depreciation of plant and equipment
- Overhead (rent, utilities, maintenance, etc.)

- Insurance
- Storage
- Inventory costs
- Marketing (promotion, delivery, selling, and so forth)
- Services provided

Once these costs have been calculated, the next step is to add the "plus." Owners need to determine how much profit they want to make from each product sold. The amount needed to cover both cost and profit constitutes the price of the item. For example, $1.99 for a seven-ounce tube of toothpaste covers the following costs: raw material and labor is 99 cents; selling and general expenses are 37 cents; the manufacturer realizes a profit of 34 cents; and the retailer's markup is 29 cents.

Cost-plus pricing seems to be a relatively simple process, but there are some drawbacks to this pricing method. The following are a few of the principal shortcomings: allocating joint costs to specific products is difficult; elasticity of demand is ignored; profit goal or market share objective may be unrealistic; competitor strength and reaction is often underestimated; determining "fair return" is difficult; and many costs vary with volume, and volume depends on price charged.[22]

DISCOUNTING. Some small business owners believe that discounting (selling the product at a lower-than-normal price) is the best way to increase market share and volume. The problem with discounting, whether it takes the form of rebates, coupons, or special sale price, is that it becomes habit forming. Customers refuse to buy a product at its "regular" price (automobiles are a good example). Instead, they wait until the product has been discounted. Business owners who choose to periodically discount should do it carefully (see Exhibit 12-4) and not too frequently.

Increasing Prices

We mentioned earlier that some pricing strategies such as penetration and leader pricing were temporary. They are usually short-term strategies designed to attract customers. Once customers have been attracted, prices are raised. There are other reasons why small business owners need to raise prices. Any of the following can lead to price increases: basic costs are higher than estimated; product demand outpaces supply; or competitors have left the market. Regardless of cause, price increases should be instituted carefully to avoid losing customers. The following suggestions make price increases more palatable:

- Raise prices when everyone else does.
- Raise prices gradually and infrequently.
- Reduce some prices while raising others.
- Look after your key accounts.
- Provide sound—and true—explanations.[23]

EXHIBIT 12-4 The Dos and Don'ts of Discounting

DO	DON'T
Keep your aim in mind	Offer discounts because everyone else does
Make surcharges if they won't pay	Offer settlement discounts if there is another way of getting yourself paid
Be creative with your discounting	Copy everyone else
Use discounts to clear stocks	Discount when there is no need
Put time limits on the deal	Publish discounts for all time
Discount for extra business	Let them stick in the dealer's pocket
Make sure discounts are passed on	Give them away automatically
Discount only to survive in a mature market	Discount with a new product
Use different discounts for different groups	Use one discount for all purposes
Keep flexibility, keep reviewing	Let the boss give the money away

SOURCE: John Winkler, *Pricing for Results* (New York: Facts on File Publications, 1984), 99. Used by permission of Butterworth Heinemann, Oxford, England.

The last suggestion may be the most important. If customers do not under-stand or accept the reasons for a price increase, they may buy elsewhere. The following are a few ways to overcome pricing objections: (1) justify a higher selling price by emphasizing greater value for each dollar spent; (2) if cus-tomers claim to have a lower quotation, ask for a copy of the quote; (3) point out the dangers of dealing with the lowest bidder; (4) compare the features and quality of your product with those of the competition; (5) have an order alternative that affords customers a lower price based on some larger volume formula; and (6) provide the buyer with an extended period of time in which the product may be bought at a guaranteed price.[24] Of course, these problems do not exist when prices are decreased.

Cutting Prices

Certain pricing strategies such as skimming are fairly short lived. When com-petitors catch up, prices need to be cut. There are other reasons, including the following, for cutting prices:

- Sales have not met expectations.
- Competitors have introduced a more attractively priced product.
- Costs are lower than estimated.
- Lower prices will attract different market segments.
- The company is carrying too much inventory.
- Some products are about to become obsolete.
- Reduced prices will drive out marginal producers.

Price-cutting should be done carefully so as not to send the wrong signal to customers. If prices are cut too drastically or too frequently, customers will decide the company is in trouble and might wait for even lower prices. Or,

The Way It Is

12-9 COMPETING ON PRICE

Jan Bell Marketing Inc., a seller of private label jewelry, is exceptionally price conscious. The company sells mostly to wholesale clubs, which expect to buy at rock-bottom prices. It is not one big idea that allows Jan Bell to sell for less than its competitors. Rather, at each step along the way Jan Bell does at least one thing that allows it to cut costs. First, the company buys raw material in bulk from the source (no wholesaler to mark up the supplies). Second, the company always pays cash. "If you don't ask your suppliers to be your banker, they're willing to shave somewhere between 3 and 5 percent of the purchase price," says company cofounder and cochairman Isaac Arguetty. Third, unlike other jewelry companies, Jan Bell buys raw material throughout the year (saving between 10 to 15 percent on the cost of materials). Finally, there is no inventory. Jan Bell workers convert the raw material into jewelry and it is shipped out within forty-eight hours. The result of the slavish devotion to price is a six-year-old company whose sales and earnings have increased steadily since its founding. In 1989 Jan Bell reported income of $16 million, up 55 percent on sales that rose 51 percent.[25]

customers might equate price reduction with inferior merchandise and refuse to buy even at lower prices.

Importance of Price

There is no doubt that price is one of the most important Ps in the marketing mix. Setting the wrong price for products, either too high or too low, can lead to business failure. However, relying solely on price as a competitive strategy can also lead to failure. Customers who always see terms such as *manufacturer's list price, deep discount, invoice price,* and *sale* have become quite skeptical. Customers want quality, good service, and quick delivery. However, if companies chose to compete on price, it must drive every other decision made (see The Way It Is 12-9).

The Robinson-Patman Act

Robinson-Patman Act

Prices are generally determined by market, customer, and competitor analysis; however, there is legislation that affects companys' pricing strategy. The **Robinson-Patman Act** requires that prices charged to the same kind and class of account be equal, with the exception of cost-justified and competitively-justified discounts. Companies can charge customers different prices only if they base the decision on volume discounts, frequency of purchase, and so forth.

Within the constraints of the Robinson-Patman Act, companies can charge what they want for their products. Sometimes companies discover that their products are not selling at the listed price. When this happens, businesses can lower the price, raise the price (reposition the product), reduce costs, discontinue the product, or change the product to make it different from competing products.

SUMMARY

For small businesses to grow and be profitable, their owners need to appreciate the importance of marketing. The four Ps are the heart of an effective marketing program. Business owners should continually research their products, sales, consumers, and promotion in order to keep ahead of the competition. If customers do not get the products or services they want at the right price and place, they will go elsewhere. Small business owners who neglect marketing or minimize its importance should not expect to be the owners of thriving businesses. Effective marketing also requires owners to pay attention to effective packaging and pricing.

Most marketing experts agree that an attractive package alone will not sell products. However, they also agree that well designed and produced packages certainly enhance the appeal of products. Besides providing containment and protection, packaging performs the following functions: information, identification, convenience, aesthetics, and safety. Companies have found that designing new packages for established products can increase the sales of those products. Package design communicates through the following basic components: color, copy, illustration, typeface, and container. Small businesses that cannot afford in-house designers can use package design consultants who can provide all necessary packaging services.

Packaging costs, along with other costs associated with manufacturing and marketing products, determines the price of products. The following are some of the pricing strategies that small business owners can use: competitive pricing, penetration pricing, oddball pricing, prestige pricing, skimming, leader pricing, and odd-number pricing. Setting the right price for products is critical. Either too high or too low prices can lead to business failure. By wisely timing price increases and decreases, business owners can be competitive, minimize inventory, and maintain customer loyalty.

QUESTIONS FOR REVIEW AND DISCUSSION

1. Briefly explain the components of market research.
2. Why do so many new products fail?
3. What are the five categories of products?
4. Briefly describe the channels of distribution.
5. Why is packaging such an important part of the marketing mix?
6. What are the functions of packaging?
7. Identify three consumer products that you believe have well-designed packages. Why are they well designed?
8. What is price elasticity and inelasticity?

9. What are the different pricing strategies?
10. What are the drawbacks of cost-plus pricing?
11. What are the provisions of the Robinson-Patman Act?

KEY TERMS

competitive pricing   prestige pricing
convenience goods   price
Four Ps   price elasticity
leader pricing   product
new products   promotion
oddball pricing   Robinson-Patman Act
odd-number pricing   shopping goods
opportunistic pricing   skimming
penetration pricing   speciality goods
place   unsought goods

CASE
Knickers in a Twist

After Peter Barnett left Shiplake College in England, he worked in the wine business until he and his employer parted ways. Peter decided to go into business for himself. The first part of the business he decided on was the name—Knickers in a Twist. The British use the phrase "knickers in a twist" to imply that they are confused or undecided. Once the name had been chosen, Peter had to come up with a product for his business to manufacture or sell. He decided on knickers (ladies underpants).

The knicker would be designed by Aura, a leading lingerie design firm whose designs fill the shelves of well-known English shops. The design is known technically as high-leg mini, which is sexier than most types of knickers. Although the name Knickers in a Twist provides the company with a marketing edge, the company would not be successful unless the product is different and well made. In conjunction with Aura, Knickers in a Twist has designed a brief that is similar to one currently marketed on the continent but not widely distributed in England.

The packaging of the briefs should complement the name of the product; therefore, Peter decided to twist together two knickers of different colors and package them in a transparent tube six inches long and two inches in diameter. A three-color label, using the distinctive Knickers in a Twist logo, would be affixed to each tube. The tubes will be placed in a plastic dispenser that can hold twenty tubes. The dispensers will be located near cash registers throughout a store. This location would make it easier for men to buy the product for their lady friends or wives.

Peter had decided on packaging and distribution, but he was not sure how much to charge for his product. He knew that the cost of the product would be £1.20, and he knew competitors charged the following prices:

Marks & Spencer	Pack of 3	£2.99
Sock Shop	Tube of 3	3.99
Selfridges	Single brief	2.99
Richard Shops	Single brief	1.99
Debenhams	Single brief	0.99

Peter thought that he could sell his knickers for a suggested retail price of £ 4.95. At that price, he would have a gross profit of £ .67 if he sold the product to retailers for £ 1.87.

At the lowest price he would accept, £ 4.15, his gross profit would be £ .35 because he would sell to retailers for £ 1.55. Peter knew if he set the price too high or too low his business would not be successful.

QUESTIONS
1. What do you think about Peter's packaging?

2. Would men buy more knickers if they did not have to go into the lingerie section of a store?

3. How can Knickers in a Twist be sold for so much more than competitors charge for their product?

4. What price would you recommend for the product? Why?

ACTIVITIES

1. Answer the questions in this creativity quiz to learn how innovative you are. (Answers and explanation are at the end of this section.)

Entrepreneurial Innovation Self-Test

Read each statement carefully, then respond by marking the answer that most accurately describes your behavior, feeling or attitude as it actually is, not as you would like it to be, or think it should be. Try to mark your first reaction.

Agree Disagree

___ ___ 1. My parents encouraged me to take an interest in discovering things for myself.

___ ___ 2. At least one of my close relatives is an entrepreneur.

___ ___ 3. Throughout my education, I had many part-time jobs.

___ ___ 4. One or both of my parents had many unorthodox or unconventional ideas.

___ ___ 5. If I were stranded in an unfamiliar city without friends or money, I would cope quite well.

___ ___ 6. I am curious about more things than most people are.

—   —   7. I enjoy ventures in which I must constantly keep trying new approaches and possibilities.

—   —   8. I always seek challenging problems to solve.

—   —   9. I am not too painstaking in my work.

—   —   10. I am able to work for extended periods of time, frequently to the point of exhaustion.

—   —   11. When faced with a problem, I usually investigate a wide variety of options.

—   —   12. While working on one project, I often think of the next one I want to tackle.

—   —   13. Before taking on an important project, I learn all I can about it.

—   —   14. When confronted with a difficult problem, I try solutions others would not think of.

—   —   15. Once I undertake a new venture, I'm determined to see it through.

—   —   16. I concentrate harder on projects I'm working on than most people do.

—   —   17. I cannot get excited about ideas that may never lead to anything.

—   —   18. When brainstorming with a group of people, I think up more ideas quicker than others.

—   —   19. I have broader interests and am more widely informed than most people.

—   —   20. When the chips are down, I display more personal strength than most people do.

—   —   21. I need social interaction and am very interested in interpersonal relationships.

—   —   22. I find it easy to identify flaws in others' ideas.

—   —   23. I regard myself as a ''specialist,'' not a ''generalist.''

—   —   24. When evaluating information, I believe the source is more important than the content.

—   —   25. I am easily frustrated by uncertainty and unpredictability.

—   —   26. I can easily give up immediate gain or comfort to reach long-term goals.

—   —   27. I have great tenacity of purpose.

—   —   28. Things that are obvious to others are not so obvious to me.

Always	Often	Sometimes	Rarely	Never	
_____	____	_____	_____	____	29. I get a kick out of breaking the rules.
_____	____	_____	_____	____	30. I become upset if I cannot immediately come to a decision.
_____	____	_____	_____	____	31. Ideas run through my head at night to the point that I can't sleep.

_____ _____ _____ _____ _____ 32. I get into trouble because I'm too curious or inquisitive.

_____ _____ _____ _____ _____ 33. I am able to win other people over to my point of view.

_____ _____ _____ _____ _____ 34. I tolerate frustration more than the average person does.

_____ _____ _____ _____ _____ 35. I rely on intuition when trying to solve a problem.

_____ _____ _____ _____ _____ 36. I can stick with difficult problems for extended periods of time.

_____ _____ _____ _____ _____ 37. My problem-solving abilities are stronger than my social abilities.

_____ _____ _____ _____ _____ 38. A logical step-by-step method is best for solving problems.

_____ _____ _____ _____ _____ 39. I can readily allay other people's suspicions.

40. Below is a list of adjectives and descriptive terms. Indicate with a check mark 12 words that best describe you.

ENERGETIC	PREDICTABLE	OPEN-MINDED	PERSUASIVE	SELF-CONFIDENT
TACTFUL	OBSERVANT	INFORMAL	INHIBITED	FASHIONABLE
DEDICATED	ENTHUSIASTIC	FORMAL	ORIGINAL	INNOVATIVE
PERSEVERING	QUICK	POISED	CURIOUS	GOOD-NATURED
ACQUISITIVE	CAUTIOUS	HELPFUL	PRACTICAL	HABIT-BOUND
PERCEPTIVE	ALERT	RESOURCEFUL	COURAGEOUS	FORWARD-LOOKING
EGOTISTICAL	STERN	ORGANIZED	INDEPENDENT	CLEAR-THINKING
UNEMOTIONAL	EFFICIENT	FACTUAL	THOROUGH	UNDERSTANDING
DYNAMIC	MODEST	POLISHED	REALISTIC	SELF-DEMANDING
INVOLVED	ABSENT-MINDED	FLEXIBLE	SOCIABLE	WELL-LIKED

SCORING INSTRUCTIONS

To score the test, circle and add up the values for your answers.

	Agree	Disagree		Agree	Disagree
1.	4	1	15.	4	1
2.	3	1	16.	4	1
3.	4	1	17.	1	4
4.	3	1	18.	4	1
5.	4	1	19.	4	1
6.	4	1	20.	4	1
7.	4	1	21.	1	4
8.	3	1	22.	3	1
9.	0	4	23.	1	4
10.	4	1	24.	1	4
11.	4	1	25.	1	4
12.	3	1	26.	4	1
13.	4	1	27.	4	1
14.	4	1	28.	4	1

	Always	Often	Sometimes	Rarely	Never
29.	2	3	5	1	0
30.	0	2	3	5	1
31.	2	4	5	3	0
32.	3	4	5	1	0
33.	3	4	5	1	0
34.	3	4	5	1	0
35.	5	4	3	1	0
36.	4	5	3	1	0
37.	4	5	3	1	0
38.	1	2	5	3	0
39.	3	4	5	1	0

40. The following characteristics score 2 points each:
    energetic, observant, persevering, resourceful, independent, dedicated, original, perceptive, enthusiastic, innovative, curious, involved, flexible.
    The following score 1 point each:
    self-confident, forward-looking, informal, courageous, thorough, open-minded, alert, dynamic, self-demanding, absent-minded.
    The rest of the characteristics score zero.

SOURCE: Eugene Raudsepp, "What's Your IQ?" *Entrepreneurial Woman*, March 1992, 56–59. Reprinted with permission from Entrepreneurial Woman Magazine, March 1992.

INTERPRETING YOUR SCORE

125–186. If you scored in this range, you are probably a highly innovative person. Ideas come readily to you and you have a keen awareness of and concern for unsolved problems. On the whole, you take an innovative approach to solving problems. You also discern possibilities and opportunities in areas where others find little potential. You are original and individualistic, and you have no problems resisting pressures to conform. You have the courage to pit yourself against uncertain circumstances and you have the innovation to come out ahead.

77–124. A score in this range indicates that you are moderately innovative. While you lack some of the autonomy, self-sufficiency, and self-confidence of the highly innovative entrepreneur, you compensate with your predilection for method, precision, and exactness. You also have faith in the successful outcome of your present and future entrepreneurial efforts. While entrepreneurs with an innovative flair may succeed in a variety of enterprises, they are sometimes surpassed by other less creative entrepreneurs who possess keener abilities in marketing, deal-making, negotiations, finance, and human relations. So although you need to beef up on innovation, your abilities in other areas will still help you succeed.

27–76. If you scored in this range, you may be more successful operating a franchise or working for someone else than you would be starting your own business. However, remember: Innovative abilities can be developed and cultivated, either through self-training, or by attending workshops or seminars. So if you are determined to own your own business, don't give up!

2. Take any consumer product you use and determine if it is effectively packaged. The questions in this section will help you make that determination.

Effective Packaging

	Yes	No
1. Is the package made of the most appropriate material?	___	___
2. Is the design directed toward the target market?	___	___
3. Are the "right" colors used on the package?	___	___
4. Is the design new and modern looking?	___	___
5. Are there several different package sizes?	___	___
6. Are instructions clearly displayed on the package?	___	___
7. Are the ingredients listed on the label?	___	___
8. Does the package contribute to the company's image?	___	___
9. Is the brand name appropriate?	___	___
10. Will the packaging material harm the environment?	___	___
11. Can the package harm the product users?	___	___
12. Could the package harm small children?	___	___
13. Can the package be reused?	___	___
14. Is the package distinctive?	___	___
15. Is warranty information clearly displayed?	___	___
16. Can packaging material be recycled?	___	___
17. Is the product overpackaged (too much packaging)?	___	___
18. Is packaging material biodegradable?	___	___
19. Can you suggest packaging improvements?	___	___

3. Complete the pricing analysis, using a friend's business or one you might open later.

Pricing Analysis

	Yes	No
Have you determined to price below, at, or above the market?	___	___
Do you set specific markups for each product?	___	___
Do you set markups for product categories?	___	___
Do you use a one-price policy rather than bargain with customers?	___	___
Do you offer discounts for quantity purchases, or to special groups?	___	___
Do you set prices to cover full costs on every sale?	___	___
Do the prices you have established earn the gross margin you planned?	___	___
Do you clearly understand the market forces affecting your pricing methods?	___	___
Do you know which products are slow movers and which are fast?	___	___
Do you take this into consideration when pricing?	___	___
Do you experiment with odd or even price endings to increase your sales?	___	___
Do you know which products are price sensitive to your customers, that is, when a slight increase in price will lead to a big drop in demand?	___	___
Do you know which of your products draw people when put on sale?	___	___
Do you know the maximum price customers will pay for certain products?	___	___
If the prices on some products are dropped too low, do buyers hesitate?	___	___
Is there a specific time of year when your competitors have sales?	___	___
Do your customers expect sales at certain times?	___	___
Have you determined whether or not a series of sales is better than one annual clearance sale?	___	___
Have you developed a markdown policy?	___	___

Do you take markdowns on a regular basis, or as needed? ___ ___

Do you know what role you want price to play in your overall retailing strategy? ___ ___

Are you influenced by competitors' price changes? ___ ___

Do any of your suppliers set a minimum price below which you cannot go? ___ ___

Do you issue "rain checks" to customers when sale items are sold out so they can purchase them later at the sale price? ___ ___

SOURCE: Michael W. Little, "Marketing Checklist for Small Retailers," U.S. Small Business Administration, Management Aids Number 4.012.

13 PROMOTION

LEARNING OBJECTIVES

After you have read this chapter, you will be able to do the following:
- Understand the importance of selling
- Explain the function of promotion
- Explain promotion techniques
- Understand the importance of advertising
- Select the best advertising media for small businesses

We are now ready to discuss promotion, the last P in the marketing mix. It is difficult to isolate any one of the Four Ps as the most important because they are all important. However, we can state that most small businesses will not thrive if they have an ineffective promotion program. After all, customers need to be convinced to patronize one business at the cost of others, and promotion is how they are convinced. Dull, boring advertising programs are not likely to lure customers to retail establishments or induce them to buy a manufacturer's product. There are numerous aspects of promotion that, when skillfully combined, create an effective promotion program, which leads to growth and profits.

In earlier chapters, we discussed types of products and different sales roles. In this chapter, we will again look briefly at the importance of selling. We will also discuss promotion in two parts. First, promotion will be discussed as periodic, special-event activities. Then, our focus will be on advertising—the long-term, consistent attempt to keep customers' attention and loyalty. Our discussion of advertising will include creation of an advertising plan, media selection, advertising copy, budgets, and helping agencies.

THE MARKETING-COMMUNICATIONS MIX

marketing-communications mix

Marketing is basically a means of communicating with customers. Small businesses have a product or service that they want consumers to purchase and use. Advertising is one important element of the **marketing-communications mix;** however, there are other elements that can be used in conjunction with or instead of advertising. Those other elements include the following: direct marketing, packaging, personal selling, trade shows, public relations, point-of-purchase displays, and sales promotion. We have discussed packaging in the previous chapter, and we will discuss most of the other elements of the marketing-communications mix in the remainder of this chapter.

PERSONAL SELLING

In Chapter 12, we discussed channels of distribution, types of salespeople, and other aspects of selling. In this section, we will focus on several selling techniques and some selling methods that are quite important. The two selling methods discussed in this section, telephone and direct selling, are increasing in importance because more families have two income earners. Before examining telephone and direct selling, we will discuss sales planning and making personal sales calls.

Sales Planning

Every business with products to sell needs people to do the selling. Effective salespeople are those who have planned their work. They know what they want to accomplish, and they know how to manage their time. The following are suggestions to help salespeople plan their work:

1. Planning should be considered a top priority. Plans created to meet supervisors' requirements are usually quite meaningless.
2. Planning is an ongoing process; therefore, a regular place and time should be established for planning.
3. Every salesperson should set realistic, attainable goals that will give him or her direction.
4. Goals should be fairly simple and should reflect the amount of time a person has to accomplish them.
5. Plans should be flexible, but changes should be made only when absolutely necessary.
6. Plans should be evaluated regularly so they can be modified if changing circumstances so dictate.
7. Salespeople should be thoroughly familiar with their product and company policy about service after the sale.
8. Once a sales plan has been established, salespeople should keep records of their accomplishments.[1]

Sales Calls

Once sales plans have been established, salespeople need to make contact with their customers. In retail establishments, salespeople wait for customers to come to them. However, manufacturers, wholesalers, sales representatives, and others must call on the customer to make a sale. One of the main difficulties in making sales calls is being allowed to see the "key" decision maker in the buying company. Some sellers have come up with some effective ways of making appointments with the right buyer. For example, Tony Frederick, CEO of Frederick-Seal Inc., encourages his salespeople to send postcards to customers a week before calling on them. The postcards are printed with a list of all the items the company sells, by category, and carry the message that the salesperson looks forward to a visit the following week.[2] Frederick claims that the postcard makes the customer feel obligated to see the salesperson. Other companies have discovered more ingenious ways of getting customers' attention (see The Way It Is 13–1).

Direct Selling

With more women working outside of the home, many companies are turning to direct selling as their major sales method. Companies such as L. L. Bean and Lilian Vernon have relied on catalog sales for years. These companies sell to a fairly well-defined target market, and their customers appear to do much of their shopping from catalogs.

For sellers, direct selling has the following advantages: distributors are eliminated; overhead is minimized; products are paid for before delivery; very little inventory is needed; a wide range of products (see a Lilian Vernon catalog) can be offered; few items are returned; and catalogs are not intrusive. Although most direct sellers have offered traditional items such as clothes, kitchenware, gardening supplies, and so on, some manufacturers sell unusual products directly to customers. Vintner Daryl Sattui, for example, has eliminated distributors.

Unlike many wine makers, Daryl Sattui's vineyard showed a profit its first year. Today, V. Sattui Winery in Napa Valley produces thirteen wines that sell for $5.75 to $30 a bottle. Thirty thousand cases earned $4 million in 1988. Sattui has made a splash in the industry by selling his wines direct to

---

The Way It Is

13–1 A BIRD IN THE HAND

Larry Cahill is a busy man. He is the president of Larkin, a motel developer and franchiser. His secretary, Diane Claussen, knows not to waste his time with frivolous matters. So when a cage, containing a homing pigeon, addressed to him arrived at the office, she hesitated before showing it to him. Cahill accepted the package and looked over the accompanying letter from Homewood Suites, an extended-stay hotel franchise. Homewood Suites' marketing people thought Cahill would be a good prospect if only they could get his attention. Following the letter's instructions, Cahill released the bird and called Homewood's development director. Now he is looking for just the right spot to build a Homewood Suites hotel. Homewood marketing chief Jennifer Burgess is sold on the pigeon ploy. She says, "You just can't ignore a live bird."[3]

customers. There's only one way to buy a Sattui wine—at the winery or through the mail. Cutting out the distributor boosts Sattui's net margins by about 25 to 30 percent per bottle.[4]

Direct selling is not without its drawbacks and frustrations. The following are a few of the disadvantages of selling directly to customers: it is expensive to maintain large mailing lists; only a small percentage of people who receive catalogs buy any of the advertised products; catalog production and distribution is expensive; many people will not purchase products they cannot touch or try on; customers usually need no reason for returning products; and too many companies are relying on direct selling, increasing competition to an uncomfortable level.

Telephone Selling

Some companies resort to telephone selling because it is less expensive than other methods. Using the telephone also allows businesses to reach customers at home or in their offices. Although this method of selling might be beneficial to companies, it often irritates customers. Because customers can very easily hang up telephones, people using this sales method should learn good telephone selling techniques. For example, telephone salespersons should be prepared, speak distinctly, be courteous and not argumentative, build confidence, and control the conversation.

Listening

Almost all sales methods require good listening skills. Listening is an art that most of us have not mastered but could with a little effort. The art of listening effectively is especially important for salespeople who have direct contact with customers. Salespeople who wish to enhance their listening ability can use some of the following skills:

- Limit your own talking
- Be interested and show it
- Tune in to the other person
- Think like prospective customers
- Ask questions
- Look and listen for buying signals
- Listen for ideas, not just words
- Use interjections
- Prepare in advance
- React to ideas, not to the person
- Observe nonverbal language
- Do not jump to conclusions
- Take notes
- Get feedback[5]

PROMOTION

Promotion generally refers to a company's attempt to make the public aware of the advantages of its products. In this chapter, however, we are separating promotion into two sections—promotion and advertising. The promotion section will deal primarily with the special-event, one-time activities used to grab customers' attention. Advertising, on the other hand, will be defined as the long-term, consistent tactics used by companies to keep customers' attention and loyalty.

Types of Consumers

Before business owners can develop promotion programs, they need to be aware of the types of customers they are trying to attract. Just as there are different types of products, there are also different types of consumers. Consumers cannot be perfectly categorized, but the following categories are often used by marketers: **innovators** (2 to 3 percent of customers); **early adopters** (12 to 15 percent); **early majority** (33 percent); **late majority** (34 percent); and **laggards** (12 to 15 percent).

innovators

Innovators. Innovators are willing, and have the income, to buy new products. These consumers are usually upper class, well-traveled, and self-confident. They do not need peer approval of the products or services they purchase. If innovators do not buy new products, it is unlikely that other customers who often emulate innovators will purchase the product either.

early adopters

Early adopters. Usually well-educated upper-middle class, early adopters are those consumers who have earned their own wealth and are willing to spend it for quality products. These consumers are not sufficiently confident to buy new products until they see someone else buy them. However, once they see innovators using new products, they quickly purchase the same products.

early majority

Early majority. These consumers are less educated and not as wealthy as innovators or early adopters. They may be small business owners or nonmanagement white-collar workers who identify strongly with their own kind. This group, influenced by the early adopters, will only purchase new products after they have seen other people using them for some time after introduction.

late majority

Late majority. This group is composed of skilled workers who are basically upper-lower or lower-middle class. They lack the confidence to decide if they should purchase new products, so they wait until the product has been purchased by a considerable number of people (the early majority) before they make their decision.

laggards

Laggards. Laggards are people with unskilled or menial jobs who tend to live only for the present. They are impulse buyers who purchase mainly necessities.

Small business owners who find it difficult to identify customers based on the above classifications might prefer Peter Hart's categories of shoppers. He came up with these seven types of shoppers by doing a cluster analysis of the data from his poll on consumer buying habits and attitudes.[6]

Agreeable shoppers (22 percent). These consumers are especially susceptible to advertising and are most likely to shop at discount stores.

Practical shoppers (21 percent). These are smart shoppers who research their purchases and look for the best deal. They would shop at a store that sells off-price, name-brand clothing.

Trendy shoppers (16 percent). These impulse buyers love to shop and stay up with the latest fads. Expect to find them at fashion boutiques.

Value shoppers (13 percent). These are cost-conscious shoppers who believe the best products are those that have stood the test of time. They shop at mid-priced department stores.

Top-of-the-line shoppers (10 percent). These buyers put a premium on a product's reputation for quality and believe they have earned the right to buy the best. They usually shop at upscale department stores.

Safe shoppers (9 percent). These people shop for familiar products that make them feel comfortable. They are likely to shop at the well-known mass merchandisers.

Status shoppers (5 percent). For these shoppers, a day without a new gadget is a day without joy. They love to buy designer labels.

Appealing to Customers

A well-designed promotion program should convince consumers to purchase a firm's products, which is done by making products appealing to customers. This can be done by using the following types of appeal: status appeal, humor appeal, statistical appeal (studies, surveys, etc.), sex appeal, economic appeal, natural ingredients appeal, youth appeal, and health appeal. A promotion program can be developed that uses more than one type of appeal, and a program can be developed that uses a type of appeal unsuccessfully. For example, a company may develop a program to appeal to consumers' humor only to find that the campaign is not funny. To avoid costly promotion errors, business owners should know what causes consumers to buy and how they make their purchases (see Exhibit 13–1).

Promotion Techniques

Promotion programs are usually directed toward either dealers or customers. In some instances, a firm may choose to assist dealers with their selling activities, or it may direct most of its promotional effort at the consumer. Promotion activities primarily for dealers include dealer displays, dealer premiums, cooperative advertising, advertising materials, dealer discounts, promotional material, push money (money paid to the dealer to emphasize or "push" the firm's products), sales training, and trade shows.

If a firm decides to promote its products directly to the consumer, it can provide samples, demonstrations, cents-off coupons, premiums, rebates,

EXHIBIT 13–1 A Simplified Model of Consumer Purchasing

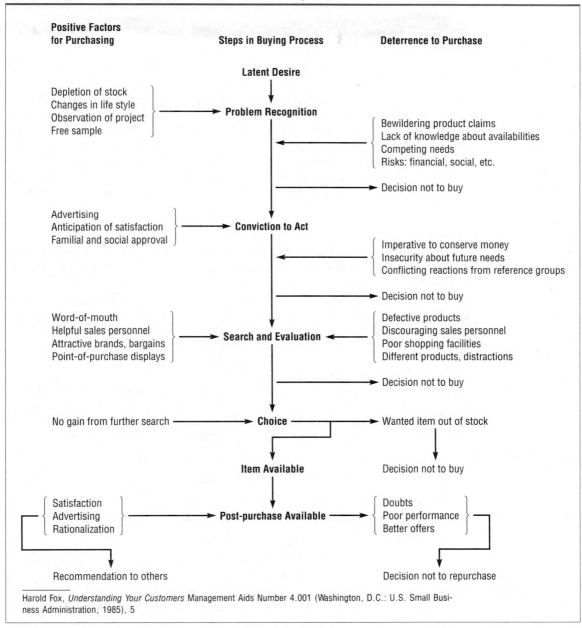

warranties or guarantees, and service contracts. Business owners should be sure that they do not give too many promotional "goodies" to consumers. Too many giveaways might lead consumers to buy only when they have some tangible inducement.

ADVERTISING

Advertising is one of the most creative and productive marketing functions. Small businesses spend billions of dollars on advertising, and they want a reasonable return on their investment. Businesses receive the most return for their advertising dollar when they create effective advertising programs. Effective advertising programs can be created by analyzing and segmenting the market, setting definite objectives, establishing reasonable budgets, developing creative strategies, choosing appropriate media, and evaluating advertising results.

Analyzing the Market

Business owners need to know their market and their customers because advertising directed at everyone is virtually useless. Good advertising should get attention, be interesting, create desire, and suggest action (AIDA), and it should be targeted toward a specific market segment. Targeting can only be done once a company has determined who its customers are, where they are, and why they buy. Having identified potential customers, business owners can proceed to establish specific advertising objectives.

Advertising Objectives

We know that the purpose of advertising is to sell products. Although this is an acceptable goal, it is not specific enough to guide or control an advertising program. Advertising objectives should be specific, accepted, achievable, and measurable. The following are a few acceptable advertising objectives:

- Increase the number of customers by 150 this year
- Have a 10 percent sales increase this year
- Increase average order value by 10 percent
- Increase store traffic by 12 percent this year
- Improve lead-conversion rates by 10 percent

There are many other advertising objectives a company could set for itself. Some other objectives include product or brand awareness, company image, sales promotion, and consumer information or education (see Exhibit 13–2 for ways to determine long-range advertising objectives for retailers).

Advertising Budgets

Objectives can be met only if businesses allocate sufficient money to their advertising programs. The problem is deciding how much money is enough. Small businesses may need to allocate more money to advertising than larger

EXHIBIT 13–2 Checklist for Determining Your Long-Range Campaign Objective

- Your goal is establishing visibility if:
  - —You are a new business.
  - —Your research shows that few people have heard of you.
  - —You are an established business, but are opening a store in a new area.

- Your goal is building an image if:
  - —You already have good visibility among your target areas.
  - —Most people in your target market are already aware of who you are and what you do.
  - —You want to refine your advertising in order to attract a specific type of customer.

- Your goal is changing an image if:
  - —Your research tells you that people have a wrong idea about your prices, style, clientele, etc.
  - —You have made changes designed to upgrade your store, or reduce prices, etc.
  - —You have taken steps to correct previous image problems and need to communicate that change.
  - —Your target market is changing, and you need to communicate an image that appeals to that changing market.

- Your goal is increasing store traffic if:
  - —Business has leveled off, and you feel that it can be increased.
  - —Changes in your business now allow you to handle more volume.
  - —Changes in your business will appeal to new and different target markets.
  - —Because of changes in the market, you feel that people can now be convinced to buy your product or use it more often.

- Your goal is explaining complicated ideas or products if:
  - —No one else offers the type of product or service that you have.
  - —Your product or service is something entirely new.
  - —Your product or service solves a specific problem, but people need to be made aware of the need to solve the problem.
  - —Using your product requires technical expertise.

- Your goal is maintaining visibility if:
  - —Your business is well established, and most people know who you are and what you do.
  - —You already have a definite (and positive) business image.
  - —You are satisfied with the volume of business you are now doing, and only want to maintain that level.
  - —You have no new competitors that threaten to cut into the market that you have captured.

companies just to stay competitive. The following are some methods companies use to determine how much money to budget for advertising:

Advertising/Sales ratio method. This often-used method allocates a percentage of expected sales to advertising. For example, in stable industries it might be customary to allocate 5 percent of sales revenue to advertising. However, in rapidly growing industries, it might be necessary to spend 20 percent of revenue on advertising. Some advantages of this system are that managing the budget allocation is relatively easy, the formula to determine how much to spend is easy to use, and more funds are allocated to advertising when sales increase. The drawbacks of using this system are that it is often difficult to forecast sales and it is often necessary to increase (not decrease) advertising expenses when sales decline.

Mathematical models. A number of formulas have been used to determine how much to spend on advertising. For example, the Hendry Corporation describes the interrelationships between advertising, share of market, and profits. From this, Hendry is able to determine how much money should be spent on advertising to maximize profits and how much could be spent on advertising to maximize market share.[7]

Match the competition. Many small businesses try to determine how much their competitors spend for advertising. Then they plan to spend the same amount—if it works for the competition, it will work for us. The primary obstacle that has to be overcome is finding out how much money the competition is allocating to advertising.

Experiments. The change in sales associated with different advertising budgets, while controlling for other important influences on sales, can be measured.

Whatever is left. Small business owners who cannot or will not allocate money to the advertising budget simply spend what is left over. Once all other expenses have been covered, business owners spend the remains on advertising. This, or any other method examined, is fairly imprecise because of all the unknown variables.

Allocating money to advertising is difficult because many of the costs are not predictable. For example, media costs depend on frequency of advertising, time of advertising, size of the advertisement, and so forth. Advertising agencies also have rates that depend on the value of the customer, services required, and ability to pay. At least one advertising agency is trying to eliminate some of the price fluctuations (see The Way It Is 13–2).

Creative Strategies

Once business owners determine how much to spend on advertising, they need to get help from an advertising company. There are a number of different kinds of companies involved in various phases of promotion. The following are some of the companies that can be consulted.

ADVERTISING AGENCIES. These companies provide all the advertising services required by small businesses. Advertising agencies can create the ad-

13–2 FIXED-PRICE ADVERTISING

Elizabeth F. Harris, president of Harris Edward Communications Inc. (HEC), is trying to revolutionize the advertising industry. To get her revolution started, Harris released a 28-page catalog offering fixed prices for more than 100 different types of advertising projects. The following are some of her fixed prices: a 10-second straight-announcer radio spot at $414; a one-page news release at $515; and a 30-second television spot at $15,320. This is heresy in an industry in which compensation is negotiated on a case-by-case basis. So is Harris's introduction of discounts for volume purchases. Businesses, says Harris, need advertising budgets they can understand and count on, which is precisely what her plan offers.[8]

vertisement, select the appropriate media, and monitor the effectiveness of the advertisement. Even though the agency can provide small businesses with a complete advertising package, business owners should be active in their advertising campaign.

Selecting the best agency is not always an easy task. Small business owners should ask their peers to recommend an agency; then they should look at several examples of that agency's work before hiring the company. Finally, small business owners should negotiate the cost of their advertising campaign. The fees are often determined by a company's ability or reputation, but as we have seen earlier (see The Way It Is 13--2), at least one agency has fixed, published rates for its services. Another interesting approach to setting fees is to make the agency's fee contingent on advertising results (see The Way It Is 13–3).

MEDIA AGENCIES. As the name implies, these agencies specialize in selecting the best media mix for a company's advertising campaign. These agencies provide no creative services, so they should be used only by business owners able to do most of their own advertising.

ART SERVICES. Some agencies only handle the art needs of small business clients. These companies provide a much needed service to small businesses that can develop their own advertising themes but do not have the capability to do the necessary artwork.

RADIO AND TELEVISION STATIONS. If small business owners choose to use radio and television advertising, they can contract with the selected stations to produce their advertisements. Ads created by these stations often cost less than comparable ads created by an advertising agency.

MAGAZINES. Magazines selected to run a company's advertisements can also produce those advertisements. As with radio and television ads, adver-

The Way It Is	**13-3** THE PUT-UP-OR-SHUT-UP STRATEGY

Jim Quest's advertising agency, Posey Quest Genova Inc., beat out five other agencies for the Murphy's Oil Soap account. The problem was that the agency was not making any money on the account. Quest went to Paul Murphy, great-grandson of the company founder, and asked to renegotiate the fee. After some discussion, the men agreed on what Quest called his put-up-or-shut-up strategy. If the agency's advertising campaign increased Murphy's sales, it shares in the profits. The program works like this—Say Posey Quest Genova charged most customers $75 an hour for its time. Under the agreement with Murphy's, it might get $65, but will receive a bonus, based on the increase in Murphy's sales. If sales increase 20 percent, so does Quest's fee. Instead of $65 an hour, the agency will make $78. If sales stay flat, or decrease, the fee stays at $65.[9]

tisements produced by magazines may be cheaper than those created by advertising agencies. However, advertising produced by agencies is probably more creative and effective because that is the company's speciality.

Advertising Media

An important step in the advertising program is deciding which media to use. A small business owner may elect to use only one advertising medium or several different media. The following media make up the advertising mix:

print media

broadcast media

position media

point-of-purchase displays

word-of-mouth

- **Print media** (direct mail, newspapers, magazines, etc.)
- **Broadcast media** (radio and television)
- **Position media** (billboards and transportation advertising)
- **Point-of-purchase displays**
- **Word-of-mouth**

Small business owners should evaluate each medium and decide which meet their needs. Selecting the most effective medium is not easy because all have advantages and disadvantages that must be considered. Listed below are some of the advantages and disadvantages of advertising media.

YELLOW PAGES. This form of advertising is used by virtually every small business because not being listed in the yellow pages can be fatal. The following are some advantages of yellow pages advertising:

- Most shoppers use the yellow pages.
- Advertisements are relatively inexpensive.
- Business owners can create their own ads.
- The effectiveness of the ad can be measured.

The following are some of the disadvantages of the yellow pages:

- All competitors are also listed in the yellow pages.
- Small ads are often ignored.
- Most businesses have to be listed under several categories (increasing the cost of advertising).

NEWSPAPERS. Newspaper advertising is advantageous because

- It is timely.
- It provides good market coverage.
- It benefits from the use of color.
- Coupons and inserts can be used.
- It can be read and reread.
- It is relatively inexpensive.

The disadvantages of newspaper advertising include:

- Audiences cannot be segmented.
- Advertising is good for a short period of time.
- Too many advertisements cause clutter.
- Newspapers have limited pass-along value.

MAGAZINES. The following are some of the advantages of magazine advertising:

- The market can be segmented.
- People pass along their magazines to other readers.
- Magazines offer excellent color reproduction.
- Coupons and inserts can be used.
- Magazine layout is orderly so ads do not get lost.
- Magazines serve as a reference source.

The limitations of magazines include the following:

- The frequency of advertisement exposure is limited.
- Businesses need to plan fairly far in advance to have their ads placed in monthly magazines.
- Ads usually cost more than similar ones in newspapers.

DIRECT MAIL. An increasingly popular form of print advertising, direct mail has the following advantages:

- Advertising is targeted to those most likely to buy the product.
- Advertisements can be as long as necessary (there are no space limitations).
- It is difficult for competitors to know in advance what another company is advertising.

The drawbacks of direct mail include the following:

- It takes time to create, print, and mail advertisements.
- Mailing lists are expensive and often inaccurate.
- Many people consider this form of advertising to simply be junk mail. However, one CEO found a way to overcome that prejudice. A business can spend thousands on a direct-mail campaign only to find that most mailings ended up in the trash basket. Polymer Plastics, a seller of printer circuit-board products, found a way to bypass the circular file. "If customers got a videotape in the mail, I figured they were going to have to look at it," says CEO Larry Stock. They do not just look. Stock estimates that when video catalogs accompany the paper catalog, they generate twenty times the response of paper catalogs sent alone.[10]

RADIO. The oldest form of broadcast media, radio advertising offers small businesses the following advantages:

- Ads can be targeted toward a specific audience.
- Selecting appropriate time slots allows the same audience to hear advertisements several times.
- Good copy can hold listeners' attention.
- A relatively short lead time is needed to have ads included in selected programs.
- Radio advertising is fairly inexpensive.
- Announcers can add personality to advertisements.
- Listeners cannot "skip over" or ignore ads as they can with print advertisements.

Radio advertising has the following disadvantages:

- Ads usually cannot exceed sixty seconds.
- There is competition for the best time slots.
- Professional help is needed to develop and deliver ads.
- Using several announcers can confuse the intent of the advertisement.
- Listeners who are working or driving do not pay careful attention to radio advertising.
- Listeners cannot refer back to advertisements.
- Too many ads aired at the same time create clutter.

TELEVISION. Television advertising offers the following advantages:

- Television programs reach a large audience.
- Audiences consider television to be a prestige medium.
- People learn better by seeing than by hearing.
- Well-known people can be used to endorse products.

- Products can be demonstrated on television.
- Audiences can be segmented by selecting appropriate programs.
- There is a sense of immediacy to television advertising.

The following limitations make television advertising inappropriate for some small businesses:

- Television advertising is quite expensive.
- Stations usually air several ads together, thereby lessening the impact of each one.
- Businesses usually need professional help to develop effective advertising.
- Ads must be aired repeatedly to have maximum effect.
- Advertising copy may offend some viewers.
- Viewers leave the television set when commercials are shown.

Unusual Media

The media described above are quite traditional and tested. There are, however, some indications that companies are utilizing some rather unusual media for their advertising. The following are some examples of unusual advertising media that have been tested:

Trash bins. Keith Clayborne has created Ad Bins. These are trash receptacles that he covers with advertising and places outside convenience stores.

In stores. Now advertisements appear on aisle directories, in-store videos, shopping carts, and refrigerators.

Near captive audiences. People cannot escape ads on telephone hold or on airport scheduling screens. Ads are also showing up in restrooms, cinemas, and phone booths.[11]

On envelopes. Barry Fribush, founder of Bubbling Bath Spa & Tub Works Inc., puts advertisements on all letters mailed from his company. Each envelope he mails contains this message: "Mr. Postman: Thank you for delivering this valuable letter from the Bubbling Bath . . . at the end of the day you should relax in a Jacuzzi"—which Bubbling Bath just happens to sell.[12]

Clothing labels. When Elizabeth Andrews, CEO of the Baby Bag Co., began selling her infants' clothing, she made sure buyers could find her even if they could not find a store that carried her goods. She stitched her new company's address and phone number right on every Baby Bag's label.[13]

Creative Use of Media

Not all business owners can find new and unusual media for their advertising, but they can use existing media creatively. The right timing or astute positioning can increase the effectiveness of advertisements. The following are a few examples of creative media usage (although most examples are from large companies, the concepts also apply to small businesses):

American Express. When American Express wanted customers to use their cards to buy theater tickets, it ran its commercials during the Tony Awards presentation seen on national television.

No-Doz. The stay-awake pill maker with a small advertising budget purchased time on late night radio — the right medium for an appropriately timed message aimed at tired drivers.

Contac. Contac increased its advertising budget for its hay fever pill at the time that the pollen count started to rise.

Open Pit. Open Pit was positioned as a barbecue sauce during the short summer selling season. Ten-second identification commercials were aired in prime time for quick reach and heavy frequency. To extend the media concept into the winter, when the brand was positioned as a cooking ingredient, the company used small-space newspaper advertisements that looked like recipe cards.[14]

Publicity

Our discussion of advertising media focused on advertisements for which small businesses must pay. However, everyone knows that sometimes the best advertising is free. For small businesses, that normally means articles or news releases featured in local newspapers. It is difficult to interest newspaper editors in an individual business, but owners can make it easier to have their company noticed. The following are a few hints on being interesting to newspapers:

- Examine the paper in which you are interested to learn what it covers and how it gets its stories.
- Be brief when writing press releases.
- Make sure you verify all facts.
- Place your name and phone number at the top of the release.
- Do not quit. If one release does not get printed, try again.
- Use the telephone to follow up when you have something to add to your release.
- Write thank-you letters when you get good coverage.
- Do not take rejection of your article personally. Keep writing.[15]

Creating Advertisements

Many small business owners choose to do much of their own advertising. If not done correctly, in-house advertising can be disastrous. Think of some of the worst broadcast ads you have seen or heard. Do most of them feature the business owner, his or her employees, or his or her children? It is usually acceptable for owners to write advertising copy, assist in advertisement production, and select the media, but very few owners have the talent to star in their commercials. In this section, we will discuss making effective advertisements.

ADVERTISING IDEAS. Business owners who have a creative flair may develop ideas and write copy by themselves. Others may choose to involve their employees or friends in the process. Group idea generation is referred to as brainstorming. This activity encourages everyone to come up with as many ideas as possible in a given time period. Successful brainstorming sessions depend on the following factors:

- Everyone should know the purpose of the session.
- Participants should be encouraged to generate crazy ideas.
- As many ideas as possible should be generated—quantity not quality is important.
- Ideas should not be analyzed or evaluated (that comes after the session).
- No person should be inactive during the brainstorming session.
- All ideas presented should be recorded.

Once the session is over, ideas can be evaluated and the most promising ones can be further developed. Once an idea for an advertisement has been developed, it is time to begin writing the copy. Writing copy begins with the headline because that is probably the most important part of the advertisement.

HEADLINES. If headlines cannot get a person's attention, the remainder of the ad will not be read. In addition to getting attention, headlines stimulate interest, entice people to read the entire ad, summarize the selling message, identify the product or service, and offer some benefit. The best headlines are usually short and to the point. The following are examples of headlines shortened to be more effective:

- Original title: Hot Tips on Heating Your Home
- Revised title: How to Cut Fuel Bills
- Original title: A Smart Shopper's Guide to Bargains
- Revised title: Shopper's Guide to Bargains
- Original title: Three Ways to Mothproof a Marriage
- Revised title: 3 Ways to Save a Marriage
- Original title: Which Diet Tips Pay Off?
- Revised title: Diet Tips that Pay Off[16]

Sometimes headlines may need to be lengthened or reworded. Once the headline is right, it is time to write the copy for the advertisement.

COPYWRITING. Creative headlines get attention, but good copy sells the product or service. Copy is interesting and effective if sentences are short and the right words are used. Advertising experts have identified the words that work best in advertising. In his book *Confessions of an Advertising Man*, David Ogilvy said the following words work wonders:

suddenly	miracle
now	magic
announcing	offer
introducing	quick
improvement	easy
amazing	wanted
sensational	challenge
remarkable	compare
revolutionary	bargain
startling	hurry

These words are used frequently by advertisers, and they do make copy more interesting and effective. (For more information on copywriting, see 37 Tips on Copywriting in Appendix 13–1.)

COLOR. Although copy is important, many experts agree that color is probably the single most important ingredient in advertising. We have already noted the importance of color in packaging, and we explained factors associated with different colors. Now we will see how color affects advertising. The following factors are associated with the use of color in advertising:

- The addition of color in newspaper advertising provides significant benefits for the costs incurred.
- Color is particularly important when advertising food, film, furniture, automobiles, cigarettes, and cosmetics.
- Color is used in more than 95 percent of television, poster, and transit advertising.
- Color is more important in ads directed toward women.
- People achieve higher recall scores when full color is used.
- The use of a second color in magazine ads is seldom worth the additional cost.[17]

Advertising Effectiveness

advertising
effectiveness

Once advertisements have been created and aired in the appropriate media, how can business owners determine **advertising effectiveness?** Unfortunately, there is no way of measuring exactly how effective an ad was, but the following methods can help measure effectiveness:

Surveys. Surveys conducted at the point of sale help determine why customers purchase certain items.

Coupons. The number of redeemed coupons or inserts included with advertisements indicate an ad's success.

Comparison of sales. Business owners can compare sales immediately after a major advertising campaign with those of an earlier period to determine the campaign's effectiveness.

The
Way
It Is

13-4 WHO'S CALLING?

Richard A. Gagne, owner of Dental Horizons, never knew which of the many places he advertised generated the most business. Then he started listing different phone numbers—his office has several lines—in any advertisements running concurrently. "Now, we always track which ads are drawing phone calls," says Gagne. He compares response rates to ads in different publications, and then allocates his advertising budget accordingly.[18]

Sales signals. Customers who mention a name or word from an advertisement are an indication of how successful the ad was.

Miscellaneous. Some companies have developed their own effectiveness measures. L. L. Bean, Inc., for example, uses different return addresses in the magazines and newspapers in which it advertises. For that company, the most frequently used address indicates which magazines are best for its advertising. A business could achieve the same results by using different telephone numbers (see The Way It Is 13-4).

Some Unsuccessful Advertising

One of the principal ways of determining advertising effectiveness is to measure the brand loyalty that ads help to create. Consumers are very loyal to some products but have very little loyalty to others. A recent survey[19] found the percentage of users of the following products who were loyal to one brand: cigarettes (71 percent), toothpaste (61 percent), coffee (58 percent), beer (48 percent), soft drinks (44 percent), tires (33 percent), athletic shoes (27 percent), canned vegetables (25 percent), and garbage bags (23 percent). Business owners who sell athletic shoes, canned vegetables, and garbage bags could not be very encouraged with the results of their advertising efforts.

Advertising Criticism

Besides being ineffective, some advertising is criticised for its content, its quantity, the products advertised, and its influence on human behavior.[20] Product advertising that is criticised include the following products: tobacco products, alcoholic beverages, condoms and other sexually related products, medical products and services, and personal care and hygiene products. Advertising content can be silly or insulting, in poor taste, exaggerated, negative, insensitive, or manipulative. Finally, some claim that advertising causes people to buy goods they otherwise would not purchase, promotes materialistic values and life-styles, and lowers values and moral standards.

Advertising Travesties and Tragedies

Advertisements created by business owners or agencies are not always successful. Something goes wrong, and there is no response to the ad. The problem could be with the advertisement, the media selection, or the philosophy of the advertising campaign. The following are some advertising travesties and tragedies:

- Advertising can sell anything, anywhere, anytime.
- Television always gives the biggest bang for the buck.
- Mass, not class, is important.
- Clever copy gets thoroughly read.
- Pictures sell better than copy.
- Sex can sell anything.
- Entertainment can sell anything.
- Sales are down, so cut the advertising budget.
- Sales are up, so cut the advertising budget.
- Creativity is more important than media selection.
- If it's beautiful, they'll read (watch) it.
- The agency is always right; they are the professionals.
- The advertisement (campaign) has run long enough.
- Positioning is for big business.
- Research is expensive; we know the ads are working.[21]

Regulating Advertising

Because of the criticism of advertising and the deception practiced by some business owners, advertising is regulated by several federal agencies. The following are some of the agencies charged with keeping advertisers honest:

Federal Trade Commission

- **Federal Trade Commission**—Controls unfair business practices of advertisers and takes action on false and deceptive advertising. This is the most important agency in the regulation of advertising and promotion.

Food and Drug Administration

- **Food and Drug Administration**—Controls the labeling of food, drugs, cosmetics, medical devices, and potentially hazardous consumer products. The FDA also monitors the advertising of prescription drugs.

Federal Communications Commission

- **Federal Communications Commission**—Regulates broadcast media advertising. Stations that air noncomplying advertising could lose their broadcasting license.

Postal Service

- **Postal Service**—Regulates all material that goes through the mails.

Department of Agriculture

- **Department of Agriculture**—Controls advertising for seed, meat, and insecticides.

Securities and
Exchange
Commission

Library of
Congress

· **Securities and Exchange Commission**—Regulates advertising of securities.
· **Library of Congress**—Protects copyrights.

SUMMARY

For most small businesses, marketing is an extremely important function. Selling, promotion, and advertising are integral aspects of marketing. To have effective sales programs, small business owners need to plan their sales effort and make sure that they or their salespeople make sales calls professionally and successfully. To save time and money, some small businesses are relying more on telephone sales and direct selling. These can be successful selling methods; however, many potential customers are annoyed by telephone sales calls.

Special promotion programs can be very effective for small businesses if they are executed properly. Companies can help their dealers' promotion programs by offering displays, premiums, discounts, promotion materials, or push money. Customers can be encouraged to buy products by receiving samples, discounts, cents-off coupons, premiums, rebates, or service contracts. Promotional giveaways are only effective for a short time; after that it is a company's advertising campaign that keeps customers coming back for repeat purchases.

Effective advertising campaigns can be created after business owners know who their customers are, where they are, why they buy, and how much they buy. Companies need advertising objectives and a reasonable advertising budget. If the budget is sufficient, owners may choose to have advertising agencies develop and present their campaign. If an advertising agency is too expensive, business owners can be helped by media agencies, art services, or radio and television stations. Whoever does the advertising for a small business will have to choose the most appropriate media to use. The five media that comprise the marketing mix are print, broadcast, position, point-of-purchase, and word-of-mouth. Once advertisements have been created and used, their effectiveness should be measured so they can be improved or replaced.

QUESTIONS FOR REVIEW AND DISCUSSION

1. How can salespeople plan their work?
2. What are the advantages and disadvantages of direct selling?
3. Who are the different types of consumers?
4. What is push money? Do you think using push money is ethical?
5. If you owned a small business, what would your advertising objectives be?
6. What are the different sources of advertising assistance?
7. Which advertising media do you think would be most effective for small businesses?

8. Can you think of any unusual advertising media other than those mentioned in the chapter?
9. How can small business owners get free publicity for their companies?
10. Why are advertisement headlines so important?
11. How can you measure an advertising campaign's effectiveness?

KEY TERMS

advertising effectiveness
broadcast media
Department of Agriculture
early adopters
early majority
Federal Communications
   Commission
Federal Trade Commission
Food and Drug Administration
innovators
laggards

late majority
Library of Congress
marketing-communications mix
point-of-purchase displays
position media
Postal Service
print media
Securities and Exchange
   Commission
word-of-mouth

CASE
Survival Aids, Ltd.

Nicholas Steven is the founder and owner of Survival Aids, Ltd., a seller of outdoor clothing and camping equipment, located in the north of England. The company sells primarily through catalogs, which it sends to approximately 100,000 people. There are also two retail outlets for the company's merchandise. Nick favors direct selling for the following reasons:

- Full price is paid.
- Cash is received in advance.
- There are few bad debts.
- The wide range of customers eliminates dependence on major accounts.
- Cash sales and credit purchases reduce working capital requirements.

Direct selling does have its drawbacks. The following are some of the disadvantages associated with catalog selling:

- Small orders may be uneconomical to process, especially if paid for by credit card.
- Returns can be expensive.
- Customers cannot really "examine" products before they purchase them.
- It is necessary to maintain a large and growing mailing list.

Survival Aids has been quite successful over the years, but Nick wants to explore other means of selling. He is also looking for new ways to advertise the quality merchandise sold by Survival Aids. The largest group of customers is civilians who enjoy outdoor activities. The other group is military personnel who find Survival Aids' merchandise superior to equipment they are issued. The company has advertised in several media to attract both civilian and military buyers. Advertisements are placed in weekly, monthly, and quarterly magazines such as *Soldier* and *Great Outdoors*. Survival Aids also offers survival seminars, and its employees speak before various outdoor or civic groups. Nick thinks that there may be better ways to advertise his company's products, but he is not sure what other media to use.

QUESTIONS

1. Do you think direct selling is the best way for Survival Aids to sell its merchandise?

2. Can you suggest other ways to sell to both civilians and military personnel?

3. Should Survival Aids turn to outside agencies to do its advertising? If so, which kind of agency do you suggest?

4. What do you think Survival Aids can do to improve its advertising effectiveness?

ACTIVITIES

1. A number of sentences used in advertisements are listed below. Try to rewrite them so they are more effective. The rewritten sentences are listed in "Sentences That Sell, Part 2."

Sentences That Sell, Part One

Ad for Stainless Steel Cookware

1. The covers fit snugly.
2. These utensils have a hard surface of stainless steel.
3. These utensils have molded, heat-resistant handles.

Ad for a Folding Cot

1. This cot has a rigidly braced, tubular aluminum frame.

Ad for a Traveling Bag

1. This bag has a cover of grained vinyl laminated to cotton.

Ad for a Book on Memory Training

1. This magic key opens up the memory-storage cells in your mind.

Ad for a Car Loan Plan

1. Now you can get a forty-eight-month car loan.

Ad for a Set of Books

1. The first volume is yours free.

Ad for a Book on How to Win Friends

1. This book tells you nine ways to influence people.

Sentences That Sell, Part Two

Ad for Stainless Steel Cookware

1. The covers fit snugly to seal in moisture and health-building vitamins and minerals.
2. These utensils have a hard surface of stainless steel for easy cleaning and lasting beauty.
3. These utensils have molded, heat-resistant handles that won't turn or loosen or burn the hands of the user.

Ad for a Folding Cot

1. This cot has a rigidly braced, tubular aluminum frame that provides strength without weight . . . can't rust.

Ad for a Traveling Bag

1. This bag has a cover of grained vinyl laminated to cotton that is easy to care for . . . just wipe clean.

Ad for a Book on Memory Training

1. This magic key opens up the memory-storage cells of your mind and enables you to perform amazing feats of memory.

Ad for Car Loan Plan

1. Now you can get a forty-eight-month car loan that gives you more months to pay, so you pay less each month.

Ad for a Set of Books

1. The first volume is yours free, with no obligation to buy anything.

Ad for a Book on How to Win Friends

1. This book tells you nine ways to influence people without giving offense or arousing resentment.

SOURCE: From the Book: How to Make Your Advertising Make Money By: John Caples © 1983. Used by permission of the publisher, Prentice Hall Press/A Division of Simon & Schuster, Englewood Cliffs, NJ.

2. Select the best headline in "A Quiz for Headline Writers." The answers are at the end of the quiz.

A Quiz for Headline Writers

1. A. If you are a careful driver, you can save money on car insurance.
   B. How to turn your careful driving into money.

2. A. How to make your food taste better.
   B. How to get your cooking bragged about.

3. A. How to build an attic room.
   B. How to build your own darkroom.

4. A. How to do your Christmas shopping in 5 minutes.
   B. The gift that comes 12 times a year.

5. A. How to get a loan of $500.
   B. When should a family get a loan?

6. A. To every woman who would like a career in Interior Design.
   B. Can you spot these 7 common decorating sins?

7. A. Announcing an important revision of the Bible.
   B. Most important Bible news in 340 years.

8. A. How to make chocolate pudding in 6 minutes.
        (Illustration: Picture of pudding being mixed in a
        bowl)
    B. Tonight serve this ready-mixed chocolate pudding.
        (Illustration: Picture of a smiling woman eating pud-
        ding)

9. A. Good news for men who want attractive, well-
        groomed hair.
        (Illustration: Picture of man being admired by attrac-
        tive woman)
    B. Will your scalp stand the "Fingernail Test"?
        (Illustration: Picture of a man scratching his head
        and looking at his fingernails)

10. A. Girls . . . Want Quick Curls.
        (Illustration: Picture of a girl looking in a mirror, set-
        ting her hair)
    B. Does he still say . . . "You're lovely"?
        (Illustration: Picture of a girl being admired by a
        man)
    Answers: 1-A, 2-A, 3-A, 4-A, 5-A, 6-B, 7-B, 8-B, 9-B,
    10-A.

SOURCE: From the Book: How to Make Your Advertising Make Money By: John Caples © 1983. Used by permission of the publisher, Prentice Hall Press/A Division of Simon & Schuster, Englewood Cliffs, NJ.

APPENDIX 13-1

37 Tips on Copywriting

12 WAYS TO GET STARTED

1. Don't wait for inspiration
2. Start with something easy
3. Write as if talking to a companion
4. Write a letter to a friend
5. Forget the "do's" and "don'ts"
6. Describe the product
7. Make a list of benefits
8. Write what interests you most

9. Get inspiration from others
10. Copy successful copy
11. Start by writing headlines
12. Write fast and edit later

11 Ways to Keep Going

1. Make an outline
2. Choose the writing tools that work best for you
3. Work in comfortable surroundings
4. Avoid noise and interruptions
5. Read what you wrote yesterday
6. Set a deadline
7. Solve writing problems
8. Avoid self-criticism
9. Avoid heavy meals before writing copy
10. Avoid liquor when you are writing
11. Take advice from famous writers

14 Ways to Improve Your Copy

1. Write more than one headline
2. Choose the best headline
3. Do an opinion test
4. Write more copy than required . . . then cut
5. Omit introductory remarks
6. Omit unnecessary wordage
7. Ask for action
8. Use judgment in revising copy
9. Read it aloud
10. Ask someone else to read it
11. Invite criticism
12. Give your critic a choice
13. Aim for the stars
14. Write every day

SOURCE: From the Book: How to Make Your Advertising Make Money By: John Caples © 1983. Used by permission of the publisher, Prentice Hall Press/A Division of Simon & Schuster, Englewood Cliffs, NJ.

PART FIVE

ACCOUNTING, FINANCIAL, AND INVENTORY MATTERS

14 ACCOUNTING RECORDS AND PROCEDURES

S mall business owners must have a method of determining the financial health of their business. Sound and accurate accounting records provide the best measure of a firm's health and may be used by both management and financial analysts to determine the direction the firm is heading. In effect, financial records may be used both as a control tool and a preventive checkup to chart the firm's progress. The objective of this chapter is to introduce the elements of a basic accounting system and to introduce the different types of accounting systems that all small firms should consider.

This chapter will emphasize why a sound accounting system is needed and how it can be maintained to provide up-to-date and accurate financial information. The analysis of financial statements is also covered in this chapter with an emphasis on how these statements may be used by the small business owners to help make their firms more efficient and more profitable. The final section discusses a wide variety of accounting software packages that have been developed especially for small firms.

THE NEED FOR ACCURATE FINANCIAL RECORDS

Too many small business owners view accounting records as mere bookkeeping (the maintenance of accounting records) and assume that accounting is really no more than a score-keeping function for the firm. Too many also view the accounting function as a necessary, time-consuming, and expensive system required by the government for tax purposes. Although accounting is a score-keeping function and is required by the government, small business owners should have good accounting systems even if they were not required.

Dun & Bradstreet statistics show that most small business failures occur due to management incompetence. Management incompetence does not mean a lack of managerial intelligence but rather not knowing the firm's weaknesses and then being able to react before a weakness causes a failure. A result of several surveys of failed or failing firms by Dun & Bradstreet indicated that less than one-third of the firms prepared and used a cash budget. Almost 95 percent of the surveyed firms that sold on credit did not have any method of checking a customer's credit before the credit was extended or an efficient system of determining which customers were behind in their payments. Many times customers who were more than 120 days late on past purchases were routinely granted additional credit. For some of these firms, bad debts were as high as 10 percent of sales.

The survey also indicated that the majority of the unsuccessful firms' owners did not even know the true financial condition of their firm due, primarily, to the poor quality of their financial records. Although 81 percent of the firms produced income statements and balance sheets, only 11 percent of the owners used these two financial statements as part of their formal process of evaluation, planning, or decision making. None of the firms produced a cash flow statement on a regular basis and only 2 percent used financial analysis.[1]

Provide Accurate Financial Information for Management

The first reason for accurate financial records, therefore, is to provide small business owners with a complete and accurate picture of the financial health of their firms. With these pictures, small business owners will be able to take the action required to weather the downturn in business that many firms will eventually face. For example, if a small business owner sees that accounts receivable are rising much faster than sales and that there has not been a change in the credit terms, then an effort can be taken to determine the reason for the increase. For example, are the existing customers taking longer to pay, or is there just a group of customers who are behind? Accurate records, therefore, help in two ways. First, they indicate that accounts receivable are rising, and next they indicate which customers are slow in paying and how far behind they are. With this information, the small business owner can determine the best course of action to take before the firm faces financial problems.

An accurate and up-to-date financial record-keeping system will provide owners with information that will assist them in the efficient operation of their firm by answering such questions as the following:

1. What was the firm's income last year? Its expenses?
2. What is the total of the accounts receivable? How much is 30 days past due? How quickly are we collecting our accounts?
3. How quickly is the inventory being turned over? Do we have inventory that is not moving? How do we compare with other firms in the same line of business?

4. How much does the firm owe? When is it due?

5. What sales taxes are due the state? Have we withheld the proper amount for FICA?

6. What is the book value of the firm's building and equipment? Are we taking the maximum deduction for depreciation?

7. How much cash does the firm have? Are we expecting a cash crunch in the near future?

8. What expenses could be reduced? How do the firm's expenses compare with other similar firms?

These and dozens of similar questions can be more easily answered with good financial records than without them, and without good records the answers could be almost impossible to answer. Simply stated, good financial records allow small business owners to spot problems before they become major problems and to run firms more efficiently and more profitably.

Required by the Financial Community

A second reason for having accurate financial records is that they are required by the financial community and by the tax authorities. Small business owners will find it almost impossible to borrow money from any financial institution without standard financial records such as income statements and balance sheets. Of course, loans may be obtained based on the personal assets of the small business owner, but loans of this type are actually loans to the owners and not to the firm, and as such, the amount of capital raised will be severely limited. Under these limitations the future growth of firms will likewise be limited, and firms will be handicapped during periods of tight money.

Local, state, and federal tax personnel expect accurate documentation for everything from sales taxes to employees' income and social security taxes. Standard financial record keeping makes the task of attempting to explain a firm's tax liability a lot easier than a set of single-entry records that are backed by checkbook stubs.

Provide a Meaningful Measurement of Performance

A third reason for having accurate financial records is that the records provide a method of measuring how firms are performing against certain standards. A good accounting system will have well-defined standards by which performance can be measured. These standards must be capable of being measured on both a frequent and a continuous basis. For accounting systems this means that they should be set up in accordance with **generally accepted accounting principles (GAAP)** so that they are understandable both to the existing management and to outsiders who may be considering providing loans or credit to the firm. The accounting system, therefore, serves a dual function of providing accurate information to management and providing information to the financial community.

generally accepted accounting principles (GAAP)

From these records, management can determine how the firm is doing against some goal or budget, against the previous period (month, quarter, six months, or year), or against the competition. Without these records, management has only a rough idea of how the firm is doing, and a rough idea is usually not good enough in today's competitive environment. Of course, excellent records are of little value unless they are used by management. The small business owner must see not only that accurate records are being kept but also that those records are read and that action is taken when the records indicate such a need.

Need for the Owner to Understand the Accounting System

Small business owners all too often are so involved in the day-to-day operation of their business that they turn over the design of a record-keeping system and the actual record keeping to their bookkeepers or accountants. There are two major reasons for not doing this and becoming just as involved in the accounting aspects of running the business as with the daily operations. First, accountants will tend to set up the records to fit their needs (i.e., make the record keeping easy for the accountant), and that may not be what is needed by firms. Firms need accounting information that is accurate and timely. Accounting information delivered one to six months late is of little value in managing a firm but may be fine for tax purposes. Why should companies have accounting systems that deliver information that satisfies only the tax authorities? Yet many small firms have exactly that.

Small business owners should work with an accountant to design a system that will serve both to aid in the management of the firm and to provide the necessary accounting records. However, many small business owners do not seem to be even willing to ask their accountants to explain the accounting system to them. Although they pay for the system, they then seem reluctant to fully understand what they have bought. This is a symptom that most people have in their dealings with professionals (doctors, lawyers, and accountants). They willingly pay, but seldom ask the pertinent questions that will let them know what they are paying for or what the alternatives are, or even ask if there are any alternatives. Small business owners must ask questions until they have a good understanding of their accounting system. This does not mean that they need to know as much as their accountant, but they should fully understand the basic accounting statement. For example, if one does not know what deferred taxes or accumulated depreciation is, one should ask.

Finally, if the owner does not understand the accounting system, the possibility of fraud is increased. Small firms are especially vulnerable to fraud because they cannot or do not install the safeguards that reduce the possibility of fraud. These systems include documents to control purchasing, sales, shipping, billing, and collections. For example, with one particular shipping system, no order may be shipped without a standard consecutively numbered order form that has been initialled by designated members of the sales staff. The objective of such a system is twofold. First, only with proper documentation can the accuracy of the billing process be ensured, and second, one of the major losses due to fraud comes from merchandise that "leaves" the premise without being recorded. This system may not eliminate the shipment of unbilled merchandise, but the system certainly reduces the possibility.

FINANCIAL AND ACCOUNTING RECORDS

The previous section covered the three major reasons for maintaining accurate and up-to-date financial records. Basically, good record keeping is the first step toward the profitable operation of any business. Without accurate records, management must simply guess at firms' current financial status. For this reason almost every business has an accounting system. This section presents the basic accounting records that should be considered by all firms and a brief description of each. These basic accounting records include the cash receipts journal, cash disbursements journal, general journal, and the general ledger.[2]

Cash Receipts Journal

cash receipts
journal

The **cash receipts journal** is a detailed, daily listing of all incoming cash. The emphasis here is on cash, not sales. Included in the cash receipts journal are the cash from sales, collections on accounts, rents, interest income, cash from a loan, and cash from the sale of stocks or bonds. The number and headings of the columns in the cash receipts journal may vary from firm to firm to suit the needs of the individual business. An example of a cash receipts journal for Lone Star Technology is shown in Exhibit 14–1. The entries start at the beginning of the month and are shown in chronological order with a total for the month. In the example shown there are columns for both debits (an entry resulting in an increase in assets or a decrease in liabilities or owners' equity) and credits (the opposite of debits: a decrease in assets or an increase in liabilities or owners' equity).

At the close of each business day, the summary figures for cash deposits, sales, and the individual amounts for the miscellaneous income accounts are

EXHIBIT 14–1 Cash Receipts Journal

		Debits		Credits		
Date	Description	Cash	Sales Discounts	Account Credited	Accounts Receivable	Sales
July 1	Paid in full	3,024	30	WRA, Inc.	3,054	
1	Paid in full	748		Lexion	748	
1	Paid on account	1,000		Kenesaey Co.	1,000	
1	Cash sales	6,482				6,482
2	Paid in full	2,620		Blazers	2,620	
	Monthly totals	168,748	462		71,980	97,230

Lone Star Technology — Cash Receipts Journal

entered in the cash receipts journal. At the end of the month, each column in the journal is totaled. The total in the debit columns should equal the total in the credit columns, and these totals are then posted to their respective accounts in the general ledger (explained later in this chapter). Note the simple symmetry of this, and all other, double-entry accounting records. Debits equal credits, and if these two do not agree, the accountant knows there is an error.

Cash Disbursements Journal

cash disbursements journal

The **cash disbursements journal** is a detailed, daily listing of all cash outflows from the business. This journal is the accounting counterpart of the cash receipts journal. As with the cash receipts journal, the column headings are designed to suit the individual business. An example of a cash disbursements journal is shown in Exhibit 14–2. Again, the entries start at the beginning of the month and are entered in chronological order. The second column shows the number of the check that was used to pay the invoice. As a matter of good business practice, most cash payments should be paid by check. Between the checkbook records and the cash disbursements journal, the firm has an excellent record of its expenses. Small cash payments, however, can be made from the petty cash fund. The third column indicates the designated payee, and the additional columns are divided into credits and debits. The example shown illustrates the minimum number of columns; additional columns—for example, for different payroll deductions—could be added.

At the end of each month, each column is totaled, and the total of the credit columns should equal the total of the debit columns. These totals are then posted to their respective accounts in the general ledger.

CASHBOOK. Some small firms and many not-for-profit organizations choose to combine the cash receipts journal and the cash disbursements journal into a single journal called a **cashbook.** The debit and credit columns of the cashbook are set up to fit the particular organization and are, therefore, unique for each firm.

cashbook

EXHIBIT 14–2 Cash Disbursements Journal

			Credits		Debits	
Date	Check No.	Payee	Amount	Purchase Discounts	Account Debited	Accounts Payable
July 1	2431	Kissimee Supply	1,548	32	General expense	1,580
1	2432	Gulf Power	2,210		Utility expense	2,210
1	2433	Petty cash	250		Office expense	250
1	2434	July rent	3,600		Rent expense	3,600
2	2435	Payment in full	2,100	50	Jola Apparel	2,150
		Monthly totals	141,380	410		141,790

Lone Star Technology
Cash Disbursements Journal

General Journal

Both the cash receipts journal and the cash disbursements journal are known as special journals. As a firm and the number of accounting transactions grow, the number of special journals also increases. Typical of these special journals are the sales journal, sales returns and allowance journal, purchases journal, purchases returns and allowance journal, notes receivable register, and notes payable register. Although these special journals provide a means of recording the transactions that occur frequently, a need remains for recording transactions that do not occur frequently, for correcting entries, and for adjusting and closing entries. For these needs and for other financial transactions that do not include the immediate collection or disbursement of cash, *general journal* the **general journal** is the journal of original entry.

The general journal for Lone Star Technology is shown in Exhibit 14–3. Credit sales, credit purchases, depreciation, and amortization are some of the more common types of transactions that may be recorded in the general journal. For example, bad debts are written off in this journal, and if payment is received at a later date, then the entry is reversed (the bad debt credit becomes a debit). The entries in the first column are listed in chronological order, and the explanation or account number is shown in the second column. In the general journal a more detailed explanation of the transaction is made and compared with the description given in the special journals. The additional columns indicate the posting reference number and the now expected debit and credit columns.

General Ledger

All three journals described above are known as books of original entry, and they provide a record of firms' financial transactions in chronological order. *general ledger* The entries from these journals are then posted in the **general ledger** and to subsidiary ledgers for grouping them into asset, liability, capital, income, and

EXHIBIT 14–3 General Journal

Date	Account/Explanation	Post Ref.	Debit	Credit
	Lone Star Technology			
	General Journal			
July 1	Notes receivable	216	5,000	
	Accounts receivable—Salem Inc.			5,000
	To record receipt of 90-day note in full settlement of account			
1	Bad debts		1,280	
	Cash			1,280
	Check returned ISF— Youngstown Inc.			
2	Purchases		6,440	
	Hinkle Jobbers, Inc.			6,440
	To record credit purchases			

expense accounts. Separate sheets are provided in these ledgers for each account. Firms' financial statements (income statement and balance sheet) are then prepared from the information available in the general ledger. This posting is done each accounting period, usually each month or each quarter. An example of the general ledger is shown in Exhibit 14–4.

The general ledger consists of many pages similar to the two pages illustrated in Exhibit 14–4. The general ledger provides a running balance of each of the firm's various accounts. Each account is given a number. In Exhibit 14–4, the two accounts are Cash, with account number 100, and Office Supplies Expense, with account number 420. These account numbers will vary from firm to firm, but the following partial chart of accounts is typical.

CHART OF ACCOUNTS

Current Assets (100–120)		Current Liabilities (200–220)	
100	Cash	200	Accounts payable
105	Accounts receivable	205	Notes payable
110	Inventory	210	Sales tax—payable
115	Materials and supplies	215	FICA taxes—payable
120	Prepaid expenses	220	Withholding tax
Plant and Equipment (150–190)		**Long-Term Liabilities (250–270)**	
150	Equipment	250	Long-term debt
155	Accumulated depreciation		
		Stockholders' Equity (280–295)	
		280	Capital stock
		290	Retained earnings
Revenues (300–350)		**Expenses (400–490)**	
300	Retail sales	400	Salaries and wages
305	Service	405	Commission
310	Miscellaneous income	410	Payroll taxes
		415	Rent
		420	Office supplies
		430	Interest

As the journal entries are posted in the general ledger, the journal page from which the entry was taken is recorded, and the account balance is brought up to date. The balance in the summary accounts in the general ledger should always equal the sum of the balances of the individual accounts in the subsidiary ledgers. A trial balance is taken to verify that the debit total equals the credit total. When these accounts are in balance, the firm's financial statements may be prepared. The two basic financial statements that should be prepared for every firm on at least a quarterly basis are the income statement and the balance sheet.

Income Statement

income statement

The **income statement** (sometimes called the profit and loss statement) is a summary of a firm's sales or revenues minus expenses over a particular ac-

EXHIBIT 14–4 General Ledger

		Lone Star Technology		
		General Ledger		

	Cash		Acct. No. 100	
Date	Explanation	Debit	Credit	Balance
	Balance brought forward			10,000
July 1	Received on account	4,772		14,772

~~~~~~

		Office Supplies Expense	Acct. No. 420	
Date		Debit	Credit	Balance
July 14		690		690
July 31		410		1,100

~~~~~~

counting period. Firms are profitable if their sales are greater than their expenses, and firms are unprofitable if expenses are greater than sales. Obviously the objective of any firm is to be profitable. (That is why businesses are divided into for-profit and not-for-profit operations, with the not-for-profit types usually thought of as charitable organizations such as churches, schools, United Way, or Girl Scouts.) An example of an income statement is shown in Exhibit 14-5.

As can be seen in the income statement shown in Exhibit 14–5, the income statement is roughly divided into three parts: (1) sales, (2) expenses, and (3) the resulting summary of sales and expenses. Sales show the total (gross) sales from the business during the accounting period. Most firms differentiate between sales and cash. For the firm that sells only for cash, sales and cash are equal; but for the majority of firms that have at least some sales on credit, sales indicate that a sale was made but cash may or may not have been collected. From sales, any returns, allowances, and/or discounts must be subtracted. The result is net sales. Cost of sales (or cost of goods sold) is an accounting of what the goods sold by firms actually cost. Cost of sales may be described by a simple equation:

Cost of sales = Beginning inventory + Purchases + Freight costs
− Purchase discounts taken − Ending inventory

The difference between net sales and the cost of sales is the gross profit.

The second section indicates the cost of generating sales. This section may be subdivided into selling expenses and general and administrative expenses. Selling expenses include all the expenses incurred that are directly related to producing the sale of a firm's goods and services. These expenses include the salaries paid to the sales personnel, commissions, advertising, promotions, marketing, and any fixed overhead directly connected to sales. General and administrative expenses are those expenses not directly related to the cost of sales or the selling effort. These expenses include administrative salaries,

EXHIBIT 14–5 Income Statement

Lone Star Technology
Income Statement (000 omitted)
for the three months ended September 30

Revenue		
Gross sales		$2,968
Less returns and allowances		193
Net sales		2,775
Cost of sales		
Beginning inventory	$ 190	
Plus: purchases	1,210	
Plus: freight	20	
Less: discounts taken	10	
Less: ending inventory	185	
Cost of sales		1,225
Gross profit		1,550
Selling expenses		
Salaries and wages	120	
Commissions	130	
Advertising and promotion	150	
Overhead expense	92	
Total selling expense	492	
General and administrative expenses		
Salaries and wages	235	
Employee benefits	128	
Insurance	45	
Depreciation	52	
Overhead expense	134	
Total general and administrative	594	
Total operating expenses		1,086
Total operating income		464
Interest expense		82
Income before taxes		382
Income taxes		143
Net income		$ 239

employee benefits, utilities, rent, insurance, interest paid, bad debts, office supplies, and fixed overhead that is connected with the administration of the firm.

The final section, and the one most people look at first, shows the net income. The difference between gross sales and expenses is the firm's operating income. Operating income minus taxes equals net income. Net income, therefore, is what the owners earn from their investment in the business. The net income may be paid out as dividends or may be retained by the firms as a source of funds that help the firms grow.

Balance Sheet

balance sheet

The **balance sheet** is the second of the two financial statements that all firms should have prepared on a periodic basis. The balance sheet indicates the

EXHIBIT 14–6 Balance Sheet

Lone Star Technology
Balance Sheet (000 omitted)
September 30

Current assets			Current liabilities	
Cash	$ 36		Accounts payable	$ 113
Marketable securities	10		Notes payable	165
Accounts receivable	284		Misc. accruals	21
Inventory	185		Total current liabilities	$ 299
Total current assets	$ 515			
Fixed assets			Noncurrent liabilities	
Building and equipment	$ 410		Long-term debt	$ 278
Leasehold improvement	298		Deferred taxes	35
Less: accumulated depreciation	72		Total noncurrent	$ 313
Net fixed assets	$ 636			
			Owner's equity	
Total assets	$1,151		Common stock	$ 50
			Capital surplus	162
			Retained earnings	327
			Total net worth	$ 539
			Total liabilities and net worth	$1,151

assets, liabilities, and net worth a firm has at a particular time. Thus, the income statement indicates how a firm did over a period of time, and the balance sheet shows a firm's position at some point in time. The balance sheet is so called because it shows the assets, which are on the left side of the statement, balanced against (i.e., equal to) the liabilities and the net worth of the firm, which are on the right side of the statement. The basic equation is

$$Assets = Liabilities + Net\ worth$$

This simple equation tells a lot about the firm, because it indicates what the resources (assets) of firms are and how the firms have chosen to finance their resources.

An example of a balance sheet is shown in Exhibit 14–6. The assets (left side) of the balance sheet are divided into two categories: current assets and fixed assets. Current assets are those assets that are held only temporarily by firms and can be converted into cash in one year or less. They are listed in order of their liquidity from cash, which is the most liquid asset, to inventory, which is the least liquid current asset. Fixed assets are those assets that represent long-term (fixed) investments by the firm. These assets are not very liquid in nature. Fixed assets include such items as buildings, land, machinery and equipment, trucks, furniture and fixtures, and leasehold improvements.

The first section on the right-hand side of the balance sheet contains the current liabilities (obligations) of firms. Current liabilities are those obligations due within one year. This section also includes any part of the long-term debt that is due in the next twelve months. Accruals are obligations related to the normal operations of the businesses that have not been paid but are owed. An example is wages payable, which includes wages that firms owe employees but have not yet paid due to the date of the recording period. Thus, the date of the balance sheet may be on a Wednesday, but employees will not be paid until Friday although they have earned three days' pay.

The second section indicates the noncurrent or long-term (due in more than one year) liabilities of firms. These obligations include long-term debt such as bonds, deferred income taxes, or notes payable that have a maturity of more than one year. The final section indicates the net worth or owners' equity. From an accounting standpoint, net worth is the difference between the total assets of the firm and the total liabilities (the total of current liabilities plus noncurrent liabilities). Basically, owners' equity is the capital invested in firms by the owners of the firm plus any earnings that have been retained (not paid out as dividends) by the firm. When a business is profitable and the profits are not paid out as dividends, then the owners' equity will increase. Likewise, if firms are not profitable, then owners' equity will decrease. Although not desirable, owner's equity can be negative.

Understanding Financial Statements

Of what real value are the financial statements that were presented above? Financial statements are required by the Internal Revenue Service and needed by firms to obtain loans from legitimate financial institutions, but financial statements also are very valuable to small business owners as an indication of the financial health of firms. This section will present a brief look at some of the most common methods of analyzing the financial statements. Basically, data from the financial statements are used to determine financial ratios, which are compared with what firms have done in the past and with other similar sized firms in the same industry.

Ratios may be grouped into four major categories: (1) liquidity, (2) asset management, (3) debt management, and (4) profitability. Only a few of the most popular ratios will be presented under each category of ratios; for a more complete study, the interested reader should consult any standard financial management textbook or any similar publications available in most public libraries or bookstores. To show how the information from financial statements is used to aid management in its analysis of the firm, the income statement and balance sheet from Lone Star Technology (Exhibit 14-5 and Exhibit 14-6) will be used.

Liquidity Ratios

liquidity ratios

current ratio

quick ratio

Liquidity ratios are an indication of the firm's ability to meet its short-term obligations. The two most commonly used ratios are the **current ratio** and the **quick ratio.** The current ratio is the current assets divided by current liabilities. Referring to Exhibit 14-6, the current ratio for Lone Star is as follows:

Current ratio = 515/299 = 1.72

In this case, the current ratio indicates that Lone Star's liquid assets are 1.7 times more than its short-term obligations. The ratio, by itself, is relatively meaningless and should be compared with other similar sized firms in the same business. For example, Dun & Bradstreet's *Key Business Ratios* or *Troy's Almanac* are two well-known publications that have most of the common ratios for a large group of firms by industry and by firm size. These publications are available in most public libraries. In this case, the industry median (from *Troy's Almanac*) for a retail firm is 1.55. Thus, Lone Star is slightly more liquid than the industry average. When a firm's ratios vary a great deal from the industry averages, management must attempt to determine the reason for the variance and what, if anything, should be done to correct the problem.

Another indicator of a firm's liquidity is the quick ratio. The quick ratio is the current assets minus inventories divided by current liabilities. Thus, the quick ratio is a more severe test of liquidity because it looks only at the most liquid of the firm's current assets and compares them with the short-term obligations of the firm. For Lone Star the quick ratio is as follows:

Quick ratio = (515 − 185)/299 = 1.10

By this measure, Lone Star has a quick ratio of 1.10 as compared with the industry average of 1.01. Thus, Lone Star is slightly more liquid than the average store in this industry.

When can management and financial analysts tell that a firm may have a liquidity problem? Usually when firms are having financial problems, they start paying their bills a little later. Thus, their accounts payable and their notes payable increase faster than their current assets, and the liquidity ratios will decrease. A low or deteriorating ratio may indicate that the firm is experiencing some financial difficulties and could have trouble meeting its current obligations. Sound management practice requires the constant monitoring of these ratios and, when needed, an attempt to improve them.

For example, one way of improving the quick ratio is to have a sale, particularly to move obsolete or slow-moving inventory. The reduction in inventory and the resulting increase in cash has a positive effect on the quick ratio. If the increase in cash is used to pay off accounts payable, then the current ratio also improves. From the Lone Star example, assume that an inventory sale (a sale of slow-moving inventory at cost) results in a reduction of $30,000 in inventory and a corresponding increase in cash. The quick ratio now is (515 − 155)/299 = 1.2, and if this cash is used to reduce accounts receivable, the current ratio improves to 485/269 = 1.80. Improvements in liquidity ratios, the ratios most considered by bankers before granting a loan, can mean obtaining a loan that may not otherwise have been granted, and/or obtaining the loan at a lower interest rate.

Asset Management Ratios

asset management ratios

Asset management ratios, sometimes called operating ratios, indicate how efficiently firms are utilizing their assets to generate revenues. Some of the more popular asset management ratios are the inventory turnover ratio, fixed asset turnover ratio, total asset turnover ratio, and the average collection period.

inventory
turnover ratio

INVENTORY TURNOVER RATIO. The **inventory turnover ratio** is derived by dividing the cost of sales by the average inventory. For Lone Star the inventory turnover ratio is as follows:

Inventory turnover ratio = 1,225/185 = 6.62

In this case, the assumption is that the ending inventory is equal to the average inventory. A more precise figure could be obtained by averaging the inventory at the end of each month or quarter. This turnover compares quite favorably with the industry average of 4.34. This means that Lone Star is able to do a much better job than the typical firm in the industry of selling its products and/or managing its inventories. This could be the result of lower prices, better service, or just better marketing.

fixed asset
turnover ratio

FIXED ASSET TURNOVER RATIO. The **fixed asset turnover ratio** indicates the dollar amount of sales that is generated compared to the fixed assets of firms. The ratio is defined by dividing sales by net fixed assets. For Lone Star the fixed asset turnover ratio is as follows:

Fixed asset turnover ratio = 2,775/636 = 4.36

This turnover ratio is slightly better than the industry median of 3.85. Comparison with the industry average, however, can be misleading for several reasons. The primary reason is because the denominator in the equation, net fixed assets, may not be comparable between firms. Newer assets will result in higher net fixed assets than older equipment; firms that depreciate assets more quickly than other firms will have a smaller net fixed asset base; generally the firm with older assets will have less net fixed assets than firms with newer assets; and firms that lease assets will have a lower net fixed asset base than firms that purchase their assets. All these factors make the comparison of the fixed asset turnover ratio between firms very difficult to interpret. However, the ratio is useful as a year to year comparison for the firm.

total asset
turnover ratio

TOTAL ASSET TURNOVER RATIO. **Total asset turnover ratio** is defined as sales divided by total assets, thus including current as well as fixed assets of the firm. The ratio indicates the amount of revenues that are generated on the total resources of the firm. For Lone Star the total asset turnover ratio is as follows:

Total asset turnover ratio = 2,775/1,151 = 2.41

Again Lone Star is above the industry median of 2.23, an indication that management is employing the assets of the firm in an efficient manner.

average
collection
period

AVERAGE COLLECTION PERIOD. The final asset activity ratio is the **average collection period,** which is defined as the accounts receivable divided by the average daily credit sales. Average daily credit sales is found by dividing the firm's annual credit sales by 365. For Lone Star, which has 80 percent of its sales on credit, the average collection period is as follows:

$$\text{Average collection period} = \frac{284}{2,775(.80)/365} = 46.7 \text{ days}$$

This number compares unfavorably with the industry average of 37.2 days. For competitive reasons, the credit terms within an industry are equal, and for this industry, terms usually are 1/10, net 30. This means that the customer may take a 1 percent cash discount if the invoice is paid in 10 days; otherwise the entire amount is due in 30 days. This may mean that Lone Star's relatively higher activity ratios are related to a relaxed credit policy. Management may have decided that the way to increase sales was to grant credit to an increasingly risky (from a credit standpoint) group of customers. The effect could be both a stimulation in sales and an increase in bad debts.

A high average collection period, by itself, is not a sign of poor management; in fact, if the increase in sales is profitable, (i.e., the increase in profits are greater than the increase in the cost of managing and collecting the increase in sales), the relaxing of credit terms is a smart decision. Likewise, a low average collection period is not necessarily an indication of good management. If a firm's credit policy is too tight, then sales may be reduced as profitable, but slightly risky, customers go to a competitor with a less stringent credit policy. The key point is to determine where the increase in sales, and the resulting profit from those sales, is offset by the increase in the cost of generating those sales. The increase in costs comes from an increase in administration expenses in the credit department and an increase in loss from bad debts.

If credit terms are not changed, then the average collection period should be used as a measure of a change in either the general credit conditions of the firm's customers or the efficiency of the credit department. Thus an analysis of changes in the average collection period over time can be a good indication of developing problems. These problems may be due either to problems with the general economy or with the effort the credit department personnel are exerting in checking the credit rating of the firm's customers or maybe just the lack of effort in collecting past due accounts.

Debt Management Ratios

debt
management
ratios

Debt management ratios, sometimes called financial leverage ratios, indicate the amount of debt a firm has in relation to the amount of capital supplied by the owners of the firm. These ratios, like the liquidity ratios, are also an indication of the financial risk that a firm is taking. High debt ratios indicate a large amount of debt with its inherent fixed amount of interest payments, but high debt also indicates a potential for favorable financial leverage. Favorable financial leverage is the result of earning a higher return on borrowed capital than the cost of that capital. The difference between the return on borrowed capital and the cost accrues directly to firms' owners. The debt management ratios presented in this section include the debt ratio, the debt to net worth ratio, and the times interest earned ratio.

debt ratio

DEBT RATIO. **Debt ratio** is defined as the total debt divided by the total assets of the firm. Some textbooks and some financial reporting services define debt ratio as total long-term debt divided by total assets. The definition is not as important as realizing that if small business owners are going to compare firms within an industry, then they must be sure to determine how the debt ratio is defined. Here the more common definition using total debt will be employed. For Lone Star the debt ratio is as follows:

Debt ratio = 612/1,151 = .53

A debt ratio of .53 means that the creditors of the firm are financing 53 percent of the assets of Lone Star and the owners only 47 percent. Obviously the creditors would like the firm to have a lower debt ratio because the lower debt offers them more protection if the firm suffers financial distress. This ratio is about equal to the industry average of .51 and indicates that Lone Star uses about the same amount of financial leverage as the typical firm in the industry.

debt to net worth ratio

DEBT TO NET WORTH RATIO. The **debt to net worth ratio,** sometimes called the debt to equity ratio, is defined as total debt divided by the net worth. The ratio is similar to the debt ratio, but compares debt to net worth rather than debt to all the assets of the firm. For Lone Star the debt to net worth ratio is as follows:

Debt to net worth ratio = 612/539 = 1.14

The ratio indicates that Lone Stars' creditors are putting up $1.14 for every dollar that the owners have put into the business. This compares favorably with the industry debt to net worth average of 1.10. Like the debt ratio, the firm's creditors would like a relatively low debt to net worth figure because it gives them more protection if the firm experiences financial problems. Analysts, however, should not attempt to interpret either the debt ratio or the debt to net worth ratio without considering the industry in which the firm is located. Those industries with steady cash flows, such as utilities, can have much higher ratios than industries that experience large seasonal fluctuations in cash flows, such as most retail businesses and the construction business.

times interest earned ratio

TIMES INTEREST EARNED RATIO. The final of the three debt management ratios presented in this section is the **times interest earned ratio.** This ratio indicates the number of times that the interest charges of firms are covered by the operating income of firms. The result is an important indicator of how much a firm's operating income can fluctuate before there is a danger of it not being able to meet its interest obligations. For Lone Star the times interest earned ratio is as follows:

Times interest earned ratio = 464/82 = 5.66

Thus, Lone Star's operating income is covering its present interest expenses over six times, and this compares very favorably with the industry average of 4.88 times.

Profitability Ratios

profitability ratios

Profitability ratios are designed to indicate the type of return the firm is obtaining on its investments. These ratios are the bottom-line figures that are used to measure the result of all of management's investment and financing decisions. The profitability ratios are the ratios that most people look at first to determine how well firms are doing, whereas the other ratios tend to indicate why firms' profitability ratios are where they are. The profitability ratios presented in this section are the gross profit margin, the net profit margin, the return on total assets, and the return on owners' equity.

gross profit
margin ratio

GROSS PROFIT MARGIN RATIO. The **gross profit margin ratio** is an indication of how well firms are able to price their products in the competitive environment. The gross profit margin ratio is defined as the gross profit divided by net sales. Gross profit is determined by subtracting the cost of sales from net sales. For Lone Star the gross profit margin ratio is as follows:

Gross profit margin ratio = 1,550/2,775 = .56

Because the gross profit margin ratio for the industry is .54, Lone Star is able to obtain about the same markup on the goods sold as the typical firm in the industry. Another way of looking at this ratio is that forty-four cents of every dollars worth of goods sold covers the cost of those goods, leaving fifty-six cents to cover operating expenses and profit for the owners. Firms can increase their gross profit margin by selling higher markup goods or by providing a superior service or some other amenity that allows them to sell at higher prices.

net profit
margin ratio

NET PROFIT MARGIN RATIO. The net profit margin indicates the profit obtained after all expenses are subtracted. The **net profit margin ratio** is defined as net income divided by net sales. For Lone Star the net profit margin ratio is as follows:

Net profit margin ratio = 239/2,775 = .086

Thus, Lone Star is obtaining a net profit of 8.6 percent on its sales, and this slightly below the industry average of 9.7 percent. Because the net profit margin is calculated after both operating and financing costs are considered, a comparison with other firms in the industry is a useful measure of how well management has been able to set prices and control expenses. If firms' net profit margins are below the industry norm, then management should investigate why.

return on total
assets ratio

RETURN ON TOTAL ASSETS RATIO. The **return on total assets ratio,** sometimes called the return on investment ratio, is defined as net income divided by the total assets of the firm. This measure indicates the net profit that firms are obtaining on the total invested (in assets) capital. For Lone Star the return on total assets ratio is as follows:

Return on total assets ratio = 239/1,151 = .208 or 20.8%

Lone Star is obtaining a 20.8 percent return on the assets invested in the business, and this compares quite favorably with the industry average of 19.6 percent. The ratio is very useful to management as a comparison with other firms within the industry and as an indication of how well the firm is doing. This ratio, and the other profitability ratios, are excellent indicators of the ability of management to provide an adequate return on the resources invested in the firm.

return on owners' equity ratio

RETURN ON OWNERS' EQUITY RATIO. The final profitability ratio is the **return on owners' equity ratio,** which is defined as net income divided by stockholders' equity. The ratio is an indication of the return that the owners are obtaining on the capital they have invested in firms. This capital includes their original investment plus any of their earnings that have been retained by firms. For Lone Star the return on owners' equity ratio is as follows:

Return on owners' equity ratio = 239/539 = .443 or 44.3%

Return on equity (ROE) is one ratio that is comparable across industries, and the return obtained by Lone Star is very high; however, a high ROE is seldom attained by a firm that has any close competitors. In this case Lone Star is selling a new medical testing device that, at the current time, has no close competition.

Because ROE is a very important ratio for management to use as an overall assessment of how firms are being managed, a further look at this ratio may be worthwhile. ROE is the culmination of several actions taken by management to obtain a high return on the resources employed by the firms. The ratio is determined by a combination of one of each of the three major management ratios: an asset management ratio, a debt management ratio, and a profitability ratio. In fact the ratio may be stated as a multiplicative equation as follows:

ROE = Net profit margin × Total assets turnover × The equity multiplier

The first two ratios have been defined previously, but the equity multiplier has not. The equity multiplier is defined as total assets divided by owners' equity. The ratio, therefore, is a variation of a type of debt management ratio and is an indication of the total size of firms in relationship to what the owners have put into the firm. The equity multiplier is, therefore, a leverage ratio. The usefulness of ROE as an analytical device for management can then be seen by inspecting each of the three ratios that make up the ROE. ROE may be stated mathematically as follows:

$$ROE = \frac{\text{Net income}}{\text{Sales}} \times \frac{\text{Sales}}{\text{Total assets}} \times \frac{\text{Total assets}}{\text{Owners' equity}}$$

On the right-hand side of the equation, sales and total assets cancel out leaving net income divided by owners' equity or ROE. What this equation shows is that improvements in ROE come from an increase in the net profit margin, in the turnover of assets, or in leverage and that each of these ratios has a powerful multiplicative effect on ROE. The ratio, therefore, may be used by management to see where it may improve its results; also, a comparison of each of the three individual ratios with other firms in the industry may be a good indication of where it may start looking for improvement.

EXHIBIT 14–7 Lone Star Technology
Summary of Financial Ratios

Ratio	Lone Star	Industry Median
Liquidity		
Current ratio	1.72	1.55
Quick ratio	1.10	1.01
Asset Management		
Inventory turnover	6.62	4.34
Fixed asset turnover	4.36	3.85
Total asset turnover	2.41	2.23
Average collection period	46.7 days	37.2 days
Debt Management		
Debt ratio	.53	.51
Debt to net worth	1.14	1.10
Times interest earned	5.66	4.88
Profitability Ratios		
Gross profit margin	56%	54%
Net profit margin	8.6%	9.7%
Return on total assets	20.8%	19.6%
Return on owners equity	44.3%	

SUMMARY OF FINANCIAL RATIOS. One method to determine where to improve a firm's results is to calculate a group of ratios and then compare them with the industry averages. The objective is to determine where the firm's results vary from those of the industry and then take the appropriate action to improve the weak areas or to strengthen the strong areas. A summary of the financial ratios for Lone Star Technology and the industry is presented in Exhibit 14–7. A summary page such as the one presented in Exhibit 14–7 is usually the quickest method of comparison. In this case each of the ratios has already been discussed previously and will not be reiterated here.

MAINTAINING ACCOUNTING RECORDS

In the early stages of most small businesses, the maintenance of the accounting records can be accomplished by small business owners or by hiring part-time bookkeepers or accountants. Interestingly, a recent survey indicated that about 35 percent of the small business owners surveyed did their own internal bookkeeping, but 90 percent used an outside accounting service for at least some of their accounting needs.[3]

The advantage of having owners keeping the accounting records early in the life of a new firm is that they will learn the accounting function when the firm is small and will have a better appreciation of what the accounting system is and can do for the firm. More importantly, small business owners will learn the language of accounting and will be comfortable using accounting terms when discussing the financial status of the firm with the financial community, including their accountants or accounting firms. The primary disadvantage of having small business owners keeping the accounting records is that the task can be time consuming and take time away from tasks that small business owners cannot as easily delegate to others.

A part-time accountant or bookkeeper is probably a good solution for most small businesses. In fact, even the smallest companies are eventually faced with the need to hire a bookkeeper or an accountant.[4] Part-time help can be either someone employed part-time by the firm or the accounting services from a firm that offers accounting services for small businesses. The advantage of having the accounting records maintained by professional part-time help is that they are usually knowledgeable about accounting techniques and will do a professional job of keeping firms' records in compliance with the generally accepted accounting practices. There are, however, two major disadvantages to having the accounting records maintained by an outside accounting service.

The first disadvantage is that part-time accounting services are not known for the speed or timeliness with which they deliver accounting records and financial statements. In all fairness, they have a near impossible task of trying to deliver each firms' month-end reports near the beginning of each month, but many services deliver financial statements two to three months after the end of an accounting period. This is far too late to be of any managerial help to the small business owner. This problem of timeliness leads to the second major disadvantage. Part-time accountants tend to set up accounting systems that make the accounting task easier, and they are not set up to provide financial information that could be useful in managing a more efficient operation. Unfortunately, management usually acquiesces in this arrangement by not using the financial statements for anything but financial reporting and tax information.

What Accounting Should Do

All firms need accounting systems that keep accurate records of their financial status. This includes such relatively obvious tasks as verifying and posting bills and keeping accurate records of employees' time and the resulting pay, sales and sales tax collected, deposits made and checks written, invoices written and payments recorded to the correct accounts, and dozens of other similar day-to-day tasks that must be completed for the firm to operate. In addition to these tasks, an accounting system should be designed to provide the normal financial statements plus allow management to develop reports such as cash flow projections, budgets, actual versus budget, cost accounting, and standard cost reports. Firms' accounting systems must be designed so that they will provide the reports needed by management.

What the firm needs, when the initial accounting system is established, is someone who has set up accounting systems in the past, not someone who has merely kept books at other firms. The initial set up is all-important, because after the system is in place, then a bookkeeper may be hired to keep the system running. However, as the firm grows, the need for an accountant to manage the accounting system increases. An accountant has the ability and knowledge to develop cash flow projections, budgets, and cost accounting systems that most bookkeepers do not know how to do. In addition, the accountant can assist management by writing specialized reports that may originate from accounting data.

Auditors

Most entrepreneurs misunderstand what auditors do, believing that an auditor's job is to find problems with a firm's accounting records. Because they are paying for the auditor, they tend to resent the negative comments. Actually the auditor's job is to examine firms' accounting and control procedures and determine if they are both adequate and complete. Thus, the auditor's job is to give small business owners reports on the firms' accounting system and to indicate how it may be improved. In the process of checking, the auditors will verify some of the accounts receivable, accounts payable, inventory, and other documents that may materially influence the value of firms' assets.

When the auditor completes the examination, an opinion is issued. Auditors' opinions are based on their objective examination of the accounting records and expresses their view as to the fairness of the presentation of the financial position (balance sheet) and the results of the firms' operations (income statement). Because audited reports are based on both the integrity of the firm's financial statements, for which management has the prime responsibility, and the completeness of the auditor's examination, for which the auditor has the responsibility, they are used by the financial community with complete confidence. Financial statements that are not audited carry very little weight in the financial community.

CHOOSING AN ACCOUNTING COMPUTER SOFTWARE PACKAGE

The small business accounting market is growing faster than any other software market due primarily to the many attractive features of the programs. There are literally dozens of excellent accounting software packages designed for small businesses. The typical package will not only provide very good accounting information but also be easy to use. Specialized accounting packages are available for a wide variety of businesses from gas stations and video rental stores to retail clothing stores. These specialized packages provide much more information than just accounting records, and this information can assist small business owners in the efficient operation of their enterprises.

Small business owners should consider the purchase of an accounting package if they are spending more than one hour a day on the accounting records of their firms. Also, if firms have payrolls of more than twenty people or more than fifty accounts receivable, then a computerized accounting system may be advantageous. With microcomputers costing between $1,000 and $4,000 and software packages selling for $100 to $500, the cost of obtaining and maintaining up-to-date and accurate records is relatively inexpensive for most small businesses.

Selecting a Software Package

There are two primary ways for owners to select an accounting package for their small business. The first is to read the advertisements in their trade journals and obtain additional information on those that sound as though they may fit their particular businesses. In looking for software, small business owners should seek accounting software designed for small business owners rather than for accountants. According to one expert, short manuals with few charts tend to be better than long manuals with many charts.[5] In addition, they should check with other managers on their experience with accounting packages.

The second method is to visit the local computer store or the local computer software store. Many times the best advice will come from the sales personnel in software stores specializing in business software. They know which packages have problems because the purchasers have called them complaining or asking for help. Before purchasing a software package from any source, small business owners should check with local owners to see if they are satisfied with the results they have obtained. (Appendix B contains information on specific accounting software programs that are suitable for small businesses.)

SUMMARY

There are many reasons for managers of small businesses to set up and maintain accurate financial information records. First, accurate records provide owners with a picture of the financial health of the firms. Second, accurate financial records are required by the financial community, and finally, accurate records provide a meaningful measure of performance. Excellent records are of little value unless they are used by owners, and they tend to be used when management understands the basic accounting system.

The basic accounting system for small firms includes the maintenance of the cash receipts journal, cash disbursements journal, general journal, and general ledger. The cash receipts and cash disbursements are detailed, daily listings of all incoming or outgoing cash. General journals are used for financial transactions that do not include the immediate collection or disbursement of cash, for correcting entries, and for adjusting and closing entries. Entries from the journals are posted to the general ledger in order to group them into asset, liability, capital, income, and expense accounts.

Two basic financial statements, the income statement and the balance sheet, should be prepared for firms at least every quarter. The income statement is a summary of a firm's revenues minus its expenses over a specific period of time, whereas the balance sheet indicates the firms' assets, liabilities, and net worth at particular points in time. Financial information from the income statement and balance sheet are used to determine financial ratios, and these ratios may be used to analyze the firm. These ratios are grouped into four major categories: (1) liquidity, (2) asset management, (3) debt management, and (4) profitability ratios.

Small business owners must set up accounting systems that gives them the information they need to intelligently manage their firm. The actual record keeping may be done either in-house or by employing accountants part-time. In addition, there are many excellent accounting software packages that may aid owners in maintaining accurate accounting systems and provide the firms' managers with timely and useful information that may be employed in decision making.

QUESTIONS FOR REVIEW AND DISCUSSION

1. Why does the small business manager need to understand the firm's accounting system?
2. How can a timely and accurate financial report help the small business manager avoid liquidity problems?
3. Are high debt ratios always a negative sign for a small business? Explain why or why not.
4. Why are return on equity (ROE) ratios comparable across industries?
5. If a firm has liquidity ratios that are above the industry average, does this indicate that the firm will not have trouble paying its current liabilities? Explain your answer.
6. Give three reasons why a small business should maintain accurate financial records.
7. Why is a high average collection period, by itself, not necessarily a sign of poor management?
8. Why do most people look at the profitability ratios before looking at the other financial ratios?
9. How can a firm increase its gross profit margin?

KEY TERMS

asset management ratios
average collection period
balance sheet
cashbook
cash disbursements journal
cash receipts journal
current ratio
debt management ratios
debt ratio
debt to net worth ratio
fixed asset turnover ratio
general journal
general ledger

generally accepted accounting principles (GAAP)
gross profit margin ratio
income statement
inventory turnover ratio
liquidity ratios
net profit margin ratio
profitability ratios
quick ratio
return on owners' equity ratio
return on total assets ratio
times interest earned ratio
total asset turnover ratio

CASE
Rowe Enterprises, Inc.

S ue Rowe has just received her company's annual financial statements and thought that she should complete a ratio analysis of her firm and compare it with the industry averages. Her primary interest was to see how her company was doing and if there were any obvious areas of concern. She had the following statements and industry averages:

Rowe Enterprises Balance Sheet
December 31, 19xx

Cash	$ 120,000	Accounts payable	$ 190,000
Accounts receivable	160,000	Notes payable (9%)	210,000
Inventory	520,000	Other current liabilities	25,000
Total current assets	$ 800,000	Total current liabilities	$ 425,000
Net plant & equipment	400,000	Long-term debt (10%)	400,000
Total assets	$1,200,000	Stockholders' equity	375,000
		Total liability & stockholders' equity	$1,200,000

Income Statement
for the Year Ended December 31, 19xx

Net sales (all on credit)	$1,500,000
Cost of sales	900,000
Gross profit	600,000
Selling, general and administrative expenses	430,000
Earnings before interest and taxes	$ 170,000
Interest	58,900
Earnings before taxes	111,100
State and federal taxes (35%)	38,885
Net income	72,215

Industry Averages

Current ratio	2.5 times
Quick ratio	1.1 times
Inventory turnover	2.4 times
Total asset turnover	1.4 times
Average collection period	35 days
Debt ratio	67 percent
Times interest earned	3.5 times
Net profit margin	4.0 percent
Return on owners' equity	16.8 percent

QUESTION

1. Evaluate Sue's firm using ratio analysis and compare the results with the industry averages. What are the strengths and weaknesses of her firm?

ACTIVITIES

1. Go to a local computer software or office supply store and see what accounting software packages they have for sale. Have them explain the advantages and disadvantages of the most popular package and then present your findings to the class. Would the package be equally suited for a service firm as well as a retail firm? Why or why not?

2. Read the ratio analysis case (Rowe Enterprises, Inc.) and answer the question at the end of the case.

15 PROFIT PLANNING AND CASH-FLOW MANAGEMENT

LEARNING OBJECTIVES

After you have read this chapter, you will be able to do the following:

- Set up a profit plan for a firm
- Forecast asset requirements
- Determine a firm's cash break-even point
- Set up and monitor a firm's cash flow
- Improve operating cash flow

This chapter emphasizes planning for two very important aspects necessary for the good health of any firm but particularly for the new and/or growing firm. The planning for and control of cash and profits are absolutely paramount to the long-term well-being of any firm. First, cash is needed to pay employees, the rent, the utility bill, the insurance premiums, as well as to purchase supplies and many other items required to run a business. Simply stated, cash pays bills that, if not paid, will cause the company to close its doors. Second, profits are needed for the long-term health of the firm. Although a firm cannot operate without cash, it can operate without profits for a short period of time. Certainly many firms are not profitable in their start-up stage, and most firms experience some non-profitable periods during their life.

PROFIT PLANNING

Although a profit plan should include a well-defined statement of goals and strategies, in reality most small business owners do not have the time or the inclination to develop formal written plans. They usually are highly involved in the day-to-day operation of their businesses, and they have a good idea of whether they have the cash to pay the next bills that are due. To many small business owners, profit is having the cash to pay those bills and having enough left over to pay themselves something for their effort. Fortunately as the business grows, planning for profits starts taking more of the small business owners' time as they realize that hard work deserves a good return for the effort.

At this point profit planning can have dramatic results. Owners realize that if they increase advertising or decrease expenses profits will grow, and they are the recipients of those increases. Unfortunately, many owners will not reach this point because they do not take the time early enough to study their revenue sources and expenses and to make the business decisions necessary to insure survival and profitability sooner.

Definition of Profit Planning

profit
planning

What is **profit planning?** In its simplest form, profit planning is no more than establishing a revenue and expense budget. The budget shows what revenues are expected from the sales of goods or services and what expenses will be incurred to obtain those revenues. The beauty of establishing the budget is that it forces the small business owner to sit down and take a look at the firm's expenses; such a process can yield insight into where it is possible to reduce expenses and, therefore, increase profits. In addition, profit planning gives managers a guide to follow as well as a measuring devise against which they can measure their progress toward profitability or, hopefully, toward greater profits.

An effective profit plan should meet three requirements. First, the profit plan needs to involve as many people in the firm as possible. By involving as many employees as possible, the plan becomes their plan and not management's plan. Second, the plan should be as quantitative as possible. The plan should be stated in dollar amounts and time spent rather than qualitative terms such as "improve sales." Finally, the plan should provide an effective mechanism for feedback. A plan is of little value unless employees are given information on how they are doing. The obvious example is giving salespeople a record of their daily and/or weekly sales figures and comparing these figures to the budget. Employees should be asked how sales can be improved. Another example is to give the production supervisor a daily record of hours worked and actual production output versus the budget, or ask the supervisor why hours were higher than budgeted or why costs were below budget.

Reasons for Profit Planning

There are several reasons for profit planning. First, the profit plan is very specific in terms of both revenue and expense expectations for the period of time covered in the plan. Thus, both the owner and employees know exactly what is expected from a sales effort standpoint for the firm to be successful and what the limits on expenses are for the firm to meet its goals. With a profit plan, therefore, the amount of money that can be spent on new inventory or advertising is specified, and the potential problem of going over budget and, thereby, under projected profits is reduced.

A second reason for the profit plan is that it can help build a sense of family and teamwork if the employees are brought into the planning process. When employees are part of the planning process, they tend to work harder to see that their plan is successful. To be part of the process, employees can be asked for suggestions on what they think purchases should be or what they need to be more successful in whatever their part of the enterprise may be. Each person has a specific task or tasks and probably has thought of possible improvements.

A third reason for having a profit plan is that it stimulates the thinking process and promotes planning for the future. The thinking process involves considering each item in the expense budget and evaluating its need and worth. The thinking process also forces the owner to set a sales goal and to at least think about how that goal will be reached. For example, will additional advertising increase sales, or will a looser credit policy help? The answers to these and similar questions will help the owner devise a budget that will serve as a guideline for his or her actions over the next few months.

A final reason for having a profit plan is that it allows the small business owner to constantly check how the firm is doing in relation to the budget. The profit plan, therefore, is important because it provides a means of identifying and treating the problem and not just the symptom. For example, if sales are behind the budgeted sales figure, the firm has time to increase advertising or promotions, or to cut expenses, whichever of these actions seem appropriate given the business environment at that particular point. For example, if sales are below budget and sales in the local economy are off, increasing promotions may help somewhat but cutting expenses may be more prudent. If, however, sales are above the budgeted figure and customer service seems a little slower than normal, the manager could consider hiring additional employees, even if only part-time help, to maintain the quality of service for which the firm is noted.

Limitations to Profit Planning

There are, however, limitations to profit planning. Probably the most severe limitation is that profit plans are specified in dollar terms, but many functions affecting profits cannot be measured in dollar terms. For example, a training program promoting better customer service by helping employees improve their listening skills has a cost that is measurable, but the results are not easily measurable in dollar terms.

A second limitation of a profit plan is that it must be viewed as a dynamic plan and not a static one. Business conditions change—sometimes dramatically. In times of slow economic growth, achieving sales goals may be impossible, and employees, realizing this, may tend not to work as hard to obtain what sales they can given the economic conditions. On the other side, in times of strong economic growth, sales goals are very easy to meet, and employees again may not work hard to obtain additional sales when they find it so easy to meet their goals. The small business owner must constantly monitor the plan to determine how the firm is doing and to take appropriate action in response to changing economic and local business conditions.

Video Station, Inc.: An Example of Profit Planning

Video rental stores have been one of the real growth industries during the late 1980s and early 1990s. Like many industries, the industry started with the so-called mom-and-pop stores, grew to include bigger stores and multistore companies, and is now attracting the interest of large organizations. These organizations are establishing chains of stores that feature video libraries containing over 10,000 tapes. Video Station, Inc., is a relatively small firm that has grown to five stores located in three towns in a single county.

Video Station is now facing competition in two locations from Blockbuster Video, the biggest video rental firm in the United States. One new Blockbuster store will open in late March and another in mid-June. Video Station expects to have its now strong profit picture changed in the near future. Although the owner of Video Station has had a profit plan during his first three years of operation, the increased competition makes planning and following a budget more imperative now than in the past.

Video Station has two major expenses: the first is the purchase of new-release videos, and the second is the salaries of its employees. Both of these expenses can have a great effect on sales and profits. If purchases are reduced, then customers will go to the competing store for their video rental needs. If too many videos are purchased, then they remain on the shelf unrented. If too many employees are brought in during expected rush periods, customer service (check out time) will be excellent, but the cost of providing this service will be high. If too few employees are working during a rush period, then customers have to wait in long lines to check out, and they tend not to return for additional rentals.

To help the planning process, the owner of Video Station keeps a daily record of rental sales. With this record, the day-by-day fluctuations are evident. Monday through Thursday is very slow, whereas Friday through Sunday are the peak days. Peak time occurs between 6 and 10 P.M. The weather plays havoc with planning because sales increase during bad weather and decrease during good weather. Given these variables, Video Station has established weekly revenue and expense budgets, and these budgets are combined into monthly budgets. Monthly budgets are established six months in advance, and, from these monthly budgets, weekly budgets are established for the current month. An example of Video Station's monthly budget is shown in Exhibit 15–1. The budget's expected revenues and expenses are based on what Video Station has experienced in the past, with revenues dropping slightly as the weather is more conducive to being outdoors in the late spring. The budget makes no allowance for the impact of the new Blockbuster Video stores.

A look at Exhibit 15–1 shows the value of a profit plan. At first glance Video Station is expecting to experience strong profits over the next three months, but this plan is a budget, and the results are predicated on the expected revenues. If revenues drop by 20 percent due to the strong competition from the new Blockbuster store, then unless expenses are reduced, Video Station would face a profit of only $560 in April, a loss of $1,810 in May, and a larger loss in June of $3,310. (See short form of the budget below.)

Total revenue	$48,320	$43,600	$42,000
Total expenses	47,760	45,410	45,310
Profit before taxes	$ 560	($ 1,810)	($ 3,310)

EXHIBIT 15–1 Monthly Budget

Video Station, Inc. Revenue and Expense Budget April–June 1992			
	April	May	June
Revenue:			
Video rental	$54,500	$49,000	$47,200
Video sales	4,800	4,500	4,350
Miscellaneous sales	1,100	1,000	950
Total revenue	$60,400	$54,500	$52,500
Expenses:			
Purchases	$12,000	$11,000	$10,800
Salaries	13,000	12,000	12,000
FICA & payroll tax	2,100	1,900	1,900
Lease payments	5,400	5,400	5,400
Utilities	1,600	1,750	1,850
Telephone	860	860	860
Interest	4,800	4,800	4,800
Selling & administration	2,100	2,000	2,000
Miscellaneous store	5,900	5,700	5,700
Total expenses	$47,760	$45,410	$45,310
Profit before taxes	$12,640	$ 9,090	$ 7,190

The value of the budget is now apparent. In this case, it is quickly apparent that the owner of Video Station must monitor his revenues very closely and be ready to reduce purchases and salaries if revenues are greatly reduced due to the increased competition. Of course, there is a real Catch 22 here, in that if the owner of Video Station reduces purchases of new releases and does not have enough for his existing customers, then his customers will go to the competitor's store for the video. In like manner, if employee hours are reduced and customers find that customer service is affected, they will also go over to the competitors' store. Profit planning, therefore, does show the effect of changes in revenues or expenses on profits, but it does not point to simple solutions. It does, however, provide a very useful tool for the entrepreneur in her or his planning.

FORECASTING ASSET REQUIREMENTS

As a firm experiences growth in sales, its need for additional assets will also grow. As assets grow, the means for financing those assets must grow. As sales increase, inventories and accounts receivable will probably increase. If an increase in production is needed, then more equipment may have to be purchased to increase the capacity of the firm. In both of these cases assets will grow and, therefore, the liabilities (debt and/or equity) to finance those assets must also grow. Think of a firm that expands from a single store to a second store. The amount of cash, inventories, accounts receivable, and fixed assets will increase, and the liability side of the balance sheet (accounts payable, notes payable, equity, etc.) must also increase. The business owner must plan for these increases to determine the amount of capital that will be needed to finance the expected growth.

Expansion of plant facilities and increases in inventories and accounts receivable are not reflected in the profit plan, but both require the use of cash or borrowed funds. Planning for these additional funds is often forgotten by small business owners, but it is very important to have time to seek the correct financing (from a cost and type standpoint) to support this growth. Several methods are available to help determine the amount of additional funds that will be needed to support growth, including the percentage-of-sales method, the regression method, multiple regression, and trend analysis.

Percentage-of-Sales Method

percentage-of-sales method

The **percentage-of-sales method** is a popular method for estimating the additional funds that will be needed to support growth in sales because it is relatively straightforward to use and understand. The logic behind the percentage-of-sales method is simply that all assets will grow proportionately with sales. Thus, a 10 percent growth in sales will require a 10 percent growth in inventories or accounts receivable. Certainly there are exceptions (fixed assets, for example, tend to grow in large blocks) to this rather simplistic approach, but the approach is general enough in execution to allow for exceptions. The method can best be explained through the use of an example.

Sports Unlimited: An Example of the Percentage-of-Sales Method

Sports Unlimited (SU) is a general sporting goods store that opened five years ago. SU is owned by three individuals, one of whom works at the store as general manager. SU sells to both the individual and the team markets. Sales to individuals are for cash or credit card, and sales to local high-school and college teams are payable in 45 days. Sales have been growing at a brisk 12 percent a year, and SU is considering opening a second store a year from now in a town located 20 miles from the present store. Sales in the new store are expected to be about half of current sales. The determination of the additional funds needed to finance this year's growth of 12 percent and next year's expansion may be illustrated.

The balance sheet for SU is presented in Exhibit 15–2. The assumption of the percentage-of-sales method is that all current assets will increase proportionately with sales. Thus a 12 percent increase in sales should result in a 12 percent increase in all current assets. The logic behind this assumption is that the firm is being efficiently managed at the present time and that the current level of cash, accounts receivable, and inventory is what is required to support current sales. In any business, fixed assets may or not increase with an increase in sales, but the manager should know whether an increase is required. In this illustration, a capital expenditure of $35,000 is expected in 1993 to support increased sales.

EXHIBIT 15–2 Balance Sheet

SPORTS UNLIMITED Balance Sheet December 31, 1992			
Current assets:		Current liabilities:	
Cash	$ 34,480	Accounts payable	$184,210
Accounts receivable	161,210	Notes payable	178,000
Inventory	348,735	Accrued expenses	24,380
Total current assets	$544,425	Total current liabilities	$386,590
Fixed assets (net)	182,100	Long-term debt	120,000
		Net worth	219,935
Total assets	$726,525	Total liabilities & net worth	$726,525

On the current liability side of the balance sheet the percentage-of-sales method assumes that only accounts payable and accrued expenses will increase proportionately with sales. Notes payable will not increase unless the owner goes to a financial institution and requests and receives an increase. The same logic applies to long-term debt. Long-term debt will not increase as sales increase unless the owner borrows additional long-term capital. The final item on the balance sheet is the owners' equity, or net worth, section. Net worth is the amount of capital that the owners have supplied to the firm. The capital comes from two major sources: (1) capital supplied directly by the owners, and (2) retained earnings. Retained earnings are the accumulated net income of the firm. (For some new firms, this figure could be negative.)

Last year SU had sales of $1,215,065, and sales are expected to increase 12 percent this year to $1,360,873. Given this increase in sales, what additional funds, if any, will be required to finance this growth? The percentage-of-sales method for SU is presented in Exhibit 15–3. The balance sheet information from Exhibit 15–3 is set up in the first column in tabular form for ease of illustration. The second column shows those items that are expected to increase proportionately as a percentage of last years sales. For example, last year cash was $34,480, and sales were $1,215,065; cash, therefore, was 2.84 percent (34,480/1,215,065) of sales. Fixed assets, notes payable, and net worth will not increase proportionately with sales and, therefore, are not given a percentage-of-sales figure.

The third column shows the pro forma balance sheet as of the end of the year. With sales expected to be $1,360,873, all current assets are expected to be the same percentage of new sales as they were of last year's sales. Thus, cash is expected to be 2.84 percent of $1,360,873 or $38,649 as shown in the third column. All other current assets are determined in the same manner. Fixed assets are expected to increase $35,000 to $217,000. Total assets are expected to be $826,908.

On the liability side, accounts payable and accrued expenses are expected to remain as the same percentage of this year's sales as last year's. Notes payable, which are a line of credit from the bank, are expected to remain

EXHIBIT 15–3 Percentage-of-Sales Method

	Balance Sheet 12–31–92	% of Sales	Pro Forma Balance Sheet 12–31–93
Assets:			
Cash	$ 34,480	2.84%	$ 38,649
Accounts receivable	161,210	13.27	180,588
Inventory	348,735	28.70	390,571
Total current assets	544,425	44.81	609,808
Fixed assets (net)	182,100	NA[a]	217,100[b]
Total assets	$726,525		$ 826,908
Liabilities:			
Accounts payable	$184,210	15.16%	$ 206,308
Notes payable	178,000	NA	178,000
Accrued expenses	24,380	2.01	27,354
Total current liabilities	$386,590		$ 411,662
Long-term debt	120,000	NA	120,000
Net worth	219,935	NA	263,483[c]
Total liabilities & net worth	$726,525	Funds available	$ 795,145
		Funds required	31,763
			$ 826,908

[a]Not applicable
[b]Increase in 1993 will be $35,000
[c]Net worth = $219,935 + .032 (1,360,873) = 263,483

unchanged in this initial calculation. Long-term debt also is expected to remain unchanged. Net worth will change as SU expects to earn a net profit of 3.2 percent of sales. The net profit margin has fluctuated from year to year, but has averaged 3.2 over the last three years. Because SU's owners do not pay themselves any dividends, all earnings of the firm are used to finance growth. Given these figures, net worth will increase by $43,548 ($1,360,873 × .032) to $263,483.

Adding up the total liabilities and net worth shows that funds available will total $795,145. Because total assets were $826,908, SU will require an additional $31,763 to finance the expected growth in sales. The next and obvious question is where will the $31,763 come from? The owner in any business needs first to know how much she or he is expected to need and then to look at the potential sources of funds to determine the most likely source. (Sources of financing was addressed in Chapter 7.)

As can be seen from the example above, the percentage-of-sales method is fairly straightforward, but it leaves room for flexibility. For example, an increase in sales may not require an increase in fixed assets. In that case, the figure in the pro forma balance sheet would be the same as the current balance sheet figure (minus the current year's depreciation) for fixed assets. On the other hand, if the firm is producing at full capacity, any increase in sales may result in a large increase in fixed assets this year, but none for the next few years. In either case, the owner should know if an increase in fixed assets is required and should add the additional costs to the current figure to obtain the expected pro forma fixed asset total.

On the liability side of the balance sheet, the entrepreneur should look at notes payable, long-term debt, and net worth to determine the best potential source of capital to finance the firm's growth. If the firm is up to its limit in debt, and the owners cannot put up additional capital, then the solution may be to limit growth—a simple but often overlooked solution.

Percentage-of-sales is a popular forecasting method that is used by many small business owners. A major problem with this method is that all the projections are based on an expected sales forecast, which may or may not be accurate. This problem can be overcome by realizing that changes in sales expectations will cause changes in the pro forma figures, and as the changes become apparent, the owner can adjust the pro forma balance sheet. The percentage-of-sales method is not intended as a one-shot calculation but as an approximation that is subject to change.

VARIATION ON THE PERCENTAGE-OF-SALES METHOD. Another method that may be employed to forecast asset requirements is just a variation of the percentage-of-sales method. In this method all assets are not assumed to increase in the same proportion with sales. Cash, for example, may only increase at half the rate of sales and inventories at 75 percent of sales, whereas accounts receivable may increase at the same rate of the sales increase. The owners who have been keeping up with their business could make these approximations by looking back at different sales levels and determining the level of cash, receivables, and inventories that were required at each level. These percentages could then be used for each current asset in the determination of the pro forma balance sheet.

Regression Method

regression
method

For the more mathematically inclined entrepreneur, the **regression method** is an excellent approach to forecasting asset requirements. With this method a simple regression is derived by regressing an independent variable, sales in this case, on a dependent variable, such as cash. The resulting equation is a linear relationship between the two variables that allows the analyst to see by how much cash increases with sales. Thus, whereas the percentage-of-sales method assumes that all current assets move proportionately with sales, regression analysis indicates by how much each individual current asset moves with sales.

For example, the percentage-of-sales method assumes that if sales go up by 10 percent, then each current asset will also go up by 10 percent. Regression analysis may show that for a 10 percent increase in sales, cash goes up only 6.5 percent, accounts receivable go up 8.9 percent, and inventories go up 7.8 percent. Regression analysis, therefore, is a more exact method of forecasting asset requirements than the percentage-of-sales method, but it also requires either a microcomputer or a statistical-type hand-held calculator to do the necessary calculations.

A big advantage of regression analysis is that the entrepreneur, or manager, has to think about what variables affect the levels of each current asset. Before a regression is run, the analyst must specify the independent variable. In simple regression, the independent variable (e.g., sales) is the single most important factor that affects the level of the dependent variable (e.g., inventories). Thus, the analyst must think what factor really is the major determinant in the level of each asset. This thinking process will help the business owner better understand what variables are affecting the asset levels, and, more importantly, which ones can be controlled by management decisions and which ones cannot.

An assumption of regression analysis is that the relationship between the variables is linear. The results of the regression, however, may not be linear or the strength of the relationship may not be very strong. To determine the strength of the relationship, a *coefficient of determination* (sometimes called the R-square) may be derived. The calculation may be performed using a hand-held calculator or by a statistical program run on a computer. The closer the coefficient of determination is to 1, the stronger the relationship. If the coefficient is near zero, the indication is that there is no relationship between the variables. To determine if the relationship is linear, the variables may be plotted and a visual check can be made on the relationship.

Multiple Regression

multiple
regression

An additional forecasting method that may used by small firms wishing a more sophisticated technique is multiple regression. Multiple regression is similar to simple regression except there are more than one independent variables. Thus, the change in accounts receivable may be explained by changes in sales, unemployment rates in the city (or region or state), and interest rates.

Trend Analysis

trend
analysis

Trend analysis is the use of past levels of some financial variable to predict the future value. For example, to forecast the expected level of inventories, the analyst would plot the level of inventories over the past 5 to 10 years (inventories on the vertical axis and years on the horizontal axis), and then extend a line through these points into the next year. The trend is the extension of the plotted data points, and this line may indicate either a linear or nonlinear trend. For the analyst, this visual look at the past can be of real benefit in helping him or her to understand the relationship between different financial variables and, therefore, should provide a better understanding of what the future levels could be.

Although trend analysis can be a useful financial forecasting technique, one of its major limitations is that the technique assumes that past trends will continue into the future. This may be a valid assumption unless there is some other economic event that may have a major impact on this trend. For example, if there is a change in the industry's credit policy toward a longer period, then accounts receivable may suddenly increase without a corresponding increase in sales. The use of trend analysis would not have forecast this increase, but the entrepreneur who is aware of what is happening in her or his industry would have known and made adjustments for it.

CASH BREAK-EVEN POINT

cash
break-even
point

The **cash break-even point** may be defined as the sales level at which total revenues equal total operating costs; thus, at this level sales are just covering the operating costs of the firm. The calculation of the cash break-even point is used to assist the firm in its cash-flow forecasting. The cash break-even point is calculated by subtracting the depreciation (*Dep*) charges (a noncash outlay) from fixed (*F*) operating costs and dividing by the difference between the selling price (*P*) per unit and the variable cost (*V*) per unit:

$$\text{Cash break-even point} = \frac{F - \text{Dep}}{P - V}$$

The cash break-even point measures the volume of output, in the number of units, required to cover a firm's fixed cash operating expenses. Fixed operating expenses are all those expenses that a firm has that do not change with sales. These expenses include such items as salaries, insurance, rent, and lease payments.

For a video rental store, assume that fixed operating cost per month is $26,000, depreciation expense is $1,800, the price per unit is $2, and the variable cost per unit is $0.30. The cash break-even point (*CBP*) would be

$$\text{CBP} = \frac{26,000 - 1,800}{2 - 0.30} = 14,235 \text{ rentals}$$

For the video rental store, the cash break-even point is 14,235 rentals. After this point, the store would experience a positive cash flow from each additional rental. The difference between the selling price (*P*) and the variable cost (*V*) is sometimes referred to as the contribution margin. The contribution margin measures how much each unit of sales, in this case each rental, contributes to covering the fixed costs of the firm.

In terms of dollar sales, the store needs sales of $28,470 (14,235 × $2) before reaching the cash break-even point. This point may also be calculated from the following equation:

$$\text{Cash break-even sales} = \frac{F - \text{Dep}}{1 - (V/P)}$$

For the example given above, the cash break-even sales (*CBS*) point would be

$$\text{CBS} = \frac{\$26,000 - 1,800}{1 - .30/2} = \$28,470$$

The answer is, of course, exactly what was expected. The *V/P* ratio is known as the variable cost ratio. This ratio indicates the variable cost per dollar of sales. The smaller the ratio, the greater the contribution margin.

Break-even analysis is most useful as a technique to help owners assess the firm's exposure to operating risk. The higher the break-even point, the higher the risk because the firm has less chance of obtaining the high sales level required for the break-even point. The lower break-even point indicates less risk because the firm has a greater chance of obtaining the lower sales level required to obtain the break-even point.

Limitation of Break-Even Analysis

There are, however, several limitations of break-even analysis. The most obvious limitation is the assumption that both the selling price and the variable cost per unit will remain constant. Although the constant price assumption may be valid over the firm's normal sales range, it may not be constant at either end. For example, one way to obtain greater sales is to reduce the per-unit price, and this may be done to increase sales during a slump or when sales are already quite strong. In addition, variable costs tend to decrease as more units are produced. The firm operates efficiently until the extra production becomes harder to obtain and the variable cost per unit starts to rise again.

A second problem stems from attempting to classify the operating costs of the firm into either fixed or variable costs. Some costs, such as utilities, are semivariable in that part of the cost is fixed and part is variable. There will be a charge for most utilities regardless of sales, and as sales and/or production increase, then the utility costs will increase. Another limitation of the break-even model lies in the assumption of a single product or a constant mix of different products; in fact, most firms have more than one product, or their product mix changes over time. An additional limitation of the model is that it is only intended as a short-term planning model. The results should not be assumed to be valid beyond one year. A final limitation is that the analysis is only valid for a single product or product mix. If fixed costs, price, and variable costs can be broken out for each product, then this limitation is not a major problem.

MANAGING CASH FLOW

Probably for the new and growing firm, no financial analysis has more immediate potential benefit than the cash budget and the use of that budget to manage a scarce commodity — cash. The new venture, for example, must pay particular attention to its cash flow, and this can be accomplished by using weekly cash-flow projections (cash budgets). Interestingly, a recent survey of small businesses found that 33 percent cited uneven cash flow as their greatest financial obstacle.[1] This percent was more than twice the second greatest financial obstacle, which was getting outside capital.

This section is divided into three parts. First, the mechanics of setting up a cash budget will be presented. Second, using that budget to monitor how the firm is doing with respect to expected cash inflows and outflows is discussed through the use of an example. This section discusses when the owner should request an increase in the firm's line of credit and when that line may be reduced. The final section will present several ways to improve cash flows.

Cash Budgeting

Cash budgeting is a simple but very effective means of determining the expected cash inflows and outflows for a firm over a specific period of time. The results indicate when the firm is expected to have a surplus of cash and when a shortfall in cash is expected. If a surplus is expected, the manager can plan to invest the surplus either in short-term investments or in additional tangible assets. If a shortfall is expected, then the manager can attempt to speed up cash inflows, slow down cash outflows, and/or obtain additional funding such as an increase in the firm's line of credit.

The cash budget begins with a forecast of sales, or revenues, over a specific period of time and a forecast of when those sales will be collected. The second section of the cash budget shows the expected cash expenditures over the same period of time. The final section compares the expected difference in cash inflows and outflows with the minimum balance the firm wishes to maintain and indicates whether a loan is needed to maintain that minimum or a surplus is expected. All firms should maintain monthly cash budgets, and, the larger the firm, the more frequent the budgeting period with the largest firms utilizing daily budgeting. Typically the smaller firm should maintain monthly cash budgets for at least the coming twelve-month period. Larger firms may have daily cash budgets for the next month, with weekly budgets for the following three months, and monthly budgets the remainder of their twelve-month planning period.

The first section of the cash budget is the most difficult because it entails a forecast of sales. By its very nature, a forecast is an estimate of something that will happen in the future and as such is certainly subject to error. Although this situation sounds like a fatal flaw in the cash budgeting system, the users of the cash budget must remember that the budget is predicated on the sales forecast. As the forecast changes, then changes can be made in some of the expenditures. In effect, this is the strength of the cash budget. It sets up a cash-flow scenario based on the expected sales, but as that scenario changes, then the manager can make the needed changes to maintain the financial integrity of the firm. In other words, the cash budget gives the manager a starting point for her or his planning, and then as the actual sales levels become apparent, the manager can attempt to make changes in the cash expenditures that reflect the actual sales levels.

Once the sales forecast has been determined, the manager must calculate when those sales will be collected. For the firm that sells only for cash, the estimate of cash collection will be the same as the sales estimate. For all those firms that extend credit, an estimate of when those sales will be collected must be determined. The best way to obtain this estimate is from experience with the firm's customers. For example, past experience may show that 30 percent of sales is collected in the month of the sale, 45 percent is collected the following month, 20 percent in the month after that, and 4 percent in one additional month. In this example, 1 percent of the sales are never collected. With this information, the owner could then estimate cash collection in each month.

The second section of the cash budget, cash expenditures, is a fairly straightforward record of the expected cash expenditures over the budgeting period. One of the main advantages of completing this section is that the owner must develop an accurate accounting of all the firm's expenses. Typically, owners will initially be able to list most of the cash expenditures during any given budgeting period and add them to this section. The "forgotten" expenses will soon become apparent during the first month as invoices are presented that must be paid. The next budgeting period will more accurately account for expenditures as the owner becomes more aware of all the costs faced by the firm.

This section serves another very useful purpose—helping the small business owner focus on the individual expenses and, therefore, question their relevance to the goals of the firm. Are they really needed? Could they be reduced without affecting the sales level or the productivity of employees? Which expenditures are vital, and which are merely nice? The answers to these questions are usually brought into sharper focus when the firm faces a large cash shortfall and all expenditures must be questioned.

The final section is simply a determination of the net cash flows and a determination of whether the firm can expect a cash surplus or will need to borrow additional funds. This section also indicates when any borrowed money can be paid back. These three sections can best be explained through the use of an example showing the cash budget for California Spas.

California Spas: An Example of the Cash Budget

California Spas is a manufacturer of portable spas. The company manufactures about twenty different models of portable spas, and its customers consist of a group of about twenty-seven distributors located throughout the southeastern region of the United States. Although the company produces to order, it also produces to keep a more even balance in monthly production because sales seem to peak in two periods each year—once in the late spring and again in October when distributors are stocking up for the holiday season. The manufacturing process consists of blowing a fiberglass compound over a mold that gives the spa its shape. The fiberglass dries, then the spa is smoothed to give it a finished look. The entire process takes about one week. The finished product is then stored in a warehouse ready for shipment to the distributors.

Due to the cyclical nature of sales and the relative simplicity of the manufacturing process, many firms have entered this business, and many have exited. For this reason, banks are very reluctant to lend money to firms in this line of business and will lend money only to those that seem to have excellent management. California Spas is determined to be one of the survivors and in an effort to maintain control of its cash flows, has been using a cash budget for over two years. Their cash budget is set up on a monthly basis. The cash budget for the next six months (January–June) is presented in Exhibit 15-4.

California Spas had sales of $440,000 in October, $390,000 in November, and $390,000 in December. The sales forecast for January through June of next

EXHIBIT 15–4 Cash Budget

	California Spas					
	Cash Budget (thousands of dollars)					
	Jan	Feb	March	April	May	June
Forecasted sales	$ 300	$ 340	$ 370	$ 410	$ 440	$ 390
Collections:						
Cash sales (10%)	30	34	37	41	44	39
Paid in 30 days (35%)	126	105	119	130	144	154
Paid in 60 days (40%)	156	144	120	136	148	164
Paid in 90 days (13%)	57	51	47	39	44	48
Total collections	$369	$334	$323	$346	$380	$405
Payments:						
Purchases (25%)	$ 90	$ 75	$ 85	$ 93	$103	$110
Wages (35%)	105	119	130	144	154	137
Direct factory (5%)	15	17	19	21	22	20
Administrative expenses (4%)	12	14	15	16	18	16
Selling expenses (8%)	24	27	30	33	35	31
Taxes	48			33		
Equipment		165	70			
Total payments	$294	$417	$349	$340	$332	$314
Net cash flow	75	(83)	(26)	6	48	91
Beginning cash	40	115	32	6	12	60
Ending cash	115	32	6	12	60	151
Minimum cash desired	25	25	25	25	25	25
Surplus cash	$ 90	$ 7			$ 35	$126
Cumulative borrowings			$ 19	$ 13		

year, shown on the first line of Exhibit 15–4, is based on an estimated 15 percent increase from last year's sales. This increase is less than the 22 percent increase that the company experienced during the present year, but, with the weak economic forecast for the Southeast next year, management feels that the sales increase will not be as strong as in past years. To determine cash collections for the budgeted period, California Spas uses the average collection experience from the past two years. This experience shows that 10 percent of each month's sales will be paid in cash, 35 percent will be paid in 30 days, 40 percent will be paid in 60 days, 13 percent in 90 days, and 2 percent will not be collected. Using these estimates, management derives total collections as shown on the sixth line of Exhibit 15–4.

For cash payments, management has found that purchases are about 25 percent of the previous month's sales, wages are 35 percent of the current month's sales, direct factory costs are 5 percent of this month's sales, and administrative expenses and selling expenses are 4 percent and 8 percent of the current month's sales. Taxes are estimated to be $48,000 in January and $33,000 in April. New equipment and warehouse renovations will require cash payments of $165,000 in February and $70,000 in March. Total payments are estimated to be as shown on line 14 of Exhibit 15-4.

The final section of this cash budget report indicates the difference between total collections and total payments (net cash flow) and adds that difference to the cash on hand at the beginning of the month. In this case California Spas had $40,000 on hand at the beginning of January. The result of this addition is the ending cash balance, and from this figure the minimum cash desired is subtracted. The minimum cash desired is the minimum amount of cash the firm's management thinks it should have for the operating needs of the firm. In this case, the minimum cash desired is shown as $25,000 each month, but this amount could have varied from month to month depending on the past cash-flow experience of the firm. The difference between the ending cash balance and the minimum cash desired is either a cash surplus or an amount that the firm needs to borrow to maintain the desired minimum cash balance.

For California Spas, the expectation is to have a cash surplus of $90,000 in January, but, with the heavy cash payments in February, this surplus will be reduced to $7,000. In March, the firm will need to borrow $19,000; it will be able to pay back $6,000 of that loan in April and the remainder of the loan in May and have a surplus of $35,000.

With this type of report, the advantage of establishing a cash budget can easily be seen. Small business owners can go to its bank officer in early January and ask for a line of credit to cover the expected shortfall in March. The bank officer is much more likely to grant such a request when he or she can see that the firm normally maintains a healthy cash surplus and, therefore, has a high probability of repaying the loan. In this case, the firm seems to have a conservative estimate of expected sales, and this point also helps establish a good working relationship with commercial loan officers. Another advantage of this report is that it establishes a guide for management because the report shows what cash flows are expected given the sales forecast. If, however, this forecast is incorrect, then management can look at the budget and determine what steps must be taken to maintain the desired cash flows. California Spas may, for example, decide to postpone the installation of some of the equipment in February and March if sales are not up to forecast. Decisions of this type are much easier to make when a cash budget report establishes a clear road map of where both cash collections and cash payments are made.

Improving Cash Flows

The cash budget is designed to help management plan for both cash collections and cash payments. When the budgeted figures are not being met, then it is up to management to see how the cash flow of the firm may be improved. One simple, yet often overlooked solution, is to free up capital through the liquidation of excess inventories. There are very few ways that are quicker routes to alleviating a cash-flow problem than selling excess or slow-moving inventory. Following are several additional ways that cash flow may be improved.

REDUCE VARIABLE EXPENSES. The first and most obvious way to improve cash flow is to reduce variable expenses. When sales are not up to expectations, then expenses that are variable with sales should go down. There is a tendency, however, for business owners to believe that the sales decline is only temporary and that the sales force, advertising and promotions, and all the other variable expenses should be maintained at their budgeted levels. In many cases this may be correct, and the owner who is too quick to reduce variable expenses could actually hurt future sales. When to reduce variable expenses is a question that honest people can disagree on, but if there is a serious cash-flow problem, then expenses must be reduced before the entire firm is in financial distress.

MAIL INVOICES AS QUICKLY AS POSSIBLE. Cash flow may also be improved simply by reducing the time between the shipment of goods or the rendering of services and the time the customer is invoiced for these goods and/or services. The ideal is to mail the invoice the same day that the goods are shipped or that the services are provided. The objective is to speed up the inflow of cash to the firm. The sooner the customer receives the invoice, the sooner the invoice will make its way through the customer's payment process, and the sooner the payment will be received.

DEPOSIT CHECKS AS SOON AS POSSIBLE. Many firms let checks accumulate until the end of the week and then make one big deposit. For firms with very few checks to deposit or drafts of small amounts to deposit this may be an excellent procedure. For most firms, however, more frequent deposits may be very beneficial. As with the invoicing procedure, the quicker the check starts making its way through the bank's check clearing process, the quicker the funds will be available to the firm.

From a practical point of view, waiting to deposit checks is seldom to the advantage of the holder. Until it is deposited, the check is of no value to the firm, but once the check has been cleared it can be of great value. First, the funds are available for the firm to pay its invoices. Second, if there is excess cash, then it may be placed in an interest-bearing account. Some banks have "sweep" accounts that automatically remove all funds over a designated minimum amount into an interest-bearing account. Thus, all monies above those needed for immediate use by the firm can start earning interest. Third, and not an insignificant reason, is that larger cash balances improve the creditworthiness of the firm. Potential lenders, either suppliers of capital or suppliers of goods and services, look at a firm's balance sheet before making lending decisions. For short-term loans, larger cash balances are usually better than smaller balances because the liquidity ratios (current and quick ratios) are improved.

A final reason for making deposits on a more frequent basis is that the owner of the firm will be going to the bank more often. Although trips to the bank may seem like a waste of time, they do give the business owner time to become familiar with the bank's personnel and to establish a solid working relationship with them. The owner will find that it is much easier to obtain a loan or a line of credit when the loan officers already know him or her through frequent trips to the bank than when they know the firm only through the employee who makes a deposit at the drive-up window.

COLLECT PAST DUE ACCOUNTS. Past due receivables often create cash-flow problems that can subsequently threaten the success of a business. The first step toward an effective collections program involves setting a policy for handling past due accounts that specifies timing, procedures, and responsibility. Most small business owners are much more interested in selling their product or service than they are in collecting those sales. Few owners are interested in calling customers who are late with payments; however, a sale not collected is a sale not made. Small business owners can turn an unpleasant task into one that can build better relationships with customers and benefit the financial well-being of the firm.

If a firm sells goods or services on terms, then the firm must have a method of determining who has not paid when the invoice was due. The most common method of obtaining this information is through an aging schedule. An aging schedule shows which customers are late, how much they owe, and how late they are. An example is shown in Exhibit 15–5. The aging schedule shows only those customers who are late because the owner only should be interested in these exceptions. An aging schedule enables the owner to quickly see which accounts need the most attention and from this list determine which course of action needs to be taken to collect these accounts.

The correct course of action will vary greatly with the industry in which the firm is located, the general economic conditions, and the personality of the small business owner involved. The credit standards of the industry will have a major impact on what terms the firm will offer, but whatever those terms, the owner should always make sure that the firm's customers are aware of the due date. In good economic times, the owner must strive to follow up on past due accounts, for if she or he spoils customers (i.e., not following up or allowing them to pay late) during the good times, then collections will suffer immeasurably during the bleak ones.[2]

Finally, the personality of the small business owner has an impact on the success of collecting past due accounts. Some people have the type of personality that allows them to call customers, ask them how their business is doing, and at the same time, ask them for payment of a past due account. They can do this without offending them and even build a stronger relation-

EXHIBIT 15–5 Aging Schedule

			Accounts Receivable June 30, 1992		
	Total	0–30 days	31–60 days	61–90 days	Over 90 days
L. Beatty	$1,549.30	$ 514.20	$ 814.90	$	$ 220.20
C. Decosta	504.75	320.75	184.00		
S. Gombers	680.25	402.15		278.10	
A. Hessin	708.70	180.80	362.50	165.40	
F. Hua	1,340.80			398.20	942.60
A. Marcus	740.10	740.10			
Total	$5,523.90	$2,158.00	$1,361.40	$841.70	$1,162.80

ship for future sales. Other people simply cannot ask for payment without making the customer angry. Of course, the personality of the customer also has something to do with the reaction. If the owner is comfortable calling customers, then that is probably the best method of both speeding up the payment of past due accounts and building a stronger relationship to increase future sales. A disadvantage of calling is that one may hear a long list of excuses and problems of the creditor's firm.

If calling customers is not a good option, then the owner must write the debtor and ask for payment of the past due account. One disadvantage of writing is that the letter may be set aside by the reader, or the letter may not even be read by the correct decision maker. Letters are easier to ignore than a person who is on the telephone. Regardless of the method, the firm must develop a consistent policy of how past due accounts will be followed up. If customers ignore repeated calls and/or letters, the firm must also have a policy of when to turn them over to a collection agency, an attorney who specializes in collections, or the small claims court. These are not pleasant alternatives, but not collecting owed money can have unpleasant effects on the firm also.

SLOW DOWN CASH DISBURSEMENTS. A final method of improving cash flows is to slow down the disbursement of funds. If a bill is due in thirty days, then pay it in thirty days and no sooner. Some companies write all their checks at the end of the week. This is acceptable if only those bills that are due or will be due next week are included. The objective of improving cash flow is to speed up the cash flowing into the firm and to slow down the cash flowing from the firm. Paying bills ahead of time gives the firm no real advantage and certainly contributes to a poorer cash-flow position.

If the need to conserve cash flow is critical, then some firms resort to paying their bills late. Although this may be a solution to a temporary cash crunch problem, it is not recommended without notifying the supplier first. Paying invoices late can brand a firm as a late payer, cause future credit problems, and ultimately have a high cost through a bad credit rating and the resulting higher interest rates on borrowed funds. In addition, in the future "slow payers" may find that their special requests (for an early shipment, or for technical help, etc.) may not be given a high priority.

THE USE OF COMPUTERS IN PROFIT PLANNING

As small firms grow, the small business owner often is pulled away from the hands-on decision making about each detail of the business. As the owner finds there is less and less time to give personal attention to these details, a computer can be used to help organize much of the firm's financial data. With the right software a computer can give the owner the information that is needed for sound decisions.

Many software packages are on the market today to help business owners make budgets, compare budgets with actual results, and make financial projections. Some of these programs will generate revenue forecasts, balance sheets, income and cash flow statements, and break-even projections.[3] Spreadsheet programs, such as Lotus 1-2-3 and Quatro Pro, have been used by small businesses to aid in profit planning and cash-flow management. (More on the selection on a business computer and related software will be presented in Appendix B at the end of the textbook.)

SUMMARY

Profit planning is the establishment of a revenue and expense budget for the purpose of maintaining the financial health of the firm. The profit plan should be very specific in terms of both revenues and expenses and should be developed by allowing employees to be part of the planning process. The profit plan can be used by owners to constantly monitor the firm's progress toward specific goals and provides time for corrections in the plan when sales revenues are either above or below expectations.

Companies need to plan for the inevitable growth in assets that will occur as sales increase. The percentage-of-sales method is one relatively straightforward technique that can give management an indication of the funds that will be required to support the growth in assets. Other methods include regression analysis and trend analysis.

Cash break-even analysis is another technique that may be used to assist the firm in its cash-flow forecasting. The cash break-even point measures the unit volume required to cover the firm's fixed operating expenses. The break-even point is also useful as a measure of the firm's exposure to operating risk, with the higher break-even point indicating higher risk than a lower break-even point.

Setting up and using a cash budget is probably the most useful of all the financial analysis techniques discussed. Cash budgeting is the determination of the expected cash inflows and outflows for the firm. The results show whether a cash surplus or deficit is expected, and with this information management can determine if it will be necessary to increase cash inflows, decrease cash outflows, or increase its line of credit from a local bank.

There are several ways to improve cash flows. One of the best ways is to reduce variable expenses. A second method is to mail invoices as quickly as possible and to deposit checks as soon as feasible. Another method to improve cash flow is to develop a good method of aging accounts receivable, and a final method is to slow down cash disbursements.

QUESTIONS FOR REVIEW AND DISCUSSION

1. Determine the funds required for SU in the second year (1994) (see Figure 15-2). Assume a capital expenditure of $130,000 is required in 1994 to support the increase in sales.
2. Can SU manage very much growth if no additional external funds are available (i.e., can 12% growth can be managed internally)?

3. Why should a small firm have a profit plan? What are some of the limitations of profit planning?
4. From a management standpoint, what is the best reason for using percentage-of-sales as a forecasting technique?
5. The percentage-of-sales method assumes that all current assets will change proportionately with sales. Why is this a valid assumption?
6. From an operational viewpoint, what is the importance of operating at or above the cash break-even point?
7. What do you think is the primary purpose of a cash budget?
8. How can a firm improve its cash flows?
9. To conserve cash flow, some firms resort to paying their bills after they are due. What are some of the disadvantages of paying late?

KEY TERMS

cash break-even point	profit planning
multiple regression	regression method
percentage-of-sales method	trend analysis

CASE
Lyles Enterprises

CASH BUDGET/CASH FLOW

Tim Lyles started building recreational trailers in 1978 as a custom builder for a local distributor of recreational vehicles. His first trailer, built with the help of one other worker, took over a month to build. From this very modest beginning, Tim's business has grown to where this year Lyles Enterprises, as his business is now known, will produce almost 4,000 custom-built trailers for dealers throughout a four-state region.

BACKGROUND

From the beginning, Tim, who had a background in engineering and production, emphasized the building of quality trailers in as an efficient manner as possible. In this endeavor he was very successful, and he developed a reputation for producing high-quality trailers at a reasonable cost. From a financial standpoint, the business was successful. The trailers were custom built on a cost-plus basis, and, because the trailers were already sold and were simply being customized, the dealers paid Tim on the delivery of the completed product.

After three years of building only custom-built trailers, Tim realized that he was building only eleven basic models that had very minor variations within the basic model. He also believed that the manufacturing process could be much more efficient if he built on a semi-assembly line setup. He visited several similar operations in other parts of the United States and then decided that he could build trailers at a much lower cost than at present. He also believed that the sales potential in the four-state area he was presently serving offered him room to easily expand his output. Because most consumers were not willing to wait while a trailer was built for them but purchased whatever was available that was close to what they really desired, there was a bottleneck is sales. Tim's goal was to produce a quality trailer at a price that would be about 20 percent less than his existing custom-built price.

With this goal in mind, Lyles Enterprises built a plant that could ultimately manufacture 1,000 trailers per month and employ 40 people. This was a rather ambitious undertaking for an operation that employed 10 people and was building 20 trailers per month. Tim believed that the production setup would allow him to efficiently expand production and add employees gradually.

New Plant

Since moving into the new plant and getting the bugs out of the production process, Lyles has started building trailers for inventory and begun selling to dealers from that inventory, and customizing the standard model when requested by the dealer. The terms of sale were changed to 2/10, net 90. Tim believed that these terms would encourage dealers to stock his trailers in larger numbers than if the terms required payment sooner. He also hoped that the discount would encourage several dealers to take the discount and pay by the tenth day. Tim was partly correct in that dealers did order more trailers than they had in the past, and he was able to sell to a growing group of new dealers, but he found that only about 10 percent of his sales were paid for in 10 days, and most of those were from dealers who requested special custom work.

As sales grew, Tim realized that he had asked for several increases in his line of credit at the bank, but this fact had not concerned him because his accountant kept telling him that his business was very profitable. Because he assumed that a growing business required more cash, Tim would have remained unconcerned with the situation if his banker, Will Brawley, had not commented that he was technically bankrupt. When Tim asked Will what he meant, Will replied that Lyles had a large, and growing, cash-flow problem that could increase to the point that Lyles may not have the cash needed to pay his suppliers and other creditors. This situation would occur if Lyles experienced an increase in the time dealers took to pay him or if his lenders would not increase his lines of credit.

Tim was amazed that he could be profitable yet face the very real prospect of going bankrupt. He had always assumed that if he had an efficient operation, produced high-quality trailers, and watched his costs, there would be no financial problems. What Will was telling him was that as his business grew, he was increasing the possibility of having financial distress and that more growth would only increase the financial pressure on his firm. The bottom line was that as Lyles sold more trailers each month his financial situation grew worse, not better, even though he was running a very profitable operation.

To help Tim understand what he was talking about, Will asked Tim to provide him with the information that would allow him to develop both a pro forma profit and loss statement and a cash-flow budget for the next three months. These two statements would be based on Tim's forecast of sales as $163,700, $178,400, and $192,000 in July, August, and September, respectively. The profit and loss statement for the last three months (April–June) is shown below. Tim estimates that the cost of sales will stay very close to 62 percent of sales and that the G&A expense will average 8.8 percent over the next three months. Depreciation and interest expenses will remain unchanged over the next three months and taxes (federal and state) will average 38 percent.

Lyles Enterprises never had a cash budget, but Lyles' accountant had set up an excellent system for keeping the records of collections and payments. From these Tim learned that about 10 percent of sales are paid for in the month of purchase and 75 percent of the sales are paid about 90 days after the sale. Another 12 percent are paid within 120 days, and 3 percent are written off as uncollectible. That last number surprised Tim. He knew that a few dealers had not paid due to disagreements over damaged trailers and a couple of dealers had gone out of business, declared bankruptcy, or were seeking protection from creditors under the protection (under Chapter 11 of the bankruptcy laws) of the courts.

To determine the cash outflow, Tim learned that purchases were about 32 percent of each month's sales, and that salaries were $4,200 per month. Wages averaged 19.5 percent of sales, direct factory expenses were 4.9 percent of sales, and administration expenses (which were $11,000 in June) were rising $500 per month. Selling expenses were constant at 7.8 percent of sales, and Tim's accountant told him that he had a lease payment of $19,000 in July and an expected tax payment of $19,800 in September. Lyles had tried to maintain a minimum cash balance of $15,000, and by the end of June the firm had borrowed $57,000 on its $60,000 line of credit from the bank. (March sales had been $112,255.)

QUESTIONS

1. Calculate the cash-flow budget and a pro forma profit and loss statement for Lyles Enterprises for the coming (July–September) quarter.

2. How much increase in his line of credit will Lyles need for the (July–September) quarter? If the increase is not granted, what can Tim Lyles do?

3. If sales are 20 percent greater than the (July–September) forecast, what will be the dollar effect on the cash flow and the profit and loss statements?

Lyles Enterprises
Profit and Loss Statement

	April	May	June
Net sales	$123,480	$135,830	$149,518
Cost of sales	76,558	84,215	92,701
Gross profit	$ 46,922	$ 51,615	$ 56,817
G&A expenses	11,113	12,002	12,962
Depreciation	14,430	14,430	14,430
Interest	7,917	7,917	7,917
Income before taxes	$ 13,462	$ 17,266	$ 21,508
Taxes	5,116	6,561	8,173
Net income	$ 8,346	$ 10,705	$ 13,335

4. If sales are 20 percent less than the (July–September) forecast, what will be the dollar effect on the cash flow and the profit and loss statements?

5. In an attempt to encourage dealers to pay sooner, Tim offered terms of 2/10, net 90. Do you find it surprising that only 10 percent of his customers took advantage of the discount and paid within 10 days? Defend your answer.

6. Tim apparently thought that high profits guaranteed adequate cash to pay any bills as they came due. Explain to Tim the difference between "profit" and "cash flow." In particular, explain how even a profitable, highly efficient firm can experience cash crunches and have a need for outside capital.

7. Do you think that a cash budget is a more important financial tool for a small firm such as Lyle's or a very large firm such as General Motors? Defend your position.

8. What happens to the cash-flow budget and pro forma profit and loss statements if sales are 20 percent less than the original (July–September) forecast and a slowdown in the economy results in 75 percent of sales being paid in 120 instead of the expected 90 days, and 12 percent are paid in 150 days. Assume that 10 percent of sales are still paid in the month of purchase and 3 percent will be written off. (February sales were $92,180.)

ACTIVITY

1. Read the case "Lyles Enterprises" and answer the questions at the end of the case.

BUDGETS AND WORKING CAPITAL MANAGEMENT

LEARNING OBJECTIVES

After you have read this chapter, you will be able to do the following:

- Understand the need for budgets
- Know different types of budgets
- Prepare a working expense budget
- Appreciate the importance of working capital
- Understand the concepts of working capital
- Know how to control working capital
- Manage accounts receivable and payable

For the small business, budgeting is usually thought of as either a cash or an expense budget. The cash budget is an estimate of cash receipts and cash expenditures. (Cash budgeting was discussed in detail in the previous chapter.) The expense budget is a statement of estimated expenses over a specific period of time. These budgets must be written so that there is both a commitment to the budget and the means to communicate that commitment to employees. The budget is an estimate of what the firm expects to happen, but estimates also indicate that even well-thought-out plans may not be realized. Working capital, sometimes called net working capital, may be defined as the difference between a firm's current assets and current liabilities. Working capital is frequently used as a measure of a firm's ability to meet current obligations.

This chapter on budgets and working capital management will emphasize both the importance of an expense budget to all small businesses and how a budget can help the small business owner keep the firm on a course designed to promote sustainable growth. The presentation will center on setting up and maintaining a workable expense budget.

In addition, the chapter will address working capital management from the standpoint of how to best manage the firm's short-term assets and liabilities. Working capital policy is the determination of the level of working capital that management is willing to accept. The level is important because there is a risk-return trade-off between accepting a lower risk (from high levels of working capital), with the resulting lower expected returns, and higher risks (from lower levels of working capital), with the resulting higher expected returns.

BUDGETING

The overall objective of budgeting is for the owner to set the level of forecasted expenditures below the level of forecasted revenues, at least over the long run. Revenues will fluctuate from month to month and are harder to control than expenses, but the owner must have some budgeted revenue figure in mind and, to be profitable, should attempt to keep expenses under that estimate. Budgets, in addition to helping the small business owner keep the profit objective in mind, also help employees understand what is expected for the firm to be profitable. Most employees understand that a firm must be profitable for them to have employment, and that they have some role in the process. Budgets, therefore, communicate to employees what the firm must do to be profitable. How much of the total budget is communicated to the employees of a firm is up to the owner, but he or she must make sure that each employee understands her or his role in insuring the future of the firm.

A simple way of maintaining a budget is to establish an overall sales/revenue goal for the firm each week or at least each month. One easy but effective method is to keep a chart of cumulative sales similar to the one shown in Exhibit 16–1. A chart of this type is easy to update and simple to understand by all employees. A fact that is often overlooked by small business owners is that employees know when sales are off because there is less work, but what they do not know is how much are they off. A cumulative sales chart, such as the example shown in Exhibit 16–1, communicates that information to them. (This chart could easily be expanded to include more weeks.) This method is most effective in maintaining or controlling the budget when the employees to whom this information is provided have some control over sales and the sales effort.

Sales (revenues), however, are but one part of the profit equation. Expenses are the second part and the part that is most controllable by the owner/manager. With an estimate of revenues, owners should plan for the expenses that will help the firm obtain those revenues.

EXPENSE BUDGET

expense budget

There is a general reluctance among small business owners to set up and maintain an **expense budget.** To most small business owners a budget is a waste of time because they have a plan in their head and that plan can be flexible as the business situation changes. They do not wish to take the time to write a budget, and they do not wish to feel tied to a budget. In a one-person operation or a very small firm, this may be true, but most small businesses need, and should maintain, an expense budget.

What is an expense budget? The family budget makes a good analogy. Most families do not have an expense budget. They know how much money is received each month and about how much they spend. This method seems to work for many families especially those that tend to spend less than they

EXHIBIT 16–1 Actual Sales versus Forecasted Sales

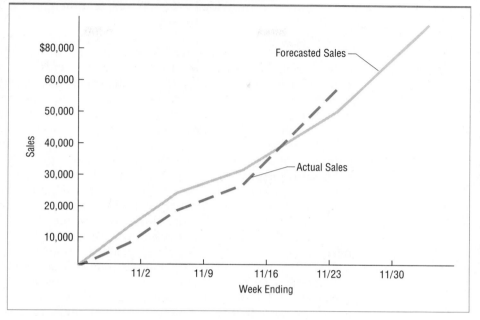

make. For those families that spend more than they make, there is an uncertainty about how, or where, they can cut expenditures. Each spouse tends to blame the other for spending too much or for allowing the children to spend too much. Without a budget and an adequate record-keeping system, this argument will seldom be resolved and instead leads only to future arguments. The only way out of this dilemma is to set up a mutually acceptable budget and keep track of actual expenses. With a budget, arguments over money tend to decrease and expenses are usually reduced to the point that they are less than income.

For the small business, an expense budget is designed to give the small business owner an indication of the amount of expenses that are expected over a particular period of time. The budget is designed to enable the owner to control expenses, and these expenses should be based on forecasted sales. The expense budget is a plan that is expressed in dollar terms, and this plan has several purposes.

Purposes of an Expense Budget

The first purpose of an expense budget is as a planning tool for the owner/ manager. As a planning tool, the budget provides a guide to the amount of money that may be spent on individual expenditures. If owners plan on a specific dollar amount of total expenditures, based on expected revenues, then each individual expense item can be allocated a specified amount. For example, advertising expenses may be budgeted for $1,200 and office supplies at $300. With very specific individual figures, owners have a much better opportunity to control total expenditures, and therefore, a better opportunity to make their budget and to be profitable.

The second purpose of an expense budget is as a method of communication with all employees who have anything to do with purchases. The budget spells out exactly what the owner expects in unambiguous terms in each expense category. For example, if the small business owner tells the head of maintenance to cut back on his or her expenses for the next quarter, the head of maintenance is uncertain about how much expenses should be reduced. With a budget, however, the maintenance manager can look at the budget and know exactly what the owner expects expenses to be in the maintenance department over the next month or quarter.

A third purpose of an expense budget is its use as an evaluation device. When budgets are set, they spell out what is expected of individuals. The budget represents a standard against which actual performance may be measured. If the budget represents what the owner expects must be done to accomplish the overall goal of the firm, then each individual must control those expenses that she or he is responsible for in order for the business to be successful. With a budget, individuals may be evaluated on how well they manage the resources for which they are responsible or over which they have some control. For the budget to be useful as an evaluative tool, the individuals must have goals that are both attainable and understandable. To have understandable goals, the best budgets will have been developed by the individuals involved and not just a number that was handed down by top management.

For the very small business with few employees, the expense budget serves less as an evaluation instrument than as a road map for the small business owner. By specifying what individual expenses must be for the firm to be successful, the owner is helping to control his or her own impulsive spending. This is accomplished by forcing an examination of any purchases above the budgeted amount in the light of the overall success of the firm in meeting its goals.

Setting Up an Expense Budget

An expense budget may be prepared on a weekly or a monthly basis for three months to a year ahead. The frequency of budget preparation depends on the dollar amount of the total expenditures of the firm. The larger the business, the more frequent the budgeting preparation. Smaller firms, for example, may employ monthly budgets and have budgets set up only three to six months in advance. A larger firm may have weekly budgets set up for the next four weeks and monthly budgets for the following eleven months.

The first effort at budgeting is seldom a successful one because the writers of the budget overlook too many expense items. Consider how many family budgets must begin. The first month a budget is attempted, many items are not included, but the next month the budget is closer to an accurate description of planned expenditures. In each succeeding month the budget becomes more accurate, and the users are more certain of what their expenses will be. The same is true for the small business. Regardless of the effort, the first month that a budget is attempted will not be as accurate as the succeeding months.

This first effort, however, is not wasted because the budgeting process forces the owner to think about each of the firm's expenses. The time spent in the determination of each expense gives the manager time to think about its value to the overall goal of the firm. For example, calculating that office supply expenses will be $900 for the month of July generates a mental picture of the office supply items that will be purchased. For example, supplies may be purchased in different quantities at a more economical price, or the owner could check with different suppliers to see if better prices are available. Each expense item should make the writer think about both the cost and the use of that item and determine if an alternative is available.

Once the budget has been set up, then each actual expenditure should be credited to one of the expense items, and then these should be summarized at the end of the budgeting period. An example is shown in Exhibit 16–2. There are three columns for each expense item. The first column is the budgeted amount for each expense item, and the second column shows the actual amount of expenditures. The third column is the difference between the actual and budgeted amounts. In addition, the budget should show the year-to-date costs for each expense item. The year-to-date columns are necessary to indicate whether a monthly spending variance is part of a trend or only a one-time or unusual occurrence that is not likely to be repeated.

The beauty of the expense budget is that the small business owner can see at a glance which expenses are over budget and try to determine the reason for the variance. Many times the reasons will be already well known, but other times the owner may wish to find out why the variance occurred. The variance by itself is not a bad sign because it may have occurred due to the expense of attracting a new big customer or processing a large order, but the owner must guard against allowing expense items to go over budget

EXHIBIT 16–2 Monthly Expense Report

	June			Year to Date		
	Budgeted Cost	Actual Cost	Variance	Budgeted Cost	Actual Cost	Variance
Purchases	$ 6,000	$ 6,300	(300)	$ 36,000	$ 35,040	960
Employee wages	5,000	5,800	(800)	30,000	31,200	(1,200)
Owner's salary	1,500	1,500		9,000	9,000	
Interest	1,400	1,400		8,400	8,400	
Utilities	800	920	(120)	4,800	4,580	220
Telephone	430	410	20	2,580	2,410	170
Lease—store	2,000	2,000		12,000	12,000	
Lease—office equipment	400	400		2,400	2,400	
Lease—automobile	520	520		3,120	3,120	
Legal and accounting	500	100	400	3,000	3,300	(300)
Miscellaneous	250	90	160	1,500	1,830	(330)
	$18,800	$19,440	(640)	$112,800	$113,280	(480)

without either a very good explanation or prior approval. A budget is worthless if it is not followed or is generally disregarded, and if it is not a managerial tool for controlling expenses.

Small business owners must both hold their expenses to the budgeted amounts and also require others to do the same. If the owner sets up and maintains an expense budget similar to the one shown in Exhibit 16–2, and questions both overage and shortages from the budget, then he or she will be well on the way to managing a profitable company. To help maintain up-to-date budgets, small business owners should consider the use of any of several easy-to-run computer programs that are available. The standard spreadsheet programs such as Lotus 1-2-3 and Excel are great for this type of record keeping.

Flexible Budgets

The budgeting process presented above indicates that each expense item in the budget is fixed for the budget period. The nature of some businesses, however, lends them to flexible budgeting where at least some of the expense items are either flexible or measured as a cost per unit of sales or per units produced. For the manufacturing plant, for example, material costs may be set as a cost per 1,000 units produced, and direct labor costs may be set at a certain amount per hour.

flexible
budget

In developing a **flexible budget,** costs must be separated into fixed and variable components. Although few costs are either truly fixed or variable over a firm's entire range of possible operations, most expense items can at least be broken into a fixed and variable portion. For example, electric power expenses for a manufacturing plant can be broken into a fixed cost per month and a variable cost per unit produced. Thus, the budget would show both the fixed cost and a variable cost that is based on the number of units produced during the budgeting period.

WORKING CAPITAL MANAGEMENT

working
capital
management

Working capital management is the management of the level of a firm's short-term assets and liabilities. Decisions on how much inventory to have on hand or on the credit terms that are extended to the firm's customers are based on the working capital policy established by management. The *conservative approach* to working capital management is to maintain a high level of current assets relative to current liabilities. Because current assets are the more liquid assets that a firm has, the firm is, therefore, maintaining a high degree of liquidity. The *aggressive approach* to working capital management is to maintain a relatively low level of current assets and, therefore, a relatively low liquidity. Thus, working capital policy is a conscious decision on the risk and return that small business owners are willing to take in managing their short-term assets.

Risk-Return Concept

The risk in the working capital management is derived from choosing to maintain a relatively low level of short-term assets (cash, inventories, and accounts receivable) and taking the risk of actually being short one or more of those assets. The risk of being out of inventory means that sales are not made, customers are not served, or manufactured units are not produced. The risk of being out of cash means that accounts are not paid, and the risk of maintaining a low accounts receivable indicates that the firm is not granting credit to some customers and is losing potential sales. Basically the risk is related to the degree of liquidity that management decides it is willing to accept.

The return in working capital management is derived from choosing to maintain a relatively low level of short-term assets and, thereby, needing fewer liabilities. Because all assets must be financed by either short- or long-term liabilities and equity, a low level of current assets means a lower level of liabilities, and thus a lower financing cost. The aggressive approach to working capital management is to maintain a relatively low level of current assets, incurring low financing costs. This approach is a high-risk and high-return approach. On the other hand, the conservative approach to working capital management is to have a high level of current assets, maintaining a high degree of liquidity, low risk, and low returns. The difference between these two approaches can easily be seen in Exhibit 16–3. A policy that is between the aggressive and conservative approach may be called the middle approach.

Alternative Working Capital Policies

A look at the alternative working capital policies shown in Exhibit 16–3 indicates that the firms are alike in every way except for the amount of current assets they maintain. The only other difference is the assumption that the increase in current assets is financed through increases in long-term capital. Thus, the increase in current assets is financed with increases in long-term debt and common equity in the proportions that are necessary to maintain the ratio of debt to total assets at exactly 50 percent. The reason for maintaining the debt to total asset ratio constant is to prove that the change in the return on equity is not due to a change in leverage but due only to the change in working capital. In addition, the financing is shown as long-term capital and not short-term capital to indicate the permanence of the policy.

Under the aggressive working capital policy, current assets are held to the minimum that management thinks is required for the firm. This minimum is based on its belief that it can control the level of current assets through constantly monitoring the levels of each. For example, this type of manager believes in using daily cash budgets, having zero balances at its bank, following up promptly on all past due accounts, and controlling inventory through such techniques as a just-in-time inventory system. The conservative approach keeps more current assets than are needed through either a less aggressive approach to the management of the current assets or a genuine belief that more current assets are needed to produce the highest amount of sales and profit.

The final assumption in this example is that the net sales and operating expenses of the two firms should not be different just because they have different working capital policies. Given these fairly realistic assumptions, the operating earnings of the firms will be equal and the difference in the net income will be due to the difference in interest expenses paid to finance the

EXHIBIT 16–3 Alternative Working Capital Policies

	Aggressive	Middle	Conservative
Cash	$ 50	$ 75	$ 100
Accounts receivable	200	300	400
Inventories	250	375	500
Total current assets	500	750	1,000
Fixed assets	750	750	750
Total assets	$1,250	$1,500	$1,750
Accounts payable	$ 180	$ 180	$ 180
Notes payable @ 10%	125	125	125
Accruals	20	20	20
Total current liabilities	$ 325	$ 325	$ 325
Long-term debt @ 12%	$ 300	$ 425	$ 550
Common equity	225	350	475
Retained earnings	400	400	400
Total liabilities and equity	$1,250	$1,500	$1,750
Net sales	$1,700	$1,700	$1,700
Operating expenses	1,400	1,400	1,400
Operating earnings	300	300	300
Interest expenses	48	64	79
Earnings before taxes	252	236	221
Taxes @ 40%	101	94	88
Net income	$ 151	$ 142	$ 133
Current ratio	1.5	2.3	3.1
Return on equity	24.2%	18.9%	15.2%
Debt to total assets	50 %	50 %	50 %

difference in current assets. Although the liquidity of the more aggressive policy is very low compared with the more conservative approach, the return on equity is much greater. Thus, the increase in return comes with the increase in risk.

This example shows that working capital management can influence the rate of return on equity and that working capital management is basically the control of the level of current assets. In the following sections, we will look at how management can reduce the level of current assets and what is required for its efficient management.

CASH MANAGEMENT

cash
management

The use of cash budgets as a **cash management** tool was discussed in detail in the previous chapter. In addition, some methods for improving cash flow were also presented. Cash management, however, is more than keeping track of cash flows; it is determining the level of cash that is optimum for the firm. Cash is a sterile asset in that it does not produce income, but cash is just as necessary to the proper functioning of a firm as accounts receivable or inventories. The problem is determining how much cash is enough and how much is too much. All individuals have the same basic problem. How much cash do they keep in their checking accounts? With most checking accounts, no interest is earned on the account balance, yet people keep more money than they need in the account to cover unexpected cash needs or because they never really stopped to think that they could manage their cash a lot better than they do.

The problem for the small business owner is exactly the same. How much cash should be kept in the firm's checking account? Too much cash means that the excess could have been put into an interest-bearing account or used to purchase inventory or capital equipment. Too little cash means that some expenses may not be paid on time or that the firm is not able to take advantage of special investment opportunities.

Reasons That Firms Need Cash

The first question, therefore, is to determine why firms need cash. There are four basic reasons for holding cash. The first is for *transaction purposes.* Cash is needed for the day-to-day payment for purchases and expenses that a firm must make to keep the business operating. These needs usually are not steady either throughout the month or over seasonal or economic cycles. Bills do not arrive at a regular and predictable time each month because purchases arrive throughout the month and suppliers' billing cycles are not coordinated with each other. An ordinary expense such as the utility bill will vary from month to month because, for example, May was hotter than expected, or March was colder than expected. The small business owner must decide how much cash is needed at any time during the month and how much will be needed over the next seasonal business cycle.

The second reason for holding cash is for *emergencies.* A small business owner finds it more difficult to borrow money on short notice than the owner of a larger corporation. All firms at one time or another are faced with unexpected requirements on their cash flows. A boiler may need extensive repairs, a vital piece of machinery may have to be replaced, or insurance may not completely cover storm damage to the firm's store. For these and similar emergencies, the small business owner must have access to cash.

The third reason for holding cash is to meet known *future expenditures.* Most small business owners know about most of their large and irregular expenditures well in advance. These expenditures include such things as quarterly income tax payments, construction progress payments, bond sinking fund requirements, or the repayment of a short-term loan. The small business owner must either build up cash in advance of these payments or have a line of credit already in place to cover such payments.

Finally a firm's bank may require that the firm maintain a *compensating balance.* As one of the conditions for granting a loan or a line of credit, many banks require that the firm maintain a minimum balance in its checking account. This minimum balance is known as a compensating balance and is often quoted as a percent of the loan amount. Thus, if a small business owner was granted a short-term loan for $100,000 and the bank required a 10 percent compensating balance, then the firm would be required to maintain a minimum checking account balance of at least $10,000. This minimum may be an absolute minimum or an average minimum balance based on the daily closing balance over some specified period of time (e.g., each month).

Optimal Cash Balance

optimal cash
balance

The small business owner must try to determine the **optimal cash balance** that her or his firm should maintain. Some people may argue that many small businesses are so short of cash that this is a moot question, but the objectives of this text are to discuss the proper management of the small firm and to help the owner improve the operation of the firm. In addition, many small firms, like many individuals, do keep too much cash on hand or in their checking account. Given these arguments, what is the optimal cash balance for a small business?

If a firm has a minimum compensating requirement with its bank, this balance may constitute the lower limit on the amount of cash held by the firm. If a firm does not have to maintain a compensating balance, the minimum that the firm has held may be determined by looking at the lowest amount shown on the firm's monthly checking account statement. The lowest balance shown each month may not be the optimal cash balance, but it is a good place to determine whether the lowest balance is still too high. The personal checking account balance analogy may help explain this situation. Assume that an individual must maintain a minimum of $1,000 is his or her checking account to retain free checking. However, the statement from the bank each month indicates that in the last three months the lowest balance was actually $2,700. The $1,700 above the minimum could have been invested in a savings account earning interest.

Cost of Maintaining Excess Cash

When a firm holds cash in excess of the minimum required, it incurs an *opportunity cost*. An opportunity cost is the amount of interest or operating income that the firm forgoes by not investing excess dollars in its next best opportunity. This opportunity may be as simple as placing the excess dollars in an income-generating money market fund or by purchasing additional inventory or equipment. The more cash that is held above the optimal minimum, the greater the opportunity cost. By reducing the opportunity cost, the firm is increasing its return on assets.

If an increase in the return on assets is the result of reducing opportunity costs, why should a firm hold any cash above some required minimum? The answer is that the additional cash is needed to help the firm avoid the *shortage cost* or the cost of not having the necessary cash to operate the firm efficiently. Shortage costs include the following:

- Not being able to take cash discounts
- Not having the cash to pay expenses by their due date

EXHIBIT 16–4 Optimal Cash Balance

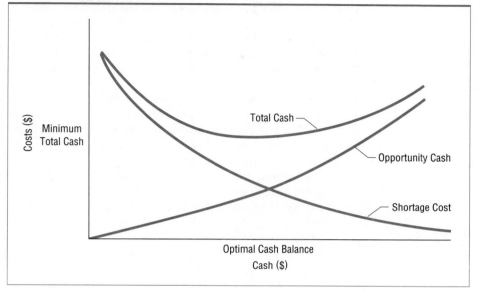

- Deterioration of credit ratings based on low liquidity
- Having to pay higher interest rates on borrowed funds due to low liquidity

The optimal cash balance, therefore, is a trade-off between the opportunity cost and the shortage cost. This trade-off is depicted is Exhibit 16–4. As the firm increases its cash balances, opportunity cost increases, but the shortage cost decreases. The optimal cash balance is where the total cost (shortage cost plus opportunity cost) is minimized.

Cost of Forgoing Cash (Trade) Discounts

For example, if a firm does not have the cash on hand to pay an invoice that offers terms of 3/10, net 40, the shortage cost to the firm is quite high, and yet it is this type of cost that is too often forgone by small businesses. The cost of not taking cash (trade) discounts may be calculated by the following equation:

$$\text{Cost} = \frac{\text{Discount percentage}}{100 - \text{Discount percentage}} \times \frac{360}{\text{Costly credit period}}$$

Using the terms of 3/10, net 40:

$$\text{Cost} = \frac{3}{100 - 3} \times \frac{360}{40 - 10} = 37.11\%$$

The costly credit period shown in the equation is that period of time that the purchaser is actually borrowing from the supplier. The supplier is saying, in effect, that there is not cost (in the above example) if the invoice is paid in ten days, but if one wishes to take an extra thirty days to pay, then the cost of the invoice is higher. The costly credit period is the time between when the discount could have been taken and the due date. The cost may be viewed in another way. If the firm does not have the cash on hand to take the discount, and if the interest cost of a thirty-day loan is cheaper than 37.11 percent, then the firm should borrow and pay the invoice on the tenth day and repay the loan on the fortieth day when the invoice would have been due anyway.

COST OF NOT PAYING BILLS WHEN THEY ARE DUE. The cost of not having the cash to pay a bill or an expense when it is due cannot as easily be calculated as the cost of not taking cash discounts. When a firm starts paying bills late, a number of direct and indirect costs are incurred. Certainly the greatest cost is the threat of being forced into bankruptcy. At first, when a firm falls behind in paying its debts, most creditors will be patient and forgiving. However, when a firm continues to fall behind in its payments, some creditors demand immediate payment and threaten legal action if payment is not forthcoming. The threat is real and can result in the delinquent firm's liquidation.

Other costs of paying late are less overt. Some suppliers will simply start shipping to delinquent firms later, taking care of all other customers first. The resulting late deliveries can result in lost sales or in shutting down the production line for a short period of time. A similar tactic is to ship only part of an order or to ship only COD to late customers, putting further pressure on cash flows. Still other suppliers will be slow in responding to calls for technical assistance from late payers. The result of each of these actions is to put the slow-paying firm into an ever more precarious financial position.

DETERIORATION OF CREDIT RATINGS. Most firms that grant credit use credit information from a local or national credit agency. The job of the credit agency is to rate creditors on their past credit history, and this history includes when and how much they borrowed and any record of late payments. Some credit agencies merely record this information and make it available to their subscribing members. Other credit agencies, such as Dun & Bradstreet, give a letter or numerical rating to the creditors in their files. The larger the debt in relationship to total assets and the later a debt is paid, the lower the credit rating given. This information can be invaluable in aiding the small business owner in his or her decision about what, if any, credit terms should be offered to a potential credit customer. This same information, of course, works against small business owners when they are behind in their payments and requesting additional credit.

HIGHER INTEREST RATES. Deteriorating credit ratings result in higher interest rates. Lenders, particularly banks, will demand a higher rate of return from borrowers with lower credit ratings or poorer credit histories to compensate them for the increased risk they are taking. Many lenders have a standard interest rate, sometimes referred to as the prime rate, that they charge their best customers (those with the best credit ratings), whereas all other customers pay a higher rate. The terminology is usually stated as the prime plus a stated percent. For example, a triple A rated firm may be charged the prime rate, say 10 percent, whereas a single B rated firm will be charged the prime rate plus 2.5 percent.

Choosing the Optimal Cash Level

The small business owner is faced with the risk-return trade-off between holding enough cash to maintain adequate liquidity but not holding excess cash, which does not increase the creditworthiness of the business and actually decreases the return. The owner is faced with a dilemma that does not have a precise solution but instead may be solved by assuming that the optimal cash level is actually a range within which the cash level should be maintained. One method of determining the correct range is to determine what cash levels other similar businesses maintain. This method assumes that firms that have been in business for several years have been successful in determining the correct level of cash needed. A list of several well-known firms with their level of cash as a percentage of total assets is shown in Exhibit 16–5.

The firms shown in Exhibit 16–5 are not small businesses, but their cash levels do give small business owners an idea of what may be the correct level for their firm. The range of cash to total asset ratios indicates the vast differences between different industries. The range within the retail industry, however, is quite narrow; therefore, small business owners should examine the

EXHIBIT 16–5 Ratio of Cash to Total Assets

Firm	Industry	Cash/Total Assets
Dairy Mart	Convenience store	3.5%
Dart Group	Discount auto parts	52.4
Deb Shops	Specialty retailer	50.4
Dreyer's Grand	Premium ice cream	4.2
Drug Emporium	Discount drug store	21.6
Duration	Truck bed liners	0.7

RETAIL STORES

Firm	Cash/Total Assets
Dayton-Hudson	1.1%
Dillard Department Stores	1.3
Dollar General	1.8
Family Dollar	1.3
K mart	2.0
Pic N Save	5.3
Wal-Mart	0.1
Woolworth	1.2

ratios other firms in their industry maintain to determine approximate figures for the optimal cash balances to maintain.

An even better source of information could be the firm's local banker. If the small business owner has maintained a fairly close relationship with her or his banker, then the banker will know the firm's business and will usually know the approximate level of other similar firms. Bankers tend to be conservative in the amount of liquidity that they think a firm should have, and, therefore, will usually recommend the maintenance of a relatively high level of cash.

A second method of determining the level of cash to maintain is to monitor the firm's actual level of cash over a period of one year. Is there some level of cash that the firm never goes below yet is above the compensating or minimum balance required by the bank? If so, the cash level may be reduced toward this minimum. (The minimum should include a safety factor.) Is the firm maintaining a high level of cash during most of the year and only experiencing a couple of periods of much lower cash levels? If so, the owner may wish to consider reducing the cash levels during the surplus periods. This may be accomplished by investing the surplus cash in short-term marketable securities such as Treasury bills or a money market account. Either of these investments allows the business to earn interest on the excess cash during periods where the additional cash is not required by the firm and yet gives the owner almost instant access to the funds if they are needed.

Another method to reduce the excess cash during periods of relatively high cash balances is for the small business owner to set up a line of credit with his or her bank to increase cash balances during periods of high cash outflow. This would allow the firm to maintain lower cash levels during the year. The cash that is released through this arrangement could be used to purchase more productive current or fixed assets.

MANAGEMENT OF ACCOUNTS RECEIVABLE

The final section on working capital management presents the management of accounts receivable. Several surveys of working capital management practices of small business owners in North America indicate that approximately 95 percent of the surveyed firms that sold on credit tended to sell to anyone who wished to buy and only 30 percent subscribed to a regular credit reporting service. Most firms had no credit checking procedures, and only 52 percent enforced a late payment charge.[1] Small business owners tend to neglect working capital management, yet the efficient management of these assets can be the difference between a profitable firm and an unprofitable one.

For the business that does not extend credit to its customers and sells everything for cash, there is no need to consider the management of accounts receivable. However, most firms do sell goods and/or services on credit because for most firms, credit sales greatly increase their total sales. The decision to sell on credit, however, should be based on careful consideration of the pros and cons of credit sales. The biggest reason for selling on credit is that most firms prefer to buy on credit, and this preference leads them to do business with firms that grant credit. Firms buy on credit for the following reasons:

- Payment of an invoice provides a written transaction of the purchase.
- Purchases on credit are a source of financing because payment is deferred.
- The time from the receipt of goods or services until the bill for them must be paid allows the firm time to verify both the quantity and quality of those goods and services.
- In many cases a credit purchase is quicker and easier to make than a cash purchase.

Realizing why customers prefer to buy on credit helps small business owners understand the need for extending credit to their customers. In addition to understanding the need for extending credit there are two excellent reasons for extending credit. First, the competitive environment may require the extension of credit. If the competition is offering credit, then the small business owner may be forced to do the same. Of course, a lower cash price or better service may offset the extension of credit as a method of increasing sales.

A second reason for extending credit is that credit customers have a greater tendency to become regular customers than cash customers do. Cash customers tend to shop price and will buy where they can obtain the lowest price, but credit customers tend to establish a long-term relationship with the seller. As a simple example, consider gasoline credit cards. Holders of gasoline credit cards tend to use these cards and to purchase gas primarily from their cards' brand, but individuals purchasing with cash tend to buy their gas wherever the price is lowest.

Disadvantages of Extending Credit

There are several disadvantages of extending credit, and most of them are based on the cost. The primary disadvantages include the following:

- Cost of credit checking
- Cost of keeping records (accounts receivable) of credit customers
- Bad debt write-offs
- Added interest cost of financing accounts receivable
- Cost of collecting delinquent accounts

These disadvantages should not be viewed as negative but as a cost of doing business just like paying the rent or the utility bills. The cost of extending credit should, however, be weighed against the increased profits from the extension of credit. The management of credit and the determination of the cost-profit trade-off is the subject covered in the remainder of this chapter.

Extending Credit

If the small business owner decides to extend credit, an effective credit system must be established. To develop an effective credit system, the owner should do the following:

- Establish a credit policy for the firm
- Use a standard credit application form
- Analyze a customers' credit application before extending credit
- Set a limit on the amount of credit granted each customer
- Establish a system for monitoring accounts receivable
- Develop a standard collection policy for delinquent accounts

credit
policy

ESTABLISH A CREDIT POLICY. Most experts agree that the first step toward an effective collection program is the establishment of a **credit policy.**[2] An effective policy should specify the timing, procedures, and responsibility for collections. The timing refers to the length of time that the small business owner is willing to let an account go before starting the collection process. Policy procedures specify the method of collecting accounts receivable that the firm will employ. The responsibility for collections can be divided among different individuals. Accounts receivable personnel should be assigned low-dollar accounts, but the owner should handle the large-dollar accounts.

credit
terms

Small business owners should establish a credit policy for their firms that clearly specifies the credit terms and the standards required before credit is extended. **Credit terms** refer to the amount and timing of payment. Typical credit terms could be "net 30," which means the entire amount of the bill is due in thirty days of the invoice date. Typical terms that include a discount for prompt payment could be "1/10, net 40" indicating that a 1 percent discount may be taken on the gross amount due if paid within ten days of the invoice date, or, if the discount is not taken, then the entire amount is due by the fortieth day. To avoid possible charges of discrimination, a firm should offer the same credit terms to all of its customers.

credit
standards

Credit standards refer to the financial characteristics required of an individual or business before credit is extended. For example, the credit standard may be that the local credit bureau's records indicate that the potential credit customer is not delinquent on any current debt. Other examples of credit standards for individuals could be as simple as the determination that the customer has a full-time job, has held a job with the same employer for over a year, has an income greater than $20,000 per year, or simply has a valid credit card such as Visa or MasterCard. If credit is extended to other firms, the standards could be a Dun & Bradstreet rating of A or better, net assets of $100,000, or a TRW report that shows the firm is not currently delinquent on any debt. Although the standards may be changed from time to time, the same standards should be applied to all customers regardless of race, sex, or age.

USE STANDARD CREDIT APPLICATION FORM. Many types of businesses require the potential credit customer to formally apply for credit before credit is extended. Standard credit application forms can be purchased from almost any office supply store, or the firm can develop its own application form. Typically the form should not be more than a single page in length and should include the following:

- Name of the business/individual, address, and telephone number
- Type of business, or, for individuals, their employer's name
- Years in business or length of employment
- Bank references including types of accounts and bank officer
- Details of credit history including the names of current credit accounts

For business applicants additional information may include the following:

- Financial statement for past one to three years
- At least three trade references
- A statement concerning any past filing of bankruptcy

ANALYZE THE CREDIT APPLICATION. The information collected through the application process is of little value unless it is analyzed before credit is extended. The first step in the analysis of the application should be to verify the data given by the applicant. The verification usually can be quickly completed through a check with the local credit bureau. Local credit bureaus are typically owned by a small business owner who collects credit information on customers who have obtained credit from the local businesses that subscribe to its services. This information is complied on each creditor and represents a fairly extensive credit history. A credit check can be completed for subscribers who, for a small fee for each request, will receive a current report on the individual or business. The report typically includes all the information on the standard credit application form plus a history of the amount of credit that the customer has been extended and her or his record of payment.

The second step in the verification process is to ascertain that the credit applicant meets the credit standards set by the firm. The credit check, focusing on the customer's history of late payments, must be completed before the sale/shipment is made.[3] The final step is to notify the customer that his or her application has been accepted and to state the terms of the acceptance.

SET CREDIT LIMITS. One of the main terms of acceptance should be the notification of the credit limits that the customer has been granted. Thus, each customer should be told the specific dollar amount of her or his credit limits. These limits can vary with different customers because those customers that have more assets or income may be given higher credit limits. Individuals are familiar with this arrangement if they have a credit card. When they received the credit card, the limits were plainly stated, and those individuals with better credit histories or higher income levels were granted higher credit limits. There is no discrimination in this case as long as the different limits are income-asset based and not based on such things as age, sex, or race.

ESTABLISH A MONITORING SYSTEM. Once a firm has decided to extend credit to its customers, a system for monitoring those customers must be set in place. The first step in the monitoring process is to provide an invoice that records the transaction and states when payment is due. An invoice should include the following information:

- Name and address of the customer
- Name, address, and telephone number of the seller and/or the address of where the payment should be sent
- A unique invoice number (This number may be the customer's account number or simply consecutively numbered invoices.)
- A description of the goods or services purchases
- Price of goods or services purchased and the date purchased
- Shipping cost, if any
- Date that the invoice was prepared
- Trade credit terms
- A statement of any past due balances

The purpose of the invoice is to provide a record that both notifies the customer of the date payment is expected and provides the seller with a record of the billing. The second step in the monitoring process is to have a set policy on when invoices will be mailed. The small business owner may wish to have the invoices mailed daily, weekly, biweekly, or even monthly depending on the type of business the firm is in, the number of invoices mailed, or the amount of the invoices, but a regular schedule is paramount to establishing a workable monitoring system. Obviously the sooner invoices are mailed, the quicker the payment will be received.

The third step in the monitoring process is to construct a system that allows up-to-date and accurate monitoring of which customers have paid, and, more importantly, which customers are past due. In fact, the lack of an ongoing review of accounts receivable has been cited as one of the major inadequate administrative procedures that lead to the early demise of many new businesses.[4] The aging of accounts receivable is an excellent system for accomplishing this step. The aging of accounts receivable means dividing accounts receivable into those that are current in their payments, those that are 0 to 30 days past due, 31 to 60 days past due, 61 to 90 days past due, and those that are more than 90 days past due. An accounts receivable aging schedule is shown in Exhibit 16–6. This schedule shows the customer's name, the amounts that are current, the amounts past due, and the number of days past due all in a simple, easy-to-read format.

The objective of the aging schedule is to indicate which accounts need the most attention so that they do not fall even further behind in their payments.

EXHIBIT 16–6 Aging Schedule

Customer Name	Balance	Current	0–30 Days	31–60 Days	61–90 Days	Over 90 days
Aging of Accounts Receivable September 30						
M. Carey	$ 582	$ 582				
A. Chafin	348	—	$ 348			
J. Chin	1,022	—	—	—	—	$1,022
T. Clair	140	140				
R. Clark	414	—	200	$214		
D. Coons	188	—	188			
A. Costello	2,120	—	820	500	$640	160
J. Crecine	874	874				
S. Crouch	628	510	118			
Totals	$6,316	$2,106	$1,674	$714	$640	$1,182
Percentage	100%	33.3%	26.5%	11.3%	10.1%	18.7%

Several easy-to-use personal computer software programs that produce aging schedules have been developed for small businesses. Some of these produce full aging schedules or only those accounts that are past due. For many small businesses, the best programs are those that produce only the past due accounts because these are usually the only ones of interest to the owner. A second objective could be the restriction of sales to those customers that are past due. This restriction could be that all additional sales will be for cash only or COD until the arrears are paid or simply a restriction on the purchase amount. These objectives lead to the final requirement for the establishment of an effective credit system, a standard collection policy for delinquent accounts.

collection policy

DEVELOP A COLLECTION POLICY. A credit **collection policy** is needed to provide the small business with a procedure to follow in its attempt to collect past due accounts. A standard procedure is necessary to provide guidelines that treat all delinquent customers equally and that provide a standard system for following up on past due accounts. A collection policy might include the following:

· Mail the first "past due" statement when the account is ten days past due.

· Mail a second past due notice when the account is thirty days past due with a statement that indicates they perhaps have not received the original statement.

· Call the customer when the account is forty-five days past due. For most small businesses this is a job that should be handled by the owner for the best results. The owner should try to determine the reason for the delinquency and attempt to establish a payment schedule.

The Way It Is

16-1 HIRING COMMERCIAL COLLECTORS

A prerequisite for successful collections is choosing the right collection agency. The two types of collection agencies are known as either a consumer or a commercial agency. When one company owes another company money, a commercial collection agency usually has the better chance of collecting the account because collecting from businesses is its specialty. Many small firms hire consumer collection agencies, but their expertise is in the area of collecting from individuals who are late on credit-card payments, charge accounts, doctors bills, and so on. Small businesses have very little clout in attempting to collect overdue accounts and normally are not skilled in the psychology or the tactics of business collections. Most reputable commercial collection agencies operate on a contingent basis, charging 20 to 25 percent of the amount collected. Although this fee may sound steep, collecting 75 percent of an account is surely better than writing off an account as a bad debt.[5]

- When the account is sixty days past due, notify the customer that if payment is not received within fifteen days the account will be turned over to a collection agency or to the firm's attorney.
- Turn the account over to a collection agency (see The Way It Is 16–1) or to the firm's attorney after the seventy-fifth day. There is a point when the small business owner must not spend additional time and effort trying to collect a past due account. Hoping for eventual payment is usually fruitless.

The above represents only a guideline, and small business owners must be flexible in the management of their accounts receivable. The flexibility stems from realizing that different industries may have very different credit policies and that collection policies may have to be less stringent in economic recessions. There are also times when a normally good customer may fall behind in his or her payments. That is the main reason that the owner should personally contact past due customers and establish a line of communication with them on the reasons for the delinquency and the possibilities for payment.

Two major points should be kept in mind here. First, there is a high probability that the small business owner may some day find that he or she is behind in his or her payment, and prompt communication with the seller can alleviate a lot of potential problems. Second, a few customers are deadbeats, and extension of credit and time to make payment merely puts off the day when the account must be written off. The small business owner must set a policy that recognizes both of these conditions. The collection of accounts receivable must be monitored with an understanding about both the temporary conditions that force a customer into late payments and those conditions

The Way It Is

16–2 GETTING PAID

Alan Burkhard, president of The Placers Inc., a Wilmington, Delaware, temporary personnel firm, watched his company grow 100 percent a year for seven years by concentrating on increasing sales and paying very little attention to receivables. "Every week we had to pay salaries and payroll taxes for every temp we placed . . . but it was taking us 60 to 90 days to collect our bills." Burkhard had fallen into a mental trap that ensnares many owners of growth companies: get sales now; worry about profit margins tomorrow. In Burkhard's case, he found that he would make a profit only if he collected within 45 days. He was, therefore, losing money on every sale.

With this realization, Burkhard put the same effort he had previously put into sales into billing and collections. Two people were hired and thoroughly trained to handle accounts receivable. The training included scripts to follow that insured a uniform approach to all customers. These scripts, although "customer friendly" in their approach, directed the conversation toward the objective of collecting overdue accounts.

To improve communication between Placers and its clients, Burkhard had his sales personnel explain the payment terms to new customers and request credit references. Placers' accounting personnel verified all references, checking the clients' financial health as well as their payment histories. In addition to the up-front customer education, customer service reps called the clients ten days after invoices were mailed to make sure they were satisfied with the temps' performance and to ask when Placers could expect payment. Burkhard's efforts paid off as Placers was able to reduce delinquent bills to 5 percent of sales and reduce the average payment date from 60 to 90 days to 30 to 45 days.[6]

that indicate that a customer may never pay. What is needed, therefore, is a very tough policy administered with a little understanding of changing or temporary financial conditions (see The Way It Is 16–2).

SUMMARY

The objective of budgeting is to help the small business owner set the expected level of expenditures below the expected level of income. The purpose is to help the owner maintain a profitable business operation by establishing revenue and expenditure goals. The expense budget serves as an expense guide to the owner, a means of communicating expense constraints to employees, and as a standard against which actual performance may be measured.

Working capital management is the determination of the level of a firm's short-term assets and liabilities. The conservative approach to working capital management is to maintain a relatively high level of current assets, whereas the aggressive approach is to maintain a relatively low level of current assets. The decision on the level of working capital to maintain is based on the risk of maintaining low liquidity and a corresponding high expected return versus maintaining a high liquidity and expecting a lower return.

Cash management is the determination of the level of cash that is optimum for a firm. Firms need cash for current transaction purposes, emergencies, future expenditures, and, if required by the firms' bank, to maintain a compensating balance. The optimal level of cash is a trade-off between the opportunity cost of forgone income for not investing excess cash versus the shortage cost of not having the necessary cash to operate the firm efficiently.

The management of accounts receivable focuses on the establishment of a credit policy, the use of a standard credit application form, the analysis of the credit application, the setting of credit limits, the establishment of a credit monitoring system, and the development of a collection policy.

QUESTIONS FOR REVIEW AND DISCUSSION

1. What are the purposes of an expense budget?
2. When should the small business owner consider using a flexible rather than a fixed budget?
3. Do all small businesses need to have a budget? Why or why not?
4. Which type of businesses could safely choose to maintain a relatively low liquidity with respect to its working capital?
5. Which type of businesses should maintain a relatively high working capital liquidity?
6. Should a firm with a low working capital level expect to have the same sales level as a firm with more working capital?
7. Why do firms need cash?
8. What is the cost of not taking a cash discount of 2/10, net 30?
9. Give some examples of the opportunity cost of holding excess cash.
10. Why would a firm that maintains a low level of cash expect to have higher interest rates than a firm with a higher cash level?
11. Why would a small business owner wish to have a listing of only past due accounts rather than a complete accounts receivable aging schedule?
12. When should an overdue account be turned over to a collection agency?
13. A firm generates $4,000 per day in sales and has a 55-day average collection period. If the average collection period can be reduced by 10 days, what is the annual dollar savings if the carrying cost is 18 percent?

KEY TERMS

cash management

collection policy

credit policy

credit standards

credit terms

expense budget

flexible budget

optimal cash balance

working capital management

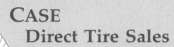

CASE
Direct Tire Sales

Direct Tire Sales has terms of net 30. Barry Stein, the owner of Direct Tire Sales, does not have an aging of accounts receivable schedule but thinks he should set one up. Given the following information, construct an aging schedule as of September 1 showing the percentage of accounts that are current; those that are 1 to 30 days past due, 31 to 60 days past due, and 61 to 90 days past due; and those over 90 days past due. Assume 30 days in each month.

Invoice Date	Amount Due	Invoice Date	Amount Due
July 15	$2,528	June 12	$2,320
June 14	1,295	August 20	1,458
June 20	841	May 5	980
July 12	4,360	July 28	450
April 5	784	July 14	4,805
July 9	5,120	June 10	1,052
June 25	489	August 2	1,002
August 20	6,595	July 16	728

ACTIVITIES

1. Prepare and turn in a personal budget for the next month. During the month keep your actual expenses and then report the differences between the budget and actual expenses.
2. Construct an aging schedule for Direct Tire Sales.

17 CONTROLLING INVENTORY AND SHRINKAGE

Inventories are assets that are purchased by a firm and held for sale. Almost all firms, except for those businesses that are in the service industry, have inventories of some type. Retail firms purchase goods that are held for resale. For retail firms, gross profit margin is the difference between the purchase price and the selling price. For the manufacturing firm, inventories are materials that may have value added by the manufacturer through their transformation into a different or more complete product. For manufacturing firms, profit comes from the value added to their inventories. In both cases, the purchase of the correct type and amount of inventory can greatly enhance the profitable operation of the business.

Small business owners need to develop a system that gives them an accurate picture of their inventory. Such a system will show what inventory is moving, what is not moving, and what the profitability of the different inventory items is; it will also serve as a tool for determining shrinkage. Owners of a one- to two-person operation may not need an inventory system if they have only a few items of inventory, but most other small businesses need some type of effective inventory control system.

This chapter will discuss the different types of inventory that are needed for different types of businesses and present methods for determining how much inventory the business should carry. In addition, several techniques for managing inventory will be discussed to help small business owners efficiently control their firms' inventory.

Types of Inventory

Inventory can be in many forms. When most people think of inventory, they think of all the products they see in retail stores. Inventory to them is all the items for sale in a grocery store or the shirts and sweaters in their favorite clothing store. This type of inventory is known as **finished goods** inventory. They are called finished goods because they are ready for sale to the consumer or end user. All businesses have finished goods; even a manufacturer's final products are finished goods although the product may be an unfinished good to another manufacturer.

finished goods

Although most people think of finished goods as inventory, in reality all inventories start out as **raw materials.** Raw materials take many forms from the raw wool that is sold to a manufacturer that spins wool into thread, which in turn, is sold as a raw material to a textile mill. Raw materials include basic commodities such as iron ore, oil, timber, coal, cotton, and oranges. These raw materials can be turned into steel, gasoline, lumber, thread, and frozen orange juice that are the raw materials for other manufacturers who may turn these items into raw materials for still other manufacturers. Raw materials may also be motors, clocks, transmissions, speakers, and other completed products that are only components in another manufacturer's assembly process. Thus, what is a raw material to one manufacturer may be a finished product to another.

raw materials

Work-in-process is a third form of inventory. **Work-in-process** is those raw materials that have been partly transformed into a finished product but that are not yet completely through the manufacturing process. The work-in-process inventory has three components that add to its value: the cost of raw material, the cost of labor that has been expended into the partially completed product, and the cost of overhead that is allocated in the manufacturing process. There is a purpose and a cost for each of these three forms of inventories.

work-in-process

Purpose of Carrying Inventory

RAW MATERIALS. Almost all manufacturing operations must maintain an inventory of raw materials, because raw materials are part of the manufacturing process and firms must have them on hand to insure an efficient production process. An efficient production process requires that raw materials be on hand when required by production and that the process not be slowed or delayed because a particular item is lacking. The problem, of course, is that all materials do not arrive at the manufacturers' plant on schedule; delays may occur due to strikes, weather, shortages, imbalances in shippers' orders, and so on. The manufacturer, therefore, must have enough inventory on hand to act as a buffer against the uncertainties of fluctuations in both raw material deliveries and in the demand for the final manufactured product.

A small business manufacturer may also purchase more inventory than required for an efficient operation because purchasing larger quantities may significantly reduce the unit price. These reductions may come through quan-

Almost all manufacturing operations must have raw materials on hand to insure an efficient production process.

standard
shipping unit

tity discounts, reduction in total ordering costs resulting from fewer orders, and savings in freight costs due to purchase in quantities at least as large as a standard shipping unit. A **standard shipping unit** is a minimum size that a seller will ship without a surcharge. For example, the standard shipping unit may be 1,000 pounds, 100 cartons, 25 rolls, a carload, or a barrel, and any orders for less than this standard unit, called a broken unit, will cost more.

WORK-IN-PROCESS. Many manufacturing operations require that raw materials be turned into finished goods in a single day's production, and, therefore, no work-in-process inventory exists at the end of the operating day. The baker, for example, would not leave a partially mixed batch of ingredients for making bread overnight. On the other hand, in most assembly line operations, the manufacturer would always have partially completed products waiting the next stage of assembly. For example, a furniture manufacturer would have some wood that has been cut to specified lengths or that have been cut on a lathe into a particular shape. In both cases, the partially completed product is called work-in-process inventory, and it is required to keep the flow of work moving through the manufacturing process.

Work-in-process inventory is also needed in piecework operations to keep all workers fully supplied so that they do not have down time waiting for work to arrive at their station. In the typical clothing operation, for example, the production of a shirt begins with one operator who cuts the cloth into various shapes; these cloth pieces are then fed to individual operators. One operator sews on the collar, another sews on the buttons, and another attaches the front to the back. Each of these operators completes his or her step in the total process of making a shirt, and then the partially completed shirt is moved to the next step. Because operators are paid by the number of pieces that they complete each day, they do not wish to stop and wait on someone else to complete the preceding step. Piecework operators love to have a stack of work at their station so that they may continue work.

In other operations, work-in-process inventory is needed for flexibility in the planning process. In many assembly-type operations, some parts may be used in several different final products. Consider the manufacturer of lawn mowers, for example; assembled gas engines may be used on several different models. The manufacturer may have an assembly line producing gas engines that are then stockpiled near other assembly lines to be used when different models are being produced. In this case, the inventory is used to keep both the gas engine line and the completed lawn mower operation moving efficiently.

FINISHED GOODS. The purpose of maintaining an inventory of finished goods is to ensure that the seller has enough of a product on hand to meet customer demand. Because customer demand may fluctuate over time, sellers must maintain extra inventory to act as a buffer against these fluctuations. In many businesses, if a product is not on hand when a customer wants it, the sale is lost because the customer goes to a competitor's business for the product. In addition, future sales may also be lost as the customer may continue shopping elsewhere. Finished goods inventory is also needed for display purposes both to attract shoppers and to show them different sizes, styles, colors, and so on. Finally, finished goods inventory is the result of ordering the most economic quantity from both a unit price and a shipping cost standpoint. (This aspect of ordering will be covered in detail later in the chapter.)

Cost of Carrying Inventory

There is a cost to maintaining inventory regardless of the type. These costs, called carrying costs, include the cost of financing, obsolescence, shrinkage, handling, insurance, and taxes.

Financing. The cost of financing is the most obvious; any asset held by the business must be offset on the balance sheet by a liability. Only in those rare cases where a business is able to purchase inventory that can be sold and the cash collected before the due date can the finance costs be eliminated. For example, if a firm purchases goods on terms of net 30 and can sell that inventory for cash within 30 days, then the financing costs would be zero. For the majority of firms, however, the cash flow from the sale does not occur before the payment is due. In effect, inventory is purchased, and the money used to pay for the inventory has a cost to the firm.

Obsolescence. Another cost of inventory is the cost of obsolescence. When small business owners purchase inventory, they assume that the inventory will be either used in the manufacturing process or sold, but this is not always the case. For the manufacturer, the demand for the final product may decrease or a new or better product may simply replace it. Think of how many times this has happened in the computer industry, particularly with the disk drives. New drives with more memory and faster speeds replaced older models that were state-of-the-art drives just a few months earlier, and manufacturers were left with obsolete drives that could not even be sold for scrap. Retailers face the continual challenge of ordering what they think consumers will want to purchase knowing that demand and styles can change rapidly. Retailers can reduce obsolete inventory through sales. These semiannual and/ or inventory-reduction sales serve as a method to reduce the loss from carrying obsolete inventory, for even selling inventory at a loss is better than not being able to sell it at all. Wholesalers accomplish the same thing by offering greatly reduced prices on inventory that has gone out of style or is not moving fast. The objective in both cases is to move the inventory, even at a slight loss, before it is impossible to sell at any price.

Shrinkage. Shrinkage can come from many sources including theft and deterioration. If goods are stolen, the cost comes from purchasing inventory that is not sold, whereas the cost of shrinkage from deterioration results in not being able to sell the inventory, reducing its price before it may be sold, or not being able to use all or part of the inventory in a manufacturing process. Shoplifting and employee theft are the two main sources of shrinkage for most retail businesses. How these losses may be reduced will be covered later in this chapter. Shrinkage from deterioration is a major cost in many manufacturing industries. The shrinkage from deterioration can also come from loss of quality such as would be expected when holding fresh fruits and vegetables for sale.

Handling Costs. Normally when inventory is purchased, it is delivered to the purchaser. When the inventory is received, an employee must physically check the shipment against the invoice, and the goods must then be placed in storage or on the shelves for display. If the goods are stored, there is a cost for the maintenance of the storage area and a cost for the employees involved with the control of the storage area. In many businesses, a periodic physical count of the inventory is required. Handling costs, therefore, include all the costs of receiving and storing the inventory before it is sold or used in the manufacturing process.

Taxes and Insurance. Most small business owners will have insurance to cover their inventory and will pay taxes on the inventory. (Taxes and insurance are covered in Appendix C.) Taxes are typically paid on the amount of inventory as of a particular date each year, and many consumers have benefited from inventory-reduction sales as businesses reduce the inventory prior to the tax date.

The cost of carrying inventory is the total of all the above costs. The exact dollar cost may be difficult to determine because of overlap between inventory and the manufacturing or the retailing functions. Insurance, for example, may cover both the inventory and the fixed assets of the firm. The employee working in the warehouse may also work on the assembly line or in maintenance. The cost of obsolescence, although very real, is also difficult to determine if there are many different items in inventory. Estimates have shown that the cost of carrying inventory is about 25 percent of the cost, but these estimates are averages that vary greatly from one type of industry to another. The important point is that there is a cost of carrying inventory, and, the more inventory a business has, the greater the total dollar cost to the firm. Due to the high cost of carrying inventory, most small business owners, make a determined effort to determine the optimum inventory for their firm.

DETERMINE INVENTORY NEEDS

Small business owners are well aware that if they carry too little inventory, they can lose sales and customers. If they carry too much inventory, they incur unnecessary carrying costs that reduce their profits, or in some cases, make the firm unprofitable. The optimum inventory to carry, however, should not be thought of as an exact number, but as a range within which the firm should try to operate. In this section, several methods for determining the inventory needs for small businesses will be presented. The discussion will center on some basic inventory methods that have been successfully employed by small businesses and then look at the determination of the inventory needs for those small businesses in manufacturing or those who are in retailing/wholesaling.

Basic Inventory Methods

For many small businesses, particularly those that need relatively few items in inventory and have a supplier located nearby, the basic inventory method is as simple as looking at the current inventory and ordering any inventory that will be needed for the next day or next week's operations. An example of this method is the typical automobile repair shop. Almost no inventory is maintained by the owner with the exception of the common and/or low-priced items such as tires, headlights, fan belts, oil filters, and spark plugs. All the major parts are purchased from a local wholesaler as they are needed for the repair of a particular car or truck. Interestingly, the wholesaler uses the same method, except they have a larger selection of the most requested parts and they order from regional or national parts warehouses, which can normally ship any needed part for delivery the next day. The use of 800 numbers and shippers such as Federal Express who promise delivery the next day make such an inventory system both simple and inexpensive.

For other small businesses, such as a video rental store, the determination of the amount of inventory to carry is more art than science. How many copies of the newest video release should the owner purchase? Studies have not shown a high correlation of rental sales with the popularity at the box office. Video rental store owners must make an educated guess based on their knowledge of the local consumers' past preferences in videotapes. Most businesses, however, have inventory needs that are between the two extremes presented above.

Inventory Needs for Manufacturing

The inventory needs of small manufacturing firms can vary from the simple to the complex. Manufacturers using very few materials or parts do not need a complex inventory system but can order additional inventory based on their knowledge of the current usage. Many other manufacturers, however, cannot easily maintain the optimum inventory without a systematic method of determining the amount of inventory on hand, the expected usage rate, the normal time between the order and the delivery of parts or materials, and the amount that constitutes the most economic order quantity. Methods for determining the amount of inventory on hand will be discussed in a later section of this chapter, but there are three popular methods for determining the expected usage rate for manufacturing firms. These methods are materials requirements planning, the use of just-in-time philosophy, and the use of an accounting system.

materials requirements planning

MATERIALS REQUIREMENTS PLANNING. **Materials requirements planning** (MRP) is based on the forecasted demand for an end product. The forecasted demand is made up of both the firm customer orders and a forecast of demand from random customers. The forecasted demand is then broken into a demand for the product or products manufactured by a firm into their component parts. An MRP system generates a complete list of all parts and subassemblies required to produce the end product along with a list of when these parts and subassemblies must be ordered. For example, the manufacturer of bicycles could break the finished product into one handlebar, one seat, two wheels, two tires, and so forth.

The main purpose of an MRP system is to determine and control inventory through the planning for production. The production plan is based on forecasted demand. The objectives of MRP may be stated as follows: (1) to improve customer service through having the product ready to ship on time, (2) to minimize inventory investment through ordering only those materials that are needed to satisfy the production plan, and (3) to improve production efficiency through having the parts on hand when needed for assembly. Some users of the MRP system have claimed that they have reduced inventory as much as 40 percent.

To illustrate how the MRP system works, a brief but simple example will be presented. Assume that a manufacturer of racing bicycles has firm orders for seventy-five bikes in five days and another 40 bikes eight days from today. Based on past demand, the manufacturer can expect a random demand that is about 25 percent of the firm orders. In this case, total orders are expected to be 100 bikes in five days and another 50 bikes in eight days. From this forecast, the manufacturer knows that a total of one frame, one handlebar, one gear assembly, and one seat must be ordered for each bike. In addition two wheels and two sets of brake assemblies must be ordered. The MRP for completing the production of these bikes is shown in Exhibit 17–1. Note that the lead time, the time between when an order is placed and when the supplies are delivered, for each part is given.

A look at Exhibit 17–1 shows when each part must be ordered so that the part will be on hand in time for the final assembly. MRP also includes the breakdown of the subassemblies, such as the brake, into its component parts in the same fashion as was illustrated for the final product. Thus, the brake assembly would have its own chart showing when each of the components must be ordered to have the completed brake system ready for the final assembly. Based on the example given, the system seems very simple, but the system adapts easily to more complex manufacturing operations. In fact, computer programs have been written for small manufacturers that quickly perform the calculations and print a chart similar to Exhibit 17–1 along with a schedule of order quantities and dates. For the more complex manufacturing system, the logic of the MRP system is the same as presented in the simple example above; there are just more parts.

JUST-IN-TIME PHILOSOPHY. Although the implementation of the **just-in-time (JIT) philosophy** has been presented as a technique for large manufacturing firms, it has also been very successful in small manufacturing firms. In a recent survey of small manufacturing firms, 75 percent reported that they were successful in implementing the JIT technique. More importantly, 80 percent of these firms were able to report decreases in their raw materials, 58

just-in-time philosophy

EXHIBIT 17–1 Material Requirements Plan

		Day								Lead Time (Days)
		1	2	3	4	5	6	7	8	
Frame	Required amount					100			50	
	Order placement	100			50					5
Handlebar	Required amount					100			50	
	Order placement		100			50				4
Seat	Required amount					100			100	
	Order placement				100			100		2
Wheels	Required amount					200			200	
	Order placement	200			200					5
Brake	Required amount					200			200	
	Order placement			200			200			3
Gear	Required amount					100			100	
	Order placement		100			100				4

percent reported decreases in their work-in-process inventory, and 56 percent reported a decrease in their finished goods inventory.[1]

The JIT system is a relatively new approach for controlling inventory that became popular as a response to the increased international, primarily Japanese, competition for manufactured goods. A reduction in inventory costs was one of the methods that the Japanese manufacturers were utilizing to reduce their costs. The reduction in inventory costs with the JIT systems stems from reducing the amount of inventory that a firm has on hand. The success of the system is measured by how much or how little inventory a firm maintains. The ultimate objective is to have the inventory arrive at an individual workstation just as it is needed and not have inventory stacked all around the work floor.

JIT works best in repetitive manufacturing situations where both the demand and production can be forecasted fairly accurately (e.g., assembly operations, metal fabrication, and food processing). The three key principles of JIT are: (1) the elimination of waste, (2) total quality control, and (3) employee participation in decision making. The elimination of waste comes from a reduction of damaged or obsolete goods that may occur when greater quantities are stored on the premises for long periods of time. The improvement on quality control occurs from working closely with the supplier to deliver goods according to both the exact specifications and the schedule required by the manufacturer. Employee participation comes from utilizing their input to streamline the production process and reduce setup times, from their participation in quality circles and acceptance of greater responsibility, and from their suggestions for modifying the plant layout.[2]

Implementation of the JIT system involves reducing inventory and improving quality of goods produced. The aim is to improve the quality of incoming inventory and to have frequent deliveries. An assumption of JIT is that the rate of production on the assembly line is fairly steady so that inventory may be ordered and delivered on fairly predictable schedules. Certainly this assumption does not fit all manufacturing firms, but for those that it does fit, the savings can be substantial. In the traditional manufacturing plant, materials are ordered to replace depleted inventory, but with JIT materials are ordered according to production schedules. This requires close coordination among production, purchasing, and suppliers. In some cases, the firm employing JIT will even give its principal suppliers its production schedules in advance.

ACCOUNTING SYSTEM. For most small manufacturing firms, the traditional accounting system is still the preferred method of controlling inventory. With an accounting system, an inventory record is maintained on each item. The inventory record keeps a daily record that indicates how much inventory is on hand, how many were sold or used, and how many were received. A typical inventory record card is shown in Exhibit 17–2. For most small businesses, a simple inventory record system may be designed for the individual inventory items that are unique to the firm. Certainly an elaborate computer system is not required for those firms that have very few inventory items. For firms that

EXHIBIT 17–2 Inventory Record Card

		Order Quantity: 800		
Item: Brake drum for 1-ton truck			Reorder Point: 250	
Date	**Received**	**Used**	**Balance**	**Note**
11/18		40	320	
11/19		60	260	
11/20		40	220	Ordered 800 PO# 1601
11/21		50	170	
11/22		40	130	
11/25		50	80	
11/26	800	40	840	
11/27		60	780	
11/28		60	720	
11/29		50	670	
11/30			672	Physical inventory

Primary supplier: Ozark Castings
100 Industrial Park Road
Smithfield, MO
Contact: John Stuart (417) 782-5500

do have a large inventory problem, inventory cards and inventory systems are available in most office supply stores. In addition, office supply stores or computer supply stores usually have a wide selection of specialized computer inventory systems. These systems have been adapted for businesses such as gasoline stations, video rental stores, and most retail stores.

To be effective, an inventory record card should include several features. First, each inventory item should have a clear and unambiguous description. A unique description helps reduce the possibility that one item could be confused with another. Adding a catalog number to the description also helps reduce the possibility of error in inventory record keeping. A note on the minimum order quantity; the name, address, and telephone number of the supplier; and the name of the contact person is the second feature of a useful inventory card. A third feature is a note on the reorder point. This alerts the person maintaining the inventory record card when an item should be ordered.

The fourth feature that every inventory record card should have is the transaction section. This section should contain a column for the date of each transaction, the quantity received, the amount sold or used, and the remaining balance on hand. A final feature is a column for recording when an item is ordered, the amount ordered, and the purchase order number.

The main advantage of the inventory accounting system is its simplicity, which makes it useful for those businesses that do not carry a large inventory. The major disadvantage is that the system requires that the cards be updated each time inventory is received, used, or sold. The system also requires a periodic physical inventory to insure accuracy, because employees may have used the wrong item or not recorded the usage; also items may have been stolen or misplaced. In addition, a physical inventory helps uncover damaged parts on the inventory record card that are not usable or salable.

ECONOMIC ORDER QUANTITY

economic order
quantity

In the previous section, three systems were presented that could help small business owners determine their inventory needs. What was not discussed was how much to order. The **economic order quantity** (EOQ) method may be used to answer that question. The EOQ, a simple technique that has proven effective and easy to use, solves the trade-off problem between the ordering cost and the carrying cost.

The ordering cost is the cost of actually placing the order. This cost includes the cost of recording the order (the physical entry of the order on a purchase order or a call to the vendor), warehousing, inventory record keeping, receiving department costs, and purchase department costs. Some of these costs are variable, which means that they vary with the number of units ordered, and some of these costs are fixed, which means that the costs are the same regardless of the number of units ordered. Typically the cost of placing a single order is about the same regardless of the size of the order, therefore, fewer orders would result in a lower total annual cost and a lower cost per unit. The annual ordering cost may be expressed as follows:

Annual ordering cost = Orders per year × Cost of each order

This relationship indicates that the greater the number of orders per year, the higher the cost.

Carrying cost represents the cost of carrying the inventory. This cost includes shrinkage (losses due to damage, deterioration, and pilferage), finance charges, handling charges, taxes, insurance, and the cost of storage. Obviously carrying costs will vary directly with the size of inventory carried. This relationship may be expressed as follows:

Annual carrying cost = Average total inventory
× Carrying cost in percent

These two costs are represented graphically in Exhibit 17–3.

Because the objective with any expense is to reduce the total cost, the graph indicates that the lowest total cost is a trade-off between ordering cost and carrying cost because these two costs make up the total cost. This trade-off may be solved utilizing the economic order quantity formula, which may be stated as follows:

$$EOQ = \sqrt{2NS/PI}$$

where:

- EOQ = economic order quantity in units
- N = number of units required annually
- S = ordering cost per unit

EXHIBIT 17–3 Graphic Representation of *EOQ* Model

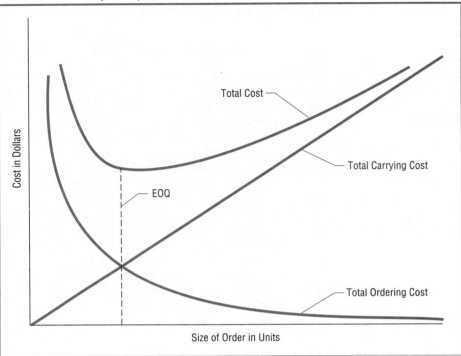

- P = price per unit
- I = annual inventory carrying cost, in percent

For example, assume that a manufacturer of trailers forecasts that the business will require 3,600 brake drums for the coming year. Also assume that the average cost to process an order is $70 and the price of each brake drum is $120. If the firm's inventory carrying cost is estimated to be 20 percent, what is the economic order quantity?

$$EOQ = \sqrt{(2 \times 3{,}600 \times 70)/(120 \times .20)} = 144.9 \text{ or } 145 \text{ units}$$

Although the EOQ model seems simple to use, three points should be remembered when considering its use. First, ordering too little usually costs more than ordering too much because a shortage may result in shutting down the assembly line or, in the case of finished goods, lost sales. Second, a change in carrying costs has a big effect on the EOQ. If carrying costs were actually 30 percent in the above example, then the EOQ would be 118 units, almost a 19 percent reduction in the number of units ordered. A third point to consider is that the standard shipping unit may be different than the EOQ. A standard shipping unit is the number of units that a supplier will ship at a set charge, and they either will not break a unit or will charge more for less than the standard unit. This problem may be overcome by rounding the EOQ up to or down to the closest standard shipping unit.

Potential Problems with the EOQ Model

One of the biggest potential problems with the EOQ model is that the model assumes that inventory is used at a uniform, constant rate. This assumption is close to reality in many manufacturing and assembly line operations but seldom is true in a retail sales store. However, the assumption may be true even in retail stores where sales are constant over an ordering cycle.

A second potential problem stems from the calculation of both the ordering cost and the carrying cost. Very few companies have an accounting system that allows them to accurately determine the cost of placing an order or the carrying cost. The individuals who place the orders normally have many other tasks especially in most small businesses. The costs, therefore, must be estimated. Most proponents of the EOQ model do not see this as a fatal limitation because a fairly accurate estimate could be made.

A third potential problem comes from the blind use of the EOQ model. The EOQ does give the optimum order number in units, but a glance at Exhibit 17-3 should indicate that the EOQ could be a range of units rather than a precise number. Thus, the difference between ordering 350 units and 365 units probably is not material. The point is that the EOQ results should be considered as a close approximation of the number of units that should be ordered.

A fourth potential problem involves changes in unit price. The EOQ model assumes that the cost per unit (P) does not change, regardless of the number of units ordered. In reality many suppliers offer quantity discounts. In this case, the lowest cost order quantity could be determined by calculating the total cost for each price break. For example, assume the price per unit decreases as shown in column 2 of Exhibit 17–4. In addition, assume that 3,600 units will be ordered next year, that the average cost to process an order is $70, and the firm's carrying cost is 20 percent of the total inventory value.

In this example, columns 2 and 3 indicate the cost per unit and the number of orders, respectively, that the firm must place each year to obtain the 3,600 units that it expects to be required for its operations. Column 4 is the average value of the inventory, and column 5 is the total carrying cost based on the estimate of 20 percent. Column 6 is the total ordering cost, which is

EXHIBIT 17–4 Order Quantity with Volume Price Discounts

(1)	(2)	(3)	(4)	(5)	(6)	(7)
	Cost		Average			
Order	per	Number	Inventory	Carrying Cost	Ordering Cost	Total Cost
Size	Unit	of Orders	(1) /2 × (2)	(4) × .20	(3) × $70	(5) + (6)
100	$120	36	$ 6,000	$1,200	$2,520	$3,720
150	120	24	9,000	1,800	1,680	3,480
200	120	18	12,000	2,400	1,260	3,660
250	115	14.4	14,375	2,875	1,008	3,883
300	115	12	17,250	3,450	840	4,290
400	110	9	22,000	4,400	630	5,030
600	100	6	30,000	6,000	420	6,420

based on the number of orders that will be placed each year times the $70 cost per order. Column 7 is the total cost, which is the carrying cost (column 5) plus the ordering cost (column 6). In this example, the EOQ of 150 units that was calculated earlier is still the optimal order quantity, but a change in the carrying cost or the order cost can quickly change the optimal order quantity. Although this example is intended to show only how to determine order quantity when a firm is offered quantity discounts, the calculation of total cost is a very useful method of determining the minimum cost under a variety of cost structures.

INVENTORY MANAGEMENT

Most small business owners want an effective inventory system that allows them to manage their inventory with the least amount of effort. Other small business owners need an inventory management system that delivers accurate and daily information on how much inventory is on hand, how much was sold, what has been ordered, and when another order should be placed. The difference in the system needed depends on both the difference in the type of goods sold and the difference in manager's skills.

inventory
management

The basic problem in **inventory management** is knowing how much inventory is currently on hand, being able to calculate the rate of usage, and determining when an order must be placed for additional inventory. One method is to maintain a system that records each sale and indicates the remaining inventory of each item. Systems of this type are used frequently in retail clothing, music (tapes, compact disks), and appliance (household and electric) stores where the cost of the individual items is relatively expensive and the cost of lost sales is important. Another method is to divide inventory into two groups: relatively expensive and relatively inexpensive. The expensive items are inventoried on a continuous basis, and the inexpensive items are inventoried periodically.

The method of dividing inventory into two groups is valid for many small businesses where a few relatively expensive items account for a large percentage of the total cost of inventory. This method is sometimes called the 20-80 method, because 20 percent of the number of items carried by a firm account for 80 percent of the cost of inventory. The objective is to spend time and effort keeping an accurate inventory of the expensive items and spend much less time with the less expensive items. In this section, several different inventory systems will be presented that will provide practical solutions to inventory management for both the expensive items and the inexpensive ones. Typically, most small businesses would not use a single system but a combination of systems depending on both the size and the type of business. These systems may be divided into informal and formal systems.

Informal Inventory Systems

For many small business owners, an informal inventory management system is all that is required for the efficient operation of their business. Visual control, a two-bin system, ABC management, and blanket ordering are four informal systems that have proved effective for many businesses.

VISUAL CONTROL. As mentioned earlier, in some businesses a visual control system is all that is necessary when there are relatively few items in inventory and the owner is on the premises most of the time. Where owners see the inventory being used or sold, and know how much and when new orders must be placed, a more formal inventory system is not required. Visual control is nothing more than a daily visual check of all inventory, knowledge of the rate of usage, and knowledge of when and where orders should be placed for replacement inventory. This system works best in one- to five-person firms where the owner is either the main salesperson or actively involved in the manufacturing process.

two-bin inventory system

TWO-BIN SYSTEM. The **two-bin inventory system** works best in businesses where small items with a low unit cost are sold in large quantities. The two-bin system is popular in hardware stores, wholesale businesses, and discount retail stores. In a two-bin system, two bins (containers or boxes) are maintained for each item. Usually one box is on top of the other, but they could be side by side. When one box is sold out, the second box is opened and an order is placed for another box. A variation that is used frequently in book stores, where books are stacked with the cover facing the customer, is to place a reorder card in a book near the back. When the book is purchased, the reorder card is removed and an order for additional books is placed.

ABC inventory management system

ABC MANAGEMENT SYSTEM. The **ABC inventory management system** recognizes that the degree of inventory control depends on the dollar value of the inventory. The ABC system classifies inventory items into three groups according to their relative cost as follows:

- **Group A** consists of items that make up approximately 70 percent of the total dollar value of a firm's inventory.
- **Group B** consists of items that make up approximately 20 percent of the total dollar value of a firm's inventory.
- **Group C** consists of the remaining inventory items.

After the small business owner has classified the firm's inventory into three groups, the next step is to establish the type of control that each group requires. Group A items, for example, may require an inventory system that continually updates the inventory level after each sale, or the system may require a physical count at the end of each day. Inventory systems for Group A items are either a visual control system or one of the more formal systems presented later in this chapter. Ordering for Group A items may also take place daily. Group B items need to be inventoried and ordered on a less frequent basis, and Group C items may be inventoried and ordered utilizing an informal inventory system such as the two-bin system or the blanket order system.

blanket
purchase order

BLANKET ORDER SYSTEM. A **blanket purchase order** is a general agreement between a buyer and the supplier listing a description of the items covered, the price, and the period of time covered by the agreement. A blanket order is used for high turnover items that need to be replaced frequently. For items such as office supplies (printer ribbons, copying paper, etc.) and retail items such as film, the inventory items are ordered from a local distributor's catalog. The advantage of a blanket order, in addition to fixing a price for the terms of the agreement, is the savings in ordering time. Blanket orders reduce paperwork because inventory may be ordered quickly over the telephone by catalog number. The buyer gets an invoice but saves the time of writing and sending an order.

stockless
purchasing

A technique that is similar to blanket ordering is known as stockless purchasing. With a **stockless purchasing** agreement between the buyer and a supplier, the supplier agrees to maintain the inventory level of specified items in the buyers' store. The inventory belongs to the supplier and the buyer is charged only for what is sold. Stockless purchasing is frequently used in grocery stores for such items as bread, pastries, soft drinks, and paperback books. Stockless purchasing reduces the amount of capital needed for inventory yet provides the small business owner with a constant supply.

Formal Inventory Systems

The informal systems presented above were classified as informal because they did not require either a computer or a rigorous accounting system. The systems presented in this section normally would require the use of a computer and specialized software. The systems presented are the point-of-purchase system, bar coding, and electronic data interchange. Each of these systems can provide small business owners with an economically priced but sophisticated inventory control system that can greatly improve their ability to efficiently manage their business.

point-of-
purchase
systems

POINT-OF-PURCHASE SYSTEMS. **Point-of-purchase systems** are available, inexpensive, and for many small businesses indispensable software programs that have been developed for almost every type of retail business. The typical point-of-purchase program records each sale and subtracts the item that is sold from current inventory. In effect, a complete and current up-to-date inventory is maintained. For example, in a book or music store, owners want to know what book or compact disc is selling, how many are left, and when should they order more. A good point-of-purchase program can provide an answer to all these questions, allowing owners to quickly replenish those items that are the most popular.

Point-of-purchase programs are advertised in almost all trade journals and are demonstrated at trade conventions. Before choosing a program, small business owners should make sure that the program they are considering will do the job that they need for their business. A good source of information is from owners of similar businesses, particularly those who are not in direct competition. Reviews in trade journals are another good source of information. A good review will discuss both the advantages and disadvantages of a system and define the type of business for which the program is best suited.

bar coding

BAR CODING. Point-of-purchase systems can be made even more effective through the use of **bar coding.** Bar codes are those black-and-white parallel bars that seem to be printed on almost everything purchased in a retail store. The bar code is much more than a system for speeding up the checking-out process at the local grocery store. In effect, the same bar code that sends a message to the register at the grocery store that a box of Cheerios costs $1.77 also updates the inventory and notes that another case of Cheerios needs to be ordered. At some time during the day, store owners can check their computer program, and with the touch of a few keys, determine what items need to be ordered.

The basic bar code system includes a personal computer, a laser scanner, a decoder, and the bar code symbols. The program and training for a system that would be adequate for most small retail businesses costs between $5,000 and $15,000. The key element in a bar code system are the bar codes. Small business owners can purchase preprinted bar codes or print their own, as long as they obtain high-quality labels.

Any business that requires repetitive and accurate data entry could profit from using bar code technology. Bar coding can reduce the amount of inventory kept on hand and save time in the inventory and ordering process. For example, Chuck Wallington, of Christian Supply Inc., a book store, lowered his investment in inventory by $50,000 in the first year after a switch to bar coding.[3] Small business owners can learn more about bar coding by subscribing to *ID Systems*, the major journal of the bar code industry. The journal is published by Helmers Publishing Inc., 174 Concord Street, P.O. Box 874, Peterborough, NH 03458.

electronic data interchange

ELECTRONIC DATA INTERCHANGE. **Electronic data interchange** (EDI) is a system that transmits inventory data from the retailer to the supplier. In the typical EDI system, the retail sales information that is collected using bar code technology is analyzed by the retailer, an order is generated, and the data is electronically sent to the firm's supplier. The supplier ships the order to the retailer using the normal distribution channels, but the billing and account information may be sent electronically.

EDI has been used by national retailers such as K mart, Wal-Mart, May Stores, and Sears for several years, but the system is now affordable for small businesses. A direct linkage between retailers and their suppliers can be achieved through the use of computer modems, an e-mail (electronic mail) connection, or third parties such as Geisco, CompuServe, or Prodigy. In addition to the direct linkage mentioned above, the data transfer can be achieved by mailing a diskette, with the data encoded, to the supplier. The savings resulting from the use of EDI come from an increase in inventory turnover, a decrease in the amount of inventory required, and the elimination of frequent ordering, demand forecasting, and/or calculation of EOQ.

Thus, the EDI system improves profitability for both the retailer and the supplier.[4]

EDI is also used in manufacturing where a large manufacturer wishes to be connected with its suppliers to improve efficiencies. For example, Texas Instruments (TI) is connected with more than 1,600 of its suppliers, many of which employ fewer than 100 people. TI gives the EDI software to its suppliers, provides technical support, and even offers training in order to implement the advantages of EDI. In addition, EDI is the perfect technique to improve the use of other systems such as just-in-time.[5]

Turnover Analysis

For many small retail firms, inventory is the largest single asset and their only true earning asset. Inventory turnover analysis can indicate how efficiently that asset is being utilized. The basic objective is to have inventory available when the customer wants it but not to have inventory that does not move quickly from the shelves or warehouse. Inventory turnover is an indication of how quickly inventory is moving, and inventory turnover analysis is an indication of whether the small business owner can improve the turnover and ultimately the profitability of this asset.

The inventory turnover ratio (cost of sales/average inventory) was presented in Chapter 14, but its use in inventory management was not discussed. The inventory ratio for the firm can give small business owners an idea of how efficiently they are managing their inventory. This fact, by itself, makes only a minor contribution in the total effort of maintaining the optimal inventory level because the ratio compares the firm's utilization of all inventory and not the individual items. Inventory turnover analysis, therefore, may be used to compare the firm with other firms from a total inventory turnover standpoint and, by the firm, to analyze the inventory turnover of individual items.

TOTAL INVENTORY TURNOVER. Inventory turnover analysis may be used as an indication of the efficiency of the firm's utilization of inventory assets. The first step is to compute the inventory turnover and compare it with similar firms. For example, assume that the owner of a health products store, Functionalized Nutrition, Inc. (FNI) has an annual sales volume of $480,000, an average investment in inventory of $90,000, and a cost of sales of $312,000. The annual inventory turnover for FNI is computed as follows:

$$\text{Inventory turnover} = \text{Cost of sales/Average inventory}$$
$$= 312,000/90,000 = 3.47$$

Thus, FNI turned, or sold, each item in its inventory an average of 3.47 times during the year, or FNI turned its products every 105 (365/3.47 = 105.2) days.

If the standard inventory turnover for retail nutrition supplement stores is 5.1, or 71.6 days, then FNI should be able to improve its turnover.[6] Usually the first step in making an improvement is the recognition that the firm is not up to standard. In this case, if the owner of FNI can improve turnover to the industry standard, the firm will need less inventory and be more profitable.

For example, if FNI can increase its inventory turnover rate to the 5.1 standard, the average inventory would decrease to only $61,176 (computed as follows: cost of sales divided by inventory rate = $312,000/5.1 = $61,176), an inventory reduction of almost $28,824 from the current average of $90,000. If FNI's average cost of financing inventory is 17 percent, then the annual dollar savings is $4,900 ($28,824 × .17 = $4,900). Thus, an improvement in inventory to the industry standard would result in better cash flow and higher profits.

ITEM TURNOVER. To improve the total inventory of any firm, the objective is to determine which individual items are the slow-moving ones. Typically, in any business, some items are selling very quickly and others are not moving as well, creating the excessive investment in inventory. For example, if the owner determines that there is no need to stock any major item above the level to meet the sales demand in 60 days, then an analysis can be accomplished by comparing the number of units of each item on hand with the number sold in the last 60 days. An illustration of how this could be accomplished is shown in Exhibit 17–5.

Certainly the analysis of individual items should be performed only on the larger cost items carried in inventory. In the example in Exhibit 17–5, an analysis of several items that are sold in a small appliance store are shown. The description column could be by model, catalog number, and/or brand name because the objective is to separate each individual item into its own category. Thus, the owner is not as interested in how many electric fry pans are being sold, as in how many of each particular size and model are being purchased.[7]

The other information shown in Exhibit 17–5 is self-explanatory, but the simplicity of the system belies the real value of the information to the small business owner. The item turnover analysis quickly indicates which items can be reduced in the number of units carried and which could be eliminated. The problem with many inventory systems is that they provide for replenishment of existing stock. Thus, if six items are sold, six are ordered for replacement.

EXHIBIT 17–5 Item Turnover Analysis

Description	Number on Hand	Number Sold Last 60 Days	Excess	Action
10" electric fryer	20	34	(14)	Increase
12" electric fryer	27	18	9	Decrease
14" electric fryer	14	5	9	Decrease
8" waffle iron	15	16	(1)	Leave as is
9" waffle iron	12	7	5	Decrease
8" Belgium waffle	17	5	12	Decrease
9" Belgium waffle	9	2	7	Eliminate

The system presented above provides a method of determining whether the existing stock of each item is currently too high. The reduction of unnecessary inventory will increase inventory turnover, reduce the owners' investment in inventory, and increase profits.

DETECT AND REDUCE SHRINKAGE

Many small business owners have no idea of how much they lose to shoplifting or to theft by vendors and employees. In fact, most small business owners do not even think much about security and often look at security as an extra expense that does not return anything on investment.[8] With these attitudes, small businesses may be even more susceptible to losses from theft than larger businesses who maintain better internal control systems and sophisticated alarm systems that discourage shoplifting. In fact, the scenario illustrated in The Way It Is 17–1 is all too typical. This section will present ways to reduce shoplifting and discourage employee and vendor theft.

Shoplifting

Shoplifting is estimated as costing U.S. retailers about $12 billion dollars a year. Other estimates indicate that retail businesses lose approximately 3 percent of their inventory to shoplifting. In terms of cost, if a store has a net profit margin of 4 percent, $2,500 worth of goods (100/.04 = 2,500) must be sold for every $100 worth of merchandise that is stolen. How can the scene illustrated above in The Way It Is 17–1, which is played out in shopping malls all over the United States, be changed? The first problem is that many small business owners hire minimum-wage employees and then give them few instructions except on the use of the sales register. In contrast, most larger businesses have training sessions for new employees that concentrate not only on how to serve the customer, but also on how to discourage shoplifting.

The Way It Is

17–1 SHOPLIFTING

It was 7:30 on Friday night at the K & S News store located in a corner of a popular shopping mall. Jim Carter, a high-school student, was the only employee working, and he was busy reading a sports magazine. While he read, three different customers came into the store and browsed among the rows of available magazines. Jim was so engrossed in the article he was reading that he never even looked up as they entered. Two customers found what they wanted and took them to the counter and paid for their selections. The third person put three magazines from the adult magazine section in a shopping bag and walked out past Jim, who continued reading his article.

One of their prime instructions is to give each customer personal attention by greeting them and asking if they can help them. Thus, small businesses can reduce shoplifting by following the method used by larger stores and giving their new employees more training.

An alert sales force is an excellent deterrent to shoplifting. Shoplifters are looking for those stores where the employees are not attentive to the customers but are busy talking to friends, reading, or putting up stock. Too many small business owners see the cost of hiring additional employees as an unnecessary expense. What they do not see is the savings that can result by having enough employees in the store to discourage shoplifting. Additional measures that discourage shoplifting are the installation of convex mirrors that allow employees to see more areas of the store and visible video recorders. In addition, electronic tags may be placed on merchandise. These tags will set off an alarm if an employee does not remove the tag before the merchandise passes a detector located near the store exits. This type of security system is relatively expensive, but if the store carries merchandise that is both expensive and easy to steal, the system can quickly pay for itself in reducing potential losses.

Reducing Employee and Vendor Theft

Employee and vendor theft can be reduced through the development of a sound security program. The different parts of the security program that a small business should have are listed below. Some will pertain only to employees, others to vendors at either a retail or a manufacturing facility. All, however, have some validity for most small businesses. A sound program should include the following:

1. Before employees are hired, their references from past employers should be thoroughly checked. This simple, yet too often ignored, step would probably do more to reduce employee theft than any other single program.

2. The physical location of the shipping area should, if at all possible, be located completely removed from the company's receiving area. When the shipping and receiving departments are located in the same area, the control of materials is much more difficult, and the possibility of theft is increased.

3. There should be an inspection of all inventory as it is both received and shipped/sold. The inspection of the receipt of inventory should be a physical count and, where possible, a check as to model number. When inventory is shipped or sold, again a physical check should be made. For the retail store, the check is through the checkout counter, and, with the wholesaler or manufacturer, the check should be made before the inventory is loaded for shipment. Particularly, the shipping personnel must check what is being shipped against the bill of lading. Another common checkpoint in manufacturing facilities is the scrap area where good inventory may be added to the scrap before the scrap is sold or removed from the premises.

4. The business should build or arrange the inventory facilities with security in mind, particularly with restriction of the flow of people through the facility. In retail stores, the checkout counter is located near the exits and inventory is located where employees can see it at all times. Most stores limit entrances and exits to specific areas. In manufacturing facilities, the employee parking lot should not be located near exits that allow employees to leave unnoticed. These restrictions may be seen as a fire hazard, but additional emergency doors can be available if they open only from the inside.

5. For some facilities, a closed-circuit television may be installed. After one well-known national doughnut chain installed closed-circuit television in its stores to deter potential robbers, sales increased over 20 percent. Obviously the constant monitoring by the television camera was enough to deter more than nonemployee robbery.

6. A final step in a security program is communication with employees about what is happening. Known losses should be explained to them, and they should be told what they can do to reduce these losses.

For the most part, the above steps are nothing more than commonsense approaches to reducing employee and vendor theft. Having a good inventory management system, described earlier in the chapter, is also very important because the small business owner has an accurate idea of inventory losses. This knowledge can indicate whether more expensive security programs are needed. Usually the simple steps reduce the need for more expensive programs.

SUMMARY

Inventory may be classed as raw material, work-in-process, or finished goods. Each type of inventory has its own purpose and its own cost structure. In the manufacturing process, raw materials are changed into a product that may be sold to another manufacturer or to the ultimate consumer. Businesses realize that there is a cost of carrying inventory due to obsolescence, shrinkage, handling, financing, insurance, and taxes.

Manufacturers can determine the amount of inventory they need by first forecasting the demand for their product. Materials requirement planning, just-in-time, and the use of an accounting record are three systems that help manufacturers determine their inventory needs based on the planned rate of production.

The economic order quantity (EOQ) is the quantity of an inventory that should be ordered to minimize total inventory costs. The EOQ model assumes that both demand and lead times are known with certainty, and the model performs well under those conditions. The EOQ model should not be used if suppliers offer quantity discounts, and the lowest cost order quantity can be determined by calculating the total cost for each price break.

An effective inventory management system provides small business owners with information on how much inventory is on hand and how fast that inventory is moving. Informal inventory systems include visual control, two-bin system, ABC management system, and the blanket order system. Formal inventory systems include computer-based programs that utilize the computer's data storage capabilities to maintain a current inventory record. Point-of-purchase systems, bar coding, and electronic data interchange have been very successful for small businesses.

Turnover analysis is also considered a necessary part of effective inventory management. Turnover analysis includes a study of both total inventory turnover and the turnover of individual items. Finally, small business owners need to be aware of methods to detect and reduce inventory shrinkage. Well-trained employees are the best deterrent to shrinkage, but other measures include the use of convex mirrors and video recorders and the installation of electronic tags on merchandise.

A program to reduce employee and vendor theft should consider a check on all employees before they are hired, separation of the shipping and receiving areas, physical inspection of all inventory when it is received and before it is shipped, the arrangement of inventory facilities with security in mind, and constant communication with employees about potential or actual inventory problems.

QUESTIONS FOR REVIEW AND DISCUSSION

1. Why do manufacturers carry inventory?
2. Why does the manufacturer wish to reduce inventory, whereas piecework employees wish to maintain high inventory?
3. Give some examples of how a retail clothing store could have obsolete inventory.
4. Is there a financing cost if the retail store owner purchases goods for sale on terms of net 45?
5. Specify how material requirements planning helps manufacturers determine their inventory needs.
6. How does the use of just-in-time improve the quality of finished goods?
7. What are some disadvantages of using an accounting system as a means of determining the amount of inventory needed?
8. Using the information in Exhibit 17-4, determine the order quantity that results in the lowest total cost if carrying costs are 15 percent and ordering costs are $100 per order. Assume all other variables do not change.
9. Is the exact determination of the order cost a major factor in the EOQ model?
10. What are four potential problems with the EOQ model?
11. How should small business owners deal with the potential information overload of having a daily printout of all inventory balances in their business?

12. List several things that Jim Carter (see The Way It Is 17-1) was doing wrong as an employee of K & S News.

13. What do you think is the main advantage of installing video recorders in retail stores?

14. Some small business owners believe that one of the most effective ways to keep their employees honest is to keep them in the dark concerning the possible existence of accounting checks. Do you agree or disagree with this philosophy?

15. Indexx pays $10 per electronic card and uses 15,000 cards per year. Indexx's inventory carrying costs are 20 percent. Each time an order is placed, Indexx incurs an ordering cost of $40. Use the EOQ formula to calculate the economic order quantity for Indexx. If the supplier gave a 10 percent discount for orders in excess of 1,500 cards, would this change the EOQ?

16. JIT and EOQ are often competing, incompatible systems between which the manufacturing firm must make a choice. Give a manufacturing situation where JIT may be the best system, and one where EOQ may be the correct system.

KEY TERMS

ABC inventory management system	materials requirements planning
bar coding	point-of-purchase systems
blanket purchase order	raw materials
electronic data interchange	standard shipping unit
economic order quantity	stockless purchasing
finished goods	two-bin inventory system
inventory management	work-in-process
just-in-time philosophy	

CASE
K & S News

Howard Skolnik is the owner of five stores that sell paperback books and magazines. Each store contains 1,400 square feet of retail shopping space arranged with two rows of books down the center of the store and racks for the magazines on each wall. The stores are located in medium-sized shopping centers, with one door that opens onto the regular mall traffic. Customers must enter and leave the store through the one door, and the checkout counter is located near the door. The store contains no convex mirrors, does not have video recorders installed, and does not install electronic tags on any of the merchandise.

All of Mr. Skolnik's employees are hired on a part-time basis, and they work only twenty-five hours a week at the minimum wage. Employee training consists of an explanation on the arrangement of the books and magazines. Magazines are arranged by interest groups with the sports in one section, news in another, and so on. Books are arranged in four broad categories (popular, romance, novels, and general interest) alphabetically by author except for the current top ten, which are in a rack located near the front of the store.

Mr. Skolnik does all the ordering of inventory for each store, but the books and magazines are delivered almost daily from a distributor. Mr. Skolnik, therefore, explains the check-in system for accepting these deliveries to each new employee. This system consists of counting the number of each title and comparing with the number on the delivery invoice. There is no urgency to this count, so the employees are instructed to check the new supplies in when there are no customers in the store.

From an inventory standpoint, the only other instructions Mr. Skolnik gives his new employees is on the use of the checkout register. The K & S system records only the dollar amount of each sale.

ACTIVITY

1. Read the expanded version of the K & S News case. From an inventory management standpoint, what is the owner doing right and in what ways could the owner improve the training of his employees?

PART SIX

SPECIAL TOPICS

18 GOVERNMENT REGULATIONS AND INTERNATIONAL TRADE

LEARNING OBJECTIVES

After you have read this chapter, you will be able to do the following:
- Explain how government makes and enforces regulations
- Define government's role as a competitor of small business and as a buyer of goods and services from small companies
- Explain the advantages and disadvantages of international trade
- Determine the difference between direct and indirect exporting
- Decide where to go for international trade assistance

One of the rewards of starting or buying a business is the ability to make decisions without consulting the "boss." Entrepreneurs believe that their business is an extension of themselves and its success or failure depends on their abilities. Although business owners may not have bosses, they do not have total freedom to operate their companies as they see fit. The government has something to say about how businesses will be operated and what happens to owners who disregard its rules and regulations. Government—federal, state, and local—is not a homogenous body that always knows what each agency is trying to accomplish; therefore, small business owners should expect conflicting rules from different governmental bodies.

Business owners typically think of the government as an overbearing, bureaucratic body that exists to make their lives miserable. Although there is some truth to that belief, the government can also provide valuable, low-cost assistance to small businesses. In fact, government plays four roles for small business owners—regulator, competitor, buyer of services, and provider of assistance. In this chapter we will see how each role affects small businesses.

The government also has an important role in international trade. The opportunities to do business with other countries are limitless, yet the U.S. Commerce Department estimates that only 250 American companies account for 80 percent of all exports. In this chapter we will discuss ways of becoming involved in international trade. The majority of the section devoted to international trade will deal with exporting, in particular, when exporting is appropriate for small businesses, how companies can start exporting, and how exports can be financed.

GOVERNMENT AS REGULATOR

Until the last decade of the nineteenth century, American industry was essentially allowed to do as it pleased. Men like Rockefeller, Carnegie, and Mellon amassed huge fortunes from unregulated businesses that could expand at will. Business owners firmly believed in Adam Smith's "invisible hand" theory, and government attempts at regulation or control were vigorously resisted. However, the government finally proved to be more powerful than industrial tycoons, and industry was regulated. The first regulatory agency, the Interstate Commerce Commission (ICC), was established in 1887 to regulate the railroads. Other regulatory agencies have been established since then, with most regulatory growth occurring in the 1960s and 1970s. The regulations of these agencies affect all but the very smallest businesses.

Objectives of Regulation

The intent of government regulations was to encourage competition by eliminating or regulating monopolistic practices. More specifically, regulations were enacted to accomplish the following objectives: prevent excess profits; hold prices down to costs (including reasonable profit); avoid economic allocative waste—that is, minimize shortages and surpluses as well as allocate resources to areas of greatest demand; eliminate inefficient production methods; and insure administrative ease.[1] Government regulations were intended to protect the public from unfair or illegal business practices; however, the effects of regulations have not always been beneficial.

Benefits of Regulation

Developing, enacting, and enforcing regulations is a costly business that does not always provide the intended benefits. Abiding by the myriad of federal, state, and local regulations has increased the cost, paperwork, and frustration level of thousands of small business owners. However, regulations have provided some noneconomic benefits, including disclosure and publicity; protection from cartelization of industries; containment of monopoly and oligopoly; promotion of safety for consumers and workers; and legitimization of the capitalist order.[2] Consumers have benefited most from government regulations, but protecting them has not been a simple process. During the height of regulatory activity, 1962 to 1975, at least ten major consumer protection laws were enacted (see Exhibit 18–1).

Regulatory Legislation

From the beginning of this century until the late 1970s, it appeared as though the government would never stop devising more regulations; however, the Reagan years brought a period of deregulation rather than regulation. The Reagan administration preferred deregulation, because enacting regulations is a cumbersome, expensive process that tends to stifle and burden smaller businesses.

Another problem with the enactment of regulatory legislation is the political conflict. Each government agency has its own territory or "turf" to

EXHIBIT 18–1 Consumer Protection Laws, 1962–1975

Year of Enactment	Law	Purpose
1962	Food and Drug Amendments	Requires the pretesting of drugs for safety and effectiveness
1965	Cigarette Labeling Act	Requires labels disclosing hazards of smoking
1966	Fair Packaging and Labeling Act	Requires producers to state what a package contains and how much it contains
1967	Wholesome Meat Act	Offers to states federal assistance in establishing inspection standards
1968	Consumer Credit Protection Act	Requires full disclosure of terms and conditions of finance charges in credit transactions
1968	Wholesome Poultry Products Act	Increases protection against impure poultry
1970	Public Health Smoking Act	Extends warnings about hazards of cigarette smoking
1970	Poison Prevention Packing Act	Authorizes the creation of standards for child-resistant packaging of hazardous substances
1972	Consumer Product Safety Act	Establishes commission authorized to set safety standards for consumer products
1975	Consumer Product Warranty Act	Establishes warranty standards to which business firms must adhere

protect and enlarge; therefore, there is considerable infighting among agencies to determine which will develop and enforce the most regulations. There can be several agencies that have regulatory responsibility for the same industry or organization. For example, when legislation to protect the nation's barrier islands was being proposed, it turned out that the following federal agencies had some responsibility for those islands:

- Department of the Interior
- Heritage Conservation and Recreation Service
- National Park Service
- Fish and Wildlife Service
- Bureau of Land Management
- Army Corps of Engineers
- General Services Administration
- Environmental Protection Agency
- Department of Housing and Urban Development
- Department of Energy
- Council of Environmental Quality
- Federal Emergency Management Agency
- Federal Insurance Administration
- Office of Disaster Response and Recovery
- Office of Coastal Zone Management

- Economic Development Administration
- Federal Highway Administration
- U.S. Coast Guard
- Farmers Home Administration
- Small Business Administration

No wonder small business owners are confused and overwhelmed by this process.

Finally, many regulations are formulated with almost total disregard of the cost or the severity of the problem. The following examples illustrate that disregard:

- A new study by a Johns Hopkins professor for the National Acid Precipitation Assessment Project shows that there is no difference in environmental gains from reducing sulfur-dioxide emissions by 12 million tons over reducing them by only 6 million tons, but the added cost to consumers is more than $6 billion a year.
- The National Transportation Safety Board proposes to force airlines to require that all children under age two be seated separately in toddler safety seats. The FAA estimates this would have saved one infant life since 1978. The cost of this regulation to consumers would be $205 million a year. The cost per life saved would be over $2 billion.
- The EPA administrator announced the phaseout of a whole class of fungicides known as EBDCs, at an economic cost of more than $2 billion a year. Yet according to the FDA's own studies, the risk to the public from EBDCs is less than half of one cancer risk per year.
- In the late 1970s the EPA and the HHS said that airborne asbestos in buildings was killing nearly sixty thousand Americans a year. By 1989, careful scientific review and epidemiology had cut that estimate to fewer than five deaths a year. By this time the EPA was carrying out what could be a $50 to $100 billion program to rip asbestos out of schools. Now the EPA says that was never its intention and agrees that such removal could do more harm than good.[3]

Regulatory Enforcement

Once regulations have been enacted, agencies need techniques, such as the following, to insure compliance:

jawboning

Jawboning. Jawboning is an informal method of applying government pressure to convince a business or industry to comply with enacted regulations.

licensing

Licensing. Regulatory agencies can use **licensing** to insure compliance by threatening to revoke operating licenses from noncomplying businesses. For example, radio or television stations that fail to comply with federal regulations can have their licenses revoked by the Federal Communication Commission.

economic
incentives or
disincentives

Economic incentives or disincentives. Agencies can encourage compliance by using such **economic incentives or disincentives** as subsidies or taxation.

rate of return

Rate of return. In some cases, mainly for national monopolies, agencies stipulate what **rate of return** a business is allowed.

public
enterprises

Formation of public enterprise. If the government requires complete compliance with its regulations, it can establish **public enterprises** such as the Tennessee Valley Authority (TVA) to operate under its control.

Regulatory Outcomes

Most regulations are developed to protect business, consumers, and the general public, but intentions and reality are not always synonymous. In some instances, regulators who insist on absolute compliance cause more harm than good. The following are a few examples of the regulatory process run amok:

· Mr. Ocie Mills, 55, of Pensacola, Florida, and his son are currently serving a 21-month jail term for having dumped 21 loads of sand preparatory to building Mr. Mills's retirement home on his 65-by-200-foot building lot. They were convicted of filling "natural wetlands."

· A Los Angeles bank faces a $22 million environmental Super Fund clean-up bill for a debtor's 1944 to 1979 effluents, because the bank operated the company for eight days in 1981 in an attempt to liquidate its $900,000 loan. Banks around the country are getting out of industrial lending to avoid similar EPA "deep pockets" suits.

· Consumers of electric power in Phoenix face $4 billion in higher rates because the EPA and the National Park Service are attempting to blame visibility problems in the Grand Canyon on a clean-coal power plant 170 miles downwind of the canyon.

· An environmental group sued the Gillette Company and forced it to remove its correction fluid from the market because it contains TCE, whose cancer risk (unless ingested in large volumes) is too infinitesimal to discern. The company settled because fighting the suit would have been more costly than reformulating the product.[4]

These regulations are enacted and enforced by agencies charged with protecting businesses and consumers. There are too many agencies (see Exhibit 18–2) to examine in this section; however, we will look at one that affects small businesses—the Occupational Safety and Health Administration.

Occupational Safety and Health Administration

Occupational
Safety and
Health Act

The **Occupational Safety and Health Act** of 1970 created the Occupational Safety and Health Administration (OSHA), which enforces regulations designed to keep America's workplaces safe. Many employers are opposed to OSHA, not because they think safety is unimportant, but because they perceive this agency to be meddlesome and petty. Small business owners tend to

EXHIBIT 18–2 SELECTED REGULATORY AGENCIES

	Agency	Regulatory Purpose
1887	Interstate Commerce Commission	Control some surface transportation such as railroads, oil pipelines, and barges
1914	Federal Trade Commission	Control monopolies and unfair sales practices
1931	Food and Drug Administration	Insure the purity and usefulness of food and drugs
1934	Federal Communications Commission	Control broadcasters
1934	Securities and Exchange Commission	Regulate stock exchange activities
1948	Federal Aviation Administration	Monitor air traffic control and safety systems
1966	Federal Highway Administration	Set safety standards for interstate trucking services
1970	The Environmental Protection Agency	Establish environmental quality standards
1972	The Consumer Protection Agency	Establish product safety standards
1973	Occupational Safety and Health Administration	Insure safe workplaces and work practices

think that they are exempt from OSHA regulations, and they are partially right. Companies with fewer than ten employees are exempt from routine program and record inspections; however, they are still subject to enforcement inspections if OSHA receives a complaint or if there is a fatality. The Way It Is 18–1 illustrates the advisability of voluntarily complying with OSHA regulations.

THE OCCUPATIONAL SAFETY AND HEALTH ACT. Section 5(a) of this act states that "each employer shall furnish to each of his employees employment and a place of employment which are free from recognized hazards that are causing or are likely to cause death or serious physical harm to his employees." This act, which covers all private establishments, was passed in the Senate by an 83-to-3 vote and in the House by a 384-to-5 vote. The original act seemed simple and straightforward; however, numerous other agencies questioned various OSHA standards, causing the addition of hundreds of pages of explanation or modification.

FUNCTIONS OF OSHA. There are two ways for OSHA to inspect workplaces to insure compliance with the act's standards. First, if employees contact OSHA to report unsafe working conditions, an OSHA inspector is dispatched to investigate these allegations. Second, inspectors are supposed to make periodic, unannounced inspections of workplaces. Employers became so annoyed with these unannounced inspections that they lobbied for some type of relief. In May 1978, the Supreme Court ruled that an employer may refuse admission to an inspector who does not have a search warrant. Because of this requirement and a shortage of inspectors, periodic inspections are not common.

ESTABLISHING OSHA STANDARDS. OSHA continues to add health and safety standards to the original act whenever they seem to be necessary. These standards cannot be arbitrarily established without allowing employer comment; therefore, the following steps are required to make proposed stan-

18–1 AVOIDING WORKPLACE HAZARDS

One California small business owner was purchasing bulk chemicals, putting them in smaller containers, and selling them. There was a lot of concentrated sulfuric acid on site, and one day there was a bad spill. The owner's daughter tried to deal with the spill, slipped, and fell in a pool of acid. There was no safety shower, and the woman ran around, her skin burning, until the fire department came and hosed her down. Had this business owner voluntarily complied with OSHA regulations, a safety shower not only would have been in place, but might have been unnecessary, because the spill would have been less likely to occur in the first place.[5]

*Federal
Register*

dards part of the act: (1) a proposed regulation is submitted to OSHA; (2) an advisory committee is established to consider the proposal; (3) the proposed regulation is published in the *Federal Register;* (4) public hearings are held; (5) time is allowed for post-hearing comments to be made by interested parties; (6) the final regulation is published in the *Federal Register;* and (7) the proposal becomes a regulation.

Sometimes OSHA employees develop standards and regulations that are not really necessary. Take Harvard neurologist Michael M. Segal's recent discovery for example. Here is a company's advisory about a chemical: "After contact with skin, wash immediately with plenty of soap and water. . . . Special Firefighting Procedures: Wear self-contained breathing apparatus and protective clothing to prevent contact with skin or eyes. . . . combustible solvent and burn in a chemical incinerator equipped with an after-burner and scrubber. Observe all federal, state and local environmental regulations." This "hazardous" chemical is paraffin wax—what ordinary candles are made of.[6]

ENFORCING REGULATIONS. Once OSHA has established standards, it must develop enforcement techniques that will encourage compliance. Because OSHA only recommends penalties for noncompliance, the actual enforcement proceedings are conducted by the Occupational Safety and Health Review Commission (OSHRC), an agency separate from OSHA. Fines or other penalties are designed to reflect the severity of the violation. OSHA has identified the following types of violations:

- Minor. This type of violation has no direct relationship to job safety or health; therefore, a notice is issued to the employer, but no penalties are imposed.

- Nonserious violation. In this case, safety or health may be affected, but the violation is not likely to cause serious injury or death. A fine of up to $1,000 may be levied for these violations.

OSHA-required safety equipment within a small manufacturing plant.

- Serious violation. Serious violations are those that are likely to cause serious injury or death. For this type of violation, a mandatory fine of up to $1,000 is imposed.
- Imminent danger. When conditions exist that could reasonably be expected to cause death or injury, the employer is asked to voluntarily correct the situation. If voluntary action is not taken, OSHA can obtain a temporary restraining order, or an injunction may be secured from a U.S. district court.

GOVERNMENT AS COMPETITOR

The government regulates small business, it competes with small business, and it buys products and services from small companies. Most small business owners want government to continue purchasing their goods and services, but they do not want the government to continue providing competing goods and services to other government agencies. Owners of small businesses contend that they cannot compete with government agencies that provide similar goods and services at subsidized prices.

Competing with Government

All levels of government own and operate facilities that produce goods and services consumed by government. For example, most airports are government owned, and government units own utilities, which produce water, gas, and electricity for towns and cities. Governments own transportation systems, housing units, garbage companies, and large fleets of vehicles. Some services and products are supplied by government to government or the public because no private company is willing or able to provide them. However, there is pressure on the government to contract out those services best provided by the private sector.

Office of Management and Budget (OMB) Circular A-76 stipulates that agencies rely on the private sector for commercial-type services unless the federal government can provide them at a lower cost. Advocates of "contracting out" point to it as economically prudent, buttressing their position with the argument that government should not be involved in commercial-type activities that the private sector can provide. Opponents' criticisms focus largely on the lower quality of services that contractors often deliver and on the employment concerns of federal workers threatened by layoff. Some also see contracting out as giving an illusion of a smaller, less costly government.

Many government units, particularly local, are taking the opportunity to privatize government services (see The Way It Is 18–2). A study of 288 municipalities with more than 50,000 residents found the following percentage of services that had been privatized:[7] refuse collection (49.7%), vehicle towing and storage (76.9%), animal control (13.1%), street maintenance (23.7%),

---

The Way It Is   18–2 PRIVATIZING

privatization

Privatization—turning functions or property in the government's domain over to private management or ownership—is in transition. The once-radical idea that private business can manage prisons and collect garbage is now commonplace. But privatization is moving into whole new areas, from managing libraries, municipal golf courses, and military airfields to helping bring free enterprise to government operations in Eastern Europe. Small companies get a big slice of these operations, such as service jobs that federal agencies contract out to private businesses. The following are some recent government service contracts won by private firms: Seattle, solid-waste recycling (Recycle America Inc., Seattle, and Recycle Seattle Inc., Seattle); Starr County, Texas, jail (Pricor Inc., Murfreesboro, Tennessee); 21 percent of Denver transit system (Mayflower Contract Services Inc., and others); and Veterans Administration mail services (DDD Company, Landover, Maryland).[8]

transportation (25.9%), health care (26.9%), and park landscaping (23.7%). Services privatized by fewer municipalities were tax collection, waste water treatment, police protection, fire protection, and building inspection.

GOVERNMENT AS BUYER OF GOODS AND SERVICES

When government units follow OMB Circular A-76 and purchase goods and services from the private sector, they often solicit bids from small businesses. In fiscal 1988, small businesses provided nearly one-third (32 percent, or $62.3 billion) of the $194.9 billion in goods and services purchased under contract by the federal government. Approximately 90 percent of these contracts were awarded by the Department of Defense (DOD), the Department of Energy (DOE), and the National Aeronautics and Space Administration (NASA).[9]

Winning government contracts can be fairly lucrative, but it is often difficult to comply with all the stipulations accompanying the contract. It is even difficult to put the bid in the correct form; however, one company has developed software to help small business contractors bid for government jobs (see The Way It Is 18–3). Once a bid is won, business owners must comply with all extant government regulations such as filing an affirmative action plan, paying workers the "going rate," and not engaging in discriminatory employment practices.

Realizing that its business dealings with small companies have not always been positive, government enacted some laws to improve those relations. For example, there are laws governing prompt payment for services or goods and laws to reduce the paperwork required by government. These laws plus the near certainty of payment make government contracts alluring to many small businesses. So alluring, in fact, that some companies become nearly totally reliant on government contracts. Government contracts may be lucrative, but small business owners should not rely heavily on those contracts. Once a

---

The Way It Is

18–3 GOVERNMENT-SPEAK

There is a new software program out that helps people write in government style—whatever that is. San Francisco-based Reference Software International, which produces Grammatik writing-improvement software, found they had many customers who were government contractors. Unfortunately, Grammatik kept complaining that their favorite phrases were jargon. So Reference Software International obligingly produced a government edition. The company diplomatically promises that "where government writing guidelines conflict with standard writing rules, Grammatik cites both."[10]

contract has been completed, there is no assurance that a replacement contract can be won from another government unit.

GOVERNMENT ASSISTANCE

Small business owners often feel that they come in contact with governments only when they are being regulated, inspected, taxed, penalized, competed with, or told to do business differently. However, governments at all levels do have programs designed to assist small business owners. Some of these programs are direct, some are indirect, and some are so obscure that few business owners even know they exist.

Information

The government has books, pamphlets, and brochures that address virtually every aspect of planning, starting, and operating a small business. These sources of information are available from the Superintendent of Documents for a nominal cost. A useful reference in locating available government programs is the *Handbook for Small Business: A Survey of Small Business Programs of the Federal Government*. Other useful information is provided by such federal agencies as the Internal Revenue Service, which provides useful pamphlets such as the following: *Tax Guide for Small Business, Your Federal Income Tax*, and *Information for Business Taxpayers*.

The Small Business Administration

Small Business Administration (SBA)

The **Small Business Administration (SBA)** was created by the Small Business Act in 1953. The purpose of this agency is to assist small businesses in any way possible, but particularly with the acquisition of capital. The SBA is authorized to provide small businesses with two types of loans—loans for plant construction and the acquisition of land, equipment, and materials, and disaster loans to business concerns that suffer financial loss from floods, hurricanes, or other natural disasters. The SBA is also responsible for helping small companies secure a larger share of government contracts for materials, construction, and research and development. The SBA is responsive to changing conditions.

Responding to the needs of women who are small business owners, the government passed the Women's Business Ownership Act of 1988. The act authorized the SBA to institute a number of programs to increase opportunities for female entrepreneurs. Through its Office of Women's Business Ownership (OWBO), the SBA provides assistance in financing, procurement contracting, and training. Through its Demonstration Project Program, OWBO also established long-term training and counseling facilities for women.

Other Government Agencies

The Small Business Administration is not the only federal agency that provides assistance to small businesses. Other agencies such as the Department of Labor, the Department of Commerce, and the Department of Energy have

The
Way
It Is

18-4 GOVERNMENT ASSISTANCE

For Karakian Bedrosian, the magic number was $97,300. That is the amount of money he received from the Energy Related Inventions Program (ERIP) grant that enabled him to bring his TomAHtoes to market. ERIP offers funding and development assistance to help inventors and small business owners develop energy-efficient inventions with commercial potential. The program, which started in the spring of 1975, is a joint operation of the Department of Energy (DOE) and the Department of Commerce through its National Institute of Standards and Technology (NIST).

Bedrosian's dream was to bring consumers summer-fresh tomatoes all year long. His idea was to substitute a low-oxygen environment for low temperatures. Reducing the amount of oxygen in the air around the tomatoes helps them stay fresh without refrigeration and ripen faster. His first experiments failed and he ran out of money. Just when it looked as if his idea was doomed, Bedrosian received his ERIP grant.[11]

assistance programs for small businesses. The problem with the programs offered by these agencies is that they are often so obscure that few small business owners learn about or qualify for them (see The Way It Is 18-4).

Energy Related Inventions Program (ERIP)

Grants such as the **Energy Related Inventions Program (ERIP)** offered by the Department of Energy and the Commerce Department's National Institute of Standards and Technology (NIST) are difficult to obtain. From 1975 through 1990, the ERIP processed 27,558 applications. Of those, 531 were recommended to DOE, and only 337 were funded. One good thing about ERIP is that it is absolutely free. There is no application fee, no fee for technical evaluation, and no fee for the funding. Another good thing is that those whose applications are turned down can gather more information or correct any problems with the project and resubmit their application.

Assistance from States

Many states offer direct and indirect services to small businesses. Some states make low-interest loans to small businesses, some set aside a percentage of state services for small businesses, and most offer counseling services to small companies. Several states also offer matchmaking services to small businesses and prospective clients. A matchmaker agency seeks out prospective purchasers of goods and services and pairs them with existing businesses in the state. Agencies use a wide range of sales and marketing tactics to find out about pending contracts. Then, after canvassing businesses in the state, they solicit bids and even help negotiate deals.

All states have a vested interest in assisting small businesses because it is small companies that create most new jobs and provide services that large companies cannot profitably offer.

Miscellaneous Assistance Programs

The government helps small business in a number of ways. In addition to the programs already discussed, the government has the following programs that help small companies:

"Buy American" provisions. The Buy American Act of 1933 mandated that federal agencies purchase American goods for domestic use if the goods were available at a reasonable price.

Interest-free loans. Companies cannot apply directly for interest-free loans; however, the government's progress-payment plan serves almost the same purpose. Small businesses doing work for the government can request partial payment before the job is completed, thereby having the use of "unearned," interest-free money.

Trade inducements. The government has tried to encourage small companies to export by establishing agencies that insure exports, make loans available to exporters, and provide information about which goods are in demand in other countries.

Import restrictions. The government protects small businesses by limiting the amount of certain goods that can be imported. However, many experts do not believe that establishing quotas for imported goods is a very effective method of protecting domestic businesses. For example, they point out that when quotas were established for Korean shoes, the Koreans began importing rubber footwear, which was not covered by the original trade agreement. Another significant problem with restricting the importation of foreign goods is that other countries tend to retaliate and limit the amount of American goods that can be imported into their countries.

TRADING INTERNATIONALLY

The United States is the world's largest economy, the largest market, and the leading exporter and importer. In 1990, merchandise exports contributed about three-fourths of real U.S. gross national product growth. Although exports are increasing, imports continue to increase leaving the United States with an annual trade deficit of approximately $100 billion. The federal government constantly searches for ways to encourage exports and discourage imports in an effort to reduce our trade deficit.

U.S. Trade Facts

The following U.S. trade facts were compiled and published by the Commerce Department for the years 1989 and 1990:

- U.S. two-way trade totaled $890 billion in 1990, with exports of $393 billion and imports of $497 billion.
- The 1990 U.S. trade deficit shrank to $104 billion, 32 percent below the 1987 deficit peak.
- U.S. merchandise exports rose to 7.2 percent of the nation's GNP in the first nine months of 1990 from 7.1 percent in 1989.

- In 1989, the United States accounted for 13.2 percent of the world's merchandise exports and an estimated 16.5 percent of the world's merchandise imports.
- Merchandise exports accounted for nearly seven million jobs in the United States in 1989.
- About one in six U.S. jobs in manufacturing was probably due directly or indirectly to exports in 1989.
- From 1891 through 1970, the United States had an unbroken string of trade surpluses. After 1970, it had deficits in every year except 1973 and 1975.
- The Commerce Department estimates that roughly one-third of U.S. manufacturing companies export goods.
- Two-thirds of U.S. merchandise exports are by American-owned multinational corporations, with over one-third of these exports being shipped by the U.S. parent to its foreign affiliate.[12]

International Trade Advantages

Before more small business owners can be convinced that trading internationally will benefit them, they need to be shown that trade advantages outweigh the disadvantages. The primary advantage of trading internationally is that a company's market is expanded significantly and growth prospects are greatly enhanced. Other advantages include the following: idle capacity can be utilized; cyclical or seasonal slumps can be minimized; owners can become acquainted with manufacturing technology used in other countries; owners can learn about products not sold in the United States, and they can learn about other cultures; growth capital may be more readily available in other countries than in the United States; and company owners have ample opportunity to travel for business and pleasure.

International Trade Disadvantages

Most small business owners who avoid international trade do so because they believe it is too complicated and fraught with bureaucratic red tape. They also believe that international trade is only profitable for large companies that have more money and personnel than smaller businesses. Some other disadvantages include the following: a company may become too dependent on international trade; foreign government instability could cause problems for domestic companies; tariffs and import duties make it too expensive to trade in other countries; products manufactured in the United States may need significant modification before they are accepted by people in other countries; and foreign cultures, customs, and languages make it difficult for Americans to do business in some countries.

Entering International Markets

Many business owners are finding that trade advantages do outweigh the disadvantages, and they are committing their companies to the international arena. For most business owners, beginning to market their products internationally is an evolutionary rather than immediate process. Companies are started and remain domestically oriented until some trigger such as market saturation prompts their owners to consider international trade. Having made that decision, owners next have to decide how to enter other countries and which ones to enter. Owners usually select one or a few countries to begin trading with before they are willing or able to trade with several countries at the same time.

International Trade Barriers

Sometimes it is not particularly easy to become an international trader. Foreign companies, foreign governments, U.S. companies, and the federal government consciously or inadvertently erect barriers that hinder international trade. The two major categories of barriers include tariff and nontariff barriers (see Exhibit 18–3). **Tariff barriers** determine how much money a company pays to import or export goods, which goods are subject to tariffs, and so forth. **Nontariff barriers** are less straightforward and may seem capricious to exporters and importers. Either type of barrier may prevent many small businesses from becoming involved in international trade.

tariff barriers

nontariff barriers

The U.S. government also hinders trade by explicitly prohibiting the export of certain technologies and products. Since 1949, the government has restricted the export of weapons and dual-use technologies with potential for both military and commercial applications. This export control system currently applies to 40 percent of all U.S.-manufactured exports, as well as to technical data, and covers virtually all U.S. advanced technology. It has been estimated that these export controls cost U.S. companies $9.3 billion a year.[13] Because of the export control system, the United States is losing numerous trade opportunities in Eastern Europe and the developing world. U.S. companies choosing to export a product must first determine if the product is subject to export controls and then which of eleven government agencies administers the controls in question.

Coordinating Committee for Multilateral Export Controls

The political changes in Eastern Europe have caused the **Coordinating Committee for Multilateral Export Controls** (COCOM—the NATO allies except Iceland plus Australia and Japan) to reconsider their ban on certain exports. The number of high-technology items that cannot be exported to the former Soviet Union and what was the Warsaw Pact have been cut in half. In May 1991 the allies agreed, after nearly one year of negotiations, to lift restrictions on the export of almost all personal computers, some semiconductor-manufacturing equipment, and most civilian aircraft and civilian aircraft engines. COCOM is also recommending more favorable licensing for exports to Eastern Europe and is creating a core list of controlled goods and technologies to replace the current COCOM list.

EXPORTING

Business owners who choose to become international traders can either export their products to other countries or physically establish branches of their companies in those countries. Most people new to international trade find

EXHIBIT 18–3 Trade Barriers

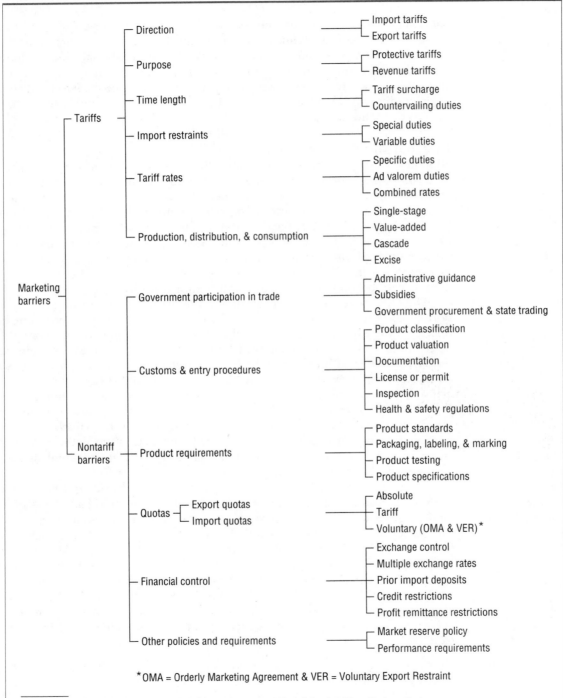

*OMA = Orderly Marketing Agreement & VER = Voluntary Export Restraint

that exporting is easier and less expensive than manufacturing and marketing products in other countries. Most international trade neophytes need to be convinced that they will benefit financially from exporting. They are intimidated by the supposed complexities and intricacies of exporting and need to have the reasons to export explained to them.

Small business owners are finding that exporting is not as difficult as they imagined. In fact, many owners have found that all they really need to become an exporter is a fax machine and an 800 telephone number. The following are a few small companies that have begun exporting: Life Corporation, emergency oxygen kits (sales less than $5 million with exports accounting for 50 percent of total sales); Treatment Products, auto wax ($5 million/25 percent); Midwest Tropical, aquariums ($5.5 million/25 percent); and Sharper Finish, laundry/ironing equipment ($3 million/60 percent). The small companies that export are typically private, closely held, or family owned.[14]

Reasons for Exporting

The Commerce Department, the federal agency primarily responsible for fostering international trade, has identified the following reasons for exporting:

- Increase overall sales volume
- Enlarge sales base to spread out fixed costs
- Use excess production capacity
- Compensate for seasonal fluctuations in domestic sales
- Find new markets for products with declining U.S. sales
- Exploit existing advantages in untapped markets
- Take advantage of high-volume foreign purchases
- Learn about advanced technical methods used abroad
- Follow domestic competitors who are selling overseas
- Acquire knowledge about international competition
- Test opportunities for overseas licensing or production
- Contribute to the company's general expansion
- Improve overall return on investment
- Create more jobs[15]

If these reasons convince business owners to try exporting, they then have to decide which method of exporting—indirect or direct—is most practical.

Indirect Exporting

Indirect exporting, using intermediaries, is the easiest method because someone else does most of the work for business owners. Business owners choosing to export indirectly need to decide which of several different intermediaries they will use. The decision often rests on services rendered, location, and cost of the intermediary. The following are individuals and companies that offer export services: commission agents; export management companies; export trading companies; export agents, merchants, or remarketers; and piggyback marketing.

commission
agents

COMMISSION AGENTS. When foreign firms or governments need certain products, they hire buying or **commission agents** to locate and purchase those goods in the United States. These agents cost American business owners nothing because their commission is paid by the foreign firm or government; however, the likelihood of being "found" by an agent is extremely small. Small business owners who need steady export services cannot rely on commission agents.

export
management
company
(EMC)

EXPORT MANAGEMENT COMPANIES. An **export management company (EMC)** serves as the export department for one or several noncompeting companies. For a commission, a salary, or a retainer plus commission, an EMC will arrange to sell a company's products to foreign buyers. Some large EMCs will arrange financing for client companies or buy their products for resale at a later date. Because most of the 2,000 EMCs are quite small, they usually specialize either by product or by foreign market. This specialization allows EMCs to remain thoroughly informed about their products and markets, and it allows them to establish reliable foreign networks.

export trading
companies
(ETC)

EXPORT TRADING COMPANIES. **Export trading companies (ETC)** are similar to EMCs; however, they generally provide more services than EMCs, and they are more likely to take title to a client's products. The goals of the Export Trading Company Act of 1982 are to stimulate U.S. exports by

1. promoting and encouraging the formation of export trading companies,
2. expanding the options available for export financing by permitting bank holding companies to invest in export trading companies and reducing restrictions on trade finance provided by financial institutions, and
3. reducing uncertainty regarding the application of U.S. antitrust law to export operations.[16]

export agents

EXPORT AGENTS, MERCHANTS, OR REMARKETERS. These people purchase products directly from manufacturers, repackage and relabel the products, and sell them in other countries in their own names. In transactions with **export agents,** merchants, or remarketers, a U.S. company relinquishes control over the marketing of its product, which could have an adverse effect on future sales efforts abroad.

PIGGYBACK MARKETING. In some instances, a company that exports its products may have foreign buyers who want complementary products that it does not produce. The exporting company might contract with a U.S. firm that has the desired product to export that product to the foreign buyer. In

piggyback marketing, the original U.S. producer piggybacks its products to the international marketplace, generally without incurring the marketing and distribution costs associated with exporting.

Direct Exporting

The advantages of direct exporting, using no intermediaries, for a U.S. company include more control over the export process, potentially higher profits, and a closer relationship to the overseas buyer and marketplace. The advantages are realized only because companies take on the responsibilities of intermediaries. The direct exporter selects target countries, chooses the most effective channels of distribution, and markets and sells its product to foreign buyers. Direct exporters can use sales agents, representatives, or distributors, or they can sell directly to foreign retailers or end-users.

SALES AGENTS OR REPRESENTATIVES. In foreign countries, agents and representatives function like manufacturer's representatives do in the United States. The sales representative normally works on a commission basis, assumes no risk or responsibility, and is under contract for a specified time. Some agents or representatives are awarded exclusive territories, whereas others are not restricted by geographic boundaries. Similarly, some agents may represent several companies with competing products, whereas others offer their services exclusively to one manufacturer of a particular product.

DISTRIBUTORS. Unlike agents and representatives, distributors purchase products from exporters, add their markup, and resell the product to wholesalers, retailers, or consumers. Distributors normally provide support and service for the product and carry inventory of products and spare parts to service the product when necessary. Distributors generally do not carry competing products; however, they can carry complementary products.

FOREIGN RETAILERS. In some instances, it may be most efficient for exporters to sell directly to foreign retailers. Bypassing agents, distributors, wholesalers, and others provides maximum profit to both exporter and retailer; however, the exporter assumes more marketing responsibility than when he or she uses third parties. Selling directly to retailers means that business owners or their own salespeople must call on prospective retailers as they might do in the United States. It is possible for exporters to rely on catalogs, brochures, or trade fairs to entice retailers to buy their products, but the personal approach is likely to be more fruitful.

SALES TO END-USERS. Some exporters may be able to identify large end-users such as foreign governments, hospitals, or schools that will buy their products without the benefit of intermediaries. For exporters, this is the most profitable selling arrangement because there are no intermediaries, but it also requires the most work on the part of the exporter. Buyers can be identified at trade shows, through international publications, or through U.S. government contact programs, such as the Commerce Department's Export Mailing List Service.

Exporting Mistakes and Problems

Many small business owners who heed the call of the federal government to export rush into international trade without adequate preparation. They make mistakes, some of which can be overcome; others, however, can be terminal. The Commerce Department has compiled the following list of the twelve most common mistakes and pitfalls made by new exporters:

1. Failure to obtain qualified export counseling and to develop a master international marketing plan before starting an export business.
2. Insufficient commitment by top management to overcome the initial difficulties and financial requirements of exporting.
3. Insufficient care in selecting overseas distributors.
4. Chasing orders from around the world instead of establishing a basis for profitable operations and orderly growth.
5. Neglecting export business when the U.S. market booms.
6. Failure to treat international distributors on an equal basis with domestic counterparts.
7. Assuming that a given market technique and product will automatically be successful in all countries.
8. Unwillingness to modify products to meet regulations or cultural preferences of other countries.
9. Failure to print service, sale, and warranty messages in locally understood languages.
10. Failure to consider use of an Export Management Company.
11. Failure to consider licensing or joint-venture agreements.
12. Failure to provide readily available servicing for the product.[17]

Other observers trace export failure to managerial barriers.[18] These problems include the following:

Limited ambition. Complacent managers are satisfied with the current status of their companies and do not even look for other opportunities. Parochial managers are interested in growing, but limit their horizons to regional or national domestic markets.

Unrecognized opportunities. For the company willing to consider exporting, the first step is the acquisition of accurate knowledge. Problems can arise from both inadequate knowledge and an inappropriate interpretation of that knowledge.

Apparent lack of necessary resources. Some managers who do recognize foreign opportunities plead that they lack the necessary resources (knowledge, people, technology, capital, and/or productive capacity) to take advantage of export opportunities.

Unrealistic fears. There are fears of environmental differences (language, social customs, laws, and so on). There are also fears of operational difficulties such as travel, unfamiliar exporting procedures, financing, shipping, credit risks, and exchange-rate fluctuations.

Managerial inertia. Sometimes management fails to take advantage of export opportunities simply because no one is willing to do anything about them.

SUCCESSFUL TRADING

Small business owners who decide that their companies are ready to export need not make the mistakes discussed in the previous section. They can start exporting the same way they started their businesses—with counseling, caution, and adequate planning. Owners do not need to start exporting all of their products, nor do they need to try to export to several countries at the same time. Business owners should start exporting to one or two countries until they learn the "ropes" and feel comfortable enough to develop relations with other countries. The first order of business is to create an export plan (similar to the business plan prepared before the business was started).

Export Plans

Business owners would be foolhardy to begin exporting without some idea of what they hoped to accomplish and how they would meet their goals. An export plan, which should be only a few pages long, can provide guidelines for successful exporting. The length and complexity of the plan will depend on whether the business owner decided to export directly or indirectly. Indirect exporters will need a simpler plan than direct exporters who will do most of the work for themselves.

The components of an export plan are similar to those found in most business plans. A table of contents and executive summary are the first features of an export plan. Following these sections are a company analysis, the marketing plan, export strategies, an export budget, and background data on target countries and markets. Because export success depends largely on selecting the best country with which to trade, owners should give this aspect of the plan considerable attention.

Market Research

The principle of foreign market research is similar to that of domestic market research except that the former is more complicated. Learning about other countries includes acquiring information about language, religion, culture, and other factors not applicable to domestic markets. For an effective international market scan, owners need information about economic conditions, the political environment, the legal and technological environment, the physical and financial environment, and competitive and sociocultural conditions. This information may be somewhat difficult for novice exporters to acquire, but there are numerous agencies (see Appendix 18–1) that can provide the necessary data about countries.

Country Selection

European
Community

Effective market research should identify countries where small business owners are most likely to be able to initiate successful trade agreements. New exporters can select countries with which the United States does the most business (the five countries that buy the most U.S. goods are Canada, Japan, Mexico, the United Kingdom, and Germany), or they might want to consider the **European Community** (Belgium, Britain, Denmark, France, Germany, Greece, Ireland, Italy, Luxembourg, Netherlands, Portugal, and Spain), because exports to that market have been increasing dramatically (see Exhibit 18–4). The consolidation of the EC into one market makes it easier for U.S. small businesses to trade with European countries. Other small business owners may find it more profitable to trade with less developed or developing countries.

Small business owners need to be aware of the risk as well as the rewards of dealing with certain countries. The International Country Risk Guide ranks the following as the safest countries with which to do business: Switzerland, Luxembourg, Norway, Austria, and Germany. Conversely, the following are the riskiest countries with which to do business: Burma, Iraq, Sudan, Somalia, and Liberia.[19]

EXHIBIT 18–4 U.S. Exports to the European Community

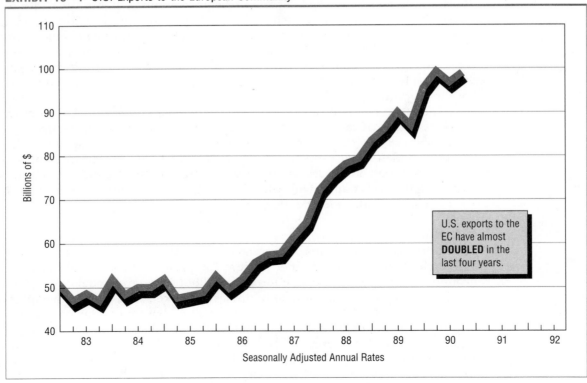

U.S. exports to the EC have almost **DOUBLED** in the last four years.

Billions of $

Seasonally Adjusted Annual Rates

Culture Shock

One of the surest ways to be an international trade failure is to be ignorant of foreign cultures. People in every country, even England, have customs, beliefs, values, religions, and languages different from those dominant in the United States. Business owners who fail to learn something about the country with which they intend to trade should expect to commit some unintended social blunders. The following are some examples of language and cultural differences in other countries (for more on this topic see *Do's and Taboos Around the World, Understanding Cultural Differences: Germans, French, and Americans,* or other similar publications):

- Never touch the head of a Thai or pass an object over it, as the head is considered sacred in Thailand.
- Avoid using triangular shapes in Hong Kong, Korea, or Taiwan, as the triangle is considered a negative shape in those countries.
- Remember that the number 7 is considered bad luck in Kenya, good luck in Czechoslovakia, and has magical connotations in Benin.
- Red is a positive color in Denmark, but represents death and witchcraft in many African countries.
- A nod means no in Bulgaria, and shaking the head side to side means yes.
- Romanians, Japanese, and Germans are very punctual, whereas many of the Latin countries have a more relaxed attitude toward time.
- The "OK" sign commonly used in the United States means zero in France, connotes money in Japan, and has a vulgar connotation in Brazil.
- First names are seldom used when doing business in Germany, but Thais address each other by first names and reserve last names for very formal occasions.[20]

Some of the cultural distinctions that U.S. firms most often face include differences in business styles, attitudes toward development of business relationships, attitudes toward punctuality, negotiating styles, gift-giving customs, greetings, significance of gestures, meaning of colors and numbers, and customs regarding titles. Business owners may also find it difficult to distinguish among gifts, tips, and bribes (see The Way It Is 18–4). Gifts and tips are acceptable, but the Foreign Corrupt Practices Act "makes it unlawful for a firm (and those acting on behalf of the firm) to offer or pay anything of value to any foreign official (and certain other foreigners) for the purpose of obtaining or retaining business."

Export Pricing

Many small business owners have difficulty setting prices for the products they sell in domestic markets. That difficulty is magnified when they attempt to price their products for export. Factors such as willingness to bargain about price, local customs, price sensitivity, and others must be considered before

The Way It Is

18-4 WHEN IS A TIP A BRIBE?

That question has puzzled travelers for centuries; therefore, it is wise to know the words for bribe in different countries.

- **Baksheesh** (bak-SHEESH) in Turkey, Egypt, India, and other Eastern countries, a gratuity or gift of alms.
- **Mordida** (mor-DEE-da) Spanish for bribe. Especially known in Mexico. Literally, "a little bite."
- **Jeito** (jay-EE-toe) commonly used in Brazil. Signifies "you do me a favor, and I'll do you a favor." Can also mean "influence" in the sense of using influence to help. Does not usually involve an actual transfer of money.
- **Dash** (dash) used in various parts of Africa. A small monetary gift that is expected when getting anything from a visa to an airplane seat.
- **Grease** (greese) also "facilitating payments." Refers to legal and permitted payments of modest sums to foreign officials for speedy action of their normal duties. Used almost everywhere, including the United States.
- **Kumshaw** (KUM-shaw) Southeast Asian term for bribe.[21]

determining appropriate prices for export goods. The following six variables have significant influence on export pricing:

Nature of the product/industry. A specialized product, or one with a proprietary position, gives the firm pricing flexibility because there are not likely to be any serious competitors in other countries.

Location of production facility. Many U.S. companies produce only in the United States and are unable to take advantage of lower production costs prevalent in some other countries. Purely domestic companies are tied to conditions prevailing in the United States.

Chosen system of distribution. Channels of distribution often dictate prices of exported products. For example, indirect exporters usually have the price of their product suggested to them by the intermediary agency. Direct exporters usually control prices only until their products reach foreign distributors, retailers, or other sellers.

Location and environment of the foreign market. Political conditions, climate, economic conditions, and other local factors can affect export prices. Currency fluctuations, which tend to be cyclical, also affect export prices. Exporters need to be creative, pursuing different strategies during different periods.

U.S. government regulations. Many exporters feel that U.S. regulations such as the Foreign Corrupt Practices Act put them at a significant competitive disadvantage.

Attitude of the firm's management. Some companies treat exporting as an extension of the domestic sales effort, and export pricing policy is established accordingly. The nuances of foreign trade dictate that business owners adapt to pricing strategies prevalent in the countries where their products are to be sold.[22]

INTERNATIONAL TRADE ASSISTANCE

Small business owners, especially those new to exporting, will need all the assistance they can get from private and public sources. They will need help in selecting countries where their products will sell, making contacts in those countries, marketing their products, deciphering trade documents, and financing their exports. Fortunately, there are numerous private and public sources of assistance; however, they are not always easy to find, and determining the appropriate source can often be an exercise in futility.

Government Export Services

International
Trade
Administration
(ITA)

The primary federal provider of export services is the **International Trade Administration (ITA),** which is part of the Commerce Department. This organization offers services such as export counseling, world traders data report, and overseas trade fairs (see Appendix 18–2 for a complete listing of services offered by the ITA). In addition to the ITA, the Commerce Department has other agencies such as the U.S. Travel and Tourism Administration and the Office of Metric Programs, which provide more specialized export assistance.

Other than the Commerce Department, federal agencies that offer export assistance include the U.S. Export-Import Bank, which extends credit to exporters; the Small Business Administration, which provides export counseling, some financial assistance, and other services; the Department of Agriculture; the Department of State; the Overseas Private Investment Corporation, which facilitates U.S. private investments in less developed nations; and the Agency for International Development. At first glance, the number of federal agencies and their scope of services seems impressive, but they are often underfunded and poorly managed.

Among major industrialized nations, the United States spends the least per capita to promote exports. Canada spent $21.44 for each inhabitant versus $1.20 in the United States. Some of the touted services offered exporters are often of little or no value to small businesses (see The Way It Is 18–5). Business owners who find working with the federal government unrewarding might try using the export services offered by their state. Most states have an agency that provides export services similar to those provided by the federal government.

18–5 EXPORT OBSTACLES

Many problems small companies encounter while trying to become exporters are domestic. Small business owners starting to export say that the single, largest source of information—the Commerce Department—is also one of the major sources of frustration. As more small firms look for foreign business, many say that their two greatest needs, reliable trade information and trade financing, are in short supply. For example, when N&N Contact Lens International Inc. of Lynwood, Washington, needed international marketing information, president Peter Snook stumped the local Commerce Department office with relatively simple questions. Asked who sells contact lenses in Caracas, Venezuela, it gave him lists of distributors of such broad categories as "medical devices." Finally, Mr. Snook called U.S. embassies in targeted nations. "We'd just ask the embassy guy on the phone, 'Where do you buy your glasses?' " said Snook.[23]

Export Financing

As we saw in The Way It Is 18–5, the two export ingredients most needed but supposedly in short supply are information and funding. Money to pay for exports is available, but may be hard to find. There are several sources, both public and private, of export funds including the following:

Export-Import
Bank of the
United States
(Eximbank)

Export-Import Bank of the United States (Eximbank). Eximbank provides the following types of financial assistance for U.S. exports of capital equipment and services that are normally financed for more than one year:

- Direct loans to public or private buyers abroad
- Loans to financial intermediaries who then make loans to international buyers
- Guarantees to lenders of foreign buyers

Small Business Administration. The SBA's International Trade Loan Program provides long-term financing to help small businesses establish or expand international operations. The Export Revolving Line of Credit Loan (ERLC) also helps small businesses export their products and services.

Overseas
Private
Investment
Corporation
(OPIC)

Overseas Private Investment Corporation (OPIC). OPIC has a lease financing program, which offers financial assistance to foreign leasing companies in which there is a significant U.S. private business interest. The Small Contractor's Guarantee Program assists small business construction and service contractors.

Agency for
International
Development
(AID)

Agency for International Development (AID). The Bureau for Private Enterprise (PRE) and **AID** will consider market-term financing for projects in developing countries through its Private-Sector Revolving Fund.[24]

Commercial Banks. Some of the larger banks that have international exposure will lend money to exporters. These banks also counsel customers and issue letters of credit.

The Language of International Trade

Some small business owners avoid international trade because they find the terms or jargon and documentation so daunting. As with the federal government, international traders seem to use a plethora of initials and acronyms. For example, what does ex works, F.A.S., or ex quay mean? These and other terms as well as methods of paying for exports are explained in Appendix 18–3.

SUMMARY

For small business owners, the government is everywhere. It regulates, competes with, assists, and buys from small business. The regulatory function appears to be diminishing as government continues to review and rescind previously established regulations. Government gives and it takes away. Besides regulating and deregulating business, government competes with small businesses by providing its own goods and services, which small firms could produce. There is a trend to privatize those government functions that can be done better and cheaper by small companies. The government also assists small business by buying some of its services and products and by making available other forms of assistance. Small business receives information, training, grants, counseling, loans, and subsidies from various government organizations.

Most small business owners have failed to take advantage of an attractive expansion option—international trade. Business owners who do choose to become international traders usually enter the arena via exporting. They can export with or without intermediaries, but they should be careful in selecting the countries with which they want to do business. Exporters need to be aware of differences in local culture, customs, and values in order to avoid embarrassing gaffes. All small business owners involved in international trade should know how to solicit assistance, finance exports, and decipher confusing trade-related documents.

QUESTIONS FOR REVIEW AND DISCUSSION

1. Why did the government believe that regulation of business was necessary?
2. How can the government enforce regulations?

3. Should the government be allowed to produce goods and services that it consumes, or should those goods and services be provided by small companies?
4. Which government functions would you like to see privatized?
5. Is the government doing all it can to assist small business?
6. Why should more small business owners consider exporting?
7. If you were a small business owner, would you choose direct or indirect exporting?
8. If you were to export a product, which country or countries would you choose to receive your goods?
9. What factors affect prices of export goods?
10. What trade assistance can one expect from the government?

KEY TERMS

Agency for International
  Development (AID)
commission agents
Coordinating Committee for
  Multilateral Export Controls
economic incentives or disincentives
Energy Related Inventions Program
  (ERIP)
European Community
export agents
Export-Import Bank of the United
  States (Eximbank)
export management company
  (EMC)
export trading companies (ETC)

Federal Register
International Trade Administration
  (ITA)
jawboning
licensing
nontariff barriers
Occupational Safety and Health Act
Overseas Private Investment
  Corporation (OPIC)
piggyback marketing
privatization
public enterprises
rate of return
tariff barriers

CASE
Natural Jellies and Juices Inc.

Like thousands of other women, Mary Grady started a business in her home making a product she liked. In 1981, Mary discovered that there were no natural (no preservatives added) fruit juices available in her hometown of Ashville, North Carolina. To rectify the problem, Mary tried making her own juices and found that she was able to produce a very tasty juice made of various berries. After considerable experimentation, Mary created several juices made entirely of natural ingredients. Because she made more juice than she could consume, Mary decided to share it with her friends and neighbors who liked it so much they persuaded Mary to make her juices available to the public.

By late 1982, Mary Grady had formed Natural Jellies and Juices Inc. to commercially produce juices and a selection of jellies that she had created. Within two years demand for the juices and jellies had increased to the point that the business had to be moved out of Mary's house. The company was moved to an 8,000 square foot facility, which was adapted to make juices and jellies. A distinct logo and marketing slogan was created for the new products, and an attractive package was developed to best display the product. Retailers in the Ashville area sold the jellies and juices, and later retailers throughout the state sold the products.

After eight years in business, Natural Jellies and Juices Inc. had grown to a $2.3 million business that employed twenty-one people. Mary was satisfied with the growth of her company and had plans to sell jellies and juices in neighboring states. Mary's expansion plans were changed when, in 1991, she was contacted by a German visiting Ashville who "fell in love" with her products. The visitor assured Mary that there would be a substantial market for her products in Germany and probably most of Europe, and he urged her to export her jellies and juices. Mary Grady knew how to manufacture jellies and juices and market them in this country, but she knew nothing about selling her products abroad.

QUESTIONS

1. Who should Mary turn to for export advice?

2. Should Mary's products be exported?

3. If she is to export, should she be an indirect or direct exporter?

4. What advice would you give Mary about financing and pricing her products for export?

ACTIVITIES

1. Visit the Small Business Administration near you and find out how many programs they have to assist small businesses.

2. Select several countries from different parts of the world, and using the country rating sheet and current information sources, rate the countries for export attractiveness or joint ventures. Ratings should be from 1 to 10 with 10 being the best. You may assume that your business makes any product you like.

COUNTRY RATING SHEET

Attributes	Country 1	2	3	4	5	6
Economic stability	_____	_____	_____	_____	_____	_____
Strength of money	_____	_____	_____	_____	_____	_____
Convertibility of money	_____	_____	_____	_____	_____	_____
Tax incentives	_____	_____	_____	_____	_____	_____
Quality of infrastructure	_____	_____	_____	_____	_____	_____
Nontax inducements	_____	_____	_____	_____	_____	_____
Political stability	_____	_____	_____	_____	_____	_____
Per capita income	_____	_____	_____	_____	_____	_____
Competition	_____	_____	_____	_____	_____	_____
Product demand	_____	_____	_____	_____	_____	_____
Legal system	_____	_____	_____	_____	_____	_____
Transportation costs	_____	_____	_____	_____	_____	_____
Labor supply	_____	_____	_____	_____	_____	_____
Labor productivity	_____	_____	_____	_____	_____	_____
Channels of distribution	_____	_____	_____	_____	_____	_____
TOTAL	_____	_____	_____	_____	_____	_____

APPENDIX 18–1

Where to Get Market Information and Trade Leads

U.S. Department of Commerce/US&FCS Commercial Information Management System/National Trade Data Bank—Local Commerce District Office specialists can tailor information packages drawing from statistical trade and economic data, market research reports, and foreign traders indices. CIMS/ NTDB house all relevant international trade publications published by ITA, including Foreign Economic Trends reports, Overseas Business Reports, and Industry Sector Analyses.
Contact: For your nearest Department of Commerce District Office, call (202) 377-4767, or see local telephone directory under U.S. Department of Commerce listing

U.S. Department of Commerce/Comparison Shopping Service—A custom-tailored service provides firms with targeted information on marketing and foreign representation for specific products in specific countries. Fee varies.
Contact: For your nearest Department of Commerce District Office, call (202) 377-4767, or see local telephone directory under U.S. Department of Commerce listing

U.S. Department of Commerce/Agent/Distributor Service—A customized search helps identify agents, distributors, and foreign representatives for U.S. firms based on the foreign companies' examination of U.S. product literature. A fee of $125 per country is charged.
Contact: For your nearest Department of Commerce District Office, call (202) 377-4767, or see local telephone directory under U.S. Department of Commerce listing

U.S. Department of Commerce/Trade Opportunities Program—TOP provides companies with current sales leads from international firms seeking to buy or represent their products or services. TOP leads are printed daily in leading commercial newspapers and are also distributed electronically via the Economic Bulletin Board. The fee varies.
Contact: For your nearest Department of Commerce District Office, call (202) 377-4767, or see local telephone directory under U.S. Department of Commerce listing; for the Department of Commerce Economic Bulletin Board, call (202) 377-1986

U.S. Department of Commerce/Minority Business Development Agency/ Minority Export Development Consultants Program—This program helps develop marketing plans, identify potential overseas markets, and trade leads for minority business. It also provides assistance in documentation, short-term financing and shipping.
Contact: Business Development Specialist, (202) 377-2414

U.S. Department of Agriculture/Economic Research Service—The staff provides economic data, models, and research information about agricultural economies and policies of foreign countries and bilateral agricultural trade and development relationships.

Contact: Bob Robinson, (202) 219-0700

U.S. Department of Agriculture/Trade and Marketing Information Centers—These centers, part of the National Agricultural Library, help locate relevant material from their large collection on trade and marketing and provide copies of research and data from their AGRICOLA database.

Contact: Mary Lassanyi, (301) 344-3704

U.S. Department of Energy/Coal and Technology Export Program—This program promotes the export of U.S. clean coal products and services by acting as an information source on coal and coal technologies.

Contact: Peter Cover, (202) 586-7297

U.S. Department of Energy/Fossil Energy-AID Database—The Office of Fossil Energy forwards prospective energy-related leads to AID for inclusion in its growing trade opportunities database in an effort to reach an extended audience seeking energy-related trade opportunities.

Contact: Denise Swink, (202) 586-9680

Small Business Administration/Export Information System—Data reports provide specific product information on the top 25 world markets and market growth trends for the past five years.

Contact: Luis Saldarriaga, (404) 542-5760

Agency for International Development/Trade and Investment Monitoring System—TIMS, a user-friendly computer-based system, provides a broad array of trade and investment information to potential U.S. investors and exporters on 42 developing countries, e.g., general economic and business data; trade and investment policies and prospects; government regulation and incentives; sources of funding and corporate tax structures; production and labor forces; and business facilities and infrastructure.

Contact: Tracy L. Smith, (202) 647-3805

Overseas Private Investment Corporation/Investor Information Service—This information clearinghouse provides "one-stop-shopping" for basic economic, business, and political information and data from a variety of sources on 118 developing countries and 16 geographic regions. This service is available for purchase in country- and region-specific kits.

Contact: Daven Oswalt, Manager, Public Affairs, (202) 457-7087

Overseas Private Investment Corporation/Investor Services—A new OPIC initiative designed to assist smaller U.S. firms with their overseas investment planning and implementation needs. Fee-based services provide counseling to American firms on business plan development, project structuring, joint-venture partner identification, and location of project financing services.

Contact: Dan Riordan, Director, Investor Services, (202) 457-7091

Overseas Private Investment Corporation/Opportunity Bank—This computer data system matches a U.S. investor's interest with specific overseas

opportunities. A modest fee is charged.
Contact: Daven Oswalt, Manager, Public Affairs, (202) 457-7087

SOURCE: "Market Entry Strategy," *Business America*, 25 March, 1991, 17.

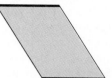

APPENDIX 18–2

Export Services of Commerce's ITA

Export counseling. Trade specialists are available at ITA district and branch offices for individualized export counseling.

Agent/Distributor Service. A customized search for interested and qualified foreign representatives will identify up to six foreign prospects who have examined the U.S. firm's literature and expressed interest in representing it.

Commercial News USA. A monthly magazine that promotes the products or services of U.S. firms to more than 110,000 overseas agents, distributors, government officials, and purchasers. Exporters may submit a black-and-white photo and a brief description of their product or service.

Comparison Shopping. A custom-tailored service that provides firms with key marketing and foreign representation information about their specific products. Commerce Department staff conduct on-the-spot interviews to determine nine key marketing facts about the product, such as sales potential in the market, comparable products, distribution channels, going price, competitive factors, and qualified purchasers.

Foreign Buyer Program. Exporters can meet qualified foreign purchasers for their product or service at trade shows in the United States. The Commerce Department promotes the shows worldwide to attract foreign buyer delegations, manages an international business center, counsels participating firms, and brings together buyer and seller.

Gold Key Service. A custom-tailored service for U.S. firms planning to visit a country. Offered by many overseas posts, it combines several services, such as market orientation briefings, market research, introductions to potential partners, an interpreter for meetings, and assistance in developing a sound market strategy and an effective followup plan.

Trade Opportunities Program. Provides companies with current sales leads from overseas firms seeking to buy or represent their product or service. These leads are available electronically from the Commerce Department and are redistributed by the private sector in printed or electronic form.

World Traders Data Report. Custom reports that evaluate potential trading partners. Includes background information, standing in the local business community, credit-worthiness, and overall reliability and suitability.

Overseas Catalog and Video-Catalog Shows. Companies can gain market exposure for their product or service without the cost of traveling overseas by participating in a catalog or video-catalog show sponsored by the Commerce Department. Provided with the firm's product literature or promotional video, an industry will display the material to select foreign audiences in several countries.

Overseas Trade Missions. Officials of U.S. firms can participate in a trade mission which will give them an opportunity to confer with influential foreign business and government representatives. Commerce Department staff will identify and arrange a full schedule of appointments in each country.

Overseas Trade Fairs. U.S. exporters may participate in overseas trade fairs which will enable them to meet customers face-to-face and also to assess the competition. The Commerce Department creates a U.S. presence at international trade fairs, making it easier for U.S. firms to exhibit and gain international recognition. The Department selects international trade fairs for special endorsement, called certification. This cooperation with the private show organizers enables U.S. exhibitors to receive special services designed to enhance their market promotion efforts. There is a service charge.

Matchmaker Events. Matchmaker Trade Delegations offer introductions to new markets through short, inexpensive overseas visits with a limited objective: to match the U.S. firm with a representative or prospective joint-venture/licensee partner who shares a common product or service interest. Firms learn key aspects of doing business in the new country and meet in one-on-one interviews the people who can help them be successful there.

SOURCE: "A Directory of Export Services," *Business America* 112, no. 2, 1991, 9.

APPENDIX 18–3

International Trade Terms and Payment Methods

TRADE TERMS

C.I.F.	(Cost, Insurance, Freight) to named overseas port of import. Quoted price includes C.I.F. to named port.
C. and F.	(Cost and Freight) to named port of destination. Quoted price includes only C. and F. to named port.
F.A.S.	(Free Alongside a Ship) at named U.S. port of export. The seller quotes a price for goods that includes charges for delivery of the goods alongside a vessel at the port.
F.O.B.	(Free on Board). The seller quotes a price for goods that includes the cost of loading them into transport vessels at a named port.
F.O.B.	(named inland point of origin). The seller is responsible for loading goods into the transport vessel, the buyer for all subsequent expenses.

F.O.B.　(named port of exportation). The quoted price includes cost of transporting the goods to the named point.

F.O.B.　Vessel (named port of export). The price includes all expenses including delivery of goods upon an overseas vessel provided by or for the buyer.

Ex　(named point of origin). For example, ex factory, ex warehouse. The price quoted applies only at the point of origin.

PAYMENT METHODS

Cash in advance.	Goods are paid for before delivery.
Open account.	Transaction payable when specified on the invoice.
Consignment sales.	The exporter retains title to the goods until they are sold, at which time payment is made to the exporter.
Sight drafts.	A draft that is payable on presentation.
Time drafts.	Payment is made within a specified time after the buyer receives and accepts the goods.
Letters of credit.	A letter of credit is issued by a bank for the buyer. It provides the issuing bank's promise to pay a specified amount of money when conditions of the sale have been met.

19 MANAGEMENT DEVELOPMENT AND SUCCESSION

There comes a time in the growth phase of many small companies when the owner is no longer capable of managing all functions of the business. He or she is always "putting out fires" and attempting to manage one crisis after another. The amount of time owners devote to the business increases, yet many essential matters are neglected. This is the time in an owner's career when he or she must admit that other people are needed to run the business efficiently and profitably. It is time to select and develop competent people who can assume management positions within the company. Once trained, these managers should be given meaningful duties, the responsibility to accomplish those duties, and appropriate rewards for accomplishing their duties.

There also comes a time when the owner of a business must pass it on to someone else. Age, poor health, other interests, or other reasons may necessitate a "change of command" from the original owner to her or his designated successor. Without careful succession planning, there may be no competent manager to replace the owner. Turning a business over to a successor can be traumatic in any business, but it can be especially painful in family businesses. There are often several second-generation family members in a company who believe that they should "inherit" the business and that their siblings should fend for themselves.

In this chapter, we will examine company growth and the changes it dictates in the management structure of a small business. We will discuss the selection and development of managers in a typical small business, and we will see how these managers can be groomed to take over the business from the owner. We will also discuss how succession can be planned and executed in family businesses. Family businesses have problems and possibilities not found in nonfamily businesses. We will discuss ways to overcome the problems and capitalize on the unique possibilities.

GROWTH

The generally accepted life cycle of a typical company consists of four phases: inception, growth, maturity, and decline. We are primarily concerned here with the growth phase. The passage from inception to growth can be either an exhilarating or excruciating experience, depending on how growth is planned for and controlled.

Stages of Growth

To be able to plan and control growth, owners should be aware of the following stages of growth: growth by innovation, growth by assignment, growth by delegation, and growth by participation.

growth by innovation

Growth by Innovation. After a company begins operating, **growth by innovation** usually occurs because the founder has a unique product or service to offer that competitors cannot or are not offering. During this period of rapid growth, the owner assumes responsibility for all phases of the firm's operations. The owner is in charge of production, sales, advertising, purchasing, personnel, and all other aspects of day-to-day business. Employees are often family or friends of the owner, and they have very little say in how the business is operated.

growth by assignment

Growth by Assignment. Growth in sales and number of employees necessitates the assignment of certain duties to other members of the company. During **growth by assignment** owners realize that they are unable to manage all the day-to-day business activities. At this point they begin to develop within the firm a management team that can assume some of their duties and functions. The new managers are expected to take care of much of the routine day-to-day activities of the business, leaving the owner more time for long-range planning.

growth by delegation

Growth by Delegation. In the previous phase, inexperienced owners often fail to make clear assignments, or they assign duties and functions to more than one manager, thereby creating some confusion and uncertainty. To eliminate confusion and uncertainty during **growth by delegation,** duties and functions and the concomitant authority and responsibility are delegated to specific managers. Delegation of authority and control often leads to power struggles among managers, who, quite naturally, want to emerge as key or dominant figures in the management structure.

growth by participation

Growth by Participation. To be successful in the long run, managers in growing firms must be able to cooperate with each other and participate equally in the operations of the business. Once managers have fought their territorial battles, they are usually willing to work together as a team to accomplish the goals and objectives of the company. During **growth by participation** the company is likely to experience the controlled growth that brings with it personal and financial success.

From Entrepreneurship to Professional Management

Entrepreneurial companies are often quite informal, lack well-developed systems, and are controlled by one person. As control is delegated to more managers, the company becomes more formal, decision making is often a group effort, and authority and responsibility are shared with selected managers. The most important differences between an entrepreneurship and a professionally managed company involve the following key result areas:[1] profit, planning, organization, control, management development, budgeting, innovation, leadership, and culture (see Exhibit 19–1 for a summary of these result areas).

Profit. In a professionally managed company, profit is an explicit goal, but in entrepreneurial companies profit is desired, however, it is usually not an explicit goal to be attained.

Planning. Most professionally managed companies have formal, written business plans, whereas entrepreneurs often prefer to "wing it" or at least choose not to write the plans that they have formulated. Managers want planning to be formalized and strategic so they will be able to determine where the company is headed and how goals will be achieved. Entrepreneurs, on the other hand, often lack planning expertise or they perceive planning to be too difficult or time consuming.

Organization. Entrepreneurial companies often have no formal structure, and employee responsibilities and duties may be poorly defined and

EXHIBIT 19–1 Comparison of Professional Management and Entrepreneurial Management

Key Result Areas	Professional Management	Entrepreneurial Management
Profit	Profit orientation; profit is an explicit goal.	Profit seen as a by-product.
Planning	Formal, systematic planning: Strategic planning Operational planning Contingency planning	Informal, ad hoc planning.
Organization	Formal, explicit role descriptions that are mutually exclusive and exhaustive.	Informal structure with overlapping and undefined responsibilities.
Control	Formal, planned system of organizational control, including explicit objectives, targets, measures, evaluations, and rewards.	Partial, ad hoc control; seldom uses formal measurement.
Management Development	Planned management development: Identification of requirements Design of programs	Ad hoc development, principally through on-the-job training.
Budgeting	Management by standards and variances.	Budget not explicit; no follow-up on variances.
Innovation	Orientation to incremental innovations; willingness to take calculated risks.	Orientation toward major innovations; willingness to take major risks.
Leadership	Consultative or participative styles.	Styles may vary from very directive to laissez-faire.
Culture	Well-defined culture.	Loosely defined, "family"-oriented culture.

SOURCE: Eric G. Flamholtz, *Growing Pains* (San Francisco, CA: Jossey-Bass, 1990), 45. Used by permission.

explained. Professionally managed firms have written job descriptions that clearly state responsibilities. There is no confusion concerning what each employee and manager is expected to do in the company.

Control. Entrepreneurs tend to control operations in informal and unexplained ways, and sometimes controls appear to be lacking or insufficient. Managers, however, install a formal, planned system of organizational controls in their companies.

Management Development. Management development is planned in a professionally managed company. Competent employees are exposed to development programs that prepare them to move into more responsible and important positions. Entrepreneurs tend to minimize the need for competent managers; therefore, they provide very little formal management development for their employees. Entrepreneurs tend to hire managers rather than develop their own, thereby saving money in the short run but perhaps costing the firm more in the long run.

Budgeting. Budgets, if they exist, in entrepreneurial companies are rather sketchy and informal, and little effort is made to explain budget variances or deviations. Budgets in professionally managed companies are detailed, but flexible. Managers' job performance is measured, in part, by their ability to operate within limits prescribed by the budget.

Innovation. One distinguishing characteristic of entrepreneurial firms is their innovativeness and creativity. The company is often built around a unique product or service created by the owner. Innovation, although it exists in professionally managed companies, is more incremental. To minimize risk, managers tend to expand the product line and have backup products in case one fails.

Leadership. Entrepreneurs tend to be dictatorial or autocratic leaders who may or may not have the best interests of employees at heart. Professional managers, on the other hand, tend more toward a consultative or participative style of leadership. Many people in management positions prefer to manage by consensus, which is not a leadership style well suited to entrepreneurs.

Culture. Culture, which is poorly defined in entrepreneurial companies, is not explicitly managed by the entrepreneur. Professional managers are more likely to create an explicit culture that is transmitted throughout the company to give the organization a competitive edge.

MANAGEMENT SELECTION AND DEVELOPMENT

When business owners realize that they need managers to assist with day-to-day operations, they have two options: they can hire new, already trained managers or they can develop their own. Hiring new managers entails considerable risk because owners may not be able to judge a person's capabilities and potential for growth. Developing managers is a less risky proposition because owners have had the opportunity to evaluate candidates' performance in nonmanagement positions. Development, however, is the more costly option, and owners have no guarantee that employees with newly acquired management skills will not leave for better jobs.

Selecting Management Candidates

If small business owners initially staffed their company correctly by employing people who could grow with the business, they should have enough capable individuals to fill management positions. By using formal or informal performance evaluations, owners should be able to assess employees' long-term potential, promotability, knowledge and skills, adaptability and capacity to learn new concepts, and adaptability to change. Owners who feel that they cannot objectively decide who should be selected for management development can use the services of outside consultants.

Using a battery of valid, nondiscriminatory tests and personal interviews, consultants can determine which employees have management potential. If a single consultant does not seem appropriate, owners may choose to send their employees to established assessment centers. These centers are staffed by a number of experts with different evaluation and counseling skills. Using tests, individual counseling sessions, and team exercises such as a "leaderless group exercise," the professionals at an assessment center can identify those candidates with management potential.

Development Techniques

Once selected, management candidates need some development before they can replace other managers or fill newly created positions. Many different development methods or techniques can be used by business owners; however, because development is usually a long-term process, most companies use a combination of the available methods. Some management development techniques are appropriate for companies with an established management structure whereas others can be used by companies just creating managerial positions.

Owners can use techniques such as job rotation and understudy assignment (letting a management candidate work with an experienced manager) to develop new managers, or they can use outsiders to do the developing. Consultants, professional groups, and universities have formal development programs that they offer to businesses. Some providers tailor their programs to the needs of small businesses, which may not need managers as specialized as those needed by larger companies. Development techniques used by providers include seminars, simulations, in-basket exercises, and case studies.

Successful Management Development Programs

A recent study of successful development programs[2] found that they met the following criteria:

1. There should be extensive and visible involvement of the owner in the program.
2. Companies should have clearly articulated and understood development policies, strategies, and philosophies.

3. Successful development programs should be directly linked to the company's business strategies, objectives, and challenges.

4. Successful development programs should include the following: an annual succession planning process; planned on-the-job developmental assignments; and customized, internal education programs supplemented by the selective use of university programs.

5. Management development should be the task of line managers.

DELEGATION

People who assume management positions want to have the power and authority to perform the duties delegated to them by the business owner. However, relinquishing power and authority is extremely difficult for most business owners who have grown accustomed to being the only decision maker in the company. Business owners often say "it takes too much time to delegate," or "if you want the job done right, do it yourself," but they may actually be concerned that subordinates can perform certain duties better than they can. Owners who are unable or unwilling to delegate their authority to subordinates will have dissatisfied managers, and their companies may stagnate and eventually fail (see The Way It Is 19–1).

Reasons for Delegating

Eventually all business owners will need to delegate some of their authority to other managers. Some of the more important reasons for delegating include the following:

1. The volume of work becomes too great for one person to comfortably manage. Business owners reach the point where they are simply not physically capable of attending to all the functional needs of their companies.

The Way It Is

19–1 INEFFECTIVE DELEGATION

Norma Rothenberg founded NAR Communications, a public relations company, after she realized that she could not achieve her goals working for her previous employer. Soon after the company began operations, Ms. Rothenberg found that she had problems delegating responsibility and authority to others. She did not want to manage, but would not let others manage. She knew that she could not do all the work herself, but she constantly meddled with the people she hired to do it. She was afraid of hiring people who might be better than she, or who might want to approach clients differently.[3]

2. In addition to increased volume, the complexity of the work being done also escalates. Many business owners are generalists who lack the ability and inclination to attend to all the technical details involved in operating a growing company.

3. Delegation may be one of the best methods of developing subordinates. All the benefits of management development programs and seminars will be of little value if authority is not delegated or is only partially delegated.

4. Preparing replacements is another valid reason for delegating authority. Even though most owners think that they are immortal, the time does come when they are no longer capable of managing their business. Owners who delegate wisely will have competent managers ready to replace them when necessary.

5. If done correctly, delegation can motivate subordinates because most people enjoy greater responsibility.

Obstacles to Effective Delegating

Although most business owners know that they need to delegate authority to their managers, some do not delegate or only do it half-heartedly. Owners who want their businesses to grow need to be aware of and overcome the following obstacles to effective delegating:

1. The tendency of owners to want to do everything themselves is quite strong. They know what has to be done and how to do it, and they feel that they can do it better than anyone else.

2. Some owners or managers do not delegate because they are afraid of being exposed. Delegation might show that operations were not being performed in the most effective manner, or that the owner was neglecting some necessary functions.

3. Some owners are concerned that delegating authority to managers might provide them with the tools necessary to leave and start their own competing business.

4. Some owners need to dominate their subordinates. It is not uncommon for owners to want to influence others, participate in all decision making, and generally be the lifeblood of the company.

5. Owners may not be willing to tolerate their subordinates' mistakes.

6. There are times when owners are willing to delegate their authority, but they have no capable subordinates to whom they can delegate.

7. Some owners feel that they should do all the work rather than "burden" their subordinates.

Learning to Delegate

Because the obstacles to effective delegating can be identified, they can be overcome. For some owners and managers the learning experience may be painful, but in the long run it will be a worthwhile lesson. There are a number of steps owners and managers can take to learn how to delegate effectively.

Create Security. Owners and managers need to feel that their position is secure and that they will not lose status or prestige if they delegate some of their power and authority to others.

Need to Delegate. Instill in managers the need to delegate in order to accomplish more work. If owners and managers realize that 50- or 60-hour weeks are more a sign of unwillingness to delegate than of dedication, perhaps they will not be so reluctant to part with some of their authority.

Eliminate Fear. Try to eliminate fear and frustration from the workplace. Managers should realize that delegation helps to build an effective management team. Delegation should be viewed as an opportunity for individual growth and development.

Do Not Meddle. Owners and managers who delegate their authority to subordinates should not hamper the efforts of those subordinates to successfully complete their assignments.

Do Not Overdelegate. Wholesale delegation or abdication of authority and responsibility is as unwise as partial delegation.

Select the Right Person. Choose the right person to receive authority. Delegating authority to the wrong person is as bad as not delegating at all.

Delegate Complete Authority. Refrain from delegating partial authority. Owners have a tendency to delegate some authority for a job, which turns out to be insufficient to effectively complete the assigned task.

Support New Managers. Provide support and assistance to the manager who has just been delegated authority and responsibility for a task. Everyone with a new job or new responsibilities can use the assistance and support of someone with more experience. There is a difference between support and meddling.

Tolerate Mistakes. Treat mistakes as a learning opportunity rather than a cause for termination. Managers who know that mistakes will not cause them to lose their jobs are usually willing to make decisions and take risks.

LEADERSHIP

One factor that contributes significantly to successful management succession is a manager's leadership ability. People should be selected to be managers because they possess leadership skills that differentiate them from other employees. The management development techniques we have discussed are designed to enhance a manager's leadership skills and enable him or her to accept more responsible positions within the company. Perhaps one of the major failings of business owners is their inability or unwillingness to encourage the development of leadership ability in their managers. Some owners subscribe to the theory that leaders are born not made and that a person with leadership ability needs no additional training. Others believe in the more realistic theory that leadership ability can be enhanced by training and development.

Leadership Styles

Leadership or management styles within a company vary from person to person. There are several different leadership styles, ranging from autocratic to participative to laissez-faire, that managers can select. Owners and managers may find that they change leadership styles to fit different situations.

Theory X

Theory Y

THEORY X AND THEORY Y. Of all the explanations of leadership style that have been formulated, McGregor's X and Y styles are probably the best known. **Theory X** (see Exhibit 19–2) assumes that employees are lazy, shiftless, devious, and unmotivated. To insure desired performance, managers must constantly supervise and watch employees. Unsupervised employees will find things to do other than their assigned tasks, or they will do their jobs in an unacceptable manner. **Theory Y,** on the other hand, assumes that employees like to work and are willing to do the best possible job in order to justify their pay. Managers do not have to tell employees exactly how to do their jobs and then watch them constantly to make sure that they do the work as prescribed. Very few owners or managers are purely X or Y; most are a mixture of both.

AUTOCRATIC STYLE. Theory X managers are usually quite autocratic or dictatorial. They do not believe in asking employees for suggestions or advice, and they usually do not accept employee input. Owners and managers have supreme authority and responsibility for accomplishing required tasks, and any employee who does not obey orders is likely to be reprimanded. Very little positive motivation is used by autocratic managers, who prefer to rely on commands and orders supported by sanctions.

BENEVOLENT-AUTOCRATIC STYLE. Unlike purely autocratic managers, benevolent-autocratic leaders care about the welfare and well-being of their employees. Decisions that might have a negative impact on employees might be avoided if possible; however, company objectives still supersede individual preferences, and employees are not invited to discuss decisions with owners or managers.

CONSULTATIVE STYLE. Consultative managers are ultimately responsible for most decisions, but they do solicit employee input. Employees are encouraged to make suggestions and comments about particular situations and incidents before managers make decisions. In some instances employees are given limited authority to make decisions that affect them directly; however, it is more likely that they will be asked for advice rather than actually given the opportunity to make decisions. In a consultative leadership environment employees are given a sense of belonging and importance without actually having responsibility and authority delegated to them.

EXHIBIT 19−2 McGregor's Theory X and Theory Y

Theory X

- The average human being has an inherent dislike for work and will avoid it if at all possible.
- Because of this human characteristic of dislike of work, most people must be coerced, controlled, directed, and threatened with punishment to get them to put forth adequate effort toward the achievement of organizational goals.
- The average human being prefers to be directed, wishes to avoid responsibility, has relatively little ambition, and wants security above all.

Theory Y

- The expenditure of physical and mental effort in work is as natural as play or rest.
- External control and the threat of punishment are not the only ways of encouraging people to accomplish organizational goals. People will exercise self-direction and self-control to accomplish goals to which they are committed.
- Commitment to objectives is a function of the rewards associated with their achievement.
- The capacity to exercise a high degree of imagination, ingenuity, and creativity in the solution of organizational problems is widely, not narrowly, distributed in the population.
- Under the conditions of modern industrial life, the intellectual potentialities of the average human being are only partially utilized.

PARTICIPATIVE STYLE. Participative management style may be the most praised and least implemented form of leadership. To be effective, participative management requires managers and owners to voluntarily delegate most of their authority to their employees, who are expected to actively participate in the management of their jobs. Employees are expected to identify problems, develop solutions for those problems, implement the solutions, and evaluate the solutions. It takes considerable time and effort to prepare employees to accept participative management (see The Way It Is 19–2).

LAISSEZ-FAIRE STYLE. This management style is on the opposite end of the leadership continuum from the autocratic style. It is essentially a "do whatever you want" approach to management. Employees receive very little direction or guidance and little or no supervision. The only time this management style is justified is if a company has highly qualified, well-trained, and self-motivated employees who know what needs to be done and need no supervision. In most situations, however, laissez-faire management results in utter chaos and confusion.

19–2 PARTICIPATIVE MANAGEMENT

One company where participative management has been successful is Action Instruments Inc., a $15 million electronics firm in San Diego. Since founding the company in 1972, Jim Pinto has developed a firm where the distinction between employees and owners is almost nonexistent. Employees are encouraged to acquire an ownership position in the firm, and they are expected to participate in the decision-making process. Job applicants who do not appear to be enthusiastic about teamwork and cooperative ownership are not hired. Action Instruments has few private offices, no personal secretaries, and no reserved parking; however the commitment of managers and employees to the concept of participative management keeps the firm growing.[4]

Selecting Management Style

Few owners or managers are likely to adopt a management style that they use in all situations. Most know that their management style should change to be appropriate for different situations. For example, autocratic management might be appropriate for a group of employees who are familiar with their jobs and do not care to participate in decision making, but it might be inappropriate for employees who are attempting a new and unfamiliar task. In the latter instance, consultative or participative styles may be more appropriate. The following variables determine appropriate leadership styles: culture, power, employee expectations, and task structure.

Culture. Companies develop a culture, or set of norms and values, that dictates the type of leadership style that will be accepted. The same is true of cultures developed among different peoples of the world. For example, the culture in Japan is essentially one of sharing and group effort. In such an environment, it would be very difficult to get employees to accept an autocratic management style. Conversely, in Germany where people recognize and respect individual authority and power, autocratic management might be preferred to participative management.

Power. The amount of power a manager has will also determine which leadership style is appropriate. For example, a manager with considerable power might choose an autocratic style of leadership, whereas a manager whose power is somewhat more tenuous may have to adopt a consultative leadership style to be effective. It may be argued that managers and owners with absolute power are in a position to select any leadership style, whereas weaker managers may have leadership styles forced on them by their employees.

Employee Expectations. If employees expect to have autocratic leaders, it would be very difficult for them to accept any other style. Many managers who have decided to initiate participative management have encountered stiff resistance from employees who are comfortable with autocratic leadership.

Task Structure. The type of task to be performed will also determine, to some extent, the type of management style that is appropriate. Routine, frequently performed tasks normally require nothing more than autocratic or benevolent-autocratic leadership styles, but unfamiliar and unstructured tasks might require consultative or participative management styles. If no one has performed the task before, it might be helpful to have everyone involved participate in planning and decision making.

Although it is possible to identify and describe the various management styles, it is almost impossible to say with any degree of certainty which is superior. Some companies are very efficient and profitable with autocratic managers, whereas others in the same industry are equally profitable and efficient with consultative or participative leadership styles. Some companies have tried participative management only to revert back to an autocratic style when the former failed.

PARTICIPATIVE MANAGEMENT

participative
management

For many small business owners, **participative management** enhances management development, motivates employees, and eliminates some succession problems. Participative management might be threatening to both owners and employees, so it should be implemented only after considerable deliberation and examination. Some owners may find that a combination of participative and consultative management is best for them. However, as we noted in the previous section, if employees expect autocratic leadership, no amount of preparation or planning will make participative management successful. Therefore, business owners should evaluate the advantages and disadvantages of participative management and determine how to implement the system.

Advantages of Participative Management

Many firms that have tried participative management have discovered several advantages. The most notable advantage seems to be increased profit; however, there are a number of more subtle advantages, including the following:

- Because employees are active decision makers, they are more committed to their recommendations.
- There is a free flow of information among employees and managers who no longer benefit from withholding information from each other.
- Because employees benefit from group activities and decisions, there is little open conflict or jealousy.
- There is no need for elaborate control procedures designed to monitor employee compliance with company procedures.

- Employees who are most familiar with a particular job will be motivated to design methods that will make the job easier to perform.

Disadvantages of Participative Management

Because many small business owners have avoided participative management, there must be some perceived drawbacks to the system. Some companies have tried participative management and have reverted back to more traditional management styles because the new system did not work. The following are some of participative management's disadvantages:

- Sometimes participative management is doomed to failure because employees do not accept the concept and will not actively participate in the management of their own jobs.
- Managers or owners are unwilling to delegate the authority necessary to successfully implement participative management. Managers feel that employees are trying to usurp their power.
- It is difficult to hold individuals responsible for group decisions or actions.
- Not all employees contribute equally, but all share benefits equally.
- Group decision making is quite time consuming, and decisions often represent compromises rather than the best option.
- Managers and owners have to accept employee decisions and recommendations that they might not have made themselves in similar situations.

Implementing Participative Management

Some owners who have experimented with participative management and found it unacceptable were unsuccessful because they implemented the system incorrectly. Like any other new system or program, participative management should not be introduced without proper planning and preparation. The following steps will help owners successfully implement participative management:

Management Support. Owners need to accept the concept of participative or shared management. If owners and managers do not support the concept of participative management, no amount of effort or explanation will convince employees that the system is expected to succeed or become permanent.

Preparation. Once owners are committed to shared management, they must prepare the employees to become involved. The system should be explained to all employees, who should be encouraged to question any aspects of the program that they do not understand. Employees should know what will be expected of them when the new system is activated and what they can expect from owners and managers.

Goal Setting. Once employees have accepted the concept of participative management, they should be encouraged to set goals for themselves and their work groups. Initially, these goals should be relatively modest and they should be accepted by all concerned. Once goals have been set and accepted, employees can devise strategies for accomplishing them.

Accountability. Employees should not make decisions and recommendations for which they are not held accountable. Although it may not be possible or desirable to hold one individual responsible for decisions, there should be some mechanism for making a group accountable for its collective decisions.

Rewards. If employees are accountable for their decisions, they should also be rewarded for success. Rewards need not be only in the form of money. Benefits, praise, and recognition are also valid forms of reward; however, whenever possible employees should participate in selecting rewards that they deem appropriate.

Timing. Some participative management programs have failed because they were implemented too rapidly. Implementing these programs gradually and patiently is more likely to insure employee acceptability and eventual success.

SUCCESSION

There comes a time in the lives of all businesses when ownership must be transferred. We have observed, in an earlier chapter, that the unexpected death of a sole proprietor often leads to the dissolution of the business. This would not have to happen if a business owner had effective succession plans that designated who would take over a business in the event of the owner's death. Succession plans are also necessary for small businesses that are formed as partnerships or corporations. In fact, it would be wise for all small business owners to identify their successors.

In this section we will examine succession from a number of different viewpoints. We will look at methods for developing succession plans in non-family-owned small businesses. These are plans not only for who succeeds the owner but also for who succeeds key managers. Then we will look at the potentially more difficult succession planning function in family businesses. In family businesses, the objectivity needed for succession planning is sometimes distorted by emotion and family responsibilities.

Succession Planning

succession planning

Succession planning is the cognitive process of creating a plan to replace managers in small businesses and also the firm's owner when the time comes. Succession plans can be extensive and elaborate, or they can be quite simple. Even relatively simple plans should include the following: a clear description of the duties and responsibilities of management positions; the characteristics and qualities suitable replacements should possess; and the search methods to be used to locate successors, for example, whether managers should be replaced with internal candidates (those whom the company has developed) or externally recruited candidates.

Clearly articulated succession plans benefit both business owners and their employees who might have managerial ambitions. The following are some of the benefits to both parties:

- There is a provision for managerial continuity.
- Employees who have participated in management development programs know that they can advance their careers.
- Succession problems are avoided because managers and owners know how vacancies will be filled.
- Owners have the opportunity to evaluate potential managers before they assume management responsibilities.
- Planning avoids equal-employment-opportunity problems.

Succession Techniques

Although management succession within a company is important, the most important successor question is who will replace the owner or owners. Sole proprietors who decide that they want out of their business typically sell it (an option discussed in the last chapter) to an acceptable buyer. However, in situations where there are multiple owners, a more formal succession mechanism is advisable. Two such succession mechanisms include formal buy-sell agreements and the creation of an ESOP (employee stock ownership plan).

buy-sell agreement

BUY-SELL AGREEMENTS. A **buy-sell agreement** enables owners to buy the company from their partners in the event of death, divorce, disability, or other serious problems, as it did for Bread Loaf Construction Company. Ronald Mainelli, the founder of Bread Loaf, sold stakes in his company to Maynard McLaughlin and John Leehman, and then created a succession plan that would take effect in the event of his death. Mainelli died in a car accident at the age of 42, but his company continued without disruption. In fact, the buy-sell agreement made succession so smooth that the company did not lose any of its customers.[5]

To be useful, buy-sell agreements should be as specific as possible. The possible events that could put the agreement into effect should be identified. The buy-sell agreement should be executed by a competent attorney who will also implement its conditions in the event of death, disability, or other stipulated events. The agreement should be reviewed whenever there is a significant change in the business such as the withdrawal or addition of a partner. People such as key managers, suppliers, and customers should be aware of the document's existence. Finally, the agreement should be complete. For example, Ronald Mainelli's buy-sell agreement was quite brief, but the one created by his successors was twenty-two pages long and has been altered at least eleven times.

As important as buy-sell agreements are, several recent studies[6] indicate that they are not deemed important by all business owners. A Coopers and Lybrand survey of 210 owners of small companies found that only 51 percent had a management succession plan in place and only 38 percent have put their plan in writing. Another survey by Buckingham Associates of 400 business owners found that 85 percent of respondents had no formal exit plan and 31 percent had no idea at all how they would exit their business.

EMPLOYEE STOCK OWNERSHIP PLANS. It is not an uncommon occurrence for business owners to want to retire and find that they have no one to replace them. These owners know that their companies might very well be bought by competitors who may close the business. To keep their companies from being closed, some owners choose an **employee stock ownership plan (ESOP),** which sells the company to the employees who then collectively succeed the withdrawing owner. For example, the survival of Diamond Saw Works Inc. was questionable when its six aging owners contemplated selling out. One owner, Thomas Ronan, felt that any buyer would close the company or curtail its operations, thereby putting eighty workers out of jobs. Instead, the company established an ESOP that will eventually own 34 percent of Diamond Saw. The ESOP's stock purchases removes pressure on the owners to sell to outsiders.[7]

employee stock ownership plan (ESOP)

Some employees may be wary of ESOPs because they believe business owners establish the plans for their own benefit. Therefore, communication with employees is essential before an ESOP is established. Diamond Saw, with the assistance of New York's Center for Employee Ownership and Participation, consulted with its employees about the benefits and responsibilities of an ESOP. The employees were told that the plan was not an attempt by the owners to obtain tax advantages or to create a market for their stock. The primary purpose of the ESOP was to provide for orderly succession as the owners retired.

SUCCESSION IN FAMILY BUSINESSES

We have seen that succession in nonfamily businesses can be planned, orderly, and rational. Succession in family businesses can be planned, but the process can become disorderly and irrational when familial relationships become entangled with business judgments. Some may argue that family businesses are not a significant portion of the economy and, therefore, do not warrant special treatment in a discussion of the succession process However, family businesses constitute approximately 90 percent of all American businesses, and about 35 percent of the Fortune 500 companies are owned or controlled by families. Nearly 40 percent of GNP comes from family businesses.

family business

What is a **family business?** The term bears definition because there is some argument about exactly what a family business is. Those who accept the broadest possible definition consider any business owned or controlled by a family is a family business. We prefer the definition of a family business as one "in which majority ownership or control lies within a single family and in which two or more family members are, or at some time were, directly involved in the business."[8] If only one family member is active in a business, succession is essentially the same as in nonfamily businesses.

Advice to Owners of Family Businesses

In the remainder of this chapter, we will examine succession in family businesses; however, it seems appropriate to begin this section with "Twelve Commandments for the Business Owner," postulated by Leon A. Danco, president and founder of the Center for Family Business in Cleveland, Ohio.

1. Thou shalt share thy dream with thy family.
2. Thou shalt inform thy managers and employees—"This company will continue forever."
3. Thou shalt develop a workable organization and make it visible on a chart.
4. Thou shalt continue to improve thy management knowledge, that of thy managers, and that of thy family.
5. Thou shalt institute an orthodox accounting system and make available the data therefrom to thy managers, advisors, and directors.
6. Thou shalt develop a council of competent advisors.
7. Thou shalt submit thyself to the review of a board of competent outside directors.
8. Thou shalt choose thy successor(s).
9. Thou shalt be responsible that thy successor(s) be well taught.
10. Thou shalt retire and install thy successor(s) with thy powers within thy lifetime.
11. Thou canst not take it with thee—so settle thy estate plans—NOW.
12. Thou shalt apportion thy time to see that these commandments be kept.[9]

Which Businesses Survive Succession

Only 30 percent of all family businesses are successfully transferred from one generation to the next. The other 70 percent retire with the owner. Companies that pass from one generation to the next exhibit the following characteristics:

- They are perceived by family members to be financially and organizationally sound, profitable, and well positioned in their industries.
- They are "family affairs" in which family members are active, informed, and committed.
- Family members come into the business with prior training and experience, which is acquired through apprenticeships, formal education, special seminars, or jobs in other companies.
- The most important ingredient for successful transitions is flexible, forward-looking leadership.[10]

Family Members in Businesses

If a family business is defined as one in which two or more family members work, which family members are these likely to be? A survey of 964 businesses[11] found that: spouses, 65 percent of husbands or wives, were the most likely family member to be in the business; 19 percent said sons were in the business; 17 percent of family members were parents; 14 percent of daughters worked in the business; 13 percent were brothers; and only 3 percent of sisters worked in the business.

The same survey found that loyalty was cited as the greatest strength of a family business, followed by willingness to sacrifice, teamwork, common goals, and sharing the wealth. However, there is a flip side to loyalty—37 percent of survey respondents claimed that loyalty contributed to the inability of family members to see each other's faults. When faults are unrecognized or overlooked, the family business could be a failure.

Failure in Family Businesses

Family businesses are subject to the same causes of failure as other small businesses, but they also encounter problems not associated with nonfamily companies. The following are some factors that can ruin a family business:[12]

1. Lack of clear goals and objectives. The absence of articulated goals and objectives causes confusion and insecurity among employees and potential family successors.

2. Conflict between business and family "systems." Rules from one system may override the more practical rules from the other when these systems conflict (see Exhibit 19–3 for an explanation of the two systems). For example, a parent may be vested with authority in a business even though he or she is not the boss.

3. Age differences. Family members who represent different generations have different ideas, values, motivations, and needs. It is often difficult for family members to agree on what is best for the company.

4. Lack of commitment. Commitment of owners to their successors and vice versa is a necessary ingredient for the effective transfer of business ownership.

5. Not letting go. Some owners, much to the consternation of other family members, stay in the business beyond their time. As owners age, they find they have no hobbies or goals to accomplish so they are reluctant to turn the business over to their designated successor.

6. Not getting out after letting go. Owners frequently turn their business over to a successor but then remain in the business "second guessing" the new owner's decisions and orders.

Separating Family and Business

As we can see in Exhibit 19–3, conflict occurs when family and business systems overlap. There are a number of steps business owners can take to keep the two systems separate.

1. Clear boundaries between personal and business lives should be established and maintained.

EXHIBIT 19–3 System Overlap

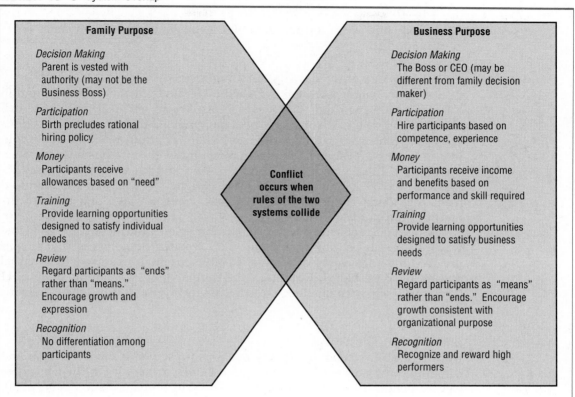

2. All family members should have some time alone away from the business.

3. Clear areas of responsibility for each family member should be delineated, and members should not meddle in each other's area.

4. Competition among family members should be kept healthy.

5. Power struggles should be avoided, and they can be when everyone has identified their area of responsibility.

6. Family members should take time to plan their business and personal relationships.

7. A system for overcoming disagreements should be established and used before serious impasses occur.

8. Personal habits, particularly disagreeable ones, should not carry over into the business.

9. Family and business money issues should remain separate and distinct concerns.

10. Finally, it is important for all family members to retain their sense of humor.[13]

Failure to Separate Family and Business

As we have already seen, the most common family members to be found in a business are husbands and wives. This can be an ideal arrangement if husband and wife are happily married, but marital difficulty can cause serious business problems, as it did for Pat and Rhonda Patterson.[14] Like many couples of the 1980s, Pat and Rhonda married and went into business together. They ran a Tulsa video production company, which blossomed. Sales increased to $700,000 and the future was bright. "It was like we produced magic," Rhonda Patterson said. The magic did not last long because the marriage did not last long.

As marital problems developed, the Patterson's business suffered. Trust was lost, battles became heated and more frequent, employees' loyalty was divided, and sales were lost before the Pattersons finally resolved their marital and business problems. Eventually the company was forced into chapter 11 bankruptcy when its liabilities exceeded assets by $200,000 and the Pattersons divorced.

Succession Planning

Failure can be avoided and family relations preserved if there is a clear and communicated succession plan in place before owners leave their business (see Appendix 19–1 for an example of how to prepare a succession plan). Although plans can smooth the leadership transition, they may not please family members. A study of 350 small business owners by the American Institute of CPAs included the following question: "What path would your company follow if ownership were to change within the next two years?" Only 22.3 percent indicated that they would pass the business to family members. The majority of respondents, 51 percent, indicated that they would sell to a larger corporation or to outside investors.[15] Although that study might disappoint owners' families, another[16] is even more disheartening. Nearly 67 percent of 1,873 business owners were not prepared to name a successor.

WHY KEEP THE FAMILY BUSINESS IN THE FAMILY? When a number of owners of family businesses were asked that question, they gave the following answers:

- 34 percent. Opportunity for children.
  Provides freedom, control of their personal destiny, and autonomy.
  Provides opportunity for personal growth, creativity, and expression.

- 21 percent. Perpetuate heritage.
Builds tradition, history, and roots.
Creates living memorial.
- 15 percent. Keep family together.
Helps family work together.
Strengthens family bond.
Allows more family time together.
- 10 percent. Generate financial advantages and wealth.
- 8 percent. Ensures own retirement and personal purpose past age 65.
- 6 percent. Protects loyal employees.
- 5 percent. Provides family with financial security.
- 1 percent. Benefits society.[17]

WHY CHOOSE AN OUTSIDE SUCCESSOR? We have seen that only a minority of business owners actually pass their business on to a family member. Some reasons for this include the following: no family member is capable of operating the business; no family member wants to own the business; family jealousies cause too many succession problems; and outside buyers make an offer too good to refuse. Perhaps the most serious problem to rectify is family jealousies, particularly sibling rivalries. To reduce, if not eliminate, sibling rivalry, owners can do the following:

- Assign specific duties and responsibilities to each sibling.
- Create an outside board of advisors who can offer independent guidance and counsel.
- Develop an arbitration system that can resolve conflicts.
- Be sure siblings understand that the continuance of the business is more important than personal aggrandizement.
- Allocate financial rewards on the basis of a person's responsibilities and duties.
- Identify as early as possible the family member who is to take over the business.

WHO SHOULD INHERIT THE BUSINESS? Because spouses are the most likely person to be in business together, it is reasonable that one succeeds the other when the time comes. The next most likely successors are sons and daughters. The former seem to be given preference in succession matters; however, a growing number of daughters seem to be replacing their fathers or mothers, and they appear to be quite capable of managing family businesses (see The Way It Is 19–3). In some cases, daughters have to make explicit their desire to take over the business, and they need the guidance and support of their father or mother.

WHEN SHOULD SUCCESSORS BE IDENTIFIED? Most business owners are reluctant to contemplate retirement or recognize their own mortality. They

The
Way
It Is

19–3 DAUGHTERS TAKING THE REINS

When 84 Lumber Company was started thirty-five years ago, conventional wisdom was that the building supply business was a man's domain. As the company's owner prepared to step down, he surprised the lumber trade by selecting his daughter to succeed him. Joseph A. Hardy Sr. built 84 Lumber into a chain of 348 stores with sales of $900 million per year before he decided to name his daughter, Maggie Hardy, as his successor. Often, brothers or sisters, or even mothers, envy the anointed daughter. Employees and customers accustomed to dealing with men have difficulty adjusting to a female boss. Maggie Hardy knows firsthand about these problems: hers is a male-dominated business; she edged out two older brothers; and she outranks three middle-aged men who might have been successors. Maggie Hardy is confident that she will overcome these problems and successfully run 84 Lumber.[18]

believe that they can extend their active business life by ignoring succession matters. However, owners must decide who is to replace them when the time comes to hand over the reins of the company. It is actually never too early to identify a successor and alternate successors who can take over in the event that the chosen successor does not stay with the business. Once identified, the chosen successor should be groomed for the position, and the owner should leave the business at the appropriate time and hand over responsibility and authority to the successor.

Transferring the Business

transferring
the business

Once successors have been identified and all other aspects of the succession plan are in place, owners must decide how they will transfer the business to their successor. **Transferring the business** is the aspect of estate planning that allows for the orderly transfer of the business at the least cost to heirs. The easiest estate planning tool may be for an heir to take over the business and pay off the former owner in cash. If that option is not acceptable, any of the following can be tried:

1. A buy-sell agreement can be created that stipulates that stock be offered first to family members active in the business before other family members, employees, or outsiders have an opportunity to buy the stock. If the company's stock has not been widely traded, an outsider will have to determine its value before any is sold to interested buyers.

2. Interest in a business can be bequeathed to a spouse to avoid estate taxes because of the unlimited marital deduction or through tax-free gifts of $10,000 per year.

3. The company can be sold to heirs over a specified period of time to reduce the value of the owner's estate. This reduces the heirs' tax burden even though they will have to pay some tax on their inheritance.

4. A business owner can establish a testamentary trust that is funded with common stock for the children to become beneficiaries. When the founder dies, a trustee runs the company until any minor children reach an age when they can take over the business.

5. A trust can be set up for family members to remove them from business operations while still providing for them to start new ventures.

6. Owners can set up a charitable foundation as a way to keep nonactive family members out of daily business operations.[19]

SUMMARY

As businesses grow management positions are created that need to be filled with qualified people. The training and development of individuals capable of filling management positions is the responsibility of the business owner. Owners should also create plans for filling vacant management positions, and they should have a mechanism for turning the company over to another owner when they retire or in the event of their death. Owners can create buy-sell agreements, which indicate who will succeed an owner, or they can establish an employee stock ownership plan (ESOP), which enables employees to assume ownership of the business.

Succession in family businesses has its own set of problems because business decisions are colored by family relationships. When sons and daughters work in businesses with mothers and fathers, it can be difficult to separate business decisions from family decisions. That is one reason why only 30 percent of family businesses are successfully passed from one generation to the next. To avoid problems in family businesses, owners should create a written succession plan that clearly identifies the person who will succeed the owner. Owners should also know when the time is right to turn the business over to their successor, and, having turned over the reins of the business, they should not meddle.

QUESTIONS FOR REVIEW AND DISCUSSION

1. What are the different stages of growth?
2. How does a business change when it transitions from an entrepreneurship to a professionally managed company?
3. Why should owners delegate to their managers?
4. How can business owners learn to delegate successfully?
5. What are the different leadership styles? Which do you think would be most appropriate for small businesses? Why?
6. What is the purpose of a buy-sell agreement?
7. What are some of the causes of failure in family businesses?

8. What are some characteristics of family businesses that are most likely to be successfully transferred from one generation to the next?

9. How can owners avoid sibling rivalry if more than one of their children expects to inherit the business?

KEY TERMS

buy-sell agreement

employee stock ownership plan (ESOP)

family business

growth by assignment

growth by delegation

growth by innovation

growth by participation

participative management

succession planning

Theory X

Theory Y

transferring the business

CASE
A Father Unable to Take Action

Dick Symanski, 55, owns a construction company in the Northeast. Despite the slowed economy in his part of the country, Dick has been able to maintain his company's substantial profitability as a result of selective bidding, minimal debt, and other good management techniques.

Even though his business is very successful, Dick is completely at a loss over what to do about two sons in the business. Alan and Harry, both in their mid-30s, have each begun to press their father for an opportunity to lead the company. But Dick has taken no action, and his sons have begun to believe that he has no appreciation for their contribution to the success of the company. They also see Dick as passive and indecisive, qualities they resent.

Alan and Harry have both demonstrated solid technical expertise over the

years, but their management skills have been untested. Dick is just not sure what their leadership capabilities are. But more than that, they are the children from his first marriage—to a woman whose alcohol abuse left scars on Dick and his entire family.

Dick is happily remarried, and children from the second marriage are beginning to push for roles in the company. Dick is afraid that giving Alan and Harry stronger roles will result in anxiety in his new family. But he is just as sure that not doing so will escalate the tension between Dick and his older sons as well as reopen wounds from the first marriage.

Dick regrets his inability to act—it reminds him of his frustration with his own father, who seemed equally indecisive when Dick worked for him in another business. Dick wants to please everyone and avoid a further split in the family. But can he?

QUESTIONS

1. Should Dick begin succession planning immediately?

2. Who should he choose to replace him?

3. What will happen to those not chosen to lead the company?

SOURCE: "A Father Unable To Take Action," *Nation's Business*, January 1991, 30. Copyright by the Family Firm Institute Inc., Brookline, MA. Used by permission.

ACTIVITIES

1. Answer the "Is Your Business Ready for Succession" questions below to learn how you feel about passing on a business.

Is Your Business Ready for Succession?

For each of the following, circle the number that most nearly describes how you feel about the statement:

1 = Strongly Agree   3 = Disagree
2 = Agree   4 = Strongly Disagree

1. The founder or senior owner of a company is the one who knows the company best and should make all final decisions about its operations.   1   2   3   4

2. The only way to learn a job is by trial and error.   1   2   3   4

3. Successive generations seldom run the company as well as its founder did.   1   2   3   4

4. It isn't necessary to plan for succession in a family business if the current owner has only one child.   1   2   3   4

5. Planning for ownership and management succession is dangerous because it keeps everyone on edge for too long.   1   2   3   4

6. A business owner's family should be told of the business's successes but not its problems.   1   2   3   4

7. Younger family members should be brought into the owner's company in top positions so that employees will respect their authority.   1   2   3   4

8. Company employees should have little or no role in planning for succession in the business.   1   2   3   4

9. Planning for succession should not begin until the current owner is ready to retire.   1   2   3   4

10. A successful business owner's sons and daughters have a natural obligation to take over the business.   1   2   3   4

Total of all numbers circled _____

A total score of 40 on this self-assessment, indicating strong disagreement with every statement, shows your readiness to begin planning for family succession in your business. A score above 30 shows good orientation for succession planning. If your score is between 24 and 30, you should reconsider your views on family involvement in the business. If your score is 23 or below, you are not likely to involve your family in the business.

SOURCE: James W. Lea, *Keeping It in the Family* (New York: John Wiley & Sons, 1991), 17–18. Copyright 1991. Reprinted by permission of John Wiley & Sons, Inc.

2. After you have read the case and answered the questions, read the analysis of the case.

Case Analysis

Thomas M. Hubler, president of Hubler Family Business Consultants.

Family influences often cloud an otherwise straightforward process of leadership selection and development. To address the management selection issues in his business, Dick needs to understand the impact of his family on the succession process. Dick should begin to explore, perhaps with the help of a therapist, the history of his own relationship with his father. By understanding its impact on him and gaining the ability to honor his own love for his father, Dick will find that he is more able to deal objectively with Alan and Harry and the demands they are making on him. The Symanskis also need to understand the negative effect that the first wife's alcoholism still has on the family.

Finally, the family should adopt rules governing members' participation in the business. A program of career development should be instituted for Alan, Harry, and the younger children so that they are prepared to offer their best to the business and so that it becomes apparent when the strongest candidate for the next generation of leadership emerges.

Paul Frishkoff, partner in Leadership in Family Enterprise.

Dick is an "analyzer" who is thorough and cautious, craving data before reaching a decision. Analyzers hate being pushed to make decisions—and his sons are pushing. It is doubtful, by the way, that Dick's interactions with his own father or the difficulties of his first marriage are the causes of his "passive and indecisive" style; rather, those rifts exacerbated a tendency that Dick already had. Further, the Symanskis are a family suffering from, and probably still unable to face, the issues surrounding the mother's alcoholism.

Dick and his sons do not trust each other at a profound level, certainly do not speak (about what really matters to them), and do not feel—or at least do not communicate about their feelings. A beginning toward a solution would be a family retreat, facilitated by a consultant or therapist. The mere opportunity to verbalize, in a neutral, safe setting, what each person wants (family peace, recognition, freedom to compete, and—underneath all this—love) will be a giant step toward resolving the succession issue and re-creating the family.

Appendix 19–1

The Succession Planning Organizer

For this organizer to be of value in building a family business succession plan, all sections of it must be completed *in writing*. All information, facts, and opinions must be accurate, honest, current, and complete.

I. A Description of the Business
1. Legal description
   a. Charter: Sole proprietorship ( ) Partnership ( )
   Closely held corporation ( ) Public corporation ( )
   Founded in 19 _____ Founded by_____
   b. Current owners and investors:
   Name: _____Ownership: _____ %
   Name: _____Ownership: _____ %
   Name: _____Ownership: _____ %
   Name: _____Ownership: _____ %
   (Continue on separate sheet if necessary)
   Officers by name: _____ President
   _____Vice-President
   _____Secretary
   _____Treasurer

   Directors: _____
   _____
   _____

2. Strategic description
   a. Nature of the business: What is this company in business to do?
   _____
   _____

   What are all of its revenue-producing activities?
   (1)_____
   (2)_____
   (3)_____
   (4)_____
   (Continue on separate sheet if necessary)
   b. Market position: By market share or rank (e.g., first, second, tenth), what is the company's position in its market?_____
   c. Reasons for success: What are the three things most responsible for its current level of success?
   (1)_____
   (2)_____
   (3)_____

      d. Strategic goals: What are the company's three most important goals for the immediate and long-term future?

        (1)_____

        (2)_____

        (3)_____

  3. Organizational description

      a. Organizational chart: What are the lines of supervision in the company? Does the business have an up-to-date organizational chart? (If not, draw one.)

      b. Working organization: Briefly describe the key jobs and duties of the owner(s), managers, and other employees in the company.

      Owner(s):_____

      _____

      Other executive(s):_____

      _____

      _____

      Manager #1:_____

      _____

      Manager #2:_____

      _____

      Other key employees (by name or job):_____

      _____

      _____

      _____

II. A Description of the Family

  1. Family boundaries: What persons are included in "the family" for purposes of planning business ownership succession?

    _____   _____

    _____   _____

    Who in the upcoming generation is likely to inherit or otherwise receive ownership?

    _____   _____

    What change will that make in the current distribution of ownership and control of the business?

    _____

  2. Family members in the business: What relatives are now involved in the business as owners and/or employees, and what are their jobs or other roles?

    Name   Role

    _____   _____

    _____   _____

    _____   _____

(Continue on separate sheet if necessary)

3. Successor qualifications: Which members of the family are qualified by training, experience, and/or interest for management positions in the company? According to the best evidence available *at this time,* for what job is each person best suited? What additional training or experience would each person need in order to become fully qualified for that job in the next generation of company management?

Name	Possible Future Position	Training/Experience Needed
_____	_____	_____

4. Family needs: What family needs—financial, career, other—will the business be expected to meet over the next 10–20 years? (Be as specific as possible.)

_____

III. Overall Goal of the Succession Plan

In clear and direct terms, describe the result that should be produced by this succession plan if it is completely successful. In other words, what should be the specific role of the family in the business, and what benefits should the business be providing to the family, 20 years from now?

_____
_____
_____

IV. Specific Succession Goals and Actions

List a minimum of five specific succession goals that must be achieved if the overall goal is to be achieved over the next 20 years. List these goals in a logical sequence (i.e., order of importance or chronological order), remembering that sustaining the business should be of greater *immediate* importance than meeting family members' needs and desires.

Under each goal, list the sequence of actions, in chronological order, that must be taken to achieve that goal. Give a target date for each action. (Continue listings of goals and actions on separate sheet if necessary)

Goal #1: The first goal is to:_____

First action:_____

_____ Target date:_____

Second action:_____

_____ Target date:_____

Third action:_____

_____ Target date:_____

Goal #2: The second goal is to:_____

First action:_____

_____ Target date:_____

Second action:_____

_____ Target date:_____

Third action:_____

_____ Target date:_____

Goal #3: The third goal is to:_____

_____

First action:_____

_____ Target date:_____

Second action:_____

_____ Target date:_____

Third action:_____

_____ Target date:_____

Goal #4: The fourth goal is to:_____

_____

First action:_____

_____ Target date:_____

Second action:_____

_____ Target date:_____

Third action:_____

_____ Target date:_____

Goal #5: The fifth goal is to:_____

_____

First action:_____

_____ Target date:_____

Second action:_____

_____ Target date:_____

Third action:_____

_____ Target date:_____

V. Succession Roles and Responsibilities

List the individuals—current owner(s), owner's spouse, owner's children, other relatives, attorneys, accountants, consultants, company employees, and others—who will play key roles in carrying out this succession plan. Describe the responsibilities that each person should take.

Name	Responsibilities in Plan
_____	_____
_____	_____
_____	_____
_____	_____
_____	_____

(Continue on separate sheet)

VI. Costs of Succession

1. Succession training: Estimate the cost of education and training that individual family members may require for succession purposes. $_____

2. Outside help: Estimate the cost of consultants and other specialists whose help may be required during the transition process. $_____

3. Successors' salaries: Estimate the cost of salaries _____
and benefits that will be paid to successors during their apprenticeship(s). Note if these salaries
will be greater or lesser than salaries and benefits payable to nonfamily employees in the same
jobs.

Total Estimated Cost of Succession $_____

SOURCE: James W. Lea, *Keeping It in the Family* (New York: John Wiley & Sons, 1991), 101–106. Copyright 1991. Reprinted by permission of John Wiley & Sons, Inc.

20 GOING PUBLIC AND SELLING THE BUSINESS

S mall businesses go through many different stages of growth and decline. Most businesses are started full of promise and great expectations for the future, but many of these will never achieve even modest success. Some will cease operations within a short period of time, and others will continue to operate just above or very near the break-even point. Others will have a short, brief burst of spectacular growth buoyed by the popularity of the original concept of the founder only to falter when either the competition increases or the concept becomes obsolete. Still other businesses will develop a market niche that may have limited growth potential but provides a product or service yielding a stable, profitable business. For a very few, growth, sometimes even fantastic growth, will continue many years because the firm is able to adapt to changing competitive and economic pressures. The owners of these last two groups may at some time consider either going public or selling the firm.

In effect, in either selling the firm or going public, the small business owner is relinquishing some or total control of the business to others. This chapter will address the reasons a small business owner may decide to either sell the entire firm or sell shares in the firm by going public. After small business owners consider both the advantages and disadvantages of selling part or all of the firm, their next step is the preparation of the firm for sale. The final step is the location of a buyer or buyers. What the owner should consider in these final two steps will be presented in the latter part of this chapter.

The previous chapters in this book have addressed the management of a small business, and the emphasis has been on methods and/or techniques that small business owners could use to survive in a competitive business environment and to increase the profitability and growth of their firms. For those businesses that survive and grow, small business owners will eventually face an entirely different type of challenge: when to give up some or total control of their firm. This decision may come from the need to raise additional capital, the desire to obtain a return on their investment, or the realization that they cannot, or do not wish to, manage the business forever.

This chapter will address these issues by first presenting the process of selling stock to the public and then looking at various ways small business owners can sell their firm. Both of these alternatives can leave current owners with various degrees of control of their business.

GOING PUBLIC

going public

Going public is the process by which a privately held firm sells a portion of its ownership to the public through a stock offering. Small business owners generally take their firms public to raise additional capital for the expected growth of the firm or to obtain a return on their investment. Going public, however, is a major change in the management philosophy of the firm, for the firm will change from a private business, run primarily for the benefit of the owner, to a public company, which must consider the returns to a large number of owners. Managing a small (private) business is hard enough, but public ownership adds a new dimension to these problems. In effect, the original owners are now responsible for running a business not just in their best interest, but for the best interest of all the shareholders, including the new shareholders. These new owners, and the general public, require time of the top managers to answer questions about the firm, its products, its expectations of earnings, and many other queries that the owners of a private firm may not have wished to share with the public.

Another major change is that public ownership means public disclosure. With public disclosure comes the scrutiny of shareholders, stock analysts, government security regulators, and lawyers. What many small business owners overlook is that going public means that not only the financial records of the firm, but also private financial information such as the salaries and stock holdings of the top executives are public. Thus, going public means that there are additional owners of the firm, and decisions made by the original owners now have to consider the interest of a much larger group of owners.

initial public offering (IPO)

Small Corporate Offering Registration (SCOR)

In taking a firm public, the existing owner, or owners, may chose one of three methods. The first is a process known as an **initial public offering (IPO)** whereby shares are sold through an investment banker to the public. A second method is for the business to sell shares directly to the public. A third, and relatively new, method is known as a **Small Corporate Offering Registration (SCOR).** The SCOR is a method designed for sales of relatively small ($1 million) amounts of stock, and the process uses some of techniques of both the IPO and the direct sales methods. The IPO process receives a huge amount of media attention and is, therefore, the best known of the three methods. In reality, the IPO is seldom the best method of going public for small businesses. Each method, however, is the best under certain circumstances, and each has its advantages and disadvantages.

INITIAL PUBLIC OFFERING

Probably no aspect of managing a small business receives more attention in the popular press than the initial public offering, almost better known through the initials IPO. As in the well-publized case of Bill Gates, the CEO of Microsoft, the IPO conjures images of instant millionaires or billionaires for those entrepreneurs/business persons who had the vision to develop the demand for a product or service. From the articles written about these modern-day heroes, one could assume that going public through an IPO was a sure sign that they had both the vision and the business acumen to be a success. Although the popular press has given the public the indication that IPOs are successfully managed small businesses, in reality, only a few of the many very successful firms should go public through an IPO. Small business owners, with the help of expert advisors and consultants, should carefully consider whether an IPO is right for them and their businesses.

An IPO may be underwritten, or it may be sold on a "best efforts" basis. In an underwritten IPO, some of the firms' shares are sold to an investment banker, who then resells them to the public. The underwriting function is the guarantee that the issuer will receive all the funds from the sale, and the risk of selling the shares to the public is with the **underwriter.** The obvious advantage of an underwritten issue is that the firm knows how much capital it will receive from the sale of shares, and this money is received up front. The risk of selling the shares is left with the underwriter. In a **best efforts issue,** the investment banker agrees to do its best but does not guarantee the sale of stock. The issuing firm, therefore, does not know how many shares may be sold and, as a result, how much capital will be raised through the public issuance of stock.

underwriter

best efforts issue

Advantages of an IPO

The most obvious advantage of an underwritten IPO is that the minimum amount of capital raised through the sale of stock is known in advance. In an IPO, the investment banker purchases a specified number of shares from the issuing firm at a specified price. The investment banker may have an agreement to purchase additional shares if the original issue is oversubscribed, but in that case, the firm will only obtain more capital than the minimum amount originally underwritten by the investment banker.

A second advantage of an IPO is that the public market provides liquidity for owners because they can easily sell their stock. Before a business goes public, the owners have stock in their firm, but they do not have a way to easily sell any of their shares. After the firm goes public, then the stock market provides both a place and a method for the sale of stock. A third advantage stems from the second: the market provides not only liquidity but also a value for the shares and, therefore, a value for the entire firm. Prior to an IPO, the value of any business is very hard to determine, but after the IPO, the value for the firm is easy to determine, for it is the price per share times the number of shares outstanding.

Another advantage of an IPO is that a publicly traded firm normally has more access to capital markets than privately held firms. Thus, the ability to raise additional capital, if needed, is enhanced. A final advantage of an IPO is that the image of a publicly traded firm, in the eyes of suppliers, customers, and providers of capital, is normally much stronger than the image of a private business. The stronger image may result in better terms and service from suppliers, more customers, and an easier access to capital markets.

Disadvantages of an IPO

Although there are many advantages of an IPO, there are also many disadvantages that small business owners should seriously consider before taking their firm public. A recent survey of firms going public referred to these disadvantages as the "dark side" of going public.[1] Certainly one of the major disadvantages for most entrepreneur/business persons is the loss of freedom. The CEO of a public firm has more managerial constraints than the CEO of a privately held firm. The IPO prospectus, for example, clearly states what the firm plans to do with the capital raised in the IPO, and this statement becomes a constraint on future managerial decisions concerning major expenditures of capital.

A second major disadvantage of going public is the cost in time and money of dealing with stock analysts, stockholders, the media, and the general public. Very few of the CEOs in the survey had any idea how much time they would have to spend answering questions about their firm and its prospects. The problem, of course, was that the time spent answering the public's questions was time taken away from managing the company. Unfortunately one of the major questions asked always seems to revolve around the next quarter's results and the effect on the stock price. This concern can force the CEO to focus more on the short-term results than on the long-term planning that had been the hallmark of their pre-IPO strategy.

A final disadvantage of going public is the potential of the firm becoming the target of a hostile takeover. Once a firm goes public, there is always the threat that a group of investors will view the firm as undervalued, purchase shares in the company, and attempt to gain control from the current management. This potential threat, along with sudden changes in the stock price, can make both management and employees of the company start worrying more about what might be happening to the firm rather than about the day-to-day running of the business.

The Mechanics of an Underwritten IPO

After the small business owner has analyzed the advantages and disadvantages of going public and decided that going public through an IPO is the best path for her or his firm, there are four steps that must be taken: (1) the location of an underwriter, (2) negotiation, (3) preparation, and (4) the sale of the shares.

LOCATION OF AN UNDERWRITER. The first step is the location of an underwriter. If the small business owner already has a working relationship with a securities firm that manages IPOs, this step may be a short one. Typically, however, the search for an underwriter will depend on the dollar size of the potential offering. Smaller offerings may be handled by local or regional securities firms, and larger offerings are handled by the large national firms, usually located in New York City.

Whether any firm will agree to underwrite a new issue will depend on the current stage of the IPO cycle in the stock market. IPO underwriting has very definite cycles that correspond with the stock market cycle. When the stock market is up, underwriters can easily sell new issues, and the market for IPOs is very strong. When the stock market is down, the demand for IPOs is almost nonexistent. For example, there were more than 1,000 underwritten IPOs in 1969, the last year of the great 1960s bull market, but there were less than 30 underwritten IPOs in 1975, the low point of a two-year bear market. Timing, therefore, is very important in locating an underwriter, and if the firm is contemplating going public, it should obtain a general idea of the current state of the market.

If the current state of the market is favorable for IPOs, small business owners must present their situation to the underwriters. This presentation is very important because owners are, in effect, selling their firms to the underwriter, and if they cannot sell their firm to the underwriter, then the underwriter will have a hard time selling the firm to the public. Jeffrey Sudikoff, the CEO of IDB Communications, for example, listened to presentations by owners of other companies that were going public to learn what they said that was of interest to the investing community. From the responses to these presentations, he learned how to market his company to underwriters.[2]

After owners market their companies to different underwriters, they then select the underwriter that shows the most interest in their firm. If the underwriter agrees, they will then issue a **letter of intent.** A letter of intent is not a legal commitment to purchase (underwrite) stock, but the intention to purchase the shares after the offering is cleared by the Securities and Exchange Commission (SEC) and/or state security regulators. The letter of intent does cover two topics that all owners should understand. The first is called a **lockup.** A lockup requires that the current owners will not sell their shares in the public market for a specified period of time, usually three to nine months, after the IPO. The purpose of the lockup is to allow the buyers of the new issue time to sell their stock at a higher price before the original owners enter the market.

The second topic is called a **"green shoe" agreement.** A green shoe agreement is an option granting the underwriter the right to purchase additional shares at the time of the IPO if the issue is oversubscribed. Typically, the underwriter will agree to purchase a specified number of shares, and this

letter of intent

lockup

green shoe agreement

number is based on the indications obtained from interested buyers after they have read the preliminary prospectus. Because the underwriter is not sure how many of these indications will result in actual purchases, the green shoe option gives them some flexibility. To keep this option from being open-ended, under current practice, the green shoe option cannot be for more than 15 percent of the number of underwritten shares. For example, the underwriter may agree to underwrite (purchase) an issue of 1,500,000 shares with the option (the green shoe agreement) to purchase an additional 150,000 shares if the issue is oversubscribed.

NEGOTIATION. The negotiation phase between the owner and the investment banker (underwriter) centers on selecting the type of securities to sell, deciding when to sell them, determining the price of the securities, and agreeing on how they should be marketed. Interestingly, the underwriters' commission is not part of the negotiation as the commission will vary with the amount of stock that is sold and the price, but the owner can expect the commission to be between 6 and 10 percent. Investment bankers are experts on financial markets and can advise the small business owner on matters of timing, pricing, and issue size. They can point out the advantages and disadvantages of selling common stock, preferred stock, or preferred stock with warrants to buy common stock based on current market conditions.

warrants

Underwriters may negotiate to obtain warrants for themselves. In this case, investment bankers may agree to underwrite a common stock issue, but require a specified number of **warrants,** which are options to purchase common stock from the issuer at a later date but at the current price. Obviously, investment bankers are hoping the future price will be higher than the option price, and they can make a profit on the difference. The issuer may be willing to give the underwriter the warrants in exchange for lower commissions, or the warrants may be required just to get the investment banker to agree to underwrite the IPO.

PREPARATION. The preparation of an IPO usually is handled by either the investment banker's attorneys or, more rarely, the firm's attorneys. These lawyers will schedule a meeting with the major players in the IPO including the corporate officers, investment bankers, accountants, and the financial printer. The purpose of the first meeting is to outline the schedule of events that will occur before the IPO and to determine who is responsible for each event. The major issues that may be covered in this first meeting include whether the name of the company should be changed, whether the makeup of the board of directors should be changed, and whether any major legal or accounting issues could affect the IPO.

prospectus

The preparation of the **prospectus** is also handled by the attorneys. The prospectus is a formal document describing the firm and its business. The prospectus includes the current and most recent audited financial statements, a written history of the firm, a description of its operations, the planned use of the capital to be raised by the IPO, and any litigation that may be pending against the firm. Also included in the prospectus is a list of its officers and directors and their salaries, an account of any money borrowed from the firm by these officers and directors and the interest rate charged on these borrowings, and the number of shares in the firm that these officials currently own. A very important aspect of the prospectus is that the underwriters and officers of the firm can be held liable for any misrepresentation or omissions in the prospectus. For example, failure to include any pending litigation, the outcome of which could materially affect the earnings of the firm, is an obvious misrepresentation that could affect an investor's decision to purchase the stock. The prospectus is an abridged version of the firm's registration statement, which must be filed with the SEC.

red herring   A preliminary prospectus, called a **red herring,** is given to potential investors of the new shares, and it includes all the information mentioned above. The red herring is printed and distributed before the final selling price of the stock has been determined and before the prospectus has been approved by the SEC. The investment banker uses the red herring to gauge potential investors' interest in the new issue.

While the document preparation is being completed by the attorneys, the investment banker and the owner go on a "road show." A road show is the presentation of information about the firm to potential investors in several major cities in the United States and, on occasion, in Europe.

The final stage in the preparation phase includes obtaining the approval from the SEC, determining the price at which the stock will be sold, and signing the underwriting agreement. With the signing of the underwriting agreement, the underwriter is legally obligated to purchase the stock. There is sometimes a point of confusion on what the SEC approval means; however, SEC approval means that the legal obligations of the prospectus have been satisfied. It does not mean that the SEC is approving the securities as suitable for all investors.

SALE OF THE SHARES. The final step in the IPO is selling the shares to the public. In the typical situation, the underwriter forms a selling group to market the issue to the public. The selling group consists of several security firms, each of which agrees to sell a specific number of shares. The advantage of the selling group is that the risk of selling the shares is divided among several firms, each with a large number of brokers working for them. Each of these brokers will call their investor clients who may be willing to purchase the shares. An example of the announcement of an IPO is shown in Exhibit 20-1. In this case, Affymax N.V. is going public, and 4,600,000 shares are being sold at a price of $20 each. The underwriters are Goldman, Sachs & Co. and Alex. Brown & Sons; the members of the selling group are Bear, Stearns, First Boston Corporation, and the others listed under the two lead underwriters. This announcement is called a *tombstone,* because the notice usually appears as a matter of record after the sale has been completed.

About three weeks before the planned IPO, the underwriter and members of the selling group will call investors who have indicated an interest in either new issues or in the shares of companies in particular industries. The ability of the selling group to sell the shares of a new issue on the day that the

EXHIBIT 20-1 Announcement of an IPO

4,600,000 Shares

affymax

Affymax N.V.

Common Shares

Price $20 Per Share

Upon request, a copy of the Prospectus describing these securities and the business of the Company may be obtained within any State from any Underwriter who may legally distribute it within such State. The securities are offered only by means of the Prospectus, and this announcement is neither an offer to sell nor a solicitation of an offer to buy

3,450,000 Shares

This portion of the offering is being offered in the United States by the undersigned.

Goldman, Sachs & Co.		**Alex. Brown & Sons** Incorporated
Bear, Stearns & Co. Inc.	**The First Boston Corporation**	**Hambrecht & Quist** Incorporated
Invemed Associates, Inc.	**Kidder, Peabody & Co.** Incorporated	**Lehman Brothers**
Merrill Lynch & Co.	**Montgomery Securities**	**Morgan Stanley & Co.** Incorporated
Oppenheimer & Co., Inc.		**PaineWebber Incorporated**
Robertson, Stephens & Company		**Smith Barney, Harris Upham & Co.** Incorporated
Wertheim Schroder & Co. Incorporated	**Advest, Inc.**	**L.H. Alton & Company**
Dain Bosworth Incorporated	**Needham & Company, Inc.**	**Pennsylvania Merchant Group Ltd**
Piper, Jaffray & Hopwood Incorporated		**Rauscher Pierce Refsnes, Inc.**
Scott & Stringfellow Investment Corp.		**Stifel, Nicolaus & Company** Incorporated
Sutro & Co. Incorporated	**Vector Securities International, Inc.**	**W.I.G. Securities**

1,150,000 Shares

This portion of the offering is being offered outside the United States by the undersigned.

Goldman Sachs International Limited		**Alex. Brown & Sons** Incorporated
ABN AMRO	**Bayerische Landesbank Girozentrale**	**BNP Capital Markets Limited**
BSI–Banca della Svizzera Italiana		**Nikko Europe plc**
S.G. Warburg Securities		**Wertheim Schroder International** Limited

December 23, 1991

firm goes public is easy to understand. Merrill Lynch, for example, has over 12,000 brokers in the United States. From their normal conversations with their investors, the Merrill Lynch brokers know which investors may be interested in certain types of issues. When these issues are available, they call those particular investors, tell them what they know about the new issue, and offer to send them a preliminary prospectus.

Brokers attempt to sell potential investors on the new stock using information received from their firm's analysts who have read the preliminary prospectus very carefully and may have attended one of the road shows. As the date for the IPO approaches, brokers again call investors to see if they have an interest in any of the shares. By the date of the IPO, the selling group usually has investor commitments for all their allotted shares, and the brokers merely call the investors on the actual date to confirm their purchase.

SELLING SHARES DIRECTLY TO THE PUBLIC

Selling shares through an underwritten IPO is more suitable for a business that is either already well known on a national level or has a product or products with the potential to interest investors nationwide. Firms whose identity and prospects are more regional in scope may not be able to interest underwriters in their firms. For these firms, selling shares directly to the public may be a viable alternative. Common stocks can be sold just like any other consumer product. To be sold, they must be properly packaged. The steps described in this section are those that will help package this product and are the same basic steps that would be taken if the shares had been sold through an IPO.

Preparing the Firm

If small business owners wish to sell shares to the public, they must start thinking of their firms as public firms. One of the first steps is to make the firm look like a public firm. As a privately held firm, owners tend to make decisions that are for their benefit. These decisions sometimes blur the distinction between business and private use of some assets. Such items as cars, boats, vacation homes, and club memberships should usually be separated from the business before going public. Potential investors who are interested in buying shares in a firm are looking for owner/managers who seem to be attempting to produce a high return on equity for all shareholders and not just a high return for the owner.

Selecting the Board of Directors

A second step is to ascertain that the board of directors is one that will inspire confidence in potential shareholders. The board of directors of too many small businesses include friends and family of the owner. From a potential investor's view, the board of directors must be able to provide independent advice to the chief executive officer of the firm, and family and friends usually cannot provide that independence. In addition to independence, members should bring a high level of competence in some particular area to the board. This competence could be in marketing, manufacturing, finance, or some other technical area that would benefit the firm. A final mark of a good board is that the members have a high level of commitment to the firm. Commitment can be demonstrated by the number of shares they own. Potential investors tend to be more confident in a board that demonstrates its confidence in the firm through a commitment of not only their time, but also their own capital.

Determining Shareholders Rights

Another step in preparing the firm's shares for sale to the public is the determination of the rights of shareholders. Will each share have one vote, or will there be two classes of shares with one class having more votes than other class? The vast majority of public firms have only one class of shares, and all shares have the same voting rights and the same rights to dividends. However, firms may have more than one class of stock with one class having more votes per share than the other. For example, a firm may have Class A and Class B stock with the Class A stock given one vote per share and Class B stockholders ten votes per share. There may also be a difference in the dividends paid to the different classes. For example, Class A stock may be entitled to a dividend that is 10 percent greater than the dividend granted Class B stockholders.

cumulative voting

Cumulative voting is another shareholder right that may be of interest to potential investors. Typically shareholders have one vote per share when voting for members of the firm's board of directors. If, for example, six directors are to be elected, a shareholder with 100 shares would have 100 votes for each of the six directors. If a firm has cumulative voting, then the shareholder may accumulate his or her votes and place them on one or more of the directors. In the example above, a shareholder could place 600 votes on one of the directors up for election or 300 votes on two of the directors. The advantage of cumulative voting is that it allows a small group of shareholders to have a greater opportunity to elect one or more directors. Without cumulative voting, any block of votes that contains a simple majority can elect all the directors.

Selecting an Outside Auditor

The selection of an independent outside auditor is another step in preparing the firm's shares for sale. An outside auditor is usually a certified public accounting (CPA) firm that will examine the financial records of the firm and issue an opinion as to the fairness of the presentation of financial statements. The choice of auditor can be very important to potential investors. In effect, the auditor is certifying the financial records of the firm, and having a well-known CPA firm, such as one of the "Big Six," perform the audit gives the firm planning to go public the cachet of respectability that can translate into a higher initial selling price per share.

Locating a Securities Lawyer

There are certain state and federal legal requirements that must be completed before a firm's shares can be sold to the public. A public offering must be registered according to the provisions of the Federal Securities Act of 1933. In addition, each state has its own separate registration requirements that are sometimes called blue-sky laws. These federal and state requirements are complex and very specialized laws that should be handled by a lawyer who is familiar with security registration laws and has experience with the registration process. Locating a securities lawyer can come from referrals from the firm's current attorneys or accountants or from local small business owners who have already successfully gone public.

Finding a Financial Printer

The printing of the prospectus requires a printer who can deliver a final product with speed and accuracy. Seldom can a local printer meet the speed and accuracy requirements. Speed is needed to complete the prospectus between the time that the lawyers and accountants complete their sections of the prospectus and the delivery of the preliminary prospectus to the regulatory agencies. The accuracy stems from the fact that there is virtually no room for error in any of the information that is given in the prospectus. Normally, due to the time and accuracy constraints and the ability to work with attorneys and accountants, the task should be delegated to a firm that specializes in financial printing. Many small business owners are surprised to find that financial printing may easily be the largest single expense in the entire process of going public.

Developing Shareholder Relations

After a firm goes public, the public will start asking questions concerning the current and future operations of the firm. One or two people within the firm should be designated as the shareholder relations person(s). This person can be the owner, the chief executive officer, or someone who is competent to answer a wide range of questions with both knowledge and discretion. All other employees in the firm should be discouraged from answering public questions concerning the firm, especially outside their area of expertise. As well meaning as some employees may be, information given to the public can, and does, affect the image of the firm and its products and can affect the price of the stock. Incorrect or misleading information given to the public by employees, even if unintentional, can be the basis for a lawsuit.

Selecting an Advertising Agency

Before investors will purchase shares in any firm, they need to know something about that firm. Usually the best way for potential investors to learn about a firm is through the publicity generated through the activities of the firm. An advertising agency can enhance the publicity by writing press releases and generating favorable promotions about the firm, its products, and its employees. The owner generally should not attempt to generate the publicity for the firm primarily due to the lack of media contacts and the lack of time to create well-written press releases. The owner should help the agency by indicating what products or services should be featured and making suggestions about the technical side of the products or services. Advertising agencies can generate the necessary interest in the firm so that when the firm sells its shares to the public, the selling job is much easier.

Selling the Stock

Shares of stock may be sold to the public by the owner, employees of the firm, or a broker, but whoever sells the stock must register with the Securities and Exchange Commission. The registration process is basically proving a knowledge of the securities regulations and a reference check on the individual wishing to sell securities. To sell stock in a firm going public, the registered representative must contact potential buyers and send interested individuals a prospectus. (For interest, note the small print in Exhibit 20-1 concerning the prospectus.)

Pricing the Shares

In pricing the shares, the firm is, in effect, setting a value on the entire firm. For this reason, pricing will be presented later in the chapter with a thorough discussion on selling the firm.

Selling stock directly to the public is not the most common method of raising capital for a small company, but it is a viable method that has been used by many firms. An example is given in The Way It Is 20-1. Note that each of the steps presented above was covered by American Film Technologies in its successful effort to raise capital needed for growth.

(For more information on how to sell stock directly to the public, some free information is available. *Going Public: Practice, Procedure, and Consequences* by Carl Schneider, Joe Manko, and Robert Kant is available by writing to the Director of Publications, Bowne & Co., 345 Hudson Street, New York, NY 10014.)

SMALL CORPORATE OFFERING REGISTRATION (SCOR)

In most cases, the small business owner will find that going public through an underwritten IPO is not feasible primarily due to the cost charged by the underwriter; a small new issue cost can be as high as 30 percent of the total capital raised. Because of these high costs, Congress passed the Small Business Investment Act to help small businesses raise capital. In response to this law, the SEC adopted Rule 504, which exempted small public offerings from federal registration if the owners followed state registration requirements and if they included a disclosure document for investors. To comply with the SEC rule, a committee of the American Bar Association then designed a uniform filing and disclosure form that all states could use. The form, known as the

20-1 WHO NEEDS WALL STREET?

George Jensen, the founder of American Film Technologies Inc. (AFT), had a contract for the colorization of two black-and-white movies. AFT had used its initial capital, raised through a private placement from 240 investors, of $3 million to develop the colorization technology. The process was successful, and Republic Pictures had granted AFT a $600,000 contract for two movies. Although AFT had the technology to fulfill the contract, it lacked the equipment and people to do so. To raise the needed $3.5 million, George Jensen decided to sell shares in AFT directly to the public.

AFT already had a good board of directors and an outside auditor. George Jensen hired an experienced securities lawyer, Art Hartel, to prepare a preliminary prospectus that was filed with the SEC. Massey, Wheeler & Associates, a Chicago public and financial relations firm, was hired to help AFT write quarterly reports, issue press releases, and promote the products of AFT. The cost of the public relation firm was $2,500 a month. The location of potential investors was accomplished through two avenues. The original 240 investors told their friends about the firm. The second avenue was a presentation by Jensen to the clients of a stockbroker in Westchester, Pennsylvania. In these presentations, clips of a colorized *Casablanca* or *Boom Town* were shown and eventually some 3,000 potential investors knew about AFT.

George Jensen decided to sell 3.5 million shares for $1 per share. The initial offering was sold out the first day it went on sale, and by the end of the day the stock had already doubled in price. AFT had the capital it needed to fulfill its contract with Republic and to seek additional contracts. Investors were happy because they had seen their stock double in just one day. Finally, to maintain a market for AFT stock, Jensen had received approval to have AFT listed on the Philadelphia Stock Exchange.[3]

U-7, was then approved by the North American Securities Administrators Association. The final form, adopted in 1989, was called the Small Corporate Offering Registration (SCOR).

A major feature of the SCOR offering is the U-7 form, which functions as a business plan, a state securities registration, and a prospectus that helps provide information to the potential investor and provides some protection to the issuer. The form has been adopted by many, but not all, states and is designed so that small business owners and their local attorney can fill out the form without the expense of a securities lawyer. Additionally, SCOR offerings must be priced at $5 or more, which exempts them from the SEC's tough "penny stock" rules. The current limit on equity raised through a SCOR issue is $1 million.

There are several features that help reduce the cost of raising capital using the SCOR process. First, SCOR prohibits the underwriting of a new issue and requires that the stock be sold either through direct marketing or through commissioned brokers. Second, the forms to comply with the legal aspects of the filing are uniform so that most small business attorneys can handle the registration process without having to hire special securities lawyers. A third savings comes from the fact that audited statements are not required for the first $500,000 of securities sold by the firm. A fourth savings results from the ability of most small firms to produce the necessary documents on office word processing systems, eliminating the need for the specialized and expensive services of a financial printer.

The savings along with the ability of small firms to attract capital at a reasonable cost should cause the SCOR offerings to grow in the future as their potential becomes known to small business owners and their attorneys. Several owners have already used the SCOR offering to raise much needed capital. Janelle Terry, president of CV Posi-Drive Corporation, a start-up firm that developed a transmission for bicycles to ease gear shifting, used the U-7 form in her company's $850,000 offering.[4] The offering attracted small local investors who were willing to invest an average of $2,000 to $4,000 each in a firm with long-term potential. The SCOR process is relatively new, and if small business owners, or their attorneys, are interested, additional information can be obtained by writing the North American Securities Administrators Association, 555 New Jersey Avenue NW, Suite 750, Washington, DC 20001.

SELLING THE FIRM

Entrepreneur/business persons start or buy a company for many different reasons, but at some time they will face the decision of whether to sell their firm. They may receive an offer they cannot ignore; they may be nearing retirement; they may have grown the current firm as far as they had originally planned and now wish to start another venture; they may have burned out or need out for health reasons; or they may just wish to cash out and do nothing for a while. In fact, a recent survey of small business owners who were prospective sellers showed that 54 percent wanted to sell because they were bored or had burned out, 11 percent wanted to sell because they lacked the capital to grow the firm any further, 10 percent stated that their children had no interest in running the business, 10 percent wanted to cash out, 8 percent claimed health or age reasons, and the remainder had a variety of reasons for wanting to sell.[5]

Knowing that they may sell the firm at some time, small business owners should plan ahead for when they may wish to sell their firm. Certainly part of the planning should include how to get the most for the firm (pricing), preparing the firm for the best selling price, and how to find a buyer. These three subjects are the major topics of this final section of the chapter.

How to Get the Most for the Firm

When a privately held firm goes public, the original owners sell shares (ownership) in the firm to outside investors. In this case, they have sold part of the firm, but they normally do not receive any cash at the time of the initial offering. In a typical year, only 300 or so firms may go public, but more than 18,000 privately held firms will be sold. Privately held firms can be sold to another private investor/owner or sold to or merged with another firm. In either case, the original owners can improve the value of the firm, and, therefore, the selling price, by realizing how firms are valued.

multiple-of-earnings approach

MULTIPLE-OF-EARNINGS APPROACH. There are several methods that may be used to value a privately held firm, but one of the most popular is the **multiple-of-earnings approach.**[6] (This approach is sometimes called the *price-earnings method.*) With the multiple-of-earnings approach, the buyer typically pays between six and twelve times the annual after-tax earnings of the firm. For example, if a firm had net earnings of $300,000 and a buyer offered ten times earnings, then the selling price would be $3 million. The two variables that are obviously important in this calculation are the multiple and the earnings. The multiple will vary with the type of business and the current economic conditions, neither of which the current owner can do very much about, but the earnings are something that can be improved.

The owners of most privately held firms try to keep the firms' reported earnings as low as possible for tax purposes: the higher the earnings, the higher the tax liability. To reduce earnings, many owners charge certain expenses to the firm that are really more for the benefit of the owner than for the efficient operation of the firm. Typical among these expenses are country club or other social club memberships, entertainment expenses, maintenance of a car or two and sometimes even a boat, retaining a spouse or relative on the payroll whose efforts do not materially improve the efficiency of the firm, and other similar expenses. Small business owners also may use conservative methods in accounting for their inventory, thus raising the cost of inventory and lowering the reported earnings. Although all this is legal and understandable for a privately held firm, when the time comes to sell, the buyer will look at the after-tax earnings.

Assume, for example, that a small business owner could raise after-tax earnings by $75,000 just through reducing or eliminating unnecessary (from the standpoint of the efficient operation of the business) expenses. The owner could even pay himself or herself less and pay out more in dividends (an after-tax payment). The difference in the purchase price could be dramatic. Using the example given above, if the buyer is offering ten times earnings, the difference is $750,000. The solution to obtaining the higher selling price is to "invest in taxes" in the year or two before selling. The solution, therefore, states that small business owners must decide to sell at least two years before actually selling and that they must be willing to pay a little more in taxes over that period to receive many more times that "investment in taxes" as an increase in the selling price.

The determination of the multiple used will depend on many factors, most of which are not under the control of the seller. The multiple typically will be higher during periods of economic expansion and lower during periods of economic recession. Multiples will vary among different industries.

Industries with a high potential for growth tend to have higher multiples than industries with slower growth prospects. To determine the approximate current multiple for a particular industry, the interested individual could check the latest edition of *Mergers & Acquisitions,* a quarterly magazine that can be found in most large public libraries. Other valuation sources include the major business reference publications such as any of the Moody's manuals or *Value Line.*

CASH-FLOW APPROACH. Another popular method of valuing a firm is the **cash-flow approach.** Cash flow is calculated by adding the operating income of the firm before interest and taxes and the depreciation expense. The operating income represents the income from ordinary business activities before the expense of debt financing is subtracted. The depreciation expense is a non-cash-flow expense. The cash flow, therefore, represents the amount of cash that a business is generating before any financing charges are considered. The rule-of-thumb multiple for a company with a record of fairly stable cash flows is between four and six.[7] Thus, the seller could expect the selling price to be between four and six times the annual cash flow generated by the firm.

The cash flow of a firm can be improved through the same methods discussed above under the multiple-of-earnings approach. In either case, the seller can greatly improve the selling price by planning ahead and making changes in nonessential business expenses that may be currently charged to the firm or making changes in the inventory valuation method.

OTHER VALUATION TECHNIQUES. There are two other valuation methods that are fairly popular. The first is generally called the **discounted cash flow technique.** This method is also called the capitalization or the current value of cash flow technique. Under the discounted cash flow technique, the future cash flows of the firm are discounted at the firm's expected cost of capital to obtain the current value of those future cash flows. The value of the firm is the summation of the discounted future cash flows. This method requires the estimate of two relatively hard-to-estimate variables: the value of the future cash flows and the discount rate.

Basically the future cash flows can be estimated by projecting the current growth rate of cash flows into the future. For example, if the current annual cash flow is $100,000 and cash flows have been growing 12 percent per year, the expected cash flow one year from now would be $112,000 and two years from now would be $125,440 and so on into the future. The second variable is the discount rate. The discount rate of a firm varies with the amount of risk the firm faces in obtaining its cash flows. The higher the risk, the higher the discount rate. In addition, the discount rate will vary from year to year depending on the changing economic conditions, which obviously affect risk.

Given the example above, if the discount rate was 10 percent, then the current value of the cash flows received one year from now would be $112,000 divided by one plus the discount rate or $101,818 (from $112,000/1.10 = 101,818). The $101,818 is today's (the current) value of the cash flow received

cash-flow approach

discounted cash flow technique

one year from now. The current value of the $125,440 received two years from today is discounted at one plus the discount rate squared, $(1.10)^2$, or $103,669 (from $125,440/(1.10)^2 = \$103,669$). The third year is discounted at $(1.10)^3$, year four at $(1.10)^4$, and so on until the cash flows are expected to cease.

The above is a very brief explanation of the discounted method of valuation, but a full discussion would greatly add to the length of this chapter. In addition, this valuation technique is often used by very large firms and the presentation was included here primarily to give small business owners an idea of how the technique is used by larger corporations when they value smaller firms, such as theirs, for possible purchase.

The second technique is the tangible value of the assets of the firm. If the seller is simply selling the assets of the firm, then the selling price will be the liquidation value of those assets. The liquidation value is the estimated value that would be received for the firm if it was sold minus the liabilities of that firm. In effect, the liquidating value assumes the firm is going out of business and is sold for the value of its assets after all the firm's debts are paid. This approach is usually used when the firm is having serious difficulties and cannot find a buyer who wishes to purchase the firm and continue its operations. Obviously, this method is not usually advantageous to the seller and is not one generally chosen by the seller.

BUSINESS APPRAISERS. To obtain a valuation of their firm, small business owners can hire a business appraiser. A good business appraiser can provide not only a valuation but also ideas about how to improve the value before putting the business on the market. The typical cost of obtaining an appraisal is between $4,000 and $10,000. Normally business appraisers will use the valuation techniques presented above. One of the main problems with hiring an appraiser is that, although some are very good, some are really very bad. To locate a qualified appraiser, owners should contact the Institute of Business Appraiser, P. O. Box 1447, Boynton Beach, Florida, 33435, or the American Society of Appraisers, P. O. Box 17265, Washington, DC 20041.[8]

Preparing the Small Firm for the Best Selling Price

In preparing their firm for sale, small business owners should think about marketing their firm just like they would market any product. One way to maximize the selling price is to have a product that looks good. A little time and money spent on painting and sprucing up the property can result in excellent returns. A maintenance firm could be hired to fix up little things that may have been put off such as replacing broken windows, striping the parking lot, replacing burned out lights, or cleaning the carpet. A place that is clean and neat gives a positive impression that the business is successful and well run. When the property of a business has a run-down appearance, the impression is that of a poorly managed business or at least a business that is having problems. The negative impression can easily translate into a lower offer price if a bid is even made.

One simple and inexpensive thing that can give a good impression, in addition to painting, is keeping the grounds neat. Other things that can be done to improve the image of the firm include: (1) sweeping and cleaning up the trash, (2) removing discarded material and other junk, and (3) cutting the grass. All these tasks should be part of everyday practice, but if not, they certainly should become practice if the owner is thinking of selling. Again, the idea is to give a good impression. Typically, prospective buyers will have looked at the business before ever contacting the owner.

In addition to the appearance of the property, the appearance of the employees of the firm also gives impressions about how well managed and successful the firm is. Positive impressions come from having employees that are clean and neat. In some businesses, having the employees wear uniforms can make a very positive impression. The motivation of employees is all too often evident in the manner in which they greet customers and in their actions while working. If small business owners are thinking of selling their business, they should try to look at the firm as an outsider. How does the property look? What kind of impression do the employees give to individuals outside the firm?

In addition to the physical appearance of the property and the employees, there are other areas that can affect the selling price, or whether an offer is even made. One area is that of the records of the business. The first record that a buyer may wish to see is the business plan. A business plan that is up to date makes a positive impression. If there is not a current plan, then one should be prepared. The prospective buyer wants to see that the owner is managing the firm for the future and has a plan for the future.

Although maintaining the financial records of the firm seems an obvious step just in the everyday management of a firm, many small firms are negligent in this regard. Financial records are not just an up-to-date income statement and balance sheet, but current accounts receivable records, customer records, and so on. One potential buyer backed out of a deal because the seller's sales had failed to come within 15 percent of budgeted sales in any of the previous 27 months.[9] The signal given was that if the sales were far off budget, then the entire budgeting process was suspect.

To obtain the best price, small business owners can prepare their firm for sale by doing good housekeeping on the external appearance of the property and with the maintenance of up-to-date financial and operating records of the firm. In a nutshell, owners should manage their firm the way they should be managed whether they are for sale or not.

How to Find a Buyer

Three very good ways of locating a buyer for a small business are through networking, using a business broker, or employing a regional investment banker. Probably the most popular method is networking.

NETWORKING. Networking is utilizing the contacts of the small business owner to learn of investors who may be interested in purchasing a firm. These contacts can arrange meetings between the prospective buyer and seller so that they can discuss the possibilities of a sale. The advantage of networking is that a sale can be arranged with little cost to the seller. If a contact is made and the buyer seems very interested, the owner should hire a competent professional intermediary to guide them through the negotiations.

Most small businesses demand the full attention of the owner, and this does not leave them time to handle the complex legal and technical aspects of arranging the best selling price. Decisions that need to be made during the negotiation stage are the price to be paid, how the purchase price will be financed, what happens to the existing employees, whether the current owner will stay on as a manager or as a consultant, and whether the current owner will be asked to sign a noncompete clause. The current owner should, of course, have a big part in the discussion of these matters, but the details should be left to a competent professional.

The disadvantages of networking can greatly outweigh the advantages. The best way to obtain the highest price when selling a firm is to be able to consider a relatively large group of potential buyers. The larger the number of interested investors who look at, and hopefully, are serious about purchasing the firm, the higher the eventual price. For most small business owners, their network is too small to attract a large group of serious investors. A second disadvantage of networking is the potential loss of confidentiality. Once part of the network learns a firm is for sale, the word spreads. This word spreads not only to potential investors but also to the firm's employees and the firm's competitors. When employees learn that their company is for sale, morale usually goes down, and employees start looking for jobs with other businesses, often competitors. When competitors learn that the firm is for sale, they tend to make special efforts to attract the firm's customers. If a sale is not completed quickly, the loss of good employees and customers can make the firm less attractive than before.

business brokers

BUSINESS BROKERS. **Business brokers** operate much like real estate brokers. They are paid on commission for acting as an intermediary between the seller and the buyer. They usually are paid on a sliding scale of around 10 to 12 percent for deals under $500,000, 5 percent for deals between $500,000 and $1 million, and 4 percent for deals above $1 million. These percentages, of course, can vary with the perceived difficulty in completing a sale.

Some business brokers are very good, especially those who are CPAs or lawyers, or who have excellent business and accounting skills, but many are very bad. The business brokerage business is unregulated, and many brokers, especially those who work fast to make a sale, are shady. Some brokers will distribute confidential information on the firm to a wide audience in an attempt to find a buyer quickly. Brokers should get clearance from the seller before distributing company information to potential buyers, and brokers and prospective buyers should sign nondisclosure agreements.[10] Without such protection, a seller can find that the broker has compromised the company and, in effect, lowered its potential value.

To locate a good business broker, the prospective seller should ask other entrepreneurs/business persons who have already been through the process and find out which ones they recommend. The broker chosen should have experience in brokering the type of business that is being sold as there are huge differences, for example, between cable TV franchises, ad agencies, motels, and garbage pickup routes. In addition, a broker can be located by contacting the International Business Brokers Association, 118 Silver Hill Road, Concord, Massachusetts, 01742, for a list of local or regional brokers who have earned that organizations' designation, called the certified business intermediary (CBI). The CBI designation indicates that the broker has passed an examination that covers many of the legal, financial, and ethical aspects of being a business broker.

REGIONAL INVESTMENT BANKING FIRM. If the potential price of the firm being sold is above $10 million, the small business owner may wish to consider using a regional investment banking firm. Typically the investment banking firm will ask for a retainer fee of $50,000 to $100,000, and this amount will be subtracted from the commission on the final sale price, which may be around 5 percent. The retainer is designed to discourage would-be sellers from attempting to find out what their company is worth without being serious about selling. The fee, sometimes called a business valuation, will give the prospective seller an in-depth valuation of the firm. These valuations may include an updated business plan with income projections for the next three to five years and a profile of the firm with its strengths and weaknesses.

After the evaluation, the investment banker works much as a broker using its contacts to locate potential buyers for the business. One big advantage of using investment bankers is that most have excellent reputations and do not risk the loss of confidentiality during the time the firm is up for sale. In addition, they have personnel qualified to handle all the negotiations between the seller and buyer with skill and integrity.

SUMMARY

Many small business owners who start a business look forward to the day they take their firm public as a sign of their success. Going public, however, requires a major change in management philosophy because the affairs of the firm will be open to public examination. Firms may go public through an underwritten IPO, by selling shares directly to the public, or by a relatively new method known as a Small Corporate Offering Registration.

The major advantage of an underwritten IPO is that the actual capital raised from the sale is known with certainty. Going public also provides a known value for the firm and provides liquidity for shareholders. The disadvantages of going public include the loss of entrepreneurial freedom, the cost of providing information to the public, and the potential for losing the firm to a hostile takeover. The process of going public includes locating an underwriter, negotiating with the underwriter, preparing the prospectus, and actually selling shares to the public. A small business can also go public by selling its shares directly to the public.

Before going public, small business owners should take several steps to help maximize the value of their firm. The first step is to eliminate assets that could be viewed as primarily benefiting the current owner rather than the firm. The second step is the selection of an independent board of directors who bring a high level of competence and commitment to the enterprise. Additional steps include a determination of the rights that shareholders will be given, the selection of an outside auditor, and the hiring of a securities attorney, an advertising agency, and a financial printer.

A recently approved method of selling stock is through a process known as a Small Corporate Offering Registration (SCOR). The SCOR issue allows a small business to raise up to $1 million in equity without the expense of a federal registration. The law specifically prohibits the underwriting of a new issue and requires that the stock be sold either through direct marketing or commissioned brokers.

Selling, or the prospect of selling, the firm is a decision that nearly all small business owners will eventually face. Part of the planning should include how to get the most for the firm, preparing the firm for the best selling price, and how to find a buyer. Certainly part of the preparation process should include improving the physical appearance of the property and getting the financial and accounting records up to date. Understanding the valuation methods is also part of the preparation phase. The most common methods used to value a business include the multiple-of-earnings, cash-flow, and the discounted cash flow approaches. After the firm has been prepared for sale, small business owners may use networking, a business broker, or a regional investment banker to help them locate a buyer.

QUESTIONS FOR REVIEW AND DISCUSSION

1. What are some ways small business owners could operate their firm for their own best interest that may not also be in the best interest of shareholders?

2. Why would an investment banker only sell a new issue on a best efforts basis?

3. Why would owners of a small firm wish to have shares in a firm that are sold in a public market?

4. Why could going public make the managers of the firm tend to think more about short-term results and less about long-term results?

5. After the IPO, why does the investment banker require that the original owners not sell their shares in the public market for a period of several months?

6. When is a best effort public offering in the best interest of the firm that wishes to raise equity capital?

7. How does a prospectus provide protection to the issuer?

8. In preparing to go public, why is the selection of the board of directors important?

9. Why might cumulative voting be an important issue to potential investors?

10. When should a small business owner consider a SCOR offering?

11. Before putting a private firm up for sale, the owner should "invest in taxes." How does one invest in taxes?
12. Do you think that such things as a clean parking lot and a fresh coat of paint really make any difference in the price that a buyer would pay for a firm? Why or why not?

KEY TERMS

best efforts issue

business brokers

cash-flow approach

cumulative voting

discounted cash flow technique

going public

green shoe agreement

initial public offering (IPO)

letter of intent

lockup

multiple-of-earnings approach

prospectus

red herring

Small Corporate Offering Registration (SCOR)

underwriter

warrants

1 DoorMate: A New Product Venture

Steven Harris and Todd Smith were admiring Smith's new automobile while standing in a student parking lot at the University of South Carolina. It was the beginning of the fall 1991 semester for the senior business majors, and Smith was proud to be returning to campus with a new Mustang convertible. The fact that he had earned the money for the car over the last three summers by operating a lawn maintenance service with his brother just served to heighten his pleasure.

As they discussed the car and their ambivalence about entering their final year in college, Smith remarked that it would be nice if there were a dependable way to keep the car from being dented in parking lots. He knew from the looks of his old car that there were many thoughtless drivers who would pull up next to a car in a parking lot and open their door into the side of the adjacent vehicle. The shock absorbing strips in place on some cars, which were designed to prevent this from causing body damage, frequently seemed to be ineffective. Smith tried to avoid parking near others in hopes of maintaining his car's new appearance, but with spaces in student lots at a premium, this was unlikely to prove successful. His alternative strategy, parking diagonally across two spaces, earned him a $20 ticket during a brief stop at the registrar's office on his first day back. As Harris and Smith joked about the selective use of antitank armor, guard services, and other such deterrents to side-panel damage, the friends left the parking lot and parted to attend to presemester chores.

Over the next several days, Harris found himself thinking about the problem. He had always been fond of tinkering and had fairly well-developed mechanical instincts. And with the job outlook for recent college graduates in the doldrums, he was beginning to think that an entrepreneurial venture might be attractive. He had learned in his marketing class about how companies develop new products, and this semester he expected to learn about small business start-ups because he had registered for a class in small business management. With this exposure, and his knack for tinkering, perhaps he could develop and market a product for the automotive market. Harris was inspired by the success of the individuals who had launched AutoShades, the cardboard panels used behind auto windshields to keep cars cool. Harris had read that there were many reasons for the success of AutoShades, but two critical factors were that the product was effective and the panels could be printed and used as sales promotion materials. Harris felt that if he could design a device to protect car doors while also serving as an advertising vehicle, he too could be successful, so he began to think more seriously about developing a product for this purpose.

THE PRODUCT

Harris experimented with a number of different product concepts before he found one that he thought would work. Initially, he considered a metal bar that could be attached to the car door and absorb the impact of another door. But this idea was not practical. The bar could not be attached easily, it took up too much space, and it might generate retaliation from damage to the other car door. Harris next tried running a cable around the entire car. The cable would protrude from the car, which would protect the body from side panel damage, and store easily in a box at the front of the car. This too was impractical because such a cable would have to extend about a foot from the car and would require a cumbersome support system.

After these initial failures, Harris mentioned his project to a friend, a recent graduate with a degree in mechanical engineering. The engineer proposed a solution in the form of a panel, perhaps made of rubber, that would attach to the outside of the car door. The panel would be lightweight, impact resistant, and waterproof. Harris bought a ¼", 4' × 4' panel of natural rubber and began experimenting. However, after spending many hours on this prototype, Harris found out that a section of rubber large enough to protect the door would be too expensive and weigh over 50 pounds. Finally, after talking to numerous suppliers of resilient materials and visiting several trade shows, Harris located a unique type of foam that showed promise. A local firm manufactured the product, called MiniCell 200 (M200). It was lightweight, impact absorbent, relatively thin (½ inch), and could be rolled up for easy storage. But it also had several drawbacks. M200 was expensive ($2.90 for a ½", 1' × 4' sheet), could not be exposed to sunlight, and tore easily. Still, Harris thought that he could resolve these problems and he pressed on with M200.

Harris next turned to the question of a fabric cover for the foam that would not tear easily and would accept printing. He selected a material supplied by an Alabama company. The fabric had a sunlight blocker, high tear resistance, and came in a variety of colors. The one remaining problem was that the material could not be easily screen printed. In Harris's view, this was necessary for the project's success. Also, the material cost 75 cents per square yard, a factor that would have a bearing on the price of the finished product.

Harris put the material issue aside and started experimenting with how to attach the panel to a car. He first tried to use clips, which would be attached to the side of the door with cables. He dropped this idea, finally, because the clips were difficult to attach to the car, and scratched the paint. Instead, he decided to use magnets because they could be easily attached to both the foam and the car. He felt that easy attachment was critical because buyers of the product would require ease of use—one of the advantages associated with AutoShades. The magnets would cost about 30 cents per foot.

Still, the product was not complete. Without using the clips, what would keep the panels from being stolen? After several unsuccessful ideas, Harris decided to use a cable, which was attached to the foam. The user would attach DoorMate to the door, toss the cable inside the car door, and lock the door. If anyone were to try to steal the panel, the panel would be torn and rendered useless. The cable cost 15 cents per foot, and 3 feet were needed per panel (see Exhibit 1 for a schematic of DoorMate).

Harris finally faced the problem of screen printing the material. Fortunately, the supplier had developed a new way of treating the material that

EXHIBIT 1 Schematic of DoorMate

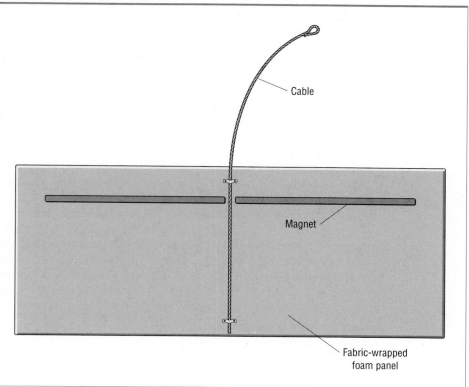

EXHIBIT 2 Illustration of DoorMate with Logo on Door*

*DoorMate was large enough to extend slightly beyond the door on a two-door car; on a four-door car it would just cover both doors.

rendered screen printing feasible. With this problem solved, Harris felt he had developed the perfect product. It would absorb impact from other car doors, was theft resistant and waterproof, stored easily, and would accept screen printing (see Exhibit 2 for an illustration of DoorMate in use).

Although Harris was pleased to have solved his material and design problems, he was surprised at how much time (four months) had passed. To accelerate the process, and due to the amount of time, talent, experience, and money he knew it would take to manufacture the product, Harris decided to contract for production of the product. To try to cut costs, he decided to stay away from contract manufacturers. Instead he sought organizations, such as Jobs for the Handicapped and Goodwill, that would assemble products less expensively. Harris finally found an organization that could do everything he needed, including the screen printing. They would charge between $3 and $4 per set of two panels to assemble and print the product.

Harris now felt that he was ready to proceed, except for a name for his product. The brand selection process consisted of little more than Harris sitting down and thinking of names that appealed to him. There were several names evaluated, such as DoorGuard, DDent, AbsorbaDoor, and DoorMate. On sheer instinct, Harris choose DoorMate.

Almost as an afterthought, he considered price. He remembered that cost-plus pricing was discussed in his marketing class last year, and he worked up a schedule of costs (see Table 1). Based on a total cost of $14.74 per complete set of two panels, Harris used a 100 percent plus markup on cost (and a little psychological pricing) to arrive at a suggested retail price of $29.95 per set. He next began to consider the market he was planning to enter.

THE MARKET

Harris knew that he should do some research on market potential, but he believed he had little to go on to develop a reasonable estimate of DoorMate's

TABLE 1 DoorMate Costs/Price

Material Costs

M200 foam panel:	$2.90 per panel
Fabric covering:	.75 per sq. yd.
Magnets:	.30 per ft.
Cable:	.15 per ft.
Misc: (screen print, packaging)	.50 per panel
Assembly:	1.50 per panel

Cost per panel

M200 ½" 1' × 4'		$2.90
Material 1 ½ sq. yds.		1.12
Magnets 3'		.90
Cable 3'		.45
Misc.		.50
Assembly		1.50
	Total	7.37
Cost per set of two panels		$14.74
Retail price per set*		$29.95

*100% markup on cost

sales potential. Nevertheless, through secondary sources he found that there were 122.8 million cars in use at the start of 1990, and that nearly 80 percent of these vehicles were at least three years old; 50 percent were at least six years old.[1] Harris was not sure what portion of the owners of those cars would purchase the product because there were not any other products he could directly compare to DoorMate. AutoShades was the only product where Harris could see any parallel; but he felt it would not be a good comparison due to the huge difference in cost. AutoShades cost from $1.49 to $6.00; DoorMate would cost nearly $30.00. Many companies gave sunshades away as advertising specialties, few companies would do that with Door-Mate.

Nevertheless, Harris was convinced that DoorMate was entering a wide-open market and that with the right marketing approach, DoorMate would be a winner. He knew that new-car sales in the United States in 1989 totaled 9,853,000.[2] Few of the buyers of these cars purchased body "protection" options from the factory, opting instead for factory-installed fancy radios, air conditioners, and cruise control, for example. Harris was sure that a person paying $15,000 or more for a car would want to protect it if he or she could do so inexpensively and were given the proper motivation. He felt that this helped to explain the success of AutoShades, a product introduced by two inventors with little knowledge of the industry. Sales started slowly for the initial sunshade, which was merely a piece of plain cardboard. But once the two creators decided to add graphics and messages to their products, AutoShades sales "heated up." In 1988, sales exceeded $20 million. Harris wondered if he could expect sales as spectacular as these. If he could capture only 5 percent of the new-car market, he would sell nearly 500,000 sets. And only

5 percent of the 122,800,000 cars on the road would generate additional sales of 6,100,000 sets of DoorMate. With this potential in mind, Harris began to think of the details involved in bringing DoorMate to the market.

THE MARKETING APPROACH

Knowing that he had limited knowledge of production and marketing, Harris wanted to proceed cautiously. He decided to consult an attorney to get information regarding legal issues in introducing the product. The attorney told Harris that the first thing to do was to patent the product and referred him to a local patent attorney. The patent attorney told Harris that she would have to conduct a patent search before applying for the patent. The search would cost Harris $500, and the application process would cost another $1,500 to $2,000.

Harris decided to investigate the patent process himself and discovered ways around the normal procedure. To begin with, he found that anyone could perform a patent search; no attorney was necessary (every state has a depository for patents). All one had to do was visit a depository and conduct a computer search to see if any similar patents existed. Harris also learned that it took an average of two years for a patent to be approved. During that period a competitor could copy and sell the product. The inventor could sue the competitor after the patent was approved, but many gave up their projects or had insufficient funds to bring suit. Harris decided to seek the patent on his own.

Harris next began to think about how to distribute the product and considered three different approaches. One was retail distribution. Harris thought that perhaps he could interest a national retail chain such as Sears or K mart. Both had large auto supply sections. Harris also considered catalog sales. Two catalog companies that he was familiar with, Sharper Image and Brookstone, seemed to be possible distributors for his product. Catalog companies had less overhead and therefore less markup, and these catalogs reached people who could afford to purchase DoorMate. The third idea was to go directly to large companies such as R. J. Reynolds or Anheuser-Busch who could offer the product as an advertising specialty or premium item. If car owners accepted DoorMate as they had AutoShades, a large market would be tapped. Further, because of these companies' association with auto racing, Harris thought they would have an interest in the product.

Harris was undecided about which of these avenues to pursue, or if others should be considered. And with the pressures and costs of his senior year, his time and resources were scarce. Harris realized at this point that he had no idea of how to proceed. He was also beginning to learn that marketing DoorMate was not going to be an easy task. He was convinced that DoorMate could be a great product, but he had not realized how complicated it would be to bring it to the market.

SOURCE: This case was prepared by Thomas H. Stevenson, The University of North Carolina at Charlotte. Used by permission.

AQUAPARK

INTRODUCTION

Even though it was late, Kevin Nett felt a rush of excitement as he poured over the marketing research report on his desk. Working as an engineer had been satisfying to Kevin, but he had always wanted to be his own boss and manage his own business. Maybe this idea of a water park was the answer. The timing certainly seemed right. Kevin was single with no financial obligations. He was only 26, had several excellent business contacts in the community, and was eager to make his mark in the business world.

Kevin graduated from the University of Alabama four years ago with a double major in engineering and personnel management. Although he had been promoted to director of CAD/CAM Systems in a local engineering firm, he began to experience dissonance. The job was challenging but the firm was making too many demands on his time. Kevin was being asked to work nights and weekends, and he began to realize that he would not have time to pursue his dream of developing his own business if he continued to work under those conditions.

Kevin sat back in his chair and thought about all the people he knew who loved water sports. While he was in college, he and his friends had made numerous trips to various types of amusement and theme parks. Many of his fondest memories were of his visits to water parks. Unfortunately, there were only two within driving distance of Tuscaloosa. White Water, located north of Atlanta, and Point Mallard, located in north Alabama near Decatur. Kevin thought about all the young people and families in the Tuscaloosa, Birmingham, and Montgomery population centers, and he envisioned a recreational facility that would be an immediate hit.

When Kevin mentioned his idea to a number of family and business friends, they were enthusiastic and supportive. In fact, several of them told Kevin that if he was "really serious" about the water-park venture, they would help him locate both land and financing for the project.

All of a sudden, this distant dream was beginning to move closer to reality. Kevin began to develop his plan. He designed several layouts with land and equipment needs. He also was able to locate construction firms who specialized in building amusement and theme parks and obtained cost and time estimates for actual construction as well as the water requirements needed to support various size parks.

The more he worked, the more involved the process became. Kevin felt pulled in so many directions that he almost gave up on a number of occasions. Of course, he still had his regular job, which was taking more and more of his already limited free time—time he needed to work on his new venture.

Kevin could see that he was coming to a crossroads. He would not be able to continue to handle both jobs for much longer. He wanted to be upfront with his employer, but did not want to quit his job until he was fairly certain that his venture had a reasonable chance of being successful. Certainly, he would not be able to obtain the financial backing he needed without additional research and data.

From his previous discussions with potential financial backers, Kevin realized that he would have to present a business plan complete with a market analysis and pro forma financial statements. Although he felt somewhat comfortable with his estimates for land, equipment, labor, and insurance costs, Kevin had no formal training or experience in marketing. He was somewhat unsure about estimating a marketing budget, developing a promotional strategy, and determining ticket prices. In addition, he had little basis for developing the revenue forecast he would need for the financial statements. Faced with all these uncertainties, Kevin decided to get started by summarizing the information he did have and to address the other issues later.

TYPE OF PARK AND LOCATION

Kevin's sole interest has been the development of a water park, and he has only considered locations in or adjacent to Tuscaloosa, Alabama. His love for water sports and the community's lack of water facilities convinced him that such a water park would be an immediate hit in the local community. He believes that the park would attract a broad range of singles and families.

The water park will be named Aquapark and is projected to be developed in three phases. Phase I will consist of a kiddie pool with slides and water toys, three combined water slides, free fall and speed slides, a river run, and sunbathing areas. There will also be a picnic and lounging area near the main building. These facilities will be located next to the kiddie pool so parents can watch their children from these areas.

Phase II would consist of a wave pool, surf pool, and bumper boats. Phase III would feature an advanced river run and other possible future additions such as a party area, which could be reserved for birthday parties and family gatherings.

Kevin believes that the variety of attractions will contribute greatly to the success of Aquapark and influence repeat business. He plans to open the park during the spring of 1992. The park will be open in May from 10 AM to 6 PM and from 10 AM to 9 PM during the summer months. Kevin believes that the park's productive season will be from May 1 through Labor Day weekend.

LAND SITES

Three possible sites in the Tuscaloosa area have been recommended to Kevin. Based on his park configurations, the park will require approximately 35 to 60 acres to accommodate all three phases.

One location is near the Northport suburb, north of the Black Warrior River and Highway 69 in the northeast part of Tuscaloosa. The site is 44 acres of wooded, rolling terrain. This location has a selling price of $4.8 million. Highway 69 is a major artery through Tuscaloosa. There is one factor that could decrease the value of this site. I-359 currently does not extend to that part of town, and the scheduled extension to be built includes no provision for an interchange near the water-park site. This situation would have to be studied to determine the impact on the water park before this site could be selected.

The second location is at the south end of town on Highway 82. This site offers 85 acres of heavily wooded, flat, swampy terrain. The land sells for $13,600 per acre and can be subdivided for $20,000 per acre. A major racetrack and a national forest are located nearby, so there is a moderate flow of tourist traffic in the area. Several hundred thousand dollars in earth-moving costs would be incurred in adapting this site.

The third location is on Highway 11, east of town. There are 52 acres of slightly rolling terrain available for $890,000. New houses are being constructed in the area and the city seems to be expanding in that direction. The location is three miles off of I-59, the major interstate highway linking Birmingham, Tuscaloosa, Meridian (Mississippi), and New Orleans.

All three locations are sufficiently close to adequate sources of water. In addition to this prime consideration, Kevin has a strong affiliation with the university and local community. He is also convinced that Tuscaloosa is a prime location sufficiently close to several large population centers connected by adequate road systems. He had considered locating the park closer to Birmingham, because it is more centrally located in the state, but could not locate any sites with a sufficient water supply and easy access to major highways.

ORGANIZATION AND STAFFING

Kevin and two assistant park directors and a small office staff will start work approximately four months prior to opening. The two assistants will be responsible for hiring all other park employees (see Exhibit 1 for his proposed

EXHIBIT 1 Organization Chart

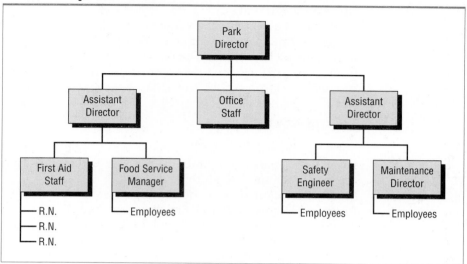

organization chart). Kevin has several friends who have expressed a strong interest in working as his assistant directors. One of them has retail experience and another has successfully managed a small business for several years. Unfortunately, none of his associates has any experience working in or managing an amusement park or directing the marketing activities for such a venture. Although Kevin has made numerous inquiries, he has not been able to find anyone with the right combination of experience and qualifications. However, Kevin feels confident that when news of his venture begins spreading, qualified people will be attracted to his organization.

Initially, Kevin plans to employ approximately thirty-five people to run the park. Sixty percent of these employees would have to be certified lifeguards or water safety instructors for safety purposes and to meet insurance requirements. A lifeguard must be present at all times at each attraction in case of an emergency.

COSTS

Construction and equipment costs for Phase I are projected at $2.5 million. Land costs will vary depending on the location selected. These start-up costs will be considered long-term debt covering ten years. Annual operating costs will include insurance, employee wages, water/energy costs, and all marketing and promotional costs. Kevin's initial estimate for first-year operating costs ranges from $600 to $700 thousand dollars.

The average pay for lifeguards would be $4.55 per hour and $5.05 per hour for water safety instructors. Employee hours will vary depending on the work load. Approximately 60 percent of the employees will be full time. The remainder will work only part time, mainly during busy weekend times such as Friday, Saturday, and Sunday.

Insurance policies for recreational facilities are very costly. The high costs reflect potential safety hazards for the large number of people who will be visiting the park. A $1 million policy carrying a $1,000 deductible per claim costs approximately $42,000 per year. Insurance costs are projected to increase 10 percent per year.

SOURCES OF FUNDING

Kevin has several realistic sources of funding for the water park. He has approached both Coca-Cola and PepsiCo with a proposal for sponsorship, and both provided very positive signals that they would be interested. Kevin projects that negotiations can be finalized within six months of the completion of his business plan.

Kevin is also seeking financial support from private investors. He has received very positive interest from one investor who would be willing to invest up to $2 million dollars as venture capital. He would become a "silent partner" with Kevin running the business full time. This investor has identified a 60 percent return on his investment within seven years as his financial goal. Neither Coca-Cola nor PepsiCo has indicated what their financial expectations are.

Kevin also has financial backing from his family. His parents have indicated a willingness to provide two to three hundred thousand dollars as a bridge loan to help get this venture off the ground. Kevin sees this support as his backup and prefers to limit their involvement if at all possible.

MARKETING ISSUES

As Kevin looked over his business plan, he began to realize that there were many marketing issues that he had not addressed or that he had simply estimated with little data to support his projections. After approaching several local marketing firms, Kevin decided to see what the local Small Business Development Center could do for him. A team of senior business students from the University of Alabama were assigned to his case. Joe Patch, Sandy Smith, and Kate Jones took on the project as part of their capstone business class. The next section describes some of the research that they conducted to gather information that Kevin could use to develop his business plan and marketing strategy.

RESEARCH NEEDS

Kevin told the team that his primary needs were to determine the level of demand for a water park and to identify the characteristics of consumers in the target markets so that effective promotional and pricing strategies could be developed. Both Kevin and the research team felt that a multi-step research process would be necessary to gather all the information that he wanted. Initially, the team gathered as much secondary information as it could on population and market statistics as well as information on direct and indirect forms of competition. Later phases involved gathering primary data to determine the recreational patterns and preferences of potential and actual users of water-park facilities.

SECONDARY RESEARCH

Market Size and Composition

Kevin told the team that he believed the water park would attract patrons from as far away as 100 miles from Tuscaloosa (see Exhibit 2 for a county map of Alabama outlining 50- and 100-mile radiuses). Exhibit 3 provides county population figures and approximate distances to Tuscaloosa. Although these figures represent an estimate of market potential, both Kevin and the research team agreed that market demand would be much less than total potential. They felt that usage rates (both initial and repeat visits) would be strongly influenced by travel distance and ease of access to the water park. In addition, the research team also stressed that promotional costs would be strongly influenced by the promotional reach Kevin would want over the 100-mile radius.

Initially the team divided the market into three segments. The city and county of Tuscaloosa comprised the local market. Residents within a one-hour drive (approximately 50 miles) were identified as the primary market, and anyone living between 50 and 100 miles of Tuscaloosa were identified as the secondary market. The research team recommended that these market divisions be verified by conducting market surveys to measure interest, intended usage rates, and the distance respondents would be willing to drive to reach the water park.

Competition

The Tuscaloosa area has an array of recreational activities for its citizens and visiting tourists. Indirect competition includes bowling, skating, and golf. Fortunately, direct competition is limited because of distance. Point Mallard is a 750-acre comprehensive recreational park located about 140 miles away. The Point Mallard facility contains a wave pool, three flume water slides, an olympic pool, sand beaches, ball fields, tennis courts, campgrounds, a golf course, miniature golf, and a recreation center. It also contains the Deep South's only outdoor skating rink, which is open during the winter months. White Water, north of Atlanta, is over 200 miles from Tuscaloosa. Kevin and the research team did not view either site as direct competitors with Aquapark because they were not close to any of the major population centers that Aquapark was targeting. For example, Point Mallard is convenient to North Alabama residents and to tourist traffic flowing along I-65 from Nashville to Mobile. The research team did not believe that Aquapark would be able to pull significant tourist traffic from I-65 because of its distance from Tuscaloosa (approximately 65 miles).

EXHIBIT 2 Alabama County Map

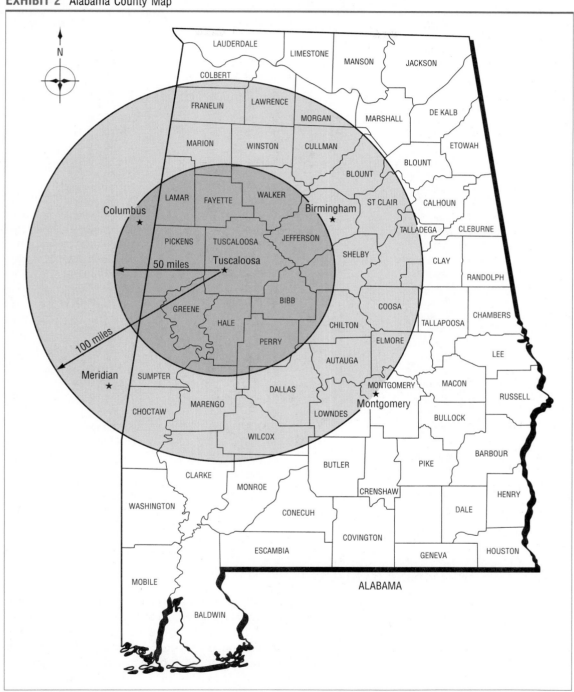

EXHIBIT 3 County Population and Distance to Tuscaloosa

Country	Population	Distance to Tuscaloosa
Autauga	35,500	60–80 miles
Bibb	16,800	20–45 miles
Blount	40,200	70–100 miles
Chilton	32,100	40–80 miles
Choctaw	16,840	70–115 miles
Coosa	11,200	70–100 miles
Cullman	67,500	60–100 miles
Dallas	53,900	50–80 miles
Elmore	49,400	80–115 miles
Fayette	19,100	20–40 miles
Franklin	28,350	80–110 miles
Green	11,200	20–40 miles
Hale	15,400	20–45 miles
Jefferson	678,000	30–75 miles
Lamar	16,700	20–60 miles
Lawrence	30,100	80–120 miles
Lowndes	13,200	70–110 miles
Marengo	24,800	45–80 miles
Marion	30,900	40–70 miles
Montgomery	214,600	80–130 miles
Perry	15,000	30–60 miles
Pickens	21,900	20–35 miles
Shelby	83,800	30–70 miles
St. Clair	41,205	75–110 miles
Sumpter	16,700	30–70 miles
Tallageda	73,800	70–110 miles
Tuscaloosa*	148,800	0–25 miles
Walker	69,700	25–60 miles
Wilcox	14,300	60–100 miles
Winston	21,500	50–75 miles
Mississippi Cities		
Columbus	31,900	60 miles
Meridian	47,800	90 miles

*Tuscaloosa County includes the city of Tuscaloosa, which has a population of 120,400.

PRIMARY RESEARCH

Both Kevin and the research team felt that usage trends and repeat purchase behavior data should be collected and analyzed. Team members traveled to Point Mallard on a weekend and randomly surveyed customers as they waited in line to buy tickets. The team also collected secondary data on park attendance from 1985 to 1989. According to park officials, the downturns in attendance were related primarily to decreases in secondary market traffic and lower repeat visit rates. One official commented on the difficulty of

EXHIBIT 4 Market Research—Point Mallard

FACTS:	Opened August 1970
	First park in U.S. to have a wave pool
	750-acre park with multiple activities including water sports, beach, golf, tennis, camping, and ice skating
	Since its opening, over 160 wave pool locations have opened in the U.S.
ATTENDANCE:	
	Mid 80s—Averaged 200,000 per year
	1988 — 176,600
	1989 — 166,700

	Local	Primary	Secondary
Estimated market penetration	40–60%	25–40%	5–10%
Percent doing multiple visits per year	50–60%	30%	1–5%
Percent families	60%		
Percent singles	40%		

CONCLUSIONS:

1. Secondary market appears to be declining.

2. Repeat visits from primary and secondary markets appear to be declining.

3. Most popular attraction: wave pool.

keeping the park's image "fresh and exciting" in order to remain competitive (see Exhibit 4 for survey results).

The team also collected consumer preference data for a water park versus other recreational facilities as well as information concerning distances people were willing to travel, repeat visits, attitudes toward pricing alternatives, and media habits.

Based on background research, three population groups with decision-making ability and influence were identified as target respondents for the survey. They were high-school students, college students, and area house-holds. Respondents from each of the three segments were selected in the following manner:

High-school students. Tuscaloosa was divided into three sections. Each section contained at least two high schools. One school was randomly selected from each of the three areas. Central in the North section, Jones in the Southeast section, and Southern from the Southwest section. Prior to administering the survey to the high schools, approval was obtained from the head of the Board of Education. The surveys were then given to the principals of each school, who in turn gave them to one teacher from each grade (freshman, sophomore, junior, and senior). A letter of introduction briefly explained the reason for the survey and asked the teachers to administer the survey to a randomly selected English class from each grade. English classes were surveyed because all students are required to take English. Exhibit 5 includes the letter of introduction and a copy of the survey.

College students. The student team administered the survey in the Student Union cafeteria at the University of Alabama in Tuscaloosa. The team felt that the respondents would fairly represent the student body at the University. Respondents were randomly selected Monday through Friday and also among morning, afternoon, and evening time periods. In addition to the information collected from the high-school students, the college students were asked for home town, marital status, and number and ages of children in the household.

Area households. The research team opted to survey families at the East Side Mall, the largest mall in Tuscaloosa. Team members randomly selected people as they approached the mall entrances. Team members canvassed people all seven days of the week and at various times during mall hours to obtain a good cross-section of shoppers. Respondents were asked the same questions

EXHIBIT 5 Market Research Survey

COVER LETTER
ACCOMPANYING SURVEY*

You have just received a survey that asks questions about your preferences for six different recreational activities. Some are seasonal and some are year-round.

Please rank the six choices in the order of your preference. Also, indicate the average number of times *per season* you would go, how far you would be willing to travel (in miles), and how much you would be willing to spend for the tickets to each activity. One ticket would provide access to the activity for one full day.

At the bottom of the survey, please indicate the area of town you live in, your age, and your preference for type of music.

This survey is being conducted by a student team for the University of Alabama, and they thank you in advance for completing this survey.

---

*SOURCE: Read by teachers after the survey had been distributed to students in randomly selected English classes.

RECREATIONAL ACTIVITY SURVEY

	Rank 1–6	How often would you go?	How far would you travel?	What price would you pay?
ICE PALACE				
WATER PARK				
SKATEBOARD PARK				
LASER TAG				
MINIATURE GOLF				
ATV PARK				

In what area of Tuscaloosa do you live—NW, NE, SW, SE? _____ (If not Tuscaloosa, identify the town you live in and the distance to Tuscaloosa.) _____ How old are you? _____
What type music do you like? (Identify up to three choices.) _____

including household composition, age of children, and occupation. The three population segments yielded 586 usable questionnaires. They were split as follows: high-school students, 230; college students, 233; and families, 123.

Some of the results are provided in Exhibits 6 through 14. The tallies in the exhibits do not include respondents who indicated little or no interest in visiting a water park. Those percentages were used, however, to project penetration levels for the first year of business.

DEMAND PROJECTIONS

Market Potential

After numerous discussions with Kevin and extensive analysis of the research findings, the team concluded that it was reasonable to segment the market by travel distance. As planned, they divided the total market into three segments consisting of a local market, a primary market, and a secondary market. The demand forecast was based on projected penetration and repeat purchase rates derived from the survey respondents' replies.

Census data[1] were used to identify population figures for each county and metropolitan area in the three geographical markets. Population data were then divided by age and grouped into three categories: (1) high-school-age customers, (2) college and young adults (18 to 24), and (3) households with primary and middle-school-age children (see Exhibit 15 for market potential estimates).

EXHIBIT 6 Comparison of Price, Visit Frequency, and Distance Willing to Travel by Water Park Ranking

| | WATER PARK—FIRST CHOICE | | | | |
	14–17 years	18–24 years	25–34 years	35–44 years	45 & up
Admission price	$9.45	$9.31	$10.35	$14.19	$7.79
Visits per season	3.8	2.7	2.1	1.6	1.0
Distance	34 miles	27.6 miles	21.3 miles	22.5 miles	16.4 miles

| | WATER PARK—SECOND CHOICE | | | | |
	14–17 years	18–24 years	25–34 years	35–44 years	45 & up
Admission price	$8.87	$8.59	$18.31	$25.00	$8.00
Visits per season	3.5	3.0	1.4	.8	.2
Distance	26.6 miles	25.8 miles	27.3 miles	15 miles	30 miles

| | WATER PARK—THIRD CHOICE | | | | |
	14–17 years	18–24 years	25–34 years	35–44 years	45 & up
Admission Price	$7.48	$6.71	$11.67	$8.50	$10.80
Visits per season	2.3	1.5	.8	.9	0
Distance	22.9 miles	26.1 miles	16.7 miles	13.3 miles	26.7 miles

EXHIBIT 7 Overall Ranking of a Water Park

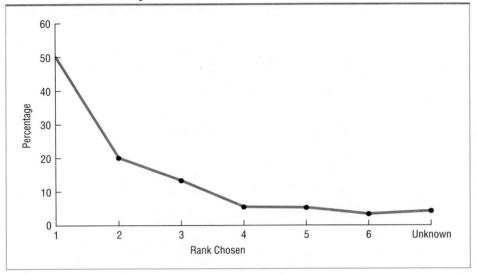

EXHIBIT 8 Distance Respondents Would Travel (Top Three Choices Only)

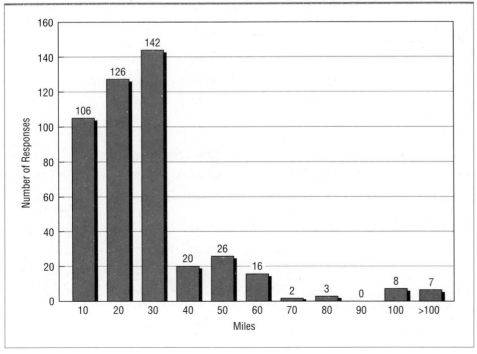

EXHIBIT 9 Visits Per Season (Top Three Choices Only)

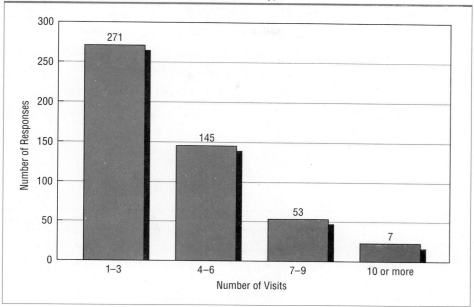

EXHIBIT 10 Top Three Choices From Survey

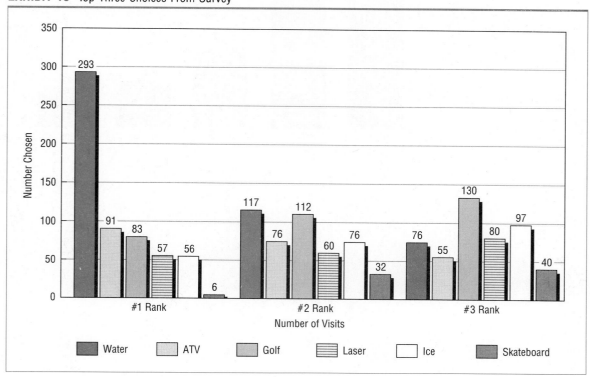

EXHIBIT 11 Overall Averages for Water Park

- Average number of visits per season—2.1
- Average distance willing to travel—26.8 miles
- Average admission price—$9.44
- Average age of those surveyed—22
- Average number of children of those surveyed—1.7

EXHIBIT 12 Age Groups

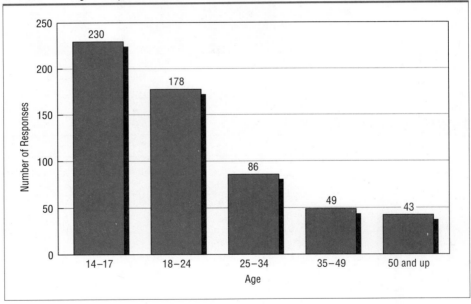

EXHIBIT 13 Average Number of Visits by Age Groups

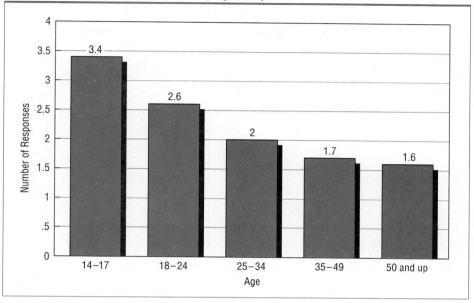

EXHIBIT 14 Music Preference

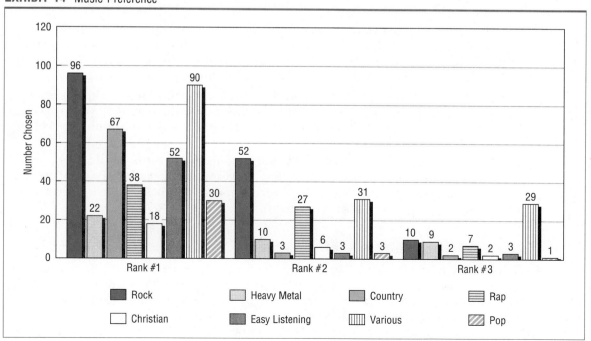

EXHIBIT 15 Market Potential Estimates

		Demographic Profile			
		Pop	**%**		
		TOTAL	100.0		
		Under 6	7.8		
		6 to 13	13.0		
		14 to 17	8.7		
		18 to 24	13.6		
		25 to 49	27.3		
		50 to 64	19.3		
		65 & over	10.3		

	Market Potential (000)	
Local	**Primary**	**Secondary**
150.0	505.1	1,080.7
11.7	39.4	84.3
19.5	65.7	140.5
13.1	43.9	94.0
20.4	68.7	147.0
40.6	137.9	295.0
29.0	97.5	208.6
15.7	52.0	111.3

The Local Market. Market potential was estimated at approximately 94,000 (ages 6 to 49). Penetration of this market in the first year of operation was projected at 30 percent with 40 percent of the "user group" indicating intentions to visit the park at least one additional time.

The Primary Market. Market potential was estimated to be approximately 315,000. Penetration of this market in the first year of operation was projected at 20 percent with 30 percent indicating intentions of repeat purchase behavior.

The Secondary Market. Market potential was estimated to be approximately 675,000. Penetration of this market in the first year of operation was projected at 10 percent with 0 percent repeat purchase behavior. Exhibit 16 shows first-year demand estimates.

PRICING STRATEGY

Kevin was unsure of his pricing structure. The team's research indicated that parks charge a broad range of prices. The large, multiattraction parks charge $20 to $30 per day. In addition, survey respondents suggested a wide range of prices. Point Mallard charges $5 for children between the ages of 5 and 13 and $7 for adults. Kevin felt that his prices should be comparable, but he also believed that the demand for recreational activities was somewhat price in-

EXHIBIT 16 Estimated Demand for the First Year (000)

	% of Demand	Local	Primary	Secondary	Total
YEARLY TOTAL	100	39.5	82.0	67.5	189.0
MONTHLY TOTALS					
MAY	10	3.95	8.2	6.75	18.9
JUNE	25	9.88	20.5	16.88	47.26
JULY	28	11.06	22.96	18.9	52.92
AUGUST	28	11.06	22.96	18.9	52.92
SEPTEMBER	9	3.56	7.4	6.08	17.04

elastic in the $8 to $12 range. Therefore, Kevin planned to charge $5 for children and $8 for adults. If demand materialized as projected, he would consider raising prices the second year to test his assumption of price inelasticity.

Kevin did not want to get heavily into promotional pricing because he was wary of his high fixed costs, and he wanted to be sure that his contribution margin would not be squeezed. However, he also recognized the need to generate initial consumer interest and thought about sponsoring several promotional programs to enhance awareness and trial, especially from the secondary market. He also thought about offering a multivisit package at a reduced price. This program would target primarily the local market.

PROMOTIONAL ISSUES

Kevin was feeling fairly comfortable with the student team's report until he came to the section that addressed the promotional issues. Together, he and the students had identified several objectives that they all felt were important to the success of the water park. They had discussed the importance of not only gaining awareness, but also creating interest and trial among the three target segments of the market if projected revenues were to be achieved.

Kevin felt confident that if people would come and experience the atmosphere and excitement of the park, they would not only return, but also spread the word to friends. Originally, Kevin had budgeted $18,000 for the April to August time frame, including a pre–Labor Day promotion.

The student team strongly recommended that Kevin increase his promotional budget by at least three or four times that amount for the first year. Because he had no advertising experience, he felt extremely uneasy about the team's recommendations in this area. He scanned the information they provided, including representative costs for newspaper ads, television and radio spots, and billboard coverage. Exhibit 17 shows some of this information.

Kevin leaned back in his chair. His feelings about this venture ran hot and cold. This was the opportunity he had been dreaming about. And yet, he felt concerned about controlling costs, especially the marketing expenses. He ran some pro formas with total first year operating expenses of approximately

EXHIBIT 17 Advertising Information

NEWSPAPERS

Splash Ads — 3 columns by 5 inches		$ 265
Daily	1/4 page	583
	1/2 page	1,167
	Full page	2,335
Sunday		
(Color-Season)	1/4 page	1,200
	1/2 page	2,000

Special Deal One

Sunday (Color-Season)	1,200
Get 1 Saturday or Monday (same ad)	500

Special Deal Two

Buy ad in Leisure	1,300
Get Showtime at ½ off	620

TELEVISION

Days	Time Period	Number of Spots
Monday—Friday	5:30 A.M. to 5:30 P.M.	34
Monday—Friday	5:30 P.M. to 10:30 P.M.	6
Monday—Friday	10:30 P.M. to 1:00 A.M.	15
Saturday and Sunday	12 noon to 6:00 P.M..	5
TOTAL (60 spots)		$3360

BILLBOARD POSTER (monthly)

100% exposure	$7,753
75% exposure	5,812
50% exposure	4,140

RADIO

WXYZ

Drive Time Rates: 30–60 second spots	$ 125 to 195
Wed–Fri: Drive time in available spots	115 to 185
Mon–Sun: 5 A.M.–8 P.M. (Station's choice)	100 to 170
Run of the Station (any spot available)	80 to 150
News Sponsorship/Traffic Report	125
Remote-Boom Box (3 hours)	1,500 to 2,200

WABC

60 sec. run-of-the-station	$ 26
30 sec. run-of-the-station	21
60 sec. you pick the time	29
30 sec. you pick the time	23
Remote Broadcast	950
News sponsorship	29

$700,000. Based on his demand estimates, it looked as though the business would be able to reach the break-even point within one to two years. Exhibits 18 through 20 identify first year pro formas for the March through February time frame.

Even with these fairly optimistic pro formas, Kevin felt uncomfortable. He looked over the estimated demand and wondered if he would be able to defend those forecasts when he presented them in his business plan. After checking his financial projections, Kevin believed he would be able to withstand operating losses of two times his projected operating expenses or approximately $1.4 million. If this were to occur, his contingency plan would be to delay construction of Phases II and III until the financial picture became more profitable.

He stared at the pages of the document and his own calculations long into the night. After all, he was a risk taker and the opportunity looked feasible. "Nothing ventured, nothing gained," he thought to himself as he dozed off to sleep.

SOURCE: This case was prepared by Professor Kenneth J. Burger, The University of Alabama in Huntsville and Professor Craig Tunwall, Ithaca College. Used by permission.

SOURCE: [1]Based on the 1980 Alabama Census of Population and Profiles and an updated 1989 projection.

EXHIBIT 18 Income Statement: Aquapark

	3/9X	4/9X	5/9X	6/9X	7/9X	8/9X	9/9X	10/9X	11/9X	12/9X	1/9X	2/9X
Net Revenues	$ 0	$ 0	$135,000	$315,000	$375,000	$375,000	$120,000	$ 0	$ 0	$ 0	$ 0	$ 0
Cost of Sales	0	0	40,500	94,500	112,500	112,500	36,000	0	0	0	0	0
Gross Profit	0	0	94,500	220,500	262,500	262,500	84,000	0	0	0	0	0
Operating Expenses:												
Salary and wages												
Salaries	7,000	10,000	38,020	50,890	50,890	50,890	12,852	10,000	10,000	10,000	10,000	10,000
Payroll taxes and benefits	2,450	3,500	13,307	17,812	17,812	4,498	3,500	3,500	3,500	3,500	3,500	3,500
Occupancy expenses												
Insurance casualty	3,500	3,500	3,500	3,500	3,500	3,500	3,500	3,500	3,500	3,500	3,500	3,500
Utilities	1,000	2,000	5,000	5,000	5,000	5,000	2,000	500	300	300	300	300
Rent	0	0	0	0	0	0	0	0	0	0	0	0
Repairs and maintenance	1,000	2,000	2,000	2,000	2,000	2,000	1,000	500	500	500	500	500
Operational expenses												
Advertising and promotion	0	5,000	6,000	2,000	2,000	3,000	0	0	0	0	0	0
Depreciation	50,833	50,833	50,833	50,833	50,833	50,833	50,833	50,833	50,833	50,833	50,833	50,833
Office expense	500	200	200	200	200	200	200	100	100	100	100	100
Professional fees	300	100	250	250	250	250	250	250	250	500	250	250
Stationery and printing	300	100	100	100	100	100	100	100	100	100	100	100
Telephone	300	200	200	200	200	200	200	150	150	150	150	150
Other 1	0	0	0	0	0	0	0	0	0	0	0	0
Other 2	0	0	0	0	0	0	0	0	0	0	0	0
Other 3	0	0	0	0	0	0	0	0	0	0	0	0
Total operating expenses	67,183	77,433	119,410	132,785	132,785	120,471	74,435	69,433	69,233	69,483	69,233	69,233
Operating Profit (Loss)	(67,183)	(77,433)	(24,910)	87,715	129,715	142,029	9,565	(69,433)	(69,233)	(69,483)	(69,233)	(69,233)
Interest Expense	12,338	12,290	12,242	12,193	12,144	12,094	12,043	11,992	11,941	11,888	11,835	11,782
Net Income (Loss)	$(79,521)	$(89,723)	$(37,152)	$ 75,522	$117,572	$129,935	$ (2,478)	$(81,425)	$(81,174)	$(81,371)	$(81,069)	$(81,015)

EXHIBIT 19 Balance Sheet: Aquapark

	3/9X	4/9X	5/9X	6/9X	7/9X	8/9X	9/9X	10/9X	11/9X	12/9X	1/9X	2/9X
Assets												
Current Assets:												
Cash and equivalents	$ 167,231	$ 124,211	$ 133,715	$ 255,844	$ 419,973	$ 583,102	$ 626,082	$ 591,063	$ 556,243	$ 521,174	$ 486,355	$ 451,535
Accounts receivable, net	0	0	0	0	0	0	0	0	0	0	0	0
Other current assets	0	0	0	0	0	0	0	0	0	0	0	0
Total current assets	167,231	124,211	133,715	255,844	419,973	583,102	626,082	591,063	556,243	521,174	486,355	451,535
Property and equipment, net												
Property and equipment, cost	3,600,000	3,600,000	3,600,000	3,600,000	3,600,000	3,600,000	3,600,000	3,600,000	3,600,000	3,600,000	3,600,000	3,600,000
Less: Accumulated depreciation	50,833	101,667	152,500	203,333	254,167	305,000	355,833	406,667	457,500	508,333	559,167	610,000
Total property and equipment, net	3,549,167	3,498,333	3,447,500	3,396,667	3,345,833	3,295,000	3,244,167	3,193,333	3,142,500	3,091,667	3,040,833	2,990,000
Other Assets	0	0	0	0	0	0	0	0	0	0	0	0
Total Assets	$3,716,398	$3,622,544	$3,581,215	$3,652,511	$3,765,806	$3,878,102	$3,870,249	$3,784,396	$3,698,743	$3,612,841	$3,527,188	$3,441,535
Liabilities and Stockholders' Equity												
Current Liabilities:												
Accounts payable	$ 0	$ 0	$ 0	$ 0	$ 0	$ 0	$ 0	$ 0	$ 0	$ 0	$ 0	$ 0
Current portion of long-term debt	7,500	7,500	7,500	7,500	7,500	7,500	7,500	7,500	7,500	7,500	7,500	7,500
Accrued expenses	0	0	0	0	0	0	0	0	0	0	0	0
Total current liabilities	7,500	7,500	7,500	7,500	7,500	7,500	7,500	7,500	7,500	7,500	7,500	7,500
Long-term debt	1,045,918	1,041,798	1,037,611	1,033,384	1,029,109	1,024,783	1,020,407	1,015,980	1,011,501	1,006,970	1,002,386	997,748
Stockholders' Equity:												
Contributed capital	2,742,500	2,742,500	2,742,500	2,742,500	2,742,500	2,742,500	2,742,500	2,742,500	2,742,500	2,742,500	2,742,500	2,742,500
Retained earnings (deficit)	0	0	0	0	0	0	0	0	0	0	0	0
Current earnings (deficit)	(79,521)	(169,244)	(206,396)	(130,874)	(13,302)	103,319	99,842	18,417	(62,757)	(144,129)	(225,198)	(306,213)
Total stockholders' equity	2,662,979	2,573,256	2,536,104	2,611,626	2,729,198	2,845,819	2,842,342	2,760,917	2,679,743	2,598,371	2,517,302	2,426,287
Total liabilities and equity	$3,716,397	$3,622,554	$3,581,215	$3,652,510	$3,765,807	$3,878,102	$3,870,249	$3,784,397	$3,698,744	$3,612,841	$3,527,188	$3,441,535
Does the Balance Sheet balance?	YES	YES	YES	YES	YES	YES	YES	YES	YES	YES	YES	YES

EXHIBIT 20 Cash Flow Statement: Aquapark

	3/9X	4/9X	5/9X	6/9X	7/9X	8/9X	9/9X	10/9X	11/9X	12/9X	1/9X	2/9X
Cash Received (Inflows)												
Receivables collected:												
Base period accounts receivable collected	$ 0	$ 0	$ 0	$ 0	$ 0	$ 0	$ 0	$ 0	$ 0	$ 0	$ 0	$ 0
Period revenues collected	0	0	135,000	315,000	375,000	375,000	120,000	0	0	0	0	0
Total cash receipts	0	0	135,000	315,000	375,000	375,000	120,000	0	0	0	0	0
Cash Disbursed (Outflows)												
Base period accounts payable paid	0	0	0	0	0	0	0	0	0	0	0	0
Period expenses paid	6,900	13,100	57,750	107,750	125,750	126,750	43,250	5,100	4,900	5,150	4,900	4,900
Salaries and wages paid	9,450	13,500	51,327	68,702	68,702	68,702	17,350	13,500	13,500	13,500	13,500	13,500
Total cash disbursements	16,350	26,600	109,077	176,452	194,452	195,452	60,600	18,600	18,400	18,650	18,400	18,400
Operating Cash Surplus (Deficit)	(16,350)	(26,600)	25,923	138,548	180,548	179,548	59,400	(18,600)	(18,400)	(18,650)	(18,400)	(18,400)
Less: Notes Payable Interest Payments	12,338	12,290	12,242	12,193	12,144	12,094	12,043	11,992	11,941	11,888	11,835	11,782
Less: Notes Payable Principal Payments	4,082	4,130	4,178	4,226	4,276	4,326	4,376	4,427	4,479	4,531	4,584	4,637
Add: Beginning of Month Cash Balance	200,000	167,230	124,210	133,713	255,842	419,970	583,098	626,079	591,060	556,240	521,171	486,352
Cash Balance Before Funding	$167,230	$124,210	$133,713	$255,842	$419,970	$583,098	$626,079	$591,060	$556,240	$521,171	$486,352	$451,533
Additional Funding												
New equity	0	0	0	0	0	0	0	0	0	0	0	0
New debt (notes payable)	0	0	0	0	0	0	0	0	0	0	0	0
Ending Cash Balance	$167,230	$124,210	$133,713	$255,842	$419,970	$583,098	$626,079	$591,060	$556,240	$521,171	$486,352	$451,533

3 Krueper Engineering & Associates, Inc.

In 1965 Harry Krueper and Robert Weddle founded Krueper (pronounce like "Creeper") Engineering and Associates, Inc. Due to family constraints, Robert Weddle did not remain in the business for long. Harry Krueper continued, and like many entrepreneurs had financial problems in the firm's early days. Later as the reputation of Krueper Engineering widened, the company began to thrive. The number of employees rose from about six individuals in 1972 to the current number of forty-three in 1988. The company has been in its present physical facility since 1972.

Krueper Engineering and Associates specializes in six specific types of consulting studies: land development, urban planning, land surveying, civil engineering, accident evaluation, and traffic engineering. Local or state agencies are about 30 percent of their clients with developers, insurance companies, and attorneys as the rest.

The firm does no advertising. Yet, client growth is constant. Harry Krueper attributes demand for land analysis studies to the rapid expansion in the Inland Empire of Southern California. Others within the company attribute Krueper Engineering's growth to the outstanding reputation of Harry Krueper.

According to Harry Krueper, the most pressing issue facing his firm is the computerization of the accident reconstruction industry. Computers are revolutionizing the way his business operates. Some equipment (both hardware and software) was less than eight months old in 1988. Harry Krueper states that he is less enamored with computers than some of his employees, but he realizes that he must computerize his business to stay competitive.

An underlying, but equally important, issue is the management of growth, and Krueper's future as a sole proprietorship. Harry Krueper, as the company's only registered traffic engineer, provides 95 percent of the firm's expert testimony in court cases. Every traffic accident study must have his final approval. According to some employees, Krueper Engineering needs more people capable of delivering expert testimony in court for two reasons. The first reason is to grow larger and the second is to have better control over the firm's backlog of accident reconstruction reports. "We have real growing pains," expressed one member of the company.

COMPANY HISTORY

A framed newspaper clipping hangs in the reception hall at the present location announcing the original formation of Krueper Engineering in 1965. At that time, Harry Krueper joined surveyor Robert Weddle to open an office specializing in traffic engineering and land design. When the firm started, Harry Krueper was a Cal Poly Pomona engineering professor.

In the beginning, Krueper Engineering had the usual difficulties of an infant company trying to establish itself in a traditional market. This occurred in both time and money. Harry Krueper's first obligation was to his teaching job in Pomona. Thus he devoted only part of his time to the company. Then in 1968 a geographical change caused additional strain within the firm. Weddle had moved to Apple Valley. This meant the two partners commuted about 40 miles one way to provide their professional talent to each other.

Thus, to help the firm, Harry Krueper ended his teaching duties in 1970 to work full time in the company. However, the geographical separation of the two partners continued to place pressure on the company. Finally in 1974, the partnership ended. Harry Krueper hired Carson Storer, a surveyor living in San Bernardino, to replace Robert Weddle.

After 1970, the firm grew constantly as a result of the increased importance of traffic planning and accident reconstruction, concepts of intensifying legal complexity. Many cities and public entities recognized the significance of traffic planning for reducing potential liability. New clients in Southern California and other western states spurred the enlargement of Krueper Engineering.

The firm earned a solid reputation for thoroughness in accident reconstruction and report preparation of a very high ethical standard. Krueper Engineering would not prepare a report that intentionally favored a client. The firm would present only the engineering facts, and these would be very carefully double-checked. Harry Krueper established himself as an expert witness in court testimony and cross-examination. By 1988, accident reconstruction generated 50 percent of the annual work load handled by the firm with the balance in land development studies, and so on. Harry Krueper currently holds engineering licenses in Arizona, California, Oregon, and Nevada.

COMPANY MISSION

One employee when asked to define the mission of Krueper Engineering stated: "to provide the best service to our clients. That's it." Another person remarked, "I don't think where we are today was ever planned. I don't think any of us really wanted to reach this point." A 1985 brochure puts the mission this way:

> "Krueper Engineering is devoted to seeking the optimal balance between the needs of the human systems. This is achieved through creating innovative designs, as well as efficient solutions.
>
> "Krueper Engineering has proven its proficiency in dealing with today's complex problems by providing dedicated, specialized assistance in over forty-five hundred jobs for over two thousand separate clients in both the public and the private sector. With these requirements in mind, Krueper Engineering looks for the best people, then turns them loose on tough problems. They keep coming up with solutions that work.
>
> "Krueper Engineering's family begins with a staff of over forty, employing professional civil engineers, land surveyors, traffic engineers, and land planners. It is further diversified with highly qualified associates in structural engineering, geology/oils engineering, architecture, landscape architecture, photogrammetry, and other related areas. Together, they are capable of handling the widest possible range of client requests.
>
> "With today's constantly changing social, economic, and physical environment, the primary objective of Krueper Engineering is to keep pace with these changes; thereby, achieving our goal of providing our clients with optimal solutions in their best interest, as well as promoting the public's health, safety, and welfare.
>
> "Krueper Engineering has the capabilities to complete large-scale projects; however, it is the objective of this company to ensure that every client, regardless of the size of the project, receives attention and services on a personal, one-to-one basis."

Yet when asked to state a major objective of Krueper Engineering for five years hence, one person said, "to keep Harry Krueper alive."

ORGANIZATIONAL STRUCTURE

As the decade changed into the eighties, continued growth of Krueper engineering caused problems in its structure and coordination. In 1987, Krueper Engineering decided to examine its organization structure. This led to the development of a formal organization chart that showed the flow of authority. As shown in Exhibit 1, Harry Krueper is president and principal engineer. Carson Storer holds the second position of command as vice-president and principal surveyor. The remaining personnel are under six departments: engineering, land development, accident evaluation, planning, secretarial, and bookkeeping. The first three functions contain the technical areas, and the latter three provide support services to the firm.

Two individuals represent the engineering department, which specializes in designs of subdivisions, sewers, and traffic systems. Fred Babbitt, a registered civil engineer, first became acquainted with Harry Krueper in 1970 while

EXHIBIT 1 Organization Chart

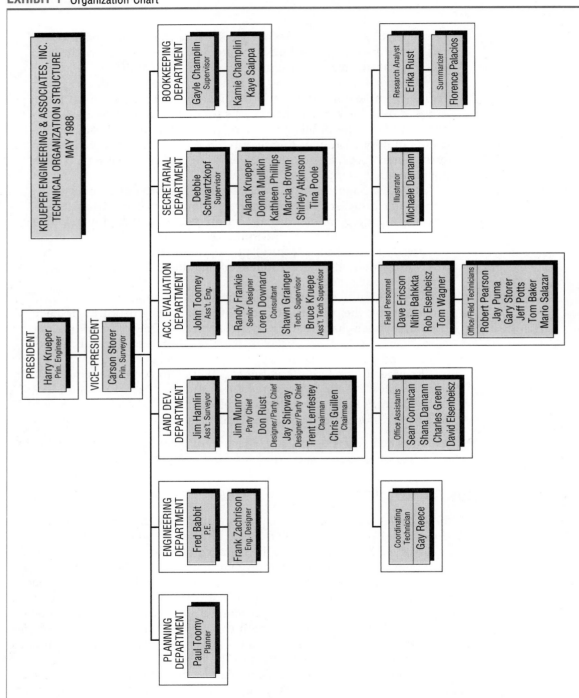

working as systems analyst. After securing a civil engineering degree from Cal Poly Pomona in 1972, Babbitt began working full time for Krueper. He has remained in his position as project manager. He enjoys the freedom and flexibility of a smaller firm.

Originally, accident reconstruction used the services of the engineering department. As the work load of accident reconstruction increased, the latter became its own department with its own people. Engineering then returned to its more traditional types of civil engineering projects.

Vice-president Carson Storer heads the land development department. He has one assistant surveyor and field crew of five. Their surveying work concentrates on land use planning as well as the parcel map development for new subdivisions. Krueper Engineering no longer performs soil engineering due to the high level of specialization needed in this field.

The land development and accident reconstruction functions of Krueper remain separate entities with independent support staffs. Harry Krueper heads the accident reconstruction function as its chief principal civil and traffic engineer. John Toomey, an assistant engineer, coordinates the department's staff in gathering and condensing all the information required in each report. The division includes twenty-three other employees responsible for completing all phases required in the preparation of a complete legal engineering document.

Toomey's supervisory responsibilities include technical and design supervision. He also supervises office technicians, office assistants, field crews, draftsmen, an illustrator (artist), a deposition researcher, and a summarizer. Recently, Toomey has delegated much of his field and office supervisory duties to Shawn Grainger, a technical supervisor. This allows him more time to coordinate each final accident reconstruction presentation with Harry Krueper, Randy Frankie, and Loren Downard. Randy Frankie is a senior designer and Loren Downard is a traffic consultant.

The support functions of planning, secretarial, and bookkeeping have faced many challenges keeping up with the constant growth of Krueper Engineering. For example, Gayle Champlin, supervisor of bookkeeping, noted that annual billings amounted to about $1.75 million in 1987 compared with $200,000 in 1973. Champlin has been responsible for changing the initial accounting methods. The original simple bookkeeping procedures have been changed to a computerized system of tracing payments and balances.

INDUSTRY

Even though Krueper Engineering provides six types of consulting studies, basically it has only two primary markets. One market is accident evaluation; a second market is civil engineering services. In the former, there is a consensus within the company that Krueper Engineering is unique. There are probably only four or five companies within the western states capable of providing accident reconstruction work and only one—Krueper Engineering—that provides so complete an analysis. One individual stated that Krueper Engineering is number one in sales for this area.

On the other hand, the civil engineering market is very competitive. There are over one hundred firms capable of doing studies similar to Krueper Engineering. Land planning, land development, urban planning, and land surveying are interrelated. Also a problem occurs because the law states engineers and land surveyors cannot advertise. Thus, Krueper Engineering only lists its name in the yellow pages of the phone book.

ACCIDENT RECONSTRUCTION

Accident reconstruction (the largest department with twenty-three people) is the heart of the company. The firm receives all its business through word of mouth built on the twenty-plus-year reputation of Harry Krueper. All employees agreed Krueper Engineering attains more business in this area than they can handle. Clients, mostly attorneys and insurance agents, will call Krueper Engineering and seek an opinion about possible liability after an accident has occurred. Krueper Engineering does a complete study of the accident site including detailed drawings and analysis. These accidents usually involve some combination of automobiles, trucks, mopeds, and pedestrians. On a rare occasion, Krueper may cover the unusual accident such as when a customer slips and falls in a client's location. When a client calls in Krueper Engineering, the problem invariably concerns a very serious injury with medical complications.

In terms of overall causes of accidents, "driver inattention is probably one of the biggest factors in traffic accidents," states Harry Krueper. The other two major factors are road conditions and the vehicle involved.

Krueper Engineering actually goes on-site to the physical location where field employees take various measurements. Because safety of the field crew is a number-one concern, Krueper Engineering provides their personnel with orange vests, safety cones, and signs. In sixteen years of roadwork, Krueper Engineering reports no accidents involving their personnel.

Attention to safety can be especially important because night work is particularly hazardous. An accident that occurred at night must be analyzed under similar circumstances. Lights are checked according to city and county standards. Krueper Engineering measures the lights' high and low values. To get those values, personnel have to stand in the road under darkness conditions. Sometimes, they have to bend down to do work at ground level. On roads with heavy traffic, such measurements can possibly be quite dangerous. At least once a year, the issue of hazard pay arises from the field personnel. This is because Krueper has no special issue compensation called "hazard pay." However, Carson Storer did not feel this was a significant issue. At most only six people go out into the field.

LAND DEVELOPMENT

Krueper Engineering performs every type of lot survey from a single unit to a 200 industrial lot survey. If a developer has a 40-acre lot and wants to put ten lots on it, Krueper Engineering could provide the land planning and layout.

This would involve streets, grading, water, and sewer plans. The major clients are developers, real estate agents, and individual property owners. Competitors vary in size. Some are one-person firms; others may have fourteen or fifteen engineers. Krueper Engineering considers itself as a medium-size firm to offer land development services.

One major past project encompassed the mapping and parceling of the land when Kaiser Steel went bankrupt. Another project included a parcel of 218 acres being developed into an industrial park.

Carson Storer stated that land development once generated about 50 percent of Krueper Engineering's revenue. Now, this area generates roughly 30 percent. He personally would like to see this area generate 50 percent of the revenue again. He feels land development could handle more work.

STRESS AND WORK OVERLOAD

Employee stress and work overload is a major issue at Krueper Engineering. More than one individual stated they have more work than they can handle. About one-third of the accident reconstruction reports have missed their due date because all the work cannot be completed on time. Frequently, a client will wait nine months to one year to receive a report. Some clients have taken up the strategy of calling once every two weeks to be sure their reports are given attention. Krueper Engineering has a backlog of six months in accident reconstruction. Carson Storer indicated the "ideal" backlog would be one month for an accident reconstruction.

Part of the problem is a function of the personality of Harry Krueper. One employee stated that Harry Krueper "doesn't have *no* in his vocabulary." Attorneys, for example, know if they call on Sunday, Harry Krueper will accept the job if he answers the phone. On the other hand, Harry Krueper commented the firm does turn work down. He refuses to accept business from lawyers he considers unethical. However, he feels that about 70 percent of the lawyers are honest and ethical. Harry Krueper rarely turns down long-time clients. Krueper Engineering accepts about 85 percent of the inquiries into its firm.

PERSONNEL PRACTICES

Krueper Engineering offers a generous benefit package. This includes full medical coverage, life insurance, profit sharing, four-week annual vacation allowances for long-term employees, sick leave, holidays, flexible work hours, pregnancy leave, and travel expenses. Employees work four ten-hour days, and many employees have been with the company for more than five years.

The firm schedules numerous company activities throughout the year to encourage the sense of belonging. Past outings have included golf tournaments, ski trips, picnics, camping trips, and Christmas parties. Carson Storer mentioned that these group activities have built the company's dedication and tenacity. This helps the company succeed and has pulled Krueper through difficult periods in the past.

Raises are based on a performance evaluation. A new employee will be on probation for three months. Wages are hourly, and a new person would probably start at $6 per hour. After three months, he or she could be earning $7 per hour and after five years, around $10 to $12 per hr. One individual implied that wages at Krueper Engineering were better than average for comparable jobs elsewhere.

Also everyone receives a raise if the company is doing well. For example, Krueper Engineering gave two across-the-board raises in 1988. Due to the financial health of the company, Krueper issued one raise in January and another one in September. Employee turnover is greater than Krueper Engineering would like, but lower than companies of comparable size.

ORGANIZATIONAL CULTURE

The atmosphere of Krueper Engineering revolves around the tone set by Harry Krueper. He is the firm's only stockholder. He appears to make a concerted effort to create a family-type atmosphere.

Krueper Engineering faces many interpersonal challenges similar to small firms as they grow. One revolves around Harry Krueper who wants to keep the high-quality image by which Krueper Engineering is known. However, he also cannot relinquish control. Employees describe Harry Krueper as "a brilliant and ethical man of very high integrity," who also has compassion for his clients. He wants to charge very reasonable fees so the average person can afford his product. One board member stated Krueper could easily double its reports accessible to the average person. Another person described Harry Krueper as a minimalist or someone who wants or needs very little. The casewriter noted a deep respect for Harry Krueper throughout the company.

Yet frustration appears to exist under the surface. With fifteen employees, each felt they could have a special place with Harry Krueper, and they did. With forty-three employees, such is not the case. Harry Krueper is frequently out of the office testifying for various cases as he is the firm's only expert witness. He relies on the reports produced by the firm, which he personally wants to review and supervise. He has not been able to relinquish control especially in the accident reconstruction area. Sometimes he has overruled or undermined decisions of his managers and department heads. He has also accepted client work later when others in the firm originally turned the work down. One individual described Harry Krueper as a workaholic.

The responsibility for handling the day-to-day organizational climate rests with Carson Storer, appointed chief of personnel. He finds about 75 percent of his time spent in resolving personnel conflicts or promoting goodwill throughout the company. To illustrate, a recent incident of the company's soda fund provides a sign of how personnel issues consume his time. An issue arose because individuals taking soda cans from the refrigerator were not properly repaying the soda fund.

Two employees implied that acclimating to the structure of office politics was far more difficult for them than performing their duties. One mentioned that in 1987 a real morale problem existed. People felt that the lines of command were unclear. Everyone thought he or she should report to Harry Krueper directly. This uneasiness lead directly to the new organization chart (Exhibit 1) instituted in May of 1988.

FINANCES AT KRUEPER ENGINEERING

By 1987 Krueper Engineering had seven main sources of revenues. Revenues show a constant upward trend except for the year of 1980. Because Krueper Engineering sells a service, the firm has also developed a standard rate schedule (see to Exhibits 2 and 3).

The net income for 1987 was $219,068 on a total sales of $1,781,701 for a net profit of 12.3 percent. The firm is essentially debt free. Krueper Engineering owns the two-story building where it is located.

COMPUTERIZATION AT KRUEPER

Accident computerization is a major concern faced by Harry Krueper as he testifies in court. Drawings done on the computer have become increasingly important, and attorneys expect Harry Krueper to be knowledgeable in this area.

Bookkeeping has already been computerized by the use of PCs, which are networked together. The other half of the firm, engineering, has its own network system, which is 80 percent complete. Computerizing Krueper Engineering has taken longer than expected. The firm spent over $70,000 in 1987 for computers, and the firm decided to do its own customized programs. Some wonder how much longer it will take to finish the job. Paul Toomey, who spearheaded the computerization, wonders if the firm could have approached the computerization project in a different manner. Harry Krueper wonders: how far should they let the computer do the work? He expressed much less faith in the computer than some others in the firm. "I have much more faith in people," he added. It is a continual test for him to see which is the more dependable and more accurate: people or the computer.

Krueper Engineering stores its case files on floppy disks. One employee noted that if a fire were to destroy the building, the firm would not have the means of reconstructing their records.

PLANNING AT KRUEPER

Staff and the board of directors develop the policies and procedures for the firm through meetings, which are fairly spontaneous. Because all board members are also employees, Harry Krueper will just call those individuals into his office if a major decision needs to be made. Staff meetings are usually held twice a month, and may last one to two hours. Discussions focus on office activities, new ideas, personnel, or operations problems. Lately, discussions have focused on the implementation of the computer system.

EXHIBIT 2 Billing Analysis

Krueper Engineering & Associates, Inc.
Billing Analysis
January 1, 1978 — September 30, 1987

	12 MONTHS ENDING 12-31-78	12 MONTHS ENDING 12-31-79	3 MONTHS ENDING 3-31-80	6 MONTHS ENDING 9-30-80	12 MONTHS ENDING 9-30-81	12 MONTHS ENDING 9-30-82	12 MONTHS ENDING 9-30-83	12 MONTHS ENDING 9-30-84	12 MONTHS ENDING 9-30-85	12 MONTHS ENDING 9-30-86	12 MONTHS ENDING 9-30-87
Accident studies	$135,178	$190,623	$ 65,225	$165,088	$332,270	$472,165	$614,868	$665,453	$ 702,009	$1,038,538	$1,160,275
Land development	114,305	106,682	37,666	55,819	189,225	99,580	107,612	91,111	141,901	186,677	332,130
Survey/staking	74,759	73,829	26,389	55,029	77,581	51,130	36,189	65,276	114,143	80,949	205,941
Traffic studies	20,432	33,369	13,009	14,976	10,346	22,221	22,814	6,405	25,800	7,121	2,442
Architectural plans	11,902					30,975			1,769		
Structural analysis evaluation	13,310	7,018	1,254	6,322			5,425	9,330	14,744	18,534	
Traffic design	10,259	10,382	8,116	3,323	5,511	3,561	245	24,347	22,973		7,176
Sewer/water	6,748	20,344	3,161	5,358	5,732	2,426	2,480	2,615	6,943	12,063	31,533
Construction inspection	5,075			788							
Percolation test sewer inspection	1,193										
Miscellaneous	907	2,797	282	1,025	5,018	5,539	868	60	149	1,125	
Drainage study		21,219	6,930	10,330	11,104	5,966	1,728	14,780	7,231	6,449	18,778
Urban planning									2,339	10,654	
Annual total	$394,068	$466,263	$162,032	$318,058	$636,787	$693,563	$792,229	$879,377	$1,040,001	$1,362,110	$1,758,275

EXHIBIT 3 Krueper Engineering Standard Rate Schedule

Job Code	Job Description	Regular Hourly Rate
OAT	Principal Engineer—Planning Comm./Council Mtg.	$ 96.00
OCT	Principal Engineer—Court/Arbitration Appearance	$ 96.00
ODT	Principal Engineer—Deposition**	$88/132.00
1A	Registered Engineer—Consulting	$ 80.00
1B	Registered Engineer—Design/Calculations	$ 68.00
2A	Staff Engineer—Consultation/Design/Report	$ 56.00
2B	Staff Engineer—Support Consultation	$ 48.00
2L	Licensed Land Surveyor—Consultation/Calculations	$ 48.00
2P	Staff Planner—Consultation/Design	$ 40.00
2R	Research/Investigation	$ 36.00
2S	Staff Planner—Support Services	$ 32.00
3A	Design Drafting	$ 40.00
3B	Delineation	$ 32.00
3C	Drafting Support Services	$ 20.00
3D	Model Making	$ 20.00
4A	Principal Engineer—Site Inspection	$ 80.00
4B	Engineer/Planner—Site Inspection	$ 48.00
4C	Assistant Site Inspection	$ 32.00
5A	2 Man Survey Crew	$ 88.00
5B	2 Man Field Crew	$ 68.00
6A	3 Man Survey Crew	$ 100.00
6B	3 Man Field Crew	$ 88.00
7A	Clerical Services	$ 20.00
7B	Clerical Support Services	$ 16.00
9MR	Mileage	$ 0.30
9MS	Mileage—Survey Truck	$ 0.40
9T1	Travel Time—Principal Engineer	$ 52.00
9T2	Travel Time—2 Man Crew	$ 48.00
9T3	Travel Time—3 Man Crew	$ 60.00
9T4	Travel Time—Engineer/Surveyor/Planner	$ 36.00
9T5	Travel Time—Technician	$ 20.00
Exp	Expenses	Cost + 10%

**   First 3 hours @ $88/hr., $132/hr. for each hour or portion thereafter.

Attachment( )   Rev. 10/85

Sitting on the current board of directors are Harry Krueper, Carson Storer, Fred Babbitt, John Toomey, Paul Toomey, and Jim Hamlin, all insiders. Board meetings are short. Members do not get involved in setting objectives or goals. The idea of having an outsider member has not yet been considered. Occasionally though, an accountant or an attorney will attend a board meeting in an advisory capacity.

EXHIBIT 4 Operating Expenses

Krueper Engineering & Associates, Inc.
Operating Expenses
September 30, 1987

Subcontracts	55,829
Field supplies	6,210
Repair & maintenance, field equipment	1,528
Drafting supplies	25,073
Photographs and reproductions	16,219
Telephone	21,104
Advertising	15,686
Equipment rental	1,000
Travel expenses	27,146
Entertainment	5,192
Filing and recording fees	1,149
Payroll service expense	894
Salary expense	704,910
Officer salary expense	196,742
Payroll taxes	69,968
Computer software	15,969
Office supplies	27,553
Repair & maintenance, office equipment	7,209
Repair & maintenance, vehicles	8,913
Gasoline, oil & service—vehicles	7,767
Depreciation expense	56,373
Copy machine and supplies	34,030
Licenses, DMV and business	6,764
Contributions	1,840
Education, publications and dues	3,900
Insurance—General	54,177
Insurance—Employee	37,175
Interest and bank charges	3,166
Professional fees	5,168
Rent	85,875
Miscellaneous	6,784
State income tax	200
Subtotal Operating Expenses (Cash Basis)	1,511,513
A/C Payable / Quarterly Taxes	1,000
Less Estimated A/C Payable 09/30/86	−8,500
Salary Accrual (1 Week)	12,000
Less Estimated Payroll 9/30/86	−14,250
Total Operating Expenses	1,501,763

Physical Resources

Krueper Engineering is located on the entire second floor of a small two-story office building in San Bernardino, California. It also has four offices on the first floor of the same building. Remodeled in 1986, the Krueper Engineering suite is organized according to its six departments. Clerical functions appear off the left-hand corridor and technical functions off the right-hand side from the reception area.

EXHIBIT 5 Balance Sheet

Krueper Engineering & Associates, Inc. Balance Sheet September 30, 1987		
	Cash Basis	Accrual Basis
CURRENT ASSETS		
Cash in banks	38,945	38,945
Prepaid interest	2,555	2,555
Other receivables	1,200	1,200
Suspense—Refund due client	<308>	<308>
A/C receivable (Net)		438,459
Notes receivable (Net)		36,286
Work in process (70%)		208,486
Total Current Assets	42,392	725,623
FIXED ASSETS		
Furniture and equipment	209,030	209,030
Automobiles and trucks	69,674	69,674
Less accumulated depreciation	<184,406>	<184,406>
Microfiche library	912	912
Deposits held	<11,640>	<11,640>
Total Fixed Assets	83,570	83,570
TOTAL ASSETS	125,962	809,193
LIABILITIES		
American Ntl. Bank (Auto)	3,714	3,714
Telephone lease payable	6,568	6,568
American Ntl. Bank (Equipment)	3,941	3,941
A M C payable (Auto)	6,896	6,896
A/C payable / taxes		1,000
Payroll payable (1 Week)		12,000
Total Liabilities	21,119	34,119
CAPITAL STOCK		
Capital stock issued 4,1,80	11,000	11,000
Retained earnings	70,687	388,894
Profit (Loss) to date	23,156	219,068
Additional capital stock (1)		156,112
Total Capital	104,843	775,074
TOTAL LIABILITIES & CAPITAL	125,962	809,193

In the middle between the two long passageways are conference rooms where staff can meet with customers. Three short hallways connect these two corridors. In these hallways are closets containing technical manuals used for more day-to-day operations. At the back of the suite is a large combination library-conference room with an adjoining outside deck with patio chairs. The patio overlooks a parking lot in San Bernardino.

All the offices have light blue walls and blue carpeting. Most people have either plants or pictures or both. There is also an assortment of drafting tables, computers, and specialized equipment. Picture collages of the employees from various picnics and golfing events hang on the walls of the reception area and the corridors. Harry Krueper stated he wants the atmosphere to seem informal.

Harry Krueper expressed no problems with the firm's physical ability to expand. When the opportunity presented itself in 1974, Harry Krueper bought the building. The downstairs area of his building houses the offices of various community organizations. These include the League of Women Voters, San Bernardino Police Officers' Association, Legal Specialists of Smith & Peckben, Att'y, U.S. Railroad Retirement Board, the Sierra Club, and a local driving school.

FUTURE OF KRUEPER ENGINEERING

One recurring concern shared by the employees is the issue of the firm's future without Harry Krueper. Because the firm has been unable to train a suitable successor, the loss of Harry Krueper would deprive the accident reconstruction team of its only expert witness. Some fear the pressure of a constant and excessive work load may eventually lead to Harry Krueper's retirement. The employees do not want the firm to cease operation in his absence. Although it is not a widely known fact within the company, Harry Krueper does carry "key man" insurance.

Harry Krueper has also been described as a perfectionist and to date his standards are so exacting that a successor has not yet been trained. Yet Harry Krueper said that he would like to have sixty people in the company within three years. He also hopes to have others do courtroom testifying, and he would like to hire an administrative manager within the next year. He would like to get more into research and be able to offer seminars in traffic accident investigation.

> "I never thought we would be as large as we are. We have 44 people now. I set initially a goal not to go over about 30, but the pressure of the needs of the engineering field are constantly expanding so you have to expand with them or you are lost. So you have to grow, but in a controlled manner . . . it's a lot different handling five people than 15. The ability to get someone under you to assist you to break this pyramid [is important] . . . I am now desperately looking for someone else to do [courtroom testifying] with me but very few want that kind of stress of going into court and fighting with the attorneys . . . There are people here who will do it but I don't want to force anybody into doing it . . . They would rather not get into that controversial area . . . but I do take staff people with me to court."

At this point, Harry Krueper wonders: what is the best way to proceed? Should he try to promote someone from within to be an administrative manager? Should he ask Carson Storer to do this? If he does get into presenting seminars, how often and how many should he give? He has not raised his rates in three years, should he do it now? How can he best protect his computer system? Should he store some records off-site? If yes, which ones? Finally, all his people seem to be technicians. How can he develop them as managers? Who should be on his management team?

SOURCE: This case prepared by Sue Greenfeld, California State University, San Bernardino. Distributed by the North American Case Research Association. Used by permission.

4 APA PUBLICATIONS

Hans Hoefer has guided his company from a fledgling venture started in 1971 with one travel guide to a multiproduct corporation with nearly 150 titles and other related products. Building and managing APA Publications has been enjoyable and profitable for Hans Hoefer, but now he needs to develop strategies for the next five years. He could continue to diversify APA's product line, prospect for attractive acquisition targets, take the company public, or sell APA Publications to a larger publisher or travel-related company. Hans knows that the final option, continuing business as usual, is also a viable option because his company has been so successful for the past twenty years.

HISTORY OF APA PUBLICATIONS

This company, like so many founded by entrepreneurs, came into being because of one person's desire to convert a hobby into an income-producing business. The new company's first product, a travel guide about Bali, was very successful and gave Hans Hoefer the confidence to create travel guides about other countries. His guides were originally written about Asian countries, but after a decade of existence APA Publications began producing books about European and American countries.

Hans Hoefer

Hans Hoefer was born near Stuttgart, Germany, in 1943. Upon completion of high school in 1959, he began an apprenticeship in printing and typesetting at a publishing house in Krefeld. By 1963 he had completed his apprenticeship and had earned a master's degree in printing. The same year, Hans entered the Fachhochschlue fuer Design (Technical University for Graphic Design) in Krefeld, which espoused the Bauhaus principle of "form follows function." He specialized in graphic design, photography, graphic printing techniques, and art history. During his stay at the university, Hans won three national awards for graphic design.

Like many people who came of age in the 1960s, Hans Hoefer wanted to travel and experience new places and people. He also wanted to record on film the places he visited, and he became quite an expert at both travel and photography. To finance his wanderings, Hans would buy a Mercedes-Benz in Germany, take it to Turkey or other Middle East destinations, and sell the car for considerably more than he paid. The proceeds from the sale of the Mercedes were used to purchase rugs that he sold in Europe for a substantial profit, which financed his next trip. Hans was also able to finance his travels by selling his paintings and photographs.

Start-up

In 1967, Hans Hoefer began an overland trip through Asia, which ended in 1969 when he settled in Ubud, Bali. He set about taking thousands of photographs of the island and making copious notes about the people, food, climate, and so forth. The result of this monumental effort was the first Insight Guide (Bali) published in 1970, which was an instant success and won several awards. That book was to be the prototype for all the other Insight Guides published since 1970.

In the following year, 1971, Hans Hoefer founded APA Publications (Hong Kong) Ltd., which was incorporated in Hong Kong, a site selected because of its favorable tax laws and strong copyright protection laws. Hans named the company APA because "old friends in many parts of Asia greet each other with the salutation 'Apa Khabar' (ah-pah car-bar). They are saying 'How are you?' and 'What's new?' In the Malay-Indonesian tongue, 'Apa' is a word that denotes a question. That is why we are APA Publications. Our books are designed for a traveler with an enquiring mind, who wants to get beneath the skin of a place and find out what goes on beneath the surface."

Preferring to work in Singapore, Hans incorporated another APA company in that country to be a color laboratory, photo studio, picture library, and design workshop. The principal activities of the Singapore company were to

a. oversee the print production of the books;
b. market the books; and
c. sell advertising space for inclusion in the books.

Similarly, the principal activities of the Hong Kong company were to

a. act as copyright holder of its publications, and
b. carry on the business of commissioning authors/photographers to create new books and to update and revise existing books (books are usually revised annually).

During the formative years, Hans wore many hats—he was the photographer, designer, and publisher of the Insight Guides. To accomplish his varied tasks, Hans spent about six months in Singapore, and the remainder of the year he traveled to new countries to gather material for the next Insight Guide.

Growth

Because APA Publications was essentially a one-man company, growth was quite slow. During the first ten years of operation, APA Publications produced only ten Insight Guides. Geometric growth began in the early 1980s, and by 1986 the company had forty-eight titles published in seven languages, which were distributed in over thirty countries. Growth continued, and by early 1991 the company had nearly 150 titles (see Exhibit 1).

The company's growth began to infringe on Hans's time, so in 1986 he hired Yinglock Chan, the company's banker, to become the managing director

EXHIBIT 1 APA Publications Titles

Algarve	New York City
Athens	Paris
Bali	Penang
Bangkok	Phuket
Brittany	Rhodes
Chiang Mai	Rome
Cote d'Azur	San Francisco
Jakarta	Sardinia
Kuala Lumpur	Singapore
Malacca	Tenerife
Mallorca	Turquoise Coast
Munich	Tuscany
Nepal	Yugoslavia
New Delhi	

Amsterdam	Lisbon
Athens	London
Bangkok	Los Angeles
Barcelona	Madrid
Beijing	Miami
Berlin	Melbourne
Boston	Munich
Budapest	New York City
Buenos Aires	Oxford
Calcutta	Paris
Delhi, Agra, Jaipur	Prague
Dublin	Rome
Düsseldorf	Rio
Edinburgh	San Francisco
Florence	Singapore
Glasgow	Sydney
Istanbul	Tokyo
Jerusalem	Venice
Kathmandu	Vienna

Alaska	Loire Valley
Alsace	Mallorca & Ibiza
American Southwest	Malaysia
Argentina	Malta
Australia	Mexico
Bahamas	Morocco
Bali	Native America
Barbados	Nepal
Bermuda	Netherlands
Brazil	New England
Brittany	New York State
Burma	New Zealand
Crossing America	Norway
Canada	Pacific Northwest
California	Northern California
Caribbean	Pakistan
Catalonia	Peru
Channel Island	Philippines
Chile	Portugal
China	Provence
Continental Europe	Puerto Rico
Crete	Rajasthan
Denmark	Rhine
East African Wildlife	Rockies
East Asia	Scotland
Egypt	South America
Florida	Southern California
France	Southern Spain
Gambia & Senegal	South Asia
Germany	South East Asian Wildlife
Great Britain	South India
Great Barrier Reef & Queensland	Spain
Germany	Sri Lanka
Gran Canaria	Sweden
Greece	Taiwan
Greek Islands	Tenerife
Hawaii	Texas
Hong Kong	Thailand
Hungary	Trinidad & Tobago
India	Tunisia
Indian Wildlife	Turkey
Indonesia	Turkish Coast
Ireland	Tuscany
Israel	USSR
Italy	Vietnam
Jamaica	Wales
Kenya	Waterways of Europe
Korea	Yemen

of APA Publications. Chan graduated in accountancy in 1972 from the University of Singapore (now the National University of Singapore) and began working in the fields of cost and financial accounting in public accounting firms in London and Singapore before going into merchant banking as head of corporate finance. Hans gradually relinquished day-to-day control of his company to Chan; however, he continues to set directions and to oversee most aspects of the design and publication of the company's products.

THE COMPANY

In twenty years APA Publications has grown from a small company with just one travel guide to one with nearly 150 titles and other complementary travel-related products. The companies continue to be the product and possession of Hans Hoefer, but they are now professionally managed by a very capable management team.

Location

APA Publications has, in addition to its Singapore location, two other offices. APA's London office staff is responsible for the editorial activities in Europe, the Americas, and North Africa. The office staff in Munich is primarily responsible for translating the travel guides into German. The Singapore office staff is responsible for editorial activities in Asia, Southern Africa, and the Pacific as well as production and sales.

In 1989, the Singapore operation moved into new facilities large enough to accommodate future growth, and it now employs 130 people to manufacture its product line and do work for other clients. The top floor of the building is used for administrative offices and assembly of manuscript material (desktop publishing is now used to prepare manuscripts for production). There is an open-office layout, and most offices and open spaces are decorated with oriental carpets collected by Hans Hoefer. The first floor of the building is dedicated to print production and storage of inventories. There is also a small employee lounge, used mainly for lunch and tea breaks, on the first floor.

Ownership

Hans Hoefer had, until 1989, owned all of APA Publications. In that year, the need for additional capital arose, and Hans and Chan began searching for a venture capital company that would take a minority position in the company. A subsidiary of the Prudential Insurance Company agreed to acquire a 15 percent stake in all the companies, and by an ordinary resolution passed on 28 August 1990, the respective company's authorized share capital was increased. During the year, new shares were issued at a premium for a total consideration of approximately US$19,943,180. Exhibit 2 depicts the ownership and primary functions of the APA companies. The venture capital company, according to Chan, bought the shares for investment only and is not interested in becoming involved in APA's operations and management.

EXHIBIT 2 Ownership and Functions of APA Companies

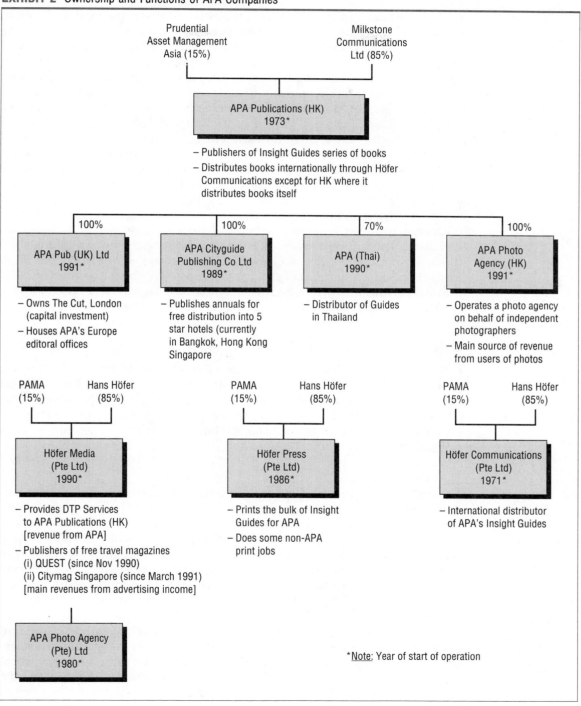

Prudential
Asset Management
Asia (15%)

Milkstone
Communications
Ltd (85%)

APA Publications (HK)
1973*

– Publishers of Insight Guides series of books
– Distributes books internationally through Höfer
  Communications except for HK where it
  distributes books itself

100%

APA Pub (UK) Ltd
1991*

– Owns The Cut, London
  (capital investment)
– Houses APA's Europe
  editoral offices

100%

APA Cityguide
Publishing Co Ltd
1989*

– Publishes annuals for
  free distribution into 5
  star hotels (currently
  in Bangkok, Hong Kong
  Singapore

70%

APA (Thai)
1990*

– Distributor of Guides
  in Thailand

100%

APA Photo
Agency (HK)
1991*

– Operates a photo agency
  on behalf of independent
  photographers
– Main source of revenue
  from users of photos

PAMA
(15%)

Hans Höfer
(85%)

Höfer Media
(Pte Ltd)
1990*

– Provides DTP Services
  to APA Publications (HK)
  [revenue from APA]
– Publishers of free travel magazines
  (i) QUEST (since Nov 1990)
  (ii) Citymag Singapore (since March 1991)
  [main revenues from advertising income]

APA Photo Agency
(Pte) Ltd
1980*

PAMA
(15%)

Hans Höfer
(85%)

Höfer Press
(Pte Ltd)
1986*

– Prints the bulk of Insight
  Guides for APA
– Does some non-APA
  print jobs

PAMA
(15%)

Hans Höfer
(85%)

Höfer Communications
(Pte Ltd)
1971*

– International distributor
  of APA's Insight Guides

*Note: Year of start of operation

Organization

APA Publications in Singapore is composed of three separate organizations housed in the Singapore corporate headquarters and one located in a building in downtown Singapore. The first, Hoefer Media, is primarily responsible for APA's desktop publishing functions. The second, Hoefer Press, prints the company's products and contracts to print material for other companies. The third company located at the Joo Koon Road facility (the main Singapore location) is Hoefer Communications, which deals mainly with product distribution. The fourth affiliated company, located at 23 Emerald Hill Road, is APA Photo Agency, which is the archive for contributing photographers' photographs.

The organization structure at APA is quite flat. Hans Hoefer is the Executive Chairman, and Yinglock Chan is the Managing Director. The other divisions—editorial, marketing, finance, production, and administration— are controlled by managers who report to Chan. Most management personnel are university graduates or have the technical training necessary for their positions. Turnover is quite low because working conditions are favorable, and there is not much demand in Singapore for people with publishing skills (there are not many other publishers in the country). Along with four other men, Hans Hoefer and Yinglock Chan serve as APA's board of directors. The board is primarily advisory, because Hans controls approximately 85 percent of the company's stock.

PRODUCTS AND MARKETS

For many years, APA Publications was a one-product company. It grew and profited on the consumer acceptance of its premier product, the Insight Guide series. In the mid and late 1980s, however, additional publications were added to APA's product line. APA Publications also profited from its ability to satisfy the needs of its target market while besting its competition in most parts of the world.

Insight Guides

The company's staple product, Insight Guides, continues to be its major revenue producer. The books are special because of Hans Hoefer's dedication to good photography, journalism, and design. He says of Insight Guides, "Each guide is produced by a team of creative photographers and journalists—some are seasoned professionals, others are talented young people at the start of their career. All have an intimate knowledge of their subject and are motivated by the challenge of capturing the spirit of a place: not only to produce a thoroughly practical guide but also to convey a sense of what it is like to be one of the people who live there.

"That is why, when you turn the pages of an Insight Guide, you will find pictures full of people—not posing for the camera but going about their everyday life and work. That is why you will read articles on subjects as diverse as pub culture in Dublin, the art of political compromise in Brazil, or the movie industry in India—each one providing a real insight into what makes each place and its people unique. We view our readers as true explorers, people who travel in order to learn."

Although most Insight Guides sell well, some sell better than others. Over the years, the following have been APA's best sellers:

1. Thailand
2. Florida
3. Australia
4. Hawaii
5. Kenya
6. Hong Kong
7. India
8. Crossing USA
9. Germany
10. Continental Europe

Although it is nice to have best-sellers, APA Publications needs to add new titles to continue growing.

Hans is constantly looking for new countries or regions about which to write. Recent interest in the former Soviet Union has led APA to investigate the market for Russian Insight Guides. In fact, APA is responding to the need for information on this vast country with three new guides: Insight USSR (already available) and Cityguides Moscow and Leningrad. There is also a brand new Vietnam guide, which was produced when the government invited APA Publications to send an editorial delegation to explore the country and produce the first-ever modern guide. Contributions to the guide came from professors and staff of Hanoi University's Institute of Anthropology. Finally, APA is beginning to produce more thematic Insight Guides such as the Nile River guide and the East African Wildlife guide.

Insight Pocket Guides

Insight Pocket Guides, a smaller version of the original Insight Guides with detailed sightseeing itineraries, were launched in the United Kingdom in 1991 by Harrap. Ten titles were made available to travelers—Algarve, Athens, Bali, Bangkok, Mallorca, Nepal, New Delhi, New York City, Paris, and San Francisco. Since the original offering, the following titles have been made available:

Brittany
Chiang Mai
Cote d'Azur
Jakarta
Kuala Lumpur
Malacca
Munich
Penang
Phuket
Rhodes
Rome
Sardinia
Singapore
Tenerife
Turquoise Coast
Tuscany
Yugoslavia

Pocket Guides are meant to supplement rather than replace Insight Guides. Hans explains that Pocket Guides came into existence "as a result of my experience with many travelers arriving in Singapore over the years. Be they friends, journalists, or travel experts loaded with guidebooks in their bags, they would still ask me 'What should I be doing in Singapore?' It struck me then that it is very important to have a local host whom you can depend on to show you the local sights, color, and experience. Pocket Guides fulfill this requirement. Designed to help travelers make the most of a short stay at any particular destination, they offer a selection of set itineraries from which they can choose (see Exhibit 3). Each itinerary includes many quaint and interesting places to go and things to do. It is as good as having your own personal guide right next to you.''

Citymag Singapore

Citymag Singapore is a new weekly publication endorsed by the Singapore Tourist Promotion Board targeted mainly for tourists to the island. The inaugural issue was launched on 8 March 1991 on Orchard Road. Two models dressed in full Chinese opera costumes—to duplicate the cover photo of the

EXHIBIT 3 Contents Page of Pocket Guides

first issue—strolled along busy Orchard Road during lunchtime distributing hundreds of copies of the magazine to amused and surprised tourists passing by. Citymag is packed with the latest news and views on the local scene, with many color graphics, photos, newsy editorials, and current attractions—all tailored to meet the needs of tourists arriving in Singapore.

Regular features include shopping, nightlife, entertainment, movie previews, the arts, a weekly calendar with selected daily listings of events and attractions in the city, places of interest in neighboring countries, and more. With a print run of 20,000 copies per week, Citymag is readily available, free of charge (production costs are offset by advertising revenue), at airport arrival halls, STPB brochure racks and information centers, as well as at all major hotels and selected shopping centers in the city. If Citymag Singapore is successful, it will be duplicated in Hong Kong and other major cities.

Quest

Quest, the other magazine published by Hoefer Media, was acquired from Pacific Publishing & Exhibitions Pte. Ltd. toward the end of 1990. Basically a travel and entertainment magazine for the ASEAN region, Quest has a print run of 27,000 copies per issue and is circulated in Singapore, Malaysia, Thailand, Indonesia, the Philippines, and Hong Kong. The bulk of the magazines are to be found in most five-star hotels and resorts, with a smaller percentage on sale at newsstands and available by subscription. The 112-page magazine, with a new layout and design, focuses on Southeast Asia and runs regular features on things Asian, food, getaways, travelogues, fashion, personalities, life-style, and more.

Hotel Guides

Hotel Guides, which are large-format copies of Insight Guides, can be found in the better hotels in Hong Kong, Bangkok, and Singapore. The information and photographs are the same as those in Insight Guides for Hong Kong, Bangkok, and Singapore; however, Hotel Guides are fully financed by advertisements (there are very few advertisements in Insight Guides or Pocket Guides). If these Hotel Guides continue to be profitable, similar guides will be produced for hotels in other major tourist cities.

Sagarmatha Book

Not all of APA Publications' activities are profit-oriented. Hans described a charitable undertaking to help people in Nepal, "A special international launch of the Sagarmatha book is being planned for this fall. This will be a charity event in which funds will be raised to help rebuild the Thyangboche Monastery in Nepal—the focus of the Sherpas' spiritual and cultural world. This revered and magnificent monument burned down on 19 January 1989, together with its irreplaceable frescoes and ancient Buddhist scripts.

Sagarmatha is the first official fund-raising book and features breathtaking photographs of the Himalayan mountains, the people, and the flora and fauna of the region. The book's introduction and text is written by Sir Edmund Hillary, and royalties from the book will be given to the Himalayan Trust for its work in the rebuilding of the monastery and for its ongoing work in the Sagarmatha National Park."

APA Photo Agency

Although not a product like the other publications, APA Photo Agency is a vital part of the guides and magazines produced by APA Publications. This is the archives for all the photographs that are used in different APA products. APA Photo Agency began a total revamp in 1990 under a new team headed by APA Villa's new manager, Vivian Kang. Hans explained that "the stock library is now being recatalogued to make for easier access and search by clients." The photo library also greatly enhanced its selection of stock pictures when it signed up to represent Superstock, a large New York-based photo library.

Under this program, APA Photo Agency will have an additional 10,000 slides added to its current selection of 200,000 slides. In addition, an APA Photo Agency Hong Kong was established in 1991 to capture the expanding Hong Kong market. Although not as extensive in its collection of photo selection as its Singapore counterpart, it will provide the same kind of quality service and will be headed by Paula Cheung.

Target Market

When Hans Hoefer started his company, he knew his product would not appeal to all travelers. In fact, he did not want to try to produce guide books that tried to "be all things to all people." Insight Guides are for the affluent, independent traveler who wants to know more about a country than merely where to stay and eat. Hans knew he had to have a focused target market, just as the creator of the Lonely Planet Guides knew he wanted to develop a product that catered to backpackers. Travel guides that appeal to the masses are usually too general to be of value to serious travelers.

The people for whom APA products were created are financially able to afford better accommodations, and they choose to travel independently. Some purchasers of APA's travel guides do not even leave their homes. Instead, they buy the books because they enjoy reading the guides even though they have no intention of visiting the country described. Hans is pleased that his books are interesting enough to be purchased simply for their entertainment and instructional value.

Competition

There are numerous travel guide companies selling books describing most countries, regions, and cities of the world; however, Chan feels that APA Publications has no direct competition. Looking through the catalog from Book Passage, a large mail-order firm that sells numerous travel-oriented products, one can see that there are more Insight Guide titles than those of any other competitors. Chan believes that the large selection of Insight Guide, and now Pocket Guide, titles gives APA Publications the competitive edge.

Although the number of Insight Guides sold continues to increase (approximately 1.6 million in 1990), there are other companies that do compete with APA for upscale travelers while also offering products for the average traveler. The following are some of the major guidebook sellers that compete with APA Publications: Frommer Guides, Birnbaum Guides, Blue Guides, Baedeker's Guides, Michelin Guides, Fodor Guides, and Berlitz Guides. Although these companies may not be able to match APA title-for-title, they do pose serious threats in countries where they and APA have competing guides.

OPERATIONS

During its formative years, APA Publications was like most small entrepreneurial companies—it had a constant shortage of capital and human resources. Hans Hoefer's personal funds supported the company until an Insight Guide could be published and sold, and he was responsible for most of the steps in the production process. However, growth has necessitated delegation and a certain amount of formalization. APA Publications is now a professionally managed, mature company with annual turnover (revenue) in 1990 of slightly more than US $6 million.

Personnel

APA Publications employs 130 people, many of whom are high-school graduates. Most people in technical and managerial positions are college graduates or have acquired appropriate qualifications through other recognized academic or vocational institutions. Blue-collar workers are generally recruited with newspaper ads, whereas professionals are referred by APA employees or by their universities. APA Publications also offers internships to university students who often stay with the company after their internship is over. New employees are trained by the company and receive additional training when new technology or production processes are introduced.

Singapore has no law that stipulates a minimum wage; however, the labor market is so tight that employers must pay at least the "going rate" to attract qualified employees. Chan indicated that APA employees were paid slightly above the going rate, and they received an annual bonus equivalent to one-and-a-half to two months' pay (this practice is quite common in Singapore where even public sector employees received an additional three months' pay in 1991). Office personnel are paid annual salaries, and marketing personnel receive commissions in addition to their salaries. Employee benefits include health care, vacation time, sick leave, and subsidized lunches.

Production

The production process begins with the publisher (Hans Hoefer) and the senior editor in London jointly deciding how many new titles to produce in the coming year (as many as thirty new titles are produced in a year). The new titles are then divided among the managing editors who select project editors for each title. Project editors are usually people in the subject country who can tap their networks for talented photographers and journalists. All Insight Guides follow a standard format—the section headings in each book are similar, the photographs are similar, and each book contains approximately 260 pages.

The first section of each guide is a history of the country, region, or city. Hans believes that "the perspective of time is an integral part of any destination. Learning about the past teaches much about the present. That's why APA guides begin with a section on history, providing readers with a brief time capsule of the most significant dates, characters, and events of a place's past." Insight Guide background articles are written in an engaging, easy-to-read style. The second section deals with people, because "people are the life and soul of a destination. They, and all the attendant activities and themes they entail, such as culture, religion, cuisine, art, architecture, and fine arts, are discussed and explored in several chapters of an Insight Guide."

The third section is the places and activities section, which "is the 'meat' of any Insight Guide, where your journey actually begins. It encompasses a systematic coverage of the various parts of a region, country, or city that holds the most interest for a visitor, and also the less obvious places as well. Rather than taking the reader by the hand and leading him through an endless list of sights and locations, we present a wide range of options that help him to make certain choices about his vacation." Next, there is a section on special features peculiar to the destination, for example, the wines of the Napa Valley in the guide to California. The final section is the travel tips section, which is a compendium of essential information. Visa regulations, transportation, what to bring, hotel and restaurant listings are all included in this black-and-white section.

Once project editors have compiled the necessary information and photographs, they forward it to Singapore where it is prepared for printing using the latest desktop publishing techniques. Finished copy is sent to the printing room where copies are run off on paper purchased mainly from Holland and Brazil. There is minimal inventory of finished goods because APA Publications guides are made-to-order rather than produced for inventory. Finished Insight Guides and Pocket Guides are palletized and prepared for export (only about 10,000 of the 1.6 million books produced in 1990 were sold in Singapore).

Distribution

APA Publications has distributors in major countries (see Exhibit 4) who are responsible for marketing and distribution to local booksellers and retail chains. In some countries distribution methods are somewhat unorthodox—in Taiwan, for example, Insight Guides are sold door-to-door. When new titles are published, a distributor is selected for that country, or the book is handled by an established distributor in the region. Because distributors typically handle products of several companies, they do not always give as much attention to individual products as manufacturers would like. APA Publications has

EXHIBIT 4 APA Publications' Distributors

- Australia and New Zealand: Prentice Hall of Australia
- Benelux: Utigeverij Cambium
- Brazil and Portugal: Cedibra Editora Brasileria Ltd.
- Denmark: Copenhagen Book Centre Aps.
- Germany: RV Reise-und Verkehrsuerlag Gmbh.
- Hawaii: Pacific Trade Group, Inc.
- Hong Kong: Far East Media, Ltd.
- India and Nepal: India Book Distributors
- Indonesia: Java Books
- Israel: Steimatzky Ltd.
- Italy: Zanfi Editori SRL
- Jamaica: Novelty Trading Co.
- Japan: Charles E. Tuttle Co. Inc.
- Kenya: Camerapix Publishers International Ltd.
- Korea: Kyobo Book Centre Co. Ltd.
- Philippines: National Book Store
- Singapore: MPH Distributors (S) Pte. Ltd.
- Switzerland: M.P.A. Agencies-Import SA
- Taiwan: Caves Books Ltd.
- Thailand: Far East Publications Ltd.
- United Kingdom, Ireland, and Europe (others): Harrap Ltd.
- Mainland United States and Canada: Prentice-Hall, Inc.

hired a liaison in New York to keep its U.S. distributor, Prentice-Hall, Inc., actively promoting Insight Guides.

Distributors order the number of copies they expect to sell, and this figure determines the production runs for individual titles. In most cases APA piggybacks orders for its guides. When a large distributor such as Prentice-Hall orders titles for the United States (which accounts for approximately 30 percent of sales), APA employees then call smaller distributors and ask for their orders of the same titles. By combining orders from several distributors, APA Publications' pressruns can be longer and more cost effective.

Marketing

APA has traditionally relied on its distributors to market its products; however, in the last two years, the company has decided to take a more proactive marketing stance. APA began advertising in the International Herald Tribune and in its own company publications such as Citymag (see Exhibit 5) and

EXHIBIT 5

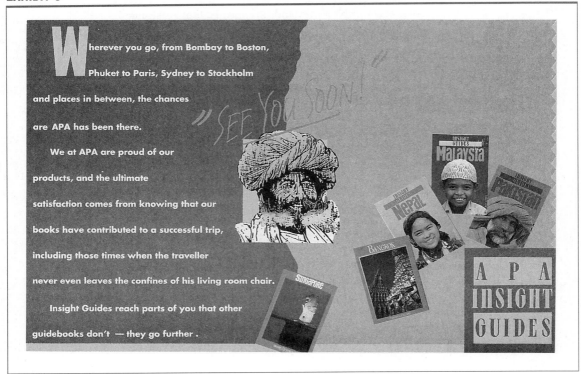

Wherever you go, from Bombay to Boston, Phuket to Paris, Sydney to Stockholm and places in between, the chances are APA has been there.

We at APA are proud of our products, and the ultimate satisfaction comes from knowing that our books have contributed to a successful trip, including those times when the traveller never even leaves the confines of his living room chair.

Insight Guides reach parts of you that other guidebooks don't — they go further.

"SEE YOU SOON!"

Quest. There are also plans to advertise in upscale magazines targeted to top executives. APA Publications also entered a trial relationship with Virgin Atlantic Airways to market its guides to the airline's affluent travelers.

Since November 1990, first- and business-class passengers flying into London have been able to enjoy copies of Virgin Insight Guide: London—a special edition of APA's Insight City Guide: London. Virgin Atlantic pays a small fee, enough to offset production costs, for each book that it makes available to its passengers free-of-charge. The Virgin Insight Guide is one example of the kind of "customizing" that can be done for clients by APA's special sales team.

Other major special sales clients include VIVA Holidays (VIVA is a subsidiary of Qantas and is Australia's largest outbound tour operator to Asia) and Meirs Weltreisen (Germany's largest outbound tour operator). Tour operators place their logo on the cover of Insight Guides and make them available to their customers. These Insight Guides are purchased wholesale with the understanding that they cannot be resold.

APA Publications is also using celebrity endorsements to market its books. For example, Sir Edmund Hillary says the following about the Insight Guide series: "I was first drawn to the Insight Guides by the excellent Nepal volume. I can think of no book which so effectively captures the essence of a country. Out of these pages leaped the Nepal I know—the captivating charm of a people and their culture. I've since discovered and enjoyed the entire Insight Guide series. Each volume deals with a country or city in the same sensitive depth, which is nowhere more evident than in the superb photography."

Finances

APA Publications was started with Hans Hoefer's money, and every cent of profit has been reinvested annually. A venture capital company injected additional funds in 1990 to enhance growth in return for control of 15 percent of the company's equity. Short-term loans from two banks satisfy the companies' working capital requirements. APA Publications' 1990 turnover was approximately US$1.3 million less than in 1989 (see Exhibit 6), a shortfall that is attributed in part to the decrease in travel caused by the Persian Gulf situation. The large difference in inventories from 1989 to 1990 is not unusual in the publishing industry. According to Chan, "those figures represent work-in-progress and not physical inventories." The entries for "amount due to subsidiaries" and "amount due from subsidiaries" reflect monies transferred among APA Publications, Hoefer Media, Hoefer Press, Hoefer Communications, and APA Photo Agency.

WHAT'S NEXT?

APA Publications has been a successful publishing company with award-winning products and a very capable staff. Hans Hoefer has the satisfaction of having created a respected travel guidebook company, which is likely to continue to grow and prosper. Hans must decide whether he and his company need to change direction to facilitate more rapid growth. APA can continue to add new items to its product line or search for acquisition targets that would complement its product line. Hans could take the company public, or he could sell it to a larger publisher or travel-related company.

SOURCE: This case was prepared by Robert L. Anderson, College of Charleston. Used by permission.

EXHIBIT 6 Financial Statements for APA Publications

APA Publications (HK) Limited
Profit and Loss Account
Year Ended 31 December 1990

	1990 US$	1989 US$
Turnover	$6,173,437	$7,527,943
Profit for the Year	1,259,629	1,319,700
Retained Profits Brought Forward	2,795,525	1,600,825
Profits Available for Appropriation	4,055,154	2,920,525
Dividends	—	(125,000)
Retained Profits Carried Forward	$4,055,154	$2,795,525

ABA Publications (HK) Limited
Balance Sheet—31 December 1990

	1990 US$	1989 US$
EMPLOYMENT OF CAPITAL		
Fixed Assets	$97,813	$18,956
Investments	114,381	20,422
Current Assets		
Inventories	5,757,013	1,254,765
Due from a subsidiary	230,021	—
Due from related companies	1,521,089	1,619,288
Due from a director	268,498	55,900
Accounts receivable, deposits, and prepayments	747,284	404,457
Bank balances	284,315	1,054,493
	8,808,220	4,388,903
Current Liabilities		
Due to related companies	326,838	465,160
Accounts payable and accruals	1,707,923	668,915
Proposed dividends	—	125,000
	2,034,761	1,259,075
Net Current Assets	6,773,459	3,129,828
	$6,985,653	$3,169,206
CAPITAL EMPLOYED		
Share Capital	442,045	373,681
Share Premium Account	2,488,454	—
Retained Profits	4,055,154	2,795,525
	$6,985,653	$3,169,206

Approved by the Board of Directors on
On behalf of the Board

_____)
　　　　　　　　　　　　　　　)
　　　　　　　　　　　　　　　)　Directors
　　　　　　　　　　　　　　　)
_____)

EXHIBIT 6 *(continued)*

APA Publications (HK) Limited
Statement of Changes in Financial Position
Year Ended 31 December 1990

	1990 US$	1989 US$
SOURCE OF FUNDS		
Operating profit before taxation	$1,259,629	$1,319,700
Adjustment for item not involving the movement		
of funds: Depreciation	18,305	2,381
Total generated from operations	1,277,934	1,322,081
Funds from other sources		
Shares issued	2,556,818	—
Loan repaid from associated company	17,785	—
	3,852,537	1,322,081
APPLICATION OF FUNDS		
Investment in subsidiaries	111,744	—
Investment in associated company	—	17,785
Dividends paid	125,000	200,000
Purchases of fixed assets	97,162	21,337
	333,906	239,122
INCREASE IN WORKING CAPITAL	$3,518,631	$1,082,959
Made up as follows:		
Inventories	4,502,248	686,067
Amount due by a subsidiary	230,021	—
Amounts due by related companies	(98,199)	244,640
Amount due by director	212,598	(145,695)
Accounts receivable, deposits and prepayments	342,827	99,115
Amounts due to related companies	138,322	(422,818)
Accounts payable and accruals	(1,039,008)	(18,935)
	4,288,809	442,374
Movements in net liquid funds:		
Bank balances	(770,178)	640,585
	$3,518,631	$1,082,959

EXHIBIT 6 *(continued)*

APA Publications (HK) Limited
Profit and Loss Account
Year Ended 31 December 1988

	1988 US$	1987 US$
Turnover	$4,735,091	$2,786,860
Profit for the Year	825,063	659,126
Retained Profits Brought Forward	900,762	565,966
Profits Available for Appropriation	1,725,825	1,225,092
Dividends	(125,000)	(75,000)
Capitalized to Issue Bonus Shares	—	(249,330)
Retained Profits Carried Forward	$1,600,825	$900,762

APA Publications (HK) Limited
Balance Sheet—December 1988

	1988 US$	1987 US$
NONCURRENT ASSETS		
Investments	$2,637	$2,825
CURRENT ASSETS		
Work-in-progress	568,698	477,369
Due from related parties	1,374,648	776,148
Due from directors	201,595	163,923
Accounts receivable, deposits, and prepayments	305,342	203,425
Bank balances	413,908	368,913
	2,864,191	1,989,778
CURRENT LIABILITIES		
Due to related parties	42,342	22,202
Accounts payable and accruals	649,980	524,850
Proposed dividends	200,000	75,000
Bank overdrawn—unsecured	—	96,108
	892,322	718,160
NET CURRENT ASSETS	1,971,869	1,271,618
	$1,974,506	$1,274,443
CAPITAL AND RESERVES		
Share capital	373,681	373,681
Retained profits	1,600,825	900,762
TOTAL CAPITAL AND RESERVES	$1,974,506	$1,274,443

Approved by the Board of Directors on August 29, 1989

On behalf of the board

```
                              )
                              )
                              )      Directors
                              )
                              )
```

EXHIBIT 6 *(concluded)*

APA Publications (HK) Limited
Statement of Changes in Financial Position
Year Ended 31 December 1988

	1988 US$	1987 US$
SOURCE OF FUNDS		
Operating profit before taxation	$825,063	$659,126
Adjustment for noncash item: Write-off of unlisted investment	188	—
	825,251	659,126
Funds from other sources		
Shares issued	—	50,897
Sale of investment in subsidiary	—	50,100
	825,251	760,123
APPLICATION OF FUNDS		
Purchases of investments	—	(2,637)
Investment in subsidiary	—	(50,100)
INCREASE IN WORKING CAPITAL	$825,251	$707,386
Represented by:		
Work-in-progress	91,329	(46,370)
Due from related parties	598,500	(157,101)
Due from directors	37,672	140,096
Accounts receivable, deposits, and prepayments	101,917	110,604
Due to related parties	(20,140)	3,169
Accounts payable and accruals	(125,130)	389,549
	684,148	439,947
Movements in net liquid funds:		
Bank balances	44,995	363,547
Bank overdraft	96,108	(96,108)
	$825,251	$707,386

A SAMPLE BUSINESS PLAN

CONFIDENTIAL

LOX & BAGELS, INC.
BUSINESS PLAN

This business plan is being provided on a confidential basis to selected individuals known by the principals of Lox & Bagels, Inc. The contents of this plan are proprietary and confidential. It is not to be copied or duplicated in any way. This document is not intended to and does not constitute an offer to sell or the solicitation of an offer to buy securities in Lox & Bagels, Inc.

Property of
Lox & Bagels, Inc.
102 Wampee Curve
Summerville, SC 29485
(803) 875-3585
Copy 4 of 4

CONTENTS

EXECUTIVE SUMMARY

Business Description

Lox & Bagels, Inc., a closely held South Carolina corporation (also referred to as "The Company" or "The Restaurant"), will be located in Mt. Pleasant on Coleman Boulevard. Lox & Bagels will be a small restaurant business catering to the breakfast and lunch clientele. Our main restaurant traffic will be morning commuters and midday business lunches. The breakfast menu will include a variety of bagels, muffins, and croissants, along with other pastries and side orders. The luncheon menu will include deli meats, soups, sandwiches, and so forth. There will be inside dining as well as carryout. A variety of beverages will also be available. The restaurant will also offer prepared trays for "to go" catering. The primary focus, hence the name, will be freshly prepared bagels of various flavor varieties.

Business Advantage

The bagels will be baked fresh daily on site using custom equipment designed specifically for kosher bagel preparation. This is our primary competitive advantage because there are no other local competitors that have fresh-baked bagels. Additional utilization of equipment will be gained through baking prepared and frozen loaves of high-quality breads and muffins. We will be purchasing high-quality croissants, sandwich breads, and deli meats. Also, a limited selection of specialty cakes, pies, and pastries will be offered.

Principals

The principals of the company are Kristina G. Bowen, BSBA, College of Charleston, Charleston, South Carolina; W. Jenkins Hidell, Jr., BSBA, College of Charleston, Charleston, South Carolina; and Theresa L. Waters, MBA, USC, Columbia, South Carolina.

- Ms. Bowen has extensive retail background with Sears, Roebuck & Company and is currently an associate with the accounting firm of Hoke Greiner CPA.

- Mr. Hidell is the partner with extensive experience in food preparation and restaurant management. His family owned a regional chain of small restaurants/pubs based in Charlotte, North Carolina. Mr. Hidell grew up in the family business—starting as crew-boy and cleanup. He progressed through all training and was most recently responsible for the family's business being bought by a national food company and being franchised nationally.

- Ms. Waters is president and CEO of Terrapin Enterprises, a construction and renovation consulting firm based in Rutherfordton, North Carolina, and also has extensive experience in the retail grocery business, having owned and operated a grocery store in Johnsonville, South Carolina, for several years.

Marketing Survey Report

Market survey demographics studied for three southeastern cities—Charleston, South Carolina; Savannah, Georgia; and Charlotte, North Carolina—indicate that a location in Charleston, South Carolina—most particularly in the suburb of Mt. Pleasant—would present the most ideal situation of population, population growth, and highest per capita income of the cities studied.

Business Partners' Investment

The total investment needed for a turnkey operation is approximately $210,000. Principal Bowen is contributing $30,000 to the initial investment and will be accountant for the enterprise at no fee for first three years of operation. This is projected to save The Company $30,000 in accounting and tax costs. Principal Waters is contributing $30,000 cash to the enterprise and additionally her construction firm will do all leasehold improvements to the leased building at no charge to the new business. This will save an additional $35,000 in working capital. Principal Hidell is contributing $50,000 to the enterprise. Additionally, he will provide on-site management to the enterprise for the first two years of operation at minimal cost to the business. This is expected to save the business $20,000 during the first two years to offset management salary.

Additional Financing

Principals anticipate needing $70,000 capital to be financed by commercial bank with SBA guaranty. Because two women are on the board of directors, and are principals, as well as Ms. Bowen being president and Ms. Waters being CEO, the firm qualifies for minority consideration in dealing with the SBA. Projected income statements will reflect a five-year payback. Each principal will pledge personal assets as well as corporate assets to secure and collateralize this capital funding. SBA will guarantee 85 percent of the loan amount, 15 percent will be secured by asset pledge to cooperating bank for all untitled goods.

PURPOSE AND BACKGROUND

Uniqueness

Lox & Bagels, Inc., is a unique concept due to our fresh, homemade bagels and freshly baked muffins and breads prepared daily, catering predominantly to the breakfast and lunch clientele for sit-down dining and carryout, business office catering, walk-in bagel and deli purchases, as well as contracts with local food stores and restaurants for bulk purchases of fresh bagels.

Strengths

The company's strengths lie within the determination of the owners and employees to give the public personalized service, which includes learning clientele's names and order preferences and keeping records on corporate accounts as to the types of previous orders in order to anticipate their future needs. Additional strengths lie in the business experiences of the founding partners. All have been involved in industries that cater to quality service to customers, most particularly the managing partner with extensive and successful restaurant experience.

Additionally, we have contracted with several food purveyors locally and in nearby cities to provide them with fresh bagels for their own resale. We have been quite careful to insist on the use of our name when they advertise this offering and also not to sell to local establishments that could be in direct competition with our own marketing strategy.

Our primary strength and focus of the business is to make and provide premium quality bagels to the consumer. We will emphasize this by continually stressing to our customer the healthful nature of what we specialize in—bagels. These are a no-fat, no-cholesterol bread that can be used in a variety of ways.

Weaknesses

One of the company's weaknesses is the ease of entry into our market, but this is partially lessened because we are both capital and labor intensive. Another weakness is that this is a relatively new concept to the area.

At first impression it might seem that we are entering a saturated market due to the quantity of restaurants in the area. But because of our uniqueness and our aim at a specialty niche, as well as our aim to provide outstanding service, we feel confident that the community will respond to our offering. There are plenty of run-of-the-mill restaurants with average fare; ours will be directed toward those seeking a different taste.

Nature of the Industry

The bagel industry in Mt. Pleasant is primarily maintained by supermarkets who sell only frozen and prepackaged bagels. All grocery chains carry bagel products, which shows there is a demand for this product line. However, no one in the area handles freshly prepared product; they are all premade at off-site "factory" locations. We also anticipate doing approximately 25 percent of our business in carryout, primarily in bulk bagel purchases. Additionally, another 20 to 25 percent will be done in supplying prepared trays for catering commercial and private functions. This catering will only involve supplying trays, food, and supplies for customer-managed events; we will not supply personnel. We will carry only the freshest ingredients, deli meats, cheeses, smoked fish, and vegetables.

Market Size

The Mt. Pleasant area is home for approximately 35,600 individuals, which expands over 13,000 households. Primarily we are targeting the 18 to 55-plus age group. The Mt. Pleasant composite breakdown is as follows:

- 18–24 years of age—in 49 percent of households
- 25–34 years of age—in 82 percent of households

- 35–44 years of age—in 49 percent of households
- 45–54 years of age—in 38 percent of households
- 55+ years of age—in 57 percent of households

We will also be pulling clientele from the Sullivan's Island and Isle of Palms area. Commuters from these two communities must pass our business location on the way to Charleston as well as returning home. This broad consumer base will provide the necessary diversity from which to attract a large and steady customer flow daily and weekly. The household income figures from our target area indicate more than enough income possibilities for success of this enterprise.

Pricing Strategy

Our company has a competitive pricing strategy when compared with other specialty niche restaurants/deli/bakeries in the metropolitan area. As for the fresh bagel portion of the business, we are premium priced in relation to large-scale competition (i.e., supermarkets). We are NOT targeting this convenience market directly but are aiming at the market with a larger disposable income that demands quality in a product and thus will pay a higher price. The other portions of the business—breakfast and lunch menu, desserts, deli meats, and catering—demand that we be competitive with larger operations. In this, however, we can remain premium priced but still remain competitive—only because of the premium service we will offer. It has been the experience of all partners that the market targeted will pay premium price for quality goods and services.

Location Strategy

The location of our company was selected after much labor and research into traffic patterns studies. Determining factors included the following:

- A large percentage of our target market resides in Mt. Pleasant, Sullivan's Island, and Isle of Palms.
- Approximately 75 percent of the population earns over $25,000 annually.

This business is directed toward an upper-middle-income clientele that is upscale and mobile. This is provided by the choice of Mt. Pleasant, South Carolina. The studies and other resources indicate that consistent growth of at least 30 percent per year is very likely. This growth will allow rapid repayment of all incurred debt and insure expansion of the original site and further expansion to new (additional) locations within three to five years. We plan to locate on Coleman Boulevard in the city of Mt. Pleasant, South Carolina. Local competition for breakfast includes several fast-food restaurants, such as Burger King and McDonalds, as well as Krispy Kreme donuts, and all-night "greasy spoons," such as Alex's. This competition is actually welcome to The Company in that we are targeting people who are looking for a more quality breakfast and a quieter location, and those who are more health conscious and want to eat that way. Bagels are a no-cholesterol and no-fat alternative to the local competition.

Lunch competition is broader in scope than breakfast. The area has up-scale restaurants in the Shem Creek area offering the business lunch with alcohol. There is also Pizza Hut, Skoogies Hot Dog Place, and the above-mentioned fast-food restaurants. Again, we will aim for a different crowd—one that is health conscious, wants a quality meal at a competitive price, and gets personal service from someone who cares that the customer is there.

Offical highway department numbers show that Coleman Boulevard is one of the most heavily traveled thoroughfares in the Charleston area. At last survey in excess of 38,232 vehicles pass our proposed location each day. This traffic flow will help insure the possibility of a successful enterprise.

Management

The Company will be managed by Bill Hidell, who will oversee all production and distribution for the first two years. Mr. Hidell is the partner with extensive experience in food preparation and restaurant management. His family owned a regional chain of small restaurant/pubs based in Charlotte, North Carolina. His desire is to start over and rebuild another "family" business. This desire, combined with his friendly attitude with people and his own personal drive and ambition to succeed, helps us foresee a profitable future.

Profitability

We plan to run a profitable business that is capable of expanding into new locations. In the future we will add to and change our product line to have the best possible product mix. Our mission is to provide freshly made, premium quality—actually the best—bagels, and to develop and maintain a substantial market share while keeping quality and service as our main concern.

THE MARKET

Type of Market

The target market that will be pursued by The Company is multisegmented, yet the type of person(s) pursued will be essentially the same. We are locating in a very upscale, growing area that is home to both families with a good deal of disposable income and growing active businesses that require in-office catering on a regular basis. The families are of an income level where a good deal is spent on dining out and/or in-home parties that are catered. These same people also manage and/or own the businesses that we will target for our catering services. If good food and service is experienced at The Restaurant by these people in one aspect of their life, they will feel very comfortable in dealing with the same firm for the other aspects that require similar services.

Marketing Strategy

The Company will have a three-directional marketing strategy to insure the continued growth and success of the endeavor. With each partner working in unison toward all three, but concentrating on one phase each of this strategy, we will be assured of continued and complete coverage of our efforts. The three directions are as follows:

1. The first marketing approach is the operation of the restaurant as a stand-alone business. We will concentrate efforts in giving quality food and service in a clean, businesslike atmosphere, one that will attract business people for breakfast and lunch hours, yet will not be so "stuffy" as to make singles and families feel unwelcome or uncomfortable dining in. This task will fall to the managing, on-premise partner.

2. The second marketing approach will be promoted by one of the other partners. This will involve selling the outside catering services of The Restaurant to local businesses—concentrating on those with consistent need for quick-response catering or those with regular catering needs but require work within budgets and/or varied menus. Our efforts will be directed toward preparing and offering our clients a variety of menus from which to choose.

3. The final marketing strategy will involve the third partner who will be involved in the ongoing advertising and promotion of The Restaurant. This will certainly overlap with responsibilities with the other two partners as to scheduling and contracting with various offers.

Promotion and Advertising

Our advertising efforts will be concentrated in several areas: newspaper, radio, yellow pages, and mail/hand-delivered flyers. Radio and newspaper will play an important part in the grand opening promotion for The Restaurant to gain the maximum exposure in the shortest possible time. This will be backed up by distribution of hand-delivered flyers to local businesses that will use our breakfast and lunch offerings and catering services.

Newspaper and flyers will primarily be concentrated on offering coupons for redemption in discount pricing of loss leaders to stimulate customer traffic. This will have the effect of creating additional sales of full-markup items to complement the loss leaders. Couponing will be directed by location—a particular offering for household needs and a different offering for the business clients. Residential coupons will offer discounts on volume bagel purchases, by the dozen, and cents-off coupons for deli meat purchases. Commercial coupons will target high-ticket spending with discounts on prepared trays, with larger discounts offered on higher priced orders. Also, commercial coupons will offer an "office bagel breakfast" consisting of bagels, cream cheese, juice, and utensils for the entire office at a greatly reduced rate. This will stimulate higher ticket sales and expose our product more quickly to a wider market. As a variation on a well-used theme, we will have a business card drawing weekly for this above-described "office bagel breakfast."

Radio will be used as an effective tool to stimulate traffic during the morning and afternoon rush hours. Driving and eating seems to be a national pastime that we intend to capitalize on. A trick for good radio advertisement is to provide station personalities with samples to try—they then give personal endorsements and testimonials for The Company.

RECIPE

The recipe for our bagel is based on that used in a well-known French restaurant. This recipe was published in *Bernard Clayton's New Complete Book of Breads*. A little background is as follows:

> More than half of the half-million French Jews live in Paris—and all at one time or another eat and shop at the large Jo Goldenberg restaurant-deli at *7 rue des Rosiers*. It is a Paris institution in a neighborhood surrounded by four synagogues and half again as many Catholic churches (the Cathedral of Notre Dame is less than a mile away). The district is old, worn, and well past its prime.
>
> One should have a mission to go there, and a Goldenberg bagel is mine whenever I visit Paris.
>
> The Goldenberg bagel can be made as varied as the imagination will allow—onion, sesame seed, poppy seed, white, rye, salted, plain, whole wheat, caraway seed, and on and on. Bagel lovers are fiercely partisan to their water or egg positions.

This recipe comes with a significant following and history. The recipe produces a high-quality bagel that is excellent for shelf life as well as taste to the most discerning palate. Using different variations for flavor and different flours, we will be able to produce a bagel that should generate a following in the Charleston area—hopefully as successful as the reputation from the Goldenberg restaurant!

Report Summary
Study for Lox & Bagels, Inc.

ANALYSIS PROCESSED on 4/4/1992 for Income/Balance on 01/01/93

ASSETS	($)
Cash and Equivalents	36,000
Accounts Receivable	0
Inventory	10,000
All Other Current	575
Total Current	46,575
Fixed Assets (Net)	126,005
Intangibles (Net)	0
All Other Noncurrent	145,000
TOTAL ASSETS	317,580
LIABILITIES	
Notes Payable—Short Term	0
Current Matured Long-Term Debt	10,750
Accounts Payable	10,100
Income Taxes Payable	0
All Other Current	3,050
TOTAL CURRENT	23,900
Long-Term Debt	59,250
Deferred Taxes	0
All Other Noncurrent	0
Net Worth	234,430
TOTAL LIABILITIES & NET WORTH	317,580
INCOME DATA	
Net Sales	657,239
Gross Profit	365,930
Operating Expenses	285,642
Operating Profit	80,288
All Other Expenses (Net)	26,771
Profit Before Taxes	53,517
CASH MARKET VALUE	409,540
BREAK-EVEN POINT	526,937
OPERATING CAPITAL	35,900
RATIOS	
CURRENT RATIO	1.9
QUICK RATIO	1.5
SALES/RECEIVABLES	inf
COST OF SALES/INVENTORY	29.1
COST OF SALES/PAYABLES	28.8
SALES/WORKING CAPITAL	29.0
EBIT/INTEREST	7.1
CASH FLOW/CURRENT MATURITY (LTD)	7.8
FIXED/WORTH	0.5
DEBT/WORTH	0.4
% PROFIT BEFORE TAXES/NET WORTH	22.8
% PROFIT BEFORE TAXES/TOTAL ASSETS	16.9
SALES/NET FIXED ASSETS	5.2
SALES/TOTAL ASSETS	2.1
DEGREE OF OPERATING LEVERAGE	2.81
Z-SCORE PREDICTOR	5.53

Income Statement
Study for Lox & Bagels, Inc.
Period Ended 01/01/93

	Period Data 8.33% of Annual ($)	Annual ($)
GROSS SALES/REVENUES	56,333	676,267
Less: Discounts & Returns	1,585	19,028
NET SALES/REVENUES	54,748	657,239
Less: Cost of Goods Sold/Cost of Contracts	24,266	291,309
GROSS PROFIT	30,482	365,930
Other Income	0	0
TOTAL RECEIPTS	30,482	365,930
OPERATING EXPENSES		
Advertising & Promotion	1,500	18,007
Bad Debts	0	0
Bank Services Charges	15	180
Car & Delivery	0	0
Commissions	0	0
Amortization of Intangibles	0	0
Depreciation/Depletion	2,500	30,012
Dues & Publications	20	240
Employee Benefit Program	0	0
Freight	0	0
Insurance	575	6,903
Laundry & Cleaning	100	1,200
Leased Equipment	0	0
Legal/Professional	0	0
Office Expense	25	300
Outside Labor	0	0
Pension/P.S./Payroll Taxes	2,388	28,667
Rent	1,500	18,007
Repairs & Maintenance	500	6,002
Operating Supplies	500	6,002
Taxes & Licenses	25	300
Travel & Entertainment	0	0
Utilities & Telephone	975	11,705
WAGES		
Salaries—Officers	0	0
Payroll	6,700	80,432
	0	0
	0	0
WASTE	6,471	77,683
	0	0
TOTAL OPERATING EXPENSES	23,794	285,642
INTEREST	730	8,764
MISCELLANEOUS EXPENSES	1,500	18,007
TOTAL EXPENSES	26,024	312,413
PROFIT (LOSS) BEFORE TAXES	4,458	53,517
TAXES	0	0
NET PROFIT (LOSS) AFTER TAXES	4,458	53,517
DIVIDEND/DISTRIBUTION	0	0
RETAINED EARNINGS	4,458	53,517

Balance Sheet
Study for Lox & Bagels, Inc.
Period Ended 01/01/93

	($)	($)
ASSETS		
Cash & Equivalents	36,000	
Accts Receivable Trade (Net)	0	
A/R Prog. Billings	0	
A/R Cur. Retention	0	
Merchandise Inventory	10,000	
Cost & Estimated Earnings in Excess of Billing	0	
Prepaid Expenses	575	
Other Current Assets	0	
TOTAL CURRENT ASSETS		46,575
Fixtures	5,165	
Vehicles	0	
Equipment	115,840	
Leasehold Improvements	35,000	
Buildings	0	
Land	0	
Accumulated Depreciation	(30,000)	
TOTAL FIXED ASSETS		126,005
JOINT VENTURES & INVESTMENT		145,000
INTANGIBLES		0
OTHER NONCURRENT ASSETS		0
TOTAL ASSETS		317,580
LIABILITIES & OWNERS' EQUITY		
Accounts Payable (Trade)	10,100	
Accounts Payable (Retention)	0	
Current Portion LTD	10,750	
Notes Payable (Short Term)	0	
Billings in Excess of Estimated Earnings	0	
Accrued Expenses	2,475	
Income Taxes Payable	0	
Other Current Liabilities	575	
TOTAL CURRENT LIABILITIES		23,900
Notes Payable (Long Term)	59,250	
Bank Loans Payable	0	
Deferred Taxes	0	
Other Loans Payable	0	
Other Long-Term Liabilities	0	
TOTAL LONG-TERM LIABILITIES		59,250
TOTAL LIABILITIES		83,150
Retained Earnings	234,430	
Capital Stock	0	
NET WORTH		234,430
TOTAL LIABILITIES & STOCKHOLDERS' EQUITY		317,580

Break-even Analysis
Study for Lox & Bagels, Inc.
ANALYSIS PROCESSED ON 4/4/1992 FOR INCOME/BALANCE ON 01/01/93

	($)	(%)
SALES/REVENUE	657,239	100.00
VARIABLE DISBURSEMENTS		
Cost of Goods Sold/Cost of Contracts	291,309	44.32
Advertising	18,007	2.74
Bad Debts	0	0.00
Car/Delivery	0	0.00
Commissions	0	0.00
Freight	0	0.00
Taxes/Licenses	300	0.05
Travel and Entertainment	0	0.00
WASTE	77,683	11.82
	0	0.00
TOTAL VARIABLE DISBURSEMENTS	387,299	58.93
CONTRIBUTION	269,940	41.07
FIXED DISBURSEMENTS		
Bank Services Charges	180	0.03
Amortization of Intangibles	0	0.00
Depreciation/Depletion	30,012	4.57
Dues & Publications	240	0.04
Employee Benefit Program	0	0.00
Insurance	6,903	1.05
Laundry & Cleaning	1,200	0.18
Leased Equipment	0	0.00
Legal/Professional	0	0.00
Office Expense	300	0.05
Outside Labor	0	0.00
Pension/P.S./Payroll Taxes	28,667	4.36
Rent	18,007	2.74
Repairs & Maintenance	6,002	0.91
Supplies, Operating	6,002	0.91
Utilities	11,705	1.78
Salaries—Officers	0	0.00
Payroll	80,432	12.24
	0	0.00
	0	0.00
Interest	8,764	1.33
Miscellaneous Expenses/(Income)	18,007	2.74
TOTAL FIXED DISBURSEMENTS	216,423	32.93
PRETAX PROFIT	53,517	8.14
DOLLAR SALES BREAK-EVEN POINT	526,937	

DEGREE OF OPERATING LEVERAGE	2.81
Z-SCORE PREDICTOR	5.53

Operating Capital Analysis
Study for Lox & Bagels, Inc.
ANALYSIS PROCESSED ON 4/4/1992 FOR INCOME/BALANCE ON 01/01/93

	($)
Sales/Revenue	657,239
Cash	36,000
Accounts Receivable	0
A/R Prog. Billings	0
A/R Cur. Retention	0
Inventory	10,000
Accounts Payable (Trade)	10,100
Accounts Payable (Retention)	0
Average Sales per Day (Based on 365 days per year)	1,801

	(DAYS)
CASH ON HAND / AVERAGE DAYS SALES	19.99
RECEIVABLES / AVERAGE DAYS SALES	0.00
INVENTORY / AVERAGE DAYS SALES	5.55
TOTAL TRADING CYCLE	25.55
PAYABLES / AVERAGE DAYS SALES	5.61
NET CASH CYCLE	19.94
OPERATING CAPITAL	$35,900

Cash Market Value Analysis
Study for Lox & Bagels, Inc.
ANALYSIS PROCESSED ON 4/4/1992 FOR INCOME/BALANCE ON 01/01/93

BOOK METHOD	
Book Value of Assets Less Liabilities	$ 234,430
CAPITALIZATION OF EARNINGS METHOD	
Last Year's Earnings	$ 53,517
Less 8.0% Return on Book Value	− 18,754
Excess Earnings	= 34,763
Value of Goodwill (Excess Earnings/0.150)	$ 231,754
Book Value	+ 234,430
Total Value of Business	$ 466,184
STRAIGHT CAPITALIZATION METHOD	
Last Year's Earnings	
Capitalized at 15.0% (Last Year's Earnings/0.150)	$ 356,783
YEARS OF INCOME PURCHASED METHOD	
Last Year's Earnings	$ 53,517
Less 8.0% Return on Book Value	− 18,754
Excess Earnings	= 34,763
5 Years' Excess Earnings Purchased	$ 173,815
Book Value	+ 234,430
Total Value of Business	$ 408,245
PREVIOUS VALUATION METHOD	
Previous Valuation	$ 0

METHOD	VALUE	WEIGHT
BOOK METHOD	234,430	0.5
CAPITALIZATION OF EARNINGS METHOD	466,184	2.5
STRAIGHT CAPITALIZATION METHOD	356,783	1.0
YEARS OF INCOME PURCHASED METHOD	408,245	1.0
PREVIOUS VALUATION METHOD	0	0.0

WEIGHT FACTORED VALUATION FOR 7500	$409,540
WEIGHT FACTORED VALUATION FOR STND # 581A1	0
COMPARATIVE CASH MARKET VALUE ADVANTAGE	409,540

Financial Statement Projections
Income Statement
($000)

DATE	01/01/93	YEAR +1	YEAR +2	YEAR +3	YEAR +4	YEAR +5
NET SALES	657.2	723.0	795.3	874.8	962.3	1058.5
Cost of Goods	291.3	322.0	356.0	393.6	435.1	481.0
Gross Profit	365.9	400.9	439.2	481.2	527.2	577.5
Other Income	0.0	0.0	0.0	0.0	0.0	0.0
TOTAL RECEIPTS	365.9	400.9	439.2	481.2	527.2	577.5
Variable Costs	96.0	105.7	116.4	128.1	141.1	155.4
Contribution (GP-VC)	269.9	295.2	322.8	353.1	386.1	422.1
Depr/Depl/Amort	30.0	30.0	30.0	30.0	30.0	6.0
Other Fixed Costs	174.1	174.1	174.1	174.1	174.1	174.1
TOTAL EXPENSES	300.1	309.8	320.5	332.3	345.2	335.4
Before Tax Profit	65.8	91.1	118.7	148.9	182.0	242.1
Income Taxes	0.0	25.5	33.2	41.7	50.9	67.8
AFTER TAX PROFIT	65.8	65.6	85.5	107.2	131.1	174.3
DIVIDENDS	0.0	0.0	0.0	0.0	0.0	0.0
RETAINED EARNINGS	65.8	65.6	85.5	107.2	131.1	174.3

Balance Sheet
($000)

DATE	01/01/93	YEAR +1	YEAR +2	YEAR +3	YEAR +4	YEAR +5
ASSETS						
Cash	36.0	120.5	225.3	351.9	502.4	671.9
Accts Rcvbl	0.0	0.0	0.0	0.0	0.0	0.0
Inventory	10.0	11.0	12.1	13.3	14.6	16.1
Prepaid Expenses	0.5	0.5	0.5	0.6	0.6	0.6
Other Current	0.0	0.0	0.0	0.0	0.0	0.0
Fixed Asset Net	126.0	96.0	66.0	36.0	6.0	0.0
Other Noncurrent	145.0	145.0	145.0	145.0	145.0	145.0
TOTAL ASSETS	317.5	373.0	448.9	546.8	668.6	833.6
LIABILITIES						
Accts Payable	10.1	11.2	12.3	13.6	15.1	16.7
Curr Port LTD	10.8	10.8	10.8	10.8	10.8	10.8
Accrued Expenses	2.5	2.0	2.0	2.1	2.2	2.1
Income Tax Payable	0.0	0.0	0.0	0.0	0.0	0.0
N/P Shrt Term	0.0	0.0	0.0	0.1	0.0	0.0
Other Current	0.5	0.5	0.5	0.5	0.5	0.5
N/P Long Term	59.3	48.5	37.8	27.0	16.3	5.5
Other Long Term	0.0	0.0	0.0	0.0	0.0	0.0
TOTAL LIABILITIES	83.2	73.0	63.4	54.1	44.9	35.6
NET WORTH						
Retained Earnings	234.4	300.0	385.5	492.7	623.7	798.0
Capital Stock	0.0	0.0	0.0	0.0	0.0	0.0
TOTAL LIABILITIES & NET WORTH	317.5	373.0	448.9	546.8	668.6	833.6

**Projected
Cash-Flow Analysis
Base Date 01/01/93**

DATE 4/4/1992

	YEAR 1	YEAR 2	YEAR 3	YEAR 4	YEAR 5
CASH FLOW FROM OPERATIONS:	$ 000	$ 000	$ 000	$ 000	$ 000
PROFIT AFTER TAXES	65.6	85.5	107.2	131.0	174.3
PLUS:					
Depr/Depl/Amort Expense	30.0	30.0	30.0	30.0	6.0
WORKING CAPITAL FROM OPERATIONS	95.6	115.5	137.2	161.0	180.3
PLUS:					
INC (DEC) VS. PREV PER IN-					
Accounts Payable	1.1	1.1	1.3	1.5	1.6
Accrued Expenses	−0.5	0.0	0.1	0.1	−0.1
Other Current Liabilities	0.0	0.0	0.0	0.0	0.0
PLUS:					
DEC (INC) VS. PREV PER IN-					
Accounts Receivable	0.0	0.0	0.0	0.0	0.0
Inventory	−1.0	−1.1	−1.2	−1.3	−1.5
Prepaid Expenses	0.0	0.0	−0.1	0.0	0.0
Other Current Assets	0.0	0.0	0.0	0.0	0.0
NET CASH FLOW FROM OPERATIONS	95.2	115.5	137.3	161.3	180.3
CASH FLOW FROM INVESTING ACTIVITIES:					
DEC (INC) VS. PREV PER IN—					
Fixed Assets	0.0	0.0	0.0	0.0	0.0
Other Noncurrent Assets	0.0	0.0	0.0	0.0	0.0
NET CASH FLOW FROM INVESTING	0.0	0.0	0.0	0.0	0.0
CASH FLOW FROM FINANCING:					
INC (DEC) VS. PREV PER IN—					
Short-Term Debt	0.0	0.0	0.1	−0.1	0.0
Long-Term Debt	−10.8	−10.7	−10.8	−10.7	−10.8
Other Long-Term Liabilities	0.0	0.0	0.0	0.0	0.0
Capital Stock Add/Ret Earnings Adj.	0.0	0.0	0.0	0.0	0.0
LESS: DIVIDENDS PAID	0.0	0.0	0.0	0.0	0.0
NET CASH FLOW FROM FINANCING	−10.8	−10.7	−10.7	−10.8	−10.8
TOTAL CASH FLOWS	84.4	104.8	126.6	150.5	169.5

PRO FORMA TRENDS SUMMARY

RUN DATE:

	01/01/93 $000	YEAR +1 $000	YEAR +2 $000	YEAR +3 $000	YEAR +4 $000	4/4/1992 YEAR +5 $ 000
BALANCE SHEET DATA						
Cash	36.0	120.5	225.3	351.9	502.4	671.9
Accounts Receivables	0.0	0.0	0.0	0.0	0.0	0.0
Inventory	10.0	11.0	12.1	13.3	14.6	16.1
Prepaid Expenses	0.5	0.5	0.5	0.6	0.6	0.6
Other Current	0.0	0.0	0.0	0.0	0.0	0.0
TOTAL CURRENT	46.5	132.0	237.9	365.8	517.6	688.6
Fixed Asset Net	126.0	96.0	66.0	36.0	6.0	0.0
Other Noncurrent	145.0	145.0	145.0	145.0	145.0	145.0
TOTAL ASSETS	317.5	373.0	448.9	546.8	668.6	833.6
N/P Short Term	0.0	0.0	0.0	0.1	0.0	0.0
Cur Port LTD	10.8	10.8	10.8	10.8	10.8	10.8
Accounts Payable	10.1	11.2	12.3	13.6	15.1	16.7
Income Tax Payable	0.0	0.0	0.0	0.0	0.0	0.0
Accrued Expenses	2.5	2.0	2.0	2.1	2.2	2.1
Other Current	0.5	0.5	0.5	0.5	0.5	0.5
TOTAL CURRENT	23.9	24.5	25.6	27.1	28.6	30.1
N/P Long Term	59.3	48.5	37.8	27.0	16.3	5.5
Other Long Term	0.0	0.0	0.0	0.0	0.0	0.0
TOTAL LIABILITIES	83.2	73.0	63.4	54.1	44.9	35.6
NET WORTH						
Retained Earnings	234.4	300.0	385.5	492.7	623.7	798.0
Capital Stock	0.0	0.0	0.0	0.0	0.0	0.0
TOTAL LIABILITIES &						
NET WORTH	317.6	373.0	448.9	546.8	668.6	833.6
INCOME STATEMENT						
DATA						
Net Sales	657.2	723.0	795.3	874.8	962.3	1058.5
Gross Profit	365.9	400.9	439.2	481.2	527.2	577.5
Other Income	0.0	0.0	0.0	0.0	0.0	0.0
Total Receipts	365.9	400.9	439.2	481.2	527.2	577.5
Variable Costs	96.0	105.7	116.4	128.1	141.1	155.4
Contribution (GP-VC)	269.9	295.2	322.8	353.1	386.1	422.1
Fixed Costs	204.1	204.1	204.1	204.1	204.1	180.1
Total Expenses	300.1	309.8	320.5	332.3	345.2	335.4
Before Tax Profits	65.8	91.1	118.7	148.9	182.0	242.1
Income Taxes	0.0	25.5	33.2	41.7	50.9	67.8
After Tax Profits	65.8	65.6	85.5	107.2	131.1	174.3
Dividends	0.0	0.0	0.0	0.0	0.0	0.0
Retained Earnings	65.8	65.6	85.5	107.2	131.1	174.3
Net Cash Flow from						
Operations		95.2	115.5	137.3	161.3	180.3
Break-even Point	497.0	499.9	502.9	505.9	508.9	451.4
Operating Capital	35.9	120.3	225.1	351.6	501.9	671.3

	PRO FORMA TRENDS SUMMARY *(continued)*				**RUN DATE:**	
	01/01/93 $000	YEAR +1 $000	YEAR +2 $000	YEAR +3 $000	YEAR +4 $000	4/4/1992 YEAR +5 $000
RATIOS						
CURRENT RATIO	1.9	5.4	9.3	13.5	18.1	22.9
QUICK RATIO	1.5	4.9	8.8	13.0	17.6	22.3
SALES/RECEIVABLES	inf	inf	inf	inf	inf	inf
COST OF SALES/ INVENTORY	29.1	29.3	29.4	29.6	29.8	29.9
COST OF SALES/ PAYABLES	28.8	28.8	28.9	28.9	28.8	28.8
FIXED/WORTH	0.5	0.3	0.2	0.1	0.0	0.0
DEBT/WORTH	0.4	0.2	0.2	0.1	0.1	0.0
% PROFIT BEFORE TAXES/NET WORTH	22.8	30.4	30.8	30.2	29.2	30.3
% PROFIT BEFORE TAXES/TOTAL ASSETS	16.9	24.4	26.4	27.2	27.2	29.0
SALES/NET FIXED ASSETS	5.2	7.5	12.0	24.3	160.4	inf
SALES/TOTAL ASSETS	2.1	1.9	1.8	1.6	1.4	1.3
SALES/WORKING CAPITAL	29.0	6.7	3.7	2.6	2.0	1.6

Lox & Bagels, Inc.
April 4, 1992
Start-Up Costs

Renovations	$ 35,000
Equipment	115,840
Inventory—Food	10,000
Inventory—Supplies	500
Furniture/Fixtures	6,000
Office Equipment/Supplies	100
Attorney Fees (S Corporation)	1,500
Working Capital	36,000
Deposits/Licenses	2,000
Subtotal	$ 206,940
Less: Owners' Downpayment	− 145,000
Total	$ 61,940

APPENDICES

RETAIL MARKET FACTORS—II

CHARLESTON—NORTH CHARLESTON SC SMSA

DETAILED DEMOGRAPHIC INFORMATION BY CENSUS TRACT

COUNTY: CHARLESTON

CITY NAME	ST	ZIP CODE	CENSUS TRACT	POPULATION 1980 CENSUS	POPULATION 1991 UPDATE	HOUSEHOLDS 1980 CENSUS	HOUSEHOLDS 1991 UPDATE	1991 Est. HHI 0–9.9	10–14.9	15–24.9	25–49.9	50 & OVER	AGE UNDER 18	18–24	25–34	35–44	45–54	55 & OVER	COLL GRAD	PROF WRKR	UNSK WRKR	% SFDU	% MFDU	OWNER OCC	RES % 1–2	% 3–5	% 6–9	% 10+
CHARLESTON	SC	29420	31.01	8,956	10,272	2,841	3,526	14	11	25	38	12	36	16	22	12	7	7	8	14	22	62	38	61	45	19	12	24
			31.03	6,135	9,218	1,694	2,926	9	8	21	40	22	29	27	15	12	8	9	14	26	12	47	53	72	55	24	9	12
EDISTO ISLAND	SC	29438	23	1,345	1,313	375	397	24	14	26	29	7	34	14	14	7	10	21	8	8	22	96	4	75	25	30	22	23
FOLLY BEACH	SC	29439	20.04	1,478	1,235	674	609	14	10	24	36	16	16	16	26	9	10	23	18	25	9	77	23	52	55	16	11	18
GOOSE CREEK	SC	29445	42	1,593	6,608	121	1,833	12	6	14	31	37	10	60	16	9	4	1	28	11	29	50	50	5	70	27	3	0
HOLLYWOOD	SC	29449	25	6,795	6,333	1,943	1,958	31	13	20	27	9	35	14	14	10	9	18	4	13	21	89	11	81	30	24	14	32
ISLE OF PALMS	SC	29451	46.04	4,294	7,058	1,360	2,423	11	8	19	37	25	33	12	23	12	9	11	20	25	16	69	31	73	41	31	9	16
			49	3,421	3,689	1,293	1,508	6	5	14	34	41	24	12	22	14	11	17	37	37	6	83	17	71	25	31	19	25
JOHNS ISLAND	SC	29455	21.01	6,016	6,211	1,835	2,049	19	9	20	37	15	34	12	16	12	10	16	6	16	20	90	10	84	29	28	27	16
LADSON	SC	29456	27.01	3,194	3,267	999	1,107	19	12	24	30	15	34	17	17	11	8	13	3	14	21	68	32	58	42	26	13	19
MC CLELLANVL	SC	29458	50	4,199	3,448	1,283	1,142	22	13	23	29	13	32	12	15	10	10	21	9	14	17	93	7	82	16	18	13	53
MT PLEASANT	SC	29464	46.01	2,182	1,958	613	595	26	14	23	28	9	36	13	15	12	9	15	3	7	20	85	15	86	24	35	33	8
			46.03	10,057	20,590	3,368	7,507	8	4	9	30	49	30	11	22	14	10	13	39	40	7	59	41	74	42	29	15	14
			46.04	4,294	7,058	1,360	2,423	11	8	19	37	25	33	12	23	12	9	11	20	25	16	69	31	73	41	34	9	16
			47	6,943	6,679	2,563	2,666	13	7	16	38	26	26	13	22	11	10	18	24	30	11	75	25	70	27	24	14	35
RAVENEL	SC	29470	25	6,795	6,333	1,943	1,958	31	13	20	27	9	35	14	14	10	9	18	4	13	21	89	11	81	30	24	14	32
SULLIVANS IS	SC	29482	48	1,867	1,601	731	680	8	5	13	33	41	20	14	24	11	9	22	48	41	6	76	24	66	25	24	15	36

SOME CENSUS TRACTS CROSS ZIP BOUNDARIES. THE DATA PRINTED IS FOR THE ENTIRE TRACT, NOT JUST FOR THE PORTION WITHIN A ZIP CODE.

MARKET PROFILE ANALYSIS—1991—SUMMARY DATA

CHARLESTON-NORTH CHARLESTON SC SMSA

COUNTY: CHARLESTON

CITY NAME	ST	ZIP CODE	RETAIL FACTORS		BUSINESS FACTORS		COMPETITIVE FACTORS				
			1991 POPULATION ESTIMATE	1991 HOUSEHOLD ESTIMATE	# BUSINESSES	# EMPLOYEES	COMMERCIAL BANKING OFFICES	THRIFT INSTITUT'N OFFICES	TOTAL BKING OFF. (CR UNION)	RATIO POP'N PER BKNG OFF	RATIO HHLD PER BKNG OFF
CHARLESTON	SC	29425	–	–	1	4	–	–	–(0)	–	–
EDISTO ISLAND	SC	29438	1,539	475	68	417	1	0	1(0)	1,539	475
FOLLY BEACH	SC	29439	1,327	637	58	208	–	–	–(0)	–	–
HOLLYWOOD	SC	29449	2,424	749	91	625	1	0	1(0)	2,424	749
ISLE OF PALMS	SC	29451	4,024	1,629	122	961	1	0	1(0)	4,024	1,629
JOHNS ISLAND	SC	29455	12,332	4,062	344	3,562	2	0	2(0)	6,166	2,031
LADSON	SC	29456	2,676	874	228	2,714	–	–	–(0)	–	–
MC CLELLANVL	SC	29458	2,441	809	52	376	–	–	–(0)	–	–
MT PLEASANT	SC	29464	35,603	12,967	1,132	9,480	7	8	15(0)	2,374	864
MT PLEASANT	SC	29465	–	–	21	50	–	–	–(0)	–	–
RAVENEL	SC	29470	2,898	890	75	394	–	–	–(0)	–	–

MARKET PROFILE ANALYSIS—1991—SUMMARY DATA

CHARLESTON-NORTH CHARLESTON SC SMSA

COUNTY: CHARLESTON

CITY NAME	ST	ZIP CODE	RETAIL FACTORS		BUSINESS FACTORS		COMPETITIVE FACTORS				
			1991 POPULATION ESTIMATE	1991 HOUSEHOLD ESTIMATE	# BUSINESSES	# EMPLOYEES	COMMERCIAL BANKING OFFICES	THRIFT INSTITUT'N OFFICES	TOTAL BKING OFF. (CR UNION)	RATIO POP'N PER BKNG OFF	RATIO HHLD PER BKNG OFF
SULLIVANS IS	SC	29482	1,583	672	61	254	–	–	–(0)	–	–
WADMALAW IS	SC	29487	2,554	778	36	130	–	–	–(0)	–	–
YONGES ISLAND	SC	29494	–	–	33	310	–	–	–(0)	–	–
SUMMARY TOTAL(S)			312,057	111,349	11,391	142,662	76	36	112(11)	2,786	994

Census Tract Map— Mt. Pleasant

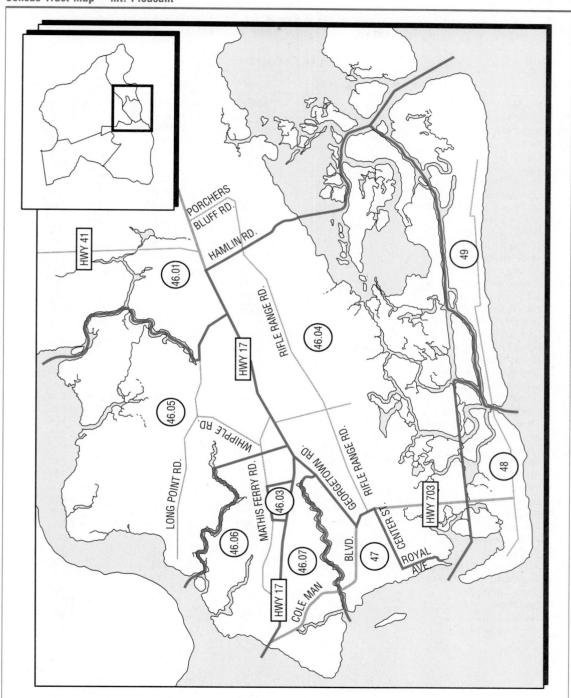

Equipment Price List

Lox & Bagels, Inc.
April 4, 1992

Equipment Price List

	Quantity	Used	New	Extended Price
Proofer	1	$3,500	$ 2,741	$ 2,741
Bagel Mixer	1		12,500	12,500
Bagel Machine	1		22,167	22,167
Kettle	1		7,240	7,240
Oven	1		17,130	17,130
Stove	1	2,500		2,500
Range Hood 4' x 8'	1		8,000	8,000
Can Opener	1		110	110
SS Pots & Pans (assortment)			1,000	1,000
Shelving-Metal Racks	6		250	1,500
Rolling Flour Bin	1		75	75
Rolling Sugar Bin	1		75	75
Work Table Plastic Top	1		450	450
SS Work Tables	2	400		800
Handsink	1	65		65
SS Triple Sink	1	450		450
Walk-in Cooler 7' x 7'	1	5,000		5,000
Shelving Racks 18" x 72"	6		128	768
Shelving Posts	12		29	348
Small Freezer 3' x 3'	1	400		400
Rolling Racks	2	150		300
Dishwasher (commercial)	1		1,500	1,500
Racks-glasses	2		250	500
Racks-plates	2		250	500
Racks-coffee cups	2		250	500
Trash Cans (55 gal cap)	3		55	165
Industrial Water Heater (100 gal capacity)	1		500	500
TNS Spray Nozzle	1		280	280
SS Trays—Full size	40		12	480
Plastic Bus Bins	3		20	60
Cash Register	1	600		600
Electronic Scale	1		1,000	1,000
Meat Slicer	1	1,500		1,500
Plastic See-Thru Bins	9		111	999
Bun Toaster	1		541	541
Tea Dispenser (10 gal)	1		226	226
Bunomatic Coffee Maker	1		330	330
Glass Coffee Pots	4		15	60
Bar Stools	10		125	1,250
Tables: 4 seaters	11	100		1,100
2 seaters	5	100		500

Equipment Price List (continued)

	Quantity	Used	New	Extended Price
Chairs	92	40		3,680
Deli Case	1		500	500
Glass Display Case	1		500	500
Stand-Up Refrigerator				
Display Case	1	1,600	2,339	2,339
Microwave	2	600		1,200
Icemaker (400# cap)	1		2,800	2,800
China Plates				
Large				
Small				
Cups				
Saucers			3,500	3,500
Bowls				
Glasses				
Water				
Juice				
Silverware				
Miscellaneous				6,366
			Total	$117,095

Menu

BREAKFAST

Includes Egg and Bagel
with Cream Cheese:

Lox & Onions	4.99
Omelette	3.49
Cheese Omelette	3.99
Peppers, Mushrooms, Onions	3.99
Bacon or Sausage	1.99

OTHER BREAKFAST

2 Eggs, Bagels & Butter	1.99
Fried Egg Sandwich	1.29
Egg and Bacon Sandwich	1.99
Egg, Ham & Cheese	2.39
Eggs Benedict	4.99
French Toast with Syrup	3.49
Cereals	.99
Hot Cakes	1.99
Waffles	3.29
Oatmeal	1.29

SIDE ORDERS

Toast	.49
Canadian Bacon	1.99
Bacon	.99
Hash Browns	.99
Sausages	.99
Grits	.99

BAGELS

with Butter	.75
with Cream Cheese	1.29
with Lox & Cream Cheese	1.99
Plain with Choice of Toppings	.49

PASTRIES

Danish	.99
Croissants	.99
Muffins	1.19
Brownies	.69

SOUPS

Chicken Noodle
Soup of the Day
Chili
All are . . . . Cup 1.99   Bowl 2.49

DRINKS

Hot Chocolate	.79
Soft Drinks	.89
Milk	.89
Fruit Juice	.89
Tea	.69
Coffee	.69

LUNCH SPECIALS

All Served with Side Order
and all Condiments

Corned Beef	4.99
Pastrami	4.99
Roast Beef	4.49
Tuna	5.49
Turkey	4.99
BLT	3.99
3 Meat Sandwich	5.99
Turkey, Ham & Swiss	5.49

DINNERS

All Include Dessert & Side Order

Corned Beef & Cabbage	6.49
Hot Roast Beef	6.39
Turkey	6.49
Hot Dog	3.99

SIDE ORDERS

Bagel Chips	2.99
Baked Beans	.89
Cole Slaw	.99
French Fries	.99
Potatoe Salad	.99
Salad	3.49
Onion Rings	1.19
Tuna Salad	3.99

DESSERTS

Apple Pie	1.99
a la mode	2.49
Cake	2.49
Cheese Cake	1.99
with Topping	2.39
Ice Cream	.69
Milk Shake	1.99
Sundae	2.39

SANDWICHES

Cold

Bologna	3.59
Cheese	1.99
Chicken Salad	3.59
Corned Beef	3.99
Ham	3.29
Egg Salad	3.29
Roast Beef	3.99
Salami	3.59
Tuna	3.59
Turkey Breast	3.89
Turkey Smoked	3.89

Hot

BLT	2.99
Corned Beef	3.99
with Pastrami	5.29
Grilled Cheese	2.99
with Bacon	3.79
with Ham	4.29
Hamburger	3.99
Hot Dog	1.99
with Chili	2.49
Pastrami	3.99
with Salami	5.29
Roast	3.99

SUBS

Deli	4.99
Italian	4.99

**LOX & BAGELS APPRECIATES
YOUR PATRONAGE**

Please try our party trays for all of
your catering needs.

All items are available for carry out
at no additional charge.

Call ahead for quick pick-up.
76B-AGEL

Coupons

Lox & Bagels

Office Breakfast Special

– one dozen assorted bagels
– with cream cheese
– one–half gallon of orange juice
– cups and plates included

All for just $9.99
Good Monday–Friday

$ $ $ $

Lox & Bagels

Two dollars off a dozen bagels

Good before noon
Monday through Friday
Located in Mt. Pleasant

$ $ $ $

Yellow Pages Ad

Lox & Bagels

Get a fresh start to your Day

Fresh Bagels
Assorted Muffins
Eggs & Bacon

Deli Sandwiches
Hot Dogs
Homemade Desserts

Open 7 days of the week
6 till 4

Located in Mt. Pleasant

Coupons

$ $

Lox & Bagels

Get a fresh start to your
DAY

99 cent Bagel with Cream Cheese

$ $

$ $

Lox & Bagels

50 cents off all deli meats

Located in Mt. Pleasant

$ $

Proposed floor plan for dining area

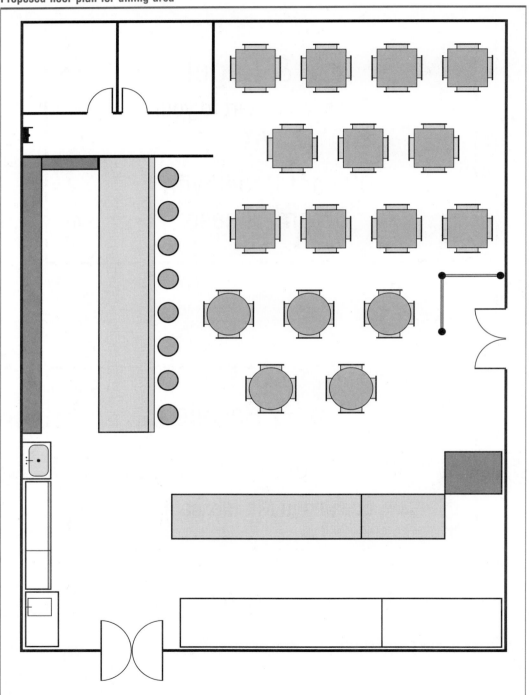

Proposed floor plan for kitchen area

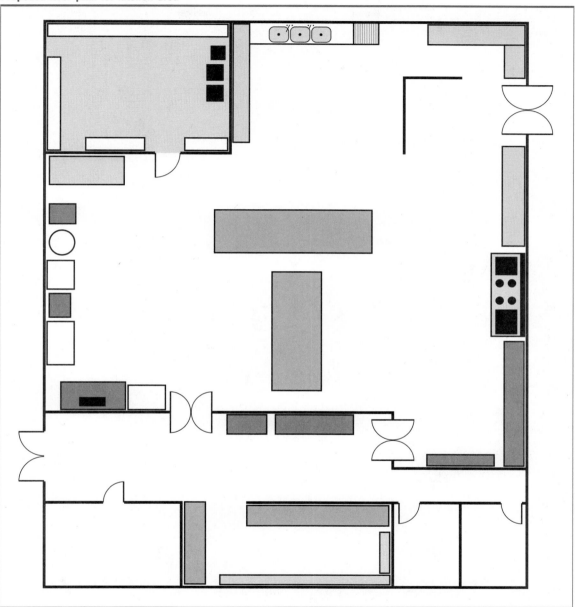

B | COMPUTERS AND PERIPHERALS

A recent survey of firms with no more than 100 employees indicated that the use of computers in small business is quite common. Almost 73 percent of the surveyed firms reported that they used a computer in their business. Although the larger the firm, the greater the propensity to use a computer, almost 64 percent of the firms with ten or fewer employees used a computer. In the construction industry, 82.3 percent of the firms used a computer, whereas only 64.3 percent of those in the service industry used a computer in their business.[1]

Given the large number of small businesses that use computers, the purpose of this appendix is to provide a brief introduction to business computers and computer peripherals. The emphasis will be on the features for which small business owners should look before purchasing computers or computer peripherals.

IS THERE A NEED FOR A COMPUTER?

Computers are designed to store and manipulate large amounts of data, and therein lies their principal use. Before deciding to purchase a computer, small business owners should look at how information flows through the company and determine where the bottlenecks are and/or where they will be in the future. After determining where the bottleneck or potential bottlenecks will be in the efficient operation of the firm, the next step is to determine if a computer will alleviate the problem. The problem could be as simple as orders that are not being quickly processed, billing that is falling further and further behind actual shipping, shipping to customers that is past due on previous shipments, or financial statements that are completed too late to be of any operating benefit to the firm. If a computer could perform these jobs faster and more accurately, then the next step is to determine what capabilities the computer, or computer system, should contain.

There are several rules of thumb that may help small business owners determine whether they need a computer for their business. First, if more than two hours a day are spent on routine and/or form letters, then a computer with word processing software will be worthwhile. Second, if the general bookkeeping is hard to keep up to date, or if the firm has a payroll of over twenty people or more than fifty accounts receivable, then a computer should be considered. Third, if more than two hours per day are spent on estimations for contracts or for pricing purposes, then a computer with spreadsheet software is a good investment. Finally, if the firm has a large database of any type (customers, addresses, products, etc.), a computer with database software will be able to search and sort through these databases for whatever information is desired much faster and more accurately than any clerk will be able to do.

Should a small business owner purchase a computer? In addition to these rules, there are several other reasons a computer should be considered:

1. Computers can save time and money.
2. Computers allow access to up-to-date information.
3. Computers reduce time-consuming payroll calculations.
4. Computers allow owners to ask "what if" questions and to see what the answers will be.
5. Computers can be used to help reduce inventories to a minimum level.
6. Computers can reduce purchases through improved purchasing histories and more accurate order statistics.
7. Computers help reduce accounts receivable problems.

A computer, however, cannot help a poorly managed firm. Before a computer system is purchased and installed in a firm, the operating and control problems must be solved. Installing a computer before correcting the operating problems merely compounds the errors that already exist. The computer, therefore, does not correct the problems; it only processes them at a faster rate. One of the common misconceptions about computers is that they can solve problems. Computers only process information and, therefore, the information that they process must be correct and in a form that is of benefit to the business.

Computer Systems

There are basically two competing business computer systems: the IBM PC and PC clones (PCs) and the Apple Macintosh (Macs). The biggest difference between these two competing systems is that the Macs are easier to learn and use and the PCs have a wider range of business software available. The Macs are easier to use because they do not require that the user memorize commands; instead the user moves a handheld device, called a mouse, around until a cursor on the computer screen is on top of an icon or on a menu item that the user wishes to perform. If a firm needs a computer for graphics or for desktop publishing in addition to basic uses such as word processing, spreadsheet analysis, and data processing, the Mac probably is the better choice. The typical Mac system costs about $500 to $1,000 more than the typical PC system, but the difference in price is not enough to warrant purchasing a system that will not provide the capabilities desired by the small business owner.[2]

The PC, on the other hand, uses a program known as a disk operating system (DOS) to control the basic functions of the computer. The PC software programs that run on DOS each have their own set of commands that the user must learn in order to operate the program. Fortunately, most of the commands are fairly easy to learn. Additionally, PC manufacturers have introduced a relatively new system that will make the PC easier to use. The new system, developed by Microsoft Corporation, is called Microsoft Windows, and it is designed to make a PC operate like a Mac. The major advantage of the PC system is that it has been considered the "business computer," and much more software has been developed for it than the Mac. In general, there is more specialized business software available on the PC; however, most of the best-selling business software is available in either a PC or a Mac version.

Computer System Features

Regardless of which system is chosen, there are certain features that should be considered before a computer or computer system is purchased for a small business. The memory capacity of a computer is an indication of its size or power. Memory is measured in the number of megabytes (MB) that are contained in the **random access memory (RAM),** where data and files are stored on computer chips. The minimum size that should be considered for a business computer is 2 MB, but 4 MB does not cost very much more, (about $100) and is the recommended size especially if the business will be using sophisticated graphics programs.[3]

random access memory (RAM)

hard disk

HARD DISK DRIVE. A business computer should have a **hard disk** drive and one or more disk drives. A hard disk works something like the compact disk (CD) player, except that in a computer, from the user's viewpoint, the information stored is in terms of numbers and words rather than music. The information is magnetically stored on the disk, which spins at very high speeds. The information on the disk is "read" from the spinning disk to the computer or "written" from the computer to the hard disk. Thus, information may be added to or deleted from the hard disk.

central processing unit (CPU)

CENTRAL PROCESSING UNIT. The brain of the computer is the **central processing unit (CPU)** where information is processed. The size or power of this brain comes from the microprocessor in the form of a chip. The speed at which information is processed is normally measured in megahertz (MHz), representing millions of cycles per second. In comparing different computers, the MHz rating gives a comparison of the speed at which the computer will operate. The common speeds available are 8, 12, 16, and 20 MHz, but speed is important only if the business application will require many applications that require large amounts of computations such as searches of large customer databases. Probably, the minimum speed that should be considered for a small business is 12 MHz.

The two basic sizes of microprocessors for business computers that will be used in small businesses are the 286 and the 386 chips. The 286 microprocessors are adequate for most business applications but should be considered only for those businesses that plan to have a very limited use of the computer for basic tasks such as word processing and relatively small database or spreadsheet applications. For growing companies, the 386 or 386SX microprocessors would be considered the minimum size, as they can run all the currently available business software. The 386 microprocessor comes in three speeds: 25 MHz, 33 MHz, and 40 MHz. The 386SX comes in three speeds: 16 MHz, 20 MHz, and 25 MHz, with the higher speeds costing about $100 more than the next slower speed.

The most powerful microprocessor is the 486, which costs much more than 386 models but is necessary for those businesses that need complex mathematical computations such as the computations required for computer-aided design (CAD).

DISK DRIVES. To be effective, the business computer requires at least one disk drive. The disk drive "reads" information from the diskette that is placed in the drive and sends this information to the computer. The drive also "writes" information from the computer to the diskette. The drive, therefore, functions as a source of additional data storage other than the data that is stored on the hard drive. Typically the hard drive contains the program and the diskettes contain the data. For example, with a word processing program, the program will be stored on the hard drive and the letters will be stored on a diskette. Most disk drives are either 3 ½-inch or 5 ¼-inch drives, but the 3 ½-inch drives are fast becoming the industry standard.

EXPANSION SLOTS. Because few computers can be designed to suit the varied needs of many different users, expansion slots are provided in most computers to provide flexibility. Expansion slots are simply a plug-in space that computer manufacturers provide within the computer housing where additional circuit boards may be attached. These boards may provide the user with the capability to connect the computer to other computers, to expand memory, or to attach a printer. For most small business applications, at least two open expansion slots should be available on any computer purchased.

KEYBOARD. The keyboard allows the user to send information to the computer. There are many different keyboard configurations, but the acceptable keyboard should have the standard "QWERTY" typewriter arrangement. Before purchasing a computer, the user should try out the keyboard to make sure that the keys are not too small or close together as to be uncomfortable for them. The keyboard should have a separate numeric keyboard and separate cursor movement keys. In addition, the keyboard should be detachable to accommodate different workspace areas and the size differences of potential users.

MONITORS. The video monitor is the last major item to consider before a computer system for a small business is purchased. For most businesses, the minimum standard should be the 12-inch screen (measured diagonally like television screens), but the 14-inch screen is common on many computers. One-color screens are known as monochrome, and the color most used in the United States is green, although the amber screen is popular in Europe and with many lap-top computers. Color screens are unnecessary for word processing and spreadsheet applications, but for those businesses that will have graphic applications or that use Windows, the VGA (video graphics array) display is required. The VGA monitor can be color or monochrome.

Some computer manufacturers have a Super VGA monitor, which is excellent for desktop publishing and CAD applications. Super VGA requires a 16- or 19-inch screen and will produce a squashed image on the 12- and 14-inch screens.

Computer Peripherals

There are two pieces of peripheral equipment that small business owners need to consider when purchasing a computer. The first is a printer, and the other peripheral is a modem. A printer should be considered as part of a computer system, as the printed results of any computer task are normally needed. The least expensive printers are the **dot-matrix printers.** The dot-matrix printer produces characters comprised of small dots in the same way that numbers and letters are formed on a scoreboard. These printers are very good for billing, invoicing, check printing, and graphics. Dot-matrix printers may be purchased for less than $200.

dot-matrix printers

The other type of printer is the letter-quality printer, and there are two basic types: the laser printers and the ink-jet printers. The **laser printers** are the most expensive type of printer, but they produce a very high quality print. A very good laser printer that would satisfy the needs of most small businesses costs around $1,000. The laser printer works like a photocopy machine and can produce characters of typeset quality as well as excellent graphics. **Ink-jet printers** are a special type of dot-matrix printer that form characters by spraying dots on the paper with a high-precision ink jet. The quality of the print depends on the quality of the ink-jet printer and can range from draft quality to almost typeset quality. A very good ink-jet printer that produces a letter-quality print may be purchased for about $500.

laser printers

ink-jet printers

A **modem** and communications software enables computers to be connected to telephone lines and through these lines to other computers. A modem is an excellent addition to a computer system if the business can profit from being able to send or receive information (data) even when the business is not open. For example, a business may subscribe to an information service such as Dow Jones News Retrieval (DJNR), The Source, CompuServe, or

modem

Prodigy. These services provide the user with the ability to search for and obtain specific information. With the DJNR, for example, a user can search for financial information or news releases from particular firms.

There are two issues to consider when buying a modem, and they concern style and speed. Modems can be either internal or external. The internal modem is a circuit board that is placed in one of the expansion slots inside a computer. The external modem is attached to the outside of the computer. They both function in the same manner, but the internal modem has the advantage of giving the work area a neater appearance because the modem and the connecting wiring are all inside the computer. The second issue is speed. The rate at which the modem can send and receive data is measured in the bits per second. This rate is commonly referred to as the baud rate, and the rates most commonly available are 1,200, 2,400, and 9,600 with the 2,400 rate the most common.[4] A modem and the necessary software will cost between $200 and $500.

SOFTWARE

Although most small business owners talk about buying a computer, what they really need is the software that makes the computer perform the tasks required by the business owner. There are software programs to suit just about every business need, but the most popular types of software for small businesses are word processing, accounting, database management, and spreadsheet analysis. Each of these popular systems will be briefly discussed along with the names of some of the most popular programs.

Word Processing

In small businesses in the United States, computers are used more for word processing than for any other single task. In addition to the normal practice of using word processors to write original letters and other correspondence, word processors can produce personalized form letters. When combined with a database program, word processors can write personalized letters to selected individuals. For example, a letter could be sent to all customers who had not made a purchase in the last year giving them a special discount if a purchase is made within the next thirty days.

The most popular word processing programs are WordPerfect produced by WordPerfect for PCs and Macs, WordStar produced by WordStar International for PCs and Macs, and MultiMate produced by Ashton-Tate for PCs. Other popular programs include Microsoft Word, Display Write, Professional Write, Mac Write, and PFS First Choice.

Accounting

Accounting programs are used to maintain the financial statements for a firm, but these programs can do a lot more than just keep the accounting records. Accounting programs can write checks, print out invoices, maintain payrolls, manage receivables, and complete many other similar tasks, all of which can save time and increase accuracy. A good accounting program should not only perform the normal essential accounting functions, but also have the ability to help owners manage their firm. For example, some programs allow the user to produce reports that list sales, returns, costs, and profits by customer. Others produce excellent aging of accounts receivable reports indicating by customer the number of days an account is late.

The best accounting programs should include the ability to maintain accounts payable, accounts receivable, the general ledger, inventory, billing, and payroll. The most popular programs are DacEasy Accounting for PCs, Peachtree Complete for PCs and Macs, ACCPAC Simply Accounting for PCs and Macs, MultiLedger and Cash Ledger for Macs, In-House Accountant for PCs and Macs, CYMA Accounting Series for PCs and Macs, Great Plains Accounting Series for PCs and Macs, and Act I for PCs.

Database Management

Database programs are designed to create a set of records (data) that can be updated by adding, deleting, or modifying those records. Data programs allow the user to search through the records and sort those that match certain characteristics. These two words, search and sort, are the key to understanding the power of database programs, because they search through the records in the systems and sort them according to the criteria specified by the user. For example, a small business owner may wish to send a notice of a special sale to all customers who had purchases in excess of $400 last year. A good database program can provide the names and addresses of those customers, and, when combined with a word processing program, can write an individual letter to each of those customers.

The most popular programs are Dbase produced by Ashton-Tate for PCs and Macs, Paradox produced by Borland International for PCs, Professional File produced by Software Publishing for PCs, PC-File produced by Button-Ware for PCs, and HyperCard produced by Apple for Macs.

Spreadsheet Programs

Spreadsheet programs are useful for those businesses that need to calculate rows and/or columns of numbers. Spreadsheets allow users to set up standard worksheet-type problems where the numbers change but the categories that the numbers represent do not change. For instance, an income statement has a standard set of categories (sales, returns, rent, telephone, etc.) that do not change from one reporting period to the next, but the numbers do change. A spreadsheet may be set up that allows the user to type in the amounts each month with the totals and subtotals instantly generated.

The advantage of the spreadsheet is that the user can perform "what if" analysis with these numbers to see what effect a change in one of the variables has on the bottom line. For example, what is the effect of a 10 percent decrease in sales on net profits, or what is the effect of a 6 percent increase in wages? This "what if" ability is also very useful when estimating a contract, because the user can determine which variables have the greatest effect on the results.

Assume, for example, that an entrepreneur is in the business of residential remodeling and that she obtained her jobs based on firm contracts. Spreadsheet analysis could allow her to estimate the cost of the work based on current prices and then determine the effect of changes in the price of critical supplies on the profitability of each job.

The most popular spreadsheet programs are Lotus 1-2-3 produced by Lotus for PCs, Excel produced by Microsoft for PCs and Macs, Quattro Pro produced by Borland for PCs, Lucid 3-D produced by DacEasy for PCs, and Wingz produced by Informix for both PCs and Macs.

KEY TERMS

central processing unit (CPU) laser printers
dot-matrix printers modem
hard disk random access memory (RAM)
ink-jet printers

C   TAXES AND INSURANCE

This appendix presents a brief introduction to some of the basic tax laws that affect small businesses. In addition, the appendix also presents a brief look at the risks faced by small businesses and the role of insurance to offset some of these risks.

TAXES

This section will provide a basic understanding of the tax laws that affect small businesses, what records must be kept for tax purposes, and how a business can arrange its way of doing business to reduce taxes to the lowest possible level.

employer identification number (EIN)

The first tax step for any business is to obtain an **employer identification number (EIN).** The EIN is required for all businesses from a single-person sole proprietorship to a corporation. Obtaining the number is as easy as calling the nearest IRS regional office. They will give any business an EIN over the telephone and then send the caller a Form SS-4, the formal application form, to be filled out. The EIN is good for the life of the business, but a new number will be required if the business changes from one form to another (i.e., from sole proprietorship to a partnership).

Tax Accounting for Business

accrual-basis method

Tax accounting is the determination of when income and expenses are computed for tax purposes. The two most common methods of tax accounting are the accrual-basis method and the cash-basis method. With the **accrual-basis method** businesses report income when earned, not necessarily when cash is received. Thus income is recognized, for tax purposes, when a service is

cash-basis
method

rendered or a product is sold, even though the customer may not pay for the service or product during the current accounting period. Similarly, expenses are recognized when incurred, although the invoice may or may not be paid during the current accounting period.

With the **cash-basis method** of accounting, income and expenses are reported for tax purposes when the cash is actually received. Thus, if a check is mailed on December 28 but not received until January 3, the income would be recorded in January. For most small businesses, the cash method may be the best method, because owners have used it for their personal tax records and therefore understand it. Businesses that may use the cash method include the following: (1) any farming business, (2) qualified personal service corporations, and (3) entities with average gross receipts of not more than $5 million. Thus most small businesses would be allowed to use the cash method.

Tax Accounting for the Sole Proprietorship

All the profit from a sole proprietorship is taxable to the owner. The three major federal tax forms that are of concern to the sole proprietorship are Form 1040-ES, Schedule SE, and Schedule C. Form 1040-ES is used to make the payment of an estimated tax each quarter. The payments are due on April 15, June 15, September 15, and January 15. Schedule SE is used for the computation of social security self-employment tax. Schedule C is used to report the profit (or loss) from the business or profession.

Tax Accounting for Partnerships

A partnership is treated as a multiple proprietorship for tax purposes. The partnership does not pay taxes, but each partner pays taxes on his or her share of the partnership's net income, whether the income is distributed by the partnership or not. For tax purposes, the partnership is merely a conduit that passes tax income to the individual partners. The partnership does, however, file an income statement on Form 1065, but this form is for reporting purposes only. The partners' shares of the income, or deductions, are reported on Schedule K or K-1, which is filed with Form 1065. As with the sole proprietorship, the self-employment (social security) tax is computed on Schedule SE.

Tax Accounting for the S Corporation

As with both the sole proprietorship and the partnership, the income earned by the business incorporated as an S corporation, is taxed only once—directly to the owners/shareholders of the corporation and no taxes are paid by the corporation. This elimination of double taxation, which a C corporation must pay, combined with the flexibility of a partnership and the advantages (such as limited liability) of a corporation, makes the S corporation a form of business every small business owner should consider.

An S corporation must divide its items of income, loss, expense, and credit into two categories: separately stated items and nonseparately computed income or loss. Separately stated items are those whose separate treatment on the shareholder's income tax return could affect the shareholder's tax liability. Separately stated items include the following: (1) capital gains and losses, (2) charitable contributions, (3) dividends, (4) tax-exempt interest, (5) recoveries of bad debts, (6) depletions on S-corporation oil and gas properties, (7) interest expense, and (8) other similar items.

Nonseparately computed income or loss consists of all gross income items of the S corporation minus all its deductible items, except separately stated items. The income tax return for an S corporation is filed on Form 1120S, and a Schedule K-1 must be filed for each shareholder. The separately stated items are allocated to the shareholders on a pro rata basis according to the number of shares of stock held by each shareholder.

Tax Accounting for C Corporations

Taxes on all the forms of business previously presented are paid by the individuals owning the business. With the corporate form of business, however, the corporation pays taxes on the income earned by the business. The corporation is a legal and a taxpaying entity. Corporations file their income taxes on Form 1120 (or short Form 1120-A, if eligible), whether or not they have any taxable income. Owners of a corporation receive income from the corporation in the form of dividends. Normally dividends are distributed to shareholders from the after-tax profits. Because all income does not flow through to the owners of a corporation, the residual left after dividends are paid is called retained earnings. Retained earnings are normally used to purchase additional capital assets or for the retirement of long-term debt.

INSURANCE

Small business owners have always had to contend with risks. Some risks such as the risk of fire, theft, or liability are well known, but other risks such as the potential loss from an interruption in business are not as well known. Risk, from a business standpoint, is the exposure to a hazard or danger of sustaining a loss. Insurance is the management of risk. The dictionary defines *insurance* as a contract binding a company to indemnify an insured party against a specified loss (or losses) in return for premiums paid. In effect, the insured agrees to pay the insurer a premium (a known, relatively small loss) for protection against the uncertainty of a large loss. A major task for small business owners is to learn to recognize risk and then learn how to manage it.

Insurance Alternatives

assumption of
risk

Small business owners have alternatives to purchasing insurance, including the assumption of risk, self-insurance, and loss prevention. The **assumption of risk** is an alternative simply because small business owners cannot afford insurance protection against every possible type of loss. A firm should assume the risk of loss when the potential loss is relatively small. A second alternative is to transfer the risk to a third party. For example, selling a building that is owned by the business and then leasing it from the new owner is

transference of
risk

self-insurance

loss prevention

the **transference of risk.** Hiring temporary personnel from an employment agency and leasing automobiles, trucks, and equipment are other examples of risk transference.

A third alternative to insurance is **self-insurance.** Self-insurance is the systematic savings of funds, just like the systematic payment of insurance premiums, except the savings are used to cover losses when they occur. Self-insurance works best for those small businesses that have several stores, so that each store can contribute to a central fund that is used to provide coverage in the event of a loss. Normally, a small business that consists of a single store or building should not self-insure. A final alternative to insurance is **loss prevention.** Loss prevention includes programs that reduce the risk of loss. Programs to prevent fires (training programs, sprinkler systems) or the spread of fires (fire doors or fire barriers) and programs to protect against burglary (burglar alarms, video monitors, and dead bolts) are examples of programs that reduce the risk of loss.

Liability Insurance

The risk of loss from a liability lawsuit is a very real threat to small business owners. A single lost lawsuit can close a small firm and has even caused several large corporations (e.g., A. H. Robbins with the Dalkon shield and Johns Mansville with asbestos) to declare bankruptcy. Liability is a civil (as opposed to a criminal) injury caused by an individual, a product, or a place of business. In a civil case, the intent to cause injury does not have to be proved, only that the injury did occur. Liability is also the financial responsibility that one party has for another party as a consequence of doing or failing to do something because of negligence or because the terms of an existing contract agreement between two or more parties was breached.

Negligence legally obliges individuals and firms to exercise reasonable, or prudent, care, such that an innocent party is not personally injured or that property is not damaged. Liability insurance provides coverage against negligence suits and losses from liability judgments, covers the expense of investigating and defending lawsuits, and even includes the cost of any court bonds or interest levied on judgments accrued during an appeal period. This protection usually is not very expensive for the small firm, but the lack of this coverage can put a small firm out of business just as quick as a fire. Unfortunately, many small business owners recognize the risk of not having fire insurance but do not fully understand the risk of liability.

Workers' Compensation

Workers' compensation insurance provides protection for employees in the event they are injured or disabled by a job-related accident. Workers' compensation insurance is required by state law, but the requirements vary from state to state and some states exempt some employers from providing workers' compensation and some states even make the coverage optional. Premiums for workers' compensation are based on the number of employees, the type of industry, the safety record of the firm covered, and the industry to which the firm belongs.

Bonding

fidelity bonds

There are two major types of bonds that a firm may secure: (1) fidelity, and (2) surety. **Fidelity bonds** protect a firm against losses from employee theft. A fidelity bond is a contract among three parties, which includes the bonding company (called the surety), the insured party (called the obligee), and the individual or entity assuming the obligation to the insured party (called the principal). In bonding, if the event insured against should occur, the bonding company pays for the loss only if the principal fails to make good on a contractual agreement. The bond, therefore, is a guarantee by the surety to the obligee that if the principal does not live up to his promise to the obligee, the surety will make good in his behalf. Most fidelity bonds cover the loss of property or money through larceny, theft, embezzlement, forgery, misappropriation, wrongful abstraction, willful misapplication, or other fraudulent or dishonest act or acts. Simply requiring employees to be bonded often discourages theft because of the thorough investigation of the employee by the bonding company.

surety bonds

Surety bonds guarantee that the named firm (the principal) will perform according to a plan or contract. Surety bonds are usually used in connection with construction contracts. They help small firms compete against larger, better financed firms because the bond creates a source of financial strength that the small firm may not possess. The insurance company (called a surety) guarantees that the principal (an individual or firm) is honest and has the ability and/or financial strength to perform according to the terms of a contract.

Life and Health Insurance

Life and health insurance should be a major consideration for all small business owners for three reasons. First, life and health insurance provide protection to the firm in the event of the death or disability of a key employee. Insurance provides the financial protection that may result from such a loss. Second, employees have come to expect life and health insurance as part of their compensation package, and the firm that does not provide it will usually encounter higher employee turnover. The third reason small businesses should consider life and health insurance is as an aid in transferring ownership rights. Sole proprietorships, partnerships, and closely held corporations often need to purchase life insurance to ease the transfer of ownership or to maintain control of a firm in the event of the death of an owner.

group life insurance

Usually group life and health insurance provides the most economical and comprehensive coverage. Group insurance can cover the employees of a single firm or can be provided for a group, or association, of firms. Although employees tend to think of life and health insurance as a single package, the two types of insurance are usually purchased as separate policies. **Group life insurance** is usually term insurance that provides coverage for employees during a specified period of time (usually a year), but the policy may be renewed at the end of the period. The typical group life policy provides protection that is related to the income of the employee, has no accumulated cash benefit, does not require a medical examination of the insured, and terminates with the end of the policy or the termination of the employee.

group health
insurance

There are four major types of **group health insurance** plans: (1) medical expense insurance, (2) major medical insurance, (3) disability income insurance, and (4) dental insurance. Medical insurance is designed to protect the insured from financial loss due to medical costs. Most policies have an annual deductible of around $200 to $400, which means that the insured pays the first $200 to $400 of her or his medical bills. Major medical insurance is designed to provide protection from the cost of catastrophic illness. These plans provide coverage after the basic medical expense insurance benefits have been exhausted. Major medical plans usually have a large deductible amount for each claim and will pay only a percentage (normally around 80 percent) of the total medical cost.

Disability income insurance is designed to replace the income of the insured should he or she become disabled. Disability due to illness or accident is one of the greatest threats to the financial security of an employee. Disability insurance is relatively low in cost yet many employers and employees overlook this type of coverage. Dental insurance is structured like medical expense insurance except that it is designed to cover those expenses arising from dental care.

Supplementary and Special Insurance Coverage

In addition to the major types of insurance coverage, there are several types of supplementary and special-purpose programs that fit the specific needs of some companies. Some of these are listed below with a brief description of their purpose.

1. Sprinkler leakage insurance is designed to protect the firm from the loss resulting from the accidental discharge of water from any part of the automatic sprinkler system that is part of the fire protection system for many buildings.

2. Water damage insurance is similar to the sprinkler leakage insurance but includes water damage from sources other than the sprinkler system.

3. Glass insurance provides protection against the loss resulting from the breakage of glass such as the plate glass windows and doors, glass countertops, glass panels, and other glass fixtures within a building.

4. Credit insurance is designed to protect a wholesaler, jobber, or manufacturer against the failure of customers to meet their financial obligations. This type of insurance is not normally available to retailers or those who lend money to commercial borrowers.

5. Rent insurance is designed to cover the loss of rent from property that is damaged by fire or some other peril.

6. Business interruption insurance is designed to cover expenses due to the loss of the use of insured property while that property is being repaired because of damage from a fire or other insured peril.

Managing the Insurance Program

This brief presentation of the many types of insurance available for consideration by small business owners indicates that the determination of the correct insurance coverage is not a simple, straightforward task. To determine what coverage is needed, small business owners should determine how the loss or damage of each of their resources would affect their ability to maintain control of their businesses and learn to manage these risks. Risk management is the determination of which risks the firm should insure against and for how much. The problem is that no firm can insure against all eventualities but most can insure against those that could cripple their business.

KEY TERMS

accrual-basis method

assumption of risk

cash-basis method

employer identification number (EIN)

fidelity bonds

group health insurance

group life insurance

loss prevention

self-insurance

surety bonds

transference of risk

NOTES

CHAPTER 1

1. Steven Solomon, *Small Business USA* (New York: Crown Publishers, 1986), 30–34.

2. Karl Vesper, *New Venture Strategies* (Englewood Cliffs, NJ: Prentice-Hall, 1990), 3–7.

3. Jill Arabas, "Corporate Layoffs Spawning Rise in Entrepreneurship," *News & Courier* (Charleston, SC), 10 June 1990, 1-J.

4. Jacqueline Mitchell, "Fear of Layoffs Spurs Employees to Launch Part-Time Businesses," *Wall Street Journal,* 25 May 1990, 1.

5. Harry Bacas, "Leaving the Corporate Nest," *Nation's Business,* March 1987, 14–22.

6. Ibid.

7. David S. Evans and Linda S. Leighton, "Some Empirical Aspects of Entrepreneurship," *American Economic Review,* June 1989, 519–535.

8. Nancy L. Croft and Dan Dickinson, "To be Young and in Business," *Nation's Business,* March 1988, 63–65.

9. Kathleen Kerwin, "An Epitaph for the EPILADY," *Business Week,* 17 September 1990, 38.

10. "The Ancestry Factor," *Inc.,* June 1989, 22.

11. "Women Entrepreneurs," *Inc.* January 1990, 105.

12. Albert V. Bruno and Joel K. Leidecker, "Causes of New Venture Failure: 1960s vs. 1980s," *Business Horizons,* November/December 1988, 51–56.

13. "Business Start-ups Not so Risky After All," *Nation's Business,* January 1990, 26.

14. Joan C. Szabo, "Small Business Update," *Nation's Business,* October 1988, 8–12.

15. Brent Bowers and Jeffrey Tannenbaum, "More Important Than Money," *Wall Street Journal,* 22 November 1991, R6.

16. "Sources of Entrepreneurial Satisfaction," *Inc.,* April 1989, 163.

17. *A Tribute to Small Business* (A Joint Publication of the U.S. Small Business Administration and Pacific Bell Directory, 1987), 57.

18. Gustav Berle, *The Small Business Information Handbook* (New York: John Wiley & Sons, 1990), 77.

19. Thomas A. Gray, *Small Business in the Year 2000* (Washington, D.C.: Office of Economic Research, U.S. Small Business Association).

20. Ibid.

CHAPTER 2

1. Lawrence Tuller, *Buying In* (Blue Ridge Summit, PA: Liberty Hall Press, 1990), 68–69.

2. Vaughn Cox, *How to Sell Your Business for the Best Price* (Chicago: Probus Publishing, 1990), 41.

3. Tuller, *Buying In,* 114.

4. Cox, *How to Sell Your Business,* 41.

5. Marisa Manly, "The Competition Within," *Inc.,* September 1988, 137–138.

6. Jay Finegan, "The Insider's Guide: Buying a Business," *Inc.,* October 1991, 26–34.

7. Nancy Croft Baker, "Franchising in the '90s," *Nation's Business,* March 1990, 61–68.

8. Jeremy Main, "A Golden Age for Entrepreneurs," *Fortune,* 12 February 1990, 120–125.

9. Bryce Webster, *The Insider's Guide to Franchising* (New York: AMACOM, 1986), 7–8.

10. Lloyd Tarbutton, *Franchising: The How-To Book* (Englewood Cliffs, NJ: Prentice-Hall, 1986), 2.

11. Croft Baker, "Franchising in the '90s."

12. Main, "A Golden Age for Entrepreneurs."

13. Helen La Van and Patrick Boroian, *Franchise Marketing & Sales Survey 1989–90* (Olympia Fields, IL: Francorp, 1990), 13.

14. Meg Whittemore, "Four Paths to Franchising," *Nation's Business,* October 1989, 75–84.

15. "Women in Franchising," *Inc.,* April 1990, 96–99.

16. "Points to Consider Before Buying a Franchise," *Venture,* July 1988, 70.

17. Robert Perry, *The 50 Best Low-Investment, High-Profit Franchises* (Englewood Cliffs, NJ: Prentice Hall, 1990), 14–15.

18. Jack Wynn, "Where the Money Is," *Nation's Business,* October 1988, 76–80.

19. Jane Furse, "Docktor to the Rescue," *Venture,* June 1988, 18–20.

20. Webster, *Insider's Guide,* 185–190.

CHAPTER 3

1. Leslie Brokaw, "Word of Mouth," *Inc.,* December 1988, 18.

2. Debbie Galant, "The Stuff Dreams are Made Of," *Venture,* January 1988, 52–56.

3. Gustav Berle, *The Small Business Information Handbook* (New York: John Wiley & Sons, 1990), 89, 196.

4. Walecia Konrad and Gail DeGeorge, "U.S. Companies Go for the Gray," *Business Week,* 3 April 1989, 64–67.

5. Joan Szabo and Nancy Croft Baker, "Hot New Markets of the 1990s," *Nation's Business,* December 1988, 20–26.

6. Galant, "The Stuff Dreams are Made Of."

7. Nathaniel Gilbert, "Breaking In: 10 Ways to Crack the Competition—Legally," *Entrepreneur,* December 1990, 147–153.

8. "Capital," *Inc.,* January 1991, 106.

CHAPTER 4

1. "A Question of Ethics," *Wall Street Journal,* 18 September 1987, 39.

2. "Insider Trading Isn't a Scandal," *Business Week,* 25 August 1986, 74.

3. Sallie Hofmeister and Jeff Shear, "The Trade Secrets Trap," *Venture,* June 1987, 53–55.

4. Gerald F. Cavanagh, *American Business Values* (Englewood Cliffs, NJ: Prentice-Hall, 1990), 2.

5. Justin G. Longenecker, Joseph A. McKinney, and Carlos W. Moore, "The Generation Gap in Business Ethics," *Business Horizons,* September/October 1989, 9–14.

6. Thomas Donaldson, *Corporations and Morality* (Englewood Cliffs, NJ: Prentice-Hall, 1982), 151.

7. Richard P. Nielsen, "What Can Managers Do About Unethical Management?" *Journal of Business Ethics* (May 1987): 309–320.

8. Donald Robin, Michael Giallourakis, Fred David, and Thomas Moritz, "A Different Look at Codes of Ethics," *Business Horizons,* January/February 1989, 66–73.

9. M. Cash Mathews, *Strategic Intervention in Organizations* (Newbury Park, CA: Sage Publications, 1988), 139.

10. LaRue Tone Hosmer, "Adding Ethics to the Business Curriculum," *Business Horizons,* July/August 1988, 9–15.

11. David Clutterbuck, *How To Be a Good Corporate Citizen* (London: McGraw-Hill Book Company (UK) Limited, 1981), 23–24.

CHAPTER 5

1. David E. Gumpert, *How to Really Create a Successful Business Plan* (Boston, MA: *Inc.* Publishing, 1990), 6.

2. Edward C. Rybka, "The Best Laid Plans . . .," *Entrepreneurial Woman*, September 1990, 74–79.

3. Rybka, "The Best Laid Plans . . . ."

4. Roger Thompson, "Business Plans: Myth and Reality," *Nation's Business*, August 1988, 16–23.

5. W. Keith Schilit, "How to Write a Winning Business Plan," *Business Horizons*, September/October 1987, 13–22.

6. Gumpert, *How to Really Create a Successful Business Plan*, 156–157.

7. Ibid., 158.

8. Stanley Rich and David Gumpert, *Business Plans that Win $$$* (New York: Harper & Row, 1985), 164–165.

9. Bob Coleman, *The New Small Business Survival Guide* (New York: W. W. Norton, 1991), 287–288.

10. Kenneth Andrews, *The Concept of Corporate Strategy* (Homewood, IL: Richard D. Irwin, 1980), 112–114.

CHAPTER 6

1. Timothy D. Schellhardt, "Small Business Monitors Statehouses, Lobbies Harder," *Wall Street Journal*, 9 May 1990, B2.

2. "Report on the States," *Inc.*, October 1989, 86–87.

3. John Case, "The Most Entrepreneurial Cities in America," *Inc.*, March 1990, 41–48.

4. David L. Birch, "RFD INC.," *Inc.*, February 1988, 14–15.

5. Otto Geier, Jr., "Site Selection and the Outsider," *American Industrial Properties Report*, December 1987, 22–23.

6. Lisa Sheeran, "Hidden Poisons," *Inc.*, February 1986, 97.

7. John Case, "Back to the Future," *Inc.*, October 1988, 33–34.

8. Troy Segal, "Feathered Nests for Your Fledgling Business," *Business Week*, 19 February 1990, 139–140.

9. Naomi Freundlich, "Business Incubators are Bringing up Baby," *Business Week*, 28 May 1990, 65.

10. Robert A Mamis, "Mother of Invention," *Inc.*, October 1989, 119–127.

11. Paul B. Brown, "The Doublemint Strategy," *Inc.*, March 1989, 121–122.

12. Ibid.

13. Nancy Brumback, "Retailing's Best-Kept High-Profit Secret," *Venture*, April 1988, 19–20.

14. Allen R. Wood, "Site Selection Trends—1989–2000," *Industrial Development*, June 1989, 12–13.

15. Hy Bomberg, "Empty Aesthetics: Your Office Is Pretty, But Is It Productive?" *Management World*, April/May 1987, 32–34.

16. Wilbert O. Galitz, *The Office Environment* (Willow Grove, PA: Administrative Management Society Foundation, 1984), 79.

17. *Small Business Location and Layout* (Washington, DC: Small Business Administration, 1980), 6.

18. Vilma Barr and Charles E. Broudy, *Designing to Sell* (New York: McGraw-Hill, 1986), 163.

19. Galitz, *The Office Environment*, p. 95.

20. David Harris, Alvin Palmer, M. Susan Lewis, David Munson, Gershon Meckler, and Ralph Gerdes, *Planning and Designing the Office Environment* (New York: van Nostrand Reinhold, 1981, 27.

21. Jacob Brandzel, "Tax Talk," *Entrepreneur*, June 1990, 40–44.

CHAPTER 7

1. Jill Rachlin, "Starting Up a Business in 1988: A Postcrash Course," *U.S. News & World Report*, 21 December 1987, 70–73.

2. Jerry Feigen, "Financing Sources for Small Businesses," *In Business*, July/August 1990, 43–44.

3. Chong Choy, "Sources of Business Financing and Financing Practices: A Comparison Among U.S. and Asian Countries," *Journal of Business Venturing*, September 1990, 271–275.

4. Elizabeth Fenner, "How to Raise the Cash You Need," *Money*, Summer 1991, 44–48.

5. John Freear and William Wetzel, Jr., "Who Bankrolls High-Tech Entrepreneurs?" *Journal of Business Venturing*, March 1990, 77–89.

6. Ellyn Spragins, "Heaven Sent," *Inc.*, February 1991, 85–87.

7. Don Nichols, "How to Woo Your Banker," *Small Business Reports*, June 1991, 41–43.

8. Joan Szabo, "Raising Capital in a Recession," *Nation's Business*, April 1991, 28–31.

9. Eileen Davis, "Selling Yourself to a Banker," *Venture*, July 1988, 77–79.

10. Don Nichols, "Factors That Let the Cash Flow," *Venture*, June/July 1989, 74–76.

CHAPTER 8

1. Eugene Carlson, "Personal Risk Becomes a Major Worry for Partnerships," *Wall Street Journal*, 3 January 1992, B2.

2. Catherine Yang, "Why an S Corp May Spell Tax Relief," *Business Week*, 15 May 1989, 160.

3. Carolyn Vella and John McGonagle, Jr., *Incorporating: A Guide for Small Business Owners* (New York: AMACOM, 1984), 49.

4. Marisa Manley, "Let's Shake On That," *Inc.,* June 1986, 131–132.

5. W. David Gibson, "Going Off Patent: Keeping the Wolves from Your Door," *Sales & Marketing Management,* October 1990, 76–82.

6. Paul M. Barrett, "Lost in Paper," *Wall Street Journal,* 24 February 1989, R5.

7. Clint Willis, "It Pays to Patent," *Venture,* October 1988, 38–39.

8. Marc Lane, *Legal Handbook For Business,* rev. ed. (New York: AMACOM, 1989), 66–68.

9. John P. Hayes, "Franchising: The Legal Issues (Part III)," *Franchising Opportunity,* October 1990, 59.

10. Bruce Posner, "Salsa Fight," *Inc.,* June 1988, 16.

CHAPTER 9

1. Marj Charlier and Wade Lambert, "McDonald's Told to Pay $210,000 Damages in Negligent Hiring Case," *Wall Street Journal,* 15 March 1991, B3.

2. "Man Fined for Hiring Illegal Aliens at Textile Plant," *News & Courier,* 2 March 1991, 14B.

3. Paul M. Barrett, "Some Specifics About the New Law," *Wall Street Journal,* 4 November 1991, B1.

4. Jeanne Saddler, "What the New Civil Rights Law Will Mean," *Wall Street Journal,* 4 November 1991, B1.

5. Kevin R. Hopkins, Susan L. Nestleroth, and Clint Bolick, *Help Wanted: How Companies Can Survive and Thrive in the Coming Worker Shortage* (New York: McGraw-Hill, 1991), 2.

6. Ibid., 2–3.

7. Harry Bacas, "Desperately Seeking Workers," *Nation's Business,* February 1988, 16–18.

8. Hopkins et al., *Help Wanted,* 3.

9. Ibid., 31.

10. Nancy Madlin, "The Venture Survey: Do Business and Friendship Mix?" *Venture,* March 1985, 27.

11. "Bring Your Friends to Work," *Inc.,* November 1988, 149.

12. Martha Mangelsdorf, "MBAs for Hire," *Inc.,* December 1990, 27.

13. "New Study Focuses on Contingent Staffing Arrangements," *The Small Business Advocate,* April 1991, 7–8.

14. "Employees: How to Find and Pay Them," U.S. Small Business Administration, Management Aids #5.002.

15. Auren Uris, *88 Mistakes Interviewers Make . . . and How to Avoid Them* (New York: AMACOM, 1988), 28–29.

16. Marvin Gottlieb, *Interview* (New York: Longman, 1988), 77–79.

17. Norman B. Sigband and Arthur H. Bell, *Communication for Management and Business*, 5th ed. (Glenview, IL: Scott, Foresman, 1991), 440.

18. J. William Pfeiffer and Arlette C. Ballew, *Using Instruments in Human Resource Development* (San Diego, CA: University Associates, 1988), 38–40.

19. John O'C. Hamilton, "A Video Game that Tells if Employees are Fit for Work," *Business Week*, 3 June 1991, 36.

20. Teri Lammers, "By the Numbers," *Inc.*, June 1989, 137.

21. Jeffrey Rothfeder, "Looking for a Job? You May be Out Before You Go In," *Business Week*, 24 September 1990, 128–130.

22. Peter M. Panken, "The Road to Court is Paved With Good Intentions," *Nation's Business*, June 1985, 45–46.

23. John J. Scherer, "How People Learn: Assumptions for Designs," *Training & Development Journal*, January 1984, 64–66.

24. Jack Falvey, "The Top Ten Sales Training Myths," *Small Business Reports*, March 1990, 68–77.

CHAPTER 10

1. Abraham Maslow, *Motivation and Personality*, 2d ed. (New York: Harper & Row, 1970).

2. F. Herzberg, B. Mausne, and B. Snyderman, *The Motivation to Work* (New York: John Wiley & Sons, 1964).

3. Victor Vroom, *Work and Motivation* (New York: John Wiley & Sons, 1964).

4. John Persico, Jr., "Employee Motivation: Is it Necessary?" *Small Business Reports*, March 1990, 33–36.

5. "The Prize Is Right," *Inc.*, January 1990, 95.

6. Raymond Katzell and Donna Thompson, "Work Motivation: Theory and Practice," *American Psychologist*, February 1990, 144–153.

7. Ellyn E. Spragins, "The Element of Surprise," *Inc.*, July 1991, 97.

8. William A. Cohen, *The Entrepreneur and Small Business Problem Solver* (New York: John Wiley & Sons, 1990), 466–467.

9. Monica Roman, "Maybe Being Your Own Boss Isn't So Hot After All," *Business Week*, 16 April 1990, 53.

10. "Boosting Productivity, and Quality Too," *Inc.*, November 1988, 148.

11. Jill Andresky Fraser, "Performance Unit Plans," *Inc.*, July 1991, 83.

12. Carla O'Dell, "Team Play, Team Pay—New Ways of Keeping Score," *Across the Board*, November 1989, 38–45.

13. Stuart Feldman, "Another Day, Another Dollar Needs Another Look," *Personnel*, January 1991, 9–11.

14. "Who Benefits?" *Entrepreneur*, August 1991, 16.

15. "Employee Benefits," *Wall Street Journal,* 11 June 1991, 1.

16. Jeffry Seglin, "Candy Is Dandy But So Is High Pay," *Venture,* May 1989, 74–76.

17. Lauren Chambliss, "Hazardous to Your Health," *Financial Week,* 21 August 1990, 20–21.

18. Jill Andresky Fraser, "Flexible Spending," *Inc.,* October 1990, 64–65.

19. *The State of Small Business: A Report of the President* (Washington, D.C.: U.S. Government Printing Office, 1990), 58–59.

20. Aaron Bernstein, "Family Leave May Not Be That Big a Hardship for Business," *Business Week,* 3 June 1991, 28.

21. Barbara Marsh, "Firms Offer Parents Help Caring For Kids," *Wall Street Journal,* 5 September 1991, B1–B2.

22. "Benefits," *Inc.,* March 1989, 119.

23. Norman B. Sigband and Arthur H. Bell, *Communication for Management and Business,* 5th Ed. (Glenview, IL: Scott, Foresman and Company, 1989), 30–31.

CHAPTER 11

1. Gary J. Zenz and George H. Thompson, *Purchasing and the Management of Materials,* 6th ed. (New York: John Wiley & Sons, 1987), 141–145.

2. "Rating Vendor Performance," *Small Business Reports,* April 1988, 48–49.

3. Tim Smart, Michele Galen, Gail DeGeorge, and Paul Angiolillo, "The Crackdown on Crime in the Suites," *Business Week,* 22 April 1991, 102–104.

4. Ibid.

5. Mark Rollinson, "Small Company, Big Law Firm," *Harvard Business Review,* November/December 1985, 6–14.

6. Marc J. Lane, *Legal Handbook for Small Business,* rev. ed. (New York: AMACOM, 1989), 124–125.

7. Erwin G. Krasnow and Robin S. Conrad, "Managing Your Lawyer," *Nation's Business,* April 1989, 70–72.

8. Milo Geyelin, "How a Small Company Fell Deeply into Debt to its Own Law Firm," *Wall Street Journal,* 8 October 1991, A1 and A12.

9. Russell R. Miller, "A Modest Alternative to Killing All Lawyers," *Wall Street Journal,* 28 October 1991, A16.

10. Michele Galen, "An Ounce of Legal Prevention," *Business Week,* 26 March 1990, 108.

11. Stephen D. Solomon, "Contempt of Court," *Inc.,* October 1989, 106–114.

12. Ellen Joan Pollock, "In a Bid to Trim Costs, Many Companies Are Forcing Law Firms to Reduce Fees," *Wall Street Journal,* 4 December 1991, B1.

13. Robert K. Mueller, *The Director's & Officer's Guide to Advisory Boards* (New York: Quorum Books, 1990), 30–31.

14. Ibid., 49.

15. Ibid., 116.

16. Brent Bowers, "Small Firms Get Help from Advisory Boards," *Wall Street Journal,* 17 October 1991, B1.

17. William A. Cohen, *How to Make It Big as a Consultant* (New York: AMACOM, 1991), 7–11.

18. James E. Suatko, "Working with Consultants," *Small Business Reports,* February 1989, 61.

19. Jeffrey Lant, "Making Your Consultant Relationships Work," *Business and Economic Review,* April–June 1991, 12–14.

20. Sabin Russell, "Living with Unions," *Venture,* February 1986, 33–36.

CHAPTER 12

1. Elizabeth Conlin, "The Peace Pop Puzzle," *Inc.,* March 1990, 25.

2. John M. Kelly, *How to Check Out Your Competition* (New York: John Wiley & Sons, 1987), 4–5.

3. Conlin, "The Peace Pop Puzzle."

4. Barbara Marsh, "Polling Picky Eaters to Boost a Restaurant's Popularity," *Wall Street Journal,* 8 May 1990, B2.

5. Geoffrey N. Smith and Paul B. Brown, *Sweat Equity* (New York: Simon and Schuster, 1986), 152–153.

6. Eugene Raudsepp, "Establishing a Creative Climate," *Training and Development Journal,* April 1987, 50–53.

7. Douglas Stewart, *The Power of People Skills* (New York: John Wiley & Sons, 1986), 129.

8. Paul B. Brown, "Mission Impossible," *Inc.,* January 1989, 109–110.

9. Paul B. Brown, "License to Steal," *Inc.,* December 1988, 141–142.

10. Echo M. Garrett, "Culture Shock," *Venture,* January 1989, 68–69.

11. Warren Strugatch, "Marketing by Design," *Venture,* October 1988, 86–88.

12. Ibid.

13. Warren Strugatch, "Marketing by Design—Part 2," *Venture* December, 1988, 94.

14. Ibid.

15. David Iushewitz, "Sudden Impact," *Entrepreneur,* November 1990, 114–120.

16. "Innovative Packaging Design Will Affect Marketing in Food Segments," *Marketing News,* 13 March 1987, 4.

17. John Pierson, "Awarding Black Marks to Un-'Green' Packages," *Wall Street Journal,* 23 May 1990, B1.

18. Sue Bassin, "Innovative Packaging Strategies," *Journal of Business Strategy,* January/February 1988, 28–31.

19. Ibid.

20. E. Jerome McCarthy and William Perreault, Jr., *Basic Marketing* (Homewood, IL: Richard D. Irwin, 1984), 173.

21. Michael Gershman, "Packaging: Positioning Tool of the 1980s," *Management Review,* August 1987, 33–41.

22. John Winkler, *Pricing for Results* (New York: Facts on File Publications, 1984), 44.

23. Ibid., 126–130.

24. Gerald B. McCready, *Marketing Tactics: Master Guide for Small Business* (Englewood Cliffs, NJ: Prentice-Hall, 1982), 89.

25. Paul B. Brown, "How to Compete on Price," *Inc.,* May 1990, 105–107.

CHAPTER 13

1. Vince Pesce, *A Complete Manual of Professional Selling* (Englewood Cliffs, NJ: Prentice-Hall, 1983), 104–105.

2. Leslie Brokaw, Teri Lammers, Stephen D. Solomon, and Ellie Winninghoff, "Drop a Line," *Inc.,* May 1989, 123.

3. Harris Collingwood, "A Bird in the Hand Is Worth . . .," *Business Week,* 10 April 1989, 38.

4. "Cutting Out the Middleman," *Venture,* April 1989, 44.

5. Pesce, *Professional Selling,* 73–74.

6. "Peter Hart's Showcase of Shoppers," *The American Way of Buying* (New York: Dow Jones & Company, 1990), 10.

7. Jim Surmanek, *Media Planning: A Practical Guide* (Lincolnwood, IL: NTC Books, 1986), 143.

8. Martha E. Mangelsdorf, "Revolution for the HEC of It," *Inc.,* September 1988, 22.

9. Paul B. Brown, "The Put-Up-Or-Shut-Up Strategy," *Inc.,* July 1988, 113–114.

10. "A Moving Picture Is Worth . . .," *Inc.,* May 1990, 100.

11. Martha E. Mangelsdorf, "Ad Infinitum," *Inc.,* May 1990, 29.

12. "Special Delivery," *Inc.,* March 1990, 92.

13. Teri Lammers, Martha E. Mangelsdorf, and Bruce Posner, "If They Can't Find It, They Can't Buy It," *Inc.,* January 1989, 106.

14. Surmanek, *Media Planning,* 149–150.

15. Ted Klien and Fred Danzig, *Publicity* (New York: Charles Scribner's Sons, 1985), 75.

16. John Caples, *How to Make Your Advertising Make Money* (Englewood Cliffs, NJ: Prentice-Hall, 1983), 139.

17. Bruce Bradway, Mary Frenzel, and Robert Pritchard, *Strategic Marketing: A Handbook for Entrepreneurs and Managers* (Reading, MA: Addison-Wesley Publishing Company, 1982), 73.

18. "Who's Calling?" *Inc.*, April 1990, 101.

19. "Faithful or Fickle?" *The American Way of Buying* (New York: Dow Jones & Company, 1990), 28

20. S. Watson Dunn, Arnold M. Barban, Dean M. Krugman, and Leonard N. Reid, *Advertising* 7th ed. (Chicago: Dryden Press, 1990), 74.

21. Bradway, Frenzel, and Pritchard, *Strategic Marketing*, 92.

CHAPTER 14

1. Arthur DeThomas and William Fredenberger, "Accounting Needs of Very Small Business," *CPA Journal*, October 1985, 14–24.

2. Joseph Dillion, "There's No Accounting for Your Business," *Life Association News*, October 1988, 77–79.

3. David Gobeli and Mary Seville, "The Small-Business-CPA Interface," *Journal of Small Business Management*, October 1989, 8–20.

4. "Even the Smallest Start-Up Needs a Bookkeeper or Accountant," *Profit-Building Strategies for Business Owners*, August 1990, 19–20.

5. Kristin Keyes, "Choosing Accounting Software," *Communications*, September 1988, 150–152.

CHAPTER 15

1. "1990 Small Business Survey" (New York: American Institute of Certified Public Accountants, 1990).

2. David Knowles, "Collection Program Fuel Cash Flow," *Small Business Reports*, July 1989, 45–47.

3. Dan Gutman, "High Finance Made Easy," *Success*, July/August 1989, 16.

CHAPTER 16

1. Richard McMahon and Scott Holmes, "Small Business Financial Management Practices in North America," *Journal of Small Business Management*, April 1991, 19–29.

2. David Knowles, "Collections Programs Fuel Cash Flow," *Small Business Reports*, July 1989, 45–47.

3. Charles Bodenstab, "The Receivables Challenge," *Inc.*, May 1989, 137–138.

4. Robert Boyle and Harsha Desai, "Basic Financial Strategies for Business Turn-arounds," *Management Review*, September 1990, 29–32.

5. "The Art and Science of Collections: How to Break the Bad Debt Cycle," *NBDC Report*, May 1991, 1–4.

6. Jill Fraser, "Getting Paid," *Inc.*, June 1990, 58–69.

CHAPTER 17

1. Damodar Golhar, et al., "JIT Implementation in Small Manufacturing Firms," *Production and Inventory Management Journal,* Second Quarter 1990, pp. 44-48.

2. L. B. Crosby, "The Just-in-Time Manufacturing Process: Control of Quality and Quantity," *Production and Inventory Management* Vol. 25, No. 4 1984, pp. 21–33.

3. Jacquelyn Denalli, "Bellying Up To The High-Tech Bar," *Small Business Reports,* May 1991, pp. 62–65.

4. Bill Stack, "Small Firms Can Reap Huge Gains With Electronic Data Interchange," *Marketing News* April 1, 1991, page 14.

5. David Waller, "EDI is Only for Large, Medium, and Small Companies," *P&IM Review,* April 1991, pp. 30 & 45.

6. Comparisons of ratios can be found in the following reference books:
   Dun & Bradstreet Corporation's *Key Business Ratios*
   Robert Morris Associates' *Annual Statement Studies*
   Leo Tryo's *Almanac of Business and Industrial Financial Ratios*

7. Bryan Milling, "Turnover Analysis Cuts Inventory Costs," *Small Business Reports,* March 1991, pp. 49–52.

8. Kevin McDermott, "Business Security: Lock the Doors and Bar the Windows," *D&B Reports,* July/August 1991, pp. 16–19.

CHAPTER 18

1. Stephen Breyer, *Regulation and Its Reform,* (Cambridge, MA: Harvard University Press, 1982), 127.

2. Thomas McCraw, "Regulation in America, A Historical Overview," *California Management Review,* Fall 1984, 114–119.

3. Warren T. Brookes, "America Dragged Down," *National Review,* 15 October 1990, 36–43.

4. Ibid.

5. Sharon Campbell, "Playing it Safe," *Entrepreneurial Woman,* January/February 1991, 12–15.

6. Michael M. Segal, "Spilled Some Salt? Call OSHA," *Wall Street Journal,* 9 July 1991, A16.

7. Harper Roehm, Joseph Castellano, and David Karns, "Contracting Services to the Private Sector: A Survey of Management Practices," *Government Finance Review,* February 1989, 21–25.

8. Eugene Carlson, "Privatization Lets Small Firms Manage Everything from Libraries to Golf Courses," *Wall Street Journal,* 2 April 1991, B1.

9. *The State of Small Business 1990,* U.S. Small Business Administration, Washington D.C., 1991, 187–191.

10. Martha Mangelsdorf, "Sign of the Times," *Inc.,* February 1991, 27.

11. Donna G. Albrecht, "The Time Is Ripe," *Entrepreneur,* April 1991, 222–225.

12. "U.S. Trace Facts," *Business America* 112, no. 2, 1991, 32.

13. Robert Kuttner, "How 'National Security' Hurts National Competitiveness," *Harvard Business Review,* January/February 1991, 140–149.

14. Ibid.

15. William J. Holstein and Kevin Kelly, "Little Companies, Big Exports," *Business Week,* 13 April 1992, 70–72.

16. *A Basic Guide to Exporting* (Lincolnwood, IL: NTC Publishing Group, 1989), VII.

17. Ibid., p. 18.

18. Ibid., pp. 85–86.

19. Christopher M. Korth, "Balance of Trade II," *Business and Economic Review,* April–June 1991, 35–36.

20. "A Global Ranking," *Wall Street Journal,* 20 September 1991, R4.

21. "Understand and Heed Cultural Differences, *Business America* 112, no. 2, 1991, 26–27.

22. Roger E. Axtell, *Do's and Taboos Around the World* (New York: John Wiley & Sons, 1985), 109.

23. S. Tamer Cavusgil, "Unraveling the Mystique of Export Pricing," *Business Horizons,* May/June 1988, 54–63.

24. Mark Robichaux, "Exporters Face Big Roadblocks at Home," *Wall Street Journal,* 7 November 1990, B1–B2.

25. "Financing," *Business America,* 25 March 1991, 18–23.

CHAPTER 19

1. Eric G. Flamholtz, *Growing Pains* (San Francisco, CA: Jossey-Bass, 1990), 44–47.

2. Julie A. Fenwick-Magrath, "Executive Development: Key Factors for Success," *Personnel,* July 1988, 68–71.

3. Tom Richman, "Personal Business," *Inc.,* April 1985, 68–72.

4. Joel Kotkin, "A Call to Action," *Inc.,* November 1983, 85–96.

5. Jill Andresky Fraser, "Life After Death," *Inc.,* February 1990, 90–92.

6. Brent Bowers, "Entrepreneurs Neglect One Type of Planning," *Wall Street Journal,* 8 April 1992, B1.

7. Udayan Gupta, "ESOPs May Be the Answer If the Question Is Succession," *Wall Street Journal,* 15 July 1991, B2.

8. Paul C. Rosenblatt, Leni de Mik, Roxanne Marie Anderson, and Patricia A. Johnson, *The Family in Business* (San Francisco, CA: Jossey-Bass, 1985), 4.

9. "Twelve Commandments for the Business Owner," *Nebraska Business Development Center Report,* May 1991, 1–4.

10. James W. Lea, *Keeping It in the Family* (New York: John Wiley & Sons, 1991), 9.

11. Echo M. Garrett, "All in the Family," *Venture,* July 1988, 16.

12. Mike Cohn, *Passing the Torch: Transfer Strategies for Your Family Business* (Blue Ridge Summit, PA: TAB Books, 1990), 10.

13. Kristin von Kreisler-Bomben, "Married with Business," *Entrepreneur,* September 1990, 46–49.

14. Barbara Marsh, "Mom & Pop Businesses Can Be a Nightmare If Mom & Pop Split," *Wall Street Journal,* 13 December 1990, A1 and A6.

15. "Sorry Kids, But Business Is Business," *Business Week,* 23 July 1990, 67.

16. "Heir Necessities," *Entrepreneur,* February 1991, 18.

17. Cohn, *Passing the Torch,* 13–14.

18. Gabriella Stern, "More Daughters Take the Reins at Family Businesses," *Wall Street Journal,* 12 June 1991, B2.

19. Barbara B. Buchholz and Margaret Crane, *Corporate Bloodlines* (New York: Carol Publishing Group, 1989), 273–275.

CHAPTER 20

1. Joshua Hyatt, "The Dark Side," *Inc.,* May 1990, 46–56.

2. Ibid.

3. Ellyn Spragins, "Who Needs Wall Street?" *Inc.,* October 1990, 159–162.

4. Martha Mangelsdorf, "Taking Stock," *Inc.,* September 1991, 24–27.

5. Beatrice Mitchell and Paul Sperry, "Selling Out," *Venture,* November 1990, 25–26.

6. Arthur Rosenbloom, "How To Add Value," *Inc.,* May 1988, 151.

7. Marc Frons, "Rule No. 1 for Selling Your Company: Don't Rush," *Business Week,* 3 April 1989, 114–115.

8. Jay Finegan, "The Insider's Guide," *Inc.,* October 1991, 27–36.

9. Fred Richards, "Preparing a Small Company for the Best Sale Price," *Mergers & Acquisitions,* September/October 1986, 62–65.

10. Sallie Hofmeister, "Quack, Quack," *Inc.,* October 1991, 27–36.

CASE 1

1. *Standard and Poor's Industry Surveys,* Standard and Poor's Corporation, New York, vol. 1, April 1991, A-82.

2. Ibid., A-81.

APPENDIX B

1. Dwight Morris and David Bradbard, "Comparison of Computer Users and Non-users Among Small Businesses," *Journal of Business & Entrepreneurship,* October 1991, 83–98.

2. Cary Lu, "Macs or IBMs," *Inc.*, January 1991, 116–117.

3. Walter Mossberg, "Personal Technology," *Wall Street Journal,* 26 December 1991, B1.

4. Walter Mossberg, "Personal Technology," *Wall Street Journal,* 9 January 1992, B1.

INDEX

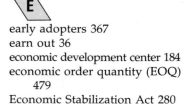

PHOTO CREDITS